America

⤳

The Life of
Francis Asbury

America's Bishop

✥

The Life of
Francis Asbury

DARIUS **L. S**ALTER

FRANCIS ASBURY PRESS
of Evangel Publishing House

Nappanee, Indiana 46550

Evangel Publishing House
P.O. Box 189
2000 Evangel Way
Nappanee, IN 46550

Toll-Free Order Line: (800) 253-9315
Internet Website: www.evangelpublishing.com

Scripture quotations are from the Holy Bible, King James Version.

Cover design by Ted Ferguson
Copyediting by Candace McNulty

LCCN 2002116574
ISBN 1-928915-39-6

Printed in the United States of America
10 9 8 7 6 5 4 3 2 1

Table of Contents

To My Best Friends

Brenda, Heather, Heidi, Tabitha, Ashley

Foreword

Children of outstanding parents often have difficulty being objective about the ones who gave them birth. There may be no greater illustration of this than the understanding of American Methodists about their founding father, Francis Asbury. His fate among his own people has been largely one of neglect. Yet he is one of the most important men in the history of the Christian church, particularly in the development of American Christianity.

John Wesley sent Francis Asbury, a young man of 26, to the American colonies in 1771. At that time there were four Methodist preachers in the thirteen colonies caring for about three hundred people. By 1813, three years before Asbury's death, official Methodist records report 171,448 white and 42,850 African-American members "in full society." By that time, according to historian Mark Noll, one out of every eight Americans—some one million persons—were attending Methodist camp meetings each year.[1] Noll continues by insisting that by 1860, Methodism had become "the most pervasive form of Christianity in the United States." Methodism, as no other single religious tradition, helped shape the character of American religious life. The key to it all was Francis Asbury. Yet his story is largely unknown, especially among his own spiritual children.

In 1951, the National Historical Publications Commission of the United States government identified sixty-six Americans whose works were considered essential to an understanding of the development of the American nation and its strategic place in world history. Asbury was listed as one of these, along with Washington, Jefferson, Adams, and Lincoln. Asbury's letters had never been collected and his journal had not been printed for over a century. Nor was there an adequate biography of him in print.

In September of that year, the World Methodist Council at Oxford, England, responded to the commission's report by endorsing the publication of Asbury's letters and the republication of his journal. The task was turned over to the Association of Methodist Historical Societies in the United States. In 1958, the two major Methodist publishing houses in Britain and America published the journal and the letters but no adequate biography appeared. It was left to L.C. Rudolph, a Presbyterian church historian, to place a serious biography on the American market in 1971, the bicentennial of Asbury's arrival in America.

We are again indebted to one who is not a Methodist for providing us with the story of this great American religious figure. Darius L. Salter, a graduate of the only college and theological institution that bear Asbury's name, has im-

---

[1]Mark A. Noll, *America's God: From Jonathan Edwards to Abraham Lincoln* (New York: Oxford University Press, 2002), 335–41.

mersed himself for a number of years in the journal, the letters, and the literature about Asbury. He has traced Asbury's journeys, researched the story of his time and circumstances, and given us a faithful report on this apostolic figure. Again, American Methodism is indebted to someone beyond its ranks for the privilege of sensing afresh the richness of our origins.

There are a number of things to commend about Salter's work. I am particularly moved by the fact that Salter has been able to grasp the essence of Asbury's theology and the glory of Asbury's passion for God. Asbury was not a published systematic theologian. He did not leave for us a body of theological writings, unlike that other giant of early American religious life, Jonathan Edwards. This does not mean though that he was not keenly sensitive to intellectual issues. Asbury found himself at odds with the prevailing currents of theological thought, but his method of response was not scholarly writing. Rather, he and other Methodist leaders produced journals, testimonies, and especially hymnbooks. Their primary methods were preaching and witnessing, so they preached and witnessed everywhere and to everybody. It was all an expression of the theology that drove them. Comparing it with the theology that came out of New England, which was symbolized by Jonathan Edwards and which dominated the American scene through the eighteenth century, Noll speaks of Asbury's theology as "heterodox" yet remarkably appropriate for the American scene.[2]

Asbury's theology, which was simply obvious biblical truth to him, was remarkably democratic. He believed as fervently as any Calvinist that all humans were fallen and lost in their sinfulness. He believed that there was no saving power for humankind apart from the atoning work of Christ. He differed however from most other Christian leaders in the new American nation in that he believed that Christ's atoning work was an answer to the need of the human heart and was available, not just for the elect, but for all human persons. In fact, he believed the sacrifice of Christ had the power to bring everyone to a perfecting in divine love that would enable one to love God with one's whole heart and one's neighbor even as oneself. This had the effect of making all persons equal before God. All are equally sinful. All are equally salvable. How then could a gospel messenger differentiate between rich and poor, educated and uneducated, black or white, politically significant or insignificant? All needed Christ, therefore all deserved the chance to know him. Every living person on the North American continent needed what Asbury had to offer, so he had a divine obligation to see that every person he could reach would have the chance to receive God's gift of grace.

Asbury's mentor said that the world was his parish. Asbury was a bit more parochial. His world was the new nation, and he gave himself for four and a half decades to reaching every American that he could. He tried to send his itinerants

---

[2]Noll, 335.

to all of the rest. He gave himself for America in the way the apostle Paul gave himself for the Mediterranean world of his day. Asbury's story is one that should not be lost.

An equestrian statue of Francis Asbury stands in Washington, D.C., as a memorial to him. At the unveiling of that monument, President Calvin Coolidge said of Asbury:

> His outposts marched with the pioneers, his missionaries visited the hovels of the poor, that all might be brought to a knowledge of the truth. . . . Who shall say where his influence, written on the immortal souls of men, shall end? . . . It is more than probable that Nancy Hanks, the mother of Abraham Lincoln, heard him in her youth. Adams and Jefferson must have known him, and Jackson must have seen in him a flaming spirit as unconquerable as his own. . . . He is entitled to rank as one of the builders of our nation.

But he was more. He was an apostle of Christ whose legacy has been a host of believers whose influence has reached beyond America and touched the world. Thank you, Darius Salter, for bringing to us again this remarkable story.

Dennis F. Kinlaw, Founder
Francis Asbury Society
Wilmore, Kentucky

Introduction and Acknowledgments

On October 15, 1924, President Calvin Coolidge unveiled an equestrian statue of Francis Asbury at the intersection of Mt. Pleasant and Sixteenth Streets in Washington, D.C. Coolidge addressed about five hundred dignitaries, including the ambassador of France. The flags of the thirteen original colonies waved in the background, the Third Cavalry band played "Behold the Christian Warrior Stands in All the Armor of His God," soldiers of Fort Myer stood at attention, the Paul Revere bell of All Souls Church echoed off the nearby buildings, and a flock of carrier pigeons was released as symbols of joy and goodwill.

On the same afternoon, Mrs. Coolidge visited the opening display of a 124-nozzle fountain installed to further grace the Lincoln Memorial. Lincoln's gleaming white marble presence, the most majestic monument in Washington, continues to preside over our nation's capital. Soot and dirt mar Asbury's bronze image in an unmanicured park, while thousands of oblivious commuters pass by daily. Only an idiosyncratic historian or an extremely devout Methodist would pause to consider the American president's claim that Francis Asbury is "entitled to rank as one of the builders of our nation." The inscription on the statue reads: "His courageous journeying through each village and settlement from 1771 to 1816 greatly promoted patriotism, education, morality, and religion in the American Republic."

Objectivity and biographical writing are strange bedfellows. The marriage is inherently incompatible. Why would someone give several years to an individual, unless the investment was driven by particular presuppositions of repulsion or attraction? I do not begin this work with any disclaimer as to my reverence for Francis Asbury. His greatness has been established by too many other people who are both knowledgeable and perceptive to begin the account with a clear slate. My bias is further augmented by having attended both a college and seminary named after Asbury.

Francis Asbury responded to and was influenced by events unique to his time and space. The American Revolution not only redefined the body politic within America, but drastically relocated all other cultural landmarks. Only by viewing Asbury within the context of the ideologies that swirled around him can we begin to understand the formation of a complex individual. Leaving the shadow of a giant intact while at the same time whittling him down to size calls for careful carving. As historian Richard Norton Smith said of George Washington, Asbury is a rare historical figure, and only by considering his humanity can we confirm his greatness.

I do not claim objectivity in my portrayal of Asbury, but I do fervently assert an attempt to examine and analyze the many facets of his historical contributions to American Christianity. This includes looking in depth at his personality, a chronological tracing of his life, an interpretation of both positive and negative relationships with other people, and engaging as many voices and faces as time and space allow.

In 1783, George Washington stated that the "Citizens of America" were "placed in the most enviable condition, as the sole Lords and Proprietors of a vast Tract of Continent, comprehending all the various soils and climates of the World….They are, from this period, to be considered as Actors on a most conspicuous Theatre, which seems to be peculiarly designed by Providence for the display of human greatness and felicity." Had Washington known both the future and Asbury, he could not have prophesied more accurately.

All that has been written about Asbury can be classified as hagiography, treatises of veneration. This is understandable, since Asbury was a person of commitment, trustworthiness, wisdom, sacrifice, religious intensity, and above all, unparalleled perseverance. But these qualities do not preempt his proclivities to recalcitrance, misperception, myopia, manipulative prowess, as well as the doubts, fears, and anxieties that create the angst which plagues all of human existence. Historian Nathan O. Hatch asks, "Why do we have no modern critical biography of the indomitable Francis Asbury, one of the most revered and influential figures in the early republic?" Fortunately, an immense amount of historical record allows us to do just that. Asbury journaled, and he encouraged his fellow laborers to do the same. Thus, they have left behind thousands of pages that introduce us to the early family of American Methodism.

L.C. Rudolf authored *Francis Asbury*, the most recent biography, in 1966. Since then scholars have discovered scores of Asbury letters, written a myriad of articles, and published new interpretive works on early American Methodism, all of which shed new light on the Asbury story. This new treatment of Asbury utilizes these newly discovered resources. Capable researchers have mined countless nuggets that invite further examination of the foremost religious leader in America at the beginning of the nineteenth century. I have attempted to melt and mold these nuggets together in an acceptable form.

This book owes its existence to an almost innumerable list of persons who have provided assistance over the last four years: Debra Bradshaw, Laurie Mehrwein, and the staff at Nazarene Theological Seminary Library; Ken Rowe, Dale Patterson, Mark Shenise, and the staff at the Methodist Archives, Drew University; the staffs of the libraries of Duke University, Vanderbilt University, Garrett-Evangelical Theological Seminary, Baker University, St. Paul School of Theology, Elon College, and of St. George's Church, Philadelphia, and Barrett's Chapel, Fredericksburg, Maryland. Overseas travel took me to the Sandwell Library, West Bromwich, England, to the John Rylands Library of the University of Manchester, and to the Nazarene Theological College Library, also in Manchester, England. A special thanks goes to Edwin Schell, unofficial dean of Methodist history, director of the Baltimore Historical Society, Lovely Lane United Methodist Church, Baltimore, Maryland.

Eric Wright, Chet Bush, David Thornhill, Eric L. Reynolds, and my daughter Heather Salter have performed the labor-intensive task of word processing. I express my gratitude to all of them.

Fred Parker, Harold Raser, and Rob Staples gave careful readings of the manuscript. Face-to-face dialogue is a must for any academic enterprise, and I thank an unnameable group of people who have offered suggestions, clarified perceptions, and traced tidbits of information. A huge debt of gratitude is owed to Elmer Clark, J. Manning Potts, and Jacob S. Payton, who in 1958 gave the world a minutely annotated edition of Asbury's *Journal and Letters*.

My sincere thanks go to my publisher, Joseph Allison, and his co-workers at Evangel Publishing House. Joe discerningly offers both firmness and flexibility, commodities which this writer desperately needs.

I am especially grateful to the five women who enrich my life and continue to love me in spite of my love for history. My wife Brenda, and daughters Heather, Heidi, Tabitha, and Ashley have attempted to tolerate patiently my neurotic attachment to libraries, cemeteries, churches, and archives. For my insular detachment I beg them forgiveness. To my twelve-year-old daughter Ashley, who proclaimed, "I'm sick of Francis Asbury!," let me confidently say, "You will recover." Perhaps even enough to read this book.

To reduce the number of endnotes, I have used parenthetical notes in the text to cite the three volumes which comprise the *Journal and Letters* of Francis Asbury.[1] The language of the characters in the following drama has intentionally remained unedited. You will hear them speak in their dialect and discover that they are not so far removed from us.

Darius L. Salter
Nazarene Theological Seminary
Kansas City, Missouri

---

[1]Francis Asbury, *The Journal and Letters of Francis Asbury*, eds. Elmer Clark, J. Manning Potts, and Jacob S. Payton (London: Epworth Press, 1958).

1. "Behold Me Now a Local Preacher"

Francis Asbury's England

The people of eighteenth-century England were a study in contrasts: wealth and poverty, independence and subservience, honesty and corruption, sobriety and debauchery, philosophical argument and trivializing sport.[1] John and Charles Wesley traveled through England convinced that these gaps could be bridged with their all-inclusive message of universal grace. No place was their optimism more tested than among the inhabitants of Birmingham and the surrounding area, the foremost producers of metal goods in the world.

Unhampered by regulations, guilds, and charters, a man who could build a fire and swing a hammer was in business to create whatever he thought marketable in the way of knives, hooks, buttons, buckles, guns, toys, jewelry, and watch chains. This unbridled capitalism was energized by twelve to fourteen hours a day of smelting iron and shaping it with anvil and hammer. Such long days left no time for theological niceties, much less the disciplines required by their adoption. At no place was the contrast between the Oxford brothers and their mission field more apparent than the Birmingham area. When John decided to become more "vile" and utilize field preaching as his primary evangelistic methodology, never did he envision such vileness.

In October 1743 the Wesley brothers first made their way to Birmingham and its surrounding communities. Nicknamed the "Black Country" because of its coal- and iron-rich hillsides, the "Midlands" was "an industrialized countryside, or rather a countryside in course of becoming industrialized; more and more a strung out web of iron working villages, market towns next door to collieries, heaths and wastes gradually and very slowly being covered by the cottages of nailers and other persons carrying on in industrialized occupations in rural Birmingham."[2] The area was the greatest producer and consumer of forge iron in all of England.[3] It was also one of the most irreligious and most resistant to the holiness demanded by the message of the Wesleys. Alfred Camden Pratt, in his work *Black Country Methodism,* states of the era and area that

> the few magistrates and constables of those days were as sleepy as the few parsons, ordained and unordained: and provided a man was ignorant enough and poor enough and stupid enough not to trouble them, they would not trouble their heads about him. Ignoramuses were almost as plentiful as heads then, poverty was more abundant than it has been since, and nobody was wise enough in those days to dam out inflowing stupidity.[4]

Just outside of Wednesbury, John and Charles were accused of singing Psalms all day and making folks rise at five in the morning. John reported that a mob "like a flood" carried him through the streets "from one end to another."[5] The popular vote was split as to whether the mob would hear him speak or "knock his brains out first." Although John "lost only one flap" of his waistcoat and a "little skin" from his hand, he managed to retain his brains and plant Methodism not only in Birmingham but in other industrial areas. Again, Pratt writes of the brick throwers, "and can we wonder that an urchin, ignorant of shoes and stockings, and whose other garments mainly consisted of a greasy pair of leather breeches, should heave a stone at him when he gave plain utterance to his uncomplimentary and unsoothing convictions?"[6] Joseph Benson, twice president of British Methodism, historically reflected that "Methodism flourished most in the manufacturing and trading towns."[7]

The spectator sports of the Black Country mainly consisted of bull baiting and cock fighting. When Charles Wesley was preaching in the bull ring of Birmingham, not only did "the mob pelt him with stones and dirt, from the cobbled streets, and with turnips from the gutter, but the bells of nearby St. Martins were set ringing to drown his voice."[8] In Wednesbury the "justice" would do nothing to protect the Methodists, and one magistrate said that he would give five pounds to drive the Methodists out of the country. Charles Wesley recorded, "No wonder the mob is so encouraged, and say there is no law for the Methodists. Accordingly, like outlaws they treat them, breaking their houses, and taking away their goods at their pleasure; extorting money from those who have it and cruelly beating those who have it not."[9]

The mob did not cease its activities once the Wesleys departed. It continued to pillage the houses, break out the windows, destroy the furniture, and do physical harm to those who openly professed their allegiance to the experiential religion and pietistic living of Methodism. When Thomas Parker's residence in West Bromwich was broken into, in February of 1744, his windows broken and furnishings ruined, he responded, "I have found nothing in my heart toward my persecutors but love. Neither could I doubt God's love to my soul. All that is within me bless His holy name!"[10] James Jones reported in June 1743 that of the four score houses in Wednesbury, many of them did not have three panes of glass left.

When John Wesley returned to the Birmingham area (Wolverhampton) on March 17, 1761, he recorded that "[n]one had yet preached abroad in this furious town; but I was resolved with God's help, to make a trial, and ordered a table to be set up in the inn yard. Such a number of wild men I have seldom seen; but they gave me no disturbance, either while I preached, or when I afterwards walked through the midst of them."[11] The English historian, Herbert Butterfield stated 250 years later that "[t]he degradation and bestialities were such that it was easy to picture this submerged populace as not human at all—not even humanizable. While they were untamed, men felt that society and civilization were built on the edge of a volcano that there were incalculable brute forces, blind as the forces of nature and capable of sudden eruption."[12]

Butterfield's assessment may not be totally accurate. Without guild or union, the mob served as a collective bargaining agency in preindustrialized England. With vigilante and often organized resistance, mobs fought any and everybody that intruded on their way of life. And the Methodists could be quite intrusive and often offensive. A Methodist preacher, Robert Williams, was especially slanderous of a local Anglican priest: "Look upon your ministry; there are dicers and carders, some blind guides and cannot see, some dumb dogs and will not bark. It might be better if all dumb ministers were hanged in their church."[13]

These violent indictments were compounded with extravagant theological claims, among them "[t]hat every person must have an absolute assurance of his salvation or he would certainly be damned."[14] This assertion Wesley later regretted and retracted. Also, as Charles Goodwin has argued, Methodism's first forays in the Black Country were during a time of intense political unrest. "The most serious riots in June 1743 and February 1744 took place during the English victory at Dettingen and the declaration of war against France respectively, when national feelings against a foreign enemy were already running very high and could be further inflamed against a religious movement that was sincerely, if misguidedly, regarded as a subversive agent of the Jacobite cause."[15]

John Nelson

One of the first Methodist preachers to face the brute forces at Wednesbury was the stonemason John Nelson, sometime in the 1740s. "I preached in an open yard to very large congregations of people, several times some of the mobbers came to hear me, but all behaved well: so he who stops the raging of the sea can stay the madness of the people."[16] No eighteenth-century English Methodist preacher was more courageous than John Nelson. He was pelted with eggs and stones, knocked down eight times at Ackham, dragged through the stones by the hair of his head for twenty yards while he was being kicked in his sides. "[S]ix of them got on my body and thighs to tread the Holy Ghost out of me, so they said."[17] Even Nelson's pregnant wife was beaten to the extent that she miscarried her child. "God more than made it up to her by filling her heart with peace and love."[18]

When Nelson was led through York as a prisoner with the crowds "huzzing" him, he declared that "the lord made my brow like brass so that I could look at them as grasshoppers and pass through the city as though there had been none in it but God and me!"[19] Nelson was arrested on the charge of vagrancy ("this is that Methodist preacher, and he refuses to take money").[20] The dungeon into which Nelson was thrown at Bradford "stunk worse than a hog-stye or little house by reason of the blood and filth which sink from the butchers who kill over it."[21] He testified that "my soul was so filled with the love of God, that it was a paradise to me."[22] Nelson died at the age of 67, an irresistible monument to Methodism's triumph in the face of enormous odds.

Family

It was in the above turmoil and unrest that Joseph and Elizabeth Asbury made a commitment to the God of the Methodists. The quest for genuine religion had already defined the Asbury home before the Methodist invasion. Because of the loss of a daughter, Sarah, in infancy and the accompanying depression, Elizabeth became a devout and somewhat melancholy seeker of spirituality. Her son recalled that she read almost constantly, standing "by a large window poring over a book for hours together."[23] Other than the memories supplied by their son, we know almost nothing of the Asburys. The name has an uncertain origin, being most common in the area of Joseph and Elizabeth's home. "Ash" signifies east and "Bury" fortress (Old English "Bur"); hence, fortified town, or east fortification.[24]

The Asburys were not status-minded people, which was fortunate, because other than Elizabeth's religious influence, the family was of little social consequence. Joseph aspired to no more than domestic labor, tending the gardens of wealthy neighbors such as Wirtly Birch,[25] Joseph Foxall, and Henry Gough. However, eighteenth-century English gardening was no mean achievement. The gardens of the large country houses were virtual parks, which came up to the windows, producing "the kind of landscape that came to be so typical of England —a landscape really selective, tidy and ordered, though appearing to have been created by nature itself."[26]

Elizabeth's maiden name of Rogers suggest that she was of Welsh descent. We do not know anything of Elizabeth's or Joseph's date or place of birth, nor has a record of their date of marriage been discovered.

Beginnings

On August 19 or 20, 1745, Francis was born to the Asburys, who, at the time, lived just north of Hamstead Bridge on the Handsworth Wood Road, four miles north of Birmingham.[27] Approximately a year later, with little Franky, they moved to Newton Village, a mile and a half away, a community later to assume the name of West Bromwich. In 1776 the town was noted as a "nailing" village, "for five or six miles . . . one continued village of nailers."[28] A contemporary, William Whitehouse, observed the town as the scene of immense manufacture.[29] West Bromwich was a hamlet making guns, buttons, metal toys, and jewelry. It was connected by the River Tame to Birmingham, a city of twenty to twenty-five thousand people.

Birmingham was renowned as England's manufacturing hub and, as noted above, the world's foremost producer of metal goods. E. Hopkins has labeled Birmingham "[t]he first manufacturing town in the world." Indeed, it was quipped that "[g]iven a guinea and a copper kettle, a Birmingham workman could make a hundred pounds worth of jewelry."[30] The area may have at that time possessed the most significantly discovered coal resource in the world. A vein of coal thirty feet thick, at places only about three feet from the surface, "stretched between Walsall three miles to the north-northeast of Wednesbury; Darlaston a mile to the northwest of Wednesbury; and West Bromwich a mile to the northeast of Wednesbury."[31]

The earliest incident that we know of in Asbury's life was related by John Wesley Bond (Asbury's last traveling companion) late in life:

> The Bishop's Father being a gardener by trade, used to put up his gardening tools, consisting of long shears, pruning saws, hoes, rakes, etc. in this place (a room attached to the house). One day Francis (the only son) was left in this upper room; nor was his danger thought of until his Father, called to his Mother said, "Where is the Lad; I heard him cry." His mother ran into the room and found he had crawled into a hole in the floor and fallen through. But by the kind providence of God the gardening tools had been recently removed, and a larger boiler nearly filled with ashes put in their place, into which he fell; this broke his fall, or the world most probably would have been forever deprived of the labours of Bishop Asbury.[32]

Elizabeth gave her son as much spiritual attention as any one child could absorb. Combined with Franky's spiritual precocity, her pedagogy produced a child who could fluently read the Scriptures or about anything else by age six. It was by far the most important education he ever received, since his formal schooling was of short duration. "Early," exact age unknown, Franky's parents sent him to school at Snail's Green, a mile from home, for the tuition of a shilling a week. Being unusually mature in spiritual matters and possessing a sobriety beyond his years, he was quickly labeled "the Methodist parson."

The Asbury family was congenial and reputable, providing a salubrious environment for Franky. They were always ready to entertain strangers. Joseph was especially generous, ready to render to both neighbor and stranger the necessities of life. Asbury quipped that "if his dad had been as saving as he was laborous, he would have become wealthy" (1:720). Both Elizabeth and Joseph were doting parents, seeing that their child had the necessities of life and amenities beyond the basics. Since Joseph was employed as a gardener for wealthy families, it may be assumed that Franky was not forgotten at birthdays and other special occasions.

Franky's surroundings were not luxurious, but his early life took root in ample provision. He recalled his parents as "people in common life . . . remarkable for honesty, and industry and had all things needful to enjoy. . . . I learned from my parents a certain form of words for prayer, and I well remember my mother strongly urged my father to family reading and prayer; the singing of psalms was much practiced by them both" (1:720).

As a young boy, Franky was popular with neither his peers nor his tutor, Arthur Taylor, whom Asbury dubbed a "great churl." Due to Taylor beating him "cruelly" and to being required to live with one of the "wealthiest and most ungodly" families of the area, Franky quit school before the age of ten.[33] Much to the disappointment of his father, the son had traded formal education for odd jobs at the surrounding wealthy manors. His education would continue through reading and studying on his own in the small four-room family house. Asbury summed up the deportment of his early years as follows:

> From my childhood I may say I have neither dared an oath nor hazarded a lie. . . . My foible was the ordinary foible of children— fondness for play; but I abhorred mischief and wickedness, although my mates were amongst the vilest of the vile for lying, swearing, fighting, and whatever else boys of their age and evil habits were likely to be guilty of: from such society I very often returned home uneasy and melancholy; and although driven away by my better principles, still I would return hoping to find happiness where I never found it (1:720).

With the arrival of the Methodists, the small four-room house became a thoroughfare for Methodist preachers as well as anyone else whom the Asburys spiritually trusted. "For fifty years" they kept their home open for Bible studies and devotional meetings, hosting as many as could crowd into their small hearth room. A series of persons came across Franky's path and registered a positive spiritual impression. Asbury recalled his first religious enlightenment taking place somewhere around the age of seven. This spiritual awareness was sufficient stimulus for him to begin Bible reading on a consistent basis. During the winter months, with only about eight hours of daylight, the small boy sat by the fireplace or candles poring over Scripture. His mother's admonition that he would "spoil his eyes" did not deter him. Asbury recalled that God began to deal seriously with him at the age of twelve, but his spiritual progress was stymied by his peers and lack of effective spiritual counseling. Uneducated Methodist preachers were ill-equipped in the subtleties of spiritual maturity.

Spiritual Awakening

When Asbury was 13, a spiritual crisis took place under the "influence of a traveling shoe maker who called himself a Baptist."[34]

> He held prayer meetings in our neighborhood, and my Mother who was a praying woman, and ready to encourage any one who appeared to wish to do good; invited him to hold a prayer-meeting at My Father's house. At that meeting I was convinced there was some thing more in religion than I had ever been acquainted

with. And at one of these meetings, held by this man, I obtained that comfort I had been seeking.[35]

But this experience did not afford the "lasting comfort" Asbury was seeking. Approximately a year later he heard John Fletcher, British Methodism's resident saint, preach. Even though some of his friends were "convicted," Asbury remembered his own response as unmoved. It was left to Alexander Mather to provide the spiritual influence that would be of a more lasting nature. Of that experience he later wrote: "I was then about fifteen; and, young as I was, the word of God soon made deep impressions on my heart, which brought me to Jesus Christ, who graciously justified my guilty soul through faith in his precious blood; and soon showed me the excellency and necessity of holiness" (1:124–5).

Alexander Mather had arrived in Birmingham in 1760 and began preaching there and in the surrounding communities.[36] He was one of Wesley's most faithful and discerning preachers. It was to Mather that Wesley wrote in 1777, "Give me one hundred preachers who fear nothing but sin and desire nothing but God, and I care not a straw whether they be clergy or laymen, such alone will shake the gates of hell and set up the Kingdom of Heaven upon earth."[37] When Mather reported to Wesley that God had called him to preach, Wesley responded, "Being a Methodist preacher is not the way to ease, honor, pleasure, or profit. It is a life of much labour and reproach. They often fare hard, often are in want. They are liable to be stoned, beaten, and abused in various manners. Consider this before you engage in so uncomfortable a life."[38]

In 1760 Mather was appointed to the Staffordshire Circuit, which included West Bromwich. Mather's ministry was so successful that "a large building" had to be rented in Birmingham in order to house the crowds.[39] Mather returned to the Staffordshire Circuit in 1763 and discovered that, in spite of Methodism's success, the mob's activity had not quieted. Evidently the Methodists had become somewhat more resistant. At Darlaston a mob was discouraged from tearing down the meeting house when "a hog butcher who lived near the house, hearing the alarm, leaped out of bed, seized his cleaver, and running out, swore death to the first that meddled with it."[40]

It was at Wednesbury that Mather specifically mentioned preaching the Wesleyan doctrine of full salvation, that is, freedom from sin. Mather recorded, "What I had experienced in my own soul was an instantaneous deliverance from all those wrong tempers and affections which I had long and sensibly groaned under; an entire disengagement from every creature, with an entire devotedness to God: and from that moment, I found an unspeakable pleasure in doing the will of God in all things."[41] John Pawson noted that Mather "took great care of, and treated with remarkable tenderness those who professed faith in Christ and who were so suddenly and powerfully brought out of darkness into light."[42] The most influential person that he nurtured was, no doubt, Francis Asbury.

Not that Mather's spiritual direction was always perceptive. When it was reported that Mather believed himself to be as happy as if he were in heaven, Asbury reflected, "I thought I was not as happy as I would be there, and gave up my confidence, and that for months; yet I was happy; free from guilt and fear, and had power over sin and felt great inward joy."[43]

Fortunately, Mather was not the only spiritual advisor in the young boy's life. Asbury had already taken the initiative to attend the Anglican All Saint's Church in West Bromwich rather than Great Barr, where he felt the priest was spiritually "blind." Here he was mainly influenced by Edward Stillingfleet, the namesake of the famed seventeenth-century Anglican bishop who was instrumental in shaping Wesley's ecclesiology.

Concurrent with the Wesleyan Revival was an "evangelical" movement within the Church of England, led by Stillingfleet, chaplain to Lord Dartmouth; William Talbot, spiritual director to Lady Huntington; Thomas Haweis, New Testament translator and commentator; and Henry Venn, author of *The Complete Duty of Man*. Asbury heard all of these men as well as others bring powerful messages from Stillingfleet's pulpit, only two miles from his house.

In fact, it was Venn, one of the best cricket players at Cambridge, who, after playing a game just before his ordination, threw down his bat, inviting anyone to take it who wanted it. When asked "why?" he responded, "Because I am to be ordained on Sunday, and I will never have it said of me, 'Well struck, parson.'"[44] Venn favored Wesley's revivalism, but grew increasingly wary of perfectionism. He wrote to his daughter Catherine, "I am not sorry you have heard Mr. Wesley— a very extraordinary man, but not to be believed in his assertions about perfection. . . . How much more good would Mr. Wesley had done had he not drunk in this air? As there are, doubtless, many excellent Christians amongst his people;—but the best are sadly harassed by this false doctrine."[45]

The Maternal Influence

Asbury believed himself to be most in debt to his mother for the spiritual formation that took place in his life through the early years. Whereas he made little reference to the religious character of his father, he spoke effusively of his mother. In fact, George Roberts, a confidant of Asbury's, said that Asbury's mother was the only family member of whom he ever heard him speak.[46] Elizabeth was the spiritual leader in the home. His attachment to her remained steadfast in spite of the miles and decades that separated them. This attachment more than anything else cast doubt (in his subsequent years) as to whether he had really done the right thing by leaving her. His guilt was partially relieved by the monthly stipend which he sent his mother, but it was intensified by the knowledge that she had been financially victimized after the death of her husband: "My dear mother was in such an advanced age that she gave her property into improper hands" (3:257).

Time served only to deepen an increasingly sentimental memory of the secure and happy days in the cottage at West Bromwich (one of two cottages attached to a "malt house"[47]). Asbury believed that because he had honored his father and mother, as the fifth commandment dictated, his own life would be lengthened. Honor to the memory of affectionate parents would have to be fulfilled via letters filled with spiritual exhortations, plans for reuniting in eternity, and financial gifts.

Above all, the maternal influence would forever be a source of Asbury's spiritual endurance and commitment. Elizabeth Asbury established many of the patterns that would stay with her son. She woke her son up at 4 a.m. in order for him to fulfill his apprenticeship obligation before his afternoon round of preaching and society leadership. More than any other single person, Asbury's mother orchestrated the rhythms and patterns that would be his for the rest of his life. She died January 6, 1802, at age 87 or 88, and upon receiving word of her death Asbury wrote:

> When she saw herself a lost and wretched sinner, she sought religious people, but "in the times of this ignorance" few were "sound in the faith," or "faithful to the grace given": many were the days she spent chiefly in reading and prayer; at length she found justifying grace, and pardoning mercy. So dim was the light of truth around her, from the assurance she found, she was at times inclined to believe in the final perseverance of the saints. For fifty years her hands, her house, her heart, were open to receive the people of God and ministers of Christ; and thus a lamp was lighted up in a dark place called Great Barre, in Great Britain. She was an afflicted, yet most active woman, of quick bodily powers, and masculine understanding; nevertheless, "so kindly all the elements were mixed in her," her strong mind quickly felt the subduing influences of that Christian sympathy which "weeps with those who weep," and "rejoices with those who do rejoice." As a woman and a wife she was chaste, modest, blameless; as a mother (above all the women in the world would I claim her for my own) ardently affectionate; as a "mother in Israel" few of her sex have done more by a holy walk to live, and by personal labour to support, the Gospel, and to wash the saints' feet; as a friend, she was generous, true, and constant (2:333–4).

Because Asbury's mother enabled his spiritual precociousness, pinpointing a specific conversion date for Francis Asbury is difficult. There does not seem to be any time in his life when he was not serious about spiritual matters. In all probability he made a confession of faith at his mother's knee. He claims to have been awakened by a "pious man" who was not a Methodist (the Baptist shoemaker?)

before he was fourteen years old. He does not specifically relate the pious man to his recalling that "on a certain time when we were praying in my father's barn, I believe the Lord pardoned my sins and justified my soul."[48] It was to this "barn" that Asbury often retreated for the purpose of private devotion or group prayer with his friends. It was quipped throughout the immediate community that Asbury's prayers kept the old barn from falling down.[49] Asbury recalled that he lost the assurance of this experience in the "father's barn" when some of his friends talked him out of it. The truth is, Francis Asbury's relationship with God was established over a period of approximately ten years via the influence of his mother, the Anglican preachers of West Bromwich, Alexander Mather, the reading of "Whitefield's and Cennick's sermons," and the many godly Methodists who lived in the northwest hamlets of Birmingham.

One thing is certain, between the Anglicans and Methodists, the latter captured Franky's curiosity and ultimately his life's devotion. Of the society at Wednesbury he noted, "I soon found this was not the church, but it was better. The people were so devout—men and women kneeling down, saying amen. Now, behold! They were singing hymns—sweet sound! Why, strange to tell the preacher had no prayer book, and yet he prayed wonderfully. What was yet more extraordinary the man took his text and had no sermon—thought I this is wonderful indeed."[50] Both the style and content of this observation remained his for the rest of his life. Asbury would model extemporaneity as a foremost and necessary tool for American preaching.

Early Vocation

In the meantime, at age thirteen, Franky had given himself to learn a "branch of business." In all likelihood, even after he was converted and began preaching, he fully believed he would retain this vocation the rest of his life. Exactly what Asbury created out of forged iron, we are not sure. Frank Baker and John Vickers are probably correct that he was apprenticed to a Mr. John Griffin, who was a chape maker. A contemporary of the Asburys, Joseph Reeves, stated that Franky was "bound and apprenticed to John Griffin. His trade was 'chape filing.'" Reeves explained that "this trade had to do with the making of portions of the scabbard 'sword-holder' and also the fitting for attaching the scabbard to the belt."[51] Whatever Franky made, he would have worked thirteen hours a day for seven to ten shillings per week. Asbury had a highly specialized job, which required minimum skill. There were 8,000 buckle makers along with 2,500 iron chape makers in Birmingham. Chape makers and chape filers "made the iron tongue of the buckle which they then passed on to the buckle maker for assembly with the buckle ring."[52]

Henry Foxall

Less historically supported is the tradition that Franky was apprenticed to Henry Foxall, a friend of the Asburys, at the Old Forge.[53] Henry was the father of the Henry Foxall, who moved to America and founded Eagle Iron Works in Philadelphia. The son gave the money for the building of the Foundry Church in Washington, D.C. Recalling his apprenticeship, Asbury stated, "During this time I enjoyed great liberty, and in the family was treated more like a son or an equal than an apprentice."[54]

Though Asbury may not have worked for the Foxalls, the Asburys and the Foxalls were close friends. The son, Henry Foxall, at whose home Asbury often stayed, represents a remarkable story in early nineteenth-century American industrialism. He made a fortune selling cannons to the United States government. After visiting Foxall's foundry, Major John Clark, "superintendent of construction" for the state of Virginia, wrote a letter to James Monroe. "From his great experience he, 'Foxall,' has made very considerable improvement in the art of making ordnance, and is acknowledged by the best judges to understand that business better than any man in America."[55] Thomas Jefferson later persuaded Foxall to move his foundry to Washington D.C. Foxall then established the Columbian Foundry along the Potomac River just above Georgetown. Preaching frequently, Foxall was ordained an elder at the Baltimore Annual Conference, March 19, 1814. According to Henry Boehm, Asbury and Foxall were like brothers.

When the British descended on Washington during the War of 1812, Henry Foxall promised God a "thank offering" for sparing his foundry. Immediately, a violent thunderstorm deterred the advance of the British. The "thank offering" provided seed money for the Foundry Church, which was completed and dedicated September 10, 1815. (Foxall stated that the word "Foundry" was not a reference to his industry, but to the first meeting place of English Methodism.)

When criticized that he gave the proceeds from making military weapons for the founding of a church, Foxall replied, "No doubt you have some reason for thinking I have sinned in turning out all these grim instruments of death, but don't you think therefore, that I should do something to save the souls of those who escaped?"[56] During 1819 and 1820 Foxall served as the mayor of Georgetown. He died December 11, 1823, in Handsworth, England. Five days earlier he had taken a carriage ride to show his third wife the childhood haunts and homes of both himself and Asbury.[57]

Whatever it was that Asbury crafted with hammer and anvil, or poured into a mold, it was pertinent training for his life's vocation. Eighteenth-century metal fabrication was not a tool and die enterprise, turning out precision parts. It was an occupation demanding innovation. The pioneer bishop would later employ this spirit of improvisation as he repaired harnesses, saddles, wagon shafts, and whatever else needed fixing on the margins of civilization. The accumulated strength in his hands and forearms would be necessary to control both beast and primitive machinery. Between reading by the light of candles and working at the metal forge, nothing was wasted in Asbury's training. He was being shaped by Providence as readily as he shaped the metal which felt the force of his hammer.

Beginning Ministry

At about age fifteen, Franky bonded with like-minded friends James Mayo, James Bayley, Thomas Russell, and Thomas Ault. James Mayo would succeed Asbury as the leader of the West Bromwich Methodist society after Asbury departed. In 1779 Mayo moved to Birmingham and was succeeded by Ault. It is from Ault we discover the group's pattern of attending four services each Sunday. "He and me [Asbury] and three or four more used to go to Wednesbury in morning of the Lord's Day to the preaching at 8 of the clock; and when this was over twice to West Bromwich church, and at 5 in the evening to Wednesbury again."[58]

Franky's first forays into public speaking involve providing some commentary at his mother's devotional meetings, which she conducted fortnightly. After preaching attempts at nearby Methodist homes, he caught the eye of Alexander Mather, who appointed him as a local preacher and the leader of a class of young people who met at West Bromwich Heath. The pious youths held meetings at surrounding houses, but these were discontinued because rioters disrupted the gathering. "I then held meetings frequently at my father's house, exhorting the people there, as also at Sutton Coldfield, and several souls professed to find peace through my labour. I met class awhile at Bromwich-Heath, and met in band at Wednesbury. I had preached some months before I publicly appeared in the Methodist meeting houses; when my labour became more public and extensive, some were amazed, not knowing how I had exercised elsewhere."[59] Henry Prince suggests that "his first sermon in this capacity was preached at the Manwood's Cottage, near 'The Manwood's,' a farmhouse built by an uncle of the famed Samuel Johnson."[60] About this time, he made friends with Richard Whatcoat, who would later loom as a critical contributor to American Methodism.

Between the ages of seventeen and twenty, Asbury traveled around the Birmingham area, preaching wherever he was asked, often several times a week. Of his successes and failures we know almost nothing. Authorized by Alexander Mather as a "local preacher," he understood himself as the "humble and willing servant of any and of every preacher that called on me by night or by day; being ready with hasty steps to go far and wide to do good; visiting Derbyshire, Staffordshire, Warwickshire, Worcestershire, and indeed almost every place within my reach for the sake of precious souls; preaching generally, three, four, and five times a week, and at the same time pursuing my calling" (1:722). On the Derbyshire "round" he preached at the home of Thomas Slater, a well-known farmhouse at Shottle. When Slater later recalled the persons who preached at his house, he referred to Asbury as a "youth not quite out of his teens with a voice like the roaring of a lion."[61]

A Methodist Preacher

For three or four years Asbury followed the tiring routine of regular preaching, leading the society meeting at West Bromwich, and working at the forge. At age 20 he finally decided that something had to give. The next step was to become a full-time itinerant for English Methodism. This transition may have been stimulated by his being requested to fill in for the local itinerant William Orpe, who had become ill. Evidently Asbury usurped some authority that, in Orp's perspective, he had not earned. This was not the last time this accusation would be leveled at Asbury.

> Dear Frank,—After having so firmly engaged you to supply Hampton and Billbrook at the end of the week I could not be surprised to hear you have turned dictator. Certainly you must either *think* I was not able to see the places properly supplied, or else that I am fickle and inconstant, and therefore you expect to hear my *new* mind. I take this opportunity of informing you that I shall not be at those two places and shall expect you to see them supplied in due time. It is true another preacher is come; but he goes immediately into the new round; in the meantime I wish you would hearken to those verses of Hesiod:
>
> > "Let him attend his *charge*, and careful trace
> > The richt-lin'd *furrows*, gaze no more around;
> > But have his mind employed upon his work;"
>
> Then I should hope to hear that your profiting would appear unto all men. You have lost enough already by *gazing all around*; for God's sake do so no more. I wish I could see you on your return from Hampton on Sunday evening. I shall be at Wednesbury if it please God. I have a little concern to mention. I hope you'll call.[62]

There is fragmentary evidence that Asbury performed his pastoral duties with competence and was beloved by his parishioners. After he left for America, several Whitebrook parishioners wrote to Elizabeth, "You have great reason to rejoice in the Lod, in that your son is also the son of God, and an heir with the Lord of glory." [63] Another parishioner, impressed by the young preacher's devotion, wrote to Asbury's mother, "I doubt not but that Franky believed that it was the will of God he should go [to America] . . . and am persuaded that God will not forget this his work of Faith and Labour of Love."[64] Jasper Winscom, a layperson in Asbury's last station in England, offered this assessment: "I think we may say he is a good preacher and a honest Christian, fitted for the work by the Lord."[65]

In August of 1767 Asbury traveled to London, where he was admitted to the Methodist Conference on trial (a probationary license to preach) and then appointed to the Bedfordshire Circuit under the direction of his senior, James Glassbrook. The next August he traveled to the Methodist Conference in Bristol, where he was admitted into "full connection," the highest recognition of ministerial authority granted by Wesley, the leader of an unofficial movement within Anglicanism. (Only the Methodist preachers who had already been ordained by the Anglican Church could serve the sacraments.) He was then stationed at Colchester as the lone circuit rider. On this circuit he stood up to one of the strong-willed society members, William Norman, who was the leader of the Portsmouth society. The details of the controversy are unclear, but the outcome was that Norman did not get his way and Asbury held firm. John Vickers states that Norman had traded ministry for marriage, and had assumed a role that neither "preacher nor people could bear."[66] Asbury ousted him from his position of authority and replaced him with another steward.

In 1769 the Methodist conference stationed Asbury at Bedfordshire, along with Richard Henderson. His appointment in 1770 to Wiltshire South was his last station on an English circuit. It was also at the 1770 Conference that the first two English preachers, Joseph Pilmoor and Richard Boardman, were appointed to America.

Over a four-year period, Francis Asbury had demonstrated administrative ability, showed leadership qualities, preached well enough to draw a crowd, quieted conflict, and endured the rigors of travel with few comfort amenities. These precursors would intensify beyond his wildest expectation.

Inner Doubts

Asbury's successes did not quiet his innermost doubts. On October 26, 1768, he wrote to his parents, "I wonder sometimes, how anyone will sit to hear me, but the Lord covers my weakness with his power" (3:4). Again in a letter to his parents, July 20, 1770: "When I meet with fighting without and fears within, my heart trembles, my courage fails, my hands hang down, and I am ready to give up all for lost. I despair almost of holding out to the end, when I think of the difficulties I have to wade through" (3:8).

Now twenty-five years of age, the young man who had grown up in the Tame River Valley, surrounded by the iron- and coal-producing hills of the Black Country, had graduated from an internship that emphasized the *doing* of ministry. At the heart of this doing was the mission of evangelism. British Methodism was not about appointing men to established churches, but rather entailed discovering persons with the evangelistic gifts for starting and establishing new churches. Impromptu proclamation was the order of the day, rather than ready-made pulpits.

In 1741 a William Hutton visited Birmingham. "I was surprised at the place," he wrote, "but more so at the people; they possessed a vivacity I had never beheld. I had been among dreamers, but now I saw men awake. Their very step along the street showed alacrity. Every man seemed to know what he was about."[67] No man ever knew what he was about more than Francis Asbury. This "aboutness" had been nurtured in a loving home, tempered in a forge mill, and modeled by sacrificial Methodist itinerants who interpreted their life's calling as the salvation of souls. He was now ready for his life's assignment, a destination that, as far as we know, until twenty-five years of age had never entered his mind. In the winter of 1770 he began to have "strong inclinations" that he should visit America.[68]

After the Bristol conference in 1771, at which Wesley appointed Asbury to America, he returned home for his farewell. The goodbye was far more final than he comprehended, for it was Asbury's original intention to return home after four years in America at the age of thirty. His father's premonition was more nearly correct: "I will never see my boy again." Friends and neighbors packed into the cottage to hear the newly appointed missionary preach.

It was an emotional scene. A fourteen-year-old boy, T. Blacksidge, was so impressed with Asbury's commitment that he began to cry because his parents would not let him go too.[69] Asbury himself could not fight back the tears. Sobbing out his final goodbye, he thrust his most precious belonging, a large silver pocket watch, into his mother's hand.

On the Sunday evening before his departure, in the meeting room on Paradise Street, Asbury took his text from 2 Timothy 2:20: "But in a great house there are not only vessels of gold and silver, but also of wood and earth; and some to honor and dishonor."[70] Seven years earlier he and some friends had bought and furnished this "Methodist Room" at which the West Bromwich Society met. This inauspicious beginning would beget thousands of churches on a continent he was yet to visit.

According to Asbury, his last preaching on English soil took as its text Psalm 61:2, "From the end of the earth will I cry unto thee." Toward the end of his life, Asbury stated to the Methodist preacher, James Quinn, "This might not have been of high interest and importance to the hearers but it was to the speaker; for often has my heart been overwhelmed during my forty years pilgrimage in America. And if I had been a man of tears, I might have wept my life away." These words were uttered with the sentiment of the home he had left, loving parents, and faithful friends. Then a smile came to his face as he said to Quinn, "[I]f I were not sometimes to be gay with my friends, I should have died in gloom long ago."[71]

On the last evening at home, Asbury and Edward Hand spent several hours reminiscing and praying together. Years earlier Asbury had preached at Hand's house in Sutton Coldfield, one of his first experiences at effective sermonizing. "[S]everal souls professed to find peace through my labours."[72] Hand's house had been set on fire twice by Methodist persecutors. Conversation with like-minded friends would be Asbury's most enjoyable entertainment for the rest of his life. On October 26, 1768, he wrote to his parents, "As for me, I know what I am called to. It is to give up all, and have my hands and heart in the work; yea, the nearest and dearest friends and I am content, and will do it, nay, it is done"(3:4).

2."I Will Show Them the Way"

The American Appeal

Thomas Taylor was one of the original trustees of John Street Methodist Church (Wesley Chapel) in New York. He was either a person who lacked means or who failed to put his money where his mouth was (or where his pen was). He subscribed only one pound for the church's construction. Nevertheless, on April 11, 1768, he wrote a letter to John Wesley that may have carried some influence. In the letter, Taylor traced the history of revivalistic religion in the colonies over the past twenty years. He highlighted the work of Methodists George Whitefield, Philip Embury, and Thomas Webb. The latter was a "point blank" preacher dressed in a scarlet coat who told his listeners that "all their knowledge and religion was not worth a rush unless their sins were forgiven and they had the witness of God's Spirit with theirs that they were the children of God."[1] Taylor implored Wesley to send an "able and experienced preacher, a man of wisdom, sound faith, and a good disciplinarian" to help the American Methodists. Taylor accented his plea that if the English could not pay the preacher's passage, "We would sell our coats and shirts to procure it."[2]

In October of 1768, John Wesley dined with Charles M. Von Wrangle in Bristol, England. Wrangle, who had been appointed by the King of Sweden as a Lutheran missionary to America, talked in animated terms of the evangelistic opportunities which the New World represented. Wesley listened intently. Wrangle pleaded with Wesley, "You need to be sending missionaries to the colonies. It is fertile ground for Methodism. The people hunger for the Gospel. The fledgling churches that have begun will die if they do not have sufficient leadership." As Wesley listened later that evening to Wrangle's "sound doctrine preached with simplicity," he mused over the Swede's exhortation.[3]

In all likelihood there were several other communications that came Wesley's way urging pastoral oversight for the three or four hundred American Methodists. Joseph Pilmoor recorded that "a few people in Maryland, who had lately been awakened under the ministry of Mr. Robert Strawbridge, a local preacher from Ireland, sent a pressing Call to the Bristol Conference in 1768, *entreating* us to send them over Preachers to help them."[4]

The First British Missionaries

At the Leeds Conference in 1770 Wesley called for volunteers, and at least two responded, Richard Boardman and Joseph Pilmoor. History would demonstrate that both offered stability to the fledgling American sect but little in the way of leadership. Boardman's wife had recently died, and part of his grief recovery was to volunteer to go "wherever God needed him." Because Boardman was older and more experienced than Pilmoor, Wesley appointed him as "assistant" or head of the American enterprise.[5] Pilmoor was the more gifted of the two, and his preaching more fruitful. He was also more judicious in discovering the temperament of the American people. Though he was committed to the Methodist doctrine, he early on decided that the Wesleyan system could not be imposed wholesale without accommodations to the American culture.

When Thomas Rankin arrived in 1773, he immediately clashed with Pilmoor. Rankin assessed Pilmoor as uncommitted to the Methodist discipline, and Pilmoor retorted that Rankin was brittle and harsh. As numbers dwindled at St. George's Church in Philadelphia, Pilmoor penned, "Such is the fatal consequence of contending about *opinion* and minute (details) of *Discipline*. It grieves me to the heart to see the people scattered that we have taken such pains to gather; but I cannot help it without opposing the measures of Mr. Wesley's delegate and that would breed much confusion, so I am obliged to go weeping away."[6] The exact date that Pilmoor "went away" was January 2, 1774. He and Boardman sailed for England; they came together and they left together. Boardman continued to serve Methodism, but he died in Ireland a scant eight years later at the age of forty-four. When Wesley left Pilmoor's name off the "legal one hundred" (English Methodism's trustees) because he had lost confidence in him, Pilmoor returned to America and was long-time pastor of St. Paul's, a Protestant Episcopal church in Philadelphia. He died in 1821 and is buried at St. Paul's.

The Planting of American Methodism

Evangelism via migration gave rise, without plan or forethought, to three locations for Methodism within the colonies. Philip Embury, a carpenter, was encouraged to "rekindle the gift that was within him" by his neighbor Barbara Heck. Before long there was a small group meeting in a rigging loft on Horse and Cart Street in Manhattan. The sixty-by-eighteen-foot upper room served as a preaching point for both Embury and Thomas Webb until a church could be built, sixty by forty-two feet, on John Street. Because Methodism had not registered with the colony as an established church, its dissenting status was circumvented by attaching a chimney and fireplace to the edifice. Philip Embury dedicated the church, which had been designed by Barbara Heck to look like a house, October 30, 1768.[7]

A former New York businessman wrote from Charleston, South Carolina, on May 13, 1769, "New York is a large place: it has three places of worship of the Church of England, two of the Church of Scotland, three of the Dutch church, one Baptist meeting, one Moravian chapel, one Quakers meeting, one Jews synagogue, one French reformed chapel. Among all these there are very few that like the Methodists."[8] The disliking had its exceptions. John Adams, future second U.S. president, said of Thomas Webb, the British captain who had lost his right eye in battle, "He is one of the most fluid, eloquent men I ever heard. He reaches the imagination, and touches the passions very well and expresses himself with great propriety."[9] Charles Wesley referred to Webb as "an inexperienced, honest, zealous, loving enthusiast."[10]

Around 1765 an Irish scrabble farmer, Robert Strawbridge, began preaching to the surrounding communities in Frederick County, Maryland, mainly in the vicinity of Pipe Creek. He was a person of limited abilities but unlimited zeal. He could barely feed his family of six children, could not write, and agreed to preaching tours only on the condition that his neighbors would work his farm. In 1765 he built a twenty-two-foot-square log house for preaching and worship. It lacked windows, doors, or floor, but in all likelihood it was the first Methodist edifice built in America.

In 1813 James Finley, one of Methodism's first historians, said he met a man traveling between Barensville and Marietta, Ohio. He was "of the most grotesque appearance, trudging along at a slow rate, half bent, with an ax and two broom sticks on his shoulder." Noting the man's poverty as well as his advanced age, he engaged him in conversation inquiring about his mission in life. "Oh yes," the man said, "in dis vorld I has noting, but in de oder vorld I has a kingdom."

"Do you know anything about that kingdom?"

"Oh, yes!"

"Do you love God?"

"Yes, wid all my heart and Got loves me."

"How long a time have you been loving God?"

"Dis fifty years."

"Do you belong to any church?"

"Oh yes! I bese a Methodist."

"Where did you join the Methodists?"

"I joined de Methodist in Maryland under dat grate man of Got, Strawbridge, on Pipe Creek—an my vife too. An Got has been my foder and my friend ever since."[11]

On May 1, 1801, Asbury held a conference at the spacious home of Henry Willis at Pipe Creek. He recorded, "Our own people, and our friends in the settlement were equally kind; and we had rich entertainment. This settlement of Pipe Creek is the richest in the state: here Mr. Strawbridge formed the first society in Maryland—and *America*"(2:294).[12] There can be little doubt as to Strawbridge's commitment to God and his sacrifice for God's flock. His devotion to Scripture along with his lack of education modeled a prototype preacher that would be characteristic of thousands of Methodist itinerants. After hearing Strawbridge preach, Freeborn Garrettson recorded, "When I retired, it was with these thoughts—I never spent a few hours so agreeably in my life. He spent most of the time in explaining and in giving interesting (and humorous) anecdotes."[13]

In 1763 a group of Reformed Germans built a church, fifty-five by eighty-five feet, for which they could not pay, at the corner of Fourth and Sassafras Streets in Philadelphia. At least some of them were jailed for their indebtedness and insolvency, which led to the church's auction in the late spring of 1770. A half-wit, *non-compos mentis*, placed the highest bid, and his father, rather than getting out of the deal by having his son legally declared incompetent, paid the bid amount of 700 pounds.[14] On June 14, 1770, a Methodist "tallow chandler" purchased the property for 650 pounds. He then talked Richard Boardman, Joseph Pilmoor, and others into assuming both the debt and the shell of a building for the sake of Methodism. The small society that had been founded two years earlier by Thomas Webb moved from a sail loft to what was to be Methodism's most spacious headquarters and most burdensome debt for years to come. Asbury referred to St. George's as "Methodism's cathedral."

Asbury Embarks for America

On Tuesday, August 6, 1771, John Wesley addressed the annual conference which met at Bristol. "Our [American] brethren call aloud for help. Who are willing to go over and help them?" Five volunteered, and two were appointed: Francis Asbury and Richard Wright.[15] (Asbury states August 7; the *Minutes* state August 6.) Both William Guirey and Ezekiel Cooper suggest that there was contention over Asbury's appointment. We may conclude that objections were raised because of Asbury's youth and inexperience. Wesley's conviction that Asbury was the right man prevailed.[16]

After returning home for a couple of weeks, Asbury returned to Bristol with "not one penny of money; but the Lord soon opened the hearts of friends, who supplied me with clothes and ten pounds: thus I found, by experience, that the Lord will provide for those who trust in him" (1:4). From the port of Pill near Bristol the two sailed on Wednesday, September 4, 1771. Asbury was immediately seasick, and possessing only two blankets for a bed he found the whole trip a trying affair. On at least four Sundays he preached to the "insensible" people on board. "Though it was very windy, I fixed my back against the mizen-mast, and preached freely on those well-known words, 2 Cor. v., 20: 'Now then we are ambassadors for Christ, as though God did beseech you by us: we pray you in Christ's stead, be ye reconciled to God'" (1:6). Asbury summed up his missionary endeavor: "Whither am I going? To the New World. What to do? To gain honour? No, if I know my own heart. To get money? No: I am going to live to God, and to bring others so to do" (1:4).

If Asbury expected his wobbling sea legs to find immediate stability on American soil, he was in for disillusionment. Subterranean fault lines were waiting to erupt: authority questioned, leisure mocked, patriarchal ideology scoffed at, aristocratic bloodlines diluted, family lineages vanishing, deference disdained, and liberty replacing obligation as the *summum bonum*. Not the least of the wavering landmarks was the identity of God. Was He an arbitrary despot ruling the earth by caprice, or was He a benevolent father dotingly watching over his children?

America, not yet a nation, was a land up for grabs, in both its political and religious dimensions. These seismic rifts would erupt in an earthquake known as the American Revolution; the earthquake would level sociological traditions that were largely inherited from England. This leveling would result in what Thomas Paine called "a blank sheet to write upon."[17]

Asbury's American Arrival

On Sunday, October 27, 1771, Francis Asbury and Richard Wright landed on the wharves of Philadelphia, America's largest and most sophisticated city, population approximately twenty-eight thousand. "When I came near the American shore, my very heart melted within me, to think from whence I came, where I was going, and what I was going about" (1:7). It was an emotional moment. That night, the pair received a warm welcome at St. George's, where they listened to Joseph Pilmoor preach. The next morning Asbury breakfasted with the class leader at St. George's, John Hood, a convert of Charles von Wrangle. Hood was also the uncle of the captain of the ship on which Asbury had just crossed the Atlantic. The captain joined Asbury and Hood for the meal. Asbury remarked, "Your nephew is quite the gentleman; but I am afraid the devil will get him for he has not got religion."[18]

The next evening Asbury climbed into the "tub" or "crow's nest" (slang terms for the raised pulpit) and preached in St. George's, the largest church in which he had ever spoken. Pilmoor recorded, "In the evening we had a fine congregation to hear Mr. Asbury, he preached with a degree of freedom and the words seemed to be attended with life."[19] Asbury noted his initial encounter with the American people: "I felt my mind open to the people, and my tongue loosed to speak. I feel that God is here; and find plenty of all we need" (1:7).

The following Sunday Asbury attended the watchnight service at which Pilmoor preached. He was impressed with a "[p]lain country man" who afterward exhorted with words that "went with great power to the souls of the people" (1:7). Two nights later Asbury preached his last sermon in Philadelphia before leaving for New York. It was, he wrote, "a night of power to my own and many other souls" (1:7). The trip to New York by stage must have been a real eye-opener. The ruts and roots in the road generally required the drivers to cry out "bear to the right" and "bear to the left" to keep the stage from tipping over, leaving travelers spattered with mud or covered with dust.

Peter van Pelt, from a prominent Dutch family, had heard Asbury preach in Philadelphia and invited him to preach on Staten Island. Here Asbury preached twice, and then went to the house of Hezekiah Wright, who was a judge in the Court of Common Pleas and also the owner of several ships engaged in trading on the east coast. Asbury preached to a large congregation, which confirmed to him both the legitimacy of Methodism and the propriety of his missionary visit.

All of these first homiletical ventures on the American continent met with positive response. Day by day, Asbury was more convinced that he was on the right course. At the same time, both outer adjustments and inner assessments were characterized with a bit of uneasiness. "I am still sensible of my deep insufficiency, and that mostly with regard to holiness. It is true, God has given me some gifts; but what are they to holiness?" (1:8).

In truth, Asbury was ready for neither the city nor the country. On June 3, 1803, he wrote, "I was born and brought up in a temperate climate with great indulgence, and lived in retirement till I was twenty one years of age" (3:261). In other words, in spite of all his past experiences, Asbury believed he had lived a sheltered life, a background which was incongruent with an urban setting. The hamlets of Birmingham were far removed from Philadelphia. The "Athens of America" was a refuge for escaped slaves, hundreds of immigrants, prostitutes, and thousands of unskilled laborers seeking employment. There were "wagoneers, farmers, and flatbed operators," who "carried flour, bread and other foodstuffs into the city and returned to the countryside laden with shoes, textiles and other processed goods."[20]

Philadelphia majored in the manufacturing of ships, which necessitated "smiths, farriers, wheelwrights, riggers, sail makers and chandlers who cared for horses, carts and boats."[21] Indeed, Philadelphia was embryonic urban America, portending late nineteenth-century industrial sprawl, with problems of sanitation, disease, poverty, and crime. As early as the 1750s Gottlibb Mittleberger stated, "Liberty in Pennsylvania does more harm than good to many people, both in soul and in body. They have a saying there, Pennsylvania is heaven for farmers, paradise for artesans, and hell for officials and preachers."[22]

Initial Doubts About American Methodism

On Tuesday, November 12, 1771, Asbury preached at John Street Church in New York "to a large congregation." It was here that he first met Richard Boardman, whom he described as a "kind, loving, worthy man truly amiable and entertaining, and of a child like temper" (1:9). He continued to be impressed with the evangelical hunger that seemed to characterize the American people. On the other hand, the churches and lay leaders with whom he met seemed to be somewhat dormant. He had not been in America a month and already he was feeling restless. The preaching stops were enjoyable, but where was the evangelistic thrust to the countryside and to the more marginalized members of society? And worst of all, there was not a plan in place; there was no organizational leadership. No one was in control, and nothing was more unsettling to Asbury than a command vacuum. "At present I am dissatisfied. I judge we are to be shut up in the cities this winter. My brethren seem unwilling to leave the cities, but I think I shall show them the way. I am in trouble, and more trouble is at hand, for I am determined to make a stand against all partiality" (1:10). The transition from Wesley's hierarchal organization to an ill-defined mission unsettled the young missionary. Wesley's own missionary experience in America had been a complete disaster. Methodism's founder was hardly equipped to provide his emissaries with a plan of action.

The formalities and niceties were over; Asbury believed that he must take the evangelistic bull by the horns and model aggressiveness. This he proceeded to do by taking a northerly route across Manhattan Island, accompanied by Richard Sause and Charles White, prominent members of Wesley Chapel. On Sunday, November 24, they prevailed with the local judge, Nathaniel Underhill, for use of the courthouse at Westchester, New York. It was here that Asbury sounded his evangelistic keynote: "'Now he commandeth all men everywhere to repent.' Seriousness sat on the faces of my hearers, and the power of God came both on me and them, while I laboured to show them the nature and necessity of repentance, and the proper subjects and time for it" (1:11). The message was delivered with clarity and conviction, hallmarks that characterized Asbury's preaching for over fifty years. The sermon was aimed at the heart, sought experiential transformation, and called for a verdict.

Asbury was so pleased with the endeavor that two weeks later he was back at the same spot, but with much different results. "[T]he noise of the children, and the ill-behaviour of the unhappy, drunken keeper, caused much confusion" (1:12). That afternoon he was informed that the courthouse would no longer be available for preaching. His disappointment was soon relieved by an invitation to preach at the home of a tavern keeper. "The power of God was with us, and many of the vilest of those present will, I trust, remember it as long as they live" (1:12). That night he lodged with the Oakley family, whom he invited to pray after supper. "They looked at one another and said there was need enough" (1:12). They later became Methodists.

On Monday evening, December 9, Asbury preached at the home of Theodosius Bartow in East Chester, where he discovered that he was "straitened and shut up; but the Lord knoweth what he hath to do with me" (1:13). Elation and depression, acceptance and rejection, the pendulum would incessantly swing throughout the next half century. The path was anything but even. The honeymoon was now over (if there had been one), and Asbury was prepared to endure the better and worse of his newfound home.

From December 10, 1771, to the end of the year, Asbury preached fifteen times, not quite averaging once a day. An uneasiness about the routine nature of his appointments increasingly gripped him. At each stop Asbury was afforded commodious hospitality, typified by the lodgings of Richard Sause, Justice Wright, and Peter Van Pelt; in other words, it was too easy. On January 1, 1772, he recorded, "I find that the preachers have their friends in the cities, and care not to leave them. There is a strange party-spirit. For my part I desire to be faithful to God and man" (1:16).

It wasn't long before Asbury's faithfulness was tested by the introduction to a New York City winter. With a cold and through the cold, "which pinched me much," he rode to New Rochelle and preached three times on January 19, 1772. The next day his throat was sore, a malady that regularly plagued him for the rest of his life. The only problem with Asbury's ideal vision for ministry was that it had to be carried out in a house of clay. The immortal call would constantly be inhibited by mortal flesh, a limitation to which the visionary was quickly introduced. "On the 23rd I came in covered sleigh to my friend Bartow's, where I took up my lodging, being unable to go any farther. I then applied to a physician, who made applications to my ears, throat, and palate, which were all swelled and inflamed exceedingly. For six or seven days I could neither eat nor drink without great pain. The physician feared I should be strangled, before a discharge took place" (1:18).

For two weeks Asbury was shut in at Anthony Bartow's, where he read "much in my Bible and *Hammond's Notes on the New Testament.*" When he took the sleigh back to the city, he found Joseph Pilmoor sick, and preached in his place at Wesley Chapel. The next day he visited a condemned criminal who was to be executed eleven days later. On February 23, Asbury preached at the home of Israel Disosway, a wealthy mill owner on Staten Island. "I preached twice at that gentleman's house to a large company. Some, it appeared, had not heard a sermon for half a year; such a famine there is of the word in these parts, and a still greater one of the *pure* word" (1:20).

On the whole, Asbury's ministry had been favorably received. In spite of the harsh winter he was beginning to feel at home. "New York is a large city, and well situated for trade; but the streets and buildings are very irregular. The inhabitants are of various denominations, but nevertheless of a courteous and sociable disposition" (1:23). Asbury was not oblivious, however, to New York's cruder side; "wandering cows and pigs were still visible at public crossings, and dead dogs, cats and rats were left to decompose in the gutters and vacant lots that turned into quagmires in rainy seasons."[23]

A Plan Evolves

On March 17, Asbury left New York and headed south through New Jersey toward Philadelphia. This was Asbury's American introduction to single-mount equestrian transportation. Up until now his mobility had been afforded by sleigh, carriage, and stage. "I set off on a rough-gaited horse, for Burlington; and after being much shaken, breakfasted at Spotswood; fed my horse again at Crosswick's, and then thought to push on to Burlington; but the roads being bad, and myself and horse weary, I lodged with a Quaker on whom I called to inquire the way" (1:24). Sore bottom, bad roads, tired horse, lost traveler, friendly host (and sometimes unfriendly); the pattern was repeated *ad infinitum.*

When he arrived in Philadelphia, Asbury was introduced to the plan that he would perfect. As Wesley's assistant, Boardman appointed the preachers: "[H]e should go to Boston; brother Pilmoor to Virginia; brother Wright to New York; and that I should stay three months in Philadelphia. With this I was well pleased" (1:25). The next day he was confronted with an issue to which, until this time he had given almost no thought; a dilemma which would continue to plague him and American Methodism. "We dined with Mr. Roberdeau who cannot keep Negroes for conscience' sake; and this was a topic of our conversation" (1:25). General Daniel Roberdeau would later arrange a meeting for Asbury and Thomas Coke with George Washington for the purpose of discussing slavery, May 26, 1785.

No job description was handed to the foreign itinerant describing how to plant Methodism in the colonies. It was a task of trial and error, and occasionally Asbury fumbled. On April 11 he tried to pray with a sick old man but was intimidated by two intruders "whose countenance I did not like." It was especially difficult for him to know how to discipline the young church. His legalistic interpretation of the "General Rules" led to the expulsion of some society members. "While I stay the rules must be attended to; and I cannot suffer myself to be guided by half-hearted Methodists" (1:28). Needless to say, Asbury was ruffling more feathers than he could smooth.

Asbury's early preaching had more of a negative than a positive cast. It was more gloom than Gospel. On May 31, he "[p]reached morning and evening with some life; but found that offenses increased." On June 4, at Gloucester, New Jersey, he preached to a "few dead" souls with indifferent results. "The word preached did not profit them, not being mixed with faith in them that heard it" (1:33). On July 1 he traveled from Trenton to Philadelphia with "unprofitable company; among whom I set still as a man dumb, and as one in whose mouth there was no reproof. They appeared so stupidly ignorant, skeptical, deistical, and atheistical, that I thought if there were *no other* hell, I should strive with all my might to shun that [congregation]" (1:35). On July 26 he preached "If I come again, I will not spare" (1:37). There were an increasing number who welcomed his leaving rather than his coming.

Asbury's next appointment was in New York, where he arrived in early August. As he listened to Richard Wright admonish the company concerning evil-speaking of others, he perceived that Wright himself was being hypocritical. "But all this was mere talk. I know the man and his conversation" (1:38). Increasingly, it was dawning on Asbury that this spiritual oversight was no human task. Asbury was attempting to discipline insubordinate society members when all was not right in his own soul. He was discovering that spirituality cannot be regulated by rules, and discerning true disciples was far more complex than issuing society tickets. "A cloud rested on my mind, which was occasioned by talking and jesting; I also feel at times tempted to impatience and pride of heart" (1:38–39).

Not only was Asbury plagued by internal conflict, but he learned that the possibility was looming that the American mission would be aborted. Saturday, August 15, was clearly a bad day. "I set out for New York on a bad horse, and met with indifferent fare on the road; but reached New York on Saturday, and there received a letter from my father and friend, Mr. Mather, who informed me of the preachers' returning to England. Preached also this evening with some satisfaction, but found broken classes, and a disordered society, so that my heart was sunk within me; but it is still my desire to commit myself to God" (1:39).

Increasing Conflict

As Asbury approached the end of his first full year on the American continent, he found himself wrestling with his core identity as pastor. Was enabling persons to realize personal and social holiness something more than preaching and imposing Wesley's "rules," strictures that had been imported from another culture three thousand miles away?[24] Perhaps a meeting "for the better ordering of the spiritual and temporal affairs of the society" would help. On Saturday, September 5, he posed queries to the society gathered at Wesley Chapel, John Street, New York. The communication was not as open and fluid as Asbury would have wished it. The society had been resistant to Asbury's leadership. The queries were an attempt by him to elicit dialogue and air out grievances. "Ought we not to be more strict with disorderly persons? Very little was said in answer to this. . . . Who will stand at the door? Not determined" (1:41).

Increasingly, Asbury feared that the growing tension would come to an impasse, but how to compromise or collaborate for the sake of resolving conflict was entirely beyond him. "It appears to me that trouble is at hand; but I fear nothing, being conscious of having acted uprightly before them all, and having no by-ends in view. Whoever has, must answer for it. Whatever comes, I am determined, while here, by the Grace of God, to proceed according to the Methodist doctrine and discipline" (1:42).

On Friday, October 9, the showdown finally came. There had been run-ins with the two most prominent laymen in the church on John Street, Henry Newton and William Lupton. Lupton was the wealthiest man in the church, the largest subscriber for its construction, and carried an imposing frame (someone said his coffin was the largest they had ever seen).[25] Newton, a bachelor, carried a note on the church and devoted much time and energy, especially in the hosting of preachers. He had become physically sick, and Asbury's badgering, according to the trustees, was to blame.

One of the items that may have most bothered Asbury was the church's purchasing of rum for both its construction and maintenance workers.[26] Lupton said to Asbury, "You will preach the people away and you are going to destroy the whole society" (1:46). Asbury said little, but he surmised that his admonition to

Henry Newton concerning the company he kept had so smitten Newton's conscience that it may well have made him physically ill.

Nevertheless, Asbury continued to hound Henry Newton about his absence from leadership meetings and his carelessness in keeping the Methodist rules. The stalemate raised doubts about Asbury's fitness for the work. Following a confrontation with Newton, he wrote to his mother, "'Tis one great disadvantage to me I am not polite enough for the people. They deem me fit for the country, but not for the cities; and it is my greater misfortune I cannot, or will not, learn, and they cannot teach me" (3:14).

Perhaps a year was enough, and the pasture back in England was looking greener all the time. To his parents he wrote, "However, you may depend upon it, I will come home as soon as I can: but he that believeth shall not make haste. As I did not come here without counsels and prayers, I hope not to return without them, lest I should be like Jonah. I have seen enough to make me sick; but if I faint in the day of adversity, my strength is small. I am under Mr. Wesley's direction; and as he is a father and friend, I hope I shall never turn my back on him" (3:13).

Increased Stature

The day after his "dialogue" with the John Street leadership, Asbury received a letter from Wesley appointing him "assistant," that is, head of the American work (1:46). On October 19, Asbury set out for Philadelphia via stage on which was a "curser" whom he rebuked. He stopped at Princeton to see the school that had been headed by Samuel Davies, Wesley's friend. Over an eight-day span he preached nine times. "Glory to God! I have found peace, and power, and love" (1:48). On October 31 Asbury made his first journal reference to money, bemoaning that the last 150 miles had cost him three pounds, which must come out of his twenty-four pounds per annum. He grumbled that the societies at Philadelphia and New York had not made any allowances for his expenses.

But what worried Asbury most was spiritual, not financial, depletion. The more the external pressures of ministry got to him, the more he was made aware of his internal inadequacy. Some sort of spiritual retreat seemed the only answer to every ecclesiastical crisis. Spiritual resourcing thus became the strategy for perseverance. The only way to manage the raw (however well-meaning) passions and opinions that surged around him was through internal control. He quickly learned that a proper relationship with God was the only route to a proper relationship with others. On November 1, he recorded, "For some days past my mind has been blessed with much peace; so that I experience a present salvation, and hope to experience that which is eternal. Thanks be to God for what I feel! Glory, glory be given to my dear and gracious Saviour!" (1:49).

On November 5, Asbury preached "to many people" in Harford County, Maryland, at the home of Richard Webster. Twenty-year-old Freeborn Garrettson recorded,

> The place was crouded [sic], however I got to the door and sat down, but he had not preached long, before I sensibly felt the word: and his doctrine seemed as salve to a festering wound. I heard him with delight, and bathed in tears could have remained there till the rising of the sun, the time passed so sweetly away: I was delightfully drawn, and greatly astonished to find a person go on so fluently, without his sermon before him.[27]

Upon hearing Asbury again, Garrettson recalled that, "He began to wind about me in such a manner that I found my sins in clusters as it were around me; and the law in its purity, probing to the very bottom, and discovering the defects of my heart, I was ready to cry out, how does this stranger know me so well?"[28]

It was here also that Asbury met the Watters family, and William Watters in particular would become a close friend. "The Lord hath done great things for these people, notwithstanding the weakness of the instruments, and some little irregularities. Men who neither feared God, nor regarded man,—swearers, liars, cock-fighters, card-players, horse-racers, drunkards, &c., are now so changed as to become new men; and they are filled with the praises of God" (1:50). While it has been claimed that William Watters was the first American native-born traveling preacher, that honor, however, goes to Edward Evans. Evans, a Whitefield Methodist, had charge of Greenwich Chapel near Gloucester, New Jersey. He died the month Asbury came to America, October 1771.[29]

On November 26, Asbury entered Baltimore, population approximately five thousand, for the first time. The city, then hardly more than a seaport village, later became the citadel of Methodism. Asbury visited it more than any other American city. As yet, Methodism had not erected a church here. Robert Strawbridge erected a crude log cabin for a church at Sam's Creek six miles outside of Abingdon, Maryland, in 1769. On December 6 Asbury preached there: "The house had no windows or doors; the weather was very cold: so that my heart pitied the people when I saw them so exposed. Putting a handkerchief over my head, I preached, and after an hour's intermission (the people waiting all the time in the cold) I preached again" (1:56).

At Bird's Tavern a letter awaited Asbury from Joseph Pilmoor, who was not in agreement with Asbury's frequent changing of the preachers.[30] Pilmoor penned in his journal, "[F]requent change . . . is never likely to promote the spirit of the gospel nor increase true religion."[31] He fumed that Pilmoor's letter "surpassed everything I ever had met with from a Methodist preacher. The Lord judge between him and me" (1:57). Asbury already had. Empathy for the diverse opinions of others never was his forte.

In Kent County, Asbury was accosted by a Mr. Reed, an Anglican priest, who told Asbury that he was without authority to preach in his parish. "I have authority over the people and am charged with the care of their souls," Reed said. "If you attempt to preach here I will take action against you according to law."

"I have come to preach and preach I will," replied Asbury. "Do you have authority to bid the consciences of the people? Are you a justice of the peace? If not, you have nothing to do with me."

"You are making a schism," warned Reed.

"I don't draw people from the church. Is your church having services at this time?" asked Asbury.

"You hinder people from their work," was the reply.

"Do fairs and horse races hinder people from their work? I have come to help you," was the response.

"I have not hired you for my assistant, and thus do not need your help," retorted Reed.

"If there are no swearers and sinners you are sufficient," added Asbury.

Mr. Reed then went into a rage, and Asbury entered the Anglican church and preached (1:58).

An Unresolved Issue

On December 22, Asbury conducted his first quarterly conference.[32] Robert Strawbridge raised a disturbing question concerning the legitimacy of Methodism's very existence. If the administration of the sacrament validates a church as a community of believers, Strawbridge argued, Methodists could not participate in the *ecclesia*, that is, the worldwide body of Christ. "Will the people be contented without our administering the sacraments?" he asked. Asbury reported: "Brother Strawbridge pleaded much for the ordinances; so did the people, who appeared to be much biased by him" (1:60).

Asbury was ill equipped to deal with the sacrament issue, historically or theologically. He could only support Wesley's fiat in the matter, "No ordinances in Methodist Societies."[33] It was a painful dilemma, especially for a leader and people attempting to obtain a coherency of direction. The sacramental question plagued the evolving institution for the next dozen years and almost obliterated its existence. Until 1784 American Methodism existed as a society, which obliged Asbury and his followers to receive the sacraments elsewhere. The Anglicans were the full-service stop of choice. On December 25 Asbury made the following entry: "I then went to Josias Dallam's; and on Christmas day attended the Church, . . . which contained much truth; and afterward received the sacrament" (1:60).

Renewed Resolve

Asbury began the new year, 1773, by reading a *History of the Quakers*. "How great was the spirit of persecution in New England, when some were imprisoned, some had their ears cut off, and some were hanged!" (1:65). The budding leader renewed his resolve, "My mind is fixed on God. I both desire and purpose to exercise fasting, prayer, and faith" (1:66). On January 10, he preached on "perfect love": "The more I speak on this subject, the more my soul is filled and drawn out in love. This doctrine has a great tendency to prevent people from settling on their lees" (1:66).

His renewed religious fervor did not prevent his homesickness. On January 25 Asbury wrote to his mother, "I am here in a strange land, nothing to depend on but the kindness of friends, am spending the best of my days, what shall I do when I am old? . . . 'Tis strange I have seen but one letter from you now these sixteen or seventeen months I have been in America; and as I am now so far from New York and Philadelphia where the letters come" (3:16–17).

Still, Asbury was finding his stride as a preacher. Both the settings and responses were varied. On January 30 he "disposed" the Word in a tavern where there was swearing and drinking; on February 10 he "foreclosed" because of the disorderliness of his congregation; on March 5 there was a "melting time" at Joshua Owing's. On March 12 he preached his first funeral sermon in America: "This was a solemn time indeed. What melting and weeping appeared among the people! There was scarce a dry eye to be seen" (1:72).

Asbury's preaching constantly had to battle the twin enemies of weather and depression. It was sometimes so cold in the Middle Atlantic States that the water from the horses' and riders' eyes froze. On March 18 Asbury was depressed "in such a manner as I hardly ever felt it before. In my journey my heart sunk within me; and I knew not why" (1:72). That night he preached with "great feeling," but could not get his "spirit free. They persuaded me to stay all night; but it was as if I had been bound in chains" (1:72).

George Shadford, with whom Asbury identified more than any other English preacher, arrived from England on April 29, 1772. He was six years older than Asbury and, in 1816, died in the same month as did Asbury. As a youth Shadford excelled in athletics, "wrestling, running, leaping, football and dancing . . . being as active as if he had been a compound of life and fire."[34] He became a traveling preacher in 1768 and, meeting Thomas Webb at the Leeds Conference in 1772, was persuaded to go to America. Upon embarking from Peel, England, Shadford remarked to Thomas Rankin, "This is the ship, the place, and the wharf, which I saw in my dream six years ago."[35] Wesley wrote him a terse commission: "I let you loose, George, on the great continent of America. Publish your message in the open face of the sun, and do all the good you can."[36] Thomas Rankin arrived on the same ship with Shadford. Asbury's failure to mention the fact in his journal is revealing.

Asbury continued to find himself in tension with the members of St. George's, Philadelphia. After a "country tour" he returned to Philadelphia on May 6 and preached on the "stony ground hearers." It seemingly had not yet occurred to

Asbury that preaching could be used for reconciliation. "Some perhaps were displeased with me. But I must declare the whole counsel of God, and leave the event to him" (1:77). On the following Monday he did some fence mending by visiting several of the church families.

Thomas Rankin

On June 3 Asbury received Thomas Rankin, George Shadford, and Thomas Webb, persons that he had not previously met. That night Rankin preached at St. George's, a performance which Asbury assessed as "good." "He will not be admired as a preacher. But as a disciplinarian, he will fill his place" (1:80).

"His place" was as Wesley's general assistant, an appointment which displaced Asbury. Asbury made no mention of any emotion in his journal, though it was certainly a blow to his self-esteem. On June 10 he recorded, "My soul has been much assaulted lately by Satan; but by the grace of God it is filled with Divine peace" (1:80). There would have been plenty of time to discuss the new arrangement, as Asbury and Rankin dined together in Trenton on Friday, June 11, and then rode to Princeton.

In a sense, Asbury both lost and won. If the societies didn't like his discipline, wait until they got a load of Rankin's. The first evidence of Rankin's whip was his displeasure with Richard Wright, whom he shipped back to England within the year. Rankin incarnated what Asbury had been attempting to implement. When Rankin laid out his philosophy of strict discipline to the New York society in no uncertain terms, Asbury responded, "This afforded me great satisfaction" (1:82).

If Thomas Rankin was not a reincarnation of John Wesley, he was at least his alter ego. Rankin said of his mentor, "I loved him superior to any man, and the cause he was, and had long been engaged in, above every other consideration below the skies. For the confidence he placed in me, and the sincere regard he had at all times evidenced toward me raised the spirit of jealousy and even in some of whom I expected better things, and a more liberal mind."[37] In all likelihood, this remark was directed toward Asbury more than any other person.

At a later date, December 3, 1773, Wesley reminded Rankin of his job description. "Improper leaders are not to be suffered upon any account whatever. You must likewise deal honestly with the societies whether they will hear or whether they will forebear."[38] Wesley then separated the sheep from the goats. "There has been good, much good done in America, and would have been abundantly more had Brother Boardman and Pilmoor continued genuine Methodists both in doctrine and discipline. It is *your* part to supply what was wanting in them. Therefore are you sent. Let brother Shadford, Asbury, and you go on hand in hand, and who can stand against you?"[39] Over the next several months the handclasp would be loosened and, in Wesley's perspective, Asbury would become more goat than sheep.

Wesley had plenty of reason to entrust Rankin with leadership responsibilities. He was a disciplined veteran, nine years older than Asbury, competent, and above all, he displayed fervent spirituality.[40] His ministry was accompanied by revival, which the societies interpreted as "divine visitations." When preaching on February 27, 1774, he reported that "the Lord visited the congregation with His almighty power. Many wept and trembled, while others were enabled to rejoice in God their savior."[41] On another occasion he recounted that "The word of the Lord ran and was glorified. Many wept and trembled under the mighty hand of God. He did indeed make it the house of God and the gate of heaven to many souls."[42] During a three-hour love feast at St. George's the "preachers were so overcome with the divine presence that they could scarce address the people . . . as for myself I scarce knew if I was in the body or not and so it was with all my brethren."[43] Rankin represented far more than the letter of the law; he had genuine concern for Christian nurture, which he exhibited with a tireless devotion.

Thomas Rankin, for the most part, found himself at home within the colonies, and in all probability adjusted more quickly than did Asbury. In the early years, Asbury's journal is almost totally oblivious to landscape, wildlife, and whatever scenery would capture the imagination. In contrast, Rankin was enthralled with the vistas that rolled out before him. "I know not if ever I felt more pleasure within and without in all my life. . . . Frederick County, where I have now been is very romantic traveling through hills, dales, rivers and woods and particularly the Blue Ridge of mountains affords a most pleasing and grand prospect."[44] He found the trip to Henry Gough's (Perry Hall) to be especially romantic: "[T]here only wanted the pen and genius of a Pope to make the verdant groves, the flowery lawns, the murmuring streams, the rising hills, the spreading trees . . . to live and flourish in song."[45] Rankin laced his journal with zoological observations as he described buffalo, elk, deer, bear, panthers, wildcats, wolves, beavers, raccoons, groundhogs, foxes, muskrats, minx, bass, sturgeon, and herrings.

The working relationship between Asbury and Rankin over the first couple of years was amiable enough. They were both outsiders and spawned common enemies. The New York church continued to threaten mutiny against both of them. Asbury's spirit was "grieved by the false and deceitful doings of some particular persons" (1:84). William Lupton accused Asbury of favoritism, that is, "winking at the faults of some." Henry Newton said to Asbury that "[h]e did not know but the church door would be shut against me" (1:84). Rankin received the same threat. His tactic was to make sure all the team members were on the same page. Thus, he called for a conference of all the preachers to meet at St. George's Church on July 14, 1773. In doing so, he imported British Methodism's practice of "conferencing," the supreme governmental reference of Methodism.

The future of Methodism would be determined by a regular gathering of clergymen. This first conference gave itself mainly to clarifying and reinforcing its boundaries, mostly in terms of negatives. There was to be no new doctrine, no administering the sacraments (except Strawbridge), no admittance to love feasts or society without becoming a member (more than "once or twice"), and no reprinting of books without Wesley's consent.[46] Overall, Asbury was pleased; it was a genuine attempt by the preachers to set their own house in order. "There were some debates amongst the preachers in this conference, relative to the conduct of some who had manifested a desire to abide in the cities, and live like gentlemen. Three years out of four have been already spent in the cities. It was also found that money had been wasted, improper leaders appointed, and many of our rules broken" (1:85).

Increased Effectiveness

Asbury was sent to the Baltimore vicinity where he remained for almost the entire year, which greatly pleased him. During the first part of August he met with the quarterly conference and found Strawbridge's determination to serve the sacraments to be "inflexible." In working with the classes at Baltimore and Patapsco Neck, he encountered contention and disorder. But all was not lost. There seemed to be an increasing awakening under Asbury's preaching. For example, "[A]serious Negro was powerfully struck; and though he made but little noise, yet he trembled so exceedingly that the house shook" (1:89). At Pipe Creek both a large number of people and the "power of the Lord" were present. Fell's Point, later to be incorporated into Baltimore, was becoming his favorite stop. It was here that Methodism built its first Baltimore chapel, located on Strawberry Alley, off Fleet Street.

Asbury's affection for the societies was growing as he became more attached and more dependent on them for his own welfare. During October he had his first extended bout with illness, which debilitated him most of the month. He was nursed by Sarah Dalton, wife of Josias, who lived in the area of Aberdeen. At the end of the quarterly meeting on November 4, "I discovered the affectionate attachment which subsisted between many of my dear friends and me. It cut me to the heart when we came to part from each other. They wept and I wept" (1:96).

Even as Asbury was becoming more reconciled to the place and people to whom God had called him, he became increasingly anxious about his inner world. Asbury had too much freedom of temper, which proceeded from a flow of what he called "animal spirits." He felt almost incessantly guilty for his tendency to joke, a reflex to the ironies of a job that he thought demanded sobriety. "My foolish mind felt rather disposed to murmuring, pride and discontent. Lord, pardon me, and grant me more grace! The next day my conscience checked me for the appearance of levity" (1:92). In others, he saw improprieties which he disliked and yet discovered in himself. He was especially pained in conscience about making disparaging remarks concerning persons who were not present. He concluded his journal in 1773 in Baltimore by writing: "I still pray, and long, and wait, for an outpouring of the blessed Spirit on this town. O that the time were come! Lord, hasten it for thy mercy's sake!" (1:100).

During the month of January, 1774, Asbury did little in the way of public ministry because he was physically indisposed. On February 2 his bed caught fire, though he was not in it, in all likelihood from the fireplace three yards away. Awaiting him was a new enterprise, the raising of money for a church, which would later become Lovely Lane Meeting-house. "I find the burden rather too heavy. However, God is my support, and my heart is with him" (1:106). He continued to struggle physically. His body had problems throwing off infection, which led to a constant bout with chills and fever. By the end of April he was feeling somewhat better and exclaimed, "What a miracle of grace am I! How unworthy, and yet how abundantly blest! In the midst of all temptations, both from without and from within, my heart trusteth in the Lord" (1:113).

On May 3 he first met Philip Otterbein, whom he had invited to Baltimore to establish a German United Brethren Church. The church he built, Old Otterbein, is still active; it conducted services in German through the 1940s. On May 16 Asbury left Baltimore and traveled to New York, which was to be his assignment for the next six months. Otterbein would serve as a faithful and honest friend. When Asbury presented Otterbein with some of his poetry, after a perusal the latter responded, "Brother Asbury, I don't tink you vas born a poet."[47]

Ecclesiastical Storm Clouds

On the way to his new station, Asbury stopped for a conference at St. George's in Philadelphia. Thomas Rankin, Francis Asbury, and George Shadford were named the American assistants in that order. Methodism reported 17 preachers and 2073 members. Pay for the preachers was set at twenty-four pounds per year.[48] In all, the business was perfunctory except for the vote to send Richard Wright back to England. Asbury and Wright had traveled to America together. It was both Asbury's and the conference's perception that Wright had played the "dandy," had not fulfilled his ministerial obligations, and had lost his relish for true spirituality. Though Asbury consented to the decision, he was troubled by the domineering attitude of Rankin, which he attempted to bear with a "meek and quiet spirit." It was this conference that demonstrated an essential difference between Rankin and Asbury. Both of them believed in discipline, but Asbury's was tinged with reprieve. He would prove himself a master of second chances. The relationship between Asbury and Rankin had seen its best days.[49]

Asbury had been in America less than three years and the prospects for future leadership development were looking bleak. He was being sent by a superior he did not like to a location he did not like. At the end of the Philadelphia conference he wrote, "My lot was to go to New York. My body and mind have been much fatigued during the time of this conference. And if I were not deeply conscious of the truth and goodness of the cause in which I am engaged, I should by no means stay here" (1:116). He arrived in New York on the heels of a letter that had been circulated against him.

Toward the end of June and during the first half of July, Asbury's strength was almost totally depleted. The chills and fevers continued. On July 14 he estimated that he had been sick for ten months, "yet I have preached about three hundred times, and rode near two thousand miles in that time" (1:122). His feeble body faltered in preaching to the extent that he became concerned about fumbled performances. "It seems strange, that sometimes, after much premeditation and devotion, I cannot express my thoughts with readiness and perspicuity; whereas at other times, proper sentences of Scripture and apt expressions occur without care or much thought" (1:126). At one point his thoughts totally left him, but there was exhortation on which to fall back. Such resorting was not uncommon for Methodist preachers.

On August 12 Asbury received a painful letter from Thomas Rankin. Also there was an unsigned, inflammatory letter waiting for him when he climbed into the pulpit at Wesley Chapel. While the ecclesiastical storm clouds gathered, there were rumors of war circulating up and down the seaboard. Asbury was so stressed as he stood in the pulpit on September 18 that he lost some of his ideas. "I was ashamed of myself, and pained to see the people waiting to hear what the blunderer had to say" (1:131). Another letter came from Rankin on September 23 accusing Asbury of injuring him. On September 29 William Lynch, one of Asbury's converts, complained of Rankin abusing Asbury.

Asbury attempted to place the best perspective on Rankin's motives, but it was impossible to keep his resentment from growing. He was feeling overwhelmed. Physical exhaustion coupled with a torrid pace was enough without the drain of administrative conflict. After having been in New York four months and maintaining a schedule that had called for preaching every day and twice on Sunday, he observed, "[I]t seems to be too much for both the people and the preacher" (1:134). By November 1 his health had deteriorated to the point that his legs, hands, and feet were swollen. Some of the society members requested that Asbury be allowed to stay beyond his appointment, in order to recover his strength. Rankin consented.

During the first part of November, 1774, James Dempster and Martin Rodda[50] arrived from England as the last pair of Wesley's missionaries. Dempster was immediately assigned to New York, which allowed Asbury to leave on November 28. On the way to Pennsylvania, he and Thomas Webb stopped at Burlington, where they visited two persons who were to be executed, "one for bestiality, and the other for abusing several young girls in the most brutish and shocking manner" (1:139). The ministers presented the Gospel to the condemned pair but left with little hope of their salvation. They visited the prisoners again before departing Burlington, but again, there was minimal response.

Rankin met Asbury and Webb in Burlington and requested that Asbury go to Philadelphia. Outwardly Asbury consented, but inwardly he longed for Baltimore. Three days later, when in Philadelphia, he presented his case to Rankin, but to no avail. Asbury recorded that they did not "agree in judgment" (1:140). Rankin jotted down the following, "Brother Asbury preached this evening and not without the divine blessing. Next day we talked over different matters respecting the work, and also removed some little and foolish misapprehensions that had taken place in his mind."[51]

Rankin had either underestimated the situation or was unwilling to face it. There was a difference in philosophy and a likeness in personality, a volatile mix. Asbury immediately wrote a letter of complaint to Wesley, which he read in Rankin's presence. "The next day Mr. Rankin appeared to be very kind; so I hope all things give place to love" (1:140). The hope was in vain. Only the American Revolution would mute the clash of egos. It would also draw a line that would decide the destiny of both men. In October of 1774 Rankin recorded, "From the first of my coming here, it has always been impressed on my mind, that God has a controversy with the inhabitants of the British Colonies."[52]

3. "I Am Determined Not to Leave Them"

Imminent War

On the eve of the American Revolution, Philadelphia was the largest city in the colonies, and it would remain so until the turn of the century. There, Gilbert Tennent, one of the architects of the first Great Awakening, had married his third wife, Sarah. Tennent had befriended evangelist George Whitefield, whom historian Harry Stout has dubbed America's "first celebrity."[1] This historical connection brought Asbury to the door of Sarah Tennent's house on January 7, 1775. After recalling the evangelistic exploits of her husband, who had died in 1764, Mrs. Tennent turned the conversation to the spiritual apathy of her son, a student at Jersey College (later Princeton), founded by Gilbert's father. Asbury was sympathetic as he listened to the widow's lament; the implications of a son's losing his father at age seven had not dawned on him. In Asbury's view, raising children was essentially a spiritual enterprise. As he headed out the door, he succinctly formulated, "While carnal parents regard only the worldly prosperity of their children, truly religious parents are chiefly concerned about the eternal salvation of their souls" (1:146).

For the first two months of the year 1775, Asbury hardly preached at all, mostly because of a sore throat, but also because of the firm conviction that he had been appointed to the wrong place, Philadelphia. He coped by reading Neal's four-volume *History of the Puritans,* and by finding sympathetic ears such as those of Thomas Webb. He incessantly wrestled with the theological reasons for his illness (from which he found some relief when he discharged, "near a pint of white matter," on January 29). Convinced he ought to be in Baltimore and feeling guilty over attitudes of insubordination, he penned, "Mr. Rankin keeps driving away at the people, telling them how bad they are, with the wonders which he has done and intends to do. It is surprising that the people are not out of patience with him. If they did not like his friends better than him, we should soon be welcome to take a final leave of them" (1:146–147). Asbury was not alone in his assessment. William Duke, whom Asbury had licensed as a sixteen-year-old, recorded on December 4, 1775, "Mr. Rankin as his manner is spoke exceeding rough to me upon some occasion so that I could hardly bear it and as soon as we got on the road I opened my mind to him. He satisfied me that his design was good."[2]

Asbury began entertaining thoughts of becoming a missionary to the Island of Antigua. Methodist missionary Nathaniel Gilbert, half brother of Sir Walter Raleigh, had died in 1774, leaving a leadership vacuum there. His widow had issued an invitation to Asbury to come to Antigua. Even before Wesley got the news that Asbury was entertaining the notion, he advised that Asbury return to England.[3] Wesley was clearly running out of patience with all the wrangling and saw no solution but the separation of the principals in the conflict. At the same time he attempted some conflict resolution with an open letter calling for continued allegiance to Rankin. "You are never in your lives in so critical a situation as you are at this time. It is your part to be peace-makers, to be loving and tender to all, but to addict yourselves to no party . . . the conduct of T-Rankin has been suitable to the Methodist plan. I hope all of you tread in his steps."[4]

Rankin finally consented to Asbury coming to Baltimore, for which he set out on February 25. Baltimore, with a population less than one-third that of Philadelphia, was immensely preferable to a man who would always esteem country and small town life over the city. The large crowd that came to hear him preach on March 5 rejuvenated him both physically and spiritually. "The power of God was present; and I had an inward witness that it was the will of God I should, at that time, be amongst those people" (1:150). He began a faithful and fruitful round of preaching, but he was becoming disturbed by the sights and sounds of encroaching war.

As the tension mounted between Great Britain and its colonies, Asbury's conversion to the American perspective was gradual. Early on he was irked by all the talk about British oppression. In a 1773 letter he penned, "One fault, I have to find with the people, they are too disloyal, there are too many murmurs against government."[5] He later wrote, "I have a natural affection for my countrymen, yet I can hear them called cruel people and calmly listen to threatenings of slaughter against them."[6]

On March 9, 1775, Asbury preached at William Lynch's home in Baltimore. Present was Captain Charles Ridgely, brother-in-law to Henry Gough, Asbury's close friend. The sisters Prudence Gough and Rebecca Ridgely were devout Methodists. Over a seven-year period, the Ridgelys built "Hampton" on a ten thousand-acre estate in Towson, Maryland. The home was so large that his wife could host a prayer meeting in one part of the house while her husband "held high carnival" in another part. Asbury noted of Charles Ridgely, "And who can tell but the Lord may reach his heart." Evidently, the Lord did not reach the captain's heart to the extent that he ceased his pipe smoking, card playing, and hunting with his hounds, such activities being anathema among Methodists. However, it should be noted that Ridgely provided a home for Robert Strawbridge at Long Green during the last years of the latter's life.[7]

The tormenting tension with Rankin continued, and Asbury was not above at least privately criticizing his ecclesiastical foe. On March 12, he recorded, "I saw brother Strawbridge and entered into a free conversation with him. His sentiments relative to Mr. Rankin corresponded with mine. But all these matters I can silently commit to God, who overrules both in earth and heaven" (1:151). However, the confidentiality of silence was an ideal which Asbury was not able to actualize. And according to Joseph Pilmoor this was an inadequacy that often plagued Methodism. After Pilmoor had broken affiliation with the Methodists he wrote that "many of them are very unfit for Familiar Friendships. . . . Through a kind of puerile simplicity they are often drawn into a sort of loquacity which proves very hurtful to the characters of individuals, and the society in general."[8]

On April 20, six men were wounded in a militia exercise, which Asbury attributed to the willful disregard of his preaching in the vicinity. There was increasing talk of politics and rebellion, so much so that Asbury was fed up with Baltimore by the time he left on March 14. On March 30, George III and the English parliament forbade the colonies from trading with any other country after July 1. They also ordered that fishing in the North Atlantic must cease after July 20. Asbury was noncommittal in the escalating tension, much more aggravated by the "hell" of being surrounded by men "destitute of religion and full of sin and politics." As he left Baltimore he absolved himself: "I hope my skirts were clear of the blood of the people in this little town, whether they reject or accept of an offered salvation" (1:156).

Wesley assumed that his order for Asbury to return to England was being carried out. On May 19, he wrote to Rankin, "I doubt not but Brother Asbury and you will part friends; I shall hope to see him at the conference. He is quite an upright man. I apprehend he will go through his work a little more cheerfully when he is within a little distance from me."[9] Providentially, at the very time Wesley wrote this letter, American Methodism was conferencing at Philadelphia. By the time Rankin received the letter, the conviction that all the British preachers should return to England preempted the singling out of Asbury. Rankin appointed Asbury to Norfolk, Virginia. Asbury was pleased with both the appointment and conference, which ended with "great harmony and sweetness of temper" (1:156).[10]

A Decision of Destiny

Throughout the summer, Asbury kept up a ceaseless round of preaching and visiting the societies, attempting to restore order and discipline, often with little results. He and the people of the Tidewater were at an impasse. The stalemate was verbalized by a Mr. Stevenson, who said to Asbury, "It is my opinion that persons should be allowed to attend society gatherings even if they do not attend class meetings. I think our real problem is you. You are much more bent on exposing the faults of the people than you are on preaching the Gospel. If you could preach more Gospel, things would change for the better around here" (1:161).

On August 7, Asbury received a letter from Thomas Rankin, not with the Wesley request that he return to England, but with a decision that Rankin, Rodda, and Dempster had decided that it would be best for all of them to return to England. Asbury's response was swift and adamant: "I can by no means agree to leave such a field for gathering souls to Christ, as we have in America. It would be an eternal dishonour to the Methodists, that we should all leave 3,000 souls, who desire to commit themselves to our care; neither is it the part of a good shepherd to leave his flock in time of danger: therefore, I am determined, by the grace of God, not to leave them, let the consequence be what it may" (1:161). Two weeks later Asbury again heard from Rankin that Rankin had changed his mind. The change of mind would prove only a delay. At the end of August Asbury got his first taste of a hurricane: "Houses were blown down; docks torn up; bridges carried away; abundance of trees broken and torn up by the roots; and several tracts of land overflowed with water" (1:163). The storm's ferocity was no greater than the turmoil in Asbury's heart.

Rankin was working through his own internal conflict between staying and leaving. Reports were beginning to circulate from the Eastern Shore of Maryland that Methodists "were dragged by Horses over stones and stumps of trees till Death put a period to their suffering."[11] Commitment to the American enterprise was an increasing struggle, especially since Rankin had ministered in England longer than had Asbury, and was much more attached to Wesley than was his junior partner. He wrote: "I cannot, I dare not countenance the measures taken to oppose Great Britain: and yet at the same time, I would do nothing to hurt the inhabitants of America. How difficult to stand in such a situation; and not to be blamed by violent men on both sides?"[12]

Perhaps Rankin's die was cast on Sunday, September 7, 1777, at a dinner party at Perry Hall (Henry Gough's home outside of Baltimore), where a certain John Stirrett of Baltimore was present. Discussion became increasingly heated concerning the war. Stirrett became so enraged that he almost punched Rankin. "He called Rankin a scoundrel Tory and reminded the company that Mr. Wesley had always employed his tongue and pen against America and that all Methodist preachers were tools of the British Government! John Littlejohn thought Stirrett would strike Rankin, who continued to be calm and polite, but Stirrett stormed out of the house."[13]

Methodism's Fragmentation

The heat, rumors of war, and general discouragement of ministry were enough to overwhelm Asbury physically and spiritually. For the entire month of September, he was almost completely incapacitated, not even able to keep his journal. Life seemed to be running headlong toward death and decline. The society at Portsmouth, which had numbered twenty-seven at Asbury's arrival, was now only fourteen, due to Asbury's expulsions. The building prospects of war had thrown Wesley into confusion, because it was now difficult to assess and give direction to the American missionary effort. With the possibilities that the English entourage would depart en masse, Wesley did not single out Asbury. On August 13, he wrote to Rankin, "I am not sorry that Brother Asbury stays with you another year. In that time it will be seen what God will do with North America, and you will easily judge whether our preachers are called to remain any longer therein."[14]

The anxiety of an uncertain future was intensified when Robert Williams died on September 26, 1775. He was American Methodism's first truly imported itinerant preacher, an instrument of revival in Eastern Virginia. He came from England as a Methodist preacher on his own accord in 1769. He sold his horse to pay his debts and stepped on the ship with the entirety of his earthly possessions in his arms: a saddlebag, a loaf of bread, and a bottle of milk. Without fare, he trusted his passage to be paid by whomever God would designate. When Williams attempted to preach while standing on a fallen tree at Perryman, Maryland, an Anglican vestryman offered a gallon of rum to anyone who would pull him down. After being knocked off his perch Williams again mounted his open air pulpit, boosted by the acclaim of his listeners, and finished his message.[15] On September 28, Asbury preached his funeral, stating that "Perhaps no one in America has been an instrument of awakening so many souls, as God has awakened by him" (1:164).

On November 1, Asbury was directly affected by the escalating political stress. A Virginia militiaman stopped and questioned him at a checkpoint in Suffolk, Virginia. "When we had given him an account of ourselves, he treated us with great kindness, and invited us to dine with him, which we did" (1:166). On November 5 he met with George Shadford, who had become his closest confidant. They were of one mind, avoiding politics, at least nationally, and wanting to be completely absorbed in the work of revival that was going on throughout the Virginia countryside. It was refreshing catharsis for Asbury to freely share his struggles and fears with one whom he could trust.

In November 1775, the loyalist governor of Virginia, John Murray Dunmoore, attempted to institute martial law in Virginia by forming a loyalist army. In response, the fourth Virginia convention ordered a nine-hundred-man militia to fortress themselves at Great Bridge, about twelve miles southeast of Norfolk. On December 9, 450 loyalists, including 150 British grenadiers, attacked the patriots' breastworks. The grenadiers had been told that patriot rifles were very unreliable, and thus, without fear, marched six abreast to the beat of two drums. The patriots held their fire until the regulars were within fifty yards. The mayhem was so great that the retreating British screamed out, "For God's sake, do not murder us."[16] One Virginian had been wounded in the finger, while 102 British were killed or fatally wounded.

Asbury's response to the first southern battle of the American Revolution was, "We have awful reports of slaughter at Norfolk and the Great Bridge; but I am at a happy distance from them, and my soul keeps close to Jesus Christ" (1:171). Distance would become increasingly difficult to keep.

Henry Gough

Arriving in Baltimore on March 4, 1776, Asbury found the city in a state of alarm because of an alleged British man-of-war off the coast. He had a lengthy discussion with Martin Rodda, who was at odds with Rankin. Asbury enabled Rodda to reframe his perception to the extent that, upon parting, Rodda "was less agitated." He spent a couple of days at the mansion of Henry Gough, which would become his favorite stopping place for the rest of his life. He prayed for its residents: "May this family evince that all things are possible with God; though their salvation should be attended with as much apparent difficulty as the passage of a camel through the eye of a needle!" (1:180).

Henry Gough's mansion was one of the most majestic homes in all of the colonies, "an imposing two-story red brick Georgian house with one-story balancing wings." On Asbury's first visit that spring, he rode up the long lane surrounded by the spacious greenery of magnificent lawns lined with budding white oak, black walnut, hickory, and locust trees. Possibly not even in England had he seen such a defining roofline with its cupolas. The house's magnificent frontage of more than 150 feet was dignified by four white columns and triple windows at the peak of the gable over the entrance. Imported cattle and sheep filled the nearby pastures. The Methodist itinerant Henry Smith said that "Perry Hall was the largest dwelling house I had ever seen and all its arrangements within and without, were tasteful and elegant, yet simplicity and utility seemed to be stamped upon the whole."[17]

In 1774, Henry Gough had purchased the thousand-acre palatial setting, at that time called the Adventure, from Archibald Buchanan. Gough quickly changed the name to Perry Hall after the residence in Staffordshire County, England, owned by the Goughs for whom Asbury's father had worked (directly related or not is anybody's guess).[18] John Rawlins, who ornamented and plastered the ceiling, was later hired by George Washington to decorate the banquet hall at Mount Vernon. Washington, however, did not go so far as to replicate Gough's bathhouse lined with marble and containing a steam room, pool, and "hot room." Gough was so renowned for his breeding of animals that he later sold livestock to Washington. In 1786, Henry Gough was elected as the first president of the Society for the Encouragement and Improvement of Agriculture in Maryland.[19]

Wesley's Political Perspective

Upon Asbury's arrival in Philadelphia there was a letter waiting for him from John Wesley. The epistle alluded to Wesley's notorious "A Calm Address to Our American Colonies." The "Address" calmed neither the American Methodists nor their enemies. Neither did it calm Asbury, who was "truly sorry that the venerable man ever dipped into the politics of America." Wesley's harangue was little more than a repeat of Samuel Johnson's "Taxation No Tyranny." Johnson had categorized the Americans as a "race of convicts" who ought to be "thankful for anything we allow them short of hanging."[20] Wesley toned down Johnson's diatribe, but not without saying, "When a man voluntarily comes into America, he may lose what he had when in Europe. Perhaps he had a right to vote for a knight or burgess; crossing the sea he did not forfeit this right. But it is plain, he has made the exercise of it no longer possible. He has reduced himself from a voter to one of the innumerable multitudes that have no votes."[21]

Wesley had put his thumb on the issue—self-determination. But forfeiture of that was clearly not an American option. If there had been any chance for the Methodist coterie on American soil to remain intact and unmolested, it now seemed sabotaged. Asbury attempted to place Wesley's political naivete in the best light. "Had he been a subject of America, no doubt but he would have been as zealous an advocate of the American cause. But some inconsiderate persons have taken occasion to censure the Methodists in America, on account of Mr. Wesley's political sentiments" (1:181). Wesley's tract had at least one positive effect: It further led Asbury to cast his sympathies with the American colonists.

Escalating War

During the months of April and May, Asbury preached in and around Philadelphia in both Pennsylvania and New Jersey. Battle reports from the undeclared war were flying about in every town, causing Asbury no little apprehension. He kept a constant schedule of preaching, with solid but less than spectacular results. It was difficult to maintain the evangelistic focus. On May 8, while Asbury was in Philadelphia, there was a report of a naval battle off the coast of Delaware. "At this news," he wrote, "the inhabitants of the city were all in commotion; and the women especially were greatly shocked. Lord, what a world is this!" (1:186). On May 27, Thomas Rankin appointed Asbury to Baltimore.

As war escalated in the North, Methodism's numbers weakened. All revivalistic vitality was now taking place south of the Potomac, especially in the area of Brunswick County, Virginia.[22] By the end of the summer, British General William Howe occupied New York City with over thirty thousand troops. A little more than a year later he took Philadelphia. Both John Street Church in New York and St. George's Church in Philadelphia were used for British barracks. Neither society reported members at the 1778 conference in Leesburg, Virginia. In fact, John Street Church disappeared from the "Minutes" for a total of seven years. Even though the patriot noose was tightening around the Methodist preachers, because they were suspected to be Tories, Asbury's efforts went mostly uncurtailed. On June 13, he recorded, "My feeble frame is much fatigued with preaching twice a day; but it must drag on as long as it can; for it is my meat and drink, yea, it is the life of my soul, to be labouring for the salvation of mankind" (1:189). The five-pound fine which he received for preaching about six miles northeast of Baltimore did not deter him.

Asbury's "Vacation"

On June 26, Asbury was doing some spiritual daydreaming, forgetting that both his horse and chaise needed some guidance. As a result, the carriage toppled over, causing little physical damage, but completely unnerving Asbury. The incident, coupled with exposure to the rain, laid him up for over a week. During this time he made up his mind that when he was sufficiently recovered he would visit the "warm springs" of Morgan County in western Virginia (later West Virginia). No doubt Asbury had heard of Berkeley Springs from Henry Gough, who owned lodging in the vicinity.

The mountainous travel was harsh for an unseasoned horseman like Asbury. "My body complains of so much traveling, for which it is almost incompetent; but the Spirit of the Lord is the support and comfort of my soul. I was thrown out of my chaise the next day, but was providentially kept from being much hurt" (1:192). In Hagerstown, Maryland, on the way to West Virginia, he attempted to penetrate with the gospel the "drinking, swearing, drumming, etc.," but with little result.

West Virginia (not yet a state) may have served as a respite, but not as a vacation. Asbury knew nothing of a holiday that did not include being "instant in season and out of season." "I could not be satisfied till I declared to the people their danger and duty: which I did from Isaiah lv, 6, 7. They all behaved with decency, though it is more than probable that some of them had enough of my preaching" (1:193).

During the days, Asbury soaked in that spring water and read biographies (Halleburton, Walsh, and DeRenty), and in the evening he conducted prayer meetings and preached. As people went in and out of the baths, he preached on the side of a hill. "[P]reaching in the open air, to a people who are almost strangers to a praying spirit, is more disagreeable to my feelings, and a much greater cross than traveling and preaching in a circuit" (1:194). Truly it was an evangelistic "vacation." Asbury attempted to preach loudly enough so that the people in the surrounding houses would hear him, thus injuring his voice (1:193).

During his almost six-week stay he worked himself into a regimen of reading one hundred pages a day, praying in public five times a day, preaching in the open air every other day, and lecturing every evening in prayer meetings. Though he had gone there to recover his health, it was difficult for him to get a good night's rest in a room twenty by sixteen feet, which housed sixteen people "and some noisy children. So I dwell amongst briars and thorns; but my soul is in peace" (1:197). Upon leaving he recorded, "I this day turned my back on the springs, as the best and worst place that I ever was in; good for health, but most injurious to religion" (1:198).

The rest of the year was spent in and around Baltimore, where there were plenty of established preaching points such as Henry Gough's and Fell's Point. Twice he preached funerals for which he refused remuneration. At times there was a "great melting of the people" and at other times spiritual destitution. The general preoccupation with the political tempest irked Asbury. On Sunday, November 24, Asbury's patience was at a low ebb due to frequent interruptions caused by the tardy people. "Why don't you people stay at home if you can't come in a more regular manner?" Asbury's English punctuality was often at odds with the American *laissez faire*. On one occasion the service was scheduled for 8:00 P.M. and did not start until 8:30 because of the lateness of the congregation. Asbury quit at 9:00 P.M., reminding the attendees that they were supposed to have been there at 8:00 P.M.[23]

The Methodist Crossroad

According to John Atkinson, early Methodist historian, Asbury, early on, was optimistic for American success against the British. In July 1776 he penned, "The English ships have been coasting to and fro, watching for some advantages; but what can they expect to accomplish without an army of two or three hundred thousand men? And even then there would be but little prospect of their success."[24]

The actual situation merited far less optimism. In the early months of the revolution, the "continental army" was a ragtag outfit, without uniforms, artillery, or any other field equipment. Shortly after George Washington's election as general (he was in full uniform at the Continental Congress before his election), he ordered spears for the American soldiers and suggested bows and arrows,[25] with the rationale that "[a]n arrow sticking in any part of a man puts him *hors de combat* till 'tis extracted."[26] Gunpowder was almost nonexistent. In December of 1775 Benjamin Franklin recorded, "When I was at the camp before Boston the army had not 5 rounds of Powder a Man. This was kept a secret, even from our People. The world wondered we so seldom fired a cannon. We could not afford it."[27]

Asbury spent the entire year of 1777 in the Baltimore area. Mobility was becoming more restricted, especially for the English-born preachers. It was becoming more obvious that the Methodist mission was the wrong fare at the wrong time at the wrong place. Missionaries were caught in a web not of their own making. The preachers of spiritual reform represented a country that was attempting to strangle freedom. The contradiction was not lost on the English emissaries nor on their American constituents. The conversation between preachers was less about mission than it was retreat. The singular question was no longer whether they were going to leave, but when.

Shadford and Asbury Remain

On April 16, between Annapolis and Baltimore, a bullet passed through Asbury's chaise. Whether he was intentionally targeted, Asbury had no idea. Nevertheless, it was becoming increasingly clear that his job description included hazardous duty. The growing crisis called for a preliminary meeting of the preachers at Perry Hall before the regularly scheduled conference. The preachers attempted to face the reality of their situation. The majority agreed to a certification of "good conduct" for the preachers who wished to return to England. Asbury objected. It was also recommended that a committee be appointed to superintend the preachers who remained in America.

American Methodism had unwittingly taken a step toward self-government. Appointed to the "superintending" committee at the ensuing conference were Daniel Ruff, William Watters, Phillip Gatch, Edward Dromgoole, and William Glendinning. American Methodism had built an administrative bridge to the future in case all of Wesley's missionaries returned to England. And it seemed there was an abundant crop to take their place as nineteen preachers were admitted on trial, including Caleb Pedicord, John Dickens, and Francis Poythress, enormous contributors to American Methodism.

The 1777 conference met at the convergence of Deer Creek and the Susquehanna River in Harford County, Maryland, and there all twenty-five preachers signed a covenant before leaving. It stated that they would devote themselves "to God, taking up our cross daily, steadily aiming at this one thing, to save our souls and them that hear us," and "to preach the old Methodist doctrine as contained in the Minutes."[28] Asbury recorded that "when the time of parting came, many wept as if they had lost their first-born sons. They appeared to be in the deepest distress, thinking, as I suppose, they should not see the faces of the English preachers any more. This was such a parting as I never saw before" (1:239).

On July 21, Asbury heard Rankin preach what was expected by his fellow preachers to be his last sermon in America. The question as to whether Asbury himself should preach his last sermon haunted him. Much of the time he was either depressed or angry. In attempting ministry in a small community in Ann Arundel County, Maryland, he pronounced, "[I]t is a miserable, stupid, careless neighborhood; so I bid it farewell" (1:244). "Shaking the dust off his feet" seemed to be the inclination more often than not. He prayed, "May the Lord direct me how to act, so as to keep myself always in the love of God!" (1:244).

Somehow Asbury managed to maintain a regular schedule of preaching, but not at the torrid pace that would be his future lot. During the week of July 6–12, he preached two times, and from July 27 to August 2 he preached three times, fairly representative weeks for his stay in Annapolis. The constant of Asbury's life was putting time to productive use. On August 1 he recorded, "I have now finished reading sixteen volumes of the Universal History" (1:245).[29]

On September 22, George Shadford informed Asbury that Rankin and Rodda had returned to England. Shadford was wrong. Actually, Rankin had placed himself at the disposal of the British, who were in the process of occupying Philadelphia, and would not return to England until the spring of 1778. Rodda was embarrassing both himself and the whole Methodist enterprise by distributing Tory tracts in the Philadelphia area. By the help of a slave he fled for his life, finding refuge on a British ship in the Chesapeake Bay. Rankin was almost as imprudent. He sealed his fate by declaring from the pulpit of St. George's that

"God would not revive his work in America until they submitted to their rightful sovereign George III."[30] So much for Rankin's prophecy.

Rankin's departure left the Methodist movement somewhat rudderless. There was not total dissolution, but neither were there immediate steps by the "committee" or anyone else to ensure momentum. The first practical implication was that George Shadford was able to define his circuit loosely, so that it included Asbury's assigned territory. The two of them worked together until Shadford's departure.

The next several months were some of Asbury's most enjoyable on the American continent. Shadford had been the chief instrument of revival in the Brunswick circuit, which added eighteen thousand Methodists in one year. Until that time Shadford was Methodism's most effective evangelist. Others like Garrettson and Abbott might have been more spectacular, but they lacked the pastoral skills to nurture the harvest. Asbury said that when Shadford exhorted, "the hearts of the people melted under the power of the word" (1:251). He recorded on October 30, "We have been greatly blessed, and seen great displays of the divine goodness since we have been together. And we have been made a blessing to each other" (1:251).

In the meantime, British General John Burgoyne was getting whipped by the Americans at Saratoga, New York. There were two battles, September 19 and October 7, which led to the October 17 surrender of Burgoyne's 5,700 troops to General Horatio Gates.[31] It took 26 wagons to carry the baggage of Gentleman Johnnie and his senior officers, which included tents, camp beds, blankets, cooking stoves, dinner china, silver and crystal, wines, personal supplies, and uniforms. Burgoyne was apparently more concerned with his immaculate dress for dinner parties than he was with doing battle. One observer described him as very merry, spending the whole night singing and drinking, amusing himself with the wife of a commissary supply officer, who was his mistress. Like him, she was fond of champagne. "Gentleman Johnnie" was America's anti-matter, the exact opposite of the desperate, buckskin-clad militia of Daniel Morgan against whom he fought. Likewise he was Asbury's antithesis, the incarnation of why the British lost the continent, and why the "prophet of the long road" would later conquer it.[32]

One Left

Asbury continued to conduct quarterly meetings, to preach wherever possible, and to meet with classes. When there was no place to preach and no one to visit, he read and prayed. On the whole, he prospered both physically and spiritually. A sense of freedom was mixed with an awareness of political doom such as he had not experienced for some time. On November 9, he jotted down these terse words, "Calm on tumult's wheels I sit" (1:251). Indeed, there was a contentment about him that was totally incongruent with the circumstances. "Commotions and troubles surrounded me without, but the peace of God filled my soul within" (1:250). On December 11 he entered the home of Judge Thomas White near Whitesburg, Kent County, Delaware. There he preached and led a class meeting. If there was any anticipation that this would be a sanctuary from the war for almost a year and a half, he did not record it.

On December 26, 1777, Asbury preached the funeral sermon of a lady and on January 1 the funeral of her daughter. The imminence of death was a specter that pastoral care continuously confronted. The Methodist preachers were burying so many people that they decided at the May conference of 1777 to preach no funerals except for "those we have reason to believe have died in the fear and favor of God." There is no evidence that Asbury ever abided by the ruling. He was intrigued by death, rarely interpreting it as solely a natural event, but rather a means for God to communicate his favor or disfavor. Death was ominous, but normally not as foreboding as this incident recorded in Asbury's journal:

> A person in the form of a man came to the house of another in the night; the man of the house asked what he wanted. He replied, "This will be the bloodiest year that ever was known." The other asked how he knew. His answer was, "It is as true as your wife is now dead in her bed." He went back and found his wife dead. But the stranger disappeared (1:240–241).

During the early months of 1778, Asbury's movements became more circumscribed. His points of reference were increasingly the homes of Thomas White and his nephew, and Edward White, M.D., which were in proximity to each other in Kent County, Delaware. Asbury chaired the quarterly conference in the latter's barn.

It was while recovering from a cold at Thomas White's, on March 9, that the dreaded separation happened. George Shadford, his faithful companion in ministry, bade him goodbye. Shadford had suggested to Asbury that they have a day of fasting and prayer in order to discern God's direction for either staying or leaving for England. At the end of the prayer vigil Shadford discerned a definite leading of the Lord to depart for the homeland. Asbury responded, "One of us must be deluded, because I feel impressed that we should stay." Shadford was unshaken in his resolve to leave:

> One of us is not necessarily deluded. God may want me to leave and you to stay. My work is here done. I cannot stay; it is impressed on my mind that I ought to go home, as strangely as it was at first to come to America.[33]

Shadford may have had doubts that night as he crawled on his hands and knees over a plank replacing a bridge that had been washed out. There was further chagrin a few hours later when he requested British General Smallwood to give him asylum. Smallwood responded, "Now you have done all the hurt you can, you want to go home."[34]

At first, Asbury transcended with a stiff upper lip. "However, I was easy, for the Lord was with me. And if he will be with me, and bring me to my Father's house in peace, he shall be my God forever" (1:263). Four days later, however, he broke down, gripped by the stark loneliness of the moment. "I was under some heaviness of mind. But it was no wonder: three thousand miles from home—my friends have left me—I am considered by some as an enemy of the country—every day liable to be seized by violence, and abused" (1:263–264).

Anyone unsympathetic to the Methodist cause considered the one remaining Methodist import a political risk. There were plenty of reasons why Asbury would be considered a political threat to the patriotic cause. It was enough that he was an immigrant Englishman and that his associate Rodda supported "mad" King George. Aggravating the situation was the fact that Wesley had extended his political nose three thousand miles. Also, there was the crazed apostate Methodist Chauncey Clowe, who, after forming a company of Royalists, sought to fight his way through Patriot militia in order to join forces with the British. Clowe was captured, tried, and executed. Maryland required an oath of loyalty that swore off all allegiance to Great Britain and bound the adjurer to "make known to the government or someone of the judges or justices thereof, all treasons, or traitors, conspiracies, attempts or combinations against the state or the government thereof which may come to my knowledge. So help me God."[35] To make such a vow was out of the question for a Christian Englishman.

Thomas White

Asbury therefore retreated to Delaware, from which he did not depart for the next eighteen months. On March 7, 1778, a rumor of militia in the area of Thomas White's home caused Asbury to take extra precaution. He lay in a swamp until darkness fell, and for the next two weeks he stayed in the home of an unidentified friend. The next step was truly perplexing. "I know not what to determine—whether to deliver myself into the hands of men, to embrace the first opportunity to depart, or to wait till Providence shall further direct" (1:267). He turned to a regimen of spiritual disciplines: fasting, praying, and Scripture reading, with particular attention to Wesley's *Notes on the New Testament*, Philip Doddridge's *Rise and Progress*, and John Bunyan's *Holy War*. He also changed his prayer methodology. "I purposed in my own mind, to spend ten minutes out of every hour, when awake, in the duty of prayer" (1:268). There would certainly be sufficient time.

In early spring of 1778 Asbury made his way to Judge Thomas White's, where he would be a guest for the next year and a half. White's house was isolated, obscured by trees in the flat country of Kent County, Delaware, on the Maryland border. The White acreage included out-dwellings in which Asbury could find solitude away from the family activity. Furthermore, Delaware did not require clergy to take an oath of loyalty to the state. However, despite these practical reasons and the fact that White was a Methodist, Asbury could hardly have jeopardized his hiding strategy more. Thomas White was a Tory, highly sympathetic to the British cause. In fact, he had been appointed by the state to the Continental Congress as one of the three conservatives, as required by the state's new constitution. Hardly anyone in the state of Delaware was more suspect than was Thomas White. The Whigs well remembered the Tory insurrection in which White had participated in 1776.[36]

Ironically, the time period in which Asbury hid out at Judge White's was a season of stalemate in the war. No major battles were fought from June 1778 to May 1780. General Howe had ensconced himself in Philadelphia, the most English of all American cities, finding plenty of Tory sympathizers to make himself at home. Since many patriots had fled the city, there was a shortage of manpower to service the ten thousand British troops. The soldiers drank, danced, gambled, and cavorted with the women while the garbage piled high in the streets. If the stench were not enough, the soldiers, housed at the State House, where the Declaration of Independence was signed, relieved themselves whenever the impulse beckoned. The barracks commander issued a general order "[t]o put a stop to such scandalous behavior and to confine any man who shall presume to make use of any other place whatever than the Privy for his Necessary Occasions."[37]

General Howe departed Philadelphia by throwing a lavish party, in which four hundred thirty people were entertained at a sit-down dinner.[38] The occasion was complete with gambling, dancing, jousting, fireworks, and a gun salute from the British warships, all at the cost of three hundred pounds. Howe packed up and left for England six days later. Asbury knew nothing of the wanton wastefulness of his countryman. Had he been informed, he would have had far less reason to worry about the future of the American Methodist enterprise. While Howe's guests were consuming twelve hundred dishes of lamb, beef, veal, pies, and puddings, Asbury penned on May 18, 1778, "My spirit was oppressed by heavy temptations" (1:272). The end of the British oppression had already begun.

On April 2 a knock rattled the front door of the Thomas White house, followed by a command: "Open up!" Delaware militia hauled the judge to Dover and there imprisoned him. They apparently did not suspect that the family was harboring the fugitive Asbury. The authorities did know that White had been friendly to Methodists, who were all under a cloud of suspicion.

Four days later, after much fasting and prayer and again preaching at Edward White's barn with "great solemnity," Asbury took to the open fields. "I then rode on through a lonesome, devious road, like Abraham, not knowing whither I went: but weary and unwell, I found a shelter late at night; and there I intended to rest till Providence should direct my way" (1:265). For most of the month of April 1778, Asbury was on the lam, not indicating his where-abouts via journal entries. On April 29 he recorded, "Ventured to leave my asylum; and under the special providence of God, came safe to my old abode (Judge White's); where I purpose spending these perilous days in retirement, devotion, and study" (1:269).

Forgotten

Asbury's spiritual disciplines did not prevent a deep depression, perhaps the most severe of his life. The trough of despair was overwhelming: "[M]y temptations were so violent, that it seemed as if all the infernal powers were combined to attack my soul" (1:269). On May 13 he preached to a "small congregation" for the first time in six weeks. At the very time that Asbury was preaching, the annual conference was being held at Leesburg, Virginia, but Asbury made no reference to the fact. If the conference made any mention of Asbury it was not recorded (perhaps intentionally). His name did not appear in the list of appointments. William Watters was listed as the first assistant, and he apparently chaired the gathering.[39] Asbury either was recognized as incognito or was simply forgotten. At any rate he was a man without official ecclesiastical identity or sanction, that is, without an appointment.

On May 30, 1778, Asbury made a twenty-mile trip south, but he found himself so unaccustomed to riding horseback and so weak of body that he actually wondered if he was going to make it. The sizable crowd that gathered to hear him brought a measure of encouragement. Upon retiring to the Whites', he was indisposed for the week with fever and boils. (He had been reading the Book of Job.) Though emaciated of body and depressed, he preached each Sunday during the month of June either in the "barn" or at a neighboring house. It no doubt did more for him than it did for the listeners. Garrettson, who had been appointed to the Kent circuit, came to see him on June 30, but Asbury did not record the gist of the conversation.

During July Asbury preached twelve times, once to "about two hundred people who appeared to be kind and willing to receive instruction; and I was enabled to fix their attention, though they were ignorant and wild" (1:276). There was a similar schedule in August, with visible results. "I enforced Acts xiii, 40, 41, at Robert Layton's, where many people were affected, and about twelve were taken as probationers into the society" (1:279). During the last several days of the month and the first half of September, Asbury was extremely ill, to the point of delirium. By the fifteenth he was mentally and physically spent. "My usefulness appeared to be cut off; I saw myself pent up in a corner; my body in a manner worn out; my English brethren gone, so that I had no one to consult; and every surrounding object and circumstance wore a gloomy aspect" (1:280). Even the continued solicitous hospitality of the Whites bothered the distressed preacher. The predicament was not lost on White's slaves. "Massa goes to the woods to feed his swamp robins."[40]

G. Hallman noted that Judge White's farm was "an ideal place to hide off the beaten track, a comfortable brick house, a heavy forest to slip into, in case of need, and a warm hearted, high minded, socially prominent family to assist. In addition, it was close to the state line."[41] Thomas and Dr. Edward White, the nephew, lived about a mile apart and often walked to one another's houses for family prayer. Thomas's wife, Mary, had been converted after walking to church because her husband refused to take her. It was Mary White who introduced Asbury to Richard Bassett, who later became governor of Maryland. In 1773 Thomas White was elected a member of the Maryland State Legislature from Dorchester County, as he owned considerable land there. Before his death in 1795, Thomas White stated in his will,

> And whereas I think it wrong and offensive and not doing as I would be willing to be done by to keep Negroes in bondage or perpetual slavery, I thereby manumit and set free those that are or have been in bondage to me.

White was a man ahead of his time. A slave to White named Leanna was later to recall that Thomas White "hid Asbury in an out-house, and used to carry his victuals to him; that the bishop used to come to the house late at night and hold prayers with the White family upstairs, in a low tone of voice."[42]

For the rest of the calendar year Asbury maintained a regular schedule of preaching, interspersed by whole weeks when he did little stirring about, occupying himself with reading a hundred pages a day, Bible study, and prayer. He again changed his prayer schedule to seven times a day. At some juncture in the fall, he received appointment to Kent, Delaware, twenty miles away. We are not told who made the assignment. He intended to keep his preaching responsibility on the last Sunday of the year, but was prevented by snow. His journal ended the year on a low note. "But alas! how is my soul abased. It is my deliberate opinion, that I do the least good in the Church of Christ, of any that I know, and believe to be divinely moved to preach the Gospel. How am I displeased with myself! Lord, in mercy help, or I am undone indeed!" (1:287).

Asbury's journal demonstrates that he was far busier in ministry during his hiatus than people knew. Some would question the clandestine manner in which he went about his ministerial labors. *Real* prophets boldly publish their message in the face of the sun, without fear nor favor of man. Instead, Asbury was slinking through the back roads of the eastern seaboard, mostly rural countryside, hoping that no one would see him. His co-workers had continued to publicly proclaim the Gospel, often facing dire consequences. Garrettson had filled an appointment for Asbury on September 5 by preaching to from five hundred to a thousand people, many coming out of curiosity. Later, Garrettson was imprisoned at the Dorchester County jail in Cambridge, Maryland, where he had "a dirty floor for my bed, my saddlebags for my pillow, and two large windows open with a cold east wind blowing upon me."[43] Phillip Gatch was tarred, having an eye permanently injured; Joseph Hartley was imprisoned, courageously preaching from his cell; and Caleb Pedicord was beaten until the blood ran down his face. Thomas Chew was condemned to spend three weeks at Squire Henry Downs's home, where he converted the whole family. And Asbury had not a hand laid on him.[44]

During the first part of December, Asbury talked himself into fulfilling his appointment responsibilities in the Sommerset and Broadcreek area in spite of ominous fears. "(N)otwithstanding all the foreboding apprehensions of my mind, no person offered me the smallest insult" (1:285). The possibilities that his inhibitions were groundless were a blow to his spiritual ego. The wound would leave him with a spiritual limp for the rest of his life. Just possibly, it was the turning point that would direct him over the next five years to American Methodism's most exalted position.

4. "The Spirit of Separation"

A Fully Converted American

Asbury began 1779 with deep forebodings, as well as an attempt to reconcile his conscience to the partial seclusion of the past year. "Upon mature reflection I do not repent my late voluntary retirement in the state of Delaware" (1:292). Once out of retirement, he began a vigorous round of preaching, family visitation, and meeting with classes. Due to inclement weather and the confined area of his labors (Kent Circuit), he had opportunity to do extensive reading: Humphrey Prideaux's *Connections of the Old and New Testaments in the History of the Jews*, James Hervey's *Dialogues*, and Wesley's *Sermons*. Out of all the books imported into America, a large percentage were both British and theological. In all likelihood, the silver lining at Judge White's house was a well-stocked library.

During the month of January, reports trickled up from the South regarding the British taking Savannah and Augusta. Because of high anxiety for both himself and the mission he represented, Asbury experienced conversion of national loyalty. In an intercessory moment he exclaimed, "O my God! I am thine; and all the faithful are thine. Mercifully interpose for the deliverance of our land, and for the eternal salvation of all who put their trust in Thee" (1:294).

Sometime before that, we do not know when, Asbury had written a letter to Thomas Rankin declaring his intention to stay in America. The essence of his declaration was that he was "so strongly knit in affection to many of the Americans that he could not tear himself away from them: that he knew the Americans; and was well satisfied they would not rest until they had achieved their independence." Thomas Ware claimed that the letter fell into the hands of American officers, and its confiscation changed their attitude toward Asbury.[1]

During the early part of April, Asbury took a definitive step toward becoming the bureaucratic leader of American Methodism. He called for a conference of "Northern" preachers to meet at Judge White's house for the purpose of "stationing." The 1778 conference, which had met at Leesburg, Virginia, and at which Asbury was not present, had designated the 1779 conference to meet at the Broken Back Church, Flauvanna County, Virginia, the second Tuesday in May. Asbury was still not politically comfortable enough to stray that far outside of Delaware.

The Search for Leadership

But there was a far more critical problem. With all English missionaries having returned to England, save one who was in hiding, the Southern preachers were distancing themselves from Wesley. It was a foregone conclusion that at the Flauvanna Conference they would authorize themselves to administer the sacraments. There they would assume an ecclesiastical identity unlike the societies that were under Wesley's sponsorship.

Because of the revivalistic impulse in Virginia, Methodism's sphere of operation had largely shifted to the South, where most of the preachers now ministered. Asbury was removed both politically and geographically. Out of the five commissioners in which leadership had now been vested, only Daniel Ruff lived north of the Potomac River. The Northern Conference stationed seventeen preachers, compared with the thirty-two in the Southern Conference. British occupation of New York and Philadelphia during the war greatly curtailed Methodist operation in the North.

The irregularly called gathering at Kent took the initiative to name Asbury as Wesley's general assistant. How they could assume that the move would be *ipso facto* accepted by the majority of the whole, including both North and South, is difficult to understand. How Asbury accepted it, considering his misgivings about his own performance, is a psychological conundrum. The only explanation that rings plausible is the conviction that by resisting sacramental authority the Northern preachers were the true Wesleyan remnant, and the remnant needed a leader. But why wasn't the leader chosen from the two of the "committee" that were present at Judge White's, Daniel Ruff and William Watters?

The overriding fact for Methodism north of the Potomac was that not all of the preachers whom Wesley had appointed to America had returned to England. One remained, and that one was willing to risk rejection in order to pursue his definition of the Methodist enterprise within the colonies. The *Minutes* of the conference gave the following reasons for Asbury's election as the general assistant: "First, on account of his age; second, because of being originally appointed by Mr. Wesley; third, being joined with Messrs. Rankin and Shadford, by express order from Mr. Wesley."[2] One thing was certain: the young sect was ripe for schism. Asbury sought conciliation via an epistle sent by William Watters: "I wrote to John Dickens, Philip Gatch, Edward Dromgoole, and William Glendinning, urging them if possible to prevent a separation among the preachers in the south—that is Virginia and North Carolina" (1:300).

The Sacramental Schism

Whether the Southern preachers who met at Roger Thompson's in Flauvanna County, Virginia, on May 18 ever received Asbury's epistle or made any mention of it, we do not know. The "Minutes" read, "Because the Episcopal Establishment is now dissolved and therefore in almost all our circuits the members are without the ordinances, We believe it to be our duty."[3] A majority of the preachers, eighteen, approved. Next a new committee was elected. The four committee members who did not favor assuming responsibility for the ordinances were voted off. Those who voted with the majority, James Foster, Leroy Cole, Ruben Ellis, and Philip Gatch, replaced the dissenters. The committee was then designated by the whole as a "presbytery," "to administer the ordinances themselves," and "to authorize any other preacher or preachers approved of by them, by the form of laying on of hands and of prayer."[4] The gauntlet had been thrown.

The news reached Asbury on June 30. "I received the minutes of the Virginia conference by which I learned the preachers have been affecting a lame separation from the Episcopal Church, that will last about one year. I pity them; Satan has a desire to have us that he may sift us like wheat" (1:304). Asbury was non-empathetic, and little did he understand the anguish with which the Southern preachers made their decision. Nelson Reed recorded, "[W]e went into Conference & endeavored to go on with business as usual but could not for their [sic] was a division in opinions about the ordinances so inquiry was made amongst all concerning the matter and there was a great majority for it. O what a soul rendering time it was hearts did Tremble many tears was shed and many prayers made to God my very soul was made to Tremble so we spent the first day and little was done."[5]

About July 15, Asbury began to travel about without a sense of inhibition. A visit to the Delaware coast proved invigorating. At the quarterly conference, held out of doors to accommodate the crowd, there was an portentous clearing of the rain and clouds. The sun broke through on the arbor that provided sanctuary for three to four hundred people. Asbury marveled at the preaching of Freeborn Garrettson. Prospects for a fresh beginning were encouraging. "We have had much of God in this meeting" (1:309).

On August 8, Asbury preached just south of Milford, Delaware, to about three hundred people. "I had uncommon light; I never spoke there with such liberty in my life." (1:309). August proved to be a month of returning to a full schedule of proclamation. During the week of August 15, Asbury preached six times. In the meantime, he continued to write to the Southern leadership in order to divert their course. He took comfort that renewed ecclesiastical duties were pressing him physically and spiritually. It was affirming to be needed, and to be needed required discipline.

> This morning I ended the reading of my Bible through in about four months. It is hard work for me to find time for this; but all I read and write I owe to early rising. If I were not to rise always by five, and sometimes at four o'clock, I should have no time only to eat my breakfast, pray in the family, and get ready for my journey —as I must travel everyday (1:311).

On September 14, Asbury visited Joseph Hartley in jail at Easton, Maryland. During his three-month imprisonment Hartley preached through the windows and was released because his persecutors feared that he would convert the whole town.[6] Hartley's perseverance and boldness challenged Asbury, causing him no small twinges of guilt. Two days later he recorded, "I am unwell and much dejected and lament the want of more grace" (1:313).

Asbury was finding greater affinity with his Anglican brethren, who were being marginalized by the war. He continued to receive the sacraments at their hands, and they reciprocated by attending Methodist meetings. Disenfranchisement loves company! Asbury's note on November 13 revealed further reason why he had alienated himself from the Southern leadership.

> I received a letter from Mr. Jarrett, who is greatly alarmed, but it is too late; he should have begun his opposition before. Our zealous dissenting brethren are for turning all out of the society who will not submit to their administration. I find the spirit of separation growing among them, I fear that it will generate malevolence and evil speaking; after all my labor, to unite the Protestant Episcopal Ministry to us, they say, "We don't want your unconverted ministers: the people will not receive them." I expect to turn out shortly among them, and fear a separation will be unavoidable; I am determined, if we cannot save all, to save a part; but for the divisions of Ruben there will be great heart searching! (1:322).

Asbury's choice to accept the sacraments from an "unconverted" minister rather than an unordained Methodist was thoroughly Wesleyan, in that the *opus operato* depended on the faith of the recipient rather than the integrity of the celebrant. No church was so apostate that it could invalidate the faith of its individual participants. Perhaps the answer was to join forces with the newly forming Protestant Episcopal Church. The musing was serious enough that Asbury conferred with his close friend, Samuel MaGaw, the Anglican Rector of Dover, about jointly erecting a "Kingswood" school in America (1:390, 468).

On the whole 1779 represented a renewed spiritual quest. Asbury longed after holiness, a pursuit marked by the ebb and tide of faith. On June 16 he recorded, "My mind enjoys great peace and sweetness in God, and I find myself much given up to Him: 'tis very seldom I feel a thought, much less a desire, contrary to His holiness" (1:303). On August 12 he renewed his covenant with God, desiring that every act and word be characterized by love. He intensely sought God for "full Christian perfection." There were plenty of opportunities to fall short. He castigated himself for lying in bed till 6 A.M. "I have not spent this day as I ought: perhaps not one in my whole life" (1:316). In spite of personal failings and Methodism's fragile state, he continued to aspire spiritually, both for himself and the movement, which was on the brink of fragmentation. The impending crisis seemed only to sharpen his vision. "I tremble to think of the cloud of the divine presence departing from us; If this should be I hope not to live to see it: and with Mr. Wesley desire that God may rather scatter the people to the ends of the earth: I rather they should not be than to be a dead society" (1:324).

The Ongoing War

The winter of 1779–80 was exceedingly cold, causing George Washington to endure even more hardship outside of Morristown, New Jersey, than he did at Valley Forge. On January 5, 1780, Washington wrote to the Continental Congress,

Many of the (men) have been four or five days without meat entirely and short of bread, and none but on very scanty supplies. Some for their preservation have been compelled to maraude and rob from the inhabitants. And I have it not in my power to punish or to repress the practice. If our condition should not undergo a very speedy and considerable change for the better, it will be difficult to point out all the consequences, that may ensue.[7]

January 1780 was a tough month for Asbury. Staying in crowded, cramped houses and preaching in unheated, unventilated churches, it was hard to concentrate, read, pray, or do anything. Asbury for the most part traveled in a carriage, not always with the best results. The topography on the Delmarva Peninsula was flat enough for the novice to negotiate, but there were plenty of woods and lowlands with which to contend. On February 4, he recorded,

I had today a providential escape: my horse started, turned round in the woods, hardly escaped running me on the trees; which if he had would have overset me, and might have broken the carriage and my limbs the ground being so hard, but thanks be to God I received no hurt (1:334).

Preaching for the first couple of months was irregular, and Asbury was experiencing the winter blahs. Again he attempted to adjust his spiritual diet; "I must spend whole nights in prayer" (1:335).

Richard Bassett

During the winter of 1778, Asbury had met Richard Bassett at Thomas White's house. Upon discovering that there were Methodist preachers in the house, Bassett announced his intention to leave. White's wife implored him to stay for dinner, at which time he entered into conversation with Asbury. After Bassett discerned that his new acquaintance was not a madman, he halfheartedly invited Asbury to stop in to see him when in Dover. Asbury took him up on it. Not wishing to be isolated with a Methodist preacher, Bassett invited the local Anglican pastor, Samuel MaGaw, and the state's governor to join them for dinner.

On September 12, 1779, Asbury stood in Bassett's yard and preached to persons who were walking to church. It was about that time that Thomas White stayed at the home of Richard Bassett. When patriots tried to drag White from the house, Bassett stood at the door armed with sword and pistol announcing to the intruders, "Over my dead body."[8] On February 27, 1780, after preaching in Dover, Asbury went home with Bassett: "A very conversant and affectionate man, who, from his own acknowledgements, appears to be sick of sin. His wife is under great distress; a gloom of dejection sits upon her soul; she prayeth much, and the enemy takes an advantage of her low state" (1:338).

Both Bassetts became ardent Methodists, opening their homes to preachers, especially Asbury, for the rest of their lives. Asbury enjoyed Bassett's estate at Bohemia Manor, Maryland.[9] Bassett, who died in 1815, served as a U.S. senator and governor of Maryland, and was a delegate to the Constitutional Congress. He did not, as Asbury predicted, become a preacher.[10]

Asbury continued to preach mainly on the Kent Circuit, not leaving Delaware for better than three months at a time. It was close quarters and he was experiencing "cabin fever." He longed to venture out to a wider domain of ministry. On March 30 he got lost in a swamp and feared he would have to spend the night there. But he miraculously wandered out. Rumors continued to fly concerning the ever-widening rift over the sacraments. Perhaps a change in the weather, for which Asbury prayed, would help. "An appearance of good weather: Blessed be God! Though when the weather was so uncomfortable, I was tempted to murmur" (1:333). All the while he pondered what to say at the Northern Conference scheduled for Baltimore on April 24. He hoped at that time to present some conditions for a partial reconciliation.

The Showdown Over the Sacraments

At first there was no evidence of a willingness to compromise. The Baltimore preachers decided to send an ultimatum to the Virginia Methodists that they were to desist from the practice of ordination and not "administer the ordinances where there is a decent Episcopal minister" (1:347). After some debate, they realized their directive sounded too harsh and so they softened the communication, requesting that the Southerners suspend the ordinances for one year.[11] Philip Gatch and Reuben Ellis, delegates from Virginia at the Northern Conference, agreed to deliver the notice. Both of them later reported that they were treated coldly by everyone except William Watters.

In turn, Asbury, Freeborn Garrettson, and William Watters were appointed as delegates to the conference at Manakintown, Powhatten County, Virginia, May 9. Watters joined them, since he was the only one who had attended both Northern and Southern conferences and seemed to have the best interests of both parties at heart. As Asbury made his way south, he pondered his predicament. There was plenty of reason for anxiety; Zion was about to split in two. "Lord give me wisdom," he prayed.

It was a great opportunity to get to know the flaming zealot who accompanied him. "Brother Garrettson will let no person escape a religious lecture who comes his way" (1:348). Along the way, they stopped at George Arnold's, at whose house Asbury would die thirty-five years later. Arnold had already made up his mind on the ordinances, much to Asbury's annoyance. On April 8, Asbury got his first taste of preaching in a tavern, a preaching stop that would be an oft-repeated event in his life. The next day, Monday, the three arrived by ferry at Manakintown, a French Huguenot settlement on the James River.

For the rest of the day, Asbury and Garrettson tried to take the political pulse of their Southern brothers. Asbury conversed with John Dickens, a man whom he would later grow to love and esteem, and found him strongly opposed to further dependence on the Episcopal Church. "Brother Watters and Garrettson tried their men and found them inflexible" (1:349).

After the conference officially convened, the Northern delegation was invited to present its case. Asbury was the spokesman. "I read Mr. Wesley's thoughts against a separation. Showed my private letter of instruction from Mr. Wesley; set before them the sentiments of the Delaware and Baltimore conferences; read our epistles, and read my letter to Brother Gatch and Dickens' letter in answer" (1:349).

The assembly responded by saying they would cease serving the sacraments if Asbury would supply men who were sufficiently qualified to serve them. Their request was out of the question, especially since so many Anglican clergymen had been displaced. During the preaching time, Asbury spoke from Ruth 2:4, stressing the mutual blessing between Boaz and his relatives. Such mutuality was not to be found on the issue which divided him and his auditors. After the sermon there was some milling about, and at the reconvening of the assembly an official response had been formulated. The Southern circuits would not stop from ordaining their own ministers, who would thus be authorized to serve the sacraments.

It was the lowest moment yet in American Methodism's existence. Asbury felt the full impact of the rejection:

> I thus prepared to leave the house to go to a near neighbors to lodge, under the heaviest cloud I ever felt in America: O! What I felt!—Nor I alone!—But the agents of both sides! They wept like children, but kept their opinions (1:350).

William Watters assessed the cleavage: "We had a great deal of loving conversation, with many tears, but I saw no bitterness, no shyness, no judging each other. We wept, and prayed, and sobbed, but neither would agree to the others terms."[12]

The North and South Reach a Compromise

Garrettson and Watters began a prayer vigil above the conference room. Asbury himself must have prayed and agonized a good deal during a sleepless night. When he returned to bid farewell the next morning, he discovered there had been a change of mind. It was the consensus that the preachers of American Methodism should cease to serve the sacraments until they could find further direction from their English father, John Wesley. The breach had been closed at least for the time being. It was music to Asbury's ears. "Surely the hand of God has been seen in all this; there might have been twenty promising preachers and three thousand people seriously affected by this separation, but the Lord would not suffer this" (1:350).

William Watters filled the final preaching slot, taking as his text, "Come thou with us and we will do thee good," followed by a love feast characterized by uninhibited emotion.

For at least once, Asbury had understated the case. The conference averted becoming two schismatic groups, which would have wandered off into oblivion. American Methodism was still too young to chart its own course, needing the incubation that English Methodism would provide over the next half-decade. They had preserved unity by choosing a greater good over a lesser good. But, ironically, they made a decision that both maintained allegiance to British Methodism and set American Methodism on its own course. "[T]here should be a suspension of the ordinances for the present year, and . . . our circumstance should be laid before Mr. Wesley and his advice solicited; also . . . Mr. Asbury should be requested to ride through the different circuits and superintend the work at large."[13] For all practical intents and purposes, Asbury was now the leader of American Methodism.

Asbury more than any other person had been the instrument of reconciliation. The result was not lost on the witnesses. Asbury was not naive, as he never was concerning his role. Heading north, he mentally replayed the preceding events.

> There seems to be some call for me in every part of the work: I have traveled it this time from north to south to keep peace and union: and O! if a rent and separation had taken place, what work, what hurt to thousands of souls! It is now stopped, and if it had not, it might have been my fault; it may have been my fault that it took place (1:351).

There was still a good deal of commotion caused by the war and fear of political intrusion. At one point American soldiers joined Asbury's service but caused no disturbance. On May 12, British General Henry Clinton had taken Charleston by capturing a 5,400-man garrison. It was America's worst defeat of the Revolutionary War. American troops were sent southward for reinforcement.[14]

Introduction to Ministry in the South

On May 16, Asbury encountered the Anglican revivalist Devereux Jarratt, whom he had not seen in over four years. Upon hearing Jarratt preach, Asbury commented that "[h]e was rather shackled with his notes" (1:351). Jarratt was not so immediate with assessment of his visitor. On August 2, he penned, "Mr. Asbury is certainly the most indefatigable man in his travels and varieties of labours, of any I am acquainted with; and though his strong passion for superiority and thrust for domination may contribute not a little to this, yet I hope, he is chiefly influenced by more laudable motives."[15]

The passage into North Carolina was accompanied by a good deal of physical pain. Asbury remedied his toothache, among other maladies, by placing tobacco upon it. He had earlier quit tobacco, but in what form he previously used it, it is not clear.[16] Near Halifax, North Carolina, he became acquainted with John Dickens, a man given to Greek and Latin, as well as to piety. Asbury referred to Dickens as a "gloomy countryman of mine, and very diffident of himself" (1:358). The two discussed plans for a Kingswood school in America that would later be established on the Halifax and Edgecomb County lines. (Established sometime before 1793, it would actually be called "Cokesbury".)[17]

On the whole, Asbury had a favorable opinion of North Carolina, finding a better place than he had assumed. The summer was his first introduction to plantation slavery, a much different situation than the domestic servitude of the north. When he let his opinions be known, he did not find receptive ears. "[T]his I know, God will plead the cause of the oppressed though it gives offense to say so here. O Lord, banish the infernal spirit of slavery from thy dear Zion" (1:355).

Making his way toward Louisburg, North Carolina, the ever improving horseman became lost. Having to ford streams and swamps while battling the oppressively hot, humid air was overwhelming. In an attempt to make it to Major Green Hill's for a preaching appointment, he discovered that he had "ridden about thirty miles out of his way" and was now "twenty six miles from the place of preaching tomorrow. Having been happy till today, but when lost I began to feel like fretting against persons and things" (1:364). At Cyprus Chapel in Franklin County, he met James O'Kelly for the first time, a man who would be imbedded in Asbury's psyche for the rest of his days. In the meantime, he would simply contend with the heat, chiggers, ticks, and whatever else a Southern summer in the lowlands could throw at him.

As Asbury journeyed through thickets and thickly treed terrain, making his own trail, he encountered persons and conditions he had not faced before. His tattered, dirty congregations, who lived in pole cabins, were more possessed by alcohol and guns than they were by religion. His poor and crude audiences challenged his perceptions of both grace and anthropology.

> [I] dwell as among briars, thorns, and scorpions: the people are poor, and cruel one to another: some families are ready to starve for want of bread, while others have corn and rye distilled into poisonous whiskey; and a Baptist preacher has been guilty of the same; but it is no wonder that those who have no compassion for the non-elect souls of people should have none for their bodies (1:369).

On the whole it was a "vile" society, a "hardened" people, adapted to robbing, stealing, and murdering. Conversions were few and far between, if not nonexistent. In Caswell County, North Carolina, the amenities of a dirt floor and a damp bed, accompanied by heat and a headache, awaited Asbury. "I knew not how to lie down, Edward Bailey [his traveling partner] lay down and slept well" (1:372).

Asbury's impressions were similar to those of the Episcopal priest Charles Woodmason, who ministered as an itinerant in the "back country" of South Carolina. The following is Woodmason's impression of the people at Flatt Creek:

> Here I found a vast body of people assembled–Such a medley! Such a mixed multitude of all classes and complexions I never saw. I baptized about 20 children and married 4 couples–most of these People had never before seen a minister or heard the Lord's prayer, service or sermon in these Days. I was a great curiosity to them—and they were as Great Oddities to me. After service they went to Reveling, Drinking, Singing, Dancing and Whoring and most of the company were drunk before I quitted the spot.[18]

Maturity through Hardship

Asbury headed north again through Virginia, beginning to sense that he was becoming a man fit for the place and time. He had now been in America almost nine years. Matured by sickness, conflict, rejection, and defeat, he thought to himself, "I have a better constitution, and more gifts, and I think much more grace. I can bear disappointments and contradiction with greater ease" (1:376). He sensed that he was in control of himself, possessing a spirit that was content in whatever circumstances. He continued to gain perspective on the American cause, bearing with patience the diatribes against his own nationality. He was also learning dependence upon Providence, a critical necessity for the vagabond life. Some friends in Virginia replaced Asbury's tattered suit with a new outfit made of "Virginia cloth."

It was during the summer and fall of 1780 that he was introduced to the great outdoors, "exposure hotel." On and off, this would be his accommodations for the next thirty-five years. Sleeping on the ground he became ill, and his traveling companion, Edward Bailey, became even sicker. Asbury left him under the care of a Dr. Hopkins, in the area of Lynchburg, but nine days later received news of his death. The loss was a precursor of future years of illness and crude medical attention, the double curse of late eighteenth-century living. "The doctors supposed a mortification took place in his bowels, inflamed by the corrosive nature of the bile. It was a sorrowful quarterly meeting for me, few people; they lifeless, and my dear friend dead" (1:384). The mission carried a huge price tag.

Asbury spent November through January of 1781 in what had become his home state, Delaware. He conducted quarterly meeting on November 13 at Barrett's Chapel, a preaching house forty-two by forty-eight feet, recently built by Philip Barrett. Asbury stated that one to two thousand were present, "[c]rowded above and below," with many not being able to get in. When one of the locals was told the purpose of the building, which was then under construction, he responded, "It is unnecessary to build such a house, for by the time the war is over a corn crib will hold them all."[19] Asbury stationed the preachers without incident except for a disagreement with Freeborn Garrettson, who did not want to return to Baltimore. Garrettson referred to the conference as a "time of distress."[20]

In December, winter rapidly descended on Delaware, resulting in a throat ailment that troubled Asbury. By the end of the first week he was depressed. His voice, the primary instrument of his profession, was greatly impaired. By the end of the month he was desperate enough to receive two blisters, one on his neck and the other behind his ear, to have blood drawn from his arm and tongue, all accompanied by a laxative. Miraculously, in spite of his medical attention, he recovered from the "putrid sore throat." The month was not a total loss; he met Thomas Haskins, who in that year had been converted from the study of law under the preaching of Freeborn Garrettson. Haskins would later become a local preacher and merchant in Philadelphia, leader at St. George's, a teacher at Cokesbury, and a founding member of the Academy Church.

There was news from the South that harmony continued among the churches, and a growing contentment with the decision that had been made at Manakintown. In the midst of war, peace was triumphing. If there had been any doubt that America would be Asbury's continuing venue, it had been dispelled over the last several months, at least in his own mind. On September 3, 1779, he had written to John Wesley,

> [I]t appears more and more plain to me that I ought to continue in the station of a preacher because God called me to and blessed me in this way, and not move one step forward or backward . . . be assured, the people of God in America are dear to me . . . the very affection and sufficiency I have had among them endear them to me, strange as it may appear, and bind me to the continent (3: 25–26).

Sometime during the month of January 1781, Asbury obtained a horse that had been used for racing. Its familiar racetrack was somewhere in the vicinity of Canterbury, Kent County, Delaware. One day, as Asbury passed by the track, the horse bolted and the preacher had the ride of his life.

During the first part of March, Asbury ventured into Pennsylvania where he had not been in almost four years. Three weeks later he traveled to Philadelphia, which was no longer occupied by the British. He then returned to Delaware, estimating that over the past ten months he had traveled nearly four thousand miles. He was becoming an itinerant preacher.

In April of 1781 a conference was held in Baltimore with several preachers from the South in attendance. There was continued agreement to abide by the no-ordinance decision that had been made in Manakintown. However, Robert Strawbridge continued to be insubordinate. Afterward, Asbury set out toward Virginia with a black man, Harry Hosier, as his traveling companion. Hearing a black man preach was a new experience for Southerners, and black Harry was a curiosity. Hosier was described as "a short and intensely black Negro, whose eyes were of unusual brilliance." Asbury was convinced that one of the best ways to draw a crowd was to announce that "Black Harry" was scheduled to preach. Thomas Coke referred to Hosier as "one of the best preachers in the world."[21]

Going through the West Virginia mountains would have been rougher without "Braddock's Road." It had been laid out by Colonel George Washington and was so named because it had been used as a retreat by the British General during the French and Indian War. Washington had accompanied Edward Braddock during the Spring of 1755 in his march against the French. When Braddock was shot through the chest, Washington helped carry the dying general off the battlefield. Washington's own life was spared because of his affliction with dysentery, which placed him in the rear of the troops.[22]

West Virginia was rough territory to travel through, especially during the summer months. There were whiskey drinkers, rocks, woods, and little houses with big families. The crowds were small and, worse yet, were full of poor listeners. When he returned to Maryland, Asbury was laid up again for a week with a sore throat. Upon arriving to preach at Bush Chapel, he found that Robert Strawbridge had died during the summer. Asbury had little good to say about him. "[P]ride is a busy sin. He is now no more: upon the whole I am inclined to think the Lord took him away in judgement because he was in a way to do hurt to his cause" (1:411). Asbury entered Philadelphia on October 12, 1781, for the first time in five years. He was immediately oppressed by all the political conversation in a city that would always be too secular for his taste. Asbury opined that Philadelphia had corrupted Harry Hosier, who declined to travel with him any longer. "I fear his speaking so much to white people in the city has been, or will be, injurious; he has been flattered and may be ruined" (1:413). Asbury was at least partially correct, as Hosier unfortunately became an alcoholic (though later recovered). In spite of his illiteracy, he impressed thousands of people, including Benjamin Rush, America's most prominent physician. Henry Boehm (Asbury's later travelling companion) said of Hosier, "He would repeat the hymn as if reading it and quote his text with great accuracy. His voice is musical and his tongue as the pen of a ready writer."[23]

The Sacramental Issue Solidifies Asbury's Leadership

It was in December 1781 that Asbury said goodbye to his base of operation, Thomas White's home. He had fallen in love with the Judge and his family. "[H]e has the most real affection for me of any man I ever met with" (1:414). Though he conducted two quarterly meetings, Asbury recorded preaching only twice in November and December. Administrative matters, including rising discontent among the Southern circuits, consumed Asbury. On December 17 he headed south to quiet the "troublesome business." Would he be able to quell the schismatic tempest one more time?

Horseback riding through northern Virginia in the dead of winter was a new experience. "In the country I have to lodge my nights in lofts, where light may be seen through a hundred places; and it may be the cold wind at the same time blowing through as many" (1:420). During a service in Charlotte's County, Virginia, the adjoining house caught fire. The congregation saved all the furniture and other valuables before the building was completely consumed. At Kimbrough, North Carolina, rain interrupted Asbury's sermon. "[T]he people seem to be more afraid of their saddles being wet than their souls being lost" (1:423). Rain and fire did not stop Asbury from focusing on the upcoming conference. Could Methodism continue to forestall the serving of the sacraments by its own ministers? Many within the ministerial fold tired of being "ecclesiastical half-breeds." Asbury gathered political support as he rode along, including pledges from Philip Bruce and James O'Kelly. Devereux Jarratt would preach at the conference, giving visibility to the newly formed Protestant Episcopal Church.

The Southern Conference met at Ruben Ellis's "preaching house" in Sussex County, Virginia, April 16–19. Again, Asbury was able to persuade the preachers to remain under the old plan, which included their obligation to John Wesley. All the preachers but one signed a "written agreement" that they would refrain from serving the sacraments. There was cause for celebration. Fifty-nine of the sixty American preachers, representing twenty-six circuits, were of one accord. The conference ended on an emotionally high note, "We had a love feast—the power of God was manifested in a most extraordinary manner—preachers and people wept, believed, loved, and obeyed" (1:424). Methodism had become a galvanized and unified force, with the current seeming to flow through one person, Asbury. He was winning his battles both privately and publicly. Victories seemed to abound for both him and the country he now called home.

The War Ends

In February 1782, the British House of Commons voted against waging any more war in America. In April, peace talks began in Paris with John Adams and Benjamin Franklin in leading roles. Strangely, Franklin is a man that Asbury never mentioned.[24] Asbury would have been strange company for the cosmopolitan Renaissance man who was a steadfast friend of George Whitefield. The meteors of both Franklin and Whitefield were a little too flashy for Asbury. At the time, Franklin may have been the most popular person in both France and the United States; at least he was popular enough to make the future president, John Adams, intensely jealous. When Adams was with Franklin in Paris 1778, he recorded that "[t]he Life of Dr. Franklin was a scene of continual dissipation. . . . As soon as breakfast was over, a crowd of carriages came to the Levy. . . . By far the greater part were Women and Children, come to have the honour to see the great Franklin, and to have the pleasure of telling stories about his simplicity, his bald head and scattering straight hairs, among their acquaintances."[25] In contrast, Thomas Jefferson opined that Franklin was the greatest man and "ornament" of the age and country in which he lived.[26]

Nevertheless, Asbury was not so obscurantist as not to record on May 10 at Colepepper [Culpepper], Virginia, "Here I heard the good news that Britain had acknowledged the Independence for which America has been contending—May it be so! The Lord does what to him seemeth good" (1:425).

At this point, Methodism had evolved into a bi-geographical legislature with houses in both the North and the South.[27] Though the travel inhibitions created by the Revolutionary War no longer prevailed, it was difficult for the pastors to journey great distances. The basic North/South pattern that had operated during the Revolutionary War continued. At the conference held May 21 at Lovely Lane Church in Baltimore, the attenders unanimously chose "Brother Asbury to act according to Mr. Wesley's original appointment and preside over the American conferences and the whole work."[28] The North made official what had been affirmed in the South.

Asbury Reflects on His New Position

Asbury had become the leader of American Methodism but had not been appointed as such by Wesley. He made no mention of his newly granted status. He did record the lack of financing for the printing of books, which would have to be suspended. All of America was in a financial crisis. The continental currency, a glut of money pumped into the economy by Congress, had collapsed. During the war a bushel of corn had inflated from five shillings to eighty dollars. In 1780 Governor William Livingston of New Jersey calculated that his salary of eight thousand pounds in currency was worth no more than one hundred fifty pounds in silver.[29]

A couple of weeks later, Asbury could be found sitting on the banks of the West River in Anne Arundel County, Maryland, simply meditating. He had begun his lifelong practice of seeking composure through retreat. He pondered the administrative scepter that had been passed to him, one he had not overtly sought, but one he had knowingly positioned himself to receive. Was this what he really wanted for the rest of his life?

During the summer of 1782, Asbury came to the conclusion that riding a horse was his best mode of transportation. The American wilderness required that he become both an equestrian and veterinarian. Finding sufficient water, food, rest, shoes, and shelter for his mount would be a perennial quest for the rest of his life. Asbury was blessed with a common sense of innovation, a giftedness that was doubtless acquired as a metal fabricator back in England. He was a master of improvisation. When his horse lost its shoe, he bound the hoof with bull hide. He constantly had to respond to moments that threatened the well-being of both himself and his steed.

The Sociology of Itinerancy

On the whole, 1782 was not an encouraging time for Asbury's preaching. A treaty of peace was yet to be signed and Americans, at least on the Eastern seaboard, were not ready for spiritual matters. Asbury was concerned that there were no "visible movings and instantaneous conversions among the people" (1:429). Most of the time he made no comment on his preaching appointments. Other times he noted that congregations were noisy, disagreeable, gospel hardened, and wild. Other times he simply recorded geographical locations.

Asbury was inclined to make blanket assessments of the sociological contexts in which he found himself. If Paul had sized up the Cretes, why couldn't Asbury also make collective appraisals? "I think the Pennsylvanians are, in general, as ignorant of real religion as any people I have been amongst" (1:433). And then there was the aggravation of having to obtain valid passes to travel as a still politically suspect Methodist preacher. At Germantown, Asbury's certificate was pronounced invalid because he did not have the proper signatures. He pleaded ignorance.

The war being over (a provisional treaty was signed November 30, 1782) and Methodism exhibiting some organizational coherency, there was now time and energy to focus on other matters. For Asbury there was a quickening of his conscience on the issue of slavery. He was a man in pursuit of understanding. What was the solution to the situation that seemed so horribly wrong, especially in a nation which had just won its freedom? Strong testimony was borne for the cause of "African liberty" at the May 7 Southern Conference.

During the week of June 8, Asbury refused to stay at a house in Montgomery, Maryland, because of "cruelty to a Negro." Soon afterward he entered into a heated conversation with John Wilson, later a trustee at Sugarloaf Chapel, who argued for slavery's propriety. "[O]ur talk had well nigh occasioned too much warmth" (1:442). Asbury was discovering that he was not automatically going to carry every conversation, even with his newfound status. American pluralism had begun long before he arrived. "The inhabitants are much divided; made up as they are, of different nations, and speaking different languages, they agree in scarcely anything except it be to sin against God" (1:443).

For the most part, Asbury's occupation in 1783 consisted of shoring up the Methodist work however he could. He was constantly on the go, recording few of his stops. He worked his way from Virginia to New York and then back down to North Carolina. On Sunday, September 14, he injured himself "by speaking too long and too loud. I rode seven miles, got wet, had poor lodgings, with plenty of mosquitoes, next day poorly as I was, I had to ride seventeen miles and spoke while I had a high fever on me. I laid down on a plank—hard lodging this for a sick man" (1:446). In August, he sent George Shadford a progress report: "I travel four thousand miles in a year, all weathers, among rich and poor, Dutch and English" (3:29). The next month he wrote to Wesley, "No man can make a proper change upon paper to send one here and another without knowing the circuits and the gifts of all the preachers unless he is always out among them" (3:31). Whatever Asbury's attributes, he possessed the true giftedness of being "among them."

Wesley Confirms Asbury's Leadership

On December 24 a letter from Wesley awaited Asbury in Hertford, North Carolina, appointing him general assistant, the person immediately responsible to John Wesley for American Methodism. He was to receive no preachers from Europe that were not recommended by Wesley, "nor any in America, who will not submit to me and the Minutes of the conference" (1:450). In January and February of 1784, Asbury met the challenge of a rugged winter. His horse fell on the ice, pinning Asbury's leg under him, an injury that bothered him over the next couple of months. In the summer he faced for the first time the heat of the Allegheny Mountains of southwest Pennsylvania, travelling as far west as the present day Washington, Pennsylvania. It was his furthermost trek west thus far.

Never had he encountered such rugged terrain or sparse accommodations. He was rewarded for his crossing by being housed three to a bed and preaching to a "wild" people. At Old Town, Pennsylvania, he preached to people who abounded in "intemperance." He was clearly out of his natural habitat. There was little relief as he returned to the oppressive August heat and humidity of New Jersey and New York. By the time September rolled around, his religious certitude had wavered. "Two things seem to dim my prospect of heaven, and point of qualification— first, I do not speak enough for God, and secondly, I am not totally devoted to Him. Lord help me to come up to my duty!" (1:468).

Duty! On the eve of his episcopal installation, Asbury was perceived as a man of duty, a man determined to discipline the flesh for the sake of "oughtness," a man given to rightness rather than momentary action or reaction. C.H. Fowler said that Asbury represented "a character whose shortest axis was always perpendicular to the plane of obligation; therefore all his motion was along the line of duty. Perhaps no man in modern time more fully than he embodied the eternal grip of oughtness."[30]

Whatever criticism and accusation of cowardice had been leveled at him because of his Revolutionary War retreat, they were now muted. Cowards normally take the path of least resistance. It was clear to those who even remotely knew Asbury that personal comfort was not a determining criterion politically, spiritually, and vocationally. He spoke when he could have remained silent, took initiative (though not impulsively) when he could have accepted resignation. He argued passionately, while controlling his emotions. Above all, he was convinced that Methodism was God's cause, a cause for which he was willing to expend everything. Even before Wesley's emissaries arrived in November of 1784, American Methodists recognized in Francis Asbury one who had made a choice concerning which there was little or no reservation. He had come to stay.

5. "What Mighty Magic"

Wesley Takes Ecclesiastical Action

The 1783 Conference of British Methodism at Bristol requested that Wesley draw up a deed giving legal status to "the Conference of the People called Methodist."[1] The "Deed of Declaration" placed British Methodism within the hands of the "legal one hundred."[2] One hundred ministers legally formed the "conference" that possessed the authority to appoint further members and to designate official preachers for the Methodist chapels. The preachers were for the most part unordained and Methodism was still a society, a church within the Church of England. Methodism would not become a separate entity in England until after Wesley's death in 1791.

The matter was much more urgent on the American side. Methodism was in danger of fragmenting, if not completely lapsing into oblivion. Secession of the largest conference, Virginia, had been narrowly averted in 1780. Seven of the eight preachers whom Wesley had sent to America had returned to Britain. The Anglican pastors who had provided the sacraments during the war had now fled or were disenfranchised. Not only had the Bishop of London refused to ordain Wesley's preachers, he and the other English bishops refused to consecrate the Anglican pastor Samuel Seabury as a bishop. Seabury's Connecticut diocese sent him to England, where he met with constant rejection. If the Anglican Church wasn't going to provide leadership for its own children, it certainly wasn't interested in ensuring the continuation of its illegitimate offspring. More important than the failure of ecclesiastical options was the new political climate, which had increasingly prevailed since the Revolution. Sidney Mead states:

> The Revolutionary Epoch is the hinge upon which the history of Christianity in America really turns. During this period, forces and tendencies long gathering during the Colonial era culminated in new expressions, which came to such dominance that a fresh direction was given to the thought patterns and institutional life of the churches.[3]

The American Methodists were now operating within a radically reworked structure of political allegiance. No anecdote better represented the independent attitude of Methodism than the repartee of the Methodist preacher Nelson Reed to Thomas Coke in 1787. When Coke interrupted Reed to say, "You must think you are my equal." Reed responded, "Yes Sir, we do; and we are not only the equals of Dr. Coke, but of Dr. Coke's king."[4]

Coke complained to Asbury that Reed was "hard" on him, but Asbury replied, "I told you our preachers were not blockheads."[5]

American subservience to the Church of England having been reduced to only a formality, John Wesley desperately turned to a measure of both control and concession. He summoned Thomas Coke, Richard Whatcoat, Thomas Vasey, and James Creighton to meet him in Bristol on September 31, 1784.[6] There he announced their assignment to America: "Being now clear in my own mind, I took a step which I had long weighed in my mind and appointed Mr. Whatcoat and Mr. Vasey to go and serve the desolate sheep in America."[7] Wesley and Creighton ordained Whatcoat and Vasey and at the same time entrusted Thomas Coke, who was already ordained, with the plenipotentiary task upon arrival in America of ordaining Francis Asbury with the office of joint superintendent. As always, Wesley was not without a rationale for his action, which was stated in an epistle that he stuck in Coke's hand.

> Lord King's "Account of the Primitive Church" convinced me many years ago, that Bishops and Presbyters are the same order, and consequently have the same right to ordain. For many years I have been importuned, from time to time, to exercise this right by ordaining part of our Traveling Preachers. But I have still refused, not only for peace' sake, but because I was determined as little as possible to violate the established order of the national church to which I belonged. . . . I have accordingly appointed Dr. Coke and Mr. Francis Asbury to be joint superintendents over our brethren in North America; as also Richard Whatcoat and Thomas Vasey to act as Elders among them, by baptizing and administering the Lord's Supper.[8]

Thomas Coke

The persuasion to act in the above manner may have been Wesley's, but the actual content of the persuasion was Coke's. On August 9, 1784, Coke wrote to Wesley:

> The more maturely I consider the subject, the more expedient it appears to me that the power of ordaining others should be received by me from you, by the imposition of your hands; and that you should lay your hands on brother Whatcoat and brother Vasey for the following reason. . . . For the purpose of laying hands on brothers Whatcoat and Vasey, I can bring Mr. Creighton down with me, by which you will have two presbyters with you. [9]

Furthermore, Coke wrote: "I do not find any the least degree of prejudice in my mind against Mr. Asbury; on the contrary, a very great love and esteem and I am determined not to stir a finger without his consent, unless mere necessity obliges me, but, rather to lie at his feet in all things."[10] Coke had never met Asbury.

At the tender age of 23, Thomas Coke had assumed duties as curate of South Petherton, a town of approximately fifteen hundred persons. Though not an "evangelical," Coke fervently preached to a complacent flock. He was later to note that the reading of John Fletcher was "the blessed means of bringing me among that despised people called Methodists, with whom, God being my helper, I am determined to live and die."[11] The more Methodist that Coke became, the more he preached outside his parish, and the more he fell out with his congregation.

Wesley stated that he first met Coke at Kingston on August 13, 1776. "Here I found a clergyman, Dr. Coke, late Gentleman Commoner of Jesus College in Oxford who came twenty miles on purpose. I had much conversation with him and a union thus began which I trust will never end."[12] From then until his death in 1814 Coke would be a faithful and ardent, if not always wise, servant of Methodism. For a quarter of a century Coke's incisive and systematic mind rendered invaluable service to American Methodism in his functions as both parliamentarian and theologian. Wesley and Coke were committed to "irregular" patterns of ministry, which rankled the establishment. Both were Oxford graduates (Coke had a doctorate of civil law) and were committed to an experiential pietism that went beyond the prevailing rational moralism of Anglicanism.

It seems that the more rankled Coke's flock became, the more he intended to incite their indignation. He traded the normally sung Psalms for Wesleyan hymns, spent the church's money without proper consent, and publicly labeled his congregants as "Devil's Trumpeters," "Satan's Agents," and "Rattle Snakes." On Sunday, March 30, 1777, Coke was dismissed. A curate was waiting in the wings to take his place, and the transition was celebrated by the pealing of the church bells. The following Sunday, he was not deterred from standing in the churchyard and preaching to his former parishioners as they left the church.

By the summer of 1777, Coke had cast his lot with Wesley, who had become his mentor. The aging Methodist founder had found his righthand man, an individual full of zeal and learning, if not political sagacity. Contemporaries described Thomas Coke as an exceptionally handsome man. His looks, combined with a gentleman's decorum and a very acute intellect, did not easily translate into a servant's attitude. His conscience rebuked him when he refused to fill his "beaver's hat" with water in order to quench the thirst of a fellow traveler who was quite sick.

Charismatic, polished, and educated as was Coke, it was difficult to recognize humility in one who smelled of aristocracy, a scent despised by Americans. William Wilberforce said that Coke "looked a mere boy when he was turned fifty, with such a smooth apple face, and little round mouth, that if it had been forgotten you might have made as good a one by thrusting in your thumb."[13] By 1782, Thomas Coke had become second in command for English Methodism, the person on whom Wesley most depended for leadership and intimate counsel. In

July of 1782, Wesley wrote, "Dr. Coke promises fair; at present I have none like-minded."[14]

Coke Informs Asbury of Wesley's Plan

Asbury first set his eyes on Coke at the famed Barrett's Chapel encounter on Sunday, November 1, 1783. After his sermon at Barrett's Chapel, Coke noted that "[a] plain robust man came up to me in the pulpit and kissed me. I thought it could be no other than Mr. Asbury and I was not deceived."[15] Coke penned his immediate impression of Asbury: "I exceedingly reverence Mr. Asbury; he has so much simplicity, like a child, so much wisdom and consideration, so much meekness and love! And under all this, though hardly to be perceived so much command and authority that he is exactly qualified for a primitive bishop."[16]

Asbury encountered in Coke a short, round cherub of a man with a ready smile. He was neatly dressed, even to the point of elegance. Civil and learned in conversation, he would prove to be Methodism's able messenger to reach segments of American society other than the crude. The downside was that Coke represented American Methodism's antithesis and was thus suspect by a ministry that sometimes prided itself in an absence of civility. Thomas Ware's first impression of Coke was that "[h]is stature, complexion and voice resembled that of a woman rather than of a man; and his manners were too courtly for me."[17]

After greeting Coke with a kiss, Asbury stated that he was "shocked when first informed of the intention of these my brethren in coming to this country: it may be of God" (1:471).[18] The pair then retreated along with several Methodist preachers to the nearby house of Phillip Barrett's widow to discuss an appropriate response. Asbury mapped out a six-week preaching itinerary for Coke, which would climax (the ensuing Christmas) in a general conference of all the preachers at Lovely Lane Chapel in Baltimore. Coke took off to preach, and Freeborn Garrettson galloped off to invite the preachers to the conference.

As Wesley's right-hand man, Coke had for some time agitated for English Methodism to shake off the Anglican yoke. When he had urged that, at least in the larger towns, Methodism should hold services during regular church hours, Charles Wesley thundered out a vehement veto accented by an angry stamp of his foot. It was said that Coke "[d]ropped into his chair as if shot and did not utter a single further word in the matter."[19] It was not the last time that Coke failed to do his political homework.

Coke's political clout on the American side was inextricably bound with the extent to which American Methodism revered Wesley. It is therefore understandable that after Methodism revoked its allegiance to Wesley in the 1787 conference, he would never again enjoy the same adulation that he had for the first three years. The loss of esteem was sealed by an acrimonious message he preached on the occasion of Mr. Wesley's death. "The leaving of Mr. Wesley's name off the

Minutes was an almost diabolical thing. No history furnished any parallel to it, that a body of Christian ministers should treat an aged and faithful minister, as Mr. Wesley undoubtedly was, with such disrespect. . . . Two of those actors in Mr. Wesley's expulsion are dead and damned, and the others, with their patron [Mr. Asbury, we suppose], will go to hell except they repent" (3:99). Coke went on to assert that Wesley's excommunication had hastened his death, which would cause one to ask how long Coke expected Wesley to live beyond eighty-seven years old.

Coke continued to carry on for a time the responsibilities of joint superintendency with Asbury over the Methodist Episcopal Church. But in 1808 Coke was relieved by the General Conference of his jurisdictional authority. Long before that, however, his responsibilities had become far more formal than practical. When in 1805 Coke accompanied Asbury to the three Southern conferences, he "was not consulted in the least degree imaginable concerning the station of a single Preacher" (3:335). When Asbury was too weak to make it to the conference at Charleston, Coke expected Asbury to request him to sit as moderator; "But he refused me, & appointed Brother Jackson to station the Preachers, & Brother Jesse Lee to sit as Moderator in the Conference" (3:336).

The Christmas Conference

Several communications paved the way for the critical event that took place in December of 1784, forever after designated "the Christmas Conference." Edward Dromgoole, who was converted from Catholicism to Methodism, had come from Ireland in 1770. For the next sixty-five years he preached mainly in Virginia, where he was also a prosperous merchant and planter. His letter to Wesley on May 22, 1783, served at least partially to counteract the negative reports that Methodism's father had received about Asbury.

> The preachers are united to Mr. Asbury, and esteem him very highly in love for his work'[s] sake; and earnestly desire his continuance on the continent during his natural life; and to act as he does at present, (to wit) to superintend the whole work, and go through all the circuits once a year. He is now well and has a large share in the affections of both; therefore they would not willingly part with him, or submit to any other to act in his place, until they have good proof of his integrity.[20]

Wesley responded on September 17, 1783. "I am persuaded Brother Asbury is raised up to preserve order among you, and to do just what I should do myself, if it pleased God to bring me to America.[21]

In two letters to Wesley, the first dated October 3, 1783, and the second March 20, 1784, Asbury greased his own political axle.

> I have laboured and suffered much to keep the people and preachers together: and if I am thought worthy to keep my place, I should be willing to labour and suffer till death for peace and union (3:32). But nothing is so pleasing to me, sir, as the thought of seeing you here: which is the ardent desire of thousands more in America. . . . Sir, it is not easy to rule: nor am I pleased with it. I bear it as my cross; yet it seems that a necessity is laid upon me (3:34).

When Asbury was informed of Wesley's plan to appoint him as joint superintendent and set the Methodist preachers free to exercise a fully orbed pastoral office, he responded with a deft political stroke, a genius that he would repeatedly exhibit. "My answer then was, if the preachers unanimously choose me, I shall not act in the capacity I have hitherto done by Mr. Wesley's appointment" (1:471). By allowing a conference (which Wesley's instructions did not call for) to vote on him, Asbury combined ecclesiastical autocracy with American democracy.

Asbury thus became the supreme head of American Methodism for over three decades. He would rule over the preachers as one of them. He was both ruler and subject, a pragmatic paradox. The hierarchy of Wesley-Coke-Asbury-American Methodism had been replaced with immediate responsibility to a conference composed of daily rank-and-file field hands. For the time being, Asbury would carry simultaneously the authority of both Wesley and American Methodism. In Edwin Holt Hughes's words, "After that unanimous election they were compelled to endure their own creation."[22]

Freeborn Garrettson, the most charismatic of all the American itinerants, was able to scare up sixty of the eighty-one American preachers (Jesse Lee, who failed to receive the communication, complained that Garrettson stopped too often to preach). Thomas Ware, who was present, peered back through fifty years of cloudy nostalgia and stated that "there was not an unkind word spoken or an unbrotherly emotion felt. Christian love predominated and under its influence we kindly thought and sweetly spoke the same."[23]

The first issue faced was the name of the new church. John Dickens, who would serve as Methodism's first publisher, suggested the "Methodist Episcopal Church," and the appellation stuck. The second issue revolved around the relationship of the newly formed church to the mother church and its founder. The stated position was that "During the life of the Reverend Mr. Wesley, we acknowledge ourselves his sons in the Gospel, ready in matters belonging to church government, to obey his commands."[24] Ware later stated, "In this we undoubtedly went too far. . . . We loved Mr. Wesley. . . . But he was a man, and was several thousand miles from us."[25]

In contrast, Asbury incarnated present and immediate leadership. Ware noted of Asbury, "There was something in his person, his eye, his mien, and in the music of his voice which interested all who saw and heard him. He possessed much natural wit, and was capable of the severest satire; but grace and good sense so far predominated that he never descended to anything beneath the dignity of a man and Christian minister."[26]

If there was a dissenting voice to Asbury's new capacity, it was silenced by the enthusiasm of the majority. On December 25, Coke, assisted by Whatcoat and Vasey, ordained Asbury deacon and on the twenty-sixty an elder. On the twenty-seventh, Philip Otterbein[27] joined Coke in the imposition of hands, the latter setting apart "the said Francis Asbury for the office of a superintendent in the said Methodist Episcopal Church, a man whom I judge to be well qualified for that great work. And I do hereby recommend him to all whom it may concern, as a fit person to preside over the flock of Christ" (1:474). Thomas Haskins recorded his reservation with the opinion that the preachers should have delayed the decision until "the next June Conference. . . ."[28] "[H]eard several preach have felt my mind much exercised yesterday & today on what was done in Conference. How tottering I see Methodism."[29]

The language Coke used in his consecration sermon, which referred to Asbury not as superintendent but as "bishop," was to have far-reaching consequences. The echo of both word and deed fell on the disagreeing ears of at least one person—Charles Wesley. The dissonant vibrations back in England were translated into verse.

> So easily are Bishops made
> By man's or woman's whim?
> W—— his hands on C—— hath laid,
> But who laid hands on him?
>
> Hands on himself he laid, and took
> An Apostolic Chair:
> And then ordain'd his creature C——
> His heir and Successor. . . .
>
> W—— himself and friends betrays,
> By his good sense forsook,
> While suddenly his hands he lays
> On the hot head of C——
>
> A Roman emperor 'tis said,
> His favourite horse a consul made,
> But Coke brings greater things to pass,
> He makes a bishop of an ass.[30]

Historians are not fully agreed as to John Wesley's intentions. He may have not thoroughly thought through the consequences. Did he envision an independent church? Was Asbury appointed to an ecclesiastical office or to a pragmatic task? Would American Methodists continue to be an appendage of British Methodism? Wesley was not present to interpret his intention and it was left to Coke and Asbury to work out the ramifications; ramifications that came to full fruition in the changing of one word in the 1787 *Minutes*.[31] Asbury and Coke explained to the conference that the term *bishop* was a more biblical term than *superintendent*, and the conference, not unanimously, agreed to let the term stand. Almost forty years later Freeborn Garretson interpreted the matter negatively when he wrote: "Mr. Wesley designed we should have a moderate episcopacy, and therefore he gave us the word superintendent instead of bishop; and the change of the word was cause of grief to that dear old saint and so it was to me."[32]

Who exactly changed the term superintendent to bishop? In all likelihood it was a collaborative decision between Coke and Asbury. Since Coke's literary skills far exceeded those of Asbury, editing the *Minutes* was left to him. It could well be that Coke requested or at least informed Asbury of the editorial change. The nomenclature had been more than hinted at when Coke chose as his sermon title at Asbury's ordination "The Character of a Christian Bishop." Asbury's ordination was indeed a quantum leap for a man who had almost no formal education and who had taken no prior steps toward such an auspicious office. It was, in a measure, a sham of which Asbury was not entirely unconscious.[33]

No pre-nineteenth-century event better represented the autonomous and populist nature of American religion than Asbury's ordination. It was a new day. Indeed, the ordination was far more American than Wesley intended. The local newspapers ridiculed Wesley's intervention, with satire and sarcasm, as theologically spurious and an infringement on the Episcopal Church. A writer to the *Baltimore Advertiser* on February 5, 1785, defended Asbury's appointment by arguing,

> Heaven be praised we live in a land of equal liberty, and are determined to exert the prerogative of rational beings, to think for ourselves and to pin our faith on no man's sleeve . . . for everyone knows that, since the revolution, there were not in the full and proper acceptation of the word, either Parishes or Parish Ministers; and til very lately scarce anyone knew or thought there were parishes at all.[34]

Asbury's job description, as stated in the 1785 *Minutes*, called for him to ordain superintendents, elders, and deacons; preside as a moderator over conferences; fix the appointments of the preachers of the several circuits, and in the intervals between conferences to change, receive, or suspend preachers as necessary; and receive appeals from the preachers and people and decide them.[35] Asbury, as Wesley's general assistant, had been fulfilling all of the above except the first before Christmas of 1784. This one additional responsibility was a monumental paradigm shift for both Asbury and the American Methodists.

The power to ordain is a sacramental task. If it did not place Asbury within "apostolic succession," it at least endowed him with the spirit of apostolicity. The rite of ordination, unlike administration and organization, is shrouded in the symbolism of spiritual mystery. The Christmas Conference ordination vested Asbury with spiritual authority that transcended both Wesley and the conference he moderated. In a quick succession of events Asbury was entrusted with an authority that derives its significance from the historical community known as the Church. Asbury's position far exceeded the infantile organism which he was to lead.

Asbury Defines the Office of Bishop

The three days of ordination left Asbury's mind swimming in a sea of bewilderment. He hardly knew how to respond. Such an official position surely demanded a clerical cassock. Within a month, Asbury had donned "black gown, cassock, and band" at Colonel Joseph Herndon's mansion in Wilkes County, North Carolina (1:481). The personal uneasiness he felt in his new garb and the stares of his fellow preachers caused him to have second thoughts. He shed his professional attire. The rough-and-tumble Jesse Lee had been especially taken aback when he observed Asbury looking more like an Anglican priest than a frontier evangelist. However, when Asbury officiated in the laying of the cornerstone for Cokesbury on June 5, 1785, he wore a clerical gown.[36] As late as 1788, when ordaining Michael Leard, he wore a "gown and band" and conducted the event from Wesley's *Sunday Service*.[37] Both dress and ritual were shortly thereafter abandoned by Asbury.

In adopting liturgical dress, Asbury betrayed his stated purpose to "shake the formality of religion out of the world." Samuel Seabury, after being rejected by the English bishops, had procured consecration by the Episcopal Church of Scotland, a church that the poet Walter Scott said had been reduced to a "shadow of a shade." After being consecrated by three Scottish bishops on November 14, 1784, Seabury returned to America carrying a tailor-made "mitre," crafted in England. An observer described his dress as a "black satin gown; white satin sleeves, white belly band with a scarlet knapsack on his back, and something resembling a pyramid on his head." A Congregational minister stated that "the appearance of a man in this habit excites as much inquiry, as the greatest novelty. It is said, he must be greater than other men, or else he is crazy."[38] Asbury eventually decided that he would not jeopardize the Methodist mission with either superiority or craziness. The liturgical garments of both Asbury and Seabury were flapping in a wind that reeked of the smell of the "last king strangled with the entrails of the last priest." Or at least that is the way Thomas Jefferson wanted it.[39]

But neither street clothes nor semantics could hide the acute change that the Christmas Conference had wrought. On December 30, 1784, the Methodist preacher, Adam Fonerdon, wrote to his friend Stephen Donaldson,

> It being now well known that in primitive times the Office of Presbyter or Elder which are synonymous Terms, & Byshop were one and the Same with only this Small difference that the Chief or prime presbyter was sometimes called a Byshop. With us, the Superintendent answers to Byshop, who is to have the Oversight of all & we think it is a better name, because *modern* Byshops being Lords are generally devourers of the flock, & a Curse to the people. & the very name conveys a disagreeable savour.[40]

Fonerdon at first defined the nomenclature as a "small difference" but then went on to explain it as a major difference. Indeed, it was not simply a semantic insignificance. *Bishop*, for many Americans, denoted an apostate church and a person of privilege rather than sacrifice. Why would Asbury risk the association? Was it a quest for power, which grew out of a perceived personal deficiency in gifts and preparation? Or was it a theological understanding that assumed a separate and superior ministerial order? Whatever Asbury's motives, he was convinced that he acted on biblical authority.[41]

The office of bishop was much more than a designation of status; it was a prescribed role, a traveling order of ministry. "It is my confirmed opinion that the apostles acted both as bishops and traveling superintendents in planting and watering, ruling and ordering the whole connection; and that they did not ordain any local bishops, but that they ordained local deacons and elders. I feel satisfied we should do the same" (3:490). The recognition of the office of bishop, in Asbury's thinking, was the validation of an apostolic office. Only a traveling apostle could ensure a traveling ministry. Asbury was convinced that an authoritative episcopacy was essential to securing a constantly itinerating ministry.[42] Plus, Asbury claimed that he could save two souls while he was saying, "General Superintendent."

Fallout with Wesley

In his ordination sermon, Coke had argued that the words *bishop, elder*, and *overseer* are synonymous terms throughout the writings of St. Paul.[43] By "synonymous" he must have meant their status rather than their entrusted responsibilities. But for Asbury, the term *bishop* was much more than an enlarged job description. The term *superintendent* would have placed him on the same ecclesiastical level as everyone else, including John Wesley.

The title *bishop* placed Asbury beyond Wesley's control. The escalating tension evidenced itself in a letter Wesley wrote to Asbury on September 30, 1785:

> At the next Conference it will be worth your while to consider deeply whether any preacher should stay in one place three years together. I startle at this. It is a vehement alteration in the Methodist discipline. We [allow no one] except the Assistant, who stays a second, to stay more than [one year].

> I myself may perhaps have as much variety of matter as many of our preachers. Yet, I am well assured, were I to preach three years together in one place, both the people and myself would grow as dead as stones. Indeed, this is quite contrary to the whole economy of Methodism: God has always wrought among us by a constant change of preachers.[44]

Asbury freely offered his historical interpretation of the term *bishop* as he sought to quiet the developing anxiety over American Methodism's relationship with its English *father*. "I can truly say for one, that the greatest affliction and sorrow of my life was that our dear father, from the time of the Revolution to his death, grew more and more jealous of myself and the whole American connection; that it appeared we had lost his confidence almost entirely" (3:545). The ultimate rub was that American Methodism had something that British Methodism did not have—a bishop. Wesley attempted to subordinate Asbury by claiming himself as *father*, that is, head of and provider for the whole movement:

> [My Dear Brother],—There is, indeed, a wide difference between the relation wherein you stand to the Americans and the relation wherein I stand to all the Methodists. You are the elder brother of the American Methodists: I am under God the father of the whole family. Therefore I naturally care for you all in a manner no other persons can do. Therefore I in a measure provide for you all; for the supplies which Dr. Coke provides for you, he could not provide were it not for me, were it not that I not only permit him to collect but also support him in so doing.

> But in one point, my dear brother, I am a little afraid both the Doctor and you differ from me. I study to be little: you study to be great. I creep: you strut along. I found a school: you a college! nay, and call it after your own names! O beware, do not seek to be something! Let me be nothing, and "Christ be all in all!"

One instance of this, of your greatness, has given me great concern. How can you, how dare you suffer yourself to be called a Bishop? I shudder, I start at the very thought! Men may call me a knave or a fool, a rascal, a scoundrel, and I am content; but they shall never by my consent call me Bishop! For my sake, for God's sake, for Christ's sake put a full end to this! Let the Presbyterians do what they please, but let the Methodists know their calling better.

Thus, my dear Franky, I have told you all that is in my heart. And let this, when I am no more seen, bear witness how sincerely I am

Your affectionate friend and brother.[45]

The appellation *bishop* was not as foreign to Wesley as he claimed. In March of 1785, he wrote, "I know myself to be as real a Christian Bishop as the Archbishop of Canterbury. Yet I was always resolved, and am so still, never to act as such except in case of necessity."[46] This authority had been granted Wesley in the 1745 conference, which stated that "their father in the Lord may be called a bishop, or overseer of all."[47]

Asbury received Wesley's epistle almost six months later while in Charleston, South Carolina. "Here I received a *bitter pill* from one of my greatest friends. Praise the Lord for my trials also—may they all be sanctified!" (1:594). The political leverage for which Asbury had opted carried a huge price tag. Wesley failed to note this price tag, and in fact had little understanding of it. Asbury was accused of many things by his fellow workers, but never of "strutting. " It is difficult to strut when one lives almost entirely outside of all normal parameters for comfort and prosperity. Asbury succinctly noted the irony of his mitre. "I am a bishop and a beggar" (3:62).

There was always a pathetic aura which kept Asbury in check. While at Camden, South Carolina, in December of 1800 he received a request to remove Joseph Everett as the presiding elder at Philadelphia. His response was, "Poor bishop! no money for my expenses. I am afflicted—my life threatened on the one hand, my brethren discontented on the other: true, I received from them a petition dipped in oil and honey; and if I approve, all will be well; but if not, drawn swords may be feared" (2:273).

New Meaning for an Old Term

Providence had placed Asbury in an office that would forever plague him with the uneasiness of ecclesiastical government and the discomfort of its primitive furnishings. After dining in the woods on a very cold, damp Saturday evening and preaching on Sunday at Augusta, Georgia, Asbury penned, "My flesh sinks under labour. We are riding in a poor thirty-dollar chaise, in partnership, two bishops of us, but it must be confessed it tallies well with the weight of our purses: what bishops!" (2:585).

It was a job *non gratis*. Asbury expended his entire resources for a job that hardly anyone else wanted. *Bishop* was the last word that would have come to the minds of those who encountered him over the three decades of riding, preaching, and governing. Asbury caricatured everything that a bishop was not. His attire was one of paradox. "I have little to leave, except a journey of five thousand miles a year, the care of more than a hundred thousand souls, and the arrangement of about four hundred preachers yearly, to which I may add the murmurs and discontent of ministers and people: who wants this legacy? Those who do are welcome to it for me!" (2:401). There were few takers.

It is not critical for us to know whether Asbury willfully sought the title *bishop* or reluctantly accepted it. The narrative of his life and its imprint on the movement he led were propelled by the job description he gave to the term *bishop*. Others before him had held like office, but never had it been defined by such severity. He stripped it of all normative appurtenances and adapted it to the culture and terrain of a new world. Joshua Soule, later bishop, said that "[o]f Bishop Asbury it may be said, he possessed the power of suffering."[48]

Final Break with Wesley

At the Virginia Conference of 1784, Asbury had read to the attending ministers John Wesley's "Reasons Against the Separation of the Church of England." One of the reasons was "[b]ecause it would be throwing balls of wild fire among them that are now quiet in the land."[49] Devereux Jarratt, who was present at the conference, later wrote, "And who would suppose, that, before the close of this same year, he and the whole body of Methodists broke off from the church, at a single stroke!—what mighty magic was able to affect so great a change in one day!—it was certainly the greatest change (apparently at least) that ever was known to take place, in so short of time, since the foundation of a Christian church was laid."[50] Jarratt may have overstated the case, but there is no doubt that the fire Wesley sought to contain had now leaped both its Anglican and English Methodism's boundaries. It was already burning out of John Wesley's control.[51]

Adolescent independence was officially declared at the 1787 Baltimore Conference when the attendees refused Wesley's order to elect Richard Whatcoat as a superintendent. The order raised the ire of the conference on several fronts. First, Coke had already ruffled the feathers of the conference by autocratically changing the date from the one previously announced. Secondly, Asbury had already set a non-Wesleyan precedent by having himself elected, not appointed. Thomas Ware was correct: "To place the power of deciding all questions discussed, or

nearly all, in the hands of the superintendents, was what could never be introduced among us—a fact which we thought Mr. Wesley could not but have known,
had he known us as well as we ought to have been known by Dr. Coke."[52] The
American preachers interpreted Wesley's initiative as a threat to Asbury's authority, even suspecting that Wesley might try to move Asbury to another continent.

The differences in governance philosophy resulted in the dropping of Wesley's
name from the conference *Minutes*. Until this time, Wesley had been listed along
with Coke and Asbury as "the persons that exercised the Episcopal office in the
Methodist Church in Europe and America." It took at least six months for Wesley
to learn of his American children's recalcitrance. On November 25, 1787, Wesley
wrote to Asbury concerning his desire that ministers be sent to the American
Indians. "But let us all do what we can, and we do enough. And see that no
shyness or coldness ever creep in between you and your affectionate friend and
brother."[53] The tone was different when Wesley wrote to Coke on July 17, 1788:
"It was not well judged by brother Asbury to suffer, much less indirectly to encourage, that foolish step in the late conference. Every preacher present ought
both in duty and in presence to have said, 'Brother Asbury, Mr. Wesley is your
father, consequently ours, and we will affirm this in the face of all the world.'"[54]

On October 31, 1789, Wesley was the first to record the Caesar-Pompey
quote attributed to Asbury (repeated by James O'Kelly and Jesse Lee). Suppos-
edly, Asbury told George Shadford, "Mr. Wesley and I are like Caesar and Pompey.
He will bear no equal and I will bear no superior." Wesley accused Asbury of
quietly sitting by "until his friends voted my name out of the American Minutes.
This completed the matter and showed that he had no connexion with me."[55]
The "no connexion," at least in terms of governance, was correct. Wesley's name
was restored to the American *Minutes* in 1789, but it was only a formality until
his passing. The parting was mutual. From 1785 through 1790, the American
appointments were read and recorded at British Methodism's annual conference.
In 1791, Thomas Coke was no longer appointed to America but was listed as
stationed in London. For that conference and all succeeding conferences, Francis
Asbury and his fellow laborers were left out of the British *Minutes*.[56]

The 1787 conference completed the ideological separation that had been
incubating in American Methodism. Even before the 1784 Christmas Conference, American Methodists voted. Voting would not take place in British
Methodism until after Wesley's death. In 1766, Wesley wrote, "But some of our
helpers . . . demand a free conference; that is a meeting of all the preachers, wherein
all things shall be determined by most votes. I answer: It is possible, after my
death, something of this kind may take place, but not while I live."[57]

From the beginning, Asbury had said that he was not in favor of the
"binding minute" to Wesley (2:106). Early on he had written, "My sentiments
are union but no subordination, connexion but no subjection" (3:63). The 1787

conference had rejected Wesley's call for a "General Conference," his appointment of Freeborn Garrettson as an assistant to Nova Scotia, and the appointment of Richard Whatcoat as a general superintendent. In essence the 1787 conference declared American Methodism's independence, and no one was more responsible than Francis Asbury. The cleavage was not without a psychological, even a spiritual price. In a 1789 letter Asbury wrote, "I am sorry our dear old Daddy is so offended with me. I have dictated too free, and expect we shall never come upon terms, especially when he has so many Elbow friends. I esteem it as one of the greatest calamities of my life so highly to grieve him, and he has made me feel very sensibly by his letters, as fallen! fallen!"[58]

6. "Live or Die I Must Ride"

Slavery Meeting with Washington

On the very day Asbury was ordained deacon by Thomas Coke, James Madison published his *Remonstrances Against Religious Assessments*. He argued that the public should not be taxed for the support of a particular religious group, or for the establishment of religion in general. The Virginia legislature voted Madison's argument into law in January 1786, and it became the basis for the first amendment to the Constitution in 1789. Though Asbury was oblivious to the political developments in Constitution Hall, he was an immediate beneficiary of the resulting disintegration of the religious establishment. The Christmas Conference adjourned into wide-open territory.

Asbury's mind was "unsettled," with thoughts swirling too fast to process. He preached the following Monday after the Christmas Conference on the Apostle Paul's prayer that the Ephesian Christians "may be able to comprehend with all saints what is the breadth and length, and depth and height" (Eph. 3:18). It was an appropriate text for a man in too deep. Being the designated leader was overwhelming, and no one was more aware of it than he: "I was but low in my own testimony" (1:479). He immediately headed south to Virginia and found lodging at an "ordinary." He held prayer in one room while some wagoners played cards in another. "I am sometimes afraid of being led to think something more of myself in my new station than formerly" (1:480). No worry. After breaking ice, fording a stream, and riding with great pain to reach Waggoner's Chapel in Rowan County, North Carolina, he found he had only nine hearers. He blamed this on the failure of the person who was supposed to publish the notice of his coming.

The new superintendent was not impervious to the numerous detractors who rejected both his ministry and his authority. Among them were Baptists, ignorant settlers, and outright pagans. By the time he arrived at Georgetown, South Carolina, he wrote, "If God has not called us by his providence into these parts, I desire and pray that we may have no countenance from the people; although we have ridden four or five hundred miles, and spent our money" (1:483). While in Charleston, Asbury tried something new: He would preach each evening for seven days at the Independent meeting house known as Circular Congregational Church. Though the inhabitants were "vain and wicked to a proverb . . . I loved and pitied the people, and left some under gracious impressions" (1:485).

Asbury headed back up the coast, where at Elizabeth Town, N.C., he offered baptism to a woman who declined. "[A]fter I came away she was distressed at her refusal, and sent her son four miles after me; myself and my horse were both weary, but I returned and had a solemn time" (1:487). The first annual conference shared by Asbury and Coke was in southern Virginia in the later part of April. The dispute over slavery agitated the whole affair, but there was enough consensus to send a petition for the emancipation of slaves to the Virginia legislature.

From the conference, Coke and Asbury made their way to Mount Vernon, where they were received by General Washington for the purpose of discussing slavery. The interview was a follow-up to a letter written April 24, 1785. In spite of Asbury's dislike for politics in general, he revered no one more than George Washington. Asbury aspired to generalship no less than did Washington. He too commanded an army (3:333). To be in the presence of America's most powerful leader elated Asbury to the point of euphoria. The reception by Washington was a vote of confidence for which the young ecclesiastical leader hungered. The original letter was lost, but the follow-up, written a year later, has been preserved.

> Honoured sir: Give me leave to present you with one of our Prayer Books, and another to your Lady. Please to accept the Sermons also to your candid perusal. Receive them as a small token of my great respect and veneration for your person
>
> Who am your most obedient friend and servant
> Francis Asbury (3:47).

Thomas Coke recalled that after dinner with "quite the plain-country Gentleman, we desired a private interview, and opened to him the grand business on which we came, presenting to him our petitions for the emancipation of the Negroes, and entreating his signature, if the eminence of his station did not render it inexpedient for him to sign our petition."[1] Washington responded that though he agreed in sentiment, he would not sign the petition. He would instead write a letter to the Virginia Assembly letting his thoughts be known. Washington invited his guests to spend the night, but they declined, saying they had to be in Annapolis the next day.

The Black servants who waited on the dinner party accented the contradiction confronting Asbury and Coke's petition. Washington eventually owned hundreds of slaves to work the five farms covering eight thousand acres that surrounded Mt. Vernon. Even though Washington resolved he would "never become the master of another slave by purchase" he was forced, in order to maintain Mt. Vernon, to purchase slave labor almost to his dying day. In 1797, Washington hosted the famed English comedian John Bernard. As they ate together, Washington extolled the virtues of American freedom as opposed to "the little of its doings" in Britain. At this point, a slave entered the dining room. Bernard broke out in a smile and Washington followed up with an ironic and hollow defense: "Till the mind of the slave has been educated to perceive what are the obligations of a state of freedom, the gift would insure its abuse. We might as well be asked to pull down our old warehouses before trade had increased to demand enlarged new ones."[2] Five months before he died, Washington stipulated in his will that his more than three hundred slaves be freed upon his wife's death.

Cokesbury College

The most significant institutional matter that occupied Asbury during 1785 was the founding and raising of funds for Cokesbury College. At Abingdon, Maryland, on June 5, Asbury stood on the ground where the building was to be erected, "warm as it was, and spoke from Psalm lxxviii, 4–8. I had liberty in speaking, and faith to believe the work would go on" (1:490). The incongruity between a man with no more than six months' formal education dressed in clerical robes was not lost on those who gathered. The historian Horace DuBose was mostly accurate when he stated, "The precincts of colleges and universities were sacred ground to Asbury, peasant-bred and diplomaless though he was."[3]

Authorization for the endeavor had been given at the Christmas Conference. Though the concept of a Methodist training school had been floating around for several years, the plan did not crystallize until the 1784 conference.[4] It would seem that the matter was discussed there, but Thomas Ware made no mention of it in his notes. There is evidence that Coke and Asbury discussed prospects for the college when they met at Abingdon on November 14, 1784. Coke recorded that "Mr. Asbury met me on this side of the Bay; between us we have got about one thousand pounds stirling subscribed for the college."[5] The main purpose of the school was to educate and house the children of Methodist itinerants, especially "boys, when they are grown too big to be under their mother's direction. Having no father to govern and instruct them, they are exposed to a thousand temptations" (3:44).[6]

The school enjoyed some prosperity, having as many as thirty students in 1789. Through most of its existence, however, it was fraught with administrative and financial troubles. Asbury wrote in August of 1788, "I received heavy tidings from the college—both our teachers have left; one for incompetency, and the other to pursue riches and honours: had they cost us nothing, the mistake we made in employing them might be the less regretted" (1:578). On December 7, 1795, the 40'x108' three-story building burned to the ground, probably by arson.[7]

Asbury deeply regretted the whole enterprise. "Would any man give me 10,000 [pounds] per year to do and suffer again what I have done for that house, I would not do it. The Lord called not Mr. Whitefield nor the Methodists to build colleges. I wished only for schools—Doctor Coke wanted a college. I feel distressed at the loss of the library" (2:75). Cokesbury was quickly relocated in an adjacent building to the Light Street Church in Baltimore, where it burned again a year later. After the first burning Asbury wrote to Jasper Winscom, his friend back in England. "We had a school. Dr. Coke in his bigness printed and nominated it a college."[8]

Education of Children

Tradition states that Francis Asbury established in 1786 the first Sunday school in America, at Thomas Crenshaw's in Virginia. The tradition is wrong on two counts. There is no historical evidence that Asbury visited Crenshaw's home after 1785. It seems that William Elliot organized a Sunday school in his home in 1785, the first Sunday school in America.[9] Elliot recorded, "All were taught the rudiments of reading, in order that they might be able to read God's word for themselves—the Bible being practically the only textbook in the school."[10]

The who and where of the first Sunday school is a matter only of curiosity. What is important is that Asbury took a genuine interest in the education of children. Asbury recorded for the South Carolina Conference on February 17, 1790, "Our Conference resolved on established Sunday school for poor children, white and black" (1:625). In 1787, a Baltimore newspaper reported that "Mr. Asbury and the council of the Methodist Church make some progress in establishing Sunday school for persons of all descriptions, free of expense."[11]

The *Minutes* of the 1790 South Carolina Conference stated, "What can be done in order to instruct poor children (white and black) to read? Let us labor, as the heart and soul of one man, to establish Sunday schools in or near the place of public worship" (1:625). Asbury left to George Daugherty, the located pastor in Charleston, "a flower garden and a kitchen garden to cultivate," with attention to be paid to the Blacks.[12] In a letter to Asbury, Daugherty wrote, "I do not only suffer the reproach common to Methodist Preachers, but I have rendered myself still more vile, as 'the negro school master.'" For work in this part of the "garden," Daugherty was almost drowned in the well by the local mob. He was saved by a Mrs. Kugley, who "rushed into the midst of the mob, and gathering up the folds of her gown with both hands, stuffed it into the spout of the pump and stopped the flow of water."[13]

In September, during a visit to New York City, Asbury ordained John Dickens. Dickens, born in London in 1747, was educated in both mathematics and the classical languages. He was well equipped to become Methodism's first publisher. He died during a yellow fever epidemic in Philadelphia, refusing to leave the city because of ministry obligations. Nothing evidences his single-minded commitment to God and the church more than a letter written to Asbury concerning publishing issues on a day his wife almost died from childbirth, January 16, 1797. After discussing with Asbury the difficulties of not being able to get paper on credit, Dickens related how the physician, finding his wife almost without pulse, resorted to "desperate measures" by opening the windows and removing the blankets. "And the Lord had mercy; so that now about six o'clock in the evening she can speak and show some degree of cheerfulness."[14]

A Dream in the Midst of Disappointment

During February of 1787, while in North Carolina, Asbury ran a splinter into his leg. The accompanying swelling and fever brought much pain, from which he felt "the power of death." At Newbern he complained of the poor accommodations. "[T]he house was unfinished; and, to make matters worse, a horse kicked the door open, and I took a cold, and had the toothache, with a high fever" (1:534). The first conference of the year was in Charlotte County, Virginia, where there were almost three thousand present. "[I]t was a solemn, weighty time" (1:537).

In June, Asbury preached to two large crowds of approximately a thousand people each at Warrick, New York, and Flanders, New Jersey. The latter occasion took place in the woods, where Asbury suffered from a cold and depression. He was so physically depleted that once again he set out for the "springs" in West Virginia hoping to find some relief. The trip only taxed his already depleted energy. "In the first place we missed our way; then my baggage-horse ran back two miles: I was tried not a little. O, how sad the reflection, that matters trifling as these should make a person so uneasy" (1:547).

While at the springs, Asbury began lecturing on prophecy. On the first day, he had more hearers than he expected, but thereafter few showed up, prompting him to conclude that "everything that is good is in low estimation at this place. I will return to my own studies: if the people are determined to go to hell, I am clear of their blood" (1:548). He penned two days later, "I feel . . . the want of more life, and more love to God, and more patience with sinners" (1:548). By November, Asbury had entered into one of his periodic depressions.

Asbury spent December in Maryland, where he experienced a series of very disappointing preaching stints. Both he and his congregations were lifeless. He was pulled out of his depression by a dream he had on Christmas night. "That night while sleeping, I dreamed I was praying for sanctification, and God very sensibly filled me with love, and I waked shouting glory, glory to God! My soul was all in a flame. I had never felt so much of God in my life; and so I continued" (1:556).

December was filled with sparse preaching appointments and uncomfortable lodging. Asbury started the year 1788 by confessing that "[d]uring the last one hundred miles of our journey we have preached very little for the want of appointments" (1:559). The preaching opportunities that did develop were disappointing. In North Carolina there was "death" at Coinjock, "cold" at Flatty Creek, "barrenness" at Knotty Pine, "dryness" at Winton, and at the quarterly meeting at Lee's "my heart melted for the people: they do not, will not pray; and if they so continue, must be undone" (1:562).

At the conference in Charleston, South Carolina, on March 14, a man started a riot at the door, causing women to leap from the windows of the church, and creating mass confusion. "Again whilst I was speaking at night, a stone was thrown against the north side of the church; then another on the south; a third came through the pulpit window, and struck near me inside the pulpit. I however continued to speak on; my subject, 'How beautiful upon the mountains,' &c." (1:564).

The "West"

In April, Asbury made what was to be the first of many trips through the Smoky Mountains. Beginning in Morganton, North Carolina, he followed the French Broad River via Elk Park, Bluff City, Elizabethton, and Bristol. The roughness and difficulty of the terrain were increased by heavy rain. As he crossed the mountains, he named them "steel," "stone," and "iron." "We crept for shelter into a little dirty house, where the filth might have been taken from the floor with a spade. We felt the want of fire, but could get little wood to make it, and what we gathered was wet. . . . Night came on—I was ready to faint with a violent headache. . . . I prayed to the Lord for help" (1:569).

The Holston Conference was held for three days in the home of Stephen Keywood, fifteen miles from Abingdon, Virginia. In spite of its being May, "[t]he weather was cold; the room without fire, and otherwise uncomfortable. We nevertheless made out to keep our seats, until we had finished the essential parts of our business" (1:572).

Toward the end of the summer there were encouraging signs of evangelistic harvest. While at the Baltimore Conference, "the Spirit of the Lord came among the people, and sinners cried aloud for mercy" (1:579). Asbury also received a letter reporting the "spreading work of God" in western North Carolina. The divine refreshings did not completely cure Asbury's bouts with depression, but they did enable him to transcend the fatigue, heat, cold, filth, hunger, and the almost impossible terrain of the "West." Crossing the Appalachians had thrust Methodism into a new world of both hardship and harvest. It was rough going.

> Near midnight we stopped at William Anglin's, who hissed his dogs at us; but the women were determined to get to quarterly meeting, so we went in. Our supper was tea. Brothers (William) Phoebus and (Valentine) Cook took to the woods; old—gave up his bed to the women. I lay on the floor on a few deer skins with the fleas. That night our poor horses got no corn; and next morning they had to swim across Monongahela. . . . My mind has been severely

tried under the great fatigue endured both by myself and my horse. O, how glad should I be of a plain, clean plank to lie on, as preferable to most of the beds; and where the beds are in a bad state, the floors are worse. The gnats are almost as troublesome here, as the mosquitoes in the lowlands of the seaboard. This country will require much work to make it tolerable (1:576–577).

Trans-Appalachia culturally shocked Asbury. It is difficult to exaggerate the roughness of both the terrain and the people. William Klinkenheard, who migrated to Kentucky in 1780, recalled that "[t]he women the first spring we came out, wo'd follow their cows to see what they ate, that they might know what greens to get. My Wife and I had neither spoon, dish, knife, or any thing to do with when we began life. Only I had a butcher knife."[15]

There was little law, and what judicial process there was swift and often macabre. When Elias Plybourn was tried for horse stealing, the Washington County court in Tennessee sentenced him to be "confined to the public Pillory one Hour. That he have both his ears nailed to the pillory and severed from his Head; that he receive at the Public Whipping Post, thirty-nine lashes well laid on; and be branded on the Right Cheek with the letter H, on his left cheek with the letter T, and that the Sheriff of Washington County put the sentence in execution, between the hours of twelve and two this day."[16]

Good Order

In his first quadrennium in office, Asbury established the "itinerancy" by an incessant traversing of a route between New York and Charleston, with one trip as far south as Savannah, Georgia. There were now 85 circuits, 166 preachers, and 37,354 members.[17] The increase of 11,500 members for 1788 had been more than twice as many as any previous year. Asbury increasingly saw himself as leading the "charge of a light brigade" that was moving inexorably toward becoming an army of transients willing to go wherever there was human habitation.

Asbury had determined to be commander-in-chief on the front line of battle. He would not "winter" at headquarters, but would live in the field and exhibit the same endurance, within the same circumstances, as he demanded of his troops. It was a plan envisioned and established by Wesley. For Wesley, the term *preacher* meant an itinerant preacher. The Deed of Declaration stated that the Methodist preaching houses would not belong to local trustees. In Wesley's view, this would destroy itinerant preaching. "When the trustees in any place have found and fixed a preacher they like, the rotation of preachers is at an end; at least till they are tired of their favorite preacher and so turn him out."[18]

Asbury's administrative style grew out of both his controlling personality and his passionate pastoral philosophy. He would appoint every preacher, sign every document, oversee every financial transaction, not to mention draw up the architectural plans for almost every church. He was obsessed with the need to arrive at every preaching appointment and conference on time. There was order in his dress, his mannerism, and above all his administration. To Thomas Sargent, the pastor of Light Street Church, Baltimore, he wrote on January 6, 1805, "My continual cry to the Presiding Elders is, order, order, good order. All things must be arranged temporally and spiritually like a well disciplined army" (3:333).

Even his preference of a horse over a buggy or a wagon bespoke Asbury's independent, controlling personality. "The pomp of a wagon is too great for me, and the danger; perhaps not one in five hundred could drive to please me, this would make me more dependant than I would wish to be; the jollies of age and sallies of youth do not always fit" (3:565). At sixty-six years of age, Asbury still preferred to be on a horse rather than in a carriage. "[I] can better turn aside to visit the poor; I can get along more difficult and intricate roads; I shall save money to give away to the needy; and, lastly, I can be more tender to my poor, faithful beast" (2:652). Even though he almost always had a traveling companion, they broke camp when Asbury decreed and went in the direction Asbury pointed. This prompted Henry Boehm to comment, "The bishop seldom stopped for rain, even if it came in torrents."[19]

Always on the Move

Perseverance in spite of all outward elements was the hallmark of his life, but the above idiosyncrasies do not fully explain Asbury's always-on-the-move *modus operandi*. Taking to the open road at times was contradictory to both efficiency and his own stated desires. His famed quote, "My brethren seem unwilling to leave the cities, but I think I will show them the way," showed his failure to recognize the opportunities that the burgeoning metropolitan areas offered. It would seem that Asbury was committed at times to just going rather than going to where the people were. He often longed for rest, quiet, solitude, and study, but when opportunities for such things came, he was restless to the point of overbearing anxiety. "I have traveled so much that it seems like confinement to rest one day" (1:383).

Whenever he was prevented from public ministry, Asbury was invariably dejected. He suffered from an inherent wanderlust that could be quelled only by movement. He complained that the pastors of the circuits always expected him to preach on arrival, and yet he referred to any Sunday that he was not standing in a pulpit as a "dumb" Sabbath. He was a man occupied not so much by being at a place as getting to the next place. "Are we riding for life?

Nay; but we must not disappoint people; we are men of our words. I feel for others in bad traveling; but little for myself" (2:628).

Evangelism

But Asbury's on-the-go methodology was more than simply a quirk in his personality. He believed the foremost task of pastoral care was evangelism. In fact, for Asbury, evangelism was not a subspecialty of pastoral theology; they were one and the same. When Caleb Pedicord informed Asbury that he was called to the ministry but not to itinerancy, Asbury sternly replied, "[N]o conviction my son that you should follow the direction of him who commissioned you to preach! Has the charge given to the disciples, 'Go and evangelize the world' been revoked? Is the world evangelized?"

Pedicord said, "I looked at the world; it was not evangelized." For Asbury, the words *evangelize* and *go* were synonymous. Asbury said "go," and Pedicord went.[20]

For the most part, Asbury's one objective was arrival at his next preaching appointment. Rarely did he take a detour for sightseeing, and he could go for weeks without making any comment on the landscape. His journal comments on the terrain had mostly to do with travel conditions. There were few good roads, and those that Asbury expected to be good did not measure up to expectations. As late as 1795, the road through the Cumberland Gap was little more than a trail. After Governor Isaac Shelby entrusted James Knox and Joseph Cracket with two thousand pounds for the purpose of building a road, there was still little improvement. Even though the road was unpaved, which allowed heavy rain to create a track of mud, the *Kentucky Gazette* bragged on October 15, 1796, that "wagons loaded with a ton of freight may pass with ease, with four good horses."[21]

Asbury gratified his curiosity on one rare occasion by turning aside to observe Natural Bridge in Virginia. Instead of being impressed by its magnificence, he contemplated the possibility of preaching under its arch. Asbury didn't quite capture Thomas Jefferson's rapturous feelings about the site when the latter exclaimed, "It is impossible for the emotions, arising from the sublime, to be felt beyond what they are here: so beautiful an arch, so elevated, so light, and springing, as it were, up to heaven, the rapture of the Spectator is really indescribable!"[22] However, Asbury appreciated a Maryland April full of blossoms, banks of evergreens along the river, and views of meadows and fields that were grand and beautiful. On the other hand, his journal is often void of comments about the Atlantic seashore, the rolling plateaus of the Piedmont, the mist-covered mountains of the Smokies, and the changing foliage of the seasons. A singular utilitarian purpose energized his travel—the salvation of the lost.

"I hope I shall travel as long as I live; travelling is my health, life, and all, for soul and body" (1:383).

One of Asbury's Best Friends

To his horse, Asbury was indeed sympathetic, as it was one of the chief tools of his labor. He developed a personal attachment to it. His horse was an extension of both himself and his ministry. He often stated in the face of foreboding weather, "God will preserve both man and beast." Perhaps he entrusted his steed a bit too much to Providence and was awash in sentiment or denial when he wrote, "Our horses are always well fed and never fail." To the contrary, his horse was known to have dropped dead in the course of a journey. Asbury estimated that he put twenty-five thousand miles on one horse (2:109).

To ride a horse fifty miles in a day over terrain that offered little respite was harder on beast than on rider. On July 13, 1782, Asbury penned, "I was much fatigued, and it rained hard; my poor horse, too, was so weak from the want of proper food, that he fell down with me twice; this hurt my feelings exceedingly— more than any circumstance I met with in all my journey" (1:429). He was not as insensitive as the pioneering evangelist Lorenzo Dow.[23] When verbally chastised for how he wore out his horse, Dow responded, "Souls are worth more than old horses."[24] The first American *Minutes* stated, "Be merciful to your Beast. Not only ride moderately, but see with your own Eyes that your Horse be rubbed and fed."[25] In spite of this injunction, the Methodist itinerant Benjamin Lakin recorded that, when riding on a winter day, "the ice cut his horse's legs until the blood ran out."[26] When Thomas Haskins' horse died, he lamented that "he forced her to travel when she was so sick."[27]

Asbury's horses often suffered from stiffness, foundering, swelling, and sweating from the intense heat, as well as going without proper rest, food, and shoes. Asbury cannot be accused of being indifferent to the welfare of his steed, but at times he drove his mount to the same extremities that he himself endured. He believed that everything—man, animal, and nature—was consumed by the evangelistic enterprise. The only problem for his beast of burden was that there would be no compensation in the next life. Boehm observed, "He was very fond of horses which he generally patted and had names for them . . . the horses frequently broke down from such extensive traveling and the bishop parted with them with a sigh and sometimes with a tear. When we parted with one in Wyoming [Pennsylvania], the bishop said, 'He whickered after us; it went right through my heart.' The bishop was a good rider, and he looked good on horseback."[28]

Any Port Will Do

Lodging was a constant problem, especially in the West, which was any place other than the Seaboard cities. Asbury begrudged any dollar that he had to expend for a meal or a night's rest. Thus, he laid his head anyplace that would put him up. When the weather and the lateness of the hour demanded, "any port in the storm" would do. Perhaps Francis Asbury visited more American homes than any one person before the Civil War. There were the constant horrors of over-crowding, too much heat, too much cold, too much dampness, but never too much cleanliness. "We were cribbed in our quarters at night—a narrow bed for two; this is no novelty for us" (2:692). "About nine o'clock we made Mr. Merwin's tavern: and here were drink, and smoke, and wagoner's—*but we closed with prayer*" (2:548). "About eight o'clock, came to a cabin, an earthen floor, and damp bed" (1:372). Crudeness was not confined to the frontiers. A traveler through Connecticut gave the following as his normal lodging experience:

> When the homely meal is served up, he (the proprietor) will often place himself opposite to you. . . . Thus will he sit, drinking out of your glass and of the liquor you are to pay for, belching in your face, and committing other excesses still more indelicate and disgusting. Perfectly inattentive to your accommodation and regardless of your appetite, he will dart his fork into the best of the dish and leave you to take the next cut. If you arrive at the dinner-hour, you are seated with "mine hostess" and her dirty children, with whom you have often to scramble for a plate, and even the servants of the inn; for liberty and equality level all ranks upon the road, from the host to the hostler. The children, imitative of their free and polite papa, will also seize your drink, slobber in it, and often snatch a dainty bit from your plate. This is esteemed wit, and consequently provokes a laugh, at the expense of those paying for the board.[29]

The stark deprivation of accommodations, often without a floor and almost always without sanitary facilities, was especially prevalent beyond the Alleghenies. Lice, fleas, insects, and whatever virus that was prevalent were often a liability. The awkwardness of being housed by strangers, sometimes even single women, was a constant trial to Asbury. There is no evidence whatsoever that Asbury ever placed himself in a compromising situation. Part of his protection was the frequent presence of a traveling companion. In 1801, it was decided that Asbury would always travel with an accompanying elder.

Sleeping arrangements required delicate protocol. "The evening brought us up at Paddock's, in Manlius [New York]. I lay along the floor, in my clothes. There was a lady in the corner, and brother Boehm in bed, like a gentleman. The female could not possibly occasion reproach, and so I was persuaded; but I wished I was somewhere else: my fear was not commendable" (2:608-

609). The following malevolent passage depicts the dire circumstance in which Asbury often found himself:

> A man who is well mounted will scorn to complain of the roads, when he sees men, women, and children, almost naked, paddling bare-foot and bare-legged along, or labouring up the rocky hills, whilst those who are best off have only a horse for two or three children to ride at once. If these adventurers have little or nothing to eat, it is no extraordinary circumstance; and not uncommon, to encamp in the wet woods after night—in the mountains *it does not rain, but pours.* I too have my sufferings, perhaps peculiar to myself: pain, and temptation; the one of the body, and the other of the spirit; no room to retire to—that in which you sit common to all, crowded with women and children, the fire occupied by cooking, much and long-loved solitude not to be found, unless you choose to run out into the rain, in the woods: six months in the year I have had, for thirty-two years, occasionally, to submit to what will never be agreeable to me; but the people, it must be confessed, are amongst the kindest souls in the world. But kindness will not make a crowded log cabin, twelve feet by ten, agreeable: without are cold and rain; and within, six adults, and as many children, one of which is all motion; the dogs, too, must sometimes be admitted (2:410–411).

Asbury's Odometer

It is almost impossible to compute with any accuracy the total miles that Asbury traveled; his method of measuring leaves us with approximations. Had Asbury traveled 6,000 miles a year, the 270,000 miles estimated by Bangs, Stevens, Tipple and others would be accurate.[30] The limited geographical sphere of the early years of his ministry, periods of sickness, the quarantine of the Revolutionary War, and the amelioration of his schedule during the last years of his life represent periods in which traveling was greatly curtailed. Throughout his journal, one finds estimates of 3,000, 4,000, and 5,000 miles a year. On more than one occasion, he refers to traveling 6,000 miles a year (2:541; 2:556). In 1814, Asbury recalled, "I have nearly finished my mission, having traveled annually a circuit of *3,000 miles* [italics mine], for forty-two years and four months; and if young again, I would cheerfully go upon another" (3:499). Did Asbury have the sudden conviction that he had previously exaggerated the extent of his travels?

Asbury constantly calculated the distance between cities, and how far he had traveled in a day. How he made his calculations is hardly ever clear. A long day's ride was 50 miles, and a long week's ride was 200. The distance between Philadelphia and Augusta, Georgia, according to Asbury, was 1,825 miles, "the route we have made" (2:525). Another time he estimated the same trip as 1,200 miles. The distance between Augusta and Norfolk was stated as 800 miles (1:428).[31] Even taking into consideration that Asbury went out of his way to eastern West Virginia and eastern Tennessee, it is still doubtful that the side trips more than doubled actual distance.[32]

At other times, his estimates were far more accurate. For example, the distance between South Carolina and East Redfield, Maine, he calculated to be 1,300 miles. On another occasion, he estimated the distance between Philadelphia and Pittsburgh as 410 miles. Given the fact that Asbury often got lost, often took divergent paths just to find lodging, and had to wind his way via both mountains and streams, the miles he estimated may not be that imprecise. But it is almost certain that he averaged less than 6,000 miles a year for the entirety of his ministry.[33]

Fording streams, traversing swamps, crossing swollen rivers, scrambling over jagged rocks and crevices, and groping through forests was precarious, especially on horseback. There was a constant danger of a startled horse's throwing him or raking him off with the limb of a tree. Asbury never drew a map or created some such device that would facilitate a return trip. "My trials are great; riding twenty miles a day, or more; rocky roads, poor entertainment, uncomfortable lodging; little rest night or day; but thanks be to God, he keeps me: the more I do and suffer, the greater the crown" (1:370).[34]

The Methodist itinerancy by Asbury was a kind of monasticism on a horse. "Live or die I must ride," he wrote to Stith Mead, reminding him that their life was "to converse with all sorts of spirits, tempers, all characters, all opinions, in all companies" (3:263). He was responding to an assertion from Thomas à Kempis that, "they that travel much are rarely sanctified" (3:263). Asbury was more akin to Francis of Assisi than he was to à Kempis. No communication was more indicative of his peripatetic life than his instructions to Joseph Benson for sending a letter: "Let them direct to any part of the United States, to myself or the junior Bishops or Bishops whose names will be known upon the minutes of any Conference" (3:552). It was more the case that Asbury would catch up with a letter than that a letter would catch up with him.

In August of 1787, Thomas Coke addressed a letter from England, "The Rev. Bishop Asbury, North America."[35] Asbury was probably the least sedentary person that America has ever known. He was convinced that the only way to heaven for him was on a horse.

7. "All Men Do Not See Alike"

The Growing Bureaucracy

During the summer of 1787, the delegates to the Constitutional Convention of the newborn republic met in an unventilated building in Philadelphia which came to be affectionately known as Constitution Hall. The debates revolved around who would wield power, as well as when and how, in the burgeoning nation. The first public census conducted by the newly formed government (1790) counted America's population at 3,930,000, which included 698,000 slaves and 60,000 free blacks.[1] How government could best serve the people would need continual reinterpretation. The ambitious yet well-intentioned quest for equality distinguished the new government from all its predecessors. William Randall refers to Jefferson's "pursuit of happiness" as a "felicitous, memorable turn of phrase, the most succinct expression ever of American political philosophy."[2]

Governing the newly formed Methodist Episcopal Church had gone smoothly enough, with only minor bumps, but that was soon to change. The institution was becoming more complicated, with a new college to take care of, along with a new publishing venture. Operating out of a saddlebag was no mean achievement. If Asbury had any expertise it was organization. As Asbury rode, he gave continual thought as to how the ecclesiastical machinery could work. Preservation of the fruit of Methodism's labors could be attained only through careful attention to detail. Bureaucratic rumination may have been part of the reason that he was so frequently lost. In South Carolina on March 2, 1787, he and Coke were so badly off course that "at last we thought we had gone far enough, and stopped at a house twenty-one miles from the place whence we started, and still farther from the place we aimed at" (1:593).

Along the way they discussed the procuring of five hundred acres of land for the establishment of a school in the state of Georgia, unkind attacks because of Methodism's abolitionist stand, the lack of money for Cokesbury, and the stationing of preachers. Asbury's mind was cluttered with a myriad of problems, which may have been a partial reason for his violent headaches. Asbury fretted over Methodism's inability to gain any sense of identity and coherency.

There were plenty of reasons for pessimism. Methodism as yet owned almost no buildings; but the lack of church edifices was not his greatest concern. "When I see the stupidity of the people, and the contentiousness of their spirit, I pity and grieve over them. . . . My body is weak; my spirits are low; and I am burdened under the spiritual death of the people: yet, O my soul, Praise the Lord!" (1:602).

The Council

The 1784 Christmas conference had been an ad hoc meeting to take care of the immediate business. There was no provision for either a plenary or delegated conference to put closure on the issues that were addressed at the annual conferences. In 1788 there were eight annual conferences and in 1789, eleven. Asbury found himself discussing the same business in each conference, and rehashing it in the next conference. By the time of the final conference of the year, preachers spent most of their time ratifying decisions on all previous business. Asbury envisioned a less unwieldy mode of operation and finally came up with the idea of an executive board called the Council. It was a solution plagued with difficulties, the object of much criticism, and one of Asbury's most humiliating political defeats. Jesse Lee preserved the council's birth certificate.

> The *Proceedings* of the *Bishop* and *Presiding Elders* of the *Methodist Episcopal Church*, in *Council assembled*, at *Baltimore*, on the first day of December, 1789. The following members which formed the Council were present. Francis Asbury, *Bishop*. *Elders* Richard Ivey, Reuben Ellis, Edward Morris, James O'Kelly, Philip Bruce, Lemuel Green, Nelson Reed, Joseph Everitt, John Dickins, James O. Cromwell, Freeborn Garrettson. After having spent one hour in prayer to ALMIGHTY GOD, for his direction and blessing, they then unanimously agreed, that a general conference of the bishop, ministers and preachers all of *America*, would be attended with a variety of difficulties, with great experience and loss of time, as well as many inconveniences to the work of God. And, as it is almost the unanimous judgment of the ministers and preachers that it is highly expedient there should be a general council formed of the most experienced elders in the connection; who, for the future, being elected by ballot in every conference, at the request of the bishop, shall be able to represent the several conferences and districts in the United States of *America*: they therefore concluded that such a council should be so appointed and convened.[3]

The annual conferences of 1789 approved of Asbury's "Council" idea, but not without reservation. The plan presented to the conferences stated that the Council would consist of the bishops and presiding elders, with at least nine persons present in order to enact business. The main political problem was that the bishop appointed the presiding elders, thus Asbury chose the members of the Council. The members of American Methodism who either possessed or desired political clout feared autocracy, and they were not afraid to voice their anxiety.

The chief opinion-makers opposing the newly created caucus were Jesse Lee and James O'Kelly, the latter a member of the Council. Asbury assessed the Council's first meeting by stating, "All our business was done in love and unanimity" (1:614). The first seating of the Council attempted to rectify governance flaws with a new procedure. Instead of a resolution needing the support of all the annual conferences, it was decided that a majority vote of the conferences would suffice. The bishop would be able to make decisions concerning the publishing house and college (as well as other urgent matters) in the interim periods between council meetings. A decision could be passed within the Council by the consent of the presiding bishop and two-thirds of the members. The bishop had sole veto power. In other words, if nine said "aye" and the bishop said "nay," a motion was defeated. When Jesse Lee complained of the system's vulnerability to abuse and fragmentation, Asbury wrote the following condescending letter.

> We are both (Asbury and Coke) grieved and surprised to find that you make so many objections to the very fundamentals of Methodism. But we consider your want of experience in many things, and therefore put the best construction on your intention. You are acquainted with the discipline of the Methodist Church; if you can quietly labor among us under our discipline and rules we cheerfully retain you as our brother and fellow laborer, and remain yours in sincere affection.[4]

The Council was Asbury's attempt to shore up his own authority, to centralize the bureaucracy of American Methodism, and to provide some type of manageable control. A motion by the Council necessitated approval by only a majority of the annual conferences for passage. Heretofore, one annual conference could undo the legislation of all the other annual conferences. Without the Council, Methodism's bishops were only moderators, not much more than bureaucratic figureheads. Yet Asbury would never be content with simply oiling organizational machinery. When he received an incriminating letter from James O'Kelly, he entered in his journal the rationale for the newly proposed methodology:

> I received a letter from the presiding elder of this district, James O'Kelly; he makes heavy complaints of my power, and bids me stop for one year, or he must use his influence against me. Power! power! there is not a vote given in a conference in which the presiding elder has not greatly the advantage of me; all the influence I am to gain over a company of young men in a district must be done in three weeks; the greater part of them, perhaps, are seen by me only at conference, whilst the presiding elder has had them with him all the year, and has the greatest opportunity of gaining influence (1:620).

Wesley's Autocratic Model

Asbury's mode of parliamentary procedure was much different from Wesley's and far more democratic. Wesley reigned by fiat. He listened to discussions and then made decisions. Thomas Ware noted of Wesley, "This he deemed the more excellent way; and as we have volunteered and pledged ourselves to obey, he instructed the doctrine, conformably to his own usage, to put as few questions to vote as possible, saying, 'If you, brother Asbury and brother Whatcoat are agreed, it is enough.'"[5] Wesley's "enough" demonstrated that his distance from the democratic mentality of the new republic was far more than geographical.

When Whatcoat and Garrettson were scuttled as superintendents in 1787, they were pawns in a power struggle. The scale had been tipped when Thomas Coke had taken the initiative to change the place and time of an annual conference (on instructions from Wesley). Instead of meeting at Abingdon, Maryland, on July 24, 1787, the time and place set a year earlier, it met at Baltimore on May 1. Even though the American preachers revered Wesley, such autocratic capriciousness rubbed them the wrong way. They were not going to be ruled by Wesley, Asbury, or anyone else.

Asbury walked much closer to parliamentary procedure than to episcopal monarchy. He possessed the sagacity to create an organization that was not so strong as to curtail the liberty of its own people and not too weak to maintain its own existence.[6] This meant giving everyone their say, including the fiery and impulsive James O'Kelly. Was Asbury going to serve the denomination only as a moderator, bogged down in the endless discussion of conflict and opinions? The Council was *a* solution if not *the* solution. It would be much easier to control a small group of men than the proliferating voices of the annual conferences. With Coke absent (which he was most of the time), Asbury seized the moment to circumvent this cumbersome machinery. The *Minutes* of the second Council stated that, "In the Intervals of the Council, the Bishop shall have power to act in all contingent occurrences relative to the Printing Business, or the Education and Economy of the College."[7] (Note that the word *Bishop* is singular and not plural.)

Political Defeat

The administrative plan Asbury had devised soon backfired. Such a revolutionary change necessitated far more political homework than he had been able to give it. Besides, there was the impossibility of communicating with the entire Methodist constituency concerning the plan. Sheer logistics prevented the taming of political backlash. The year 1790 was filled with dejection as Asbury underwent a severe lesson in humility. Nervous to the point of exhaustion, feeling abandoned, and quite willing to quit, he wrote, "I could give up the church, the college, and schools; nevertheless, there was one drawback—What will my enemies and mistaken friends say?" (1:630).

At the Petersburg conference in June, Asbury experienced a full frontal assault by the opposition. "Our conference began; always peace until the council was mentioned. The young men appeared to be entirely under the influence of the elders, and turned it out of doors. I was weary, and felt but little freedom to speak on the subject. This business is to be explained to every preacher; and then it must be carried through the conferences twenty-four times, that is, through all the conferences for two years" (1:642). Asbury sought a compromise by stating to the presiding elder O'Kelly that he was willing to move out of the episcopal chair while the Council convened. This did not stop O'Kelly from boycotting the December 1, 1790, meeting and threatening to replace it with a conference meeting that he himself would chair.

The Council met on December 1, 1790, at Philip Roger's chamber in Baltimore. Even though they argued that they "had a right to manage the temporal concerns of the Church and college decisively; and to recommend to the conferences, for ratification, whatever we judged might be advantageous to the spiritual well-being of the whole body," it was the last time the Council ever met (1:657). When Thomas Coke returned to America on February 23, 1791, Asbury noted, "I found the Doctor's regard to the council, quite changed." James O'Kelly's acrimonious letters had reached London.

Asbury told Coke that he had acceded to a general conference for the sake of peace. We do not know whether Asbury's "my motives are pure" letter found its way to Coke. We do know that Asbury did not want any decision he made to be interpreted as personal gain. "As to clothing, I am nearly the same as at first; neither have I silver, nor gold, nor any property. My confidential friends know I lie not in these matters. . . . I would not have my name mentioned as doing, having, or being anything but dust" (3:93).

Concession

On July 6, 1791, Asbury recorded, "This day brother Jesse Lee put a paper in my hand proposing the election of not less than two, not more than four preachers from each conference, to form a general conference in Baltimore, in December, 1792, to be continued annually" (1:687). Thus was initiated the General Conference, the supreme jurisdictional reference for American Methodism. O'Kelly, Lee, and Coke had triumphed and, to the credit of Asbury, he knew when to concede. The mission was more important than his ego.

Asbury clothed his political clout with political sagacity. Pleasing God, others, and himself was a precarious order. In the end, the effectiveness and permanence of Methodism were largely due to Asbury's choosing survival for both himself and the sect over personal triumph. If not humble, he was pragmatic. Joshua Marsden, a Methodist visitor from England, said of Asbury, "If he could not carry a point he did not force it against wind and tide, but calmly sat down till the blast was gone by, and with a placid dignity made a virtue of necessity, or with discriminating wisdom brought the measure forward in a less exceptional shape, and at a more convenient time."[8]

The faith and trust of both his constituency and Wesley was of extreme importance to Asbury's psychological well-being. Throughout his ministerial career, he did not easily shrug off the complaints of his co-workers. He aimed to please and thus was willing to negotiate all issues other than the ultimate mission. "I want to live in love and peace with all mankind and seek and save all the souls I can" (3:64).

The tunnel vision with which Asbury operated often made him insensitive to the desires and feelings of others. Why couldn't everyone subordinate their personal tastes and opinions to the cause of spiritually conquering the territory? Asbury's single-mindedness blinded him to the storm clouds being created by James O'Kelly. On the very eve of the thunderbolt, he wrote to Edward Dromgoole, "I am in peace with all mankind and as far as I know they love and are united to me" (3:107). Whether it was psychological denial or sheer ignorance, he was blind to the mutinous crew that was ready to take over the ship.

The Council experiment taught Asbury that no amount of placating and compromising would pacify those who were determined to live outside the constraints of his power. The people he needed most, those who were most capable and passionate in matters of the Kingdom, gave him the most acute headache. "I cannot cast them off. I cannot do without them, if they can do without me. I must continue in the ship, *storm* or *calm*, near the helm, or before the mast. As long as I can, I will be with them" (3:439).

The "Able Executive"

Unity was a must, and since the highest state of grace couldn't ensure it, Asbury attempted to provide it with a deft political hand. The success of Methodism rested on his conviction that the Kingdom of God could not survive, much less flourish, without careful administration. "We ought to teach our brethren the impossibility of existing as a people without union, and an able executive; for thousands of our people know not their right from their left hand, in government" (3:466).

Asbury was secure in the conviction that he was the "able executive." Fortunately for him, some others thought the same. Asbury's confidants were readily impressed with his ability to size up both persons and critical situations. Garrettson commented, "Few men have a greater knowledge of human nature than he had."[9] Joshua Soule, later bishop, recalled that Asbury "may probably be ranked among the most accurate observer of human nature. He appealed from a very transient acquaintance, to form as correct opinions of the talents and dispositions of men, as if he had been long intimate with them."[10]

Asbury placed profound trust in those who were close to him while at the same time expecting the worst in all persons apart from grace. Asbury's demeanor demanded respect, even reverence at times. As he presided over the conferences, there was no doubt who was in charge. After Asbury died, Garrettson wrote, "We sensibly felt the need of the wise, decisive hand of an Asbury, in the exercise of our episcopacy."[11]

Even Coke was in awe of Asbury. When the 1796 General Conference tried to oust Coke, Asbury defended him by saying, "If we reject him, it will be his ruin for the British conference will certainly know of it, and it will sink him vastly in their estimation."[12] Symbolizing the conference's decision to continue Coke in the American episcopacy, Asbury reached out his right hand to Coke, who submissively received it. No one mastered the art of simultaneously exercising inclusive participation and exclusive authority better than Asbury.

Ever-Present Conflict

In order to keep the Methodist movement cohesive, Asbury expended a good deal of energy in conflict resolution. He readily understood that unity of heart and intention did not always translate into sameness of thinking. To a church on the verge of division, he wrote, "But as all men do not see alike, in matters of church discipline, we beseech you brethren, not to suffer a difference in opinion or views, to alienate your affection from your brethren, the church, or the cause of God" (3:209).

Leadership demanded a constant effort at reconciliation. To Thomas Haskins, who was at odds with Ezekiel Cooper the Methodist book agent he wrote, "Why cannot Brother Cooper and you talk together, like Christians, men, and ministers, and men of sense, and citizens?" (3:215). At the same time, Asbury was not overly idealistic about reconciling all of the diferences between others or between himself and others.

Asbury offended most of the leaders with whom he worked, sooner or later. Resolution of will to the point of stubbornness, stern discipline of personal habit, and chronic exhaustion of body did not ingratiate him to individuals who were searching for polite compliance. In fact, he could be rather testy. After William McKendree had been elected bishop and was chairing his first conference with Asbury, the new bishop prepared an agenda for his approval. Asbury countered, "I have never done business like this before, and why are we doing it now?" In the awkwardness of the moment, McKendree responded, "You didn't have need of it, but I do."[13]

Henry Boehm, his later traveling companion, attempted to place the best interpretation on Asbury's irritability. "I grant he had rather a rough exterior. That he was sometimes stern, but under that roughness and sternness of manner beat a heart as feeling as ever dwelt in a human bosom." Boehm went on to say, "If he injured the feelings of a brother he would encircle him in his arms and ask his forgiveness."[14] But such backtracking did not prevent Nicolas Snethen, another traveling companion, from saying of Asbury, "He was not incapable of the exercise of that awful attitude of power, hard-heartedness to those individual personal feelings and interests, which seemed to oppose the execution of public plans." [15]

Asbury's Highest Administrative Priority

An administrative decision that Asbury reserved for himself, and himself alone, was the stationing of the preachers. The process could best be described as spiritual paternalism. He jealously guarded the prerogative to send the preachers wherever he saw fit. Before 1808, when the presiding elders became the official committee of consultation, Asbury clothed the whole process in an aura of mysterious autonomy. Asbury was the sender and the preachers were the sent, and there was little discussion of the matter.

At times, Asbury would state that if any desired special consideration, they should write him a note and he would attempt compliance. James Finley accordingly made his desires known through a written request for appointment in the West. When Asbury read his appointment, Finley found that he had been sent a hundred miles in the opposite direction. Finley said, "If that is the way you answer prayers, I suppose you will get no more prayers from me."

"Well," said Asbury, smiling and stroking his head, "be a good son in the Gospel, James, and all things will work together for good."[16]

Asbury normally sat throughout the conference making notes for himself while saying very little. He found out as much as he could about the preachers by both observation and consultation with the presiding elders. One preacher, John Kline, saw the note which Asbury had written about him: "John Kline, a man of small preaching talents but thought to be very pious and useful."[17] Concerning others, he was far more positive. Beside John Emory's name he jotted, "classic, pious, gifted, useful, given to reading."[18] William Thacker described the closing scene of the 1799 annual conference at John Street Church in New York as follows:

> [T]he bishop looks solemnly around upon us, the doomsday document trembling in his hand, he reads instinctively each countenance, tracing the suspense and solicitude of his anxious sons, all trembling to fly to their work, yet fearing as to the place where they shall be sent. Although the suspense was painful, the slow, solemn, concluding address of the bishop gradually rolls along, occasionally stopping in its progress until its close. Then taking the Hymn-book he reads,
>
> > The vineyard of the Lord.
> > Before his laborers lies
> > And, lo!
> > We see the vast reward,
> > Which waits us in the skies.

We sing, we kneel, and O what a prayer! What unction from heaven! We arise, and then the hidden, sealed instrument is all a revelation, the benediction is pronounced and we separate.[19]

The constant traveling of the bishops was for the purpose of having first-hand knowledge of territory, churches, and men. The bishops clearly stated their intention to make appointments impartially and justly. They would take into consideration the spiritual and temporal interests of both the appointee and the territory to which he was to be appointed. For the newly initiated, the whole affair could be quite intimidating. Henry Smith stated that the first time he saw Asbury, "He was very poorly, with a bad cold and sore throat, and hardly able to sit in conference." Smith recalled that he was alarmed by the close questions that Asbury put to the candidates. When Asbury asked for his testimony, Smith trembled and wept. "The sympathies of the preachers were worked up in my favor, and the good bishop himself appeared to be touched; for when I was done he beckoned to me with his hand to sit down and I was much relieved."[20] Later, in a 1795 conference, Smith reported, "Bishop Asbury called for volunteers to go to Kentucky and fixed his eyes upon me as one. I said, 'Here am I, send me.'"[21]

Yet Asbury was no detached autocrat when it came to making appointments. If the case was especially difficult or in any way unique, he expended extra energy to "make the rough places plain and the crooked places straight." Before Jacob Young was to be sent to Mississippi, Asbury paid him unusual attention by taking him in his arms and stroking his head. He went to Young's sleeping room and read to him the biblical narrative of Jacob's travels. After pausing for prayer, the bishop asked the young preacher how he supposed Jacob felt. "Then he got up, laid his hands upon my head, and said, 'Jacob you must go to Natchez and take charge of that district.' I began to beg off. He told me in a few words to go in the name of the Lord and do my duty, and that God would be with me."[22] When the appointments were read, Jacob Young was sent to Mississippi.

Asbury's traveling companion Henry Boehm recalled that the preachers tormented him to know where they were going. Asbury always left the conference as soon as the benediction was pronounced. "He thus avoided importunity, and no one could have his appointment changed if he desired it because no one knew where to find the bishop."[23] In 1851, David Meredith Russe, M.D., recalled the following from his boyhood days, which accurately describes Asbury's practice:

> I remember, for several successive years, waiting with other boys of about my age at the door of the Conference room, when the annual session of that body was about to close, for the purpose of taking a last look at the Bishop before he left the city. It was his custom to read the appointments of the preachers, and immediately mount his horse, and hasten out to Perry Hall,—the residence

of his friend Mr. Gough, and thus escape the solicitations of the preachers to change their appointments. Hense, on the last day of the session, Bishop Asbury would order his horse, with saddle, bridle, and saddlebags, to be brought to the door of the conference room, while he himself would be dressed for his journey, having his leggins over his pantaloons, and all ready for a start. On the reading of the appointments, he would hasten to the door, mount his horse, seldom delaying longer to recognize the boys who were waiting to see him, and, with a "God bless you" to each of us, he would be off. And yet, when he had reached his retirement, it is said that his ear was ever open to remonstrances from either preachers or people, and when he could, without injury to the work, he was always ready to change his plan. But, in those days, nobody thought of disobeying Bishop Asbury, after his decision was made.[24]

The stationing of the preachers was the *sui generis* responsibility of the bishop. It was the duty to which Asbury gave the most thought and prayer. The task demanded the wisdom of a Solomon, given the wide range of both personalities and localities. There was a constant flow of requests and suggestions, of which the rather pathetic plea from James Coleman serves as a case in point. Coleman pled for special consideration because of the feebleness and sickness of his family, and the fact that his father-in-law had given him a small piece of land on which to build a house.[25] Then there was the letter from a Mr. Gillespie that informed Asbury that since he was being sent to the Clarksburg circuit, "Not finding myself that spirit and temper, which I thought every preacher ought to feel, and observing that the people of Clarksburg were very lively; I could not persuade myself that I should be able to answer their Expectations," therefore he would decline traveling.[26]

By 1812, there were 678 Methodist preachers to be stationed. The task was dizzying and individual preferences were conflicting. Long before, Asbury had written:

> One preacher wishes to go where another dreads to be sent, and smiles at the fears of his more timid brother. "But" say the citizens, "how shall we be supplied?—such a one would be too strict, and put us out of order—a second will not keep the congregations together; and our collections will not be made—a third will not please; because he is not a lively preacher, and we want a revival of religion." Ah! the half is not told of the passions, parties, hopes and fears amongst the best of men, through ignorance and mistake (2:342–344).

Only an itinerant could send an itinerant. It was not simply a right which the conference conferred on him; it was an authority which Asbury earned. The claim to that authority would instigate a showdown between him and his foremost antagonist. Even though Asbury *won,* its aftermath would plague him for the rest of his life.

When Asbury was asked where he was from, he replied, "From Boston, New York, Philadelphia, Baltimore, or about any place you please."[27] A Methodist preacher lived a migratory lifestyle defined by any place Asbury deemed fit to send him, but the bishop never asked anyone to go where he himself was unwilling to go, and in all likelihood had not already been.

8. "Enough to Make the Saints of God Weep"

A Foreboding Trip

January 9, 1792 was a cold, snowy Monday as Asbury and Thomas Morrell made their way south in eastern North Carolina. Morrell was no stranger to bitter winter weather. Attaining the rank of Major during the Revolutionary War, he proved himself a capable military leader. A rifle ball that passed through his chest and fractured his shoulder blade at the Battle of Flatbush did little to slow him down. Converted in 1785, he became a diligent and disciplined soldier for the Methodist cause, living until the age of ninety. On January 9, both his and Asbury's life well could have been shortened. The travel plans called for riding five miles in a leaky scow that the passengers feared would sink. The horses, standing in the flat-bottom boat, were liable to be blown into the creek by the high winds. Upon arriving on land, the two of them crawled along a fence because they were unable to stand up on the sheet of ice.

Upon coming to Sapney Creek, which was an ice flow, Morrell suggested that the crossing was too dangerous and that they should turn back. "Mr. Asbury, ever fruitful in invention and quick in execution, with a fence rail undertook to break the ice." Upon Asbury's mounting his horse, the horse slipped down the bank and Asbury fell off. He then mounted a smaller horse and crossed the creek. Asbury returned to the other side, crawling on an icy log, in order to retrieve the horse which had slipped. As Asbury crossed the second time, with Morrell accompanying him, the two of them were almost swept away by the current. Both of them were in danger of freezing to death, a condition little relieved by a house "not of a very promising appearance." Morrell tersely summarized, "This day was pregnant with difficulties."[1] The assessment would have been an understatement for 1792, a year which would haunt Asbury for the rest of his life.

The Prevailing Political Climate

On October 2, 1792, George Washington met with Thomas Jefferson and Alexander Hamilton to act as a mediator between the two feuding statesmen. The rivals were irreconcilable; there was little mediating ground to be discovered between Federalism and Republicanism. The former perceived that political efficiency could be realized only via a strong centralized government; the latter interpreted strong executive powers as akin to monarchy, a yoke that had been thrown off at a dear price. The foes were implacable. Jefferson accused Hamilton of undermining and demolishing the Republic. According to Jefferson, Hamilton personified a "tissue of machinations against the liberty of the country, which has not only received and given him bread, but heaped its honors on his head."[2]

Ironically, Hamilton had cast his political clout behind Thomas Jefferson when the latter was tied with Aaron Burr in the electoral vote of 1800. Hamilton did not like Jefferson, but his animosity for Burr was far greater. Burr was a grandson of Jonathan Edwards, a ladies'man ("honey trickled from his tongue"), and at this time he was a U.S. Senator from New York. Because of the "twistings, combinations and maneuvers" that elected him, Hamilton hated Burr with a hostility of "neurotic proportions."[3] Yet Jefferson's 1800 victory, followed by further recriminations between Burr and Hamilton, would cost Hamilton his life in 1804. Politics was bloody business.

On January 13, 1790, John Wesley had written to John Mason, "As long as I live the people shall have no share in choosing either stewards or leaders among the Methodists. We have not and never had any such customs. We are no Republicans, and never intend to be."[4] After observing England's House of Lords, Wesley wrote, "I had frequently heard that this was the most venerable assembly in England. But how was I disappointed! What is a lord but a sinner, born to die."[5] Wesley's confidence in self-government was almost nil. He believed God's sovereign power was much more trustworthy, if there was only a king in power, as opposed to the unruly populace corrupted by original sin. Autocratic control was the only way to run both nation and church.

In reflecting on Wesley's attempt to stretch his administrative monarchy across the Atlantic, Asbury recalled, "I did not think it practical expediency to obey Mr. Wesley, at three thousand miles' distance in all matters relevant to Church government" (2:106). The distance between Wesley and the new Republic was even farther ideologically than it was geographically. In Wesley, Asbury faced an ideological tension far more treacherous than the icy flowing creek on January 9.

Irish Influence

Before Asbury came, American Methodism owed its embryonic soul to the Irish. Philip Embury immigrated from Ireland to New York in 1760 at the encouragement of Barbara Heck, who had also immigrated from Ireland. Both of them were part of families that had migrated from the Rhine Palatinate, which John Wesley referred to as "about the lowest type of an irreligious, swearing, drunken, community that I have ever met."[6] Embury began to preach to the Irish immigrants in 1765, forming the first gathering of Methodists in the United States. About the same time, the Irishman named Robert Strawbridge had begun preaching in Frederick County, Maryland. He built a small log church about a mile from his house, possibly the first Methodist edifice in all of America.

In 1769, Strawbridge linked up with Robert Williams (an Irish itinerant) and John King (an Oxford graduate, not from Ireland).[7] King was a ranting, raving whirlwind. Upon hearing him, Asbury stated, "In the evening John King preached a good and profitable sermon, but long and loud enough" (1:155). Wesley wrote to King in July 1775, "Scream no more at the peril of your soul. God now warns you by me, who He has set over you. Speak as earnestly as you can, but do not scream. . . . O John, pray for an advisable and teachable spirit! By nature you are very far from it. You are stubborn and headstrong."[8]

Who else could survive in the American wilderness other than the stubborn and headstrong? Asbury sized up Strawbridge as "inflexible" (1:88). Strawbridge was not going to be subject to a British ecclesiasticism imposed by Wesley's representatives. Strawbridge, born at Drumsna, Ireland, had been converted under the preaching of John Wesley sometime before he came to Maryland in 1759.

In order to avoid a showdown, the American preachers, under the chair of Thomas Rankin, voted to allow Strawbridge to administer the sacraments as an exception to all the other Methodist preachers. This concession did not prevent Strawbridge from continuing to chafe under Methodist authority and ultimately drifting away from all supervision. During the Revolutionary War, though serving as pastor of a church in Harford County, Maryland, he was totally independent of Methodist appointment. Seeds of discord were sown early.

James O'Kelly

James O'Kelly, an Irishman born in 1734,[9] immigrated to America in 1778. Being of competent ability and fervent spirit, he was immediately accepted into the Methodist itinerancy and was one of twelve elders ordained at the Christmas Conference. The next year he became a "presiding elder" in the South Virginia District, the general area where he labored for the rest of his life.

Eastern Virginia was the land of aristocracy. When the Tidewater inhabitants came to Williamsburg for the legislative session, courtly, wigged men escorted women dressed in fine silk, velvets, laces, and ribbons. No place in America rivaled Williamsburg for either fashion or, from Methodist perception, spiritual dissipation. Williamsburg was not alone. Thomas Coke noted that he preached at Richmond to the "most dressy congregation" that he had ever seen in America. Virginia was renowned for everything the Methodists were not. Asbury was repulsed by Williamsburg almost as much as he was by Charleston. One wag had written of the steeple of the Bruton Parish Church: 'Would ye not with more cheerfulness pay the assessment to have money raised upon you to mend the streets of Williamsburg . . . than to be taxed to pay for a STEEPLE which is much about as like one as the Emperour of Morocco's pigeon house, or the thing upon the Turkish mosques which they call a minaret where a fellow knocks upon a piece of wood with a mallet to call the mussulmen to prayers?'[10] Upon arriving in Williamsburg, Asbury commented "the Bedlam-house is desolate, but whether because none are insane or all are equally mad, it might perhaps be difficult to tell" (1:434).

No one would have been more incongruent with Eastern Virginia's inhabitants than O'Kelly. The year O'Kelly arrived in America, someone placed in the *Virginia Gazette* an advertisement to purchase "[a]n elegant toothpick case lately imported from Paris, with a smelling bottle and gold stopper at one end."[11] The wealth of eastern Virginia was concentrated in about one hundred forty Tidewater families and, unless a will specified otherwise, that wealth would be passed on via primogeniture. Such autocratic assumptions of both wealth and power would have brought a look of disgust, if not outspoken rancor, to James O'Kelly. To understand the Methodists' feud with James O'Kelly within any type of systemic context, cultural or political, was entirely beyond Asbury's comprehension. In his perception, personal conflicts were rooted in selfish attitudes and spiritual dichotomies. Either way, he believed, Satan and sin were the culprits. Personal conflict was no more contingent on philosophical or cultural currents than the weather. Regarding what would become known as the "O'Kelly Schism," Asbury wrote, "If the real cause of this division was known, I think it would appear, that one wanted to be immovably fixed in a district; another wanted money; a third wanted ordination; a fourth wanted liberty to do as he pleased about slaves, and not to be called to an account, &c." (2:13). In the end, he believed, God would vindicate the righteous and condemn the heretical. But that did not induce Asbury to delay his own forecast of the final outcome.

Asbury's first impression of O'Kelly was favorable. O'Kelly was a moving preacher with a deep compassion for the lost. "James O'Kelly and myself enjoyed and comforted each other: this dear man rose at midnight, and prayed very devoutly for me and himself. He cries, Give me children or I die" (1:365). It should have occurred early on to Asbury that O'Kelly was a person of great zeal, especially when voicing his own opinion. In the 1785 Virginia Conference, there was a heated debate over slavery. "[B]rother O'Kelly let fly at them, and they were made angry enough; we, however, came off with whole bones, and our business in conference was finished in peace" (1:488). A contemporary noted of O'Kelly that he was "irate, somewhat overbearing, bold to bluntness and handled personal characters ungloved" (3:517n.).

Coke Sides with O'Kelly

As has been suggested, the Asbury–O'Kelly conflict was far greater than a clash of egos. Asbury was having difficulty maintaining his administrative grip, to the extent that Coke believed a radical step needed to be taken. O'Kelly persuaded Coke that Asbury's power plays were jeopardizing the fledgling denomination. From O'Kelly's perspective, the "Council" was Asbury's attempt to shore up the fragility of his leadership. The structure was so shaky that Coke investigated the possibility of merger with the Protestant Episcopal Church. On April 24, 1791, Coke wrote a letter to Bishop White of Philadelphia asking, "[W]hat can be done for a reunion, which I wish for, and to accomplish which, Mr. Wesley, I have no doubt, would use his influence to the utmost?"

(3:95). The following, written by Coke, demonstrates the crumbling *esprit de corps* and the lack of candor between the two leaders of American Methodism:

> My desire of a reunion is so sincere and earnest, that these diffi-
> culties make me tremble; and yet something must be done before
> the death of Mr. Wesley, otherwise I shall despair of success; for
> though my influence among the Methodists in these States, as
> well as in Europe, is I doubt not increasing, yet Mr. Asbury whose
> influence is very capital, will not easily comply; nay, I know he
> will be exceedingly averse to it (3:96).

Coke learned of Wesley's death and embarked for England on May 16, 1791. Coke's immediate departure indicated two aspects of his personal perspective. First, the real epicenter of Methodism was not in Baltimore, but in London.[12] Second, someone would need to take Wesley's place—and why not Coke? He was "so agitated that he could not wait for his ship to creep up the channel to the Thames, but hired a fishing boat to land him in Cornwall, whence he took a coach to London."[13]

Before Coke left, he penned a letter to O'Kelly comparing the presiding elder situation to Esther in the Court of Ahasureus. O'Kelly was not to hold his peace but to "be very firm, and very cautious, and very wise and depend upon a faithful friend in Thomas Coke."[14] Holding his peace had never been a real problem for O'Kelly. He was still smarting over the showdown with Asbury at Petersburg, Virginia, the previous winter.

Beginning Tension

If O'Kelly's description was correct, the 1790 conference at Petersburg was one of Asbury's lowest moments. When the conference rejected Asbury's revised Council plan on April 14, he threatened them all with excommunication. O'Kelly later recalled the incident: "I was struck with astonishment to find that we were all expelled [from] the union; by the arbitrary voice of one man. For no offense, but voting according to our own matured judgement."[15] O'Kelly states that at this point Asbury, upon saying, "Ye are all out of the union," gathered up his papers and without closing prayer walked out as "one in distress."[16]

A few days later, however, Asbury repented of his peevishness and confessed that he had not treated O'Kelly with the respect that was due him. On September 21, 1791, Asbury wrote to O'Kelly, "Let all past conduct between thee and me, be buried, and never come before the Conference, or elsewhere,—send me the dove" (3:104). Over the next year, all seemed to be peaceful. Asbury did not again mention O'Kelly in his journal until the first General Conference, November 1, 1792, the jurisdictional device which had replaced the Council. Jesse Lee recalled that "the bishop requested that the name of the *council* might not be mentioned in the Conference again."[17] Asbury's open concession had allowed all the anti-councilists to triumph. It seemed that the case between Asbury and O'Kelly was closed.

But was O'Kelly, as George Wells described him, "a man possessed with a divisive spirit"? Was he an Irishman who would not or could not make truce with British hierarchy, or with any pomp and machinations that smelled of it? To O'Kelly, Asbury was "born and nurtured in the land of Kings and Bishops, and that which is bred in the bone is hard to be got out of the flesh."[18] Were Asbury's political maneuverings so manipulative prior to 1792 that O'Kelly could neither forgive nor forget? At the first Council meeting, when O'Kelly had voiced the opinion that the union of the sect could not be preserved if resolutions were binding on only the districts that adopted them, "Francis jogged my elbow and I ceased speaking."[19] Jesse Lee reported that when O'Kelly returned to Virginia, "[h]e exclaimed bitterly against the proceedings and against what he himself had done in the business. He refused to have anything at all to do with the second council."[20]

From Asbury's perspective, the conflict boiled down to O'Kelly's desire to be the primary leader of American Methodism. Not only did both Asbury and O'Kelly desire leadership positions, their leadership styles clashed. The tenor of O'Kelly's life consistently opted for free forms of both worship and church government. He had been a primary voice at the war-era conference at Flauvanna, Virginia, which opted for participation in the sacraments, uninhibited by the lack of properly ordained clergy. He claimed to have proposed that Asbury present the matter to Wesley. The Virginia Conference would suspend the sacrament while waiting for Wesley's response. O'Kelly was much more aligned to Puritan biblicism than Wesleyan Anglicanism. From his perspective, Anglicanism was personified by Asbury. Asbury was rumored to have stated, "The connection is twined around me," as he marked his fingers over his shoulders and around his body.[21] In the 1792 General Conference, O'Kelly attempted to untwine Asbury; and the string snapped.

The Showdown

On the second day of the 1792 General Conference (which convened November 1 in Baltimore), O'Kelly moved, "After the bishop appoints the preachers at conference to their several circuits, if anyone thinks himself injured by the appointments, he shall have liberty to appeal to the conference and state his objections; and if the conference approve his objections, the bishop shall appoint him to another circuit."[22] On the motion of John Dickens, O'Kelly's motion was divided into two questions, "[1] Shall the bishops appoint the preachers to the circuits? and [2] Shall a preacher be allowed an appeal?" There was little discussion about the first question, but debate on the second issue raged throughout the week and spilled over into the next.

On the day before the conference, Asbury had ridden from Annapolis to Baltimore in a driving rain after holding a district conference the day before. Even before the General Conference began, his emotional and physical energies were drained. He called the Conference to order "feeling awful," but when O'Kelly raised this particular item that dealt with him, he felt much worse. Asbury asked Thomas Coke to preside and then retreated to his room. At that point, he was anything but passive. He penned a letter that utilized a two-pronged political tactic, a tactic which characterized his office for the rest of his life. Asbury made it clear that he was the servant of the conference and was also free of ulterior motives. In Asbury's mind, he was always directed by what was best for the church, corporately and individually.

My Dear Brethren:

Let my absence give you no pain—Dr. Coke presides. I am happily excused from assisting to make laws by which myself am to be governed; I have only to obey and execute. I am happy in the consideration that I never station a preacher through enmity, or as a punishment. I have acted for the glory of God, the good of the people, and to promote the usefulness of the preachers. Are you sure, that, if you please yourselves, the people will be as fully satisfied? They often say, "Let us have such a preacher;" and sometimes, "we will not have such a preacher—we will sooner pay him to stay at home." Perhaps I must say, "his appeal forced him upon you." I am one, ye are many. I am as willing to serve you as ever. I want not to sit in any man's way. I scorn to solicit votes. I am a very trembling, poor creature to hear praise or dispraise. Speak your minds freely; but remember, you are only making laws for the present time. It may be that as in some other things, so in this, a future day may give you further light. I am yours, &c.

Francis Asbury (3:112–113).

The letter worked. While the protagonists were name-calling with no little rancor on the Conference floor, Asbury presented himself as collaborative and apolitical. His response was thoroughly American. In early American politics, one ran for office while simultaneously denying any interest in assuming the office. In the quietness of his room, Asbury's carefully weighed words had depicted a non-anxious presence free of clenched jaw, flushed face, and raised voice. The cool, rational effect of Asbury's letter represented the antithesis of O'Kelly's passion. Thomas Ware noted, "Had Mr. O'Kelly's proposition been differently managed it might possibly have been carried. For myself, at first I did not see anything very objection-able in it. But when it came to be debated, I very much disliked the spirit of those who advocated it, and wondered at the severity in which the movers and others who spoke in favour of it indulged in the course of their remarks."[23]

Ware's comments might lead one to believe that only O'Kelly's exponents displayed anger. Not so. When an Asbury supporter asked if there was anyone who had ever been wronged by an appointment, Rice Haggard answered that he knew of at least two people who had been injured by the bishop. An Asbury proponent screamed, "He has impeached the Bishop! He has impeached the Bishop!"[24] Haggard backtracked, saying that he did not mean to impeach the bishop. It was one of early Methodism's most explosive moments.

The O'Kelly Walkout

But it was ultimately O'Kelly's supporters who overstated their case and thus undermined their cause. They insisted that those who did not vote for the right of appeal "must forfeit all claims of freedom and ought to have their ears bored through with an awl, and be fastened to their master's door, and become slaves for life."[25] Asbury's supporters asked a simple question: Where would the domino effect end, once preachers started appealing for more conducive appointments? O'Kelly had no answer to this.

Acrimonious verbiage had not been O'Kelly's only problem. Coke deserted him; though he had promised his support to O'Kelly, he had instead sided with Asbury. The Monday night after O'Kelly's motion lost by a large majority, Coke agreed to meet with the offended party to repair the breach. O'Kelly told Coke point-blank that he had not only betrayed him but had treated him cruelly. When one of the offended preachers accused Coke of false assertions and pro-fane swearing, the bishop confessed his sins and asked pardon "ten thousand times."[26] A circular that Coke had written on May 4, 1791, illustrates the radi-cal nature of his about-face and shows that O'Kelly had ample reason to accuse him of betrayal.

> Five things we have in view. 1. The abolition of the arbitrary aristocracy. 2. The investing of the nomination of the presiding elders in the conferences of the districts. 3. The limitation of the districts to be invested in the general conference. 4. An appeal allowed each preacher on the reading of the stations. And 5. A general conference of at least two thirds of the preachers as a check upon every thing.[27]

After O'Kelly left the Conference, Coke asked him on what basis he would return to the church. O'Kelly responded that he would remain connected to the conference only if the right of appeal was operative. Coke said that this condition

was impossible. The impasse was irreparable. Jesse Lee described O'Kelly's departure as follows:

> Waiting in town a day or two longer, he and the preachers that
> were particularly influenced by him set off for Virginia, taking
> their saddlebags, great coats, and other bundles on their shoul-
> ders or arms, walking on foot to the place where they left their
> horses which was about twelve miles from town. I stood and looked
> after them as they went off, and observed to one of the preachers,
> that I was sorry to see the old man go off in that way, for I was
> persuaded that he would not be quiet long; but he would try to
> be head of some party.[28]

Lee's prediction was correct; O'Kelly drew off many of the Virginia and North
Carolina Methodists, founding the Methodist Republican Church. Over the next
twenty years, this group became a denomination of some twenty thousand people.
In 1808, they would merge with a party mostly composed of some anti-Calvinist
New England Baptists and the Barton Stone Christian Church to form the "Christian Connection." Such early losses to Methodism were a serious blow to its
stability. Lee wrote, "It was enough to make the saints of God weep between the
porch and the altar to see how the Lord's flock was carried away captive."[29]

On April 2, 1793, O'Kelly and his followers met at Piney Grove in Chester-
field County, Virginia, to discuss their future with Methodism. They decided to
present a petition to Asbury that "although he has not power himself to redress
us, yet if we can attain his consent to call a meeting on the subject, as requested in
our petition in order to form a permanent plan for peace and union taking the
holy scripture for our guide, We will cheerfully wait." This petition was presented at the Virginia Conference at Petersburg, November 25, 1793, by John
Barker, Robert Walthal and Thomas Goode. Asbury recorded, "Our disaffected
brethren have had a meeting at the Piny Grove, in Amelia circuit and appointed
three men to attend this conference. We gave them a long talk" (1:775). After
presenting it before the Conference, Asbury reportedly responded to the visiting
petitioners, "I have no power to call such a meeting as you wish, therefore if 500
preachers would come on their knees before me I would not do it."[30]

Continuing Animosity

Methodism eventually recovered from the split, but Asbury would never find
healing from O'Kelly's invective. During the schismatic conference, Asbury took a
cold and found relief by going to bed and sweating it out. "I am not fond of alter-
cations—we cannot please everybody—and sometimes not ourselves. I am resigned"
(1:734). But Asbury was not resigned, especially to the impugning of his character,
which had come from a person whom he perceived to be a power monger.

Asbury was convinced that any compromise of his authority would jeopardize the Methodist system. History was to prove him wrong, as O'Kelly's calls for moderation were later implemented. O'Kelly was a man before his time, a voice that would never be completely forgotten, its echoes reverberating in the "reformed party." O'Kelly's republicanism influenced the later "episcopal consultation in the making of appointments, elective presiding elders, conference rights for local preachers, lay representation in General and Annual Conference, and above all free and open debate."[31]

As soon as the 1792 General Conference was over, Asbury wrote a letter to Thomas Morrell assailing O'Kelly's motives: ambition, insubordination, subversion, and collusion. The letter served as an opportunity for Asbury to vent his anger. It may have been remorse that led Asbury, in the Virginia Conference two weeks later, to suggest that the disaffected minister still be allowed to preach in Methodist churches. Asbury also suggested that O'Kelly be paid forty pounds per year on the condition that he would not excite divisions among the people. Asbury believed this would do no harm, in view of the fact that O'Kelly "is almost worn out." Asbury's offer fell far short of placating O'Kelly and his followers. Lee said that Asbury "was more despised by them than any other man."[32]

Devereux Jarratt believed that American Methodism's self-assured independence was destined to produce an O'Kelly sooner or later. Jarratt had laughed in Thomas Coke's face when Coke produced episcopal credentials granted by Wesley, which Jarratt pronounced "farcical and ludicrous" (3:83n.). Jarratt observed, "O'Kelly does great things in the divisive way and I dare say he will make Asbury's Mitre set very uneasy on his head, so as to give sensible pain to his heart, and it may be to such a degree, that he may sincerely wish Dr. Coke had never given him a Mitre at all. Indeed I never expected that Mitre would set easy for any considerable length of time, as it was but a cobble piece of work at first—and Dr. Coke was the principal agent" (3:138n.).

The uneasiness would not go away. On July 1, 1798, Asbury wrote, "James hath turned the butt-end of his whip, and is unanswerably abusive" (2:163); and on July 22, "I am the grand butt of all his spleen" (2:165). The spleen was spilled out in O'Kelly's *Apology* (date unknown), and *Vindication of the Author's Apology*, 1801. These long rambling tracts argued for a biblically based church government as opposed to a "spurious" episcopacy. He believed that, in a "clandestine" manner, Asbury had intentionally sought to displace Wesley.

According to O'Kelly, Asbury acted unilaterally without giving sufficient reason for his actions. "But as we were men under authority, we feared to offend our superior. He would often pray that God would deliver the preachers from the curse of suspicion. This prayer had the desired effect on some of us."[33] O'Kelly made it clear that he was not against Asbury because he was an Englishman; it was quite possible to be from the land of kings and bishops and at the same time republican. However, in O'Kelly's mind, Asbury had not been Americanized to the extent that he could recognize the incongruity between his autocratic style and democratic ideals.

O'Kelly's ideals were his undoing. His rambling incoherency grew worse as he grew older. In 1805, Asbury penned, "Mr. O'Kelly has come down with great zeal, and preaches three hours at a time upon government, monarchy, and episcopacy; occasionally varying the subject by abuse of the Methodists, calling them aristocrats and Tories; a people who, if they had the power, would force the government at the sword's point. Poor man!" (2:459).[34]

William McKendree

Republican Methodism led by O'Kelly continued to be characterized by a fractious and restless mentality. In 1809, William Spencer wrote a letter to John Robinson, an O'Kelly convert, attempting to entice him to return to the Methodist Episcopal fold:

> Now it was that Hell triumphed with infernal joy! Now it was that Brother had his sword, oh! the ugly-looking sword of contention, drawn against Brother and even Sister and Sister were at it too! Was this a work of God? No! No! No! Well, what is the upshot of the whole? Let truth speak for itself. In the name of God, I ask, where is the fine Church that poor man talked so much about? I have never seen nor heard of it yet (3:420).

One who did return to the Methodist fold was William McKendree. McKendree was thirty-five years old at the time of the schism and had been under the supervision of O'Kelly almost the entirety of his four-year ministerial experience. McKendree was fed such a steady diet of diatribe against Asbury that he was biased against the "bishop and his creatures." "I really loved God, and sought the welfare of his church, and was therefore disposed to listen to her complaints. The old gentleman (M. Ok.) I looked upon as her friend, her mouth, and so great was my confidence in him that his word was next to gospel with me."[35] McKendree had been as vehement as O'Kelly on the Conference floor. Over thirty years later, Ezekiel Cooper attempted to reconstruct McKendree's words against Asbury as follows: "It's an insult to my understanding and such an arbitrary stretch of power, so tyrannical that I cannot submit to it."[36] When McKendree told Asbury he had lost confidence in him, Asbury responded, "I do not wonder at that, Brother, sometimes we see with our eyes; sometimes we see only with our ears."[37]

When Asbury was in Virginia in January of 1791, McKendree had joined him for a twenty-six-mile ride through blowing snow. Though it was extremely cold and both horses and riders much fatigued, McKendree was "astonished at the bishop's sweet simplicity and uncommon familiarity. Love appeared to sweeten all our conversation."[38] McKendree stated that his only motive for traveling with the bishop was to find out if O'Kelly's representations were accurate. "[T]o my great astonishment I found him just the reverse of what he was represented, and I was fully satisfied."[39]

Within several months after the schism, McKendree realized his error and returned to Methodism. He was elected as the first native-born American bishop of the Methodist Episcopal Church in 1808.

Nicholas Snethen

In 1800, Nicholas Snethen, thirty-one years old, was chosen to travel with Asbury. Snethen was such a capable preacher that Asbury referred to him as his "silver trumpet." Elected secretary of the general conference in 1800, he was also appointed to a committee to make reply to O'Kelly's *Apology*. Although he was the youngest of the committee, his fluency in both speech and writing determined that he would be the principal writer. When Snethen presented his response four months later, Asbury pronounced it as "soft and defensive, and as little offensive as the nature of the case would admit" (2:246–247).

Snethen's biographer, Harlan Feeman, argues that while Snethen tried to represent the thoughts of Asbury, he was really sympathetic to O'Kelly's position. "It was not Snethen's ideas, but a compilation of Asbury's [ideas] clothed in Snethen's language. . . . He believed that if O'Kelly had been less impulsive and violent in pursuit of his objective, and more patient, he would in time have achieved his goal and without separation from the Methodist Church."[40]

Feeman's argument is historically supported by the fact that Snethen became a leading spokesman and writer for the Methodist Protestants in the 1830s concerning lay representation and clerical suffrage. Snethen argued that success was not sufficient justification for autocracy. "It is, indeed, beyond all doubt, that any leader, in church or state, with absolute authority, can do more than if he were fettered by system; and yet is a universally admitted fact that no governments are liable to sink under their own weight as absolute ones."[41] It was Snethen who said, "There was nothing in this world he [Asbury] so much dreaded as a preacher who was not always in action. . . . There is a real danger on this vast continent of men travelling wild, quite wild."[42] Asbury's autocracy could produce action, but not necessarily precise thinking about ecclesiology and its relationship to social order.

An Unhealed Memory

The O'Kelly confrontation troubled Asbury for the rest of his life. In his valedictory address penned to William McKendree on August 5, 1813, he reminded the junior bishop, "We have lived to see the end of such persons who left us and set up for themselves—witness Hammet and O'Kelly." Hammet was an

Irishman whom Coke brought from the West Indies and who caused a schism in Charleston, South Carolina, in 1792. Hammet let it be known quite vocally that he was not going to be subject to Asbury.[43] Needless to say, 1792 was not a good year for the bishop, and once again Coke had proved himself a poor judge of character.[44]

It would not be the last time that Coke's judgment perturbed Asbury. In 1796, Asbury wrote, "Dr. Coke had well nigh ruined his credit by recommending one of the worst men in the continent, an adulterer, a cheat, a murderer, that he deceived me, set Dr. Coke and Mr. Wesley against me with his lies."[45] (It is not clear whether Asbury was speaking of Hammet or someone else.)

In his final conference address, written January 8, 1816, and read posthumously, Asbury referred to O'Kelly no less than three times. He observed that division was an "evil and bitter thing, a sin of sins, a mass of evils hardly to be described or enumerated," leading away persons as did James O'Kelly, "to groan upon a dying bed with a backslidden heart!" (3:534). Asbury gloated that the remnants of O'Kelly's followers were now scattered. The victory yell seemed hollow, particularly in the context of Methodism's ultimate goal, perfection in love to both God and humankind, especially fellow believers.

Perhaps the most helpful clue in understanding the Asbury–O'Kelly antagonism is found in Asbury's response to O'Kelly's letter, which followed the first Council meeting. O'Kelly asked for a one-year moratorium on the Council, or at least for Asbury to rescind his power of veto. O'Kelly warned Asbury that he would use his influence among the preachers against the bishop. On January 12, 1790, Asbury wrote to O'Kelly, "Thy letter greatly alarmed me. But pray who boldly demanded my negative? My negative is my own. *I never have received such a check from any preacher in America* [Italics mine]" (3:81). The egos of O'Kelly and Asbury could not occupy the same space; one had to go.

Final Meeting

The last time that O'Kelly and Asbury met was on Sunday, August 22, 1802. O'Kelly had taken sick and was being nursed at Winchester, Virginia. Asbury sent two preachers to see how O'Kelly was doing, and possibly to extend an olive branch. If O'Kelly desired, Asbury would pay a visit. O'Kelly extended the invitation, and a polite exchange took place at O'Kelly's bedside. The deep antagonism between the two leaders was not broached. "We met in peace, asked of each other's welfare, talked of persons and things indifferently, prayed, and parted in peace. Not a word was said of the troubles of former times:—perhaps this is the last interview we shall have upon earth" (2:359). The opportunity for healing reconciliation was forever lost.

One of O'Kelly's sympathizers, William Guirey, would become an agitator for republican reform over the next several years. He published his ideas via a periodical entitled, *The Baltimore Bull*, his nickname for Asbury. Guirey sided at first with James O'Kelly, but the two later parted over doctrinal differences. Guirey founded the Independent Baptist Church. Asbury made no mention of him, but Guirey wrote, "Should not every friend to religion, liberty and the Methodist connection, in America, lament that Mr. Asbury did not accompany the fugitive missionaries to England"[46] (3:22–23). Guirey was received on trial as a Methodist preacher in 1795 and retained his credentials only through 1796.[47] Ironically, Guirey was converted under the same Von Wrangle who persuaded Wesley to send missionaries to America.

In 1792, Asbury had printed *The Causes, Evils and Cures of Heart and Church Divisions,* extracts from the writings of Jeremy Burroughs and Richard Baxter. Burroughs (1599–1646) was a nonconformist rector at Tivets Hall, Norfolk, England. He is best known for his dissenting *Apologetical Narration*, which he presented to Parliament in 1644.[48] Baxter, nonconformist pastor at Kidderminster, was best known for his work, *The Reformed Pastor.* Asbury concluded that "[r]igid, harsh, sour, crabbed, rough-hewn spirits, are unfit for union: there is no sweetness, no amiableness, no pleasingness in them."[49] Sweetness is a commodity often in short supply in strong-willed personalities. Asbury wrote,

> When wisdom, holiness, and humility are their nature, and selfish pride and worldliness are cured, this wrinkled, malignant enmity will then cease, and an honest emulation to excel one another in wisdom, love, and all good works, will then take place; and then we shall not, like drunken men, one day fight and wound each other, and the next cry out of our wounds, and yet go on in our drunken fits to make them still wider.[50]

The day of reconciliation never came. Possibly the conflict can be best understood from the perspective that "pride makes men swell beyond their bounds; the way to keep all things in union is for every man to keep within his bounds."[51] Both O'Kelly and Asbury would have agreed. They just couldn't agree on who was going to decide the bounds.

9. "It Is for Holiness My Spirit Mourns"

The Scandal of Charleston

Asbury began 1793 in South Carolina, where he headquartered for the winter. The conference was still reeling from the schism caused by William Hammet, the Irish preacher imported by Thomas Coke. There were accusations that Asbury was the real problem because he had not fixed authority in John Wesley, therefore allowing for schismatic tendencies. All of this was compounded by the fact that the South wasn't Asbury's favorite place. The swamps, thickets, and insects in abundance, and of course, the abominable slave labor, which was more prevalent in South Carolina than in any other colony, tore at both his body and soul.

A 1765 visitor to South Carolina noted that "The laborious business is here chiefly done by black slaves of which there are great multitudes. The climate is very warm. The chief produce is rice and indigo. . . . The whites in this province are composed at about twenty thousand and the blacks at 4 [sic] times that number."[1] Free labor and huge rice plantations translated into wealth. It is said that "of the ten wealthiest men who died in the mainland colonies in 1774, nine made their fortunes in South Carolina."[2] The flow of goods, services, and money produced pretentious dress and activities incompatible with Methodism's austerity.

While in Charleston during February of 1794, Asbury wrote, "I have had a time of deep dejection of spirits, affliction of body, loss of sleep, and trouble of soul. . . . I find this to be a barren place; I long to go to my work. When gloomy melancholy comes on, I find it best to think as little as may be about distressing subjects. . . . I now leave Charleston, the seat of Satan, dissipation, and folly: ten months hereafter, with the permission of divine Providence, I expect to see it again" (2:6). Asbury's sensitivities were not entirely subjective. Preaching occasions attracted only a "few old women"; passersby hailed his small flock with insults and shouts. "I was insulted on the pavement with some as horrible sayings as could come out of a creature's mouth on this side of hell" (2:41). "What blanks are in this country—and how much worse are rice plantations! If a man-of-war is 'a floating hell,' these are standing ones: wicked masters, overseers, and Negroes—cursing, drinking—no Sabbaths, no sermons" (2:7).

Charleston was by far the leading slave post in the United States. "In 1772 and 1773 sixty-five vessels, their holds jammed with more than 10,000 black Africans, tied off Charles Town's wharfs."[3] For those who extracted the Blacks from these hellholes, the sights and smells were nauseating. Before the outbound ships could be filled with commodities, the excrement, urine, and vomit had to be cleaned out. The odor was so permeating that the ships were "smoked by dropping lead bullets into buckets of vinegar."[4] Almost all of Charleston's wealth was gained from the sweat of slaves. Typical was Colonel John Stuart, who owned over 15,000 acres of land worked by 200 slaves. His three-story house, which he built of black cypress and pine timbers at the cost of 2,350 sterling pounds, still stands in Charleston today.[5] Walter Fraser claims, "In 1791, South Carolina grew 1,500,000 pounds of cotton, a decade later 20 million, and production doubled again within the next ten years"[6]—and all fueled by slave labor.

The four-year period from 1792 to 1796 was not a prosperous time for Methodism. Membership decreased by 9,316.[7] Asbury was now approaching fifty years of age and sensed himself losing physical stamina. "Twenty years ago a rude, open loft did not affect me—now it seldom fails to injure me" (1:753). He seriously contemplated the need for another bishop who would lessen his workload. Asbury's ecclesiastical burden was compounded by the extension of the Methodist territory into the West. Not only did he have to contend with exceedingly rough terrain, but there was the added necessity of traveling in large companies because of the threat of hostile Indians.

For Asbury, the Indian danger was not nearly as annoying as the swearers and drunkards with whom he had to travel. His anxiety was compounded by the irregularity of meals, sleep, and prayer, all of which brought on severe physical and mental affliction. When he accidentally caught his clothes on fire in eastern Tennessee, he was almost to the point of despair. After arriving back in Virginia he wrote, "I have little rest by night or by day. Lord, help thy poor dust! I feel unexpected storms—within from various quarters; perhaps it is designed for my humiliation" (1:758).

Fallout with Jesse Lee

The acrimony of the 1792 walkout had not fully quieted. Jesse Lee, now thirty-four years old and of imposing frame, charismatic personality, outspoken disposition, and immense energy, was quickly becoming one of the most popular leaders within Methodism. We do not know whether Lee voted for or against James O'Kelly, but he was sympathetic to O'Kelly.[8] Lee almost always represented the party which voted for limitation of the bishop's power. His first opportunity to act out his frustration was at the New England Annual Conference, August 1793, when he refused to accept an appointment to York, Pennsylvania. Methodists at his current appointment of Lynn, Massachusetts, wanted to get rid of Lee because he had been so adamant in enforcing Methodism's outlawing of "fugue" tunes.[9] Asbury attempted a compromise by requesting that Lee go to Maine.

Lee agreed to this second request if his name would be entered into the *Minutes* as stationed in both Lynn and Maine. Ezekiel Cooper recorded his thoughts on the stalemate: "There appears to have existed a jealously between Brother Asbury and Brother Lee for some time; and probably, what has passed at this conference will not be soon forgotten; . . . I truly wonder that a man of sense should be troublesome and unreasonable and ungovernable, so stiff and set."[10] Asbury summed up the New England Conference: "Circumstances have occurred which have made this conference more painful than any one conference beside" (1:767). This event returned to haunt Lee in 1800.

The Doctrine of Entire Sanctification

During the summer of 1793, Asbury was plagued by rheumatic pains, loss of sleep, sick headaches, inflammation of the throat, fever, influenza, and a pain in his right foot. "Our roads are rough; I am sick; our fare is coarse; but it is enough— I am to die. I have been under violent temptations—Lord, keep me every moment!" (1:761). After some soul-searching, Asbury concluded, "I have found by secret search, that I have not preached sanctification as I should have done: if I am restored, this shall be my theme more pointedly than ever, God being my helper" (1:769).

"Entire sanctification" was the distinct doctrine of Methodism, and the American church had inherited it from Wesley. The first official *Minutes* of American Methodism instructed, "Strongly and explicitly exhort all Believers to *go on to perfection*. That we may *all speak the same Thing*, we ask once for all, Shall we defend this Perfection, or give it up? We all agreed to defend it, meaning thereby (as we did from the Beginning) Salvation from all Sin by the Love of God and man filling the Heart."[11] As John Peters documents, many of the early American preachers were strong exponents of the doctrine of entire sanctification. Thomas Webb preached to a New York congregation, "You must be sanctified! But you are not. You are only Christians in part. You have not received the Holy Ghost. I know it. I can feel your spirit hanging about me like so much dead flesh."[12]

By 1789, the newly formed church had included in its *Discipline* a specific statement on "perfection," a term synonymous with "entire sanctification," which made the following points of definition: 1. Entire sanctification is something that can be attained, experienced, and lived in this life. 2. The attaining is both gradual and instantaneous, that is, a regenerated person can grow in sanctification until there is a definitive point in time when a person is made perfect. 3. This perfection does not mean that a person is no longer flawed by "houses of clay," which are mired by not always speaking and acting rightly. 4. There is a direct correlation between the expecting of the work and the experiencing of the work: "the more earnestly they expect this the more swiftly and steadily does the gradual work of God go on in their souls."[13]

Also in 1789, the tiny *Discipline* was buttressed by the ninety pages of *A Plain Account of Christian Perfection, As Believed and Taught by the Reverend Mr. John Wesley from the Year 1725 to the Year 1765*. The *Plain Account* was a carefully nuanced dialectic on the doctrine of holiness. Wesley explained that experiencing entire sanctification enables a person to be blameless but not faultless, to possess purity of intention but not infallibility of performance. It gives the power to eliminate volitional transgressions against the known law of God, but not to fulfill the perfect law of God. Entirely sanctified persons do not always carry out perfect love to either God or persons; therefore they always need the intercession of Christ and his atonement. A perfect man was, according to Wesley (quoting Archbishop James Ussher), one who unceasingly offers up "every thought, word and work as a spiritual sacrifice; acceptable to God, through Christ."[14] Infirmities, human frailties, limitations, and errors of judgment would remain: pure love would govern all motives and intentions.[15]

Wesley made several distinct points in his *Plain Account* that would provide the salient staples for American Methodist preaching: 1. It is possible to experience a total death to sin subsequent to the forgiveness of sins. 2. The Spirit will witness to entire sanctification, just as distinctly as He does to justification. 3. A person who is made perfect in love is liable to both mistakes and temptations. 4. It is possible to fall from grace, even when entirely sanctified. 5. Perfection is wrought in the soul by a simple act of faith; consequently, in an instant. The instant would be both preceded and followed by growth in grace.

In summary, Wesley stated in his *Plain Account* that it was both his belief and that of his brother Charles "that we are to expect it not at death but every moment, and now is the expected time, now is the day of this salvation."[16] Making this claim, Wesley oversimplified. There was running contention between John and Charles as to whether one could experience entire sanctification before the moment of physical death. Charles Wesley tended to believe that one's dying moment marked the transition into entire sanctification.[17]

Asbury was much closer to John than he was to Charles, in that he taught and expected entire sanctification to occur instantaneously. On January 10, 1773, Asbury testified to feeling "much power while preaching on perfect love. The more I speak on this subject, the more my soul is filled and drawn out in love. This doctrine has a great lending to prevent people from settling on their lees" (1:66). On March 20, 1784, he wrote to John Wesley, "Sometimes I am ready to say, he hath purified my heart; but then again, I feel and fear. Upon the whole I hope I am more spiritual than ever I have been in time past. I see the necessity of preaching a full and present salvation from all sin. When ever I do this, I feel myself, and so do also my hearers" (3:3:34).[18]

Sanctification Experiences

Asbury pressed this doctrine on his preachers. Phillip Gatch was told as a young convert that "if the Lord would sanctify me, I should be better prepared to speak his word."[19] As he was joining his family in prayer, a great "trembling seized" him. When Gatch began to pray audibly for his own spiritual condition, a "weight of glory" pushed him face down on the floor. "[T]he Lord said by his Spirit, 'you are now sanctified, proceed to grow in the fruit of the Spirit.'"[20]

Even more dramatic was the sanctification experience of the eccentric Methodist preacher Benjamin Abbott (everything was more dramatic for Abbott). At Abbott's home, during family prayer, Daniel Ruff interceded with the words, "Lord come and sanctify this family soul and body."

> That moment, the Spirit of God came upon me in such a manner, that I fell flat to the floor, and lay as one strangling in blood, while my wife and children stood weeping over me. But I had not power to lift hand or foot, nor yet to speak one word; I believe I lay half an hour, and felt the power of God, running through every part of my soul and body, like a fire consuming the inward corruptions of fallen depraved nature. When I arose and walked out of the door, and stood pondering these things in my heart, it appeared to me that the whole creation was praising God; it also appeared as if I had got new eyes, for everything appeared new, and I felt a love for all the creatures that God had made, and an uninterrupted peace filled my breast. In three days, God gave me a full assurance that he had sanctified me, soul and body. If a man love me he will keep my words: and my father will love him, and he will come unto him and make our abode with him. John xiv. 23. Which I found day by day, manifested to my soul, by the witness of his Spirit; glory to God for what he then did and since has done for poor me.[21]

For others who sought entire sanctification, their pursuit seemed never to find spiritual certitude. William Colbert's journal is a constant elegy of human sorrow, trouble, anxiety, distress, and vexation.[22] He wrote, "I sometimes feel as if I was born to be unblessed in this world."[23] At other times, Colbert referred to himself as a "dead dog" and stated that he "loathed" himself. Nelson Reed wrote, "O my helplessness and unprofitableness how short do I come of answering the end I was made for."[24] On his twenty-fourth birthday, Thomas Haskins noted, "This is my birthday. 24 years I have numbered but to how little purpose. I have only breathed."[25] Indeed, Methodist preachers could be self-debasing.

Journeying and Journaling

Asbury's pursuit of, experience of, and preaching of entire sanctification must be understood in the context of his entire spiritual journey. The quest for holiness is the primary thesis of his journal, which is quite possibly the most exhaustive account of introspective spiritual formation that we have from any American before the Civil War. Asbury's journal offers us a detailed account of the ups and downs, defeats and victories of his perception of his relationship with God.

Asbury's lack of comment on national and contemporary events does not mean that he was oblivious to current affairs. Rather, he considered the journey of his own soul to be much more important than the endless miles on horseback. His own spirituality was his first obligation. Within the first two weeks of being in the new country, Asbury wrote, "It is for holiness my spirit mourns. I want to walk constantly before God without reproof" (1:8).

Reflecting on his youth, Asbury related the following concerning his spiritual journey: "Sometime after I had obtained a clear witness of my acceptance with God, the Lord showed me in the heat of youth and youthful blood, the evil of my heart; For a short time I enjoyed, as I thought, the pure and perfect love of God; but this happy frame did not long continue, although, at seasons, I was greatly blessed" (1:722). Analyzing this recollection calls for a couple of observations. First, there is not a clear demarcation in Asbury's thinking between that which needs to be disciplined by grace and that which needs to be cleansed by grace. Second, though Asbury understood this adolescent experience as beneficial, he did not perceive it as permanent. This may have caused later vacillation in preaching and teaching entire sanctification, at least in his earlier years as bishop.

The health of Asbury's relationship with God was vitally related to both the evangelistic and pastoral task. When Asbury wrote on April 29, 1774, "I must be sure to take care of my own soul, that is more to me than all the world and the men in it!" he was not stating a selfish prerogative. Taking care of his own soul was the only way of taking care of the souls of others. Paradoxically, personal sanctification was both an end in itself and a means to an end. Becoming holy was the means for enabling others to be holy. One could not confidently preach what one had not experienced, or at least was not diligently seeking.

Spiritual Guilt

Asbury understood that health of soul was inextricably bound to spiritual intention. Sanctification required active spiritual pursuit; hallowing life both internally and externally was something to be done by the seeker. The accomplishment of this goal was to be found mainly through prayer, studying the Scriptures, and being faithful to the mission, in spite of all the obstacles. The obstacles meant that spirituality had to be played on an uneven field. Asbury, who was obsessed by spiritual regularity, faced an uphill climb of almost constant irregularity. "I . . . deplore my loss of strict communion with God, occasioned by the necessity I am under of constant riding, change of place, company, and sometimes disagreeable company, loss of sleep, and the difficulties of clambering over rocks and mountains, and journeying at the rate of seven or eight hundred miles per month, and sometimes forty or fifty miles a day. These have been a part of my labours, and make no small share of my hindrances" (1:714).

Asbury's early ministry was plagued with guilt that he did not spiritually measure up. There was a gap between his inward devotion and his idealized spiritual self. In his personal assessment, he often had too little appetite for prayer and

Bible study. "But how is my soul troubled that I am not more devoted! O my God! my soul groans and longs for this" (1:30). That he did not measure up to the Wesleyan doctrine of sanctification (that is, being entirely holy in thought, word, and deed) was continually troubling. He often cried out, pleading that in spite of his spiritual lethargy, God would continue to be faithful to him and not forsake him. "Let me die rather than live to sin against thee!" (1:48).

On January 4, 1773, Asbury wrote, "Holiness is the element of my soul. My earnest prayer is, that nothing contrary to holiness may live in me" (1:66). Asbury exercised little faith, at least in the early days of his American ministry, that holiness of heart and life would be soon realized. "The Lord favours me with great discoveries of my defects and unfaithfulness. But, blessed be God, my soul is humbled under these discoveries. My soul panteth for more of the Divine nature. When shall I be fully conformed to his blessed will?" (1:81).

Asbury was convinced that certain characteristics of his personality were displeasing to God. His quickness to perceive the ironic and the comedic tended toward levity and at times even sarcasm. Sardonic remarks were a way of relieving stress and even venting frustration, but Asbury felt them to be weaknesses of the flesh and evidences of carnal attitudes. All of this was combined with the sheer enjoyment of telling a good story, especially in the company of peers. "I was condemned for telling humorous anecdotes, and knew not whether it was guilt or fear, lest my friends should think I go beyond the bounds of prudent liberty" (1:365).

Asbury tenaciously believed that he would be truly sanctified by cautious discipline and more careful attention to his relationship with God. "My present purpose is, if the Lord spares and raises me up, to be more watchful and circumspect in all my ways" (1:95). But his intentions were always frustrated by the natural inclinations of both flesh and temperament. "I felt some conviction for sleeping too long; and my mind was troubled on account of a conversation which had past between Mr. Rankin, Mr. S., and myself" (1:128). There was the constant longing to be holy and the plaguing guilt that he was not. "Am both grieved and ashamed that my soul is not more steadily and fervently devoted to God" (1:130).

Asbury's spiritual pursuit was filled with confessions of carelessness in his spiritual life, triviality in conversation, impatience, discontent, idle words, and lack of holy affection. He was also bothered about traveling on the Sabbath. Of course, there was always the dead-tired body to conquer. "My conscience smote me severely for lying in bed till six o'clock this morning, no indisposition of body being the cause. O! why should we lose one hour, when time is so short and precious, and so many things to be learned and taught" (1:301). False accusations, recalcitrant preachers, and stark deprivation jaded his spiritual pursuit with both despair and anger.

Asbury was theologically astute enough to know that his spiritual troubles could not be conquered by sheer effort. Discipline was futile outside of Christ and his provision. Personal holiness would have to be objectively grounded in, and personally connected to, faith in the atonement of Christ. The realization of full salvation was to be found in Wesley's synergism, a cooperation of human resolve and the resources of grace—in other words, grace enabling human effort. Holiness would be attained by the confluence of human effort and divine provision. "True, I should be daily employed in the duty of self-examination, and strictly attend both to my internal and external conduct; but, at the same time, my soul should steadily fix the eye of faith on the blessed Jesus, my Mediator and Advocate at the right hand of the eternal Father" (1:119).

The Question of Immediacy

Asbury's claim that he attempted to make sanctification the "burden and labour of every sermon" merits analysis (2:283). Asbury often incorporated the topic of sanctification into a sermon.[26] Rarely did Asbury focus any sermon exclusively on sanctification.[27] However, he preached on many texts from which we might infer that he forthrightly or tangentially treated the subject of holiness.[28] Asbury rarely if ever used the term "entire sanctification," preferring the more general expression of "sanctification."[29]

Asbury frequently noted the number of converts under his ministry and elsewhere, but he infrequently gave account of persons sanctified.[30] The exception to this was the year that Asbury announced that "our Pentecost has come in some places for sanctification" (July 20, 1806, 3:351). On November 7, 1806, Asbury calculated that there had been 4, 330 sanctified in Methodist camp meetings that year.

On more than one occasion, Asbury purposed to preach more consistently on sanctification.[31] Yet these resolutions produced no discernible pattern in his preaching, at least as recorded in his journal.[32] Several reasons for this unfulfilled ideal are readily apparent. Asbury preached mostly to non-Christians, those whom he called "insensible" and "marble-hearted." The texts for a great portion of Asbury's sermons were evangelistically geared.[33] Asbury considered perfection and sanctification as not "common placed texts"; therefore they were to be reserved for the more spiritually mature, those ready to hear and receive them. For that reason, sanctification was more often experienced at love feasts (testimony meeting) and camp meetings than at evangelistic preaching services. Asbury was well aware of Wesley's advice to preach sanctification "scarcely at all" to those who were not pressing forward.[34] But to those who were pressing forward Asbury did not equivocate. On March 4, 1809, he wrote to Mrs. John Brightwell, "You will never know heaven upon earth till you gain sanctifying grace. Seek, seek it! Seek it now, in every means by faith, and in bearing every cross" (3:405). He exhorted Thomas Coke to "preach instantaneous salvation from all sin" (3:222). To Thornton Fleming he wrote, "O, my brother, preach fully upon holiness in every sermon, where there is but one believer (3:224)."

The Ambivalence of Assurance

Throughout his journal Asbury laid claim to sanctification, but he often backed away from certitude. As early as 1773 he wrote, "He favours me with sweet peace, and sanctifies all my affections" (1:98). In 1774 he recorded, "[B]lessed be God! he fills me with peace and purity. Lord, grant that this may be my portion, increasing forever!" (1:114). In 1780 he testified that he was ready to think that God had saved him from all sin (1:338). In other words, Asbury had come to the place that, according to Wesley's definition of sin (that is, a willful transgression of a known law of God), he had power to live the holy life. The holy life was most evidenced by the ability to refrain from willful transgression of God's commandments.

Even so, Asbury was often dissatisfied with himself spiritually. On May 15, 1780, he recorded, "I am for attending my twelve times of prayer, and resisting the devil steadfastly in the faith. I am much humbled before the Lord; a blessing I want, and will not cease crying to the Lord for it" (1:350-351). On May 24, Asbury's inner being cried out, "O, for faith to be saved from all sin!" (1:353). The twenty-eighth day of the following month, Asbury was oppressed by thoughts of the Revolution, the spiritual deadness of the people, the slavery economy surrounding him, and the lack of a place of retreat that would provide a spiritual quiet time to feed his own soul. Again he uttered a piteous cry, "O, my God! when shall I be established in purity?" (1:362).

When Asbury was only thirty-five years old; his life had already been filled with conflict caused by unclear lines of authority, absence from his native country, continual anxiety about the welfare of his parents, and the responsibility to provide sufficient sustenance for the scores of preachers. As a single male, he had sexual needs that could not be fulfilled in the normal avenues of marriage. The temptations to lust, disgust, and discontent were at times almost overwhelming.

On April 1, 1780, Asbury rose at 3:30 A.M. and set out for Broad Creek, Dela-ware. As he rode along in the darkness, spiritual confidence surged through his soul. Temptation was easily defeated by prayer and meditation on God's goodness. At other times, however, Asbury was not nearly as confident. This was often due to the difficulty of separating his psychological state from his spiritual condition. He was often subject to depression and melancholy. At times, this was brought on by his rigid asceticism. After fasting on April 1, 1786, a deep dejection swept over him so that he could hardly function. At one point he blamed tea and coffee for his gloom (1:447). Whatever the cause, Asbury was aware that he had a disposition to depression. Referred to as the "gloomy dean" of American Methodism, he regarded himself as "a true prophet of evil tidings, as it suits my cast of mind."[35]

Both Asbury and Wesley faced the paradox with which many Christians have struggled. To claim holiness (to be made perfect in love) is to risk pride and presumption. To dismiss the possibility of certitude is to risk falling short of the full grace of God. The paradox begs the question: Does the full realization of holiness (being sanctified through and through) produce satisfaction, a sense of having "arrived," or does it intensify one's hunger for more of God?

Stabilizing Grace

On August 6, 1786, Asbury wrote of an "overwhelming thought" that had passed through his mind. "I was saved from the remains of sin" (1:518). On June 11, 1787, Asbury testified to having reached a new spiritual plateau. "I feel myself dead to all below, and desire to live only for God and souls" (1:542). Even during the turbulent year of 1791, with all of the conflict raging around him concerning the Council, he prayed, "O Lord, help me to watch and pray! I am afraid of losing the sweetness I feel: for months past I have felt as if in the possession of perfect love; not a moments desire of anything but God" (1:696). In 1792, as political attacks gouged him en route to survey the ruins of a split church in Charleston, he wrote, "I can praise God—my soul is happy in Him; by his grace I am kept from sin, and I still hope this dark cloud that lowers over us will yet break with blessings on our heads" (1:705).

Three years later, on June 11, 1795, Asbury stated that even though he was dejected in spirit, unwell in body, crowded with company, and under deep depression, "I am not conscious of any sin, even in thought" (2:52). Again in 1804, he gave testimony to the experience of entire sanctification. "[M]y soul is happy in God—purity of heart is my joy, and prayer my delight. I feel as if God would sanctify all the conferences in the South" (2:450). After having completed the 1805 fall conference in Kentucky, Asbury wrote that in spite of physical affliction, "perfect love, peace within, and harmony without, healed every malady" (2:482).

A careful reading of the journal indicates that sometime in 1786, at age forty-one, Asbury had a turning point in his spiritual experience. From that point on, he testified to a constancy of purity and to power over sin. This does not mean that he was no longer tempted or plagued by occasional doubts. The rigors of constant travel and physical weakness were just too much to maintain a keen spiritual edge. At times he had to confess, "My mind has been dejected; Satan has assaulted me. I could not be fixed in prayer as I desired" (1:688).

Nor did sanctification mean that Asbury would not continue to grow in grace. Sanctification was a relationship with the living God that admitted of increasing knowledge, commitment, and freedom. In 1791, Asbury gave witness to this: "My soul is in peace—I want more prayer, patience, life, and love—I walk daily, hourly, and sometimes minutely, with God" (1:690–691). He would always maintain the attitude that he had expressed as a thirty-year-old:

"My desire is to live more to God today than yesterday, and to be more holy this day than the last" (1:207).

The Primary Means of Grace

John Chalmers, who was Asbury's traveling companion in 1788–1789, recalled, "I was with him not only in the pulpit and sacramental table, but often in the closet where I witnessed his agony in secret and long stay. I wondered why he remained so long on his knees, when I prayed for all I thought I needed for myself and the world."[36] Asbury intended to pray much and *did* pray much; it was his primary means of grace. "Though I now pray not less than ten times a day, yet I find I have need to pray without ceasing" (1:298). Prayer was the vital link to God that would provide both the quality and effectiveness of life to accomplish the divine mandate. The answer to his perceived lack of holiness, dejection of spirit, attacks by Satan, suffering of body, and shortness of patience, was the resolve to pray more. If ten times a day was not sufficient, then Asbury would just pray a few more times. "I see the need of returning to my twelve times of prayer; I have been hindered and interrupted by pains and fevers" (1:357).

For Asbury, prayer was not just for the secret closet but for the whole of life. Prayer was both a response to God's grace and a discipline enabled by God's grace. Henry Boehm recounted that when Asbury asked the renowned Benjamin Rush what he owed for medical services, Rush responded, "Nothing, only an interest in your prayers." Being of quick wit, Asbury responded, "As I do not like to be in debt, we will pray now." Asbury "knelt down and offered a most impressive prayer that God would bless and reward them for their kindness to him."[37]

Out of all that Asbury did publicly, he was most remembered for his powerful prayers. Nicholas Snethen recalled,

> His prayers, on all occasions, in the estimation of his friends, exceeded any composition of the kind they had either heard or read. While they had all the perspicuity of studied, written discourse, they seem to possess the fitness of inspiration to the persons and subjects for whom they were offered up. Those who heard him daily, were surprised and delighted with his seemingly inexhaustible fund of devotional matter. It is difficult to conceive how any man could more measure up to that precept "pray without ceasing."[38]

Asbury devoted himself to intercession. He prayed much for the Methodist preachers, at times naming them all to the Lord. In 1777, he wrote, "I have given myself to private prayer seven times a day, and found my heart much drawn out in behalf of the preachers, the societies, especially the new places, and my aged parents. And while thus exercised, my soul has been both quickened and purified" (1:234). Such intercession was an obligation, a part of the job description. On April 21, 1778, Asbury penned, "I purposed in my own mind, to spend ten minutes in every hour, when awake, in the duty of prayer" (1:268).

Prayer was to be accompanied by fasting as well as by other forms of abstinence.[39] Throughout his entire ministry, Asbury attempted fasting with various degrees of success. His digestive system was given to dysentery and colitis, both complications due to bad food, bad water, and stress. He observed April 17, 1795, as a day of rigid fasting and then commented, "[T]his I cannot do more than once a month. I am frequently obliged to go on three cups of tea, with a little bread, for eight or nine hours, and to ride many miles, and preach, and perform my other ministerial labours" (2:47). As he grew older, abstaining from food became increasingly difficult. When he was forty-seven he concluded, "I feel that fasting at my time of life, if only once a month, brings on such dejection of spirits I can hardly bear up under it" (2:351).

Asbury's fasting compounded a chronic problem of irregularity. Going without food, intentionally or unintentionally, put added stress on a body that was already emaciated. "There is a contention between soul and body. I wish to fast as when young, and when fast day comes, the body has a journey of forty miles to make, perhaps, and do its part of preaching: but Christ is strength in my weakness" (2:608). Fasting normally meant that Asbury would go without food until three o'clock in the afternoon on Friday, which was Wesley's practice.

Prayer for Asbury meant more than mere intercession or abstinence. Prayer was not simply a discipline for accomplishing the supernatural task of reforming the nation and spreading scriptural holiness. Prayer was an end in itself; it was communion with the holy God. Communion with God was the *summum bonum*, the primary purpose of existence. The ever-moving itinerant preacher served a ubiquitous God. "O what fellowship have I with God as I ride along! my soul is filled with love, and I witness that the Lord can keep me alive in the day of famine" (1:404).

At the end of a week in New York in which Asbury had been plagued by cold, fever, sore throat, and "wrestling with principalities and powers," he had to stay inside on Sunday. "And O! what happiness did my soul enjoy with God! So open and delightful was the intercourse between God and my soul, that it gave me grief if any person came into my room, to disturb my sweet communion with the blessed Father and the Son" (1:136).

Nature often provided the spiritual insulation that his incessant traveling and administrative duties denied. At times, Asbury took advantage of stealing away into the woods, walking, praying, and centering the totality of his being on God. He was forever about the business of knowing God, ahead of doing the work of God. Private service to the Creator enhanced public service. After one quarterly meeting, he noted, "[T]hese public times interrupt my private devotions and communion with God. It would be very disagreeable to live so always" (1:204).

The Grand Dispensatory of Soul-Diseases

Asbury devoured Scripture. He fully fit the caricature of a "Bible moth," an appellation derisively given to Methodists. At the close of an ordination service in Albany, New York, he dramatically raised his Bible, exclaiming in a loud voice, "[T]his is the minister's battle ax; this is his sword; take this, therefore and conquer."[40] Though Asbury did not give as much time to the study of Scripture as he did to prayer, it was a definite means of grace. He was sufficiently competent to read the Old Testament in Hebrew and the New Testament in either Greek or Latin.[41] If time permitted, he would read through a lengthy book of Scripture such as Job or the Book of Revelation in one sitting (1:273).

Although these times of extensive meditation were rare, Asbury believed them to be critical to the sanctifying process. Whether Scripture was contemplated in concentrated study or snatched in fragments on the go, "the Word" was Asbury's spiritual director. It was the standard by which to measure all thoughts, dreams, visions, and impressions; above all, it was the diagnostic standard for all matters of the soul. "I see the need of a preacher's being well acquainted with his Bible, . . . the word of God is one grand dispensatory of soul-diseases in every case of spiritual malady" (1:403).

Sanctification through Suffering

A constant means of grace for Asbury was the forfeiture and sacrifice he experienced on almost a daily basis. Enduring heat, cold, filth, crowdedness, loneliness, hunger, thirst, sickness, persecution, conflict, weariness, and rejection was to him essential to God's gift of sanctification. To John Dickens's widow, Elizabeth, he wrote in 1801, "I must be made perfect in suffering, this the Lord hath shown me. I am called to do and suffer more than any others in America" (3:226). Events of hardship and sickness were always interpreted as being part of divine providence for purposes of humility and purification. Asbury was determined to translate every adverse circumstance into spiritual good. After days of riding with an inflamed foot, while being "sorely assaulted by Satan" and preaching to a "still and very lifeless" congregation just south of Washington, Pennsylvania, he wrote, "I felt the power of death, and my spirits were low. This is death—when religion and every comfortable accommodation are wanting. Lord, sanctify all these for my humiliation!" (1:514).

For Asbury, personal suffering was his link to the cross of Christ. At the heart of sanctification was crucifixion, even to the point of martyrdom. Just as Christ had given His life, Asbury would give his in ceaseless exertion and struggle. In 1811, Asbury wrote Jacob Gruber, a presiding elder of the Monongahela District, "We must prepare for martyrdom, in office, in life, if some do but little we must do the more, the work of God must not be slight" (3:453). To be entirely sanctified, in Asbury's thinking, was to be totally sold out to the call of God, and thus to fully accept whatever circumstances or hardships the call entailed.

Sanctification meant no less than exhaustion of time, energy, talents, and money in the accomplishment of one thing, the will of God. Asbury would not die from old age, he would die from placing himself on the altar of sacrifice. "I look back upon a martyr's life of toil, and privation, and pain; and I am ready for a martyr's death. . . . I groan one minute with pain, and shout glory the next!" (2:756). Sanctifying grace was enabling grace, not enablement to achieve but enablement to submit, a full surrender as a poured-out offering. Exhaustion of physical strength brought not only a deeper realization of the task being completed, but more importantly, an affirmation of divine grace. With physical strength almost entirely gone, less than two years before his death, Asbury wrote, "Six weeks confinement, almost, given up by my doctors and friends, if the gates of death were near, they were gates of glory to me! Reduced beyond measure, total loss of appetite, 16 times blistered . . . 3 times bled—heaven glory all in sight! the work of God plain to view the rectitude of my intention in all my labours, my martyr's life and readiness for a martyr's death!" (3:506).

The Asbury Contribution

Asbury played a definitive role in the Americanization of Wesley's theology of Christian perfection. The differences were not intentional but were probably created by lack of communication and by the temperamental differences between the two leaders. Wesley produced logical and polemical theological treatises, while Asbury's journal is a map of spiritual consciousness that traces one man's struggle to experience God. His journaling was a pre-Freudian look at in-depth spirituality, which Brooks Holifield refers to as "introspective cartography."[42]

Asbury's journal evidences a much greater reliance on the immediate means of prayer and individual discipline than on the mediated symbolic means that characterize the covenant community. Wesley defined "the means of grace" as the "outward signs, words or actions, ordained of God, and appointed for this end, to be the ordinary channels whereby he might convey to men, preventing, justifying or sanctifying grace."[43] Wesley was convinced that God was operative in His church through the appointed ordinances, even in the Anglican Church, in spite of its flaws. One participates in corporate grace through the assurance that God is faithful to His church. God not only sanctifies certain individuals within the community, but hallows the community as a whole. For Wesley, the objective, symbolic means of the sacraments celebrate the fact that God is creating a holy people and not simply a collection of holy individuals. Wesley was convinced that God had not forsaken

Anglicanism, and that obedience to Christ included obedience to the Church, unless the former conflicted with the latter. He defined the Church as a group of people who gathered for basically two purposes: the preaching of the Word and the administration of the sacraments.

By contrast, Asbury was not from a priestly family and had much less attachment to Anglicanism than did the Wesley brothers. His "on the go" spirituality was highly compatible with William Byrd's assessment that America "was a place free from those three great scourges of mankind, priests, lawyers, and physicians….[T]he people are yet too poor to maintain the learned gentlemen."[44] America desired an unencumbered spirituality which was "loose from despots and their minions, loose from priests and their opinions."[45]

The absence of the ordinances in American Methodism until 1784 corresponded with a prevailing American folk theology that there is a wide gap between real personal piety and empty liturgy served up by corrupt priests. This created a bifurcation in Asbury's liturgical understanding. For Wesley, outward means result in inward piety, and vice versa. Asbury did not bring this concept with him from England. After preaching in 1780, he wrote, "Two women were cut to the heart and were in agony of soul for holiness…. I see clearly that to press the people for holiness, is the proper method to take them from contending for ordinances, or any *less consequential things*" [italics mine] (1:351).

Late in life, Asbury and McKendree were at a camp meeting in Rushville, Ohio, when on Saturday night some rowdies attempted to break up the gathering. A couple of intruders were thrown to the ground by some "stout" Methodists. After order was restored, Asbury stepped to the pulpit and addressed the combatants: "You must remember that all our brothers in the church are not yet sanctified, and I advise you to let them alone. For if you get them angry and the Devil should get in them, they are the strongest and hardest men to fight and conquer in the world."[46] Asbury did not bother to consider the contradictions in his extemporaneous remarks. Unfortunately, he was a forerunner for much of American holiness preaching and teaching which lacked critical thinking. For example, theological contradiction didn't seem to be a problem for early Methodist preacher Peter Cartwright who, according to some, sang the refrains of "All Hail the Power of Jesus' Name" while he "walloped the daylights" out of a camp-meeting disturber.

One of the hallmarks of holiness theology in America is that it has been taught more anecdotally and metaphorically than systematically.[47] The loose ends of the holiness preachers' assertions were often difficult to tie together. Are unsanctified men stronger and more courageous than sanctified men? Is it better to have an unsanctified sergeant-at-arms? Should camp meeting attendees feel safer if there is at least a small percentage of unsanctified security guards? The popularization of the doctrine of sanctification—that is, the triumph of experience over dogma—would produce more such contradictions for Methodists in the years ahead.

Unfortunately, Asbury occasionally penned statements that would lead one to believe that entire sanctification was not for mere mortals. "Bishop McKendree and I travel together at present, and no earthly consideration has, and I trust never will have, for a moment, any influence on our minds" (3:402). It is true that, as he grew older, Asbury exhibited less anxiety, more inner tranquility, and greater transcendence over temporal concerns. He wrote in 1815, "But whether in health, life, or death, good is the will of the Lord: I will trust him; yea, and will praise him: he is the strength of my heart and my portion forever—Glory! glory! glory!" (2:794). Robert Coleman accurately assesses that "as he matured in faith and experience, his realization of having fulfilled the one quest of his heart grew more certain."[48] At 64 years of age, Asbury testified to "perfect love and perfect peace" and "a witness of holiness in my heart." (2:611, 614)

Though there was no definitive moment which Asbury identified as the time he received the "second blessing" or "entire sanctification," there can be little doubt that he had discovered the *telos* of spiritual hunger—total acquiescence to the will and purpose of God. More than any other person, Francis Asbury connected American Methodism with John Wesley's doctrine of entire sanctification.[49]

Asbury was certain that sanctification could not be attained by his own striving but was to be experienced only by faith in Christ. However, at times the difference between works as means and works as merit was obscured by Asbury's herculean efforts to be God's man. But then this nuance was not always clear in Wesley's thinking, either. The 1789 *Minutes* of English Methodism read, "As to merit itself, of which we have been so dreadfully afraid: we are rewarded according to our works, yea, because of our works."[50]

Asbury believed that sanctification was not a momentary gift to be experienced, it was a call to be constantly lived. Asbury's God desired fellowship and not just obedience. For that reason, Asbury's favorite spot was the secret prayer closet. Freeborn Garrettson stated of Asbury, "He prayed the best and he prayed the most, of any man I every knew. His long-continued rides prevented his preaching as often as some others, but he could find the throne of grace, if not in a congregation, upon the road."[51] The road was Asbury's sanctuary.

Upon leaving a conference in Charleston, Asbury and two traveling companions happened upon a grove of trees surrounding an old pre-Revolutionary War church. It looked like a good spot for lunch. Before feasting on their saddlebag smorgasbord, Asbury suggested that the three of them enter the church. Asbury "ascended the pulpit and engaged in prayer. The spirit of grace and supplication was poured upon him in full measure. His intercession rose to vehement pleadings with God; and he had boldness to enter the holiest through the blood of

Christ. The glory of God seemed to fill the house, and the refreshment of a special visitation from on high was realized by them all."[52]

Upon exiting the church, Asbury said to his two friends, "God has graciously fed our souls with the bread of heaven—let us take some refreshment for the body." For Asbury, God was always the first order of business, no matter how great or how small the business may have been.

10. "Go into Every Kitchen and Shop"

A Nation of Migrants

On May 18, 1796, Congress mandated that all lands in the "Northwest Territory" be surveyed for the purpose of selling 640-acre parcels at two dollars per acre. These lands, bordered on the east by the Allegheny Mountains and on the west by the Mississippi River, the Great lakes on the north and the Ohio River on the south, provided new opportunities for the vast number of American farmers. Except for the rice and cotton plantations in the South and the Tidewater tobacco farms of the gentry, farming was a crude affair. Ignorance concerning soil enrichment, by manure or anything else, and the absence of crop rotation produced more agricide than agriculture. When the soil wore out, the pioneer farmer looked for new land. Farming was not so much land planting as it was land clearing. A disgusted Richard Parker warned an English farmer that if he applied his occupation in America he "would have to chop up trees, and cultivate land by hoe and pick-axe, instead of a plow and harrows."[1]

Americans migrated as sheep without a shepherd. The shanties were crude, hygiene was not observed, the food was coarse, and roads were not yet created. The circuit rider made his way from hovel to hovel, sometimes being able to preach in one shack to several families at the same time. After being assigned to a circuit, the preacher often broke tree limbs so that the next itinerant preacher could find his way. At the turn of the nineteenth century, American settlers were both physically and spiritually destitute. An outsider noted that the migrants ate hurriedly, with little attempt at masticating the poorly cooked food. Filth, insects, absence of sanitation, and distance from civilization all produced dire deprivation. In 1790, Pittsburgh had fewer than four hundred inhabitants, and as late as 1800 no port between Pittsburgh, Pennsylvania, and Natchez, Mississippi, had more than a thousand inhabitants.

In this transient culture, Methodist preachers understood themselves to be trackers rather than shepherds. On one occasion in 1812, the itinerant preacher Richmond Nolley was following fresh wagon tracks in order to encounter new settlers. He successfully located a newly arrived family. The father, upon recognizing Nolley's clerical garb, exclaimed, "What, have you found me already? Another Methodist preacher! I left Virginia to get out of reach of them, went to a new settlement in Georgia and thought to have a long whet, but they got my wife and daughter into the church; then in this late purchase (Choctaw corner), I found a piece of good land, and was sure I would have some peace of the preachers, and here is one before my wagon is unloaded."[2] Nolley replied, "My friend, if you go to heaven you will find Methodist preachers there, and if to hell, I am afraid you will find some there; and you see how it is in the world, so that you had better make terms with us and be at peace."[3]

A Year of Pain and Disappointment

As the year 1796 began, Asbury received word that Cokesbury College had burned beyond repair. This news, along with the slow progress of the circuit-riding work and continual rain, brought "dejection of spirit" to the weary bishop. "Ah! what a dreary world is this! my mind is under solemn impressions—the result of my reflections on God and souls. I will endeavor not to distress myself above measure" (2:77). Of course, he had his usual disillusionment with Charleston, especially when denied the opportunity to preach across from St. Michael's Church. "The city now appears to be running mad for races, plays, and balls. I am afraid of being out of my duty in staying here too long: my soul is among the lions; yet Christ is mine, and I trust my supreme desire is, 'Holiness to the Lord.' My soul longeth to be gone, like a bird from a cage" (2:78). Asbury did not fit into the Charleston social elite, which one visitor said "think and act precisely as do the nobility in other countries." Charleston's exclusive ancestral pride was decidedly antithetical to Methodist egalitarianism. The prayer of a Charlestonite was represented by the doggerel: "I thank thee Lord on bended knee I'm half Porcher and half Huger. . . . For other blessings thank thee too—My grandpa was a Pedigru."[4]

Asbury, now fifty years old, made his way west, but was stopped short of the Kentucky Conference at Masterson Station because of ill health. Shaken by the death of a couple of his close friends, he was tempted to go into retirement. "I am not without fears, that a door will be opened to honour, ease, or interest; and then farewell to religion in the American Methodist Connexion; but death may soon end all these thoughts and quiet all these fears" (2:84). Almost every place seemed to be uncomfortable, as he constantly had wet feet and sleepless nights. He sought relief from his headache and fever with camphorated spirits, Bateman drops, and paregoric. On May 7, he wrote, "I expect a crown for my services. Were I to charge the people on the western waters for my services, I should take their roads, rocks, and mountains into the account, and rate my labours a very high price" (2:84).

On Monday, May 9, Asbury recorded a lengthy narrative concerning an F. Dickenson, a lady who lived in Powell County, Virginia. Indians had murdered her husband and killed all her children as she watched. The Indians, one of whom wore her husband's and children's scalps on his belt, captured her and took her on an eleven-day walking journey before she finally escaped. She discovered a settler community by following a dove. Interpreting the dove as a sign of providence, "she embraced religion, and lived and died an humble follower of Christ" (2:86–87).

Unfortunately, though Asbury's story of Mrs. Dickenson held human interest, it perpetuated the Indian stereotype that was held by most American pioneers. Historian William Barclay is tragically correct that the missionary zeal of the earliest Methodists did not express itself "in extensive effort for the conversion of the Indians."[5] On March 13, 1791, Asbury and Coke reported "visiting and preaching among the Catawba Indians." Coke seemed to have been more interested in Indian evangelism than Asbury. At the May 28, 1789, New York Conference, Coke recorded that "Mr. Asbury is to set off soon for Fort-Pitt, where we are in the first instance to build a church and a school, as the grand chief of a nation or tribe of Indians who lives not far from that Fort, and who are at peace with the states, has expressed an earnest desire of having Christian ministers among his people."[6] Either Coke failed to consult Asbury or Asbury ignored Coke's plans. When Asbury arrived in Pittsburgh less than two months later, he made no mention of the Indians.

On August 15, 1792, Asbury appointed Jonathan Newman as a missionary to the "whites and Indians on the frontier" (1:726). Newman's venture was short-lived, because he located in Saratoga, New York, in 1795. In 1789, Asbury and Coke declared their intention of "sending missionaries among the Indians and opening schools among their children" (3:169). As late as 1810, Asbury referred to Indians as "depredators." Such comments evidence little concern for the plight of the American Indian.

The October General Conference at Baltimore was conducted with "good and judicious talk," and it accomplished laying out the boundaries of the seven conferences. The attendees also established a "Fund for the relief and support of the itinerant, superannuated, and worn out ministers and preachers, their wives and children, widows and orphans of the Methodist Episcopal Church (in the United States of America)."[7] Methodism was now institutionalized to the point of having a retirement plan. This conference also enacted "teetotalism," the disallowing of buying and selling spirituous liquors, or drinking them. This injunction went beyond Wesley's alcoholic allowance in "extreme necessity."[8]

Asbury was so physically depleted that he left with a cold and a boil on his face, soon to be accompanied by another on his eye. Upon reaching Tarboro, North Carolina, on December 9, he preached to a crowd that had gathered for a dance. Arriving later in an unusually cold South Carolina, he discovered that the Methodist academy had burned. The year had begun and ended with news of fire. As always, Asbury felt that it was all according to divine directive. "The loss we sustained in the college, academy, and church, I estimate from fifteen to twenty thousand pounds: it affected my mind; but I concluded God loveth the people of Baltimore, and he will keep them poor, to make them pure; and it will be for the humiliation of the society" (2:111).

The pain and disappointment that filled the year only deepened Asbury's empathy for the people whom he daily encountered. In Asbury's mind, Methodism was not chiefly about institutions to be built and conferences to be conducted. The journey consisted of soul care, an endless parade of human contact through classes, preaching, family devotions, grief counseling, and visitation of the sick. All of it was for the purpose of moving persons along the way of salvation, an occupation which admitted of no idle moment.

Wesleyan Pastoral Care

On June 18–19, 1796, while staying at the home of Samuel Phillips in Maryland, Asbury recorded, "I was musing in my own mind how I could best spend the morning of that day. I concluded to call the family into the room, and address them pointedly, one by one, concerning their souls" (2:90). Six months later, having made a "forced march" to Newbern, North Carolina, without food and in spite of an inflammation in his ear, he wrote, "[T]o our brethren in the city stations, not to neglect the sick an hour, nor an absentee from class one week: indeed we ought to be always abounding in the work of the Lord; to attend to old and new subjects, to our work, and to every means, like men labouring to find out new means for new difficulties" (2:108).

Asbury had learned well. Wesley had written in a letter dated December 10, 1777; "[I]t is true I travel four or five thousand miles in a year. . . . Yet I find time to visit the sick and the poor; and I must do it if I believe the Bible; if I believe these are the marks whereby the Shepherd of Israel will know and judge His sheep at the great day; therefore, when there is time and opportunity for it, who can doubt but this is a matter of absolute duty?"[9] At the age of eighty-one, Wesley walked around town in ankle-deep snow begging money for the poor, which resulted in his "being laid up with a violent flux."[10]

At the heart of Wesley's *cura animarum* was preaching, often three times a day beginning at 5 A.M., to the coopers and miners as they came to work. When special needs arose, pastoral care required a physician to go, rather than to wait for the diseased to seek out the pastor. Wesley recorded, "I wonder at those who still talk so loud about the indecency of field preaching. The highest indecency is in St. Paul's church, when a considerable part of the congregation are asleep, or talking, or looking about, not minding a word the Preacher says. On the other hand, there is the highest decency in a church yard or field when the whole congregation behaves and looks as if they saw the judge of all and heard him speaking from heaven."[11]

All of pastoral care was for the purpose of saving souls. But saving souls was not to be abstracted from the Christian responsibility to the total person, "doing good of every possible sort, and as far as is possible to all men;—to their bodies, of the ability which God giveth, by giving food to the hungry, by clothing the naked, by visiting or helping them that are sick, or in prison."[12] The qualification for a clergyman, according to Wesley, was an "earnest concern for the glory of God, and such a thirst after the salvation of souls, that he is ready to do anything, to lose anything, or to suffer anything, rather than one should perish for whom Christ died."[13]

Asbury's Practical Theology

Wesley examined his ministerial candidates "in substantial, practical, experiential divinity." It was this practical theology which was transported to America. The first Methodist discipline exhorted, "Whenever the weather will permit, go out into the most public places, and call all to repent and believe the Gospel."[14] Preaching in public places was only part of the job description. "Go into every house in course, and teach everyone therein, young and old, if they belong to us, to be Christians inwardly and outwardly."[15] Pastoral care consisted of ceaseless rounds of visitation, public proclamation, and private instruction. Theology was not for the purpose of speculation or debate, but rather for practical implementation.

Questions of theology discussed at the Conferences included: "How are we to deal with a sinner? How should we treat with mourners? Which way should we address hypocrites? How can we deal with backsliders? What is best for believers?" Ezekiel Cooper recalled that Asbury's doctrines were "calculated to awaken the guilty consciences of sinners, to encourage and comfort the conflicted minds of desponding mourners, to build up and establish believers in all the graces of the Spirit, to lead and direct the souls of men, in the sure way of salvation; and to set forth the honor, the praise, and the glory of God."[16] Asbury told the ordinands that when they went into the pulpit they were to go from their prayer closets: "Leave all your vain speculation and metaphysical reasoning behind. Take with you your hearts, full of fresh spring water from heaven, and preach Christ crucified and the resurrection, and that will conquer the world."[17]

The first obligation to pastoral care was to oneself. The Methodist circuit rider needed to keep his own soul fed in order to be a healthy physician, thereby able to overcome indolence, apathy, and negligence of the duties to which he was called. In Asbury and Coke's "explanatory notes" they summarized the job description of the preacher as "to preach almost everyday, and to meet societies and classes several times in the week, and to visit the sick not only in the towns, but as far as practicable on the plantations . . . a work which requires no small degree of diligence and zeal."[18]

Herculean Expectations

Asbury believed his men to be a breed apart. When he ordained a man, he operated under the conviction that he was sending out an individual who would work more, pray more, sacrifice more, and live on less. They would all be like Valentine Cook, who wrote in a letter dated May 24, 1794, "Yesterday I walked upward of thirty miles in mud and water, being wet all day without; yet heaven was within. Glory to God! I had three temptations to encounter, the devil, the mosquitoes, and my horse, and the rain and my wet clothes were my element, and God my comforter, and victory my white horse."[19] When Enoch George complained that his circuit was too difficult, Asbury remarked that "It was good for him and all others to bear the yoke in their youth, that itinerant labours must be hard, if properly performed, and that it was better to become use [sic] to poverty and pain hunger and cold, in the days of his youth, than when he was old and gray—the task would be easy."[20]

The high and holy moment of Asbury's laying his hands on a candidate for the order of deacon or elder was memorable indeed. Nathan Bangs recalls that he was impressed with the awe-filled solemnity of the occasion. The bishop's words carried such a sense of the divine presence that they overwhelmed Bangs to the extent that his knees shook and he feared that he would fall to the floor. Asbury's "sonorous" voice reverberated throughout the church. "From the ends of the earth we call upon thee, O Lord God, to pour upon this thy servant the Holy Ghost for the office and work of deacon within the church."[21] When Asbury ordained James Jenkins, he intoned, "You feel the hands of the bishop very heavy, but the divine hand will be heavier still."[22]

Asbury determined that the Methodist ministry would be a study in contrasts. It would provide what the other sects would not. When Coke was in Virginia he noted, "The clergy in general in these parts never stir out of the church, even on a Sunday, if it rains."[23] Joseph Everett, of Queen Anne's County in Delaware, noted that Anglican preaching was a "parcel of dead morality."[24] William Williams states, "Dryly delivered sermons on the significance of moral responsibilities did little to address the needs of people whose lives were dictated by the reality of poverty, disease, deprivation, violence, and sudden death."[25] In 1773, a visitor to Charlestown was surprised to see so few present at church. He noted that the sermon was only twenty minutes long and that men conversed during the prayer and sermon time.[26]

Furthermore, the established clergy were not always moral. In the very month that Asbury arrived in America, October 1771, an Anglican church in Nansemond County, Virginia, was trying to remove its pastor, Patrick Lunan, for being of evil fame and profligate manners. It was not enough that he had disavowed his belief in Christianity; he was also accused of "profane swearing, drunkenness, adultery, and exposing himself to his congregation."[27] When Thomas Jefferson was a student at William and Mary, the Reverend John Rowe was dismissed as a teacher because of his involvement in a drunken town-and-gown street brawl.[28] Devereux Jarratt wrote to Wesley on June 29, 1773, "We have ninety-five parishes in the

colony, and all, except one, I believe are supplied with Clergymen. But alas!—
You well understand the rest. I know of but one Clergymen of the Church of
England who appears to have the power and spirit of vital religion; for all seek
their own, and not the things that are Christ's!"[29]

Universal Grace

The chief instrument for pastoral care was the Word of God. It was to be
taken to homes, jails, mills, courthouses, poorhouses, taverns, slave quarters,
public houses, and colleges. People fell under the Word, "smitten, converted,
melted down, and wounded." "[P]ower went through the congregation, and a
noble shout was heard from among the people" (1: 583). Wherever one was,
the Word of God was to be offered in keeping with the need and setting. "My
mind was powerfully struck with a sense of the great duty of preaching in all
companies; of always speaking boldly and freely for God as if in the pulpit"
(1:707–708).

Being in thousands of homes, Asbury made it his constant practice to evangelize and catechize the families. Upon asking them about their spiritual condition,
he almost always offered prayer. When weather and sickness prevented his travel,
that provided the opportunity for more sustained soul care. Held up in Charleston, South Carolina, in the middle of winter, Asbury resolved to catechize the
children himself, and purposed to visit "in every house where leisure and opportunity may permit" (2:278). Another time in South Carolina he wrote, "Besides
praying regularly after every meal in our own house, I am obliged to go through
this exercise many times, daily, with the poor Negroes" (2:487).

Richard Baxter's *The Reformed Pastor* influenced both Wesley and Asbury.
This rector of Kidderminster told how his staff took two afternoons a week to
visit homes for the purpose of catechizing the eight hundred families of his parish
over the course of a year. When he was in Baltimore in May of 1795, Asbury
"spent part of the week in visiting from house to house. I feel happy in speaking
to all I find, whether parents, children, or servants; I see no other way; the common means will not do; Baxter, Wesley, and our Form of Discipline, say, 'Go into
every house': I would go farther, and say, go into every kitchen and shop; address
all, aged and young, on the salvation of their souls" (2:51).

Asbury did pastoral care without differentiation. No family was too poor, no
house too filthy, no town too remote, and no people too ignorant to receive the
good news that life could be better. Even Wesley could not boast of such universal
interest. To him, agrarian types, especially farm laborers, were stupid and brutal.
Maldwyn Edwards states that for Wesley, they "were not only grossly stupid in
the arts of this life, but even more regarding religion and life to come. He argued
they would know as much about the Northwest Passage, as about repentance and
holiness, and that they were on the same level as a Turk or a heathen."[30]

Asbury did not select those to whom he was going to render pastoral care; he simply took care of whomever was in his path and anyone with whom he lodged. Asbury modeled pastoral care via camaraderie to the extent that few have ever practiced it. Asbury ate and slept with his flock, a commune that covered all of the United States.

Asbury often displayed the affectionate side of his personality and he was especially solicitous of children. One child exclaimed to his mother as Asbury was approaching his house, "Mother, I want my face washed, and a clean apron on, for Bishop Asbury is coming, and I am sure he will hug me up."[31] William Wrightman, who was to become a bishop in the Methodist Episcopal Church South, recalled how his mother would take him and his siblings to see Asbury whenever he was in their hometown in South Carolina. Wrightman and his two brothers noticed some apples on a mantel. "After a little religious talk suitable for our years and capacity, the venerable man put his hands on our heads, one after another, with a solemn prayer and blessing, and dismissed us, giving the largest apple to the smallest child, in a manner that left upon me a lifelong impression."[32] In 1805, Asbury had the following letter from a young boy published:

> Dear Papa Asbury, I take the opportunity to let you know that I am bound for heaven and glory; and inform you of the blessed treasure I found since I saw you—that is, the love of God in my soul. Glory, glory to my blessed Jesus, that he gave me to see that I was a sinner, and that I now feel His love in my soul. . . . I should be very happy to see you this summer. We have happy times, my dear papa. . . . I hope you will excuse my liberty in writing for I love you, and I want you to know how good the Lord is to poor unworthy me. Please to remember me in your prayers that I may be faithful unto the end.
>
> I remain your unworthy boy, John Talbutt.[33]

Asbury exhorted his preachers to include children in their work of spiritual nurture. When in a chapel in Delaware he "gave an exhortation, took down the names of the children, and spoke to some of them: I desired the preachers to meet the children when they came along;—an important but much-neglected duty—to the shame of ministers be it spoken" (1:389). Asbury's affection for children was enhanced by the fact that he had none. His idealism at times gave way to naiveté; for example, he requested mothers to list the peculiar traits and evil tendencies of their children so that the church could provide more effective nurture. He didn't quite realize that children are children. Asbury believed, however, that the family was the church in microcosm and the spiritual health of the family was vital to the spiritual health of the church.

He warned his pastors to beware of visits that tended to mere hospitality or secular conversation. The secret to pastoral oversight was to realize that every contact was to be given to soul care. The following, written to Ezekiel Cooper, reflects this stringent concept: "Your attention ought to be paid to Discipline, and visiting from house to house, but not to eat and drink. I am poignantly against that. You have a house to eat in; you need not go to feast with the Church of God. We ought to visit as doctors, or as persons to plead the cause of their souls; not as guests, to eat and drink, but as divines for souls. I am convinced it is and will be an evil" (3:132). As Asbury grew older, he himself enjoyed at times luxurious entertainment and thus became less "poignantly against that."

Asbury excelled in spiritual conversation, what Walter Brueggemann refers to as "gospel modes of discourse." Asbury chastised himself when he allowed the conversation to be diverted from Kingdom issues. "It is my present determination to be more faithful in speaking to all that fall in my way, about spiritual and eternal matters" (1:185). Not to encounter others with the living God was to him a sin of omission. In November 1802, Asbury wrote, "I have nearly finished my six thousand miles—to God be all the glory! But ah! what small fruit of my labour, since August, 1801. How little do I speak of God and to precious souls! God, be merciful to me a sinner!" (2:369).

The Condemned

In the late eighteenth century, trying, transporting, punishing, and executing criminals were spectator sports. These gathered crowds provided prime preaching opportunities. In New York in February 1772, Joseph Pilmoor preached to "seven thousand people" who had gathered to witness an execution. Pilmoor said that when the executioner pulled the cap over the man's face and launched him into eternity, "the sight was rather more than I could bear, so that I had liked to have fainted."[34]

No pastoral care was more quintessentially Methodist than that of Joseph Cromwell and Caleb Pedicord at the execution of Joe Molliner. They were instrumental in the conversion of Molliner while he was in jail for committing "despicable" deeds as a Tory during the Revolutionary War. Thousands gathered in 1781 to witness his hanging at Gallows Hill just outside Burlington, New Jersey. Pedicord stood on the wagon beside Molliner and his coffin, preached to the crowd and led them in hymn singing. An eyewitness reported that Molliner clapped his hands "exaultingly" and exclaimed, "I found Him! I found Him! Now I am ready." Molliner adjusted the rope around his neck and swung out into eternity as the wagon rolled out from under him.[35]

On May 29, 1772, Asbury made a trip to Burlington, New Jersey, to minister to a prisoner he had previously met. Asbury described the condemned as a "bull in a net" shrieking for help. "O how awful." Asbury feared that drenching the man in religion was in vain. "I saw him tied up; and then, stepping on a wagon, I spoke a word in season, and warned the people to flee from the wrath to come, and improve the day of their gracious visitation, no more grieving the Spirit of God, lest a day should come in which they may cry, and God may refuse to hear them" (1:32). In October of 1772, Asbury recorded another such incident as follows: "I went to the jail, and visited a condemned criminal, and preached to him and others with some tender feelings of mind, on those words, 'Joy shall be in heaven over one sinner that repenteth'" (1: 19).

Asbury was quick to pity those who were victims of society and/or were suffering the consequences of their own wrongdoing. In July 1779, a group of English/Scotch prisoners were being transported to New York. Asbury visited their tent and especially felt sorry for an old man from Devonshire. He "read the third of Romans, lectured to them; they seemed kind and humble" (1:305). Condemned prisoners were archetypes of those who had been forgotten or cast off—the very people for whom Christ had died. To forget them was to compromise the Church for the sake of comfort and respectability. In 1810, Asbury wrote to Nelson Reed, "My dear I feel! I feel! for the Baltimore Road prisoners. Oh that some local brother would consent to preach to them every Sabbath, one that could gain their confidence, they are degraded far below domestick slavery but their rights as they respect the Gospel, they ought not, no State should dare to rob them of this. Oh help those outcastes, those dregs of human nature, precious, perishing souls" (3:426).

Both slaves and free Blacks were a special object of the bishop's compassion. He often visited them, preached in their quarters, and expressed concern for their welfare. Observing them at worship particularly touched Asbury. As they partook of the sacraments at St. Paul's Chapel in New York, Asbury remarked, "At the table I was greatly affected with the sight of the poor Negroes, seeing their sable faces at the table of the Lord" (1:43). The injustices inflicted on the Blacks caused him endless distress. After a worship service in eastern North Carolina, Asbury commented, "It was not all agreeable to me to see nearly a hundred slaves standing outside, and peeping in at the door, whilst the house was half empty: they were not worthy to come in because they were black! Farewell, farewell to that house forever!" (2:326).

Vocal Disappointment

Asbury often expressed the futility of his attempts at pastoral care. His journal provided a means for emotionally "shaking the dust off his feet." He was not beyond labeling some he had encountered as stupid, ignorant, hard, gay, cold-

hearted, or whatever description that seemed to fit. "I am grieved at the imprudence of some people; but why should I be grieved?—the work is the Lord's" (1:
310). In 1796 in Wythe County, Virginia, he was confronted with "stupid sinners of various descriptions, to whom I preached on Joshua xxiv, 19." The place
was so despicable that Asbury not only refused to spend the night, but even to eat
bread and drink water (2:87).

Indeed, pastoral care could be quite discouraging. "I arrived at Newbern. I
felt the power of death as I journeyed along. We rode round the town, and could
get no certain information about preaching, brother Cole being absent. We were
at last taken in at Mr. Lathrop's. The place and people were in such a state, that I
judged, by my own feelings, it would be as well to leave them just as I found
them—and so I did" (1: 534). Perhaps Asbury's comments were at times far more
negative than a particular people or location deserved. Jesse Lee recalled his own
preaching in Charleston: "I often had such faith in the promises of God and such
a sense of his presence, that I could not doubt but what the Lord would revive his
work amongst the people; I frequently spoke of my feelings concerning this matter. Mr. Asbury seemed to think differently, and frequently expressed his awful
fears, that the people were growing worse and worse."[36]

Preserving and Maturing the Harvest

Asbury was as convinced as Wesley that pastoral care was not simply a service
rendered by preachers to laity. There must be a structure to allow love and grace to
flow between members of the body. A disciplining mechanism was especially critical for American Methodism, since a church often would see an itinerant preacher
but once a month, or far less. Between the time of participating in worship services,
in whatever structure that might be available, the newly minted Methodists met in
weekly classes of ten to fifteen people. The classes were the nurturing and stabiliz-
ing backbone of the church. The lay leaders were to "carefully inquire how every
soul in his class prospers. Not only how each person observes the outward rules, but
how he grows in the knowledge and love of God."[37] Classes were further broken up
into bands, four to five people who were to be even more intimate and confessional.
Asbury wrote, "In meeting the bands, I showed them the impropriety and danger
of keeping their thoughts or fears of each other to themselves: this frustrates the
design of bands; produces coolness and jealousies toward each other; and is undoubtedly the policy of Satan" (1:131).

Asbury's pastoral care honed its sights on one objective, experiencing the holy
life. The holy life was a gift of the Holy Spirit, but it also had to be nurtured on
a daily basis. Not to communicate and enforce the disciplines necessary for that
nurture was a default that Asbury would not allow, either of himself or his preachers. The character of a Methodist included not only internal righteousness, but
also outward morality.

Abel Stevens stated that the disciplines imposed upon others by Asbury were so exemplified by himself that his associates or subordinates, instead of revolting from them, accepted them as a challenge to heroic emulation.[38] Wrote Stevens: "His continual passages among them inspirited them to emulate his wonderous energy. They almost universally took a chivalric character, a military *esprit de corps*, which kept them compactly united, exalted in labor, and defiant of persecution and peril."[39] Everything about Asbury personified discipline. He did not expect any self-denial or deportment that he would not doubly impose on himself. To the preachers he stated, "Do not affect the gentleman. You have no more to do with this character than with that of a Dancing-master."[40]

Methodists were to be people that stiff-armed prestige, ridiculed honor, and forsook security and anything for which human desire craves. John Lawson has written, "It is a mistake to suppose that original Methodism had as its inspiration either a rollicking revival service, or an informal group fellowship. Methodism was altogether more severe and less popular! It was in every part a religion of exact discipline."[41] Anything that distracted from this discipline Asbury interpreted as a wound to his effectiveness. To Asbury, Bible religion consisted of "the mind which was in Christ Jesus, in a victory over sin, and a conformity to the will of God; in love, joy, peace, long-suffering, gentleness, goodness, faith, meekness, and temperance; in all the amiable virtues which centre in the moral character of Christ" (3:571).

For Asbury, pastoral care and evangelism were one and the same, perpetually bringing outsiders into the church and moving them along the order of salvation. When Billy Hibbard's wife refused to become a Methodist, the husband persuaded his spouse to attend a prayer meeting. Upon asking her how she liked the meeting, she did not respond. Upon repeating the question, "I saw tears running down her face. Seeing this I reviewed my question in a softer tone. She answered, 'O how they love one another, I never saw such a love in my life.' I said, 'My dear, that is our religion.' 'Well I believe it is a good religion,' said she."[42]

One of the most intimate glimpses of Asbury's pastoral care was given by Fanny Newell.[43] While attending the quarterly conference in Bernard, Vermont, in May 1811, she was prostrated by the "spotted fever." A physician attended her, but with the normal futility of early nineteenth-century medicine.

> One day Bishop Asbury came into the room, walked up to the bed, looked on me, and groaned, turned about, walked up and down the room, and then went out without saying a word. . . . The good Bishop Asbury came again into my room as before, looked on me, walked to the door and kneeled down, and prayed; and such a prayer I scarcely ever heard before. Blessed be God for the

prayer of faith which saveth the sick. He rose came and looked on me again, and said, "she will get well."[44]

She did.

The Sacrifice of Celibacy

In 1808, Asbury penned one of his most succinct and pungent exhortations to a Methodist preacher: "Oh brother, wisdom, moderation, energy, order, union, love, fervent prayers, fervent exhortations, unremitting diligence, frugality! Temperance, charity to the poor" (3:400). He could have added, "On call twenty-four hours, no overtime pay, no vacation pay, no *per diem*, and no wife." In 1804, Asbury gave the reasons for his celibacy, the heart of which was expressed in one lengthy sentence:

> Amongst the duties imposed upon me by my office was that of travelling extensively, and I could hardly expect to find a woman with grace enough to enable her to live but one week out of the fifty-two with her husband: besides, what right has any man to take advantage of the affections of a woman, make her his wife, and by a voluntary absence subvert the whole order and economy of the marriage state, by separating those whom neither God, nature, nor the requirements of civil society permit long to be *put asunder*? (2:423).

The key word in the above is *right*. A Methodist preacher gave up the rights to private property, a home, monetary security, and sexual procreation (and certainly sexual recreation). The unwritten job description demanded foregoing the normal engagements of life. One could not take care of the Kingdom of God and a family at the same time. To expect to do so was neither just nor generous. Few, if any, would enjoy the fortunes of Freeborn Garrettson, who prophesied that he would one day be rich. He fulfilled his prophecy by marrying a wealthy widow and completing his earthly days as a country gentleman at Rhineland, New York. This possibility did occur to Asbury. In a letter to his mother he wrote, "'Tis true if I were to marry a wife with a fortune, or was less liberal, I might have more money" (3:36).

Not that anyone would want to be married to a Methodist preacher. After noting that there were only three men in the Virginia conference who were married, he reflected, "The high taste of these southern folks will not permit their families to be degraded by an alliance with a Methodist travelling preacher; and thus, involuntary celibacy is imposed upon us" (2:591). It could be that the following, written when Asbury was approaching sixty-five, was simply "sour grapes": "Erasmus Hill may possibly sell the Gospel for a rich wife, as three or four others have done. Should I say here, And thou, Francis, take heed? Not of this sin" (2:628).

Asbury was married to the church, and there was neither time nor money to give to another spouse. In stretching his funds to support widows, orphans, and worn-out preachers (preachers did not retire, they "wore out"), Asbury commented, "I feel [the] burden, I can scarcely help seventy married preachers losing one 4th or one 3rd of their time and paid for the whole, presiding elders losing half their time or not spending more than 23 weeks a year in the districts. It is such men that bring this weighty office into dishonor" (3:438). Marriage was a distraction, "a ceremony awful as death" (2:474), a battle which Asbury often sensed he was losing. When he was only a "general assistant," he discussed with Edward Dromgoole, who was entangled with a family, the necessity of providing the wives with parsonages and dry goods, "so the preachers should travel from place to place, as when single: for unless something of the kind be done, we shall have no preachers but young ones, in a few years; they will marry and stop" (1: 356).

Asbury's radical view was not lost on either his peers or his subordinates. He wrote to George Roberts in Philadelphia that the married preachers who wanted stations would have to "wait, or stretch their loves" (3:240). The sympathy that he offered to Thomas Coke upon the death of his wife (that Coke "loved her more than God") seemed almost cruel (3:450). Nathan Bangs noted in his summary of Asbury's life that the bishop had shown too great a solicitude to keep the preachers poor and should have "encouraged measures to provide a competency for men of heavy and expensive families."[45]

James Finley recalled that "Methodist preachers were not exactly obliged to take the popish vow of celibacy, but it almost amounted to the same thing. There was such a high example for single life exhibited in the cases of the bishops, that if a preacher married he was looked upon almost as a heretic who had denied the faith."[46] On March 4, 1774, Asbury wrote to William Duke, "My dear Billy . . . Stand at all possible distance from the female sex, that you be not betrayed by them that will damage the young mind and sink the aspiring soul and blast the prospect of the future man" (3:19). Asbury's exhortation increasingly fell on deaf ears. The vow to remain single was a raging torment for many of the men, as typified by Thomas Haskins' attraction to the widow Martha Potts, whom he eventually married. "Oh what would I have given to have got away from preaching today. The cause is evident. I have not kept—my heart—Oh, my unfaithfulness, my unfaithfulness."[47]

Perhaps the bishop was not as callous as it seemed. He had scriptural texts for his response to Adam Clarke's "unchristianizing" the celibate life. Among them were Matthew 19:12, which declares that some "have made themselves eunuchs for the Kingdom of Heaven's sake." And he had some fairly reliable examples in the celibacy of Jesus and Paul. However, he believed that every man should support a woman, and this he did, regularly sending money to his widowed mother and, after her death, to the widow of John Dickens.

Jeremiah Minter took the biblical "eunuch for the Kingdom's sake" quite literally. After apparently falling in love with a married lady, Sarah Jones, he had himself surgically castrated. This was such an embarrassment to Methodism that Asbury expelled him, but later he readmitted him as a licensed preacher. On April 8, 1791, Asbury recorded that "Poor Minter's case has given occasion for sinners and for the world to laugh and talk, and write."[48]

In spite of all of Asbury's public contacts and private encounters with widows who nursed him, there was never any hint of flirtatiousness or improper conduct. Unlike Wesley, who may have sublimated his desire for intimacy by writing thousands of letters to women, Asbury's female correspondents were few. "I have once in a while to address a letter to a poor widow in distress, and once in awhile to her sister, formed of the same clay, redeemed by the same blood, a daughter of the same God" (3:371).

When wives of preachers began attending Conferences with their husbands, Asbury took it upon himself to address the women concerning their wifely obligations. But these exhortations seemed more for the benefit of the pastor than of his wife. Jacob Gruber recalled that Asbury gave the women "such direction and instruction as he saw necessary as proper, that they might not by their example pull down what their husbands built up by their preaching."[49] In 1791, Asbury suggested to Garrettson the beginning of a "female school to teach anything and everything a female ought to know."[50]

But what about Nancy Brookes? It would have been historically gratifying if he had written to her at least once. At age twenty-three he wrote his parents, "Nancy Brookes, your manner of speaking made me begin to think and wonder. . . . I do not know wherein and in regard to what [?] passed when I was over at Barr. . . . My time was short. . . . I shall think no more of it if you don't, tho it gave me some little pain" (3:4). The references are vague and one is left to read between the lines.

In 1784, he wrote to his parents, "Many things have inclined me to continue as yet in a single state. One, what once befell me in England" (3:36). Was it an affair from which he could never recover? Was he jilted? Had he committed some embarrassing impropriety? All we know is that there would never be another Nancy.

Regarding the single life he wrote, "[I]f I have done wrong, I hope God and the sex will forgive me: it is my duty now to bestow the pittance I may have to spare upon the widows and fatherless girls, and poor married men" (3:278). That Asbury never married does not identify him as a misogynist. To Thomas Coke's wife, he wrote, "Excuse me Madam. I am a friend to female followers of Jesus, possibly. I preach to millions, and am served by thousands annually, all to all, my Mother was a dear woman of and among millions" (3:409). Asbury had simply found one far lovelier, Jesus Christ. "I see no beauty in any other object, nor desire anything but thee!" (1:104).

11. "The Remedy Worse Than the Disease"

Gloomy Nervous Affections

The winter of 1796–97 in South Carolina was harsh, which may have prompted Asbury's confession on January 8, "I do not yet feel myself in the spirit of the work" (2:115). His feud with Charleston continued: "I lament the wickedness of this city, and their great hatred against us" (2:116). Since Asbury spent more time in Charleston than in any other city, it was here that he assumed more the role of a pastor by visiting the sick and making rounds to the slave quarters. Asbury was sick most of January, suffering deep depression, especially over the death of his friend Edgar Wells, first Methodist convert in the city. It was during this period that Coke and Asbury worked on their *Explanatory Notes*, which were included in the 1798 Discipline.

Asbury was even more elated than usual to leave Charleston. "On my way I felt as if I were let out of prison. Hail! ye solitary pines! the jessamin, the redbud, and dog-wood! how charming in full bloom! the former a most fragrant smell" (2:121). He made his way north, much of the time cold, hungry, and wet. By the time he reached North Carolina, he had an inflamed leg caused by infection. Crossing the mountains into Tennessee offered the normal adventure. "When we had ascended the summit of the mountain, we found it so rich and miry, that it was with great difficulty we could ride along; but I was wrapped up in heavy, wet garments, and unable to walk through weakness of body; so we had it, pitch, slide, and drive to the bottom" (2:125).

By the time Asbury reached Jonesborough, he was too spent to continue to the Kentucky Conference. Traveling north toward Baltimore, he found himself almost totally incapacitated, so debilitated that he could not even write in his journal for six weeks. Thoughts of death, his parents, and the welfare of the churches filled his mind. "My reading is only the Bible: I cannot think much, and only write a few letters" (2:127).

During most of June, Asbury was shut up in Baltimore trying to regain his strength. "The constant resort of the wealthy and poor visiting me, made me much ashamed that they should look after such a worthless lump of misery and sin" (2:128). He had a sulky made, which he referred to as his chariot, and with it he managed to journey as far north as Rochelle, New York. One of Henry Gough's servants accompanied him, and by this time his physical distress was acute. "Finding myself swelling in the face, bowels, and feet, I applied leaves of burdock and then a plaster of mustard, which drew a desperate blister. I had such awful sore feet, I knew not but that they would mortify; and only after two weeks was I able to set them to the ground" (2:131).

On September 14, 1797, Asbury noted that he had not preached for eight weeks. "I have been most severely tried from various quarters; my fevers, my feet, and Satan, would set in with my gloomy and nervous affections. Sometimes subject to the greatest effeminacy; to distress at the thought of a useless, idle life" (2:132). He worried that he would no longer be able to fulfill his administrative responsibilities and there was no one qualified to take his place. Above all, idleness was killing him. "I am left too much alone. I cannot sit in my room all day, making gloomy reflections on the past, present, and future life. Lord, help me! for I am poor and needy; the hand of God hath touched me, and I think Satan *forts* himself in my melancholy, unemployed, unsocial, and inactive hours" (2:132).

The yellow fever was so bad at Philadelphia that the October annual conference was held in Smyrna, Delaware. Asbury was so weak that he simply observed, while the presiding elders acted as moderators. The conference appointed Jesse Lee as Asbury's riding companion, and a committee was formed to review Asbury and Coke's *Explanatory Notes*. Asbury reserved his strength for preaching and ordaining. "Great times: preaching almost night and day; some souls converted, and Christians were like a flame of fire" (2:135).

That I May Die

Asbury then traveled south, taking the coastal route. He dreaded having to spend the winter in Charleston, but that was the only hope if he was to regain his strength. The thought was so depressing that he stopped in Brunswick County, Virginia, which is as far as he got for several months. He wondered if this was the time to make out his will, and if life had been reduced to looking at the four walls. At Doctor Simm's, "we sat melancholy in the house—dumb *Sabbaths!*" (2:141). Thoughts of the O'Kelly schism returned to haunt him.

The mind and body of Asbury had almost totally shut down, with sufficient strength to take only short rides. He spent the days reading the Scriptures, staring at the hearth, and contemplating the cold weather outside. And as always, there were the barbaric and futile medical remedies. "I have taken cider with *nails* put into it, and fever powders, and must take more of the barks" (2:142). When a physician assessed his physical and mental condition as "debility," he had no reason to doubt it. The discouraging year closed with Asbury recording, "I felt weakness of body and dejection of mind; and sometimes I am brought to think of requesting, as Elijah and Jonah did, that I may die" (2:145).

The year 1798 began with Asbury on a stringent diet; "drink made of one quart of hard cider, one hundred nails, and a handful of black snakeroot, one handful of fennel seed, and one handful of wormwood, boiled from a quart to a pint, taking one wineglass full every morning for nine or ten days, using no butter, or milk, or meat; it will make the stomach very sick, and in a few days purge the patient well" (2:149). Inactivity continued to the point that Asbury was reduced to winding cotton in order to escape boredom. His incapacitation prevented him from making it to worship more than two miles away. He endured an almost constant fever. He hoped that the endless purgatory procedures would cleanse his system. "I was fully resolved to take three grains of tartar emetic, which operated powerfully and brought off a proper portion of bile: in this I hope for a cure" (2:151–2).

Asbury was periodically able to muster enough energy to entertain children, take notes on Scripture, and revise his journal; but the latter only added to his depression. "I am like Mr. Whitefield, who being presented with one of his extempore sermons taken in shorthand, could not bear to see his own face" (2:152). What bothered Asbury most was that he was a "prisoner." Thoughts of death haunted him. "It oppresses my heart to think that I live upon others and am useless, and that I may die by inches" (2:152). Not even during the Revolutionary War was Asbury reduced to such ineffectiveness. "I spent my time with the women and children in winding cotton and hearing them read" (2:154). His devotional life consisted of the plaintive cry of Job: "O Lord, show me wherefore thou contendest with me!" (2:155).

Partial Recovery

Traveling north, Asbury preached for the first time in over five months at Henry Resse's, thirty miles south of Petersburg, Virginia. Upon reaching Baltimore, to preside at the annual conference, he had recovered much of his strength. He noted that the vegetable diet rather than medicine had renewed his vigor. If he could rest for the summer, he was convinced that there would be a full recovery. But resting was something for which his temperament had no toleration.

Asbury received the news of the death of his father on June 16. "I now feel myself an orphan with respect to my father; wounded memory recalls to mind what took place when I parted with him, nearly twenty-seven years next September; from a man that seldom, if ever, I saw weep—but when I came to America, overwhelmed with tears, with grief, he cried out, 'I shall never see him again!'" (2:162). On July 9, Asbury received further details from Birmingham. "He kept his room six weeks previous to his death; the first month of the time he ate nothing but a little biscuit, and the last fortnight he took nothing but a little spirits and water—he died very happy" (2:163). If the son felt any continuing or unresolved grief, he repressed it. He never mentioned his father again, at least in his journal.

Rumors abounded of the yellow fever breaking out along the Eastern Seaboard. "Most awful times in Philadelphia and New York—citizens flying before the fever as if it were the sword! I now wait the providence of God to know which way to go" (2:173). Asbury rode down through New Brunswick, New Jersey, and skirted Philadelphia via Germantown. On October 3, he received the news of the death of John Dickens, his close friend and confidant. Two days later Asbury's carriage toppled over with him under it. Skinned and bruised, the bishop noted, "O, the heat, the fall, the toil, the hunger of the day" (2:174).

The day indeed seemed dark and Asbury, upon arriving in Baltimore, utilized the gloomy atmosphere to preach on 2 Chronicles 7:14. It was here that he met with Asbury Dickens, the son of John Dickens. "For piety, probity, profitable preaching, holy living, Christian education of his children, secret, closet prayer, I doubt whether his superior is to be found either in Europe or America" (2:175). Just before he died, Dickens wrote Asbury, "Perhaps, I might have left the city, as most of my friends and brethren have done, but when I thought of such a thing, my mind recurred to that Providence which has done *so much* for me, a poor worm, that I was afraid of indulging any distrust—So I commit myself and family into the hands of God, for life or death."[1]

Asbury could hardly summon sufficient strength to chair the Virginia Conference at Petersburg, a task he had not yet turned over to McKendree in spite of his intention to do so. At Baltimore in the home of James Smith, the rumors continued to swirl about Asbury's seeming prosperity and power. Asbury was angered: "*I would not ride in the coach.* Will my character never be understood? But gossips will talk. If we want plenty of good eating and new suits of clothes, let us come to Baltimore; but we want souls" (2:632). Since suspicion breeds suspicion, Asbury wrote to the presiding elder of the Baltimore Conference, Nelson Reed, upon arriving in Maryland. "Be assured my dear son I have no jealousy of your administration, no want of confidence in you" (3:426). Asbury was as conscious of paying his political debts as of his monetary ones.

All was not lost. Upon reaching Benjamin Johnson's in Virginia, he found signs of revival. On November 5 at Edward Dromgoole's, Asbury reported a "weeping and melting" time. In Camden, South Carolina, Asbury remarked on the beauty of the meetinghouse and the kindness of the people. The last two years had been so very difficult, and his absence from Charleston so long, that his disgust of the city had cooled. "We have peace and good prospects in Charleston, very large congregations attend the ministration of the word" (2:179). Things were looking up, if only because that was the only direction they could go.

The Yellow Fever

The years 1797–98 represent the nadir of Asbury's itinerant ministry. Not until a couple of years before his death would Asbury again have such physical difficulties. It was not a good time for him, for Methodism, or for the country. Yellow fever brought death to many and deathly fear to everyone on the Eastern Seaboard. Philadelphia was hit so hard that the town was almost depopulated. Social historians write, "The horror of those times, when cities lost thousands of their residents, when corpses were hurried through the night-black streets or abandoned where they lay, when rows of houses bore the tragic chalk mark, when impromptu hospitals were rigged up at the town's edge to be tended by heroic men who volunteered as nurses, when every desperate expedient at prevention and cure was tried on hearsay, when crime flourished among the prevalent distraction—such horror could not be overstated."[2] The outward signs were yellow skin and eyes, followed by "black vomiting or purging, hemorrhages from every part of the body especially the stomach, uterus, bowels, nostrils, …deafness, excitability to touch, a considerable degree of delirium, and small purple spots."[3]

Disposal of the dead was extremely uncertain and confused. Since houses were quarantined, the dead were sometimes not found for weeks if they had lived alone. The *Methodist Magazine,* which had just lost its American editor, John Dickens, to yellow fever, reported that a three-week-old corpse was "almost devoured by vermin. Two black men were hired for sixteen dollars to take the corpse and throw it into the river."[4]

Those who were wealthy enough to possess both transportation and friends elsewhere fled the city. The Philadelphia Board of Health set up makeshift tents on the outside of the city for the purpose of feeding and clothing the fugitive poor. The physicians Benjamin Rush and Samuel P. Griffitts sent out medical advice for the treating of those who had contracted the disease. "After the pulse is reduced by bleeding and purging, if the disease has not yielded, a profuse sweat should be excited by wrapping the patient up in blankets, with five or six hot bricks wetted with vinegar applied to different parts of his body, and giving him at the same time large and repeated droughts of hot camomile or sage tea, hot lemonade or weak punch, any other hot liquor that is agreeable to him to drink."[5]

Years before, Philadelphia's most prominent citizen, Benjamin Franklin, had written, "He is the best physician that knows the worthlessness of most medicines." Unfortunately, his proverb became prophetic when the yellow fever took the life of his grandson, Benjamin Franklin Bache, age twenty-nine, on September 8, 1798. As the publisher of the anti-federalist *Aurora,* he was to stand trial one month later for criticizing the President. John Adams wrote, "Benjamin . . . in his 'Aurora' . . . became of course one of the most notorious libellers of me. But the Yellow Fever arrested him in his detestable career and sent him to his grandfather from whom he inherited a dirty, envious, jealous, and revengeful spight against me."[6] The political animosity was as ugly and malicious as the fever.

Turn-of-the-Century Medicine

Causes of disease baffled the most learned doctors; germ theory was not yet understood. Baltimore continued to supply drinking water by sinking shallow wells wherever property owners offered to pay for their installation. By 1816 the town had 290 such pumps and 59 were out of repair. The shallow wells were contaminated from surface drainage that flowed from outdoor privies dug all the way to the underground water table. Without microscopes, medicine consisted largely of wild speculations about fluids, tensions, and maladjustments to the human system.

Benjamin Rush, one of the most prominent physicians of the day, expounded a theory of bodily tension and claimed unbounded faith in bleeding. The ultimate proof of his theory was that any patient who was bled long enough would eventually relax. Rush's belief that as much as four-fifths of the body's blood could be removed without harm alienated him from much of Philadelphia's medical establishment. One historian stated that "the deed of the pen alone [has saved] him from the total disgrace of the lancet."[7] At the height of the yellow fever epidemic, Rush suggested that the worst harm was being done by doctors who did not follow his purging, bleeding remedies. "Never before did I witness such a mass of ignorance and wickedness as our profession has exhibited in the course of the current calamity."[8]

As American's most prominent physician, the principal founder of two colleges, father of American psychiatry, and a signer of the Declaration of Independence, Benjamin Rush was indeed one of the leading citizens of the new republic. He became disillusioned with federalism when he observed the greed created by the Banking Act of 1791, which allowed for an unlimited supply of "bank notes"—easy credit. He labeled the disease "Scriptomania," stating that "a new scene of speculation was produced . . . by the script of the bank of the United States. It excited febrile diseases in three persons who became my patients. In one of them, the acquisition of twelve thousand dollars in a few minutes by a lucky sale, brought on madness which terminated in death in a few days."[9] Becoming fed up with politics, Rush eventually turned to theological pathology, believing that all diseases find their origin in a "morbid accumulation of excitability."[10]

Rush was one of the first persons in America to understand and expound on the positive characteristics of religious sectarianism. The following comment demonstrated his affinity for Asbury and others outside of the "establishment": "It would seem as if one of the designs of Providence in permitting the existence of so many Sects of Christians was that each Sect might be a depository of some great truth of the Gospel, and that it might by that means be better preserved. When united they make a great whole, and that whole is the salvation of all men."[11]

Benjamin Rush, who treated Asbury, was typical of post-Revolutionary War physicians. Unfortunately, he also represented the speculative approach that was so representative of colonial medicine. Being a resident of Philadelphia, he gave particular attention to the yellow fever, believing it to be caused by diet. He was a foremost advocate of bloodletting, now used, he said, "in nearly all diseases of violent excitement . . . nor is it forbidden, as formerly, in infancy, in extreme old age, in the summer months, nor in the period of menstruation."[12] To his credit, he believed that medicine should be for the purposes of public enlightenment, so that every individual would become his or her own physician.

Though medical science did not understand the causes of communicable diseases, at least it was recognized that they were contagious. The yellow fever was so bad in low-lying, mosquito-infested Philadelphia (then capital of the United States) that Congress convened in Germantown, Pennsylvania, in 1793. Also in September of that year, Asbury, recorded in eastern Maryland that "here the people pretend to be afraid of my communicating the infection of the yellow fever, although I had been out of Philadelphia from the 9th to the 26th instant" (1:771). The fear of transmission was a serious problem for traveling preachers, but yellow fever was carried by mosquitoes, not by humans.

Apothecaries consisted of all kinds of bizarre formulas, which even included concoctions of human excrement, urine, and wood lice. In Asbury's time, the medical profession had not advanced much from Cotton Mather's 1724 report to the Royal Society in London which "advised the swallowing leaden bullets—for that miserable distemper which was called the twisting of the guts."[13] The experiment went deadly when the bullet entered the lung of a patient. In 1807, Thomas Jefferson scorned the dogmatism of physicians, noting that patients sometimes got well in spite of the medicine.

A Physically Plagued Preacher

Most of the time Asbury was simply plagued by his deprived, tortured existence: poor diet, physical exposure, emotional distress, loss of sleep, hygienic ignorance, and victimization by medical quackery. His journal records a lifelong intuitive attempt to conquer the limitations of the body via primitive physiology. That he survived to the age of seventy is a miracle.

Thomas Coke described Asbury as a plain, "robust man." What he meant by "robust" is difficult to decipher. In no sense was Asbury ever overweight; there simply was too much riding and too little consistent diet. Jesse Lee states that Asbury was of slender build. The best-known portrait of Asbury was painted by John Paradise in 1812 when Asbury was sixty-seven.[14] By then his face was somewhat drawn and emaciated. Descriptions by his fellow travelers would lead us to believe that in the last years of his life he lost considerable weight. The generally accepted picture we have of Asbury is of a person of wiry build and incredible stamina born of having to spend so much time in a saddle. At fifty-one years of age, he described himself to his parents as "healthy and lean, gray-headed, and dim-sighted" (3:143).[15] Henry Boehm, who was Asbury's longest traveling companion (1808 to 1813), gives us the most complete physical description of Asbury we have:

> Bishop Asbury was five feet nine inches high, weighed one hundred and fifty-one pounds, erect in person, and of a very

commanding appearance. His features were rugged, but his countenance was intelligent, though time and care had furrowed it deep with wrinkles. His nose was prominent, his mouth large, as if made on purpose to talk, and his eyes of a blueish cast, and so keen it seemed as if he could look right through a person. He had a fine forehead, indicative of no ordinary brain, and beautiful white locks, which hung about his brow and shoulders, and added to his venerable appearance. There was as much native dignity about him as any man I ever knew. He seemed born to sway others. There was an austerity about his looks that was forbidding to those who were unacquainted with him.[16]

One of the foremost detriments to Asbury's health was inadequate lodging. The housing was often dark, damp, dirty, and crowded, with little ventilation. Where Asbury was going to spend the night was often a source of great anxiety to him. Adequate rest was a precious commodity. In 1790, he wrote, "We have been exercised in public night and day; frequently we have not more than six hours' sleep; our horses are weary, and the houses are so crowded, that at night our rest is much disturbed. Jesus is not always in our dwellings; and where he is not, a pole cabin is not very agreeable" (1:627). In North Carolina, he said, "Our lodging was on a bed set upon forks, and clap-boards laid across, in an earthen-floor cabin" (1:751).

Often having to sleep with strangers, as many as three to a bed, on mattresses frequented by cats and dogs, the bishop often contracted skin diseases. Fleas were a constant threat, plus whatever microbes were undetectable. In eastern Tennessee he noted that at Felix Earnest's house "I found that amongst my other trials, I had taken the itch; and, considering the filthy houses and filthy beds I have met with, in coming from Kentucky Conference, it is perhaps strange that I have not caught it twenty times: I do not see that there is any security against it, but by sleeping in a brimstone shirt:—poor bishop!" (2:411). The following explanation from Henry Smith, Asbury's onetime travelling companion, is a classic description of a turn-of-the-century home remedy.

> Among other disasters that befell me I had the itch two or three times in the year. I had recourse to various remedies, till an old motherly lady, at whose house I had often put up, said she could cure me. She took sulfur, raisin, and black pepper, an equal quantity of each, beat it into powder, and the same quantity of hog's lard, and mixed it into a mass, and tied it on a rag, and hung it before a large fire. The drippings made a very pleasant salve, not at all offensive. I was told to rub my joints only with it, before the fire, at bedtime, but I was so anxious to get rid of the hateful disease, that I gave myself a pretty generous anointing. It strongly

affected my nerves, and I had a restless night, but it effectively cured me of the itch.[17]

"I Am My Own Physician"

Problems in the digestive system were to be purged, especially if they were accompanied by a fever. "As I was my own doctor, I resolved to breakfast upon eight grains of ipecacuanha; this cleansed my filthy stomach, and so broke up my disease that a fever of fifty days fled" (2:444). Asbury resorted to emetics to stimulate vomiting or to cathartics, which would act as a laxative. Tartar, derived from the juice of grapes, was most commonly used. To calm the system, Asbury resorted to wine and, if he was extremely out of sorts he took some alcohol with a tinge of opium (laudanum) (2:365). He didn't abide by the Methodist ruling on alcohol.

Often Asbury grabbed whatever was immediately available for relief: poultices, bread and milk for a skin sore, tobacco for an aching tooth, and sugar of lead for his aching, swollen feet (2:364). "[I] have been for sometime with an inflammation in my throat, we concluded to turn in at a tavern, and spend the night in pain: pain begets invention. I now began to think, What shall I do? I am my own physician. I sent for two blisters; applied both to my ears; and then began to march to Ashford" (1:768).

At times, Asbury had such pain and inflammation in his jaws and face that it was almost impossible for him to eat. He often referred to his face or jaw being swollen or hurting. Oral hygiene was almost nonexistent. In fact, it was considered effeminate to pay attention to one's teeth at all. And if one did clean his or her teeth, it was done with "snuff or a chalk rag." A toothbrush was unknown.[18] At age sixty-five, he recorded, "My good teeth fail."[19]

As early as 1784, a Philadelphia dentist advertised implanting teeth, claiming that he had "transplanted 23 teeth in the preceding six months." If anyone wanted to sell their "front teeth," the dentist would give them two guineas for each tooth.[20] When the famed Paul Revere's silversmith business was at a low ebb, he resorted to crafting false teeth. He placed advertisements in the *Boston Gazette* pointing out "that a lack of teeth affected not only a persons appearance, but also ones ability to speak in public." He promised to supply teeth that would pass for "natural."[21]

Asbury was willing not only to serve as his own personal physician, but also to freely offer medical advice to others. To one who had lost the use of his arms, he prescribed cold baths or electricity (2:360). To Mary Pilkinton, of Brunswick Courthouse, Virginia, he wrote, "May great grace rest upon you now and in the power of death. I feel for your soul and body. The latter must return to death, and dust, the former, to endless bliss. If you are not too far gone, one peck of red oak bark burnt to ashes, boiled to a very stiff substance, to make a plaster applied and reapplied till the roots of the cancer are eaten away. Then apply a soft healing salve of malorate or any healing salve. You will be well, by the blessing of God" (3:341).

Blistering and bleeding were the most macabre and consistent of all attempts at relief from pains of inflammation. Disease was an entity that must be drawn out. When Asbury was seized with a "putrid" sore throat, he "applied blisters to the back of his neck and behind his ear as well as drawing blood from both his arm and tongue." For pain in the chest, Asbury placed plaster on it in order to raise a blister; when he coughed up blood, he thought to redirect it by drawing blood from his arm. When he applied several blisters in order to relieve his rheumatism, Henry Boehm, his traveling companion in 1809, noted that the plasters were too strong and "the remedy was worse than the disease."[22]

Nicholas Snethen remarked that Asbury "was subject to the asthma and inflammatory infection."[23] In 1815, Asbury stated that he had been "more or less asthmatic for about sixty years, feeble in his limbs, but more abundantly in his lungs" (3:515). Asbury probably suffered from respiratory problems throughout his life, complicated by bronchial allergies. Preaching until he was wet with perspiration in overheated quarters and then stepping out into the cold left him with an almost constant cough and sore throat. The infection was sometimes so severe that the malady probably progressed at times into pneumonia and eventually tuberculosis. "[I] had a putrid sore throat, and two persons sat up with me every night; but I found relief from purges, and a mixture of nitre and fever powder" (1:146). At one point, Asbury's throat was so infected that he expectorated a "pint of white matter." And what caused the discharge? "The gargle which I used first, to scatter, if possible, the inflammation, was sage tea, honey, vinegar, and mustard; then that which was used to accelerate the gathering, was mallows with fig cut in pieces: and lastly, to strengthen the part, we used a gargle of sage tea, alum, rose leaves, and loaf sugar" (1:147).

At least twice, Asbury submitted to minor surgery for growths on his hand and foot. On April 13, 1801, "Doctor Smith, on whom I called, took a wart, cancerous in appearance, which had troubled me three months, from my foot" (2:291). A month later, he stated that it was still sore and was accompanied by a high fever. On May 10, Philip Physick applied a "caustic" to it. Dr. Physick later advised him that he would need further surgery because of a sinew strain. There is no record that the surgery was ever performed.

Asbury strongly believed in proper diet, in spite of the fact it was rarely available. When he was thirty-two, he stated, "As I have thought bacon was prejudicial to my health, I have lately abstained from it, and have experienced the good effects of this economy" (1:242). By the time Asbury was fifty-three, he had become a vegetarian (2:170).[24] He was a believer in the benefits of various types of teas and faithfully carried a supply. Even that did not guarantee that he would be able to enjoy it, as the following from Thomas Morrell testifies: "Francis Asbury took the paper from his saddlebags and reached it to the woman of the house requesting her to make some tea. When they sat down to the table she brought on the tea. She had boiled the whole of it, thrown away the juice, and spread the leaves all out on a plate and said, 'Help yourself to tea.'"[25]

The Wesleyan Medical Heritage

Asbury combined introspective spirituality and intuitive pathology. They were his avenues to knowing both body and soul for the purpose of rendering a living sacrifice to God. Sacrifice did not mean neglecting the structure that housed the enterprise. There was a delicate balance between expending life while at the same time taking care of it. He would have been in full agreement with Paul's exhortation to Timothy "to take a little wine for (his) stomach's sake," which the bishop did. He discovered that fermented grape juice was more healthful than fresh.

In 1795, Asbury published, *The Family Adviser or A Plain and Modern Practice of Physic for the Use of Families Who Have Not the Advantages of a Physician and Accommodated to the Diseases of America*. The book was edited by Henry Wilkins and included remedies for "hectic fever," "inflammation of the brain," "bastard or spurious pluracy," "St. Anthony's fire" and "St. Vitis's dance."[26] Wilkens was fairly well known from both his medical practice and his writings. The second edition of the *Family Adviser* included Wesley's *Primitive Physick*.[27]

The 1780 edition of Wesley's *Primitive Physick* listed 824 remedies, including goose dung and celandine for breast cancer, stuffing "strong vinegar up the nose for lethargy," and holding a madman "under a great waterfall for as long as his strength will bear." Wesley listed forty-six ailments that could be cured by a cold bath, including deafness and kidney stones, and forty-nine cures that could be affected by "electrifying," including menstrual obstruction. Wesley was cautious about bloodletting. His prescriptions were for the purpose of circumventing a profession that had become unintelligibly obtrusive, speculative, and "quite out of reach of ordinary men."[28]

The Methodist preacher Billy Hibbard described a "learned description" of a disease by a physician who applied his "remedies" to an aged woman who got better. After the doctor had felt her pulse, she asked,

"Well, doctor do you know my case?"

"O yes mem, it is a plain case."

"Well, doctor, what is it?"

"Why mem it is a scrutanutory case."

"Scrutanutory case, doctor, pray what is that?"

"It's a dropping of the nerves, mem."

"Dropping of the nerves, doctor; why, what's that?"

"Why, mem, the num naticals tizer-rizer, tizer-rizer."

"Ah doctor, you have hit my case, it is just so with me."[29]

Asbury's journal is a turn-of-the-century account of mind over matter. Believing one is doing things that make one better often causes one to feel better. If Asbury could just get rid of the "bile" through bleeding, blistering, and purging, then nervousness, excitability, irritability, and ill temper could be calmed, not to speak of the boils, headaches, and inflammations that were constantly his lot. Asbury was right in his belief that there is continuity between the welfare of the soul and the health of the body. The relationship was just too complex to be treated comprehensively by the apothecary in his saddlebag. However, no one could ever accuse him of not trying.

12. "I Am a Man of Another World"

The Bishop Resigns

Charleston did not escape winter in 1798–99. The glaze on the icy streets was as thick as the spiritual crust covering Charleston's heart. For amusement, the rowdies attempted to shut Asbury down by gathering around the church to make noise. Asbury and Jesse Lee made their departure for a cold, stiff ride north. Asbury was back in the swing of preaching but still much lacking in stamina. On February 10, the draft from the bitter cold chilled him to the extent that three days later he was unable to preach in Wilmington, North Carolina. Battling the elements proved to be more than both his physical and mental constitution could bear.

At Williams Meeting House in Currituck, North Carolina, Asbury was so weak that he asked Jesse Lee to finish his sermon. Going all day with just a biscuit, preaching in cold churches, and exposure to icy rain proved to be overwhelming obstacles. He was not able to attend the Virginia Annual Conference because of inflamed bronchial tubes and an ulcer on his chest. And of course, there was a drawing of "two pounds" of blood for the purpose of relief. The conference ordered him not to preach until he arrived in Baltimore. "I was willing to obey, feeling utterly unable. The houses that we preach and lodge in, in this severe weather, are very open. My breast is inflamed, and I have a discharge of blood" (2:191).

Asbury's physical weakness and the deadness of the Baltimore Conference must have combined to make Phillip Roger's offer of a retirement house seem very inviting. Discouragement peaked when on May 21 his horse began to sweat, swell, and tremble, then died on the road. The horse's rider was almost in the same condition. By the time Asbury reached the Dover area, two physicians advised him to desist from preaching, "fearing a consumption or a dropsy in the breast" (2:195). All of this was aggravated by a falling out with one of his closest friends, Ezekiel Cooper. Asbury had appointed him as the "agent" of the book concern to replace the deceased John Dickens. However, Cooper did not want to leave the pastorate and let his displeasure be known. By July 1, Asbury was almost fully resolved to resign the General Superintendency. In a letter to Cooper he wrote,

> It is enough! My own children are risen up against me; one of the dearest friends I had in America; his letters are like the piercing of a sword, to my breast and heart. In real tenderness to you, I have offended, fearing your strength would not be sufficient for the charge. I have suffered much of late in labour and loss of my health, horse; and perpetual crowds of brethren. My Christian doctors say *rest, rest* or death, or great danger! I have resigned the pulpit, I am weaning the conferences, I am absent whole days at a time; I keep no minutes now, never preside, seldom speak in

conference, only when called upon in a special manner by the conference (3:179–80).

The summer was as hot as the winter had been cold. Working his way from northern New Jersey, Asbury crossed the Pocono Mountains with great labor. He made it as far west as Boehm's chapel just outside of Lancaster, Pennsylvania. An earthquake struck at five in the morning on July 30. "[T]he earth is growing old; it groans and trembles; which is the necessary consequence of 'palsied eld'" (2:200–1). There was a correlation between the hand tremors and the unsettledness that increasingly gripped Asbury. He was losing his hold; but all was not lost. He had sensed a revival of religion at four of the six districts he had visited since the Baltimore conference.

After visiting the Lingamore, Maryland, grave of Sarah Dorsey, who had nursed him to health in June of 1797, Asbury wrote his letter of resignation to Thomas Morrell, pastor in Baltimore. It was to be effective at the next General Conference, which Asbury seriously doubted he would attend. "I have only to say I am writing my resignation, and apology to the General Conference for every part of my general conduct. I firmly believed I have delayed my resignation too long, it is time they were put upon ways, means, and persons for the better organization of so great a body of people" (3:182).

Hardly A Worse Year

Asbury continued to travel under a pall of despondency, obsessed by the thoughts of quitting a task that had consumed him. The resignation was partly prompted by his physical depletion and partly by spite against the barbs of criticisms he was receiving. It was hard enough to continue with positive feedback, much less constant censure. From Asbury's perspective, signs that he was doing a good job were harder to find than a brush path to a hovel in the middle of the night. The decreasing sense of fulfillment was not worth the load he had to carry.

While riding through central Virginia, he lamented, "a raw and running blister upon my breast, excessive heat, and with very little rest by night or by day: I would not live always: weary world! when will it end?" (2:205). Asbury was feeling sorry for himself, but not without cause. Even when recuperating at the comfortable home of John Spencer in Charlotte County, Virginia, he wrote, "[T]hese people have not turned me out of doors, by separation, defamation, or reproach; they have made no such return for my love and labours, although some have done it" (2:206).

By the time October rolled around, Asbury was feeling better and transcending the ills of the church. He was encouraged by the thought that his traveling had "brought thousands to hear the Gospel, who, probably, would not otherwise have heard it" (2:207). On October 9, he was grateful that one of the hooks to which the harness was attached had broken just after they crossed Hunter Creek, rather than in it. On October 28, his crossing of Horse Ford in Lincoln County was not as successful. Asbury got wet head to toe because of the large rocks over which his carriage had to pass.

The journey south was a "sick, weary, hungry" ride, "jolting over the roots, stumps, holes and gullies" (2:212). At this point in his travel, Asbury was almost constantly riding in a buggy. His traveling companion, Benjamin Blanton, seemed to be sicker than he was. The constant rain turned the Georgia roads into miry red mud. "We came down the Augusta Road, gouged up by wagons in a most dreadful manner, in consequence of which we were five hours in going twelve miles to Thomas Haine's, upon Uchee. I had great *intestine* war, having eat but little" (2:216).

Asbury's final journal entry for the year stated, "I never knew worse roads" (2:217). And hardly had he known a worse year. The weight of the task had become unbearable. On October 26, he expressed its immensity: "I tremble and faint under my burden:—having to ride about six thousand miles annually; to preach from three to five hundred sermons a year; to write and read so many letters, and read many more:—all this and more, besides the stationing of three hundred preachers; reading many hundred pages; and spending many hours in conversation by day and by night, with preachers and people of various characters, among whom are many distressing cases" (2:210).

Methodism had opened a new territory in 1799. Tobias Gibson, without official appointment, had made his way down the Mississippi River by canoe. Jesse Lee reported that Gibson had been given freedom to go where he pleased because of physical affliction that prevented him from traveling a circuit. Although Gibson had not gone in the right direction for the recovery of his health, his short but useful ministry to the Natchez settlements was another lasting monument to the itinerant preachers who made the ultimate sacrifice. Upon Gibson's death from "consumption" in April 1804, Jesse Lee stated, "He was very soft, affectionate, and agreeable in his conversation; his voice in preaching was very piercing and melting."[1]

Asbury chose Nicholas Snethen to replace Benjamin Blanton as his traveling companion. He would become a capable preacher and the official defender of Asbury against O'Kelly. As the year before, the Charleston winter was unusually cold and Asbury suffered. He and Snethen made their way north through the snow, leaving Charleston on February 10, 1800. On the eleventh, they met a wagoner whose horses were startled by Asbury's carriage and "whirled the wagon among the stumps and trees: happily no considerable injury was suffered" (2:224).

Upon entering North Carolina, the pair discovered that "the snow had fallen fifteen and eighteen inches deep, and continued nearly a month upon the ground, and had swelled the rivers, and spoiled the public roads" (2:225). Upon reaching the central part of the state, Asbury preached at the State House in Raleigh and Snethen at the University of North Carolina at Chapel Hill, where they were treated with "great respect." The University, the first state institution in the South, had opened its doors in 1795.

By the time they reached Virginia, Jesse Lee had caught up with them. They decided to hold conference north of Norfolk because of a smallpox epidemic in the city. In spite of the contagion, Asbury preached in the new church at Portsmouth and visited the "brethren" in Norfolk, where he supported the plans for a new church. "[W]onder of wonders! it is to be built on the lot adjoining that on which the old Episcopal church stands!" (2:229). The reports of revival that were filtering down from Delaware and northern Virginia encouraged Asbury. Even so, at Urbana, a county seat on the Rappahannock River, no one showed up to hear the party preach. The crossing of the river on a "leaky boat, weak hands and oars, heavily loaded in the bow with four horses" was extremely treacherous. They reached Alexandria on April 22.

The newly chosen "federal city" of Washington had not yet housed a president. The new capital was a swamp, with cattle roaming the muddy field later designated "the mall." The residents of the 372 inhabitable dwellings boasted of the excellent hunting along the street and on the new capitol building's walkways. Asbury stated that his party was lost an hour in the woods. They were not the last; the next year a group of congressmen returning from a party spent most of the night also lost in the woods. The new location of the United States government was in sharp contrast with the bustling cosmopolitan fervor of New York. One European referred to the "grotesque" and "patch work" appearance of Washington. He went on to say that "[s]peculation, the life of the American, embraced the design of the new city."[2]

The Conference Rejects Asbury's Resignation

Asbury described the two-week General Conference at Baltimore on May 1 as "much talk but little work" (2:231). Richard Whatcoat received four more votes for bishop than did Jesse Lee, but the conference would not accept Asbury's resignation. "This conference do earnestly entreat Mr. Asbury for a continuation of his service as one of the General Superintendents of the Methodist Episcopal Church as far as his strength will prevail." Asbury responded by saying that since he was now feeling better he would do "anything he could to serve the connection and that the Conference might require of him."[3] Several of Asbury's nemeses fought to make the two bishops equal in power. They failed. Asbury would continue to be the father of American Methodism.

A rumor circulated on the floor of the conference hinting that Asbury would have gotten rid of Jesse Lee if he could. It was said that, before the appointment of Benjamin Blanton, Lee had been Asbury's traveling companion for most of

1799 by "imposing himself on Asbury and the connection." Lee approached Asbury on the imposition issue, which the latter flatly denied. Asbury publicly addressed the accusation at the conference, validating Lee's usefulness and faithfulness. Asbury then offered a peace alternative, requesting Lee to be a sort of roaming assistant to attend and assist in the business of the Conferences. According to Lee, Asbury "added that if I would not consent to go, he thought that he should be forced to resign at the close of the Conference."[4] Once again, Asbury had placated a wounded political opponent.

The salary of the preachers was raised from sixty-four to eighty dollars per year. The conference authorized its bishops to ordain Black preachers as deacons. At the first conference of the new century, Methodism boasted 64,894 members, 7 conferences, and 287 preachers.[5] "The unction that attended the word was great—more than 100 souls, at different times and places, professed conversion during the sitting of conference" (2:231).

Richard Allen

Asbury ordained Richard Allen a deacon at the Baltimore General Conference in 1800. On June 29, 1794, Asbury recorded preaching at Bethel Church in Philadelphia, a church "to be governed by the doctrine and discipline of the Methodists" (2:18). The building of Bethel by Richard Allen and his followers was the result of a very unfortunate incident. Not only were the Blacks assigned to seats in the gallery of St. George's, they were accosted when they sat in the front of the gallery. When a sexton attempted to physically remove Absolom Jones during prayer, Jones responded, "[W]ait until prayer was over and I will get up and trouble you no more."[6] The sexton summoned an assistant, but by the time he arrived, prayer had concluded. The Blacks immediately formed a caucus, and years later Richard Allen recalled that "all [the Blacks] went out of the church in a body and they were no more plagued with us in the church."[7]

Allen's Bethel congregation feuded with its parent body, the Methodist Episcopal Church. Unable to appoint its own Black preachers, it attempted to pull out of Methodism. Even though the Blacks had built the church, largely with their own money, they were told they did not own the church. When Asbury sent Caucasian pastors, they were rebuffed by the Black congregation. Allen lived under the tension of his commitment to the Methodist Church, which had spiritually molded him, and his vision for a Black church uninhibited by the surrounding racist culture. When a committee from Bethel requested Asbury to appoint them a preacher (we presume a Black preacher), Asbury responded that he "did not think that there was more than one preacher belonging to the conference that would attend to those duties and that was Richard Allen."[8] Asbury's response was plagued with ambivalence in that he had ordained Allen a deacon but not as an elder. Methodism never granted Allen the authority he had earned.

As a result, the African Methodist Episcopal Church was born in 1816. The Philadelphia Conference placed Bethel Church up for auction and Allen placed the highest bid—on a building for which he already held a $5,433 lien, a building that Allen's sweat and money had brought into existence. It is no coincidence that Allen's purchase of his the church building took place during the month that immediately followed Asbury's death. In deference to Asbury, Allen waited until the bishop's death to separate himself officially from the parent body.

As the founder of America's first Black denomination, a former slave who purchased his freedom and amassed a fortune of $80,000, Allen is a remarkable example of triumph of the human spirit in the face of enormous odds. Regarding his separation from the Methodist Episcopal Church, Allen stated, "This was a trial I never had to pass through but I was confident that the Great Head of the Church would support us."[9]

Not long after the 1800 Christmas Conference, Asbury invited Allen to accompany him on his southern route through the Carolinas and Georgia. Asbury told Allen that he would not be able to mingle with the white ministers and at times would have to sleep in the carriage because of unavailable accommodations. Allen's pay would consist of food and clothing. He refused Asbury's invitation, reasoning that if he got sick no one would take care of him. He was also concerned that giving up his salt business would leave him impoverished in old age. Deep down, Allen did not feel that Asbury treated him with equality. Allen never received any monetary compensation as a Methodist deacon.

The months after the 1800 General Conference saw Asbury in greatly improved health. There were unmistakable signs of revival and renewed life within Methodism. At the annual conference in Duck Creek, Delaware, from June 1–6, a hundred people were converted. Henry Boehm reported that the people did not go home until 3 A.M., and one segment of worship lasted for forty-five hours without intermission. Both saints and sinners were stricken to the floor. Jesse Lee recorded that

> [w]hen the preachers attempted to preach, the people tried to be as quiet as possible until the sermon had ended; but sometimes they would break out into loud praises to God. So that speaker could not be heard; and when they were silent till the sermon had ended they commonly gave vent to their full hearts immediately and in a few minutes the house would ring with the songs of praise.[10]

It was a new era for Methodism. "Surely we may say our Pentecost is fully come this year, when we recollect what God hath wrought in Edisto in South, and Guilford in North Carolina. . . . My health is restored, to the astonishment of myself and friends" (2:235).

Death of Washington

It also was a new era for the United States and especially the national government. Federalism under the leadership of John Adams was in its death throes and the republicanism of Thomas Jefferson was about to be ushered in. The political honeymoon of George Washington, the patron saint of the Revolution, had given way to the petty paranoia of John Adams. When Jefferson responded to the Frenchman Abbé Raynal's charge that the Americans had not "produced one great poet, one able mathematician, one man of genius, and a single science," he noted that, though there were no American Homers or Shakespeares, the country could boast a great political and military leader in George Washington.[11] Though Asbury would not have affirmed much else in Thomas Jefferson, he at least would have said "amen" to this ascription.

Of the five presidents who served during Asbury's time, he mentions only Washington. (In 1792 he gave reference to Jefferson's *Notes on Virginia*.) Washington was Asbury's hero, a "matchless man." No president would enjoy such military stature again until Andrew Jackson. Washington was the leader of a new nation even as was Asbury the leader of a new denomination.[12] They were both commanders in charge of the troops. On January 4, 1800, Asbury paid homage to Washington, who had died on December 14, in these words: "[T]he calm, intrepid chief, the disinterested friend, first father, and temporal saviour of his country under divine protection and direction" (2:221). Asbury was particularly affected as he read in Gordon's *History of the American Revolution* of Washington saying farewell to his officers. "O how minds are made great with affliction and suffering!" (2:4).

Upon Washington's death, a pall hung over the city of Charleston, a "universal cloud which set upon the faces of the citizens . . . the pulpits clothed in black— the bells muffled—the paraded soldiery" (2:221). Asbury did not so much mourn Washington as a president as he admired him as a fearless leader, a person of sacrifice during the Valley Forge and Morristown winters. He was "not ashamed of his redeemer," and a man "who did not fear death." Washington had defeated the odds with perseverance and tenacity, virtues that Asbury sought in himself.[13]

Political Tumult

George Washington was the *exception*, because Asbury's journal is singularly quiet concerning events and persons that played out their parts on the national stage during his lifetime. He seemed almost oblivious to one of the most tumultuous periods ever in American politics, 1798–1800. America was at odds with both the British and the French. During the French Revolution, Louis XIV had been beheaded and America was rife with Jacobin conspiracy theories. President Adams sent envoys to France in 1797 to stop the raiding of American ships. The envoys were insulted when the French demanded a bribe of $250,000 and a loan of $12 million. Most Americans thought the French Enlightenment had given rise to an "evil empire," bent on transforming the world into universal anarchy. The Reverend Jedediah Morse, pastor of the First Congregational Church of Charlestown, Massachusetts, and father of the famous inventor Samuel F.B. Morse, preached that there was "an international conspiracy of Deists, Atheists, Skeptics, and free thinkers to undermine the Christian religion, to destroy the basic institutions derived from it."[14] The rumored power circle of the "Illuminati" would serve as one of America's most enduring conspiracy theories.

America was already closing its door to "wild ignorant Irishmen, invading Jews and the atheistic, anarchic French." *The Porcupine Gazette*, a Philadelphia Federalist newspaper, reported on June 22, 1798, that "Americans now have everything in danger, morals, religion, independence, liberty, civil and religious, everything that can be dear to man as a social animal. Our country has been the resort of almost all seditionists, foreigners of every distinction. . . . It is a matter of the most serious consideration in time so alarming; what is to be done with these miscreants?"[15] In spite of the fact that Colonial America became a refuge for Germans, Irish, French, Jews, and Blacks, it had already developed an Anglo-Saxon ethnocentricity. As early as 1775, John Adams wrote to his wife that

> New England has, in many respects, the advantage (over) every other colony in America, and indeed of every other part of the world that I know anything of. . . . The people are pure English blood, less mixed with Scotch, Irish, Dutch, French, Danish, Swedish, etc., than any other; and descended from Englishmen, too, who left Europe in purer times than the present, and less tainted with corruption than those they left behind.[16]

Adams Versus Jefferson

It would seem that the deistic Thomas Jefferson, with French sympathies (he had lived in Paris for five years), did not stand a chance as a presidential candidate. The years 1798–99 saw President John Adams pitted against Vice President Thomas Jefferson in one of the most raucous, mud-slinging election campaigns that America has ever experienced. Timothy Dwight, president of Yale University, preached on July 4, 1798, "Can serious and reflective men look about them and doubt that if Jefferson is elected and the Jacobins get into authority, that those morals which protect our lives from the knife of the assassin, which guard the chastity of our wives and daughters from seduction and violence, defend our property from plunder and devastation and shield our religion from contempt and profanation, will not be trampled upon?"[17]

One lady in a small town in Connecticut, fearing that all the Bibles would be destroyed if Jefferson were elected, took her family Bible to the only Jeffersonian she knew with the rationale, "It will be perfectly safe with you. They will never think of looking in the house of a democrat for a Bible."[18] But Americans had had enough of the pomp and pettiness of John Adams, whom they nicknamed "His Rotundity" for his paunchy figure. His abrasive disposition took national form in the Alien and Sedition Acts, which made it a crime to utter slanderous or malicious statements against the U.S. government or one of its officials. During Adams's administration, twenty-five people were indicted and ten imprisoned under these laws, including the journalist Thomas Callendar, who was sentenced to nine months in prison. Not that Callendar bathed his comments in benevolent kindness. He labeled Adams a "repulsive pedant," a "gross hypocrite," "one of the most egregious fools upon the continent," and a "hideous hermaphroditical character which has neither the force and a firmness of a man, nor the gentleness and sensibility of a woman."[19] As contradictory as Adams may have been, he was one of the most articulate persons to ever grace American politics. His verbal prowess, which he often employed in acerbic remarks, was surpassed by no one in the early republic. He once called Tom Paine "the Satyr of the Age . . . a mongrel between Pig and Puppy, begotten by a wild Boar on a Butch Wolf."

The dirty campaign between Adams and Jefferson proceeded by means of partisan officials' buying votes with whiskey, food, or threats. Voting was done publicly, so employees could lose their jobs if they did not comply with those who stood watch. A voting day gave any small town a circus atmosphere, which Asbury alluded to on April 24, 1799: "This is the great day of election; and there is no small stir in Virginia, about federal and anti-federal men" (2:192). When George Washington ran for the Virginia State Legislature in 1753, he had provided his 391 supporters "with 28 gallons of rum, 50 gallons of rum punch, 34 gallons of wine and 46 gallons of beer."[20]

Apolitical Asbury

Asbury did not vote. Except for his occasional journal references such as the above, we would hardly know there was an election going on, much less that American society was in a political tempest. Newspapers were readily available, but Asbury's journals do not indicate that he ever read one.[21] In 1770, the *New York Gazette* had quipped,

> 'Tis truth (with deference to the college)
> Newspapers are the spring of knowledge
> The general source throughout the nation
> Of every modern communication.[22]

The Reverend Samuel Miller wrote in 1785, "Never, it may be safely asserted, was the number of political journals so great in proportion to the population of the country as at present is ours. Never were they, all things considered, so cheap, so universally diffused, and so easy of access."[23] Often Asbury was beyond the boundaries of print civilization. However, this does not fully explain the almost total absence in Asbury's journal of any reference to a contemporary event, much less a political crisis. The omission was intentional. He believed that national events were important only as they were directed and interpreted as Kingdom events.

In simple terms, the affairs of men really did not matter. God was in control and superintended for divine purposes everything that happened. Charles Foster states, "Especially during the years 1797 through 1800, fear repeatedly swept the country, fear that one might wake some fine morning to find the young republic something else, subverted by secret agents of the French or captured by a federalist army."[24] Contrast that mood with the following, which Asbury wrote to his mother on June 28, 1799: "The coming of Christ is near, even at the door, when he will establish his kingdom. He is now sweeping the earth, to plant it with righteousness and true holiness" (3:181).

A Higher Order of Business

If there were any subverting to be done, the Methodists were going to do it; they would be the followers not of Voltaire and Robespiere but of Francis Asbury. While the Congregationalists were forming societies to send missionaries to the expanding West during 1798–99, the Methodists needed no such ad hoc agencies. They *were* a missionary society. By going up every hollow, visiting every new settlement, knocking on the door of every hovel, they sought to convert individuals and their families. They believed the redemption of the microcosm would be the salvation of the macrocosm. Systemic invasion of the whole nation, all the way to the highest echelons of power, would take place in the gospel leavening of local communities.

In the Methodist understanding, government was not a vehicle of spiritual redemption but it could provide stability and order so that the gospel might be preached without fear of reprisal. In return, the Christian community would pray for the government and recognize its authority within a limited secular sphere. The twenty-third article of American Methodism, entitled, "Of the Rulers of the United States of America," recognized secular government's legitimacy. The "Explanatory Notes" quoted Romans 13:1: "Let every soul be subject unto the higher powers; for there is no power but of God: the powers that be are ordained of God."[25]

In spite of Asbury's apolitical stance, American Methodism was the first Christian denomination to recognize the American government as an official independent entity. Asbury moved in the May 1789 New York Conference that a "congratulatory" message be sent to the new President. The conference unanimously adopted the idea and appointed Asbury to write the document. While in New York, Asbury, Thomas Morrell, and John Dickens delivered the address to the President, which expressed

> . . . [f]ull confidence in your wisdom and your integrity for the preparation of those civil and religious liberties which have been transmitted to us by the providence of God and the glorious Revolution as we believe ought to be reposed in man. . . . and we promise you our fervent prayers to the throne of Grace, that God Almighty may endue you with all the graces and the gifts of his Holy spirit, that he may enable you to fill up your important station to his glory, the good of his Church, the happiness and prosperity of the United States, and the welfare of mankind.[26]

Washington's lengthy response concluded by saying, "I take in the kindest part the promise you made of presenting your prayers at the throne of grace for me, and that I likewise implore the divine benediction on yourselves and your religious community."[27] Asbury made no mention of the event in his journal. However, the letter delivered to Washington did remove some of the British stigma that Asbury still wore. The *New York Packet* reported that the "affectionate and respective address" demonstrated that the "[w]hole society [of Methodists] are warmly attached to the constitution and government of the United States" (1:594n).

The Politics of God

For Asbury, God's blessing did not depend on which person or party was in office. There was hardly a reason to vote, much less lobby or write letters. Secular government was a lower order of business run by individuals with a lesser agenda. Asbury's agenda was otherworldly: "As I am not a man of the world, the most of the conversation about it is irksome to me" (2:129). When in the City of Washington, he wrote, "Company does not amuse, congress does not interest me: I am a man of another world, in mind and calling: I am Christ's; and for the service of his Church" (2:497). When at the home of Edward Tiffin (a physician who served as the first governor of Ohio and performed one of the first mastectomies in the United States), Asbury wrote, "O what a charming view presents itself from Doctor Tiffin's house! but these long talks about land and politics suit me not; I take little interest in either subject: O Lord, give me souls, and keep me holy!" (2:614). As sociologists have noted, "The churching of America was accomplished by aggressive churches committed to vivid other worldliness."[28]

Asbury's transcendence over the 1800 political war did not totally reflect the political philosophy of his followers. For instance, at the 1800 Annual Conference in Philadelphia there was a motion to send a partisan address in support of John Adams, which generated heated debate. The motion failed.[29] Thomas Ware's opposition to partisan politics and especially his objection to support of the Federalist party got him dismissed from the district he served on the Eastern shore.

For Asbury, the only way to national health was the salvation and sanctification of humanity, one individual at a time. Of course, revivals and camp meetings speeded up the process. These were God's tools. Legislation and government were simply aids to the prosperity of God's kingdom. When the political process got in the way of God's work, Asbury did not have much patience. When the Virginia Conference was wrangling about the nature and description of epistles sent from one conference to another, Asbury observed, "Strange, that such an affair should occupy the time of so many good men! Religion will do great things; but it does not make Solomons" (2:496). Asbury feared any kind of partisan debate over nonessentials that would create division and thus dilute the essential purpose of spreading scriptural holiness. What little good there was in party politics was negated by their tendency to divisiveness. During the election year of 1785, while in Delaware, Asbury noted, "I felt the necessity of watching against the spirit of politics, and of being more in the spirit of prayer: the people's minds are agitated with the approaching election of delegates to the assembly" (1:496).

On the brink of the Revolutionary War, Asbury wrote, "I can leave all the little affairs of this confused world to those men to whose province they pertain; and can comfortably go on in my proper business of instrumentally saving my own soul and those that hear me" (1:182). Politics profited little and was only of temporal significance. Who would rule on earth next year was not nearly as important as who would rule forever. Those decisions were not made on the battlefield, but within the human heart; there true liberty was found. In Donald Mathews' words, "When Methodist preachers rode into the American countryside to preach 'liberty' to the captives 'empowered' by the Holy Spirit, they were in a sense declaring the 'politics of God' to people who were bound by race, sex, or social conditions as well as personal predicament."[30]

Asbury was not naïve about the rights and privileges afforded by good government: "the American Government; the best upon earth" (3:416). Thus, he urged pastors to set aside fast days, days of intercession for the welfare of government—that is, its moral integrity and righteousness. Asbury held to no illusion that government would be thoroughly Christian or that America would be the new Israel, God's chosen people. His concerns were different. To become power brokers in human institutions that administer temporal affairs was, to him, not the way to establish the kingdom of God. Abstinence from political activities would keep a minister's job description pure and simple, a working premise of which church leaders needed to be continually reminded.

Reforming The Continent

Preachers were not to aspire to become senators, congressmen, or even government chaplains. Asbury knew there was more important business to take care of: the conquering of the land through the proclamation of the gospel. The resources would be found in the power of the Holy Spirit, not political leverage. Asbury reminded the church in his valedictory message that "[w]e neither have, nor wish to have, anything to do with the government of the States, nor, as I conceive, do the States fear us. Our kingdom is not of this world. For near half a century we have never grasped at power" (3:480). [31]

Russell Richey points out that American Methodism changed Wesley's dictum from "reform the nation" to "reform the continent."[32] The fourth question in the Discipline read, "What may we reasonably believe to be God's Design in raising up the Preachers called Methodists?" The reply read, "To reform the Continent, and to spread scriptural Holiness over these Lands."[33] The vision was neither cast nor limited by national or geographical concerns. God's kingdom would be spread as far as the sea of humanity extended.

Richey maintains that Asbury was much more concerned about the prosperity of Zion than he was about the welfare of America. The two kingdoms—one of America and the other of Christ—were not synonymous. Asbury awaited news of the prosperity of Zion as a commander anticipates a courier from the battlefield. "Zion" was any territory that had been claimed for the purposes of the kingdom. Richey states that "[b]y identifying with Zion, Methodists laid claim to that covenantal relation that gathered in the rich imagery of Old Testament and New."[34]

No denomination benefited more from separation of church and state than did Methodism. Ironically, the agnostic Thomas Paine in his tract "Common Sense" had popularized the phrase, "free exercise of religion."[35] Methodists fully supported that idea. Their work was not going to be curtailed by decorum, denomination, or government. As a populist religion, Methodism was the primary religious benefactor of American's independence.[36] In Paul Johnson's words, "There is no question that the Declaration of Independence was to those who signed it, a religious as well as a secular act, and that the Revolutionary War had the approbation of divine providence."[37]

A Covenantal Understanding

Even though Asbury did not assume that America had been singled out for God's special favor, he did believe that there was a correlation between righteousness and prosperity. Such covenantal understanding was both Puritan and Wesleyan. In his sermon on "National Sins and Miseries," Wesley had clearly stated the need for a nation's repentance and justice: "Then shall plenty and peace flourish in our land, and all the inhabitants be thankful for the innumerable blessings which they enjoy, and shall fear God and honor the King."[38] Asbury did not suffer from fantasies of a theocracy. He was too suspicious of human nature and too reverential of God's sovereignty. He would have been highly suspicious of Matthew Simpson's declaration a half century later, "If the world is to be raised to its proper place, I would say it with all reverence, God cannot do without America."[39]

If God blessed the righteous, Asbury believed, the corollary was also true: Pestilence, calamity, and disease were God's means of getting the attention of the unrepentant, if not of punishing them outright. During the yellow fever epidemic of 1793, Asbury wrote, "It appears to me some awful clouds hang over this once favoured continent. The inhabitants of Philadelphia were faithfully warned that God would punish them. If not with war, nor famine, yet he might [have] sent the pestilence" (3:122). Individual communities and nations were responsible to God, and it was the prophet's job to pronounce this truth.

For Asbury, the prophet and the politician were antithetical; to combine them in the same person represented a radical incongruity. In time of calamity, it was the prophet's job to call the afflicted to repentance, and woe to the one who does not receive the prophet. "I called at a certain house—it would not do—I was compelled to turn out again to the pelting of the wind and rain. Though old, I have eyes. The hand of God will come upon them: as for the young lady, shame and contempt will fall on her; mark the event" (2:610). This cause-and-effect understanding was typical of early American preaching and especially true for Methodist theology. The Methodist itinerant Benjamin Lakin interpreted "10 or 12 sudden deaths" in a 7-month period as God's "pouring out the fire on New River."[40]

"I Love America"

Asbury's love affair with the land where God had placed him was neither a form of imperialism or manifest destiny. "O America! America! it certainly will be the glory of the world for religion! I have loved, and do love America" (3:29). Thomas Ware claimed that Asbury's decision to stay in America was predicated on his love for the American people and his belief that America would win its independence.[41] America was not located in Washington, D.C., or any other capital, but in the hearts of the people whom he daily encountered. Asbury planned to extend God's kingdom as far as persons migrated. The Louisiana Purchase and the Lewis and Clark expedition meant new possibilities for expansion (3:357). As the great western revival steamrolled over virgin territory, there was reason for optimism. To Thornton Fleming, Asbury wrote in November 1806, "Oh, my brother, when all our quarterly meetings become camp meetings, and 1000 souls should be converted, our American millennium will begin" (3:357).

Asbury did not intentionally design a church that was endemic to American culture. However, his common touch and the itinerant ministry system was well-suited for a rootless, transitory society. Asbury's Methodism was paradigmatic of the whole early nineteenth century, which was growing, democratic, individualistic, and westwardly moving. Charles Ferguson stated in his prologue to *Organizing to Beat the Devil* that "the continuation of exuberance and statistics that belong to the national scene of idealism and bureaucracy, of ponderous effort and quick wit, of grandiose plans and infinite detail—all may arise out of forces of which Methodist churches in their various branches are a part, if not in deed, the chief exemplar."[42]

Frederick Norwood observes that in most cases the creation of a Methodist conference in a territory preceded its actual status as a state. This leads to his striking generalization that "these exercises in the relationship of space and time, provide a new method of placing the westward expansion of Methodism in proper context. . . . We are reminded that in this case, as in so many others, the history of Methodism is inextricably bound with the history of the United States."[43]

The Failure of Methodist Politics

Perhaps it was too inextricably bound. Asbury at times failed to perceive that making a people religious, even Methodists, was not the same as making them Christian. Methodism would not usher in the millennium, but would simply mirror the coming apocalypse that would tear a nation asunder and kill over half a million of its men. No matter how heavenly the vision to which Asbury aspired and no matter how spiritual the battle he waged, his successors would soon live in a house divided against itself. The carpet would be soiled by the footprints of dirty politics. Reforming the continent by the spreading of scriptural holiness somehow did not purify the whole.

Asbury had done his best to avoid the entanglement of the kingdom of God with the powers of earth. He did not foresee that the prosperity of "Zion" in the United States and the future of America were heading the same direction. That is not to discredit his idealism. It may be that there just were not enough individuals to share his vision of a Christian kingdom. "All the prospects of this world are dead to me, I feel not a wish for creatures or things. The glory of the Kingdom of Christ, the organization of a primitive Church of God, these are all my objects; was it possible to set a glass to my heart, you should see them engraven there by the word & spirit of the living God" (3:566).

English historians have claimed that Asbury never renounced his British citizenship.[44] The point is moot, since everyone in the United States at the time of the Constitution's ratification became an American.[45] Actually, Asbury considered himself to be neither a member of a political party nor a citizen of any earthly domain. "I often have it whispered in my ear, what certain folks are pleased to say of my being an Englishman. How can I help that; I am not ashamed of it. But I am seeking souls, and Zion's glory; heaven is my country" (2:313).

13. "Running Like Fire"

A Cake and Cider Cart

In May of 1800, Congress divided the Northwest Territory into two parts, creating what would later become the states of Ohio and Indiana. The U.S. government also offered liberal credit for purchases of land tracts of 320 acres or more. The western migration reached a fever pitch for both land speculators and settlers. The nineteenth century ushered in an all-out free market system for both land and souls.

The presence of the Methodist itinerant preacher was almost ubiquitous. An exasperated Presbyterian preacher in Kentucky commented, "[For] several days I traveled from settlement to settlement, on my errand of good, but into every hovel I entered, I learned that the Methodist missionary had been there before me."[1] He was no less bewildered than the New Yorker who exclaimed of Methodist preachers in 1788, "I know not from whence they all come, unless from the clouds."[2]

Asbury spent the heart of the summer of 1800 in New England, and even with the heat, he reported that he was refreshed in body and soul. There was enough rhythm between his surroundings and his inner being for him to wax idyllic in Fairfield, Connecticut, "We had an elegant view: the fields in full dress, laden with plenty; a distant view of Long Island and the Sound; the spires of steeples seen from distant hills—this country is one continuity of landscape. My mind is comforted and drawn out in prayer" (2:238).

In August, Freeborn Garrettson caught up with Asbury and Whatcoat as they were still in Connecticut. Garrettson had just attended the funeral of his mother-in-law, of whom Asbury wrote, "Madam Livingston was one that gave invitation to the Methodist preachers to come to Rhinebeck, and received them into her house. . . . She was sensible, conversable, and hospitable" (2:242). Some said of her daughter Catherine that "she could have married George Washington but preferred a Methodist preacher" (2:242n.). She declined to dance with Washington at a party because she was engaged at the time to another person.[3]

While the trio made its way down the Hudson, Asbury noted that "the passing and repassing of boats and small crafts, perhaps fifty in a day, is a pleasant sight" (2:243). Outside of Rhinebeck they were hosted by Garrettson's sister-in-law at a beautifully situated "country seat" with a "charming" view of the North River. The next day a long, hot ride of twenty-five miles was refreshed by the gift of a watermelon that "Mrs. Tillotson was kind enough to give us as we came by her house" (2:244).

Asbury and his companions traveled toward Baltimore, and upon reaching the mansion of the Goughs they found the residents not at home. Henry Gough was evidently backslidden at the time, and his wife both physically sick and depressed. Prudence had left a note: "I have left home, perhaps never to return" (2:246). Perry Hall was the most consistent hospice for Methodist preachers in all of Methodism. Prudence Gough was converted under the first message she heard from Asbury. It is said that "[s]he came into the congregation as gay as a butterfly, and left with the great deep of her heart broken up."[4] Out of his melancholy, Asbury wrote, "[T]he walls, the rooms no longer vocal, all to me appeared hung in sackcloth" (2:246).

At times the bishop's visit would be festive. At Rectortown in Virginia, there was "a kind of green corn feast, with a roasted animal, cooked and eaten out of doors, under a booth" (2:248). At Norman's Bridge, there was an "*old field feast* with a race tacked to it." (It is doubtful that Asbury's party participated in the latter.) When Asbury arrived at Bedford Courthouse in Liberty, "the people gathered around my carriage, as if I had a cake and cider cart; the sight occasioned a kind of shock, that made me forget my sickness" (2:250).

During the latter part of September, Asbury, Garrettson, and Whatcoat journeyed over the Blue Ridge Mountains in a "drowning" rain with Asbury getting "wet to the skin." He braced himself for the misery. "Now it was that I felt *properly* content to leave my *felicity*, so called, before it came to the wilderness" (2:252). He made the tortuous trip over Clinch Mountain in the heat of the day by riding at least part of the time, because he was too weak to walk. By the time they reached Bethel Academy in Jessamine County, Kentucky, Asbury confessed, "I was so dejected I could say little; but weep" (2:253). The Academy was financially depleted and geographically isolated. Asbury bluntly reproved the critics of Bethel: "But all is right that works right, and all is wrong that works wrong, and we must be blamed by men of slender sense for consequences impossible to foresee—for other people's misconduct" (2:253). Not least discouraging was that most of Kentucky was still not Christian. "It is plain there are not many mighty among the Methodist in Kentucky" (2:254). A stop at Mr. Hagin's on the Big Barren River in Hart County partially relieved the bleakness of the journey. Asbury enjoyed "a good house, an excellent fire to dry our clothing, good meat and milk for supper, and the cleanest beds" (2:254). He never took life's simple amenities for granted.

Periodic Kindlings

The trek through the Western Territory during the autumn of 1800 was for the most part disheartening. "I have thought, as I rode along, that in travelling nearly six hundred measured miles, we have had only six appointments; and at these but small congregations: have we wearied ourselves in vain?" (2:256). Asbury entered Nashville, Tennessee, for the first time, and just outside of Nashville he participated in his first camp meeting. The open-air stand, "embossomed by lofty beech trees," was used by both Presbyterian and Meth-

odist preachers. Blazing fires dispelled the darkness, and the shouts of the redeemed penetrated the silence. Asbury's first impression of a camp meeting was
highly favorable. Almost thirty people were converted, which evidenced heaven's
smile on the encampment.

The year 1800 ended with Asbury attempting to settle a dispute among
irate church members in Philadelphia. Presiding elder Joseph Everrett had attempted to oust some wayward church members. But when "push came to
shove," he had to back down by restoring those who had been accused of
"murmurings and mischief." Asbury sneered that the dispute did not seem to
hamper the "great congregation" or quiet their "great shoutings." He referred
to Philadelphia as his most contentious circuit. It was probably not the best
place for Everrett, a man with the subtlety of a sledgehammer, to preside. He
was noted for "the boldness, the pointedness, the plainness, and energy with
which he rebuked sin and warned the sinner of his danger."[5] The clash in
Philadelphia gave reason for Asbury to confide to his journal in South Carolina: "Poor bishop! no money for my expenses. I am afflicted—my life threatened on the one hand, my brethren discontented on the other: true, I received
from them a petition dipped in oil and honey; and if I approve, all will be well;
but if not, drawn swords may be feared" (2:273).

But 1800 was by no means a total loss. There were reports of spiritual fires
being ignited throughout the year. There was a work of God in Annapolis, hundreds of spiritual awakenings on the shores of Maryland, six hundred souls saved
since the General Conference, two hundred souls converted in the South District
of Virginia. These periodic kindlings of religious fervor were harbingers of a spiritual explosion that would soon detonate on the frontier. The coming evangelistic
conflagration exceeded even Asbury's hopeful vision.

The first six weeks of 1801 were spent meandering around South Carolina,
where Asbury found little sign of spiritual life. "O sin! O intoxication! when—
when will these people be civilized—and all be truly spiritualized" (2:278). The
gap between South Carolina and Methodism grew even wider with the latter's
condemnation of slavery at the 1800 General Conference. The rich, who had
always been at odds with Methodism according to Asbury, were asked not to
prevent their slaves from hearing the gospel. Asbury lamented, "Perhaps we shall
soon be thought unfit for the company of their dogs" (2:281). Nevertheless,
Asbury noted that he had many more friends in South Carolina than when he
had ridden "anxious and solitary" through the land sixteen years earlier. The trip
down the coast was time for more reflection. "I made my last visit to the sea. I
thought upon my friends on the other side of the great waters; my voyage to this
country; the little probability there was of my ever again seeing my dear mother,
or my native land" (2:283).

The "respectables" and "reputables" of Wilmington requested that Asbury preach in the local brick church. He complied by lecturing on Romans 10 to a "large and decent congregation" (2:284). The journey north was hampered by Asbury's leaving behind his spectacles and his horse's picking up an oyster shell in its heel. On passing through Virginia, Asbury paid homage to Devereux Jarratt, who had recently died. "He was a man of genius, possessed a great deal of natural oratory, was an excellent reader, and a good writer. . . . He was instrumentally successful in awakening hundreds of souls to some sense of religion" (2:289).

For the most part, Asbury would let bygones be bygones. Asbury and his colleagues had been critical of Jarrett's ownership of slaves. In a letter to Edward Dromgoole dated March 22, 1788, Jarrett wrote, "They tell me that I must go to hell; but I bless God I know better. . . . Once Mr. Asbury seemed to think Nothing could be done so well without me—but now he thinks I have done him more harm than all the preachers have done good—but I know to the contrary. Frank ought to have been the last man to say this."[6]

Despite the wranglings that had taken place in Philadelphia in the last year, the annual conference went very smoothly. Asbury managed to moderate even though he was crippled, having had a "cancer" removed from his foot. He ordained sixteen deacons and elders in his sleeping room because he was too lame to attend the concluding service of the conference. In spite of applying "caustic after caustic" and preaching on one knee and one foot, Asbury rejoiced in God's graciousness and the prosperity of Zion. But the rancor in Philadelphia continued. "Why should I continue my journal while here? What would it be but a tale of woe?—the society divided, and I, perforce, shut up in Sodom, without any communication with the connexion at large" (2:300).

Spiritual Eruptions

In September, Asbury crossed Clinch Mountain in eastern Tennessee and arrived at Ebenezer, the site of the Western Conference, on September 30. Revival was so intense in Kentucky that many of the preachers did not attend the conference. At the conference, "[o]n *Friday* and *Saturday evenings*, and on *Sabbath morning*, there was the noise of praise and shouting in the meeting house. It is thought there are twenty-five souls who have found the Lord" (2:308). There seemed to be the same stir in every place except South Carolina. On October 24, Asbury noted, "I cannot record great things upon religion in this quarter; *but cotton sells high*. I fear there is more gold than grace—more of silver than of 'that wisdom that cometh from above'" (2:311).

On November 18, while staying in a home in Jackson, Georgia, Asbury fell down the steps from "the upper room" and hurt his back. The fall caused his hip to ache while he rode. But the services at each stop during the week of November 22–29 were especially blessed. On Sunday the twenty-ninth, Asbury was often interrupted by singing and shouting. At Sparta, Asbury read a letter from the Reverend James McGready at the house of John Lucas. "Whilst I was reading Mr. McGready's letter, a Presbyterian-Methodist woman shouted and warned the Spartans to flee from the wrath to come" (2:316).

Upon arriving in South Carolina, Asbury found the spiritual fire extinguished. "I know not what beside [the love of Christ] should move a Christian minister to travel and labour in this country" (2:318). Asbury bolstered himself in the Lord, "[G]lory to God! I have strong faith for myself and for the prosperity of Zion. Glory, glory, glory to God! Amen!" (2:318). Even in South Carolina, as never before, Asbury felt his heart drawn to the people. He recalled Wesley's response to Thomas Coke's confession that he did not think highly of the people, "That is because you have never been there, when you are there you will think and feel for the people" (2:319).

It had been a light travel year for Asbury, but a fruitful one. "I have now ridden about seventeen hundred miles upon this tour. I have had close communion with God, and enlargement of preaching the word of life to saints, seekers, and sinners" (3:319). On September 12, he had written to Elizabeth Dickens, "The work of God is running like fire in Kentucky. It is reported that near fifteen if not twenty thousand were present at one Sacramental occasion of the Presbyterians; and one thousand if not fifteen hundred fell and felt the power of grace" (3:226).

Cane Ridge

Even though the number of people attending the camp meeting at Cane Ridge in August of 1801 has been exaggerated, it was a remarkable explosion of revivalism.[7] The meeting just outside Paris in Bourbon County, Kentucky, was marked by swooning, prostration, dancing, shouting, and much weeping. William Burke, the presiding elder of the Western Conference and one of the scheduled preachers at Cane Ridge, argued that the affair really was not a camp meeting since there were no tents on the grounds except his. He reported: "It was estimated by some that no less than five hundred were at one time lying on the ground in the deepest agonies of distress, and every few minutes rising in shouts of triumph."[8]

James Finley, future Methodist historian and presiding elder, gave one of the most colorful descriptions of the gathering. As a 20-year-old, he had ventured to Cane Ridge for entertainment. Instead he came under deep conviction and was converted. Standing on a rise some distance from the camp, Finley described the scene thus:

> A vast crowd, supposed by some to have amounted to twenty five thousand, was collected together. The noise was like the roar of Niagara. The vast sea of human beings seemed to be agitated as if

by a storm. I counted seven ministers, all preaching at one time, some on stumps, others in wagons. . . . My heart beat tumultuously, my knees trembled, my lips quivered, and I felt as though I must fall to the ground. A strange supernatural power seemed to pervade the entire mass of mind there collected. . . . At one time I saw at least five hundred swept down in a moment, as if a battery of a thousand guns had been opened upon them, and then immediately followed shrieks and shouts that rent the very heavens. My hair rose up on my head, my whole frame trembled, the blood ran cold in my veins, and I fled for the woods a second time, and wished I had staid at home.[9]

Even though Cane Ridge was considered the beginning of the "great western revival," it was not without its precedents. Revival had broken out in Logan County, Kentucky, in 1797 with a gradual increase in intensity under the unwavering efforts of James McGready. Barton Stone described him as possessing "unearthliness, remarkable gravity, a tremulous voice and small piercing eyes."[10] His gestures were "*sui generis*, quite the reverse of elegance. He appeared to have forgotten everything but the salvation of souls."[11]

McGready entered into a solemn prayer covenant with the people of his three churches. By July of 1800, the spiritual fervor on McGready's circuit had become so intense that Gasper River Church was transformed into a camp meeting. One eyewitness reported that "[l]ittle children, young men and women, and old gray-headed people, persons of every description, white and black, were to be found in every part of the multitude . . . crying out for mercy in the most extreme distress."[12]

Methodism's Response

In June of 1801, at the Hampton quarterly meeting, William Burke (one of the first itinerants appointed west of the Appalachians) reported that "several professed to get religion, and many were under deep conviction of sin, and the meeting continued from Sunday morning to Monday morning with but little intermission."[13] Following the quarterly meeting, the Presbyterians invited Burke to preach at "Salem meeting-house." "[B]efore I concluded there was a great trembling among the dry bones. Great numbers fell to the ground and cried for mercy, old and young. . . . The Presbyterian minister stood astonished, not knowing what to make of such a tumult."[14] The revival enthusiasm was so high that by 1802, Burke noted, "The Presbyterians appeared to have forgotten that they had any Confession of Faith or discipline, and the Methodists had laid aside their Discipline, and seemed to forget that they were bound to observe the rules contained therein, and as established from time to time by the General conference."[15]

In fact, denominational identity became so amorphous that at the Methodists' Western Conference, which met in Sumner County, Tennessee, Presbyterian clergymen were granted official recognition. According to Asbury's journal, two Presbyterian ministers, William Hodge and William McGee, were asked to fill the pulpit, which they did with "great fervency and fidelity" (2:364).

Since Burke had been rejected as a preacher at Cane Ridge because he was doctrinally suspect by the Presbyterians, he officially objected to the Presbyterians' being allowed to speak on the conference floor. Burke pointed out that Methodists were not allowed to introduce Methodist customs at Presbyterian gatherings. "Mr. Asbury decidedly opposed my views, and stated to the conference that I was but a young man and referred the conference to some of Mr. Wesley's views and conduct on like occasions."[16] But evidently Burke had gotten Asbury's ear. "Mr. Asbury acknowledged that I had taken the proper ground, and wrote me on the subject, stating that reciprocity was the true doctrine. . . . [A]t the next conference at Mount Gerizim, in 1803, he preached the doctrine to the conference."[17]

Strange Phenomena

Methodist worship from its American inception had been no stranger to supernatural phenomena and emotional outbursts.[18] Abel Stevens observed that Freeborn Garrettson's journal was almost a continuous record of "melted congregations" and "powerful awakenings" in which hearers were often smitten down to the ground.[19] Garrettson was given to dreams, impressions, prophecies, faintings, and battles with the "devil." He confessed, "Individuals thought me an enthusiast, because I talk so much about feelings, and impressions to go to particular places."[20]

No preacher was stranger than Benjamin Abbott. He was "no man's copy" and was "frequently, remarkably eloquent, sometimes overwhelmingly so."[21] Abbott reported that when he preached his sermon during a thunderstorm he "'lost no time, but set before them the awful coming of Christ in all its splendor, with all the armies of heaven, to judge the world, and to take vengeance on the ungodly! It may be that he will descend in the next clap of thunder!' The people screamed, screeched, and fell all through the house."[22]

Witnesses said that, when Abbott preached, there was weeping, melting, falling, screaming, screeching, rolling, shaking, and thumping. The effects were so overwhelming that many leaped out of the window and piled up at the door trying to escape. When one young man for hours "lay so dead a state, and continue so long that his flesh grew cold, and his blood was stagnated to his elbows," Abbott himself became alarmed. "I concluded to go home, and not proceed one step farther, for killing people would not answer."[23] The young man recovered.

When a thundercloud approached the place where Josiah Everett was preaching in Virginia, he prayed for it to come nearer. As the house "blazed with electric flame," there was a "great outcry for mercy." The event was so terrifying that one of the unconverted begged a magistrate to restrain Everett. After Everett had implored a second time for the Lord to come nearer, there was the conviction that had he "asked a third time, there would not have been one of us alive."[24]

When Billy Hibbard was preaching in a home during a thunderstorm, he cried out, "Oh Lord, thunder conviction to the sinner's heart." As lightning like a "sheet of fire" flashed and thunder "shook the house," Hibbard declared, "Glory to God! Glory in the highest." Two sisters who were occupants of the house passed out. After one of them lay still for two and a half hours, those present discovered she had no pulse. Hibbard observed that "she had no symptoms of life, her eyes and jaws were set and her head, neck and her arms were cold."

After crying to the Lord "with all his heart," Hibbard blew "down her throat" to inflate her lungs. Two hours later, he again attempted artificial respiration and the lady recovered. "I was very thankful to God that the extraordinary meeting house turned out so favorably that no scandal arose from it. But my fears were great at times."[25] Hibbard need not have worried. When five people were killed at Checkley's Boston meeting house in a stampede of people at the news of George Whitefield's arrival, the revivalistic fervor only intensified. Whitefield commented, "God was pleased to give me the presence of mind, so that I gave notice I would immediately preach upon the common. The weather was wet, but many thousands followed in the field."[26]

The Interpretation and Practice of Early Methodist Leaders

Though Asbury no doubt would have questioned such dramatic manipulation, he was no emotional prude. He let his colors be known early on, when he disagreed with Thomas Rankin over irregularities in American worship. Rankin argued that "a stop must absolutely be put to the prevailing wildfire, or it would prove ruinous to all we hold sacred; and that he had done all he could to suppress it, but was ashamed to say that some of his brethren, the preachers, were infected with it."[27] Asbury evidently confronted Rankin concerning his "imprudence." Asbury remarked, "The friends of order may allow a guilty mortal to tremble at God's word, for to such the Lord will look;—and the saints to cry out and shout, when the Holy one of Israel is in the midst of them. To be hasty in plucking up the tares, is to endanger the wheat. Of this we should be aware, lest we touch the ark to our own injury and that of others."[28] In May of 1789, Asbury wrote to Jasper Winscom, his friend back in England, "We have noise and shouting, and you must have the same or you will not get the work revived."[29] Asbury wrote to Coke on May 2, 1809, "[Y]ou know we American Methodists pray, and preach, and sing and shout aloud" (3:407).

Rankin was not the only early Methodist preacher to distrust the American extravagances. Joseph Pilmoor penned, "Wherever I go I find it necessary to bear my testimony against all wildness, shouting and confusion in the worship of God and at the same time to feed and preserve the sacred fire—which is certainly kindled in many hearts of the country."[30] It was a delicate balance, which would present a recurring problem for Methodism.[31]

But both Rankin and Pilmoor were advocates of heart-felt religion, which often displayed itself in emotional release. Rankin reported of one service: "The Word of the Lord ran and was glorified. Many wept and trembled under the mighty hand of God. He did indeed make it the house of God, and the gale of heaven to many souls."[32] Of a love feast in Philadelphia, Rankin wrote, "Many of the people were so overcome that they were ready to faint, and die under His almighty hand. For about three hours the gale of the Spirit thus continued to break up the dry bones. . . . As for myself, I scarce knew whether I was in the body or not, and so it was with all my brethren."[33]

Even the quintessential Englishman Thomas Coke, after witnessing such overwhelming and overt expressions of the faith, commented, "Whether there be wildfire in it or not, I do most ardently wish that there was such a work at this present time in England."[34] Coke was no stranger to the kind of spontaneity that often accompanied American Methodism's worship. After he had preached and Asbury exhorted, one service lasted until 2 A.M., with two or three hundred at the same time "praising God, praying for the conviction and conversion of sinners, or exhorting those around them with the utmost vehemence, and hundreds more were engaged in wrestling prayer either for their own conversion or sanctification."[35]

Emotional and Physical Responses to Asbury's Preaching

Early on, Asbury observed unusual physical responses in Methodist worship and in particular to his preaching. While preaching on December 12, 1773, "The power of God was immanently present, and one person fell under it" (1:99). While preaching in Virginia in 1775 to about 400 persons, one individual "was struck with convulsive shakings" (1:168). In West Virginia in July 1776 many were affected by Asbury's preaching, and "one man fell down" (1:194).

Asbury had plenty of opportunity to observe radical responses to God's grace. In Pennsylvania in 1789, "one woman, in particular, was so wrought upon that she fell to the ground" (1:606). Shortly thereafter at Milford, Delaware, there was a "great move and noble shouting." At one quarterly meeting the spiritual exuberance was so rowdy that the leadership called for more formal worship. Asbury commented, "There were very uncommon circumstances of a supernatural kind said to be observed at this meeting. The *saints of the world* are dreadfully displeased at their work; which, after all, is the best evidence that it is of God" (1:613). After "delivering his soul" at the 1793 Kentucky conference, "Some people were moved in an extraordinary manner, shouting and jumping at a strange rate" (1:757).

Congregations often responded to Asbury's preaching by a "crying aloud for mercy" (1:579), "a great power, a noble shout" (1:583), "a baptizing flame" (1:592), "a shaking" (1:665), "weeping and shouting" (1:758). At other times, congregational eruptions preempted Asbury's sermon. At a love feast in Rock Town, Virginia, "there was great shaking, and shouting, and weeping and praying: it was thought best not to stop these exercises by the more regular labour of preaching, as most of the persons present were engaged either as subjects or instruments" (2:360). His message at Manor Chapel, Delaware, was accompanied by "singing, exhorting, shouting, leaping, and praising God" (2:387).

Asbury was opposed to religious passivity. He had not hesitated to shake off the liturgical encumbrances of Wesley's *Sunday Service*. He believed the purpose of Methodism was to take the continent by storm and to shake "the formality of religion out of the world" (3:322). He would not have been in disagreement with his one-time travelling companion Henry Smith, who referred to preaching as a "holy, knock 'em down power." William Burke reported that when William McKendree was preaching at Shannon, Pennsylvania, in August 1803, the power of God "came down upon him in such a manner that he sank down into my arms while sitting behind him in the pulpit." Upon being stood up again to preach, McKendree "shouted out the praise of God, and it appeared like an electric shock in the congregation. Many fell to the floor like men slain in the field of battle."[36] When Thomas Ware visited Boehm's Chapel in 1798, there were such cries of distress and prayers for mercy that it was impossible for him to preach.[37]

Attempts to Moderate

Asbury and his troops were not naïve about the possibility of abuses, and neither were they impervious to criticism. One Thomas Wallcut, who traveled from Massachusetts to Ohio, wrote to a Unitarian minister in 1789 concerning the "enthusiasm & intemperate zeal" of the Methodists. After visiting several Methodist meetings, he observed that the gatherings were "attended with all that confusion, violence and distortion of the body, voice and gestures that characterizes such a boiling hot religion."[38] If the revival was boiling hot in 1789, it was a raging inferno in 1800. Even Jacob Young spoke of the Kentuckians who were "very superstitious in their notions—looking for miracles and things out of the common order. They expected God to tell them everything that they ought to do."[39] The inner and outer, the subjective and objective, had collapsed together so that it was difficult to differentiate between the human and the divine.

Asbury was conscious of the tension between maintaining order and not restricting the operation of the Holy Spirit. As early as 1774 he had written, "What some people take for religion and spiritual life is nothing but the power of the natural passions. It is true, real religion cannot exist without peace, and love, and joy. But then, *real religion is real holiness.* And all sensations without a strong disposition for holiness are but delusive" (1:127).

However, at times Asbury himself was given to dreams and impressions. On March 29, 1799, he wrote Alexander M'Caine, "I had an impression, upon my knees, that you would be the most acceptable person to take a station in Norfolk, in Virginia, for the present year" (3:178). At least once Asbury had a supernatural vision, which indicated the geographical direction in which Methodism should expand. In May of 1790, he dreamed that a "guard from Kentucky" came to him. The next morning, ten men showed up to escort him through the wilderness.[40]

But Asbury insisted that all dreams and impressions should be tried by the Scriptures. Both for him and for Wesley, the ultimate standard for truth was expressed in the Bible. As early as 1778, Asbury reflected in his journal,

> Dreams may arise from various causes; and even diabolical impressions may sometimes resemble those made by the Spirit of God. And it is evident that all such impressions as have a tendency to effect divisions, to interrupt the peace of the Church, to draw us off from any revealed duty, or to make us contented in a lukewarm and careless state, cannot come from God, because they are contrary to the revealed dictates of the Holy Spirit—and the Spirit of truth cannot contradict itself. Therefore all impressions, dreams, visions, &c., should be brought to the standard of the Holy Scriptures, and if they do not perfectly correspond therewith, they should be rejected (1:278).

Leaders Issue Caution

Asbury was particularly concerned about the extravagances of the revival, which lessened people's dependence upon the normative means of grace. In 1803, he argued that God would not work alone; conversion required not only experience but also instruction, preaching, discipline, and observance of the ordinances. Concerning a "mighty falling" among the Presbyterians, Asbury commented, "The people report they bark and snatch, and make strange noises. No wonder if they are left poor souls to themselves to contend with the devil and sin, and sinners" (3:269). Asbury stated that "any person who could not give an account of the convincing and converting power of God, might be mistaken; falling down would not do" (2:403).

As the revival continued throughout the first decade of the nineteenth century, Asbury both rejoiced and advised caution. After receiving a letter from George Daugharty, presiding elder of the South Carolina Conference, which reported, "serving God all manner of ways, jerking, dancing, etc.," Asbury urged communication between the presiding elders and the bishops. "[W]e ought to be wise as serpents in the management of our meetings" (3:326-7). Indeed things could get out of hand. Elijah Woolsey recalled preaching on the Oswego Circuit in New York State. "[I] might as well have preached to the walls, the cries of the mourners were so great; so I left my pulpit which was nothing more than a chair and went to the mourners and prayed for them." One young lady was "in such an agony that she tore her hair and beat her head on the hearth."[41]

Skeptics attributed the religious fervor to magic or the work of Satan. After a Black lady had fallen down, "thumped her breasts and puked all over the floor," Freeborn Garrettson responded by telling the congregation that they could be converted without "falling down and hollouring."[42] Rumors maintained that some of the preachers could read minds, heal diseases, and access the region of the damned. The Methodist Caleb Taylor wrote a tract, "News from the Infernal Regions," and Valentine Cook insisted that he had an encounter with Lucifer. The surging flow of the supernatural was difficult to keep on course. One visitor to America recalled having "seen Methodists jumping; striking and kicking, like raving maniacs; while the surrounding believers could not keep their posture of decency."[43]

Asbury himself was accused by Jeremiah Minter, a defrocked Methodist preacher, of "bowing down to and worshiping devils."[44] Thus, Asbury wanted to make sure that the work of God would be in no way attributed to Satan. He walked a fine line between maintaining a supernatural worldview and a superstitious one. From the Methodist perspective, superstition was the work of Satan. When William Colbert was on the Antalany circuit in Pennsylvania in July 1810, he noted the superstition and ignorance of the people. "Michael Brobsts told me that some of his neighbors that had brought their grain to his Mill, after he became a Methodist was afraid to let him bolt it as usual, but took it home sifted supposing they might find some thing in it that would make them Methodist or pray and shout like the Methodist."[45]

Asbury surrendered to neither rationalism nor fanaticism. Christine Heyrman argues that when Garrettson had his journal serialized in a periodical in 1794, he erased the accounts of having been assaulted by Satan, at the advice of Asbury. Garrettson had previously declared that he "saw the devil, who appeared very furious; he came near to me and declared with bitterness he would be the death of me."[46]

Asbury cautioned against any experience of religion that did not issue in a righteous life. Bible religion did not consist primarily in "the reveries of a heated imagination, nor the paroxisms of agitated passions; but in the mind which was in Christ Jesus, in a victory over sin, and a conformity to the will of God" (3:571). In short, Asbury was much more concerned about Christian character than he was about exercises of emotion. Asbury was aware, as was Jonathan Edwards before him, that a right relationship with God transforms the affections, and that the affections of love, joy, and surrender are often displayed at moments of spiritual crisis. Asbury wanted the best of both worlds, exuberance and order, "displays of the power of God, and a strict discipline" (2:732).

Lord, Send the Good

The growing revivalistic mode, which allowed for full participation and an evangelistic response from the congregants, continued to be a mixed bag for Methodism. It was difficult at times to know whether the emotional tide was an interruption or an enhancement of spiritual welfare. At one service, Thomas Rankin stated that he was "obliged to stop again and again to beg of the people to compose themselves. But they could not; some on their knees and some on their faces while crying mightily to God."[47] While Freeborn Garrettson was preaching on July 5, 1780, he testified that the Savior "paid us a sweet visit. I fear Satan got the advantage of two women, they cried out, so that I was obliged to stop and speak to them."[48]

Jesse Lee was especially negative about much of the camp-meeting extravagances. He noted of one woman "that she exhibited at some time the jerking exercise, at other times the dancing exercise, and not unfrequently the basking exercise, and taking them all together made as ridiculous a set of exercises as ever attracted the gaze of the multitude."[49]

But Jesse Lee also succinctly stated a philosophy Asbury would have endorsed: "Let the Lord work his own way. It is clear that the Lord has his way in the whirlwind. If we could have all the good without the confusion, if such there be, it would be desirable, but if not, Lord send the good, though it should be with double the confusion."[50] Lee confessed that the "women complained that I had preached so loud that it made their heads ache, and they pushed me to speak a little lower the next time I came."[51]

On one occasion, when Asbury heard Benjamin Abbott preach, "some fell to the floor, others ran out of the house, and many cried aloud for mercy, and others were shouting praises to the God of hosts, with hearts full of love divine."[52] Asbury recorded, "I met with and heard Benjamin Abbott—his words came with great power" (1:400). After Abbott's death, Asbury wrote of him, "He was seldom heard to speak about anything but God and religion. His whole soul was often overwhelmed with the power of God. . . . His life was pressed out of every pore of his body."[53]

No one joined the Methodists to experience the stillness of quietism. Methodism was a revolt against cold rationalism and all forms of external conformity that dampened the internal fervor of sincerity and commitment. George

Roberts, both a physician and Methodist pastor in Baltimore, exhorted pastors at the 1807 Baltimore Conference to guard their people "against the two great extremes in religion—dull formality and ranting extravagance. . . . Religion is a principle that is to be felt; it animates and invigorates those who possess it. . . . Guard them against ranting extravagances . . . against that abominable practice of jumping, pointing, dancing, boring, scratching in the earth, and jerking."[54] Roberts went on to explain that he was not opposed to warmth and exaltation that responded to the divine blessing, but that he was against the systematizing of such expressions. He called for both prudence and firmness.

Asbury was too much a Wesleyan, and an English Wesleyan at that, to be caught up in a radical fanaticism that would obscure common everyday tasks and virtues, which offer both meaning and dignity. Asbury desired respectability, but he also had to accommodate a frontier religion, which was as intense and sometimes as crude as the inhabitants. People who lived by physical prowess and in a constant state of crisis demanded religion equally physical and primitive. There was little to provide emotional release for women and men who worked sixteen-hour days and faced the constant threat of death. The confrontational preaching of the Word, which called for a divine-human encounter, released the emotions of guilt, anxiety, and loneliness. No one did it better than the Methodists. Asbury contrasted his battalions to churches of the German Lutheran and Calvinists: "[C]itadels of formality—fortifications erected against the apostolic itinerancy of a more evangelical ministry" (2:550).

Whatever the needs of early nineteenth-century Americans, the Methodist "Pentecost" met them more effectively than anything else. The numbers greatly pleased Asbury, though he knew that genuine Christian experience was primarily evidenced by character rather than by emotional and physical manifestations. Making the transition from the emotionalism of a camp meeting to the discipline of the class meeting may not have been as simple as Asbury assumed. Could the charismatic preachers of Methodism enable the masses to channel their emotions from public ecstasy into private devotion? Asbury may not have fully realized that the religious excitement that sweeps through a crowd may not easily translate into the nonconformity that is so vital for Christian piety.[55]

If the Second Great Awakening was the religious upheaval that Nathan Hatch claims it to have been, then Francis Asbury as much as any other person molded the shattered fragments into a vessel sufficiently identifiable and meaningful to pass on to succeeding generations.[56] Richard Carwardine states that "Methodism was whole-heartedly a revival movement; it had born out of a revival; its churches grew through revival; its ministers preached revival; and its success was talked of in terms of revival."[57] Revival in American church history has normally produced fragmentation. Asbury excelled in the gift of galvanization. David Hempton notes that the word "confusion" was frequently used to describe Methodist meetings.[58] By contrast, "All things done decently and in order" was Asbury's supreme legacy.[59]

14. "We Are Impartial"

A New Optimism

In the year 1800, if one had placed a seesaw east to west using the Allegheny Mountains as a fulcrum, only 373 of the 64,000 Methodists would have been on the western end. By 1810, not only had the total number of Methodists reached approximately 173,000 but a decidedly greater portion were on the west side of the Alleghenies, a remarkable demographic tilt.[1] While the overall population of America had increased 36 percent, Methodism had grown 269 percent. In the first decade of the nineteenth century, Methodism grew over seven times as fast as the nation's population.[2] Most of the growth had occurred in Tennessee, Kentucky, and Ohio. One observer noted of the westward migration, "now that Americans had independence from Great Britain, they wanted independence from one another."[3]

Methodism's itinerant system was ideal for the migrating masses. Asbury's stubborn insistence on the "traveling" ministry was now ready to bear its greatest fruit. "Breaking camp" was a way of life. Movement was so inherent to the Methodist ministerial philosophy that one itinerant preacher simply allowed his horse to wander, trusting both horse and Providence to locate lost souls. After noting that Richmond, Virginia, had only 50 Methodists in 1800, William Bennett remarked that "[t]he strength of Methodism lay in the free and open country."[4]

The increased prospects of Methodism provided a mental and physical antidote to Asbury's usual fretting and worrying. At no time was this more evident than at a stopover at Elijah Phillips's home near Stephensburg in western Virginia August 23–24, 1802. There James Quinn, a young itinerant, recorded a rare glimpse of Asbury in moments of leisure. With the reports of revival the bishop was especially buoyant. Present throughout the afternoon of August 24 were Dr. J. Tildon, a former captain in the Revolutionary War; Dr. M'Dowell, a former traveling preacher; the Reverend Edward Matthews, who had recently immigrated from Wales; and the Reverend Samuel Mitchell, a local preacher who had freed his slaves. The "Methodist dinner party" discussed world events, both present and future: "The Revolution in Europe, the shaking of thrones, the fulfillment of prophecy, the overthrow of the beast and the false prophet; Newton, Faber, Bengelius, and Wesley on the fulfillment of prophecy."[5] Interspersed in the conversation concerning the affairs of America and predictions that the millennium would begin in 1836 were renderings by several who could play the violin. As they were called to the dinner table, Asbury broke out in a musical blessing:

> Be present at our table, Lord,
> Be here and everywhere adored

> Thy people bless and grant that we
> May feast in Paradise with thee.

Asbury energetically participated in the conversation, both during and after dinner, seasoned by strains of several well-known hymns. The evening represented the optimism not only of a thriving church but of a nation ready to take the nineteenth century by storm. The social gathering was a microcosm of the nineteenth century's romantic idealism, which would produce various "utopian" experiments.[6] Asbury's faith was quickened as never before. Methodism was feeling more at home in its American house; there was cause for celebration.

Asbury's Changing Philosophy

The change in Asbury was more than a shot of revivalistic adrenaline. A gradual change in his thinking at least partially redefined Methodism's purpose and methodology. At the end of 1802, Asbury wrote to Thornton Fleming, his presiding elder in the Pittsburgh district, "I wish you would also hold campmeetings; they have never been tried without success. To collect such a number of God's people together to pray, and the ministers to preach, and the longer they stay, generally, the better—this is field fighting, this is fishing with a large net" (3:251).

"Large net" efficiency represented a transition from quality to quantity. It was new language for a movement that had admitted persons to its classes and societies only after careful scrutiny. In the past, only proven Methodists were allowed at love feasts. Methodism's admittance threshold had been high. This change was what Charles Ferguson calls a transition from "the mini to the mass." Ferguson writes, "Methodism moved toward the mass rather than the group as the primary form in society. It set the norm that the individual mind could be swayed and changed through dramatic exhortation and set the stage for the intensely personal appeal in politics as well as evangelism. In this happening the campmeeting had a stellar part."[7]

There was reason for optimism, even in South Carolina. Revivals during 1802 added over three thousand to the conference, which Asbury considered one of the most difficult. But the newly discovered exuberance did not end Asbury's daily trials. He spent the month of January 1803 visiting the various preaching points throughout the conference. The preaching houses were so crude and cold that he doubted the effectiveness of his ministry. Cold hearts and cold weather seemed to be corollaries. Typical was the trek to Gibson's Chapel over a muddy path. "[P]ole chapel—open as a sieve, and the weather very cold. Nicholas Snethen preached upon Phil. iv, 8. I only added a few pointed, scattering shot in exhortation" (2:377).

The ride up the coast of North Carolina was especially cold. Stops at Wilmington, Newbern, and Washington were somewhat unproductive. However, at Williamston a large crowd gathered at the courthouse within a 24-hour notice. In snow 8–12 inches deep, Asbury's newly-shod horse proved to be nearly more than the bishop could handle. However, by March 1, Asbury and Snethen had made their way to Olive Branch meetinghouse in Brunswick County, Virginia, for the annual conference. Asbury was encouraged by the concluding gathering of "two thousand" people who met at a stand in the woods, and by the love feast characterized by "order, solemnity, and life" (2:383).

Asbury was troubled to learn that Methodist meetinghouses continued to be confiscated by O'Kellyites in Virginia. The Methodists in Norfolk had built the finest Methodist church in the state, with a high pulpit to which Asbury objected; "like that awkward thing in Baltimore, calculated for the gallery, and too high for that" (2:384). Asbury and Snethen inadvertently got off the "long, intricate, muddy path" to Petersburg, extending an already long trip without food "for man or beast." Chilling and trembling, Asbury could hardly stem the cold blast, which blew in his face. "[I]n many places the route was dreadful: we worried through, feeding our horses once, and ourselves not at all" (2:385).

Uneven Ground

As Asbury passed through the Delmarva Peninsula, it seemed that the whole area was "Methodized." Their preachers were now accepted by the populace. Consistency had worn down prejudice, to the extent that even the "pagans" called the preachers when facing death. The area had come a long way spiritually since 1791, when the night services had to be abandoned in Wilimington, and even day services "were interrupted by the breaking of windows, the stoning of the pastor; and the throwing of snakes and lizards through the windows at female worshipers."[8]

Before the four-day conference at the Friends meetinghouse in Salisbury, Delaware, Asbury submitted to being bled in order to relieve his physical affliction. By the time he arrived in Philadelphia, he was so weak that he stayed indoors Wednesday through Saturday. Further distress was added by the continuing conflict at St. George's church. On June 12, 1801, a group had departed from St. George's because of differing notions about worship. The "respectables," led by Thomas Haskins and James Doughty, had left the "shouters" to form the Academy Church, which later became Union Methodist Church. The conflict continued to swirl.[9]

As Asbury journeyed through New England, he was reminded that all spiritual ground is not equally fertile. The conference was by far the smallest in Methodism; reporting only 2,941 members. "Poor New England! she is the valley of dry bones still" (2:392). The conference at Boston was dull and uneventful. Asbury recorded his negative feelings: "The great wants of Boston are good religion and good water. How can this city and Massachusetts be in any other than a melancholy state! worse, perhaps, for true piety, than any other parts of the Union: what! reading priests, and alive? O no! dead, dead, dead, by nature—by formality—by sin!" (2:393).

One event particularly caught Asbury's attention: A non-Methodist congregation had sold their pastor to another for a thousand dollars and placed the money on interest at 25 to 30 percent. Apparently, they deemed the financial return of greater value than their pastor's productivity.

But in spite of New England's religious formality, Asbury could not help but admire the Yankee thrift, efficiency, and stamina. The "habits of economy and industry" produced rich fields of barley, rye, and potatoes, with plenty of cheese, butter, milk, and fish from the millponds. Such observations challenged the notion that Methodism represented God's one supreme religious alternative. The steady New England temper needed a religion that was a little less emotionally volatile than American Methodism. For New Englanders, the nurture of souls was as methodical as the nurture of fields.

Moving westward into New York, he found drought and rough terrain. By the time he had presided over the annual conference, he was too weak to speak to the "two thousand" who showed up for the concluding service. Upon arriving at Albany, Asbury and Whatcoat discovered that the junior bishop had left Asbury's coat somewhere north of Troy. But who could blame Whatcoat? He was already loaded down with a copy of the laws for each state and copies of as many municipal laws as possible, so that they could be sure the gospel would not be unnecessarily offensive. "I bear the loss with some patience," Asbury said. It was patience that Ezekiel Cooper said the bishop most lacked.[10]

Further West

Trying to cover thirty to forty miles a day, each time gathering up his total earthly belongings, was a full-time job for Asbury. Retaining the major chores for himself, he often had to leave the minor details to others. They often were not as meticulous in their attention to details as Asbury himself was accustomed to be. By the time he had made his way across the Pennsylvania Alleghenies, the heat and ensuing dysentery had turned forbearance into resignation. "I have little to leave, except a journey of five thousand miles a year, the care of more than a hundred thousand souls, and the arrangement of about four hundred preachers yearly, to which I may add the murmurs and discontent of ministers and people: who wants this legacy? Those who do are welcome to it for me!" (2:401).

On August 19, 1803, Asbury preached at his first camp meeting, which was located on the Monongahela, about thirty miles outside of Pittsburgh (2:402). The gathering together of two thousand people, signaled by the sound of a trumpet, gave Asbury a shot of adrenaline such as he had rarely experienced. The attention they gave his preaching was in sharp contrast with the unruliness that often greeted him. Many were powerfully stricken, "[f]ainting, and falling; and crying for mercy." Asbury "fired a gun each day" and then retreated. Such intensity, he believed, was the antidote for the ills that besieged the eastern churches, especially those that were in conflict. The bishop had begun to dream about short-term solutions to long-term problems.

Upon arriving at Pittsburgh, Asbury found himself in a fight with other denominations over preaching rights at the courthouse. He preached once to about four hundred people and would have preached again, but the Episcopalians demanded their turn. "I come but once in twelve years, but they could not consent to give way for me" (2:403). At the quarterly conference in Middletown, Pennsylvania, he attempted to preach on Ephesians 4:18–20 but was thoroughly disappointed with his performance. "[I] felt the people still engaged in worship, much ashamed of the meanness of my performance . . . I saw that the excellency of such sublime and interesting subjects was beyond my reach of thought or expression" (2:404). Asbury often had to settle for less than his best because of mental and physical weariness.

As Asbury made his first trip into Ohio, he noted "Satan's grip" on the "little, wicked, western trading towns" (2:405). However, Satan's strongholds were not impervious to Asbury's proclamation. At West Wheeling quarterly conference, he had difficulty keeping the "thread" of discourse because of the people's singing and shouting, which continued all through the night. He and the brothers Daniel and Benjamin Hitt journeyed to Chillicothe, then the capital of the state. On a rainy afternoon, Asbury preached to a crowd of about five hundred at the courthouse, which also doubled as the capitol building. Asbury was intrigued in the vicinity of Chillicothe by "mounds and intrenchments which still astonish all who visit this country, and give rise to many conjectures respecting their origin" (2:408). He observed that New Lancaster "has nearly one hundred houses of all kinds, ill situated for health on a low, rich level, through which creeps the still Hockhocking" (2:408). He marveled at the effects of American enterprise and the resulting civilization wrought by the opening of the "National Road" from Zanesville, Ohio, to Covington, Kentucky.

Overcoming Prejudice

The Kentucky Conference opened at Mt. Gerizim, just outside of Cynthiana, Kentucky. In passing through Bourbon County, Asbury made no mention of the Cane Ridge revival, which had taken place there two years previously, but simply alluded to a meeting house of the Presbyterians (which still stands). In fact, he made no mention of revival fires at all, though they were still sweeping the frontier. The disorderly frontier ways of both Kentucky and Tennessee baffled his English deportment. At a tavern between Richmond and London, "there were masons, and carpenters, and gentlemen, and riflemen, and whisky topers, besides the gnats and bats, which, ever and anon, flew in and out: we quitted our purgatory upon paying two and a half dollars for three of us" (2:410).

Both country and people were rough. The flow of immigration that poured through the mountain passes startled even the most seasoned itinerant: "men, women, and children, almost naked, paddling bare-foot and bare-legged along, or labouring up the rocky hills, whilst those who are best off have only a horse for two or three children to ride at once" (2:410). Women and children crowded the filthy huts. The air was filled with smoke rising from open grates used for heating and cooking.

Asbury would probably not have claimed, as did Henry Smith, that he had conquered his "prejudice about eating, drinking, and lodging." He may have felt more like Henry Bascom, future Methodist bishop, who once said that he "[h]ad a breakfast that might have substituted [as] an emetic, prepared by the good wife who might, had she floated down the Nile, been safe from molestation by alligators, if filth would frighten them."[11] Bascom was low in spirit when he penned the following after staying with a family March 9, 1814: "Tried to study, but too much confusion, tried to pray in the family, but felt too dull—tried to eat breakfast, but the victuals were too dirty for any decent man to eat. The old man is an idiot, the woman, a scold, one son a drunkard, the other a sauce-box, and the daughter, a mother without a husband."[12]

Methodist preacher Jacob Young, who had been raised as a teenager in Kentucky, dressed in buckskin and referred to himself as a backwoodsman. But even he noted the impoverishment of his hosts on at least one occasion.

> There was no floor in the house. They had leveled off the ground and made it somewhat smooth. There were hickory poles laid across in the place of joists. Some clapboards laid on these poles constituted the upper floor. There was neither bedstead, chair, nor table in the house. Some small stakes or forks had been driven down in the west corner of the cabin; they laid two round poles in the forks, and laid clapboards on these poles. This was their bedstead. Some bedding, such as it was, formed all the sleeping place I saw for the man and his wife. The little Negro boy slept on the ground floor with a deer skin under him. I saw no cupboard, furniture, excepting some earthen bowls of inferior quality. The woman of the house was badly crippled . . . the squalid appearance of the inside of the house made an impression on my mind that never can be erased.[13]

Young stated that when he could avoid sleeping among fleas and bedbugs, he intended to do it. No doubt Asbury had the same intention. By the last of October, he was back in South Carolina. "[O]nce more I have escaped from filth, fleas, rattlesnake's, hills, mountains, rocks and rivers: farewell, western world, for a while!" (2:412). He was greeted by a new parsonage that had just been built for him and the other traveling preachers at the Bethel Church in Charleston. Asbury must have been unexpected, as he normally arrived in Charleston at a later date. Finding the parsonage completely unfurnished, he sat down on the front steps with the full intention of spending the night there. When he could not be deterred from sleeping on the front porch, the local Methodists quickly delivered some furniture. The house in Charleston was the closest thing to home that Asbury ever experienced.

The Specter of Mortality

Asbury began 1804 with a good deal of optimism, noting that the prospects "were the greatest that have ever yet been known in this land for religion" (2:422). His optimism may have been tried as he traveled north, meeting small gatherings in frigid churches. At one church, where the windows were open, "the people trembled under the cold, if not under the word" (2:427). The trip had been made so many times that there was a melancholy resulting from recalling former visits and relationships. The Peter Pelham home had been a retreat for him when he had been ill in 1798, but they had since moved to Ohio. Thomas Pelham had died since Asbury's last visit, leaving behind three children.

The reminders of his friends' mortality and his own advancing age caused Asbury to "take leave at every visit." The final good-byes were becoming a psychological and spiritual burden. The "great mortality rate among the aged" reminded Asbury of his own finitude and the heavy responsibilities he had carried the last twenty years. "I hardly bear it, and yet dare not cast it down, for fear God and my brethren should cast me down for such an abandonment of duty" (2:430).

The General Conference, which sat at Baltimore beginning on May 7, 1804, tried Asbury's patience. He was older and there was more institutional business. He later assessed, "I think never did a General Conference sit longer with more ado, and do less; and perhaps the less the better" (2:432). The prolonged argumentative debate addressed slavery and the transfer of the book business from Philadelphia to New York. The contention was so heated that Bishop Whatcoat recommended "the suppression of passion or ill will in debate" (2:431n.). Asbury said little, which was normal, but scratched out notes to the opinion makers in order to communicate his personal perspective on the various issues. Asbury made motions from the chair, but these normally addressed business matters such as designating money left to the Methodist Church by the will of a deceased person. On more critical issues, such as slavery, the power of the bishops, or the establishment of other publishing locations, he gave little direction. He did, however, moderate heated debate with a firm hand.

Asbury was especially irritated when the discussion provided "for a trial of a Bishop in the interval of the General Conference making it obligatory for the accusers to present their accusation in writing, a copy of which must be given to the accused himself."[14] It also irked Asbury that the conference required annual conferences to sit for at least a week, rather than allowing the bishop to call for adjournment whenever he perceived business was concluded. The 1804 General Conference was the first to allow women and children into the galleries to hear the debate. Their presence so distracted the conference delegates that by the middle of the week they were no longer allowed to attend. Jesse Lee noted that the meeting was barren of any genuine stir of religion.[15]

On June 2, Asbury experienced a devastating blow when his favorite horse became lame after being horned by a cow. He sent the horse to a Mr. Cooper to be sold for fifty dollars. He referred to "Jane" as half of his personal estate, and was so sentimentally attached to her that he seriously contemplated taking the mare with him in tow. Nevertheless, he somehow brought himself to say farewell. Within two days he purchased another horse for eighty dollars. But when he arrived at Philadelphia, Asbury discovered that Richard Allen, future founder of the African Methodist Episcopal Church, had already purchased him a horse for ninety dollars. He had to sell his present mount for sixty dollars. "[S]o much for my haste" (2:432). Breaking in two new horses caused him to comment three weeks later, "My chief suffering is from riding: I am under the necessity of riding soft, fearful as I am of worse effects, and my blanket makes me gall sadly; as yet I have been little affected with the piles, thanks to my good God!" (2:434). Asbury thanked God for all things great and small.

When passing through West Virginia in August of 1804, Asbury received the news of Joseph Cromwell's death. Cromwell was one of the most interesting preachers of early Methodism. George Shadford discovered Cromwell as a "madman," chained to a bed in Green Spring Valley, Maryland. Shadford shared the gospel with him, whereupon Cromwell was converted and became a Methodist preacher. Asbury referred to him as "an original indeed—no man's copy" (1:324). He later referred to Cromwell's preaching as "pretty long and rough" (1:341). His communication methodology was such a contrast to Asbury's that in 1780 Asbury considered making Cromwell his traveling partner. "If I should preach a systematical, dry sermon, he would pay the sinners off" (1:373).

Asbury and Cromwell traveled together for several months, and in 1787 Asbury appointed him as a presiding elder over the Ohio and Clarksburg circuits. Cromwell later backslid, returned to alcoholism, and died a drunk. At the height of Cromwell's ministry, Asbury said, "He is the only man I have heard in America with whose speaking I am never tired. I always admire his unaffected simplicity . . . a man that cannot write or read well and yet his words go through me every time I hear him. The power of God attends him more or less in every place. He seldom opens his mouth, but some are cut to the heart."[16]

Asbury did not attend the Mt. Gerizim Conference in Kentucky. For over a month, he was confined to Harry Stephens's home in northeastern Pennsylvania with an inflamed throat. "The fever subsided and left a cough. I have not had a more severe attack since I have been in America: the doctor was seldom right and medicines were not to be had, nor indeed, the comfort and alleviations which surround a sick bed in the cities" (2:443). Due to the roughness of the terrain, Asbury's physical condition, and the advancing age of Whatcoat (68), the trip into West Virginia was particularly irksome. Asbury carried a fever for fifty days that was finally broken by taking eight grains of "ipecacuanha." He then parted with Whatcoat, who had determined to set out to the Western Conference on his own. "Whatcoat has been of great service to me: he was still urgent to go on, and he has gone on, wandering alone through the wilderness—I am afraid, in vain: he said he had a *mite* and it must go. I fear his precious life will go." (2:444).

Briars, Thorns, and Scorpions

Francis Asbury may have had intimate contact with more persons and stayed in more homes than any other American before the Civil War. He had the opportunity to read the faces of a wide stratum of persons who gathered to hear him throughout the "civilized United States." He interpreted people both in singularity and in mass. If it is possible to assess people stereotypically, that opportunity was his. In his journal, he was not reticent about sizing people up. He often commented that they were dead, dull, wild, stupid, lifeless, rude, unawakened, and violent.

At other times, Asbury rejected people because they did not share his Christian perspective. Others he wrote off in a wholesale fashion: "I conclude I shall have no more appointments between Wilmington and Newbern; there is a description of people we must not preach to; the people of Onslow seem to resemble the ancient Jews—they *please not God, and are contrary to all men*" (2:381).

The people were so roughhewn that Asbury was often glad to be gone. After attempting to preach in Chatham County, North Carolina, in 1780, he was more than anxious to get away because of the guns and whiskey. Asbury dubbed the people there "briars, thorns, and scorpions." Asbury's early impression of Newbern, North Carolina, was highly unfavorable. He rode around the town but could get no positive response regarding a possible location for preaching. Sensing the "power of death," "I judge by my own feelings, it would be as well to leave them just as I found them—and so I did" (1:534). To Asbury's credit, he usually returned to those places where he experienced rejection, and sometimes often. He revised his assessments. Almost ten years later, he wrote of Newbern, "I know not when I have visited a place with such pleasing hopes and feelings: I trust there hath been something more than man in this. O! how greatly was my heart knit to these people!" (2:108).

Affinity with the Country

During the entirety of his American ministry, Asbury exhibited a natural affinity with the wide-open country and a prejudice against city life. He found the mannerisms and ruggedness of the frontier disagreeable; but he would have chosen the clear vistas over the amenities of city life. He referred to Philadelphia as a noisy and disagreeable place. For Asbury, cities represented the spirit of the world, driven toward complexity and avarice. Country life was simpler, and for Asbury simplicity was inherent in Christianity. Cities were concentrations of market activity, "hawkers and bell ringers, horses and hand carts," a quest which dulled the appetite for true spirituality.[17] Asbury feared that urban dwellers were distracted from what really matters, eternal values.

Charleston, South Carolina—with its bustling seaport, surrounding plantations, and its thriving slave trade—was infertile spiritual ground. In 1805, Asbury estimated that fewer than 180 whites had joined the local Methodist society in the last twenty years. The people in Charleston were characterized by "death, desertion, backsliding: poor fickle souls, unstable as water, light as air, bodies and minds!" (2:487). Asbury could not forget the socialites who had laughed at him as he held class meetings observable from the sidewalks below. Asbury identified with the marginalized people of Charleston—women, the poor, and slaves—but he was highly sensitive when others interpreted this as an inability to minister to a more socially acceptable clientele. Such accusations were difficult to bear, but Asbury tried to cover them with the grace of forgiveness. In traveling to Auburn, New York, in 1812, the evangelistic party was mocked by some men in a harvest field. "[T]his is their glory of wickedness: ours is, that the offence of the cross hath not yet ceased. My revenge was prayer that God might convert and save them for Christ's sake" (2:702–3).

A Mission to the Disinherited

Generally, in the country lived the poor who were more receptive to the Gospel. Upward mobility would be the death of Methodism, Asbury believed. To his mind, there was an exact correlation between the accumulation of finery and spiritual apostasy. As in England, American Methodism was a religion of the poor, which often accounted for the financial straits of the organization and its preachers. "We have the poor, but they have no money; and the worldly, wicked rich we do not choose to ask" (1:612). Possession of the world's goods dulled spiritual intensity. There was little threat of this west of the Appalachians. William Colbert recorded the following:

> I rode six miles before I got anything for my poor horse. At Wigdon's, at Meshoppen, I called for something for my horse, and some smoky dirty corn was brought. But as for myself, I thought I would wait a little longer before I would eat in such a filthy place. I talked to the filthy woman, who was sitting over the ashes with three or four dirty children in the chimney corner, about the salvation of her soul. She was kind; She took nothing for what I had; so I proceeded on my journey, and arrived at Gideon Baldwin's, the lowest [farthest south] house on my Tioga circuit. They received me kindly, and got me something to eat. I have traveled over hills and mountains without breakfast or dinner.[18]

Asbury continued to interpret the Methodist mission as a ministry of poor and plain preachers to poor and plain people. He would have agreed with Adam Smith, who wrote in his *Wealth of Nations*, "The clergy of an established and well endowed religion frequently become men of learning and elegance, who possess all the virtues of gentlemen; but they are apt gradually to lose the qualities, both good and bad, which gave them authority and influence with the inferior ranks of people, and which had been the original causes of success and establishment of their religion."[19]

Asbury condemned accessories of wealth, especially when they were ostentatious. In the Virginia Conference of 1814, there was a heated discussion on the extravagant dress of Methodist women, but Asbury assured the conference that in his extensive travels the dress of Methodist women, with few exceptions, was the plainest in the land. "He had seen ladies in England with every finger covered with rings, and their arms with ruffles of costly lace, from the shoulder below the finger ends. For his part, he said he would greatly prefer to see women dress even in this extravagant manner, than to see a preacher walk into the conference room with his fair top boots, and red morocco straps hanging down to his ankles, and a great gold watch chain and seal dangling from his fob."[20]

At a conference in 1807, Asbury gave a lecture on hair and conformity to the world. "I would just assume my remark would hit my right hand man, as anyone else." Sitting on his right was Thomas Coke with carefully groomed long locks. "Do you mean me sir? Does my hair offend you? If so, it shall offend you no longer." Between the morning and afternoon sessions, Coke made a trip to the barber.[21] Asbury's barbs bypassed no one. In 1811, he wrote to Garrettson, who lived in a fine manor house obtained by a prosperous marriage. "I disapproved musick at your house to show I spare none."[22]

In spite of his identification with those who lived in the open spaces, Asbury was not naïve concerning the barriers that lay between them and God. They had come West seeking not religion but land. The migrants expended their restless energy not in pursuing God, but in the clearing of land and the building of houses. In Tennessee in 1805, Asbury recorded: "We meet crowds of people directing their march to the fertile West: their sufferings for the present are great; but they are going to present abundance, and future wealth for their children: in ten years, I think, the new State will be one of the most flourishing in the Union" (2:482–3). And of course there were the crudeness, illiteracy, and filth of the frontier person (which Asbury loathed), not to speak of the crowded conditions. "Why should a living man complain?—but to be three months together upon the frontiers, where, generally, you have but one room and fireplace, and half a dozen folks about you, strangers perhaps, and their family certainly (and they are not usually small in these plentiful new countries), making a crowd" (2:315).

To those who accused Asbury of partiality—that he appointed the best preachers to the best places; that Methodism was gravitating toward pockets of prosperity—he responded, "We are impartial. We spend as much time in the extremities. We know not Maryland or Delaware, *after the flesh*, more than Kentucky, Cumberland, Georgia, or the Carolinas: it is our duty to save the health of preachers wherever we can; to make particular appointments for some important charges; and it is our duty to embrace all parts of the continent and union, after the example of primitive times and the first faithful preachers in America" (2:280).

Asbury incarnated the gospel in thousands of cabins, located in sparsely settled areas of nineteenth-century America. At times he *did* have to "grin and bear it," not questioning where he slept or what he ate. James Quinn noted that Asbury did not try to avoid staying in the most meager of circumstances, even though he "had as fair and as clear a skin as ever came from England, and in him the sense of smelling and taste were most exquisite."[23] But through it all, an empathy bonded him with Americans from all walks of life, especially with those who lived on the margins of civilization. There was little differentiation between his professional and private life, no superficial aloofness that would cause a cabin dweller to conclude, "He is really not one of us."

Henry Boehm said that Asbury would ask a blessing as fervently over a dry morsel as over some of the sumptuous dinners of the wealthy. Asbury's lodging might be a deserted cabin, a schoolhouse, a cabin without a roof, a deerskin with fleas, clapboards across tree limbs, or a plank for a bed and a bearskin for a covering. At times, a clean floor for a bed seemed like a palace. When there was no available lodging, the earth was his resting place and the sky was his canopy. In other words, Asbury's evangelism required him to be at home in any situation.

Boehm said that Asbury "could make himself at home in a splendid mansion or in the humblest cottage."[24]

However, Asbury was not indifferent to external appearances. He expected a person's internal transformation to result in external reformation; a clean heart meant clean clothes and a clean habitat. Observers noted Asbury's "fastidiousness" about his own clothing and appearance. Late in life, he stood before a frontier camp meeting and proclaimed, "I have been lodged in many a cabin as clean and sweet as a palace; and I have slept on many coarse, hard beds that have been as clean and as sweet as soap and water could make them, and not a bug or flea to annoy . . . keep your cabins clean for your health sake and your souls sake; for there is no religion in dirt and filth and fleas."[25] A religion espoused by Francis Asbury could mean no less.

15. "Millions Where Millions Are"

Validated Authority

"O what prospects opened in 1805," Asbury wrote to Daniel Hitt as he and Whatcoat spent a day at the Widow Jones's in Newbern, North Carolina, on January 26. Methodism's unbridled revivalism over the preceding four years offered to disenfranchised Americans a community of emotion and identity. The binding force was a commonality of religious experience. "Nobodies" without the social status of money, education, and connectedness could become "somebodies."[1] The new community was not particularly enticing to those who belonged to the fraternal order of somebodies. For this reason, at least once when Asbury was asked to speak at the North Carolina statehouse, he declined. He felt that such notariety was not compatible with his ministry to persons of low estate. The activities of society's elite were incongruent with Methodism's egalitarian appeal and revivalistic intensity. That appeal and intensity, combined with an efficient organizational structure, Asbury maintained as his working premises. Neither Asbury nor Whatcoat was physically well as they made their way north. Before the end of January, Whatcoat was suffering from dysentery and an infected bladder, passing blood. Asbury, plagued by pleurisy, was coughing up blood. Winter was hard on both preachers and people. Preaching engagements were uneventful and the northwest wind almost unbearable. On February 2, the duo covered thirty-two miles of treacherous terrain in swampy northeastern North Carolina in spite of Asbury's "disordered bowels," with no opportunity to stop at a house.

As they made their way through Virginia, the weather turned even colder. There were reports of five to six feet of snow in New York. At Petersburg, Asbury attempted to preach on Revelation 3:3–5, but his mind was "fettered." Yet his unbounded optimism was not dampened. He wrote to Epaphras Kibby, "I hope that there has been five hundred extraordinary meetings where 12, 20, 30, 40, 50, 100, 200 or more precious souls have been invited, converted, or restored, and sanctified at a meeting. . . . I calculate 1805 to be the greatest year that ever was known in America or the world; only let the preachers of a holy gospel, be holy, and Laborious" (3:307–8).

On March 1, Asbury chaired the Virginia Conference at Edmond Taylor's in Granville County, North Carolina. Conferences were becoming routine affairs, and at times it was difficult for Asbury to remain focused except for the stationing of the preachers. Several who had defected with O'Kelly were returning to Methodism. Asbury sent out a hortatory letter under the auspices of the Virginia Annual Conference.

> O Brethren, was there ever a time like this! Help, help by your
> prayers, preaching, and purses . . . such fields are opening, so many

preachers to preach, and so many people to pray, and such multitudes to be converted. What shall we see in twenty years to come
if the travelling and local preachers are united, preaching the same
doctrines, approving and enforcing the same discipline, and seeking by all lawful means ministerial and Christian union among
themselves and all Christian ministers and societies? (3:310–12).

Asbury and Whatcoat continued north, their patience tried by the weather,
Asbury's stumbling horse, and the prevailing Calvinistic theology. From March
21–23 they traveled a hundred miles over hilly, rutted, muddy roads, and stopped
at the small town of Washington in Culpepper County, northern Virginia. Asbury
opened the Baltimore Conference on April 1 at Winchester, Virginia. Here Asbury
admitted to the ministry Joseph Carson, a man who lived to be one hundred
years old and served Methodism for seventy-five years. Carson's long experience
of itinerancy allowed him to give a clear description of the task:

> Our physical labor was of small moment—when compared with
> the persecutions of every kind with which we met from the Uni-
> versalists, Hell Redemptionists, Seventh-Day Baptists, Free-Will
> Baptists, Deists, Atheists, and sinners of all classes. Among the
> wealthy and refined very bitter opposition to Methodism existed,
> consequently our homes were among the poor, who were scarcely
> able to supply us with the necessaries of life, to say nothing of
> comforts; but they had kind hearts and such as they had gave
> they unto us. Our food was of the coarsest kind and not the most
> cleanly. Breakfast generally consisted of coffee made of toast corn
> bread, sometimes a little pickled pork fried to a crackling, and a
> scanty supply of bread; for dinner we had a few vegetables and
> occasionally wild meat; supper was pretty much a repetition of
> breakfast; tea was made of Hemlock leaves sweetened with honey.[2]

Carson's own sacrificial spirit had been stimulated by the dedicated models
that had gone before him. The first Methodist itinerant minister he remembered
was John Talbot, who preached while stones and rocks were hurled at him until
the blood run down his face. "The first time I saw Bishop Asbury he was standing on a table, on the green, preaching."[3]

Though the conference had not adopted O'Kelly's idea that a Methodist
preacher had a right to appeal the bishop's decision, it was more and more practiced. An increasing number were willing to confront Asbury's authority. Nothing grated on the bishop more. On May 22, he braced himself with the following
notation: "I will tell the world what I rest my authority upon. 1. Divine authority. 2. Seniority in America. 3. The election of the General Conference. 4. My

ordination by Thomas Coke, William Phillip Otterbein, German Presbyterian minister, Richard Whatcoat, and Thomas Vasey. 5. Because the signs of an apostle have been seen in me" (2:469–70). The personal affirmation was of little comfort to himself and little heeded by others. "This was a sorrowful day to me; I was in sackcloth" (2:470).

Sixty Years Old

As usual, the summer trip through New England revealed the incongruity between lively Methodism and the staid New England temperament. In spite of the low state of "true religion" here, Asbury noted it was his best trip yet. There was a gracious time at Talland quarterly meeting. From Ebenezer Washburn's sermon, "Many exhortations followed, and prayers, with power. There was a great cry, and the meeting held without intermission until night" (2:473). The outdoor meeting at Lynn, which accompanied the conference session, was especially gratifying. Many were affected and several converted by the exhortations and prayers that went up on their behalf. At Lynn on July 9, a letter arrived announcing Thomas Coke's marriage. Coke exulted that his wife was indeed a twin soul to himself. "Never, I think, was there a more perfect congeniality between two human beings, than between us" (3:318). Asbury defensively replied, "Marriage is honorable in all—but to me it is a ceremony awful as death" (2:474).

Asbury rode across the southern tip of New York and into New Jersey almost without stopping, except for eating and sleeping at night. His party covered almost forty miles a day for six days. The road was hot and dusty. To add to their problems, they were not allowed entrance into New York because they had been exposed to a yellow fever epidemic in New Haven. The travelers met the same challenge at Philadelphia but were not quarantined from the city, though their ministry was curtailed. Asbury delighted that he had been able to purchase a "neat, little Jersey wagon" for $100. Needless to say, it was an unusual purchase for the frugal bishop.

As soon as the wagon was delivered, along with the minutes of the conference, Asbury headed across Pennsylvania, making it to Pittsburgh in nine days. It was a grueling trip that called for crossing three mountain ranges, the Blue, Kittatinny, and Tuscarora. Because of traveling in a carriage, Asbury had to walk down the mountain each time a range was crossed. It was torturous travel for a man sixty years old, especially in an area that was experiencing drought in the heat of the summer. "I am resolved to quit this mountainous, rocky, rugged, stumpy route. It was a mercy of God we were not—men, horses, and wagon— broken in pieces; I praise God now, but I hardly had time to pray then" (2:478). The trip was rewarded with the opportunity of preaching to "five thousand souls" at the Short Creek Campground near Bedford, Pennsylvania.

238 ∽ America's Bishop

By the middle of September, the bishops were traveling through Kentucky. On October 2, Asbury convened the Methodist conference in Scott County and there ordained Jesse Head, a local deacon. Head later performed the marriage ceremony of Thomas Lincoln and Nancy Hanks, parents of Abraham Lincoln. Instead of coming down through the Cumberland Gap, Asbury and his party chose to cross Clinch Mountain to save time, but heavy rain made the route almost impassable. The money that local citizens had spent on the "turnpike" had been wasted, in Asbury's opinion. "It was not better than it had been in its native state."

Informal Education

The attrition rate of ministers, especially for the South Carolina Conference, was high: "[S]ome are sick, some are settling in life—men of feeble minds. But let the Head of the Church see to his own work—it is not mine. Why should I despond?" (2:485). While reading missionary David Brainerd's biography, Asbury concluded that Brainerd's religion was "all gold, the purest of gold" (2:486). He had been doing so much reading that his eyes were now bothering him. "I must keep them for the Bible and the conferences" (2:486). The resolve was briefly kept. Ten days later, he noted reading a thousand pages of Charles Atmore's *Methodist Memorial.*

In Charleston, Asbury had to take care of the more mundane matters of church administration. Both the Bethel church and the parsonage needed to be enlarged. He noted that the Circular Congregation Church was building an edifice "worth perhaps one hundred thousand dollars." He could not resist a bit of sarcasm: "[T]here is a holy strife between [Bethel's] members and the Episcopalians, who shall have the highest steeple; but I believe there is no contention about who shall have the most souls converted to God" (2:487).

The year ended with reports of prosperous camp meetings in the North. "My soul greatly rejoiceth in the Lord, and exults in the prosperity of Zion" (2:488). His direction and philosophy of ministry were affirmed by reading Haweis's *Church History* (the same Thomas Haweis that Asbury, as a boy, had heard preach).[4] Asbury most appreciated Haweis's emphases that (1) the early evangelists exercised superintendency and episcopal leadership and (2) the introduction of philosophy and human learning as preparation for ministry was a serious evil.

Asbury was far more wary of formal education than was Wesley. He believed anything that distracted a minister from speaking plain truth to plain people was to be ignored. Learning as an end in itself drained a minister's time and energy away from Methodism's sole purpose—the salvation of souls. Acquisition of knowledge was to be done, not in preparation for ministry, but as one pursued ministry. Asbury stated his educational philosophy to William Duke in 1774: "Take every opportunity for getting knowledge, and always consider yourself as ignorant and as having everything to learn" (3:19). Asbury desired his preachers to be neither sophists nor ignoramuses. They were to acquire from both experience and knowledge whatever would bridge the gap between God and humanity. The notes to the 1798 *Discipline* stated:

> A taste for reading profitable books is an inestimable gift. It adds to the comfort of life far beyond what many conceive, and qualifies us, if properly directed, for very extensive usefulness in the church of God. It takes off all the miserable listlessness of a sluggish life; and gives to the mind a strength and activity it could not otherwise acquire. But to obtain and preserve this taste for, this delight in, profitable reading, we must daily resist the natural tendency of man to indolence and idleness.[5]

Asbury attempted to preach on Christmas Day 1805, but there were too many distractions. "It was not a pleasant season: *Christmas day* is the worst in the whole year on which to preach Christ; at least to me" (2:489). In a letter written on December 28 to Thomas Sargent, a Baltimore pastor, the bishop indulged in a bit of prophesying. "I calculate that the year 1806 will be one of the most awful years that was ever known in Europe or America for war and commotion, and I believe there will be thousands slain by the sword of desperate war" (3:333). Such political speculation was out of character for Asbury, but the upheaval of those days could turn even the most sane into seers.

Crisis after Crisis

The year 1806 was indeed tumultuous for Asbury, but not for the reason he had prophesied. Asbury endured the death of Whatcoat, the loss of Joseph Crawford as a traveling companion, and the asumption of a hundred-pound debt by Rankin. He also refused Thomas Coke's offer to reenter the American connection when Coke stipulated that he should have full episcopal powers. These events drained Asbury both physically and spiritually. After Whatcoat's death he was alone at the top of American Methodist governance—a position that at one time he would have desired—but Asbury found himself tottering. On November 7, he wrote to Thomas Haskins, "I have only to say I sit on a joyless height, a pinacle [sic] of power, too high to sit secure and unenvied, too high to sit secure without divine aid. My bodily and mental powers fail. I have a charge too great for many men with minds like mine" (2:356).

After closing the South Carolina Conference on January 4, he began the usual cold ride north. He would have preached at Rockingham, North Carolina, but there was a schedule conflict with a wedding. "[T]his is a matter of moment, as some men have but one during life, and some find that one to have been one too many" (2:493). Asbury contracted a cold and bronchial infection. At Wilmington's new edifice, 66'x33', there were "1,500 hearers," which may illustrate Asbury's tendency to exaggerate numbers. One thousand persons on the main floor would allow for about two square feet per person, while it would take an enormous balcony to accommodate the other five hundred hearers. Even so, there is no doubt that people packed in to hear the bishop. William Burke recalled that at the Old Stone Church in Cincinnati, because there was no stove in the sanctuary, "their breath would condense on the walls, and the water would run down and across the floor."[6]

In Beaufort, North Carolina, there had been a revival; "[T]he whole town seems disposed to bow to the scepter of the Lord Jesus" (2:494). The notation on Washington, North Carolina, was not as positive. "Joseph Crawford did not let that awful town go unwarned" (2:495). The Virginia Conference at Norfolk was comparatively uneventful and peaceful in spite of one obnoxious member who seemed to be against everything. One attendee wrung the nose of a conference preacher because he had been offended. "The preacher simply raised his hat, made him a polite bow, and walked into the Conference Room."[7] Both preaching and chairing a conference were hazardous duties. Asbury was worn out, being able to catch only about five hours' sleep out of every twenty-four.

The Case of Thomas Coke

The Baltimore Conference on March 14, 1806, voted on two issues that had to do with the episcopacy. The first was a response to Thomas Coke's proposal to return to America from England if the American Church would grant him full episcopal authority. Even though Coke affirmed his "veneration" for Asbury, he recalled that the American bishop had not previously granted him equal authority. Asbury had relegated him to an inferior role by holding "the three Southern Conferences entirely by himself; and I was to spend my whole time merely as a Preacher; and on a plan, upon which I should spend the chief part of my time in preaching to very few. The Northern States would be covered with snow. . . . Mountains of snow to ride over" (3:335).

The fact that Coke had launched the Methodist Episcopal Church in America left both the conference and Asbury with a delicate decision. Coke's 1791 letter to Bishop White, suggesting union between the Methodists and the newly formed Episcopal Church, had come to light in 1804. This subversive act was difficult to forget and forgive, even though Coke later explained that he "never intended that either Bishop Asbury or myself should give up our episcopal office if the junction were to take place; but I should have no scruple then, nor should I now, *if the junction were desirable*, to have submitted to, or to submit to, a re-imposition of hands in order to accomplish a great object; but I do say again, I do *not* now believe such a junction desirable" (3:384). Coke impressed the Americans as a person more obsessed with wanderlust than a commitment to "stay by the stuff." To give him equal footing with a man who for thirty-five years had not revisited his native country was unthinkable.

The specific overture that Coke had made in June 1805 was that the seven American conferences would be divided between himself and Asbury, "[t]hree and four, and four and three, each of us changing our division annually; and that this plan at all events should continue permanent and unalterable during both our lives" (3:319). The American Methodists were swift, specific, and comprehensive in their response: Coke had not been faithful to America because of his repeated intercontinental travel and did not intend to make America his home; Coke had not been accountable to his brethren in that he deserted his post without permission. And as to equal powers with Asbury, they flatly stated:

> We think it our duty to inform you that in case of the death of Bishop Asbury we do not believe the General Conference would ever invest any man with the same power. He has been with us from the beginning; he is the proper father under God of us, his spiritual children, and in every instance he has conducted himself as such in adversity and prosperity–in fullness and want; he knew us when we were scarcely a people, and he has traveled on with us through all our difficulties and dangers without ever flinching till we have become (more) than One Hundred Thousand in number.[8]

Coke responded by reaffirming his veneration for Asbury, but at the same time accusing him of stripping his episcopal powers and reducing him to a mere preacher. When he had not been consulted in the stationing of the preachers in the Georgia Conference, he said, "I thus saw clearly the will of my God concerning me—that I ought not labour in America, unless the General Conference should consent in some way or other to comply."[9] Furthermore, Coke did not agree with how Asbury stationed the preachers. "At the same time," he added, "I would have nothing doing or altered to grieve the mind of that venerable man."[10]

The Baltimore Conference again wrote to Coke, explaining that he had not been given responsibility for stationing the preachers because he had not sufficient knowledge of places or persons. "Right or wrong," the Conference reminded Coke that he had agreed not to interfere with Asbury's work. Although the committee of Daniel Hitt, Enoch George, and Nelson Reed kindly thanked Coke for services previously rendered, the essence of the whole communication was that the American Methodist Church no longer needed his services.

We do not know whether the American leadership was aware of Coke's letter to the Bishop of London in 1799. Had they known his continuing intention to place the American church under the auspices of British Anglicanism, they would have repudiated him long before. Coke's letter to the bishop of London would have set Asbury's teeth on edge:

May it please your Lordship.

I have felt strong inclination for more than twelve months past, to take the liberty of writing to your lordship on a subject which appears to me of vast importance: I mean the necessity of securing the great body of Methodists, in connexion with the late Rev. John Wesley to the church of England. A considerable number of our body have deviated in this instance [receiving the Lord's Supper from their own preachers], from the established church; and I plainly perceive, that this deviation, unless prevented, will in time, bring about an universal separation from the establishment.

But how can this be prevented? I am inclined to think that if a given number of our leading preachers, proposed by our general conference, were to be ordained and permitted to travel through our connexion, to administer the sacraments to those societies who have been thus prejudiced as above; every difficulty would be removed. I have no doubt that the people would be universally satisfied. The men of greatest influence in the connexion would, I am sure, unite with me; and every deviation from the Church of England would be done away.[11]

In any event, the 1806 Annual Baltimore Conference removed Coke's name from the official minutes of Methodism. The decision so unsettled Asbury that, six weeks after the Baltimore Annual Conference, he wrote a solicitous letter to Coke. Letters were his means for easing his conscience, especially when difficult administrative decisions appeared to benefit him.

Having passed my three score years, I feel the happiness of seeing each other again, can we ever forget the days and nights we have sweetly spent together; spirits sweetly joined, and not a jar; unless Diotrephes's here, or there, formed for discord, whisper'd evilly. Ah my brother the deep rivers, creeks, swamps, and deserts we have travelled together, and glad to find a light to hear the voice of human, or domestick creature; the mountain rains, and chilling colds or burning heats, to say nothing of the perils of the deep. How oft you have stemmed the flood, the vast Atlantic with Columbian courage. Only be thou faithful unto death and Jesus will give thee the crown of life, *Life eternal Life!* . . . My dear friend you are a witness to my poverty for more than twenty years or I had done more for you, but I have attended you by night and day, have fitted your horse, held your bridle and stirrup, lent you [my] own horse, and with all the attention of a servant and often in a dark night called out, where is the Doctor, nor I alone, but all my brethren. You have never had more undissembled friendship shown to you than in America (3:341–44).

Death of Whatcoat

Due to the failing health of Whatcoat, the conference proposed a specially called delegated conference in May of 1807 to elect an additional bishop. This proposal was approved by all the annual conferences until it reached the Virginia Conference, which met at Newbern, North Carolina, on February 6, 1807. It was the decision of that conference "[n]ot to be concerned with it."[12] Jesse Lee reported that "[t]he bishop laboured hard to carry the point, but he laboured in vain; and the whole business of the dangerous plan was overset by the Virginia conference."[13] It was one of many instances when Lee and Asbury found themselves on opposite sides of an issue. The defeat by one conference (primarily by one man) of a motion that had already been carried by six conferences, irritated Asbury so much that he made no allusion to the proceedings, other than noting that "much might be said" (2:530).

Whatcoat was so ill that he had to be left at Dover on April 21. He died on July 5, 1806. Upon receiving the news of his colleague's death, Asbury commented, "A man so uniformly good I have not known in Europe or America" (2:512). The junior bishop was apolitical in personality and thus was the perfect complement for his more assertive senior. His easy-going temperament was a perfect object for Asbury's ribbing. The early-rising Asbury did not fail to tease his traveling partner when he was not up before the break of day.

Whatcoat's even temper was in sharp contrast to Asbury's swinging moods. When the latter complained about the press of the crowds and constant attention that interrupted his longing for solitude, Whatcoat laconically responded, "O Bishop, how much worse we should feel if we were entirely neglected."[14] A contemporary said of Whatcoat, "I found him so fixed in the ways of God that nothing could disengage him or move his patience, so as to make him murmur in the least degree."[15] For six years he served as Asbury's subordinated equal, an office for which few would have been fitted. He knew his place and filled it well.

What a Son

Two days before the death of Whatcoat, Asbury had parted with Joseph Crawford, his traveling companion and wagon driver for the past year. Crawford had been presiding elder of the Vermont district, and Asbury referred to him as a "zealous, active young man" (3:326). Crawford was a tireless laborer serving as Asbury's stenographer and capably filling the pulpit at night when Asbury had already preached in the day. There was the affinity of a father and son between the two. When they parted at the ferry going into New York City, Crawford "turned away his face and wept." The increasingly sentimental Asbury anguished, "Ah! I am not made for such scenes, I felt exquisite pain" (2:511). Crawford's service had been so valuable that Asbury doubted he could be replaced.

The summer consisted of a long drought throughout the East Coast states. The lack of water changed Asbury's travel plans. He stopped at Crissman Springs, Virginia, for the sake of his health. At times he felt himself so fatigued that he was unable to carry on a conversation with his hosts, who were eager to pick his brain for any recent news. The bishop was always expected to have something to say, a word of wisdom or encouragement. He constantly gave to others, but got little in return. "This excessive delicacy of feeling, which shuts my mouth so often, may appear strange to those who do not know me; there are some houses in which I am not sure that I could speak to my father, were he alive, and I to meet him there—bystanders might have cause to exclaim with wonder, *What a son!*" (2:515).

The trip over the western mountains of Virginia proved almost too much for Asbury's exhausted condition. The summer air was like an oven, without "six hours" of steady rain all summer. In making his way to the Holston Conference in Greene County, Tennessee, he got lost, going twenty miles out of his way. The heat and rough roads, along with the frustration, triggered his colitis. On September 17, he recorded, "My bowels for some days past have been much disordered, and I have been otherwise ill; but constant occupation of writing, reading, and praying, has diverted my attention from my sufferings: the medicine taken to-day has done good. I am obliged to avoid the sun as I would a burning fire" (2:517).

In the middle of October 1806, he had opportunity for several days' rest at the home of John Horton at Hanging Rock, just east of the Catawba River in north central South Carolina. Here Asbury reviewed and corrected the conference Minutes, for which he always assumed personal responsibility, before sending them to Ezekiel Cooper in Philadelphia. There was also time for refreshment of his soul. "I feel full of God: glory to God!" (2:519). If he was "full of God," he was empty of mammon.

Thomas Rankin billed him for one hundred pounds, which Asbury had invested in Cokesbury, the school no longer in existence. The money had come from the sale of Wesley's books by Robert Williams, now dead, for whose will Asbury and Rankin had been appointed executors. Rankin was convinced that Asbury owed him the money, which the latter conceded in order to protect his own character (2:355).

Church for the Masses

By November 2, Asbury was in Charleston, where a letter awaited him from Daniel Hitt, the presiding elder of the Baltimore District. At the Long Calm camp meeting, 580 persons had been converted and 120 sanctified in the space of nine days. On a rainy day in Williams County, Georgia, Asbury had time to reflect and calculate. He estimated there were approximately two hundred thousand Methodists in each state, totaling an aggregate constituency of some four million people.[16] Early in the month, he had written to Thornton Fleming, presiding elder of the Monongahela District, reporting the results of various camp meetings. The numbers were impressive. In the Delaware District alone, there had been 5,368 converted and 2,805 sanctified. "Oh, my brother, when all our quarterly meetings become campmeetings, and 1000 souls should be converted, our American millenium [sic] will begin" (3:357).

Methodism's success was intoxicating. Numbers were not the only thing, but they were extremely important. Methodism's preaching, worship, pastoral ministry, and organizational structure could assimilate the masses. The only step that remained to be taken was the adoption of an effective technique of church governance. It was handed to them by the Presbyterians, and the Methodists perfected it.

In an age when many people went for years without seeing a gathering of people numbering over a hundred, the "quarterly meeting"—with food, music, and preaching—enticed many. Alienated and isolated people found great joy in attending these meetings. Quarterly meetings had been the center for revivals, but now that task was handed to the camp meetings. The camp meeting was perfectly suited to the Wesleyan theology of going where the people were. Wesley's field preaching began with the conviction that a church that does not live outside of the church building is an apostate church. Asbury had cut his spiritual teeth on this philosophy of ministry before he came to America.

Camp meeting was church for the masses, with simplified worship, vernacular preaching, and informal decorum. Everyone was welcome as long as they did not drink, fight, or intentionally disrupt. Camp meetings became vital to the preachers' intentional design for externalizing Methodism. Methodism would not be a secret order with a highly mysterious liturgy for only the initiated. Russell Richey writes, "Campmeetings stylized the conference revival, established revival and conversions as an expectation, and made what would have otherwise been an intra-Methodist and perhaps even intra-leadership occasion into a great annual public display."[17] As early as 1802, Asbury wrote to George Roberts, "The campmeetings have been blessed in North and South Carolina, and Georgia. Hundreds have fallen and have felt the power of God. I wish most sincerely that we could have a campmeeting at Duck Creek out in the plain south of the town, and let the people come with their tents, wagons, provisions and so on. Let them keep at it night and day, during the [Baltimore] conference" (3:255).

Numbers

In the competition for souls, Methodism, was leading the way by the middle of the decade.[18] Cooperative ventures between the Presbyterians and the Methodists rapidly dissolved as the revivalistic ecumenicity of 1801–02 fragmented. Asbury wrote on August 10, 1806, "Friendship and good fellowship seem to be done away between the Methodists and Presbyterians; few of the latter will attend our meetings now: well, let them feed their flocks apart; and let not Judah vex Ephraim, or Ephraim, Judah; and may it thus remain, until the two sticks become one in the Lord's hands" (2:515).

While the Baptists theologically slighted Methodism, the Presbyterians snubbed them. No one likes to be snubbed, least of all Francis Asbury. He wrote on December 5, 1806, "As to the Presbyterian ministers, and all ministers of the Gospel, I will treat them with great respect, but I shall ask no favours of them: to humble ourselves before those who think themselves so much above the Methodist preachers by worldly honours, by learning, and especially by salary, will do them no good" (2:523).

For Asbury, Methodism's *sine qua non* was the salvation of souls. For that cause he was willing to sacrifice both erudition and propriety. Under Asbury's leadership, Methodism would prove itself. The Methodists' planting of a camp meeting out in the middle of nowhere typified volunteerism and free-church worship in their purest forms, forms that were essential to the substance of American religion. American Christians believed that the harvest of souls validated that substance. Asbury was more and more given to this appraisal as the new century unfolded.

Asbury's letters are full of numbers. He had inherited this preoccupation from Wesley, but it allowed him to become unwittingly and thoroughly American. The denominations' competition for numbers was religiously motivated but was competition nonetheless. In 1791 Asbury wrote, "I am led to think the eastern church will find this saying hold true in the Methodists; namely, 'I will provoke you to jealousy by a people that were no people; and by a foolish nation will I anger you: they have trodden upon the Quakers, the Episcopalians, the Baptists—see now if the Methodists do not work their way: the people will not pay large money for religion if they can get it cheaper" (1:690). No one ever accused Asbury of ineffective marketing.[19] A regular tally was not essential to his well-being, but it was certainly helped to keep him going. On July 11, 1803, he recorded, "Our total for the year 1803 is 104,070 members: in 1771 there were about 300 Methodists in New York, 250 in Philadelphia, and a few in Jersey; I then longed for 100,000; now I want 200,000—nay, thousands upon thousands" (2:398).

Asbury did not ignore the necessity of spiritual nurture and of sanctification but he increasingly adopted a language of reaping and harvesting, an emphasis on quantity rather than quality. In 1789 the preachers were instructed "to take an exact account of the numbers in society, and bring it to the Conference."[20] Thus, early on, Methodism adopted "the spirit of numerical triumphalism."[21] To Thomas Coke he wrote, "I thought once, should I live to see preaching established in all the states, and one hundred in society in each of them, I should be satisfied. Now, I want millions where millions are" (3:268). Would there be enough class leaders for the millions? Would there be enough theologically and biblically informed teachers for the thousands, who were deep in experience and shallow in doctrine? Four hundred persons had been converted in four days at a camp meeting at Suffolk, Virginia, in 1804. The gate that was only slightly ajar in England, where only those who had tickets were admitted, had been thrown wide open. The doctrinal purity of American Methodism was now of only secondary importance.

The *Explanatory Notes* of 1798, written by Coke and Asbury, stated, "As we should, on the one hand, prefer a small congregation to a large one, if the small one produces a company of precious souls united in love to God and each other, while the large one affords none but those who live in the spirit of the world; So, on the other hand, we should prefer the largest congregation with proportionate fruit to any other consideration."[22] Asbury could not have been entirely ignorant of the fact that the larger the congregation, the more difficult it becomes to "inspect the fruit." He had possibly forgotten the statement he had written in the preface to the 1796 "Journal": "Our grand object is to raise and preserve a holy and united people. Holiness is our aim; and we pay no regard to numbers but in proportion as they possess the genuine principles of vital religion."[23] Asbury's ideal would be increasingly tested by the disjuncture between breadth and depth, a tension no American religious body has been able to negotiate.

A Technology of Religion

The camp meeting may have been the first definitive step toward a technology of religion in America. In technology, according to Jacques Ellul, "Completely natural and spontaneous effort is replaced by a complex of acts designed to improve, say, the yield."[24] Where large crowds had once gathered to hear George

Whitefield on Philadelphia streets or in open fields, they would now be gathered by standardized means to improve efficiency. Asbury began to give specific instructions for both layout and the maintenance of order in camp meetings. He had adopted a soul-winning machine and now fine-tuned it for effectiveness.

By 1807, camp meetings were as "common now, as quarter meetings were 20 years back, in many districts, happy hundreds have been converted; in others happy thousands! Glory! Glory! Glory!" (3:380–1). In 1811, Asbury wrote to Jacob Gruber, "Doubtless, if the state and provinces hold twelve million, we congregate annually 3 if not 4 million in campmeetings! Campmeetings! The battle ax and weapon of war, it will break down walls of wickedness, part of hell, superstition, false doctrine" (3:453).[25]

Sometimes the battle ax was too efficient. At one camp in Queens County, Maryland, in 1807, the commotion of distressing cries and shouts of victory were so great the preaching had to be suspended for a day.[26] With single camps reporting as many as 1,500 conversions, Asbury was not totally unaware of the problems of such mass evangelism. In 1809, he again wrote to Jacob Gruber, "Campmeetings, campmeetings. Oh Glory, Glory! But I fear backsliding among old professors, and some sudden conversions not sound nor not lasting, and many Methodist families have neither the form nor power of godliness; yea practical religion is greatly wanting" (3:411). There had been a definitive transition since Asbury charged his troops in 1791 to "keep close love feasts. . . . Oh my brother, let us purge the sanctuary."[27]

Love feasts had been closed because of their intensity; these occasions were given to candor, confession, and personal testimony. It was a menu only for the spiritually mature. One attendee defended the policy of exclusion by saying that "[t]he promiscuous crowd would so depress and awe the feelings of even the most pious as to destroy the spirituality of the meeting."[28] At the beginning of American Methodism, there had been more emphasis on community than on evangelistic appeal. People were converted at the quarterly conference, the setting of the love feast, although this was not the ostensible purpose of the meeting. Quarterly meetings had been times of great revival and subsequent evangelism. Now camp meetings assumed that function, although this removed the new converts from Methodism's grassroots governing process. In other words, revivalistic worship and the business of the church were separated. Camp meetings externalized spirituality. According to Lester Ruth, "Ever increasingly, campmeetings became the time when revival was expected and planned for. They gave an opportunity to distill certain aspects that had been part of an integrated whole at quarterly meetings—the liturgical and evangelistic aspects—and to place them in a setting not connected to the administrative aspect."[29]

On the surface, the combining of revivalism and evangelism was the perfect wedding. Asbury wrote on September 1, 1811, that the "[c]ampmeetings are like the great plough that tears up all the rocks. These meetings are our forts and fortifications, our worship and gondolier, these holy meetings are our soldiers, these, temporally and spiritually will keep for our foes, of all kinds and keep peace and liberty at home" (3:452–3). Yet a vehicle with so many uses was sure to break down sooner or later. Russell Richey states, "That unity of revival, machinery of evangelism, and organization of life and order proved difficult to sustain as Methodism grew in numbers, area, complexity."[30]

Though Asbury perceived that camp meetings met the spiritual needs of the growing, migrating American populace, the attempt to win and conserve more souls with less effort is a false hope. American religious leaders have never believed human ingenuity and the work of the Holy Spirit to be antithetical, but American evangelistic formulas have perhaps too often betrayed God's mathematics. One of Christianity's primary assumptions—more is not always better—has always returned to challenge American evangelism's integrity.

16. "Esteem Him as a Father"

Reform in the Air

The years 1807–08 held significant technological, economic, and political changes for the American people. In August 1807, the steamboat Clermont, a 150-foot paddle wheeler, ushered in a new age of transportation and manufacturing. John Jacob Astor incorporated the American Fur Company in April 6, 1808, but long before that he had monopolized the fur trade within the United States. In fact, by 1790 he had amassed a million dollars, quite possibly the greatest earned fortune in America up to that time.[1] In 1808, Thomas Jefferson turned the United States government over to James Madison. More than any other President, Jefferson had assured the United States a "republican government," ruled by the majority.

The same republican principles came knocking at Francis Asbury's door. At no period of time did Asbury spend more spiritual and psychological energy in assessing his relationship to the movement that he had birthed. The American Methodist Episcopal Church had now come of age, and the tension was awkward for both father and child, because that child was trying to experience the independence of young adulthood.

At the age of 62, Asbury was doing much thinking about his legacy.[2] He had begun to worry about leaving Methodism as an orphan. Since the death of Whatcoat, Asbury served as sole bishop of the American Methodists. On February 11, 1807, he wrote, "I do not wish to leave this connection as unorganized as Mr. Wesley from lamented necessity left the British, when we are in a free country; and may form as we think best" (3:364). Indeed the General Conference, without a constitution, was free to do as it thought best. Upon Asbury's death it might do away with the episcopacy, the itinerancy, the General Rules, or anything it pleased.

Monumental change would be even easier if the conference became delegated, that is, not open to all elders who had served at least four years. The system that Asbury had worked so hard to preserve could be suddenly terminated. This thought caused him particular torment. Reform was in the air, advocated by persons who carried a good amount of influence. It was to those who sought change that he alluded when he wrote, "We may hope for only a partial promiscuous aristocratical spiritual body under no tie by constitution, or any check from the superintendency, doctrine, discipline, or order may go, but God will preserve" (3:364).

Jesse Lee

On January 1, 1807, Asbury left Charleston, and by January 16 he was in Lumberton, North Carolina. In spite of cold temperatures, snow, and hail, he reported covering four hundred twenty miles in ten days—a remarkable pace for an elderly man who often traveled without roads, much less a traveler's conveniences. He did not preach in the new year until January 19. During the evenings he read Wesley's sermons, devouring at least thirty of them. Commenting on their author, Asbury wrote, "[T]hose who feel disposed to complain of the brevity of his Notes, should recollect the wonderful amount and variety of his literary labours, polemical and practical, besides *the care of all the churches* in three kingdoms" (2:530). The conference at Newbern defeated the proposal for a specially called conference to "strengthen the episcopacy" (2:530). It was a blow to Asbury's authority, inflicted essentially by one person, Jesse Lee.

Lee, weighing by his own account 259 pounds, was a person of indefatigable energy. He would have been elected bishop had it not been for his outspokenness, which was often tinged with facetiousness. He was so opposed to formality that he refused ordination for several years after he was eligible. His independent spirit anathematized the centralization of authority, and he often opposed Asbury's position in conference debate.

The fact that Lee had been elected chaplain to the United States Congress, after putting himself forward for the job, rankled Asbury. Nevertheless the two friendly foes, who had traveled together for three years, had profound respect for one another. Asbury had made open recommendation for Lee's election to the episcopacy. By the same token, Lee said of Asbury upon his death, "He is not left behind him many, if any, to equal him in the church to which he belonged."[3] Devereux Jarratt called Jesse Lee, who had opened up New England to the call of the gospel by preaching from under the "old elm" on Boston Common, "[t]he greatest preacher and the most pious person that I was acquainted with amongst that order of ministers."[4]

Lee's *Short History of Methodism* was the first full-length account of the founding of American Methodism, chronicling its events through 1809. Some have surmised that it was not officially published by the Methodist publishing house because of its unflattering portrait of Asbury. Lee juxtaposed Asbury's being "shut up in a friend's house" during the Revolutionary War with the sufferings of Joseph Harter and Freeborn Garrettson, who had continued to openly preach. Henry Boehm, Asbury's longest traveling companion, said that the bishop became "nervous" upon reading Lee's *History*.[5] At least he was nervous enough to correct Lee's assessment. "My compelled seclusion in the beginning of the war, in the State of Delaware, was in no wise a season of inactivity; on the contrary, except about two months of retirement, from the direst necessity, it was the most active, the most useful, and most afflictive part of my life" (2:642). Either Asbury's memory failed him or he was being overly defensive.

Depressed in Both Mind and Body

All the tramping around in the cold and snow, preaching in drafty houses, put Asbury in bed by the latter part of March with "a bilious colic and fever." Four days later, because of the large crowd at Dover, Delaware, he preached outside in a cold wind. At Joseph Cresap's house, William Monroe caught up with Asbury. Monroe recalled that Asbury complained of fatigue and remarked that his "British skin would never stand hardships and that the iron stirrups bruised and hurt his feet. Accordingly, I procured some soft leather and some wool and padded his stirrups. This seemed to afford him relief and it gave me pleasure even now to reflect that I ever added the smallest mite to the relief and comfort of that good man."[6]

The conference at Philadelphia greeted him with an impeachment trial for Richard Lyon, a distasteful part of Asbury's responsibilities. The ordeal was so taxing that it sent Asbury to bed for the latter part of the conference. Immediately upon adjournment, he traveled through New Jersey, still preaching funeral discourses in memory of Richard Whatcoat. "Sick or well, I have my daily labours to perform. I am hindered from that solitary, close, meditative communion with God I wish to enjoy. I move under great debility" (2:536). Upon departure from New Jersey, Asbury voiced gratitude for the good weather, which had permitted him to preach to 3,000–6,000 people.

The "turnpike" road north through Albany and Troy made travelling a bit easier than normal. In Vermont, the terrain became much more precarious. "When we [Asbury and Daniel Hitt] came to White River we were obliged to lead the horses as they dragged the carriage up the heights, over rocks, logs, and cavings-in of the earth" (2:538). Upon arriving at the "Narrows," they discovered that the riverbank had given way. Asbury guided the carriage while Hitt led the horses. Asbury in his weakness lost control of the carriage, banging it against a rock, which resulted in its dangling by one wheel over a fifty-foot precipice. During the alarming crisis, one of the horses stepped on Asbury's foot. "I felt lame by the mare's treading on my foot; we unhitched the beast and righted the carriage, after unloading the baggage, and so got over the danger and difficulty. But never in my life have I been in such apparent danger. O Lord, thou hast saved man and beast!" (2:538).

The preaching through New York did not go well, and Asbury observed that they were addressing "insensible" people gripped by spiritual death. Asbury was depressed in both mind and body. He took solace in the beauty of the lakes and of the fields planted in wheat, rye, and grass. Outside of Clifton Springs, he preached in a barn to about a thousand "unfeeling souls." The next day, he preached in another barn to about four hundred "unyielding souls." Asbury was confident that the communication problem was not with him. Now that he had been re-leased for a while from conducting conferences, he felt "uncommon light and energy in preaching: I am not prolix; neither am I tame; I am rapid, and nothing freezes from my lips" (2:545).

On the other hand, Asbury was not hesitant to record his bleak sociological assessments. "The heights of the Susquehanna are stupendous; the bottom lands very fertile; but this river runs through a country of unpleasing aspect, morally and physically—rude, irregular, uncultivated is the ground; wild, ignorant, and wicked are the people" (2:546). The very next day his perception was granted empirical evidence. In the afternoon of the camp meeting in Tioga County, where Asbury had preached that morning, a fight broke out between some drunkards and the town constables. The presiding elder was physically involved in the fracas and was officially charged with assault. Asbury himself was accused of fighting, but he responded, "I was quiet in my room" (2:546).

At the approximate place where the Susquehanna River flows into Pennsylvania, Asbury and Hitt turned their direction southeast. At Breakneck Hill, Pennsylvania, they came to a precipice so steep that the carriage had to be let down by a strap. In a carriage without comfortable suspension, flat land was stressful enough, but land on its end was almost unbearable. Near Forty Fort, the preachers tried to talk Asbury into staying inside. He insisted on preaching in the rain while someone held an umbrella over him. His bearing was so regal that a little girl later reported that seeing Asbury led to her conversion.[7]

A Bit of Braggadocio

Asbury was exceedingly glad to arrive at the Moravian towns of Nazareth and Bethlehem. The latter he lauded for its architectural layout. Asbury was not allowed to preach in the Moravian church, being told that ministers must perform "himselbst." Daniel Hitt was especially critical of the worship service that he and Asbury both attended, keyed by a "four thousand dollar organ." Asbury noted with some sarcasm, "It is no wonder that men of the world, who would not have their children spoiled by religion, send them to so decent a place" (2:549-50).

At Columbia, Pennsylvania, Asbury had opportunity to rest between July 27 and August 1 and to write about thirty letters.[8] It was time for reflection on persecution being leveled at Methodist camp meetings; Asbury defended his favorite instrument of evangelism by pointing to Methodism's numerical success. The success had been achieved by "poor men, and unlearned—without books, money or influence," all the more evidence that the work was of God. From Little York, Asbury wrote to Jacob Gruber, "I have compared the work in Britain, and America. See the disproportion. Methodism began in England, 1730, [now] numbers 150,974, number of preachers, 576—Methodism began in the country part of America, 1771, [now] numbers 144,590, preachers 536" (3:373).

America had almost caught up to British Methodism, although the new country only had seven million persons to evangelize, compared with Britain's thirty-eight million. There was reason for rejoicing, even if the gratitude was tinged with a bit of braggadocio. Asbury also informed Gruber of a "new and blessed thing," the sending out of missionaries from the last three conferences. Was the "new thing" to counteract all the preachers who were locating? Could Methodism no longer assume that every preacher was itinerating? Asbury closed his letter with a barb for those who accused him of imperialism. "Some think they must go to General Conference, or we shall import Rome, and Constantinople, they know not what, they sit awhile, and then beg and pray to go home, they find there is nobody, no blood to be shed or honors to be made" (3:373).

Accompanied by Daniel Hitt, the bishop made his way across the mountains, the ride being so rough that Asbury's head was bruised by being jolted into the iron rods across the carriage top. On August 19 they covered forty miles, not stopping to eat, though they fed their horses twice. In spite of having an inflamed throat and having to cross "mud, gullies, stumps and hills," Asbury worked on a new hymnal for the American Methodist Church.[9] He also ingested three thousand pages of John Marshall's *Life of Washington*. Upon leaving the conference at Chillicothe, Ohio, he headed south into Kentucky. By the end of September, he was feeling well enough to write, "I am young again, and boast of being able to ride six thousand miles on horse-back in ten months; my round will embrace the United States, the Territory, and Canada; but O, childhood, youth, and old age, ye are all vanity!" (2:556). He achieved this renewed energy "by faith in a prayer hearing, soul converting, soul sanctifying, soul restoring, soul comforting God" (2:556).

Valentine Cook

At the Mt. Gerizim camp meeting outside of Cynthiana, Kentucky, Asbury preached to two thousand people. Asbury tried to persuade Valentine Cook to become a missionary, but the very capable preacher declined. "Ah! how hardly shall they who have families growing up, enter into and keep in the travelling connexion!" (2:557). Cook had been trained at Cokesbury College and served as the principal of Bethel Academy in Jessamine County, Kentucky. As a young preacher, Cook had debated a well-known Calvinistic Scotsman, who said, "I am here in ample time to give the youngster a dose from which he will not soon recover." The Scotsman spoke first, with Cook following. While Cook replied, his opponent twice interrupted him and then tried to persuade the crowd to leave. Cook's voice, "usually soft and soothing rolled on, in thunder tones, over the concourse, and echoed far away in the depths of the forest. While his countenance lighted up, kindled and glowed, as he were newly commissioned from on high to proclaim the salvation of God."[10] The effect was so stunning that almost all the hearers were bathed in tears and left, "silent as a funeral procession."

Abel Stevens said that "Cook was so venerated for his singular piety; and it is probable that no man of his day wielded in the West, greater power in the pulpit."[11] Cook was said to have had "no symmetry in his figure, awkward appendages . . . stoop shouldered to such a degree, that his long neck projected from between his shoulders almost at a right angle, with the perpendicular of his chest. His head, which was of peculiar formation, being much larger than usual from crown to the point of the chin, seemed rather suspended to than supported by the neck."[12] Cook's eccentric appearance, combined with an unsurpassed command of the English language, created an attraction for both the curious seeking entertainment and the religious seeking piety.

A Bishop, Oh That It Was Never Named

As Asbury recuperated from the flu at the home of James Rembert at Camden, South Carolina, his mind was again on the superintendency. The words that flowed from his pen were weighed down with almost a half-century of sacrificial ministry—ministry that was not fully appreciated by his detractors. "O what a toil! But I sincerely think I shall never be an *arch superintendent* much less an *arch Bishop*. Rather like great George Washington, let me peaceably retire and lay my commission at the feet of the General Conference, and after the rapid race from 16 to 63, be supernumerary, superannuated or located" (3:377).

Again he argued for an itinerating superintendency that would visit all the conferences instead of being located in a diocesan fashion. Asbury was now the one supreme head of American Methodism, which made him all the more open to attack. "A Bishop, oh that it had never been named. I was elected and ordained a superintendent as my parchment will show" (3:378).

During the January 1808 trip north, Asbury was buoyant in spirit in spite of torturous travel, ice, and a lame horse, and the looming General Conference. By the time he and Hitt arrived in Staunton, Virginia, the weather shut them in for a couple of days. Asbury attempted some "reading, writing, praying, and planning," but was hindered by the cramped quarters. On February 2, Asbury opened the conference at Lynchburg after having preached to about six hundred hearers on Sunday. The streets of Lynchburg were so deep in mud that the slave of Stith Mead, the presiding elder, offered to carry the hefty Jesse Lee on his back across the street, and did.[13]

The mud was not nearly as discouraging as the church's debt. The normally solvent Virginia Conference had been almost a thousand dollars short of paying the preachers for the previous year. All the other conferences had also been insolvent during 1807. Asbury wrote that "last year" they had sent out six missionaries with ten dollars each to travel five or six hundred miles through the Indian country. The Lynchburg Conference had attempted to impeach a preacher for getting married, revealing that Methodism really was a mission of poverty, chastity, and obedience.

Particularly pleasing was Asbury's first sight of the new Eutaw Street Church in Baltimore, which remained one of Methodism's largest and best equipped churches over the next century. Asbury dedicated the church during the General Conference and was buried under its pulpit eight years later. Not so pleasant was the oversight of the conference proceedings, concerning the ouster of a preacher for having been accused of fathering a child, and the receipt of a letter from Nathan Bangs warning of an impostor who claimed to be a Methodist missionary in lower Canada. Such were the issues of being a bishop, of which Asbury almost never made note in his journal or letters.

As Asbury traveled through Delaware, he made one of his few references to world events. There was unrest with both Britain and France. The Embargo Acts passed by Congress essentially banned trade with all foreign ships because Britain and France would not allow importation of goods from America. The American economy suffered, smuggling increased, and small ports such as New Haven and Newbern were all but shut down. Asbury commented, "O my soul, rest in God! I am sometimes led to think the whole world will rise up against the pretensions of England to the dominion of the seas. Will Bonaparte conquer the world? He may: but will he govern it, and reign universal emperor over sea and land? No, no, no. Here I rest" (2:567).

Henry Gough

The days just before the General Conference in Baltimore were filled with bittersweet moments. Asbury and other Methodist luminaries laid to rest their friend and benefactor Henry Gough. A wave of emotion swept over Asbury as he placed his hand on a dying man whom, in spite of his weaknesses, Asbury had grown to love. Though Asbury belittled both status and wealth, it was difficult not to be solicitous of one who had both and who still made a fervent commitment to Christianity. Gough attempted to lead his entire household to Christ. He held a chapel service each day and required attendance by all.

Once while intoxicated, Henry Gough and some friends had gone to hear Asbury preach. The friends responded with disdain, calling Asbury's sermon "nonsense." "No," said Gough, "what we have heard is the truth as it is in Jesus." Hearing the prayers and praises of a slave, Gough responded, "Alas, O Lord! I have my thousands and tens of thousands, and yet, ungrateful wretch that I am, I never thanked thee, as this poor slave does, who has scarcely clothes to put on, or food to satisfy his hunger."[14] Later in life, he exclaimed, "I have found the Methodist blessing. I have found the Methodist God!"[15]

Asbury explained that "Mr. Gough had inherited a large estate from a relation in England, and having the means, he indulged his taste for gardening, and the expensive embellishment of his county seat, Perry Hall, which was always hospitably open to visitors, particularly those who feared God" (2:569). Over a month later, on June 5, Asbury and George Roberts preached Gough's funeral to over two thousand people, so many that he "spoke long, and was obliged to speak loud that all might hear" (2:570).

The 1808 General Conference

The 1808 General Conference, which met for three weeks from May 6–26 in Baltimore, was the most influential gathering of Methodism Asbury chaired in his tenure as its leader. It produced a constitution for the denomination, assured the continuation of itinerating episcopacy, provided for a delegated General Conference, and elected its first American bishop. The entire conference was a test of Asbury's parliamentary skill, political entreaty, personal popularity, and stamina. Of the 129 members present, 63 were from the conferences of Baltimore and Philadelphia, leaving just over half of the conference's representation for the other five. Politically, American Methodism was in danger of being tipped over. Indeed, it almost was in the raging debate of the 1808 conference.

Asbury displayed his first deft maneuver when a member moved that a committee be appointed for the purpose of bringing to the floor regulations for a delegated General Conference. Four of the conferences had already moved for this type of representation, since the geographically closer conferences could flood the General Conference with eligible voters (as indeed they had this year). The geographically proximate conferences of Philadelphia, Baltimore, and Virginia had failed to address this "memorial" that had been handed them by the other conferences.

When the committee was proposed, Asbury moved that it consist of an equal number of members from each of the seven annual conferences. The motion passed, and two were chosen from each of the conferences, among them Ezekiel Cooper, Joshua Soule, Jesse Lee, and Philip Bruce.

Ezekiel Cooper was then 45 years old and had been the publishing agent for Methodism for the past ten years. Cooper was tall with angular good looks. He was the most erudite and learned person within American Methodism, devouring whatever books he could get his hands on. His contemporaries referred to him as an "encyclopedia."[16] In 1803, he had sufficient clout to reject Asbury's appointment of him to Baltimore. On July 24, 1803, Asbury wrote to Cooper, "You will take your turn with others, and as there was such unanimity in the vote of the Conference, it ought to have weight with you. As an individual your going or staying is nothing to me. I have no spleen against you" (3:267). And neither did Asbury have any authority over him, at least none that he could assert without causing more problems than it would solve. Furthermore, Asbury was indebted to Cooper for defending him against Jesse Lee's antagonism in 1794.[17]

When push came to shove, Asbury always knew when to stop; yet Cooper said of Asbury, "His manner of ruling and governing the church, we have fully known. Perhaps, we might, with propriety, say of him what Levy said of Cato, 'You would suppose that he was born for the very place and thing, in which he was employed and engaged.'"[18]

A Yankee Trick

The committee of fourteen selected a subcommittee of Cooper, Soule, and Bruce, each of whom was to draft a position paper for the committee to consider. Soule, Methodism's 29-year-old prodigy, would be elected bishop at the conference of 1820. Soule was "six feet tall and muscular, had wide cheek bones, a high forehead, and a head so large that it was necessary to have extra size hats manufactured for him."[19] Bruce was one of the oldest preachers present, having begun his ministry in 1781. Both Soule and Cooper produced papers calling for a delegated conference, but with different ideas for the episcopacy. Soule advocated a continuing itinerancy of two to three bishops; Cooper argued for a diocesan plan that would station a bishop in each conference, with the possibility of a single archbishop. Soule's plan was adopted, in spite of Cooper's opposition, and was presented to the conference. Here it was stalemated by Jesse Lee, who argued for a conference with delegates appointed on the basis of seniority rather than election, as Soule had proposed.[20]

After the debate had gone on for a day without resolution, Cooper sidetracked the business at hand by introducing a new issue for consideration. He made the following motion: "Each annual conference respectfully, without debate, shall annually choose by ballot its own presiding elders."[21] The motion thrust at Asbury's ecclesiastical jugular. The presiding elders were his lieutenants; they kept him informed, they hosted him on his visitations, they carried out his pet projects. They implemented his vision for pastoral care, which included supervision of the camp meetings. These undershepherds were appointed by Asbury and perceived themselves as obligated to him. It was probably this challenge more than any other that caused Asbury to write to Thomas Douglas, a presiding elder, on the day after conference began. "Such a deliberate attempt to take away the last remains of Episcopacy, deprives us of our privileges, wholesale and retail. Ah! have I lost the confidence of the American People and preachers? or of only a few overgrown members that have been disappointed? and the *city lords* who wish to be bishops, presiding elders, deacons, and to reign without us—over us?" (3:392).

The debate on Cooper's motion, which continued throughout Tuesday, was excruciating to Asbury. To his relief, it was defeated by a vote of 73 to 52. When the motion for a delegated General Conference was returned to the floor, it was also defeated, by a vote of 64 to 57. Asbury was "profoundly affected" and the legislative body was thrown into emotional disarray, with at least one person openly weeping. Many of the preachers threatened to leave. Asbury called for peace. With the support of McKendree and Elijah Hedding, Asbury persuaded the offended ministers to tarry one more day.[22]

They actually stayed until the following Monday, when the previous motion for a delegated conference was broken down into two proposals, regarding the "who" and the "how." Enoch George proposed the "who": "The General Conference shall be composed of one member for every five members of each annual conference." The motion carried by a large majority. As to the "how," Joshua Soule moved that each "Annual Conference shall have the power of sending their proportionate number of members to the General Conference, either by seniority or choice, as they shall think best."[23] The motion passed. Lee had gotten what he wanted, a delegated conference, but his proposed methodology was defeated. After the vote, he walked up to his friend, "poked him in the side with his finger and whispered, 'Brother Soule, you've played me a Yankee trick!'"[24]

A Republican Autocracy

Joshua Soule gave American Methodism more than a position paper: he gave it a constitution that has endured to this day. Of importance to Asbury and the continuation of the episcopacy were the six restrictive rules that limited the powers of the General Conference. Rules one and three stated: "1. The General Conference shall not revoke, alter, or change our Articles of Religion, nor establish any new standards or rules of doctrine contrary to our present existing and established standards of doctrine. . . . 3. They shall not change or alter any part or rule of our government, so as to do away episcopacy or destroy the plan of our itinerant general superintendency."[25]

The only way that substantive change could take place in the episcopal office was by a joint recommendation of all the annual conferences brought to the General Conference, which would require a two-thirds favorable vote. In other words, even though he was directly answerable to the General Conference, Asbury derived his power from the annual conferences made up of elders and delegated lay representatives. Joshua Soule had enabled Asbury to achieve a republican autocracy.

Methodism admitted only clergy as elders, but now both elders and bishops were subject to the people. H. Richard Neibuhr called Methodism a "constitutional autocracy," a joining of clergy and laity in a fashion that did not appear to violate democratic principles. "Despite the fact that Asbury often expressed an autocratic spirit, he nevertheless accommodated the character of the church to the new environment, and so enabled it to become the representative frontier denomination."[26]

William McKendree

Two other events of the 1808 conference affecting Asbury are worth noting. During the three weeks of conference, the preachers dispersed to local churches for preaching and public worship. On the first Sunday morning, William McKendree preached at Light Street Church with Asbury present. The church was packed, "the second gallery crowded with colored people." Nathan Bangs described the occasion:

I looked at him not without some feeling of distrust, thinking to myself: "I wonder what awkward backwoodsman they have put in the pulpit this morning to disgrace us with his mockish and uncouth phraseology?" . . . His introduction appeared tame, his sentences broken and disjointed, and his elocution very effective. . . . [T]he congregation was instantly overwhelmed with a shower of divine grace from the upper world. At first, sudden shrieks, as of persons in distress, were heard in different parts of the house, then shouts of praise, and in every direction sobs and groans. The eyes of the people overflowed with tears, while many were prostrated upon the floor or lay helpless on the seats. A very large, athletic looking preacher, sitting by my side, suddenly fell upon his seat, as if pierced by a bullet, and I felt my heart melting under emotions which I could not resist.[27]

Asbury predicted that the sermon would make McKendree a bishop. On the following Wednesday, McKendree defeated both Cooper and Lee, garnering 95 votes out of 128 cast. Asbury could not have been more pleased. Again the legislative process had elected someone who would know how to play second fiddle.

The second event called for both Asbury's initiative and his compromise, a compromise that would later devastate both the country and the church. The conference voted that the yearly annual conferences were to make their own regulations concerning the admission of slaveholders into the church. Further, slaveholding Methodist preachers forfeited their credentials if they were unwilling to emancipate their slaves according to the laws of the state. This was such an explosive issue, especially for the South, that Asbury moved that "[t]here be one thousand forms of Discipline prepared for the use of the South Carolina Conference in which the section and rule on slavery be left out."[28] There was almost no discussion, and the motion unanimously passed. "Here were two codes of Discipline, put forth as law by the same ecclesiastical legislature, and intended to operate for the promotion of unity and uniformity among the same people."[29] Methodism had constructed a house divided against itself, of which Asbury was the chief architect.

Undisputed Leader

Asbury came away from the 1808 conference as the undisputed leader of American Methodism. He had long understood himself to be *primus inter pares*, first among equals, though he did not use the term until 1813 (3:480). To many, it seemed that he operated on the premise of inequality between the presider and those over whom he presided. On at least one occasion, Asbury had written a letter suggesting the election of assistant bishops.[30] Asbury simply assumed leadership, especially with his fellow bishops. He took the initiative to form plans, divide territory, envision the future, and station the preachers. When he referred to himself as a "senior bishop," he believed the longevity, experience, and sacrifice that validated his authority. Even when his colleagues were elected to the church's highest office, in Asbury's mind they were still apprentices learning the ecclesiastical machinery. The year after McKendree was elected, Asbury wrote, "If we had another man of equal mind I could as cheerfully give up the stationing the ministry; this I must do a little longer, the work is too great for one man: it must be divided" (3:418).

Asbury assessed his superior authority as return on an investment. He had, in his own estimation, simply given more than anyone else had. To Joseph Benson he wrote in 1816, "With us a bishop is a plain man, altogether like his brethren, wearing no marks of distinction, advanced in age, and by virtue of his office can sit as president in all the solemn assemblies of the ministers of the gospel; and many times, if he is able, called upon to labor and suffer more than any of his brethren" (3:544–5).

Asbury epitomized sacrifice. He went without food, sleep, water, comfort, money, new clothes, sex, and all other normal parameters of pleasure. Of whatever he was accused, aristocracy or dictatorship (one epistle addressed him as Superior of the Methodist Society in the United States), Asbury was never accused of taking the easy way. His dogged determinism of blood, sweat, and perseverance was truly American anti-aristocracy, long before Lincoln split rails.

Asbury was the antithesis of Charles Woodmason, an Anglican pastor who refused to drop his gentlemanly persona, as well as his gown and wig, in the South Carolina heat.[31] Woodmason would not cross the social gulf between himself and the backcountry settlers. Asbury may have often been critical of his listeners, but Woodmason was almost constantly negative. Concerning the inhabitants of Granny Quarter Creek, he wrote, "They are the lowest Pack of Wretches my Eyes ever saw or that I have met with in these Woods—as wild as the very deer."[32] His prospective parishoners disliked him so much that they set fifty-seven dogs on him while he was leading worship. On another occasion, they dressed a man in clerical garb and put him in bed with a woman so that they could accuse Woodmason of adultery. All of this Woodmason blamed on the Presbyterians. "They delight in their present low, lazy, sluttish, heathenish, hellish Life and seem not desirous of changing it."[33]

Asbury's servanthood was not lost on his contemporaries, especially his fellow preachers. When Nicholas Snethen defended Asbury's leadership against James O'Kelly and William Hammet, he wrote,

> It is not his native country—it is not merely because he is a bishop;
> we think nothing of basic titles; but our preference is founded in a
> knowledge of the man and his communication. We have tried him

in all things, and we have always found him faithful to the trust reposed in him by us. In him we see an example of daily labour, suffering, and self-denial worthy the emulation of the young preacher. In a word, we have every reason to esteem him as a father, and not one reason to suspect or discard him as a tyrant or despot.[34]

Our Interest at Heart

Asbury's influence went beyond leadership by example. In public he may have appeared austere, a commander without rival. In private there flowed from him a spirit of caressing kindness. The older he got, the more he became an affectionate father, exhibiting a patronizing yet genuine concern that communicated the thought, "I care; I can help." This charisma was not lost on the host of ministers who had been initiated and mentored by their father in the gospel. When Benjamin Abbott had been intimidated while preaching before his peers he reported that, the morning after, "Brother Asbury stroked down my hair, and said, 'Brother Abbott, the black coats scared you last night.'"[35] When William Capers had volunteered to go to the mission areas of Mississippi and Alabama, Asbury responded, "Can't send you, Billy Sugar, you won't know how to take care of yourself."[36] Billy Hibbard said of Asbury, "He sat as a father among his children, believed by everyone. When he prayed, he was as one conversing with a venerable friend in which he seemed to have our interest at heart more than his own, and encouraged us all to draw nigh to God."[37]

At the 1804 General Conference in Baltimore, Elijah Hedding (later to become bishop) requested that because of his ill health he be sent to Saratoga, New York. After sending a note to Asbury he waited in anticipation for the bishop's response. Near the close of the conference, Asbury suddenly approached Hedding and, while rubbing the young preacher's ears "briskly," whispered that he was to be sent to New Hampshire. Indeed, when the appointments were read, Hedding was stationed in the newly organized New Hampshire district. Asbury had not only cushioned the appointment with a caress, but Hedding discovered his territory to be a "resting place."[38]

When Peter Cartwright heard about his appointment to the Marietta Circuit in Ohio, he was so distressed that he begged Asbury to send someone else. "The old father took me in his arms and said, 'O no, my son; go in the name of the Lord. It will make a man of you.'" Cartwright later recalled, "Oh thought I, if this is the way to make men, I do not want to be a man. I cried over it literally and prayed too, but on I started, cheered by my presiding elder."[39]

Sanctified Sympathies

Unlike many leaders, Asbury did not fear intimacy. He easily formed friendships that lasted and grew over the years. In spite of his businesslike persona, his

psyche had enough room to absorb the personalities of thousands of his followers. Late in life he stated, "Ah, I am a mere child now. The time has been, when I
got one good look at a man's face, I could know him anywhere."[40] Often this
recognition paid off in political loyalty, but never can it be said that his relationships were a means to an end. He was often affectionate to those who had little to
offer him politically. When Henry Willis died, Asbury "kissed and encircled in
his arms the six orphaned children of his departed friend, and blessed them in the
name of the Lord, and prayed with them."[41]

Asbury was particularly fond of the United Brethren founder, Martin Boehm.
Boehm's son recalled, "Bishop Asbury and my father gave to each other the kiss
of affection, and mutually encircled each other in their arms."[42] Christian
NewComer, a United Brethren preacher, recalled his last departure from Asbury:
"This morning I took my leave from this man of God; he embraced me in his
arms, bid me carry his kind respects to Wm. Otterbein, his dearly beloved brother
as he expressed himself."[43]

Asbury's charm was disarming to all but his severest critics. Those who
knew him best loved him most. Nicholas Snethen recalled, as a traveling companion, that no one could be more agreeable. "[H]e was cheerful, almost to
gaiety; his conversation was sprightly, and sufficiently seasoned with wit and
anecdote. His manners and disposition in every family were all suavity and
sweetness."[44]

William Capers (later bishop in the Methodist Episcopal Church South),
who was spending a night with Asbury, assured him that he would have a fire
built when the bishop got up. Even though Capers, on that extremely cold night,
had used no blankets so that he would not oversleep, he failed to arise as early as
Asbury. He discovered that the bishop had already built a roaring fire. It "tickled
the Bishop," who had done his best to let the young man sleep. The one-upmanship
was particularly gleeful, since Capers had tried to build a fire the night before but
found the wood too damp. "And there was that Bishop Asbury," he said, "whom
I've heard called austere: a man, confessedly, who never shed tears, and who seldom laughed, but whose sympathies were nevertheless as soft as a sanctified spirit
might possess."[45]

One of Asbury's contemporaries remarked that he "seemed born to sway
men."[46] One cannot sway others without holding with them common values and
common goals. The mind that bound Asbury and a band of self-sacrificial men
together derived its source from a higher allegiance. His co-workers observed this
allegiance in both word and deed. Both he and they were constrained by the love
of Christ. This common affection was sufficient bond for both leader and followers. Effectiveness added to affection served only to strengthen their commitment
to God and to one another. Americans will follow just about anyone who is
effective, even if the payoff is slow in coming.

One more note on the 1808 conference should be made: It appropriated a thousand dollars to buy tracts, most of which would be distributed by Asbury and his traveling companion. The difference between a king and a colporteur would be lost only on Asbury's most biased detractors.

17. "Live and Die a Poor Man"

Increasing Sentimentality

Asbury traversed Maryland during the month of June with the echoes of the 1808 General Conference reverberating in his mind. He was grateful for the transition from the city into the rolling hillsides. Return visits to churches and persons of years past were times of veneration. No matter how feeble Asbury was, he was requested to preach. "I am kept at work by my friends; but they do what they can, Methodists and others, to pay me an affection, in attentions, in honour; Lord keep me humble and holy!" (2:571). The General Conference appointed Henry Boehm as Asbury's traveling companion, and he would become the man who served longest in that capacity. It was a congruent fit. Asbury was partial to Methodism's German friends, and especially to Martin Boehm, Henry's father. He admired both their piety and theological vigor. Henry preached fluently in both English and German and was largely responsible for translating the Methodist Discipline into German in 1807.[1] In 1814, Asbury would write to Jacob Gruber, "I am your feeble Father; and let it be known that, one of the grand acts of his life, was a capital mission to the American Germans; but lived not to finish it" (3:505).[2]

During the first full week of June, traveling was deterred by a deluge of rain, which gave Asbury the opportunity to read more of Wesley's sermons. Detainment tried his patience. The damp houses aggravated his arthritic rheumatism. Trying to concentrate with aching joints was extremely difficult.

By the time Asbury and Boehm arrived in Fayette County in central Pennsylvania, Asbury's arthritis demanded they spend the week at John Brightwell's. "I am fairly arrested in my course; my knees and feet are so disabled that I am lifted to bed. I can neither ride, stand, nor walk" (2:574). Seven months later, Asbury wrote to Mrs. Brightwell, "[M]y affliction at your house excelled, and I was afraid that I might have spoken or done something that might have grieved your mind, as you had to run to my help all hours of day and night, and in cases the most delicate even to lift me off the stools" (3:405). Asbury had somewhat recovered by the time he reached Ohio, but the pain at times was so excruciating that he wanted to "cry out." Asbury decreed never to visit the West again during the summer because of the heat and small green flies—another vow that he was unable to keep.

From Cincinnati there was a brief foray into Indiana, Asbury's only visit there. By the time he arrived in the Lexington area of Kentucky, he had to sit while preaching. The humid, hot air made breathing difficult. During the three weeks in Kentucky, Benjamin Lakin's wife traveled as Asbury's nurse. Asbury rendezvoused with McKendree at Liberty Hill, just outside Nashville, where they jointly chaired the Western Conference. Since the area west of the Appalachians was officially McKendree's territory, the new bishop took the lead making the appointments. His method of consulting the presiding elders in the stationing process was a bit unsettling for Asbury (2:580). McKendree placated Asbury by explaining that he was not as confident or capable in the matter as was his more experienced brother.

Two hundred miles east, Asbury recorded, "My sufferings have been great. I had the piles, and pains of body, and sultry weather, crowded houses and rough roads, and bad men for company; but my mind enjoyed great peace, notwithstanding my starting, stumbling horse, that ever and anon would run away with me" (2:580). At Sevierville, Tennessee, James Riggin, who had served Asbury as a guide twenty years before, traveled twenty miles to see the bishop. "[H]e wept over me and bade farewell" (2:581). It was a scene that would become more frequent.

As Asbury aged, he reminisced and became more sentimental. He almost always requested to visit the grave of a departed friend; he was especially solicitous of those who had befriended him in years gone by. He was also keenly aware of any unfinished personal business. At the November 1808 camp meeting outside of Camden, South Carolina, Asbury was reconciled to William Capers's father, from whom he had been estranged for seventeen years because of the William Hammet schism. Capers recorded, "On my father's entering the tent, he (Asbury) rose hastily from his seat and met him with his arms extended and they embraced each other with mutual emotion."[3] The reconciliation may have been partially the result of Asbury's resolution made on November 21: "This day I renew my covenant with God; to do nothing I doubt is not lawful, and at all times, and in all places to live as if it were my last hour—may God help me so to do!" (2:583). Settling relational accounts became all the more compelling with age.

Conference with the accompanying camp meeting took place near Milledgeville, Georgia, between Christmas and the last day of the year. Sixteen preachers were received on trial, including William Capers ("Billy Sugar"), who would eventually become a bishop. On December 31, Asbury preached to "three thousand people" for the love feast, a "monsterly" sermon, according to Boehm. It had been a good year for Asbury. Numerically, Methodism's exponential growth had begun to taper off. The century's first quadrennium had shown a 48,000 increase in membership, while the second was almost 10,000 fewer. Nevertheless, as Asbury glanced around Charleston, a city which he had often despised and belittled, there was reason for gratitude. "Some may think it no great matter to build two churches, buy three lots, pay fifteen hundred dollars of bank debt, and raise a growing society: this has been done in this Sodom in less than twenty-four years:—O Lord, take thou the glory!" (2:584).

Mental Lapses

The itinerant party of Asbury, Boehm, and McKendree traveled from Charleston to Tarboro, North Carolina, where they opened the Virginia Conference on February 1, 1809. The numbers were not encouraging, which Asbury attributed to racial prejudice both inside and outside the church. Most gratifying was a fraternal greeting from a society that had formed within the Virginia State Penitentiary under the leadership of the presiding elder Stith Mead. A revival had resulted in the conversion of forty prisoners. Their leader, Moses Joshua, wrote that "Mead appeared to be engaged for our own good with such fervency and sympathy as very much affected us and convinced us that he was more a friend to us than we had been to ourselves."[4]

The weather in North Carolina had been unseasonably warm, but turned cold as Asbury and company rode toward Virginia. The senior bishop lamented over the languishing state of religion, yet he was encouraged by the "manly yet meek" young men in the incoming class of preachers. According to Asbury, they were "elegant candidates in both mind and body." Ironically, Methodism could boast when God used the lowly and also when He chose the courtly. Legitimation was at least partly served by God's not always calling the second best.

The trip through Methodism's "garden" flooded Asbury with memories. Riding by the graves of Henry and Prudence Gough, visiting Barratt's Chapel, reuniting with Governor and Mrs. Bassett, were reminders of relationships that were quickly passing. Conference opened at Philadelphia on April 2. Since the General Conference had ordered all annual conferences to meet for at least a week, much of the time was spent in petty political wrangling and trivializing. The issues held little interest for the man who had presided over 250 of these regional meetings. Philadelphia, with the split at St. George's, had become a cacophony of conflicting opinions. Asbury penned, "I am not conscious of indulging or feeling wrong tempers in the mighty work at which I daily labour; but I never wish to meet the conference in the city of Philadelphia again" (2:596).

Asbury's patience was running short. Compounded with his physical infirmities, this made it more difficult for him to focus. His mind drifted; he dozed or simply chose to think about other matters. A month before the Philadelphia Conference, Asbury chaired the Baltimore Conference at Harrisonburg, Virginia. During the session he mumbled about the difficulty of stationing the preachers. At one point, he blurted out, "I would not give one single preacher for a half-dozen married ones."[5] When the married preachers started asking for locations, Asbury asked their reason. When told that he had offended them by his statement, Asbury denied having said it. "Well brethren forgive me, I will say it back."[6] Such mental lapses led Asbury to conclude that he needed to give up parliamentarian oversight. On October 22, 1809, he wrote to Jacob Gruber, "I have prevailed upon Bishop McKendree to preside on all the Conferences, it is with plea-sure and peace I retire" (3:417–8). However, it was simply another futile attempt at relinquishment.

Asbury's trip through New Jersey was rewarding. He visited places that he had not seen in twenty-five years and perceived a renewed spiritual vigor. On Staten Island, Asbury visited his old friend and former traveling companion Tho-mas Morrell. Here Asbury also made one of his few technological observations: "My attention was strongly excited by the steamboat: this is a great invention" (2:601).

Asbury found the New York Conference which convened on May 10 to be a trying time. Among other problems, several of the preachers were tried for mis-conduct. The pressing business and a large number of private conferences per-mitted only about five hours of fitful sleep a night. Asbury was so preoccupied with the church's affairs that he made no mention of a fire that broke out on the day after they arrived in New York, destroying about thirty houses. Out of the twelve deacons that were ordained, the conference reproved one of them because he was "too funny."[7]

This trip into New England was unusually warm; the beads of sweat rolled off Asbury's face. His winter garb of wool was poorly suited for the heat. Also, there was trouble with Asbury's horse, which twice bolted. Unable to control the chaise, Asbury called for Henry Boehm to take over while he mounted Henry's horse. Boehm's comment that he had no trouble controlling the horse would lead one to believe that Asbury was losing his equestrian touch. As the pair made their way up the Hudson Valley, they were accompanied by Daniel Hitt and Abner Chase. The heat and humidity smothered both man and beast. At a rest stop, Asbury spread some almonds on a tree stump and said a prayer, a blessing fit for a state dinner, after which the hungry preachers devoured their lunch.[8]

No Possessions or Babes

At Fort Walcott, just west of Newport, Asbury preached to the soldiers at the request of Captain Lloyd Beale, the commanding officer. Beale was also moderator of the corporation that operated the church at Newport. "I saw discipline, order, correctness; it was grand and pleasing" (2:604). Asbury's vi-sion for the church often took the form of a military encampment demanding discipline and privation. On this occasion, an eyewitness observed: "Bishop Asbury was thin in flesh and feeble in body in his manner, preaching he was calm and dispassionate in his discussion but when he became animated in his applications he was uncommonly energetic and he would raise his solemn and majestic voice in its highest note it sounds more like peals of thunder than any human voice I ever heard."[9]

Perspiration soaked Asbury's clothes as he rode to "wretched" Waltham, Massachusetts. At midnight he felt impressed to visit Lynn, Massachusetts.[10] There he discovered that "[t]here have been awful times here for two years past; the preachers are a burden—they do not preach evangelically, do not visit families, neglect the classes" (2:605). On the way to the New England Conference, the ecclesiastical party sang and preached at a tavern. The gathering was so congenial that the proprietor tore up the bill. Asbury moderated the New England Conference, which opened at Gloucester, Maine, on June 15. His earlier decision to relinquish parliamentarian leadership to the junior bishop was apparently forgotten; McKendree interpreted it as a lack of trust. A month later, Asbury wrote to Thomas Douglas that McKendree had gone west "through a dreary wilderness in but ill health; he seems exceedingly displeased with himself; perhaps it is best, the people think so high of him. But I am sorry to see him so cast down at times under the weight of the work."[11]

On July 16, Asbury and Boehm arrived at Auburn, New York, where they were held up by the rain. Asbury noted the slow progress of the Presbyterians, who were not able to hold up under the onslaught of Methodist camp meetings. "O, the terrors of a camp meeting to those *men of pay and show!*" (2:609). In spite of the rain, they made their way another six miles to spend the night in a "twelve feet square cabin."

Asbury estimated that he had traveled two thousand miles in the last three months, over rocks, fallen trees, and flooded roads, while enduring the lack of decent lodging. "I have no possessions or babes to bind me to the soil; what are called the comforts of life I rarely enjoy; the wish to live an hour such a life as this would be strange to so suffering, so toilworn a wretch" (2:609). They called on a house in a pelting wind and rainstorm. On asking for lodging, they were refused. Rejection was tough on Asbury's ego; a denial in moments of emergency was even more searing.

When Asbury commented on Sunday, July 23, that Henry Boehm had upset the sulky, breaking the shaft, Boehm responded that it was a wonder "we" had not upset it twenty times before. "It was well I was in the sulky instead of the old bishop, or he might have fared hard. He might have had something worse than a broken shaft: a broken limb or a broken neck."[12] Boehm later commented that traveling with the bishop was something other than "playing the gentleman." The past year had been "toil, intense toil, as much so as soul and body could bear."[13]

On July 28, Asbury and Boehm parted so that the latter could spend a few days with his parents. He did not catch up with Asbury until August 3 at Fort Littleton, Pennsylvania. Boehm felt a tinge of guilt at what he encountered. "I found him in a sad plight. He was not able to stand, preach, kneel, or pray. He needed both a travelling companion and a nurse. Suffering from rheumatism, he had applied several blisters to relieve him."[14]

If I Was Young

After a tortuous ride over the Alleghenies, Asbury and Boehm reached Pike Run camp meeting, where they were reunited with McKendree. The senior bishop preached only once, while McKendree preached four times. As the rain and wind pelted Asbury's tent, he pondered 2 Samuel 11:11: "And Uriah said unto David, 'The ark, and Israel and Judah, abide in tents; and my lord Jacob, and the servants of my lord are encamped in the open fields; and I then go into mine house to eat and to drink, and to lie with my wife? As thou livest, and as thy soul liveth, I will not do this thing.'" Asbury had raised up a host of preachers willing to "tent in the wilderness," and at the same time, he desired men with the decorum of well-mannered house guests. Such a combination was hard to find.

It was no doubt the rough-hewn and sometimes crude Jacob Gruber of whom Asbury commented when he spoke at the courthouse in Bedford, Pennsylvania: "There was but one indecorous thing observed; a presiding elder put his feet upon the banister of my pulpit whilst I was preaching; it was like thorns in my flesh until they were taken down" (2:611). Even when Asbury's English sensibilities were offended, he quickly recovered. Because of Gruber's fluency in his native German tongue, Asbury valued him highly. Asbury wrote to Gruber stating that he prayed for him twice a day.

On Asbury's last trip to the West in 1815, the two met in western Pennsylvania. Gruber climbed into the bishop's carriage for one last mentoring session. Asbury exhorted: "O, if I was young I would cry aloud, I would lift up my voice like a trumpet! O what pride, conforming to the world and following its fashions! Many of our people are going to ruin! Warn them, warn them for me, while you have strength and time, and be faithful to your duty."[15]

This was not a problem for Gruber. When Alfred Brunson, who later became a Methodist preacher, heard Gruber preach on November 27, 1808, he recorded, "I heard Rev. Jacob Gruber preach. He told me of all my sins and he was so clear and definite in it that if it had been possible for anyone of the town to have known me, I should have taken it for granted that someone had told him about me."[16]

Dip, Dive, and Go

South of St. Clairsville, Ohio, the terrain was so rough that the strain broke both the breast band and shaft of the sulky. Asbury and Boehm continued south on horseback and by September 13 had reached Peter Pelham's home at Xenia. Here Asbury rested a couple of days, catching up on letter writing and reading Wesley's sermons. He penned William McKendree a letter concerning those men who had come to be known as the "reformers," who wanted to make the church more republican by lessening the bishop's power. Asbury expressed his rancor especially for James Smith (Baltimore Smith) as one of the "un-accountables as all heretics and schismatics generally are, they dash at the most sacred truths, holiest characters and say [they] are not in sport" (3:414). Actually, James Smith was a preacher of "fervor and pathos," possessed high intellect, and was an especially able debater. James Armstrong, later a secretary of the Baltimore Conference, referred to James Smith as "eloquent in speech, charming in manners, social disposition and constant in his friendship."[17] Holiness did not prevent Asbury from evaluating those around him.

The Western Conference, which opened on October 2 in Cincinnati, was the first west of the Alleghenies and north of the Ohio River. On the first Sunday, there were "three thousand present" to hear four different preachers. Asbury recorded nothing of the conference, other than saying he gave full disclosure of his finances. Ordained were William Winans as deacon and Peter Cartwright and Samuel Parker as elders. Winans distinguished himself as a missionary to the extreme western parts of the newly acquired Louisiana Territory. Parker, because of his rich musical voice and eloquence, was later called the Cicero of the West. The highlight of the conference was Parker's sermon on Philippians 3:10 on the final Sunday, of which Asbury made no mention. Boehm said that "[t]he word ran through the audience like electricity, tears flowed, and shouts were heard."[18] Parker died ten years later at the age of 45 from "consumption," while serving as a missionary to Mississippi.

On November 28, Asbury preached in a log cabin "scarcely fit for a stable" to a group of soldiers who were stationed at Great Falls, South Carolina. Later in the week, he baptized Elizabeth Asbury Jenkins, daughter of James, whose preaching was so "thundering" he was known as "Bawling Jenkins." Jenkins was an incendiary zealot of the first order. In 1802, he had written Asbury, "Hell is trembling and Satan's kingdom is falling. Through Georgia, South and North Carolina, the sacred flame and holy fire of God, amidst all the opposition, is extending far and wide."[19]

The road toward Charleston had been reduced to gutters of mud. "We had the swamp to pass, and dip, dive, and go—we laboured through it" (2:622). In reference to the trade embargo, Asbury mused as he rode into Charleston, "Where does the cotton go, that arrives in such quantities? To England and France, in spite of the non-intercourse. I am mainly ignorant of these things, and have no wish to be wiser" (2:622). The proceedings at the South Carolina conference pleased the bishop. His last recorded act for the year included praying for his lodging host and giving him some medicine "which procured his ease" (2:623). He was ever the physician to both soul and body.

Acceptance by the Establishment

On January 5, 1810, Asbury, McKendree, and Boehm rode into North Carolina, where Asbury preached at Edenton to only twelve men and six women because of a snowstorm. Boehm, then 35 years old, took a cold that almost cost him his life. "For a fortnight I had high fevers every night; and then riding all day in the cold, my sufferings were intolerable. I became so weak that I had to be helped to my horse, and then, though I could hardly set upon him, rode thirty and forty miles a day with cold winds beating upon me."[20] Just south of Petersburg, Virginia, Boehm was so ill that he lay on a log and tried to persuade the bishop to leave him there to die. While the Virginia Conference was in session, McKendree became Boehm's nurse. "He administered medicine to me and watched over me with all the kindness of a father."[21]

Again the trip through Delaware and Maryland stirred Asbury's emotions. At the Smyrna Cemetery he commented, "Here moulder my friends of thirty years past." At Green's Chapel in Canterbury, he noted, "Most of my old friends in this quarter have fallen asleep; but their children are generally with me, and the three generations baptized" (2:633). Where there had been rejection, there was now acceptance by the establishment; "rich, too, thirty years ago, would not let me approach them; now I must visit them and preach to them" (2:635). Asbury and McKendree chaired the Philadelphia Conference at Easton, which was accompanied by a camp meeting. "What a grand and gracious time we have had!" (2:635).

People Call Me by My Name

As the weather improved, so did Asbury's health. On Friday (his normal day of fast), June 1, he went without food for twenty-four hours. With improved health there was improved preaching. On the following Sunday: "I think my words pierced the hearts of some like a sword. I neither spared myself nor my hearers" (2:639). The next Sunday, Asbury testified to the manifest power of the Word. Two days later at Somerset "I gave them a discourse—it was close preaching" (2:639).

On Sunday, June 24, Asbury preached three times, something he had not done in years. It rained so hard in Hartford, Connecticut, that Boehm joked that they were "like Noah's dove; had no place for the sole of our foot."[22] At Ruben Farley's place in the Catskill Mountains, Farley's wife complained that Asbury was not always accessible because of the crowd around him. "I told her that all who wished to see me might be indulged in the back settlement—a cabin has not always two rooms" (2:643).

On July 15, Asbury and McKendree launched the Genesee Conference in the town of Cazenovia, New York, which was previously a part of the Philadelphia Conference. Some doubted a bishop's authority to convene a conference, among them Jesse Lee and James Smith, the latter referring to Asbury's "dotage and increasing infirmities." The 1796 Discipline had granted bishops authority to appoint other yearly conferences in intervals of the General Conference. At its 1805 meeting, the Genesee Conference stormed the town of Lyons, New York, knocking on every door in the town as well as the local tavern. The evangelistic foray converted forty people. It was Methodism at its best.

Boehm and the bishop made their way southwest through Lancaster, York, Shippensburg, and Chambersburg, Pennsylvania. The normally precarious trip over the mountains through a path called the Northumberland Road required Asbury to ride on horseback and Boehm in the sulky, from which he was thrown. His leg was badly injured and bothered him for months. Asbury wrote, "O, what a life is this? My aid is lame, and I'm obliged to drive. People call me by my name as they pass me on the road, and I hand them a religious tract in German or English; or I call at a door for a glass of water, and leave a little pamphlet. How may I be useful?" (2:646).

I Cannot Do without Them

Asbury constantly felt compelled to set an example of sacrificial faithfulness, played out in miniscule details. On August 10, he wrote Lewis Meyers from Chambersburg, Pennsylvania, "We are losing the spirit of missionaries and martyrs, we are slothful, we can only tell how fields were won, but by our brethren and sisters, not by us" (3:433). The critique carried the contradiction of a coach or commander who never suggests that the players' performance is good enough. The next day he wrote to Christopher Frye, "The present year hitherto had been remarkable for conferences, congregations, crowds; building houses beyond any former year: woods meeting, campmeetings, quarterly meetings, multitudes! multitudes!" (3:435).

At Bedford, Pennsylvania, Asbury suspected the local circuit rider was not doing his duty. At Brownsville Camp he warned those who were spreading lies about McKendree, threatening to publish their names. Accusations of power-mongering continued to dog Asbury. The anti-bishop party persisted in the "poison of electioneering." The nagging suspicions of Asbury's misuse of funds continued. He addressed it twice on August 11, in letters to Henry Smith and Christopher Frye. "It is no small matter to support 2 men and horses one fourth of our time at Publick expenses, swimming, wading deep waters, hanging over hazardous rocks, black swamps, mountains" (3:434).

The negative aspects of the task were overwhelming. "I lament the ill health of Bishop McKendree, may I never be called back to hold the chairs of annual conferences. I retired for life. The Bishop's stomach and bowels fail, but he has gone on to Missouri, if he does not droop or die by the way" (3:436). As usual, Asbury pulled himself up by his own bootstraps, mustering a bit of defiant seniority mixed with humility: "I was made before *they* were; before some forward children were born or born again. I cannot cast them off. I cannot do without them, if they can do without me. I must continue in the ship, *storm* or *calm*, near the helm, or before the mast. As long as I can, I will be with them" (3:439).

Asbury's health was so good that he reveled in his ability to read and think. It was a delight when he was asked to baptize a baby (something he frequently did) named Joseph Asbury, his father's name. He went out of his way with no little effort to make it to a camp meeting in the Little Kenawaha [Kanawha] Valley of West Virginia. The bishop loved camp meetings and received great veneration when he dropped in for a day or two. Literally hundreds of thousands heard him preach during the last fifteen years of his life. Though enthusiasm for the camp meeting was great, he was not entirely ignorant of its many liabilities, which he had personally experienced. "Lord, prepare me by thy grace for the patient endurance of hunger, heat, labour, the clownishness of ignorant piety, the impudence of the impious, unreasonable preachers, and more unreasonable heretics and heresy!" (2:648).

Farewell Tones

From the camp, Asbury and Boehm crossed the Ohio River at Belpee, Ohio, where they found lodging at a Mr. Browning's. Their host's wife, who was from Connecticut, tried to impress her visitors by enumerating the religious refinements she had left behind: able preachers, elegant meeting houses, pews, organs, and trained choirs. She had left the culture of the East for the impoverishment of the West. The bishop was aware of the contrast. "O yes," responded Asbury,

> O Connecticut for all the world!
> A fine house and a high steeple
> A learned priest and a gay people.

When Mrs. Browning asked the bishop where he lived, Asbury answered, "No foot of land do I possess. No cottage in the wilderness, a poor wayfaring man."[23]

Asbury and Boehm quickly passed through Tennessee and took the Chattahoochee Trail across the mountains into North Carolina.[24] It was a new route, with a new route's accompanying challenges. Asbury referred to the Chattahoochee River, which he crossed by walking on a log, as a "foaming, roaring stream, which hid the rocks" (2:654). After they crossed Cove Creek Gap at over four thousand feet altitude, Asbury's whole body ached. He recovered enough to preach on Sunday at Newton Academy. "Had I known and studied my congregation for a year, I could not have spoken more appropriately to their particular cases" (2:655).

Asbury reveled in the hospitality he received in South Carolina, whether from Methodists or non-Methodists. It had become a place that was truly home to him. Conference opened Saturday, December 22, in Columbia at the home of Thomas Taylor, a United States Senator who was not a Methodist.[25] Asbury's opening address was in the farewell tones that increasingly marked the preaching of a man who had been in the ministry for a half century. Every conference keynote would become a valedictory, stirring the emotions of those who listened to the wrinkled, emaciated minister who had fathered them in the faith. The last day of the year, he and Boehm set off in the hail and rain, in spite of Asbury's severe bowel attack the day before. South Carolina and Methodism were now different, but Asbury was unchanged.

In the preceding January, Asbury had written to Thomas Douglas, "If we have no other mark of apostles, we shall have poverty, reproach, and hard labour."[26] It was Asbury's rule for ministry, which began with himself. He was convinced that experience, veneration, seniority, and "paying one's dues" would not lead a minister to economic luxury. Asbury would continue to validate his authority by a Spartan self-denial. There were to be no financial rewards, either for the responsibility he bore or for his length of service in the episcopal office. In 1807, Asbury wrote Mrs. Charles Ridgley, "It cannot be supposed that one hundred fifty dollars per year is sufficient. My highest claim from the 7 conferences, being twenty-four Dollars each to buy my clothing, horses and carriage, and to pay all my expenses in Traveling five thousand miles a year."[27] On May 12, 1811, he reported his income to Thomas Coke: "25 dollars from each of the 8 conferences, to feed 2 horses, travelling expenses, quarterage for me and my aid and my aid feels independent also, that if there is a deficiency it will come out of our own pockets" (3:449).

Egalitarian Ecclesiasticism

Asbury experienced the same kinds of financial hardships as his preachers. In the first six months that Jacob Gruber spent in ministry, he earned $5.60, almost starving. When William Burke was appointed to the Scott River Circuit, "A four week circuit, and between four and five hundred miles around," he received nothing except "hard times." He reported, "I was reduced to the last pinch. My clothes were nearly all gone. I had patch upon patch, and patch by patch. I received money only sufficient to buy a waist coat, and not enough of that to pay for the making during the two quarters I remained on the circuit."[28] During the first year of his ministry, James Jenkins received $22, and James Quinn estimated that at the end of his ministry he was in arrears for salary and expenses about $2,600 dollars.

Historian John Wigger states that in Asbury, "Methodists saw themselves, or rather their ideal of themselves."[29] Asbury expected an unencumbered, light-footed, highly mobile army of gospel troops, and he would lead the way. Boehm said that Asbury listed his equipment as a horse, saddle and bridle, one suit of clothes, a watch, a pocket Bible, and a hymnbook. "Henry, we must study what we can do without."[30] William Watters wrote in 1806 that, of all men he had known, Asbury was "the clearest of the love of money, and the most free to give away his all in every sense of the word."[31]

George Roberts commented, "I sometimes thought that he carried his deadness to the world too far, and entrusting to the care of divine providence over him was rather presumptuous in slighting the abiding means, by a kind of negligence almost peculiar to himself, and so much so sometimes that he must have really suffered in all human probability, if it had not been for the providential care of his friends who knew him well."[32] Roberts was accurate in his assessment that Asbury entrusted his circumstances to Providence and encouraged his preachers to do the same. He prayed, "If it is best for us and for the church that we should be cramped and straitened, let the people's hands and hearts be closed. If it is better for us—for the Church—and more to thy glory that we should abound in the comforts of life, do thou dispose the hearts of those we serve to give accordingly; and may we learn to be content, whether we abound or suffer need."[33]

Appropriate Dress

Asbury sought to exhibit frugality, especially in dress. His clothes were plain— that is, free of excess design and ornamentation. At times, when others noticed the excessive wear of his clothes, they took the liberty to re-outfit him. He would exchange new for old and requested that the old be passed on to a needy preacher. Even though Asbury feared "the dandy" and criticized preachers who wore pantaloons rather than straight breeches with "knee buckle and gaiters,"[34] he was somewhat fastidious about his dress, above all, desiring to look neat. To George Roberts, in 1801, he wrote, "I beg leave to suggest if I am to have a suit of clothes that they may be my own colour light blue, the excessive heat of this country, and we being so exposed perpetually to the sun, it must be so for my health and the important work to the east" (3:206).

Asbury's dress was theologically correct as well as being adapted to the climate. "I wonder how an ambassador of Jesus Christ can choose black for the color of his garment, when there is no analogy between that color and the glad tidings of great joy which he is commanded to proclaim to a lost world."[35] At one time Asbury requested of George Roberts to provide him clothing of buckskin rather than velvet, though there is no evidence that Roberts granted the request. When considering two coats, one for travel and another for dress, he decided on one. "I have changed my mind about two coats. I intend to have a bath cloak of black or white, and have it short so as just to touch the pommel of the saddle and to cover my arms" (3:238). In spite of Asbury's commitment to frugality he was often frustrated by lack of clothing and, more often, frustrated by clothing of the wrong kind, especially for the variety of weather that he encountered.

A Stewardship of Accountability

Going without basic amenities and the deliberate acceptance of meager circumstances defined Asbury's lifestyle. On September 21, 1809, he and Boehm had stayed at Daniel Baker's, just south of Dayton, Ohio. "I slept about five hours last night: I had excessive labour, a crowd of company, and hogs, dogs, and other annoyances to weary me" (2:615). In the mountainous area of Pennsylvania, near Eckland Township, he and Boehm had stayed in the cabin of John Brown, a mountain hermit. Boehm said that he had never felt more grateful than in the humble cabin of Brown, who "cheerfully divided his coarse fare with us," especially since the pair had only two dollars between them.

Asbury exhibited a stewardship of accountability. Coke and Asbury's *Annotated Notes* to the 1798 Discipline stipulated that "[t]he public money should be applied with the greatest fidelity. The account should be examined with the strictest scrutiny."[36] The insolvency of the conferences was a constant burden. Asbury did whatever was in his power to see that Methodism met its financial obligations, both to its own and to others. The conferences with surplus money were to provide financially for those who came up short. Rarely did a conference finish a year in the black, much to Asbury's chagrin. As to the eighty-dollar-per-year goal set for a minister's salary, Asbury commented, "[W]e seriously doubt whether it has ever been paid to more than one-sixth of our number of preachers, and that only in the most wealthy parts of our work" (3:527).

Asbury established the "mite subscription," a system of collecting one dollar each from as many individuals as possible in order to take care of the more destitute preachers. Freeborn Garrettson in his bicentennial sermon recalled Asbury requesting a "mite" from one of his friends. When offered more, the bishop replied that he would not "take more than one dollar from one person."[37] The friend then offered to give as many names as he had dollars. The practice was so habitual with Asbury and so embedded in his unconscious that on his deathbed he asked for a reading of the mite description, a list of donors, which he always carried with him.

For Asbury, Methodism was called to maintain its social affinity with the poor. He often refused to accept money from the poor. When a sixty-year-old woman, who earned her living in South Carolina by picking "oakum," brought to him a French crown because she was distressed "on my account," he refused it.[38] In Nansemond, Virginia, in 1780, the congregation took up a collection for him, but Asbury refused it. "[A] man offered me a silver dollar, but I could not take it, lest they should say I came for money" (1:353). Until 1800, preachers were not to accept fees for weddings, and if they did, they were to turn them over to the steward of the quarterly meeting. When Asbury was offered money for preaching funerals, which he often conducted, he refused it.

Asbury was delighted when he could travel a great distance on little money and grieved when his limited budget was drained for food and lodging. At times the resources were so low that he had to ask a particular conference for money. Nevertheless there were those who thought he carried around a plenteous supply. "One of my friends wanted to borrow or beg £50 of me: he might as well have asked me for Peru. I showed him all the money I had in the world—about twelve dollars, and gave him five" (2:227). When he chaired the Western Conference in 1806 the preachers were in such dire need that Asbury parted with his watch, coat, and shirt.

It is not surprising that sometimes Asbury was financially embarrassed. After being ferried across Deep River in Randolph County, North Carolina, he was unable to pay his fare. The ferryman cursed him because he had not a silver shilling (1:368). Despite often refusing money, Asbury was still at the mercy of handouts, especially from his rich friends such as Henry Gough and Henry Foxall. In 1807 he wrote, "[I]t cannot be supposed that 150 dollars per year is sufficient . . . to buy me clothing, horses and carriage, and to pay all my expenses in traveling 5000 miles a year. If I had not here and there a friend like mama Ridgely."[39]

When Asbury was at Governor Courtland's home in Peakeskill, New York, he confessed to Billy Hibbard that he had not sufficient means to pay the ferry fee across the Croton River. Before parting Hibbard attempted to give Asbury all the money he had, twenty shillings, except for "two and six pense." Because he didn't want his bishop begging money, Hibbard persuaded Asbury to accept the gift. "I thought myself well paid in being in his company so long and receiving so many lessons of instruction and good counsel from so great a Christian as he was."[40]

On the Defensive

Asbury was extremely sensitive to the accusations that he was storing up the monetary rewards of the episcopacy. He regularly sent money to his mother, and after his mother's death, to John Dickens's widow. Some of his friends included him in their wills, the monies from which he deposited in his own name for future ministry use. Supporters gave him gifts for specific projects within the church. By the end of his life Asbury had amassed a savings of two thousand dollars, which he left entirely to the church. There is no evidence that he ever used money for personal luxury. William Watters came to his friend's defense.

> Where is all that he has been heaping up for near these forty years? I confess if this was his object, he has stood so high in the

estimation of many that he might have accumulated considerably by this time, but is it so? Where is it? I have been as long, and as intimately acquainted with him as most men in America, and I must give this testimony, of all men that I have known he is in my estimation the clearest of the love of money, and the most free to give away his all in every sense of the word.[41]

The charges of hoarding money and earning money from Methodist endeavors so haunted Asbury that he called for affidavits from Methodist leaders, among them John Dickens. Dickens responded that "both from a sense of duty and respect I now declare in the most solemn manner that Mr. Asbury has never received any money from the book fund nor even dropped the most distant hint to my knowledge of desiring or expecting anything from that fund or the Charter Fund."[42] Asbury's most extensive statement concerning his financial mode of operation was written to John Dickens in 1798:

> My method for many years has been to keep an account of what has been given me without solicitation. I have also kept an account of what I have expended annually, charging the connection with my salary of sixty-four dollars per year and my travelling expenses, as another preacher. When I have wanted a horse or carriage my friends have provided for me. My friends of Maryland, Delaware, Philadelphia, Jersey, and New York have chiefly communicated this supply. As to Virginia or the Carolinas (except in a few extraordinary cases), as also Georgia, and the western and eastern States, I have visited them, taking nothing unless in extreme want on my side, or in great benevolence of my friends on the other. As to the college, it was all pain and no profit, but some expense and great labor. From the Preacher's Fund the conferences can witness for me I have taken nothing. Of the book interest you can witness I have received nothing. Of the Chartered Fund I am independent, and wish to keep so. Of money brought to conference, or collected publicly at times, it has been appropriated with the nicest equality to the wants and deficiencies of the preachers, but not any to me (3:171–2).[43]

Nothing Pertaining to This World

In James Quinn's words, Methodist ministry required the called to walk hand-in-hand with poverty. Asbury would not require other men to do what he would not. He too would live the liminal life of the prophet/priest, neither entirely of this life nor of the next. His possessions were barely more than he could place in his saddlebags, as crammed as they may have been. His creed of acquisition, which he stated years before he became Bishop, served as an enduring guidepost. "I wanted nothing pertaining to this world more than I possessed; neither clothing, nor money, nor food" (1:252). He led by example, even going to extremes to prove his detractors wrong. "[S]trange that neither my friends nor my enemies believe my demonstration, what I have ever been striving to prove–that I will live and die a poor man" (2: 227). No one ever saw him carrying a trunk; instead they heard him singing:

> Nothing on earth I call my own:
> A stranger, to the world unknown,
> I all their goods despise;
> I trample on their whole delight,
> And seek a country out of sight,
> A country in the skies (1:252).

The future bishop Robert Roberts graphically explained what it meant for a Methodist preacher to enter the itinerancy. Roberts was already married and with children when he answered the "call" to preach. In order for him to accept his appointment, he auctioned off almost all of his earthly belongings.

> Even the water gourd, the oven shovel, and a hundred unnamables will be missed. These articles too which are sold, will go mostly at a great depreciation; and hence another loss. And those that are retained, create a bill of expense by conveyance. Such inconveniences and losses are always more or less, connected with the itinerant life. But it has its moral. It cuts the man entirely loose from the world. It scatters into fragments everything out of which an idol could be made. It is a sheriff's sale of all that pertains to him on earth. And if he and his family are not prepared by these trying events to be heavenly–altogether heavenly, without even a shred of the earthly, the sensual, or the devilish, appertaining to them, either really or in appearance, then let them return whence they came and leave the itinerancy to those of the right spirit. They should neither touch, taste nor handle it. [44]

Impoverished Dignity

In spite of all of Asbury's privations he did fare better than his subordinates, especially in the aspect of clothing. The John Street Church financial records reveal that its parishioners furnished him with a new suit of clothes, including boots, hat, and surtout (a long overcoat).[45] In 1813, St. George's Church paid for eyeglasses, a hat, and a coat in the amount of $14.91,[46] and the financial records at St. George's also indicate that the church purchased a "portmanteau," a large traveling bag, for Asbury.[47]

Asbury was caught in the tension of identifying with the impoverishment of his preachers and at the same time maintaining the dignity of his office. The more well-to-do churches enabled their leader to look more like a leader. Their singular generosity may have blunted his empathy toward those who did not receive similar gifts. "I told some of our preachers, who were very poor, how happy they were; and that probably, had they any more, their wants would proportionately increase."[48]

In spite of the above, Asbury was not outfitted in a new suit of clothes at the first sign of wear. He wrote to his parents on October 30, 1795, "The coat and waist coat I now have on I have worn thirteen months, and I would not carry a second shirt if I could do without it" (3:135). Zachary Myles of Baltimore in a letter dated February 1807, reported that, "Mr. Asbury came into the city wrapped up in a blanket and habited like an Indian, with his own clothes worn out."[49] Had Asbury dressed in the fashion of the day he would have worn laced ruffles, silk shirts and hose in the summer, a red coat with plush breeches, and a vest. It was "the boast of a well formed man that he could by his natural form readily keep his breeches around his hips, and his stockings without gartering above the calf of the leg."[50] It is unlikely that Asbury ever made that boast.

The above did not mean Asbury was insensitive to the economic preference that was shown him, as contrasted with the deprivation of his troops. Before he left on an extended trip, the trustees of John Street Church urged him to accept financial help. He responded by saying, "I have need of nothing." When they insisted on knowing how much money he possessed, he threw his purse on the table, and upon examination his inquisitors found that it contained less than three dollars.[51] The dialectic of sufficiency and equality was a pressure that Asbury daily felt. The tension was resolved by a regimen of almost constant denial.

18. "Preach and Live and Live and Preach"

William Glendinning

Heading north, Asbury preached in Georgetown, South Carolina, on Sunday, January 3, 1811. He was both weary of body and dull of spirit. The people were yet duller. "I am always in fetters in this place; and were they to offer me twenty such towns as a bribe I would not visit it again; but I must do my duty without a bribe" (2:661). He was even more weary in Lumberton, North Carolina. "Sometimes I am ready to cry out, *Lord, take me home to rest!* Courage, my soul" (2:662). Courage was needed when the skiff that he and Henry Boehm were using to cross the Fear River turned over with their books and clothes. Boehm's saddlebags, with money from the book sales, floated down the river, but were later retrieved. Asbury's horse got stuck in the mud while trying to climb the riverbank. By using a rail to lift up the horse's hindquarters, Boehm helped the animal to free himself. Boehm recorded, "Bishop Asbury was much alarmed, far more so than I had ever seen him."[1]

The Virginia Conference convened at Raleigh on February 7. It was noted not for its business but for its religious intensity. About fifty people were converted, including the secretary of the state, William Hill. On Sunday, Asbury preached to "two thousand people" (Boehm says a thousand) at the Statehouse. For three nights, Asbury, Boehm, and Thomas Douglas stayed with William Glendinning. Boehm said Glendinning was quite eccentric, if not a little "cracked." He did, however, comment: "We had a very pleasant time at his house."[2] At this time, Glendinning was a Unitarian pastor in Raleigh, having parted with James O'Kelly. In 1791, Asbury had written, "As to Glendinning, I believe Satan is in him and will never come out" (3:107).

Asbury's comment on Glendinning carried a good deal of baggage. Glendinning was one of Methodism's first traveling preachers and was ordained an elder by Asbury at the Christmas Conference. Writing concerning that occasion, the young ordinand had said, "The preachers kneeled down to prayer: and while Mr. Asbury was at prayer, I felt all light of divine mercy, as in a moment, take its flight from me, and I felt as if I had been rent in two, and drove out, like an outcast from the face of the Lord. My soul then sunk into the depths of misery and despair." This was the beginning of an emotional and spiritual breakdown for Glendinning. By his own account, he made three suicide attempts, blasphemed God, and was convinced that he was irrevocably damned. On a suicide attempt, he waded out into "9 to 10 feet of water, with a large stone tied to him but the rope to the stone broke."

Upon recovering enough to begin preaching again, Glendinning spent many of his sermons relating his past apparitions, of which the following was typical: "I was certain that Lucifer was near; and I told the people that he would be there that night. Immediately there was a loud rap at the door. I opened it, and saw his face; it was black as any coal—his eyes and mouth as red as blood and long white teeth gnashing together."[3] Coke told Glendinning "[t]hat he believed all such accounts of creatures having any intercourse with beings from eternity were only imaginary."[4] Asbury warned Glendinning that the preaching houses were being shut against him. In a letter to Asbury on June 15, 1793, Glendinning stated, "I have found it resting on my mind to communicate to you my thoughts of your conduct towards me. I have viewed it as not consistent with the Christian character."[5]

Glendinning eventually left the Methodists and joined the Unitarians. His not being allowed to preach in Methodist churches raised an issue that would be controversial for Methodism in years to come. On December 18, 1794, Glendinning wrote Asbury:

> The authority you have put into your Bishops and presiding elders appears to strike at the root of free conferences, without the knowledge of most of them who assist in building your preaching houses are deeded over not to your people, but to your preachers. So that their aim is to secure the whole right to themselves; as Mr. Asbury told me at Conference, in Baltimore, 1793, that the right of the meeting houses, or preaching houses, was as much theirs as any man's house in Baltimore was his.[6]

Sought Out

At Georgetown, Asbury and Boehm lodged at Henry Foxall's. Wherever Asbury lighted between Baltimore and Philadelphia, he was shown luxurious deference. The families brought out their best china and prepared their favorite food. Asbury appreciated the hospitality, but with a bit of uneasiness. He quieted his guilt by penning, "O, the *clover* of Baltimore circuit! *Ease*, ease! not for me—toil, suffering, coarse food, hard lodging, bugs, fleas, and certain *et ceteras* besides!" (2:666). When Asbury had first headquartered in Baltimore in the 1770s, there were only six thousand people. Now it was a burgeoning seaport of some forty-seven thousand people.[7] Many of his old friends were now gone: "Three and thirty years make great changes on the surface of this world of evanescent existences" (2:669).

On May 1, just after the Philadelphia Conference, Asbury was visited by Benjamin Rush and Edmond Physick, two of the best-known physicians in the country. Few Americans were afforded such attention. "I was much gratified, aye, I ever am, by their attentions, kindness, and charming conversation; indeed they have been of eminent use to me, and I acknowledge their services with gratitude"

(2:670). But the bishop was not always on a pedestal; four days later, he preached under an apple tree. On May 9, he arrived in Asbury, New Jersey, the first town in America named after him, which would be a "pleasant place if not for the brewing and drinking, miserable whiskey" (2:672).

Wherever the bishop went, people sought him out. At the time in life when his nerves were most easily frayed and he was in desperate need of solitude, Methodists poured out their concerns to their ecclesiastical father. A steady stream of people were seeking advice, giving advice, complaining, or simply baring their souls. Asbury patiently listened into the late hours of the night, all the time wishing to retire. When asked for an immediate decision, he was almost always noncommittal. Joshua Marsden said of Asbury, "His prudence was equal to his integrity; he never committed himself; hence he had few things to undo."[8]

During the week of June 2–9, Asbury lodged at the homes of Pierre Van Cortlandt, Samuel Wilson, and Lemuel Clift, all men of wealth and residents of New York State. The fare was much different by the time he and Boehm arrived at French Mills above Plattsburg. Asbury's horse got stuck in the planking of a pole bridge as he was leading it across. The horse then sank into the mud while the books and clothes fell into the river. After recovering, they hired four Indians to transport them across the St. Lawrence River into Canada; the horses were transported by lashing three canoes together. The agreed-upon charge was three dollars, but upon arrival the Indians demanded four, since it was difficult to divide three dollars among four men.

This was Asbury's first trip outside of the United States since his arrival forty years earlier, and it turned out to be his only trip to Canada. In spite of an inflamed foot, which caused constant pain, Asbury was impressed. "Our ride has brought us through one of the finest countries I have ever seen: the timber is of a noble size: the cattle are well-shaped and well-looking: the crops are abundant, on a most fruitful soil: surely this is a land that God the Lord hath blessed" (2:678).

During the two-week stay in Canada, "Asbury was treated as the angel of the churches."[9] The trip from Kingston, Ontario, to Sacketts Harbour, New York, was treacherous, requiring three ferries. One of them was no more than an open sailboat. Being caught in a storm, they anchored on the north side of Fox Island in Lake Ontario. In order to keep the wind and rain off Asbury, Boehm fixed a makeshift tent and covered the bishop with hay. At the peak of the storm, the startled Bishop cried out, "Henry, Henry, the horses are going overboard." It was a tumultuous night, about which the Bishop recorded, "A tremendous passage we had" (2:679).

Despite being feverish with an inflamed digestive system, Asbury closed the New York Conference by preaching in the woods to about five hundred people. He then had to trade in his horse, Spark, for a new mount. Just outside of Lancaster,

Pennsylvania, Asbury preached at a camp in spite of his dysentery. Martin Boehm, Henry's father, gave him some Rhenish wine, which seemed to help. At Cady, Ohio, Asbury baptized the newborn son of James Simpson, named Matthew. He would serve as Methodism's most prominent bishop from 1852–84. As a personal friend of Abraham Lincoln, Simpson preached his funeral in both Washington and Springfield.

Men of All Descriptions

Asbury had now been in America for forty years, and it was a time for assessment. The movement had grown from 500 to185,000. Some of the annual camp meetings were running aggregate totals of 10,000 people. Methodism no longer consisted of only society's marginalized. Asbury boasted to Thomas Coke on November 27, "Many of our meetings are attended by men of all descriptions, Representatives, etc., with the single exception of the President" (3:456). The scaffolding was in place for Methodism to experience its best days yet. "I feel as if the year 1812 will be great in the new and old perhaps in grace and judgment" (3:457). John Calhoun and Henry Clay, both warhawks, had been elected to Congress. Another showdown with Great Britain (which meant Canada), with its adverse effects on American Methodism, was looming on the horizon. Nevertheless, "The bishops were in fine spirits, full of hope in regard to the future."[10]

The New Madrid earthquake was a series of tremors which shook the United States 1811–12. Its epicenter was near New Madrid, Missouri, where the most violent quake took place on December 16, 1811. The shocks were felt over a million square miles; Asbury commented when in South Carolina on November 25, 1811, "We had a serious shock of an earthquake this morning—a sad presage of future sorrows perhaps. Lord, make us ready!" (2:688).

Asbury's reaction was not as dramatic as Valentine Cook's, who lived with his wife Tabitha near Russellville, Kentucky. When his house began to tremble, Cook ran to the outside and through the street "with nothing on but his night clothes" shouting, "My Jesus is coming! My Jesus is coming!" Tabitha, trying to keep up, cried out, "O, Mr. Cook, don't leave me," to which her husband responded, "O Tabitha, my Jesus is coming and I cannot wait for you."[11]

The Virginia Conference convened in Richmond on February 20, 1812. It was a trying time for the senior bishop as charges were leveled at him for ordaining a slave. In his defense, Asbury produced a certificate proving the Black man's freedom. All was not lost. As Asbury was ordaining elders "in a solemn and impressive manner," revival broke out in the gallery, where several were converted. Boehm testified that he had never seen such a scene in a conference. On Sunday, Asbury preached at Roper's Chapel in New Kent County "some awful truths."

He then preached at Williamsburg recalling the names of Patrick Henry and George Washington.

Death of Another Friend

Asbury preached wherever asked, in spite of his failing voice, a deep cold, and cold preaching houses. Between the Virginia and Baltimore Conferences, a span of approximately two weeks, Asbury preached seven times and continued to travel through severe weather. Upon crossing the Potomac, the party was met with a hurricane. "I lifted up my heart in prayer to God. There was in a few minutes a great calm, which all those with me witnessed, but I will not say it was in answer to prayer" (2:696).

Before the Baltimore Conference ended, Asbury informed Boehm that they must depart immediately upon its finish. Asbury intended to go straight to Henry's father. When Boehm reminded him that there were prior appointments to keep, the bishop replied, "Never mind, we can get them filled; I tell you we must go right to your father's." They must not have gone "right" to Martin Boehm's, because it took them a week to make the hundred miles to Lancaster County. Upon arrival they found that Martin had died on March 23, as his son was en route.

Asbury preached Martin Boehm's funeral, giving an elaborate eulogy of his departed friend. Henry later recalled, "I had heard the venerable Asbury often when he was great, and he was particularly great on funeral occasions, but then he far transcended himself."[12] Asbury had known Martin for almost thirty years. He noted in his journal: "At rest in Jesus; and I am left to pain and toil: courage, my soul, we shall overtake them when our task is done!" (2:697). When they returned later in the summer, Henry stated that "Bishop Asbury wept for his old friend and I for my father."[13]

Reformers Continue to Challenge Asbury

The bishop's next formidable task was the first delegated General Conference, which began in New York City on May 1, 1812. After having served in the episcopacy for four years, McKendree was feeling sufficiently confident to take some innovative initiative. Without prior permission from Asbury, he began the conference with a State of the Union address, a precedent that has been followed in Methodism ever since. Among other things, the junior bishop assured the assembly of his accountability to them. Upon completion, McKendree sat down and Asbury stood up, saying, "I have something to say to you before the Conference." McKendree stood up and the two faced one another in front of the whole assembly. "This is a new thing," Asbury said. "I never did business in this way, and why is this new thing introduced?" McKendree responded, "You are our father, we are your sons; you never have had need of it. I am only a brother and have need of it."[14] McKendree's shrewd deference brought a smile to Asbury's face, and without a word he sat down. Abel Stevens said of Asbury, "He never lost his self-possession, and could therefore seldom be surprised."[15]

The single issue that took up two days at the conference was a motion for each conference to elect its own presiding elder. The delegates rehashed the decision made at the 1808 conference. Three of the conference's strongest opinion makers, Jesse Lee, Asa Shinn, and Nicholas Snethen, argued at length for the change. (Shinn and Snethen were later to become leaders in the Methodist Protestant Church and editors of its periodical.) Lee droned on the longest, so much so that Asbury, seated in the presiding chair, turned his back on him. An opponent of Lee observed that "no man of common sense would use such arguments as Lee expounded." At this point, Lee addressed the chair. Since he had been accused of not having common sense, he said, it stood to reason that he must have uncommon sense. Asbury swung around in his chair and said, "Yes! Yes! Brother Lee, you are a man of uncommon sense." Lee quickly replied, "Then, sir, I beg that uncommon attention may be paid to what I am about to say." Asbury again turned his back and Lee continued with his argument, which was once more defeated by the conference.[16]

Asbury's irritability called for some mealtime diplomacy. He invited seventeen of the preachers to dinner: "[T]here was vinegar, mustard, and a still greater portion of oil: but the disappointed parties sat down in peace, and we enjoyed our sober meal" (2:699). Present at the conference and possibly at the meal was Joshua Marsden, a British Methodist who was merely stopping over as a retiring missionary from Nova Scotia. Because of the escalating tension between Great Britain and the United States, he remained as a preacher in New York City. Marsden said of Asbury, "I should not omit his temperance, having frequently dined with him. I have been astonished how a man who ate so sparingly could perform so vast labours; an egg, a little salad, and a small piece of meat was his usual dinner."[17] After the "peace meal," Asbury noted, "We should thank God that we are not at war with each other, as are the Episcopalians, with the pen and the press as their weapons of war" (2:699).

The mealtime diplomacy did not settle all of the animosity. Laban Clark had made the motion for the annual conferences to elect presiding elders. After adjournment, Asbury wrote to Clark, "Since the conference in Pittsfield, or before your countenance appears cloudy towards me, . . . our rules say make all haste to cast the fire out of your Bosom. . . . I am thy Father, and the greatest Friend thou hast in the world, *a spiritual friend*." Clark responded, "[I] am extremely pained that your feelings have been wounded! Nothing can be more distant from me than designedly to injure the feelings of any man; especially the man whom I esteem and reverence above all other men. . . . Before that Conference ended I met with your frowns (if I judged rightly) in a most unexpected manner."[18] Clark went on to defend his motion by stating that Asbury had an interest in the connection and an influence over it that no one else could have. In other words, when a lesser person came into Asbury's station there would be even greater change if the liability to abuse was not now corrected. Part of the reason for Asbury's success was the political sagacity of those who surrounded him.

A Return Trip to England?

The four decades on the new continent were increasingly turning Asbury's mind to his native land. For some time, he had toyed with the idea of a fraternal visit to England that would both satisfy a sentimental craving and strengthen ties with the mother church. Asbury had received an official invitation from the British Conference for a visit. However, the committee on episcopacy (comprised of one elected member from each conference) recommended that Asbury "relinquish his thoughts of visiting Europe, and confine his labors to the American connection so long as God preserves him a blessing to the church."[19] The response both affirmed Asbury and reminded the conference delegates of the divided loyalties of Coke. On the same day that the "episcopacy committee" made their response, Asbury wrote them an official letter:

> My dear Brethren:
>
> Whatever I may have thought or spoken in former times upon strengthening the Episcopacy, I am not at liberty to say to you at this time, do this, or that. I am bound in duty to serve the Connection with all my power of body and mind, as long and as largely as I can; and, while I am persuaded that my services are needed and acceptable, to give up all thoughts of visits out of the American Continent. I feel myself indispensably bound to the Conference and my colleagues, never to leave them nor forsake them upon the above conditions (3:460).

In order for Asbury to take a sabbatical, the conference would have needed to elect an additional bishop, which they did not. The issue posed a conflict in Asbury's heart. He wished to be free, and he wished to be in control. On July 11, 1811, he had written to Thomas Douglas, "I wish that a trinity of superintendents might be in operation—that after forty years, I might be at liberty to travel into any part of the new or Old World, if called. I wish the Connection would do as well without me as with me, before they must do without. I fret like a father, that wishes to see his children married and settled before he dies."[20] The truth is, Asbury's ego would never allow the church to do without him before it *had* to do without him. Indispensability was his primary mind-set, and it would never allow him to be placed on a shelf. In his quieter moments, Asbury realized that he needed the church as much or more than it needed him.

Losing the Ecclesiastical Battle

Asbury left the conference both affirmed and relegated to a more egalitarian mode with his colleague. He dealt with it in the manner in which he dealt with everything; he rode. The only way to clear his mind was to be constantly in motion. Since the main business of the conference questioned Asbury's power, he was left physically and emotionally depleted. On the Monday immediately following the conference, he took an "emetic" and went to bed. By Wednesday at White Plains, he was again incapacitated, though he preached that evening. Whirling around in his mind were the thoughts that the General Conference had voted for his necessity and at the same time had elevated McKendree, a recognition earned by the latter's parliamentary finesse and platform presence.

McKendree had gained enough confidence to set his own direction. The preachers knew that the junior bishop would not appoint them on his own, unlike his senior partner. Over the strong disapproval of Asbury, he would determine their stations with counsel from the presiding elders. Seven months before the 1812 General Conference, McKendree had written Asbury, "I am fully convinced of the utility and necessity of the council of presiding elders in stationing the preachers, but you fear individuals will make it difficult, if not impracticable, for you to proceed on their plan . . . but I still refuse to take the whole responsibility upon myself, not that I am afraid of proper accountability, but because I can see the proposition included one highly improper."[21] "Refuse" and "improper" were strong words for Asbury to digest.

Asbury continued to be challenged by men who were esteemed both by the church and by him. He was being challenged by his friends, individuals to whom he referred as "great men." Their voice for reform ascended, while his grew fainter. He was losing the ecclesiastical battle. Asbury had given forty years of sacrifice and unceasing labor to maintain the confidence of those to whom he had entrusted that leadership. His peace of mind depended upon maintaining their confidence.

Asbury found some peace by visiting his old friend Freeborn Garrettson at his manor in Rhinebeck, New York. The conferences at Albany, New York, and Lynn, Massachusetts, merited only perfunctory mention by both Boehm and Asbury. The New England Conference continued to struggle financially. The "widows" of the New York Conference had collected $200 for the "poor preachers." "They have built a neat house in Lynn; but I am afraid of a steeple; and if they put this foolish addition, it must not be by Methodist order, or with Methodist money—they may pay for their own pride and folly" (2:701).

On June 19, with the support of Congress, President James Madison officially declared war on Great Britain. Asbury noted, "[B]etween our people and the English people: my trust is in the living God" (2:701).

On August 2, Asbury stopped at Joshua Kenney's, who had converted his former whiskey still into a house of worship at Black Walnut, Pennsylvania. At Wilkes Barre, he preached in the courtroom during recess, "Knowing the terror of the Lord we persuade men" (2:704). At Lehigh, he expressed appreciation for the Germans except for their addiction to alcohol. "[V]ile whiskey: this is the prime curse of the United States, and will be, I fear much, the ruin of all that is excellent in morals and government in them. Lord, interpose thine arm!" (2:704). In the meantime the war was not going well for the Americans. In September, the British captured William Hull and his 2,200-man army in Detroit.

As the pair started for the West, Asbury required Boehm's constant nursing attention. In spite of the fleas' and bedbugs' taking their toll, Asbury continued to preach wherever they stopped. On September 20, Asbury spent the entire night in prayer. This endeavor left him so weak that he hardly had strength to chair the newly formed Ohio Conference. During the conference, the bishop stayed with the Reverend Thomas Hinde, the son of Dr. S. Hinde who had put a "blister plaster" on the back of his wife's head in order to draw the Methodism out of her. She bore it so patiently that she converted her husband. In Kentucky, Asbury preached in the Statehouse at Frankfort on October 16. In Nashville on October 30, Boehm and Asbury lodged in the jail as "prisoners of hope."

A Grave, Venerable, and Dignified Appearance

On November 10 the Bishop convened the first gathering of the newly formed Tennessee Conference, which covered the largest land area: Tennessee, Southern Kentucky, Indiana, Illinois, Missouri, Arkansas, Louisiana, Mississippi, and Alabama. After conference, the traveling party (which now included James Axley) headed in the rain toward Knoxville. Axley made his mark on Methodism as an earnest, eccentric, and outspoken preacher. It was Axley who said to Thomas Morris, surveying him from head to foot after the latter had been elected bishop in 1836, "Upon my word I think they were hard put for Bishop timber when they got hold of you."[22] Axley may have been measuring the short and portly Morris against Asbury. The fullest description that we have of Asbury at this time of life is from Joshua Marsden:

> In his appearance he was the picture of plainness and simplicity, bordering upon the costume of the Friends; the reader may figure to himself an old man, spare and tall but remarkably clean, with plain frock coat, drab, or mixture; waist coat and small clothes of the same kind, a neat stock, a large, broad brimmed hat with an

uncommonly low crown, while his white locks, venerable with age, added a simplicity to his appearance it is not easy to describe. His countenance had a cast of severity; but this was probably owing to his habitual gravity and seriousness: his look was remarkably penetrating, in a word I never recollect to have seen a man of more grave, venerable, and dignified appearance.[23]

Lodging with Edward Teal just outside of Lancaster, Pennsylvania, Asbury thought of Teal's son-in-law, James Quinn, the presiding elder of the Muskingum District of the Western Conference. Six days later, Asbury wrote Quinn one of the most forceful pastoral charges that he ever gave anyone: "Move heaven with your prayers, and earth with your cries. *Cry aloud, spare not,* lift up your voice like a trumpet! Diligence, prudence, courage, perseverance. You will care for every circuit, every society, every preacher, every family, and every soul in your charge" (3:466).

When James Quinn had earlier quit the itinerancy, Asbury visited him and mused aloud that if he did not reenter he might "be taken out of the world in some way." When Quinn's startled horse spared him from being struck by a falling tree limb, he recalled the bishop's words. Quinn reentered the ministry. When Quinn heard Asbury preach in a schoolhouse in September 1810, he commented that "truly it might be said of the sermon, as I have heard him say of Harnack's great law of consideration, 'It was a dagger, to the hilt of every stroke.'"[24]

A Torrent of Preaching and Travelling

Asbury closed out 1812 with a torrent of preaching and traveling. Boehm recalled, "In those days we gave them sermon upon sermon, exhortation upon exhortation." Asbury's rheumatism necessitated that he be carried back and forth to his sulky. Boehm commented, "Never was he more feeble, never less able to travel, and yet he would go on! There was only one thing that could stop him, the pale horse and his rider."[25]

As Asbury grew older and weaker, he felt it even more necessary to preach wherever he stopped. His life's motif had been summed up in a letter to Thomas Sargent in 1805: "Oh let us preach and live; and live and preach" (3:332). Though he could reduce his efforts in other areas, referring responsibilities to the junior bishop and traveling companions, he knew he must continue to preach. His constituency wanted to hear him; it might be their last opportunity. People traveled long miles through difficult circumstances just to see and hear the aged leader of one of America's largest denominations proclaim the gospel. At this point in his life, Asbury was quite possibly the best-known person in America, at least by sight. More people had personally seen Asbury than had seen the President of the United States. Camp meetings had provided for Asbury both recognition and the opportunity for proclamation.

Wesley's men were preachers. For them, preaching was the preeminent pastoral task. Preaching was not a component of worship among other liturgical acts; it was the climactic essential of the gathered community. Even Wesley's streamlined order of worship, *The Sunday Service*, was too cumbersome for the army of zealots who invaded the American frontier with little more than a Bible. Within ten years, Wesley's instruction for worship (culled primarily from the Anglican *Book of Common Prayer)* had been almost totally forgotten.

According to the *Discipline* of 1798, the first duty of the Methodist preacher was "to preach."[26] Asbury took the lead as the exemplar of the American philosophy of ministry. He preached however, to whomever, wherever he had opportunity; at a paper mill, under a jail wall, in a prison, at an executioner's stand, at a poorhouse, at a tavern, from the door of a public house, in a courthouse, in a barn, in the woods, standing on a table, from a camp meeting stand, in a schoolhouse, in a borrowed church, in a private dwelling, in a statehouse, and at Yale. "My mind was powerfully struck with a sense of the great duty of preaching in all companies; of always speaking boldly and freely for God as if in the pulpit" (1:707–8).

Preaching As Production

Asbury did not consider himself a great preacher. He possessed neither the fluency of tongue nor command of language that would serve as entertainment or enthrall congregations. He spoke with directness and rapidity of speech, without being verbose or drawn out. He used a plainness of speech that majored in clarity rather than intellectual stimulation. Asbury's preaching was a call for action; it demanded response rather than reflection. His sermons required both a spiritual and moral verdict. His preaching was primarily aimed at transformation. He asked, "Ah! what is preaching, without living to God? It is a daily unction we want, that the word may be like a hammer and fire from our mouths, to break hearts, and to kindle life and fire" (1:316). Early on, he had prayed, "Lord, keep me . . . from preaching empty stuff to please the ear, instead of changing the heart!" (1:116).

Though Asbury knew both Hebrew and Greek, little of that was incorporated into his sermons. His method was not to give exegetical explanation or commentary. Asbury rarely, if ever, gave the historical background of a text or an elaborate explanation of the context in which the text was found. Quite often he shaped the text to the Wesleyan order of salvation, emphasizing specific points of spiritual decision making such as repentance, justification, and sanctification. His methodology was to shape the text according to his perception of his listeners' spiritual needs. He often chose his texts almost on the spur of the moment, trying to detect both the direction of the Holy Spirit and the needs of his congregation. Henry Boehm, who may have heard Asbury preach more than any other person, stated, "No man ever understood adaptation in preaching better than Francis Asbury."[27]

A sermon for Asbury could be evaluated only by its effectiveness. Did it do what the preacher intended it to accomplish? The sermon's purpose was always conversion—conversion to life, to holiness, to righteousness, to action, to perfection, and ultimately to heaven. Asbury was continually assessing his own performance in light of the congregational response. He was a lifelong student of his listeners. He often noted that they were "dull, insensible, dead, inattentive, inanimate, lifeless, still, a little affected, unfeeling, little devoted, judicially hardened, word proof, marble hearted, cold, mocking, and offended." At other times, he said, they were "feeling, gracious, profited, melting, attentive, alarming, shaking, well behaved, serious, tender," and even "stricken to the ground."

Asbury's emotions rose and ebbed with the responses of his congregation. They were to be affected, and he was the key instrument in producing the effect. Asbury predicated a sermon's validity on results, both qualitative and quantitative. The preacher's effectiveness was measured by the visible response. Nathan Bangs described Asbury in the pulpit: "His attitude in the pulpit was graceful, dignified, and solemn; his voice full and commanding; his enunciation clear and distinct; and sometimes a sudden burst of eloquence would break forth in a manner which spoke a soul full of God, and like a mountain torrent swept all before it."[28] Bangs remembered an incident in Baltimore in 1808 while Asbury was preaching on a Sabbath morning in the Eutaw Street Church in the presence of many members of the General Conference. Among others, the Reverend Phillip Otterbein sat on the platform.

> The bishop was discoursing upon the duty of parents to their children and warning against the frivolities of the world. He suddenly paused, and then said, "But you will say this is hard. Alas" he added–letting his voice which had been raised into that high commanding tone which gave such a majesty to what he uttered, suddenly fall to a low and soft key,–"It is harder to be damned!" These words, dropping from his lips in a manner which indicated the deep sensations of his heart, fell upon the audience, now brought up to the highest pitch of intensity by what had preceded them, like the sudden bursting of a cloud upon the mown grass, and they were in a moment melted into tears–sobs and groans were heard all over the house. The venerable Otterbein, noble and dignified in his appearance, was turned into a little child—the tears furrowing his cheeks—bespeaking the deep feelings of his heart.[29]

Asbury's Preaching Methodology

There are no extant sermons of Francis Asbury. In all likelihood, he never wrote out a full manuscript of any sermon he ever preached. He jotted down the dominant ideas, absorbing them to the extent that there was little reference to his notes. Most often, the dominant ideas were not shaped by the text but were derived from a particular idea within the text. Asbury's sermon structures usually consisted of topical outlines rather than an exposition of a particular Scripture text. The direction of his message was shaped more by the need to persuade his congregation than by either the content or the structure of the text.

Asbury chose his own intent for the message rather than the biblical writer's intent for the text. There was sufficient correlation between what the text said and what Asbury said to establish the authority of the spoken word. He was not systematically inductive in drawing ideas from the text in order to create the form of his message; rather, as one listener described him, "Asbury was the only preacher who preached to his text. He never preached from it. . . . With his proposition, argument, illustration, incident, everything was either immediately drawn from or directly connected with the subject of discourse."[30]

Asbury recorded almost two hundred sermon outlines in his journal.[31] His most frequently used text was 1 Timothy 1:15: "This is a faithful saying, and worthy of all acceptation, that Christ Jesus came into the world to save sinners; of whom I am chief." Asbury's journal indicates 935 texts from which he preached, 283 in the Old Testament and 652 in the New Testament. The Old Testament book from which the most texts were taken was Psalms, and from the New Testament, Acts. Since Asbury often repeated texts, he preached from Isaiah more than any other Old Testament book and from Hebrews more than any other New Testament book. There are 2,059 preaching instances recorded in the journals.[32] Asbury preached thousands more times, but not the 16,500 which has been estimated. (This number has been derived by calculating one sermon a day during his 45 years of American ministry.[33]) Actually, there were long stretches of time when Asbury did not preach at all because of sickness, confinement, weather, or lack of suitable places or audiences.

On October 24, 1779, Asbury preached on Hebrews 9:27: "And as it is appointed unto men once to die, and after this the judgement." He emphasized both death and judgment and alluded to verse 28, which should have been included as part of the text because it completes the thought. To verse 29 he gave a Wesleyan emphasis, which is a questionable interpretation (1:318). On October 23, 1803, Asbury preached on James 1:22: "But be ye doers of the word, and not hearers only deceiving your own selves." He did not deal with the text exegetically. Instead, he generalized a gospel message with a Wesleyan emphasis on Christian perfection.

On March 1, 1797, Asbury preached in a courthouse on 2 Corinthians 5:11, "Knowing the terror of the Lord, we persuade men." The intention of Paul, the writer, was to persuade Christians to persuade non-believers. In other words, the text is for Christians. Asbury utilized the passage to emphasize judgment, listing the "characters to be judged." "[T]hese are to be tried, found guilty, or acquitted;

sentenced and punished, or applauded and rewarded" (2:122). The setting, a courthouse, shaped the sermon more than did the text. During the 1806 Baltimore Conference, he preached on Isaiah 62:1: "For Zion's sake I will not hold my peace." Asbury used the text to differentiate ecclesiastical concerns from national concerns rather than to emphasize the results of not holding one's peace in the city of Zion, which is the good news of Isaiah 62.

In preaching on 1 Samuel 10:6—"The Spirit of the Lord will come upon thee, and thou shalt prophecy with them, and shalt be turned into another man"— Asbury did not apply the text to Saul's life but rather imposed the Wesleyan order of salvation. "Here I took occasion to show . . . [t]he operations of the Spirit on the heart of man—to convince, convict, convert, and sanctify" (1:152). On Luke 3:6, "All flesh shall see the salvation of God," Asbury showed "[t]he nature of this salvation in its degrees of justification, sanctification, and glorification." On Romans 12:1–2, Asbury interpreted the renewing of the mind as "[A]ll the powers of the soul be given in love and service to the Lord; in conviction for indwelling sin, the repentance of believers; in sanctification; persevering grace; perfect love; and the fruition—perfect and eternal glory" (2:465).

However, in many instances Asbury follows the text rather than imposing upon it key doctrinal themes. Concerning Peter's denial Asbury utilized a simple outline inductively drawn from the narrative. "I. He was self-confident. II. Followed afar off. III. Mixed with the wicked. IV. Denied his discipleship and then his Lord" (2:562). On Galatians 2:20, Asbury followed the order of the text: "Christ crucified—I live—yet not I, Christ liveth in me—by faith in Christ— who hath loved me, and given himself for me" (2:190). For Ezekiel 36:25–27, Asbury allowed the emphasis of the text to create the segments of his message: "I. Their stony heart. II. The blessings promised and prophesied. III. The blessed consequential effects" (2:119). For all three of these texts, Asbury utilized biblical content to inform both the substance and structure of the sermon. Asbury was more systematic and biblical in his presentation than most of his understudies.

Pulpit Style

Asbury's preaching style was animated, but not exaggerated in movement, gestures, or loudness. Robert Ayres, upon hearing Asbury, described him as "lively and close." He did raise his voice, slap the pulpit, accent with a gesture, or stomp his feet to make a point. George Roberts recalled that in the course of a sermon in a New York conference, Asbury stated, "I am afraid that some of you will methodize yourselves dead." And raising his voice still higher: "I am afraid that some of you will methodize yourselves damned,"—stomping the floor sufficiently to startle the whole congregation.[34] Thomas Morrell recalled that Asbury preached with "uncommon life, spirit, and power." In spite of these exclamatory outbursts, one congregation that heard Asbury on October 13, 1780, thought that Asbury needed more "thunder!" (1:383). This comment may have reflected Asbury's normal style, which normally demonstrated restraint. "I shall not throw myself into an unnatural heat or overstrained exertions" (1:383).

Asbury consistently critiqued his own preaching. He was often disappointed with his performance: "Dispirited," "a feeble spirit," "a feeble testimony," "cloud over me," "raged and threatened, but afraid it was spleen," "loud and long," "long and laboured." On Christmas Day, 1795, Asbury recorded, "When I have preached, I feel as though I have need to do it over again; and it is the same with all my performances" (2:70).

In contrast, Asbury was often quite confident that he had fulfilled the preaching task with deft efficiency: "I saw," "I felt," "I knew," "roared out wonderfully," "plainly and closely," "great heat and rapidity about a half an hour," "great plainness and so much fire," "spirit of liberty," "divinely ordered," "great light." On August 2, 1800, Asbury recorded, "I had liberty in preaching, and felt some tenderness of heart, and evinced it with weeping eyes" (2:243).

Assessments by Others

Evaluations of Asbury's preaching by his contemporaries are numerous. Ezekiel Cooper wrote that "[h]is language was good, his manner agreeable, his matter excellent, and his voice melodious. . . . His addresses were generally, plain and simple, yet energetic, carrying with them the impressive authority of truth."[35] Nicholas Snethen judged Asbury as a "[g]ood preacher; he was a better preacher than he was generally supposed to be. . . . He was a practical preacher, never metaphysical or speculative, never wild and visionary, never whining and fastidious."[36] Henry Boehm, who testified to having heard Asbury fifteen hundred times, said that "[t]here was a rich variety in his sermons. No tedious sameness; no repeating old stale truths. He could be a son of thunder or consolation."[37] Reubin Ellis wrote to Edward Dromgoole from Charleston on February 23, 1798:

> I think Bro. Asbury preached the greatest sermon that ever I heard from these words (Jer. 15 and 19) "If thou take forth the precious from the vile, thou shalt be as my mouth." And the word was indeed with power. A cry arose throughout the Church, almost; We turned into exhortation, and prayer, in different parts of the Church where Mourners were crying for mercy, till near 10 O'Clock.[38]

In short, Asbury was a more than adequate communicator of those spiritual truths that he perceived his congregations needed. His Scripture texts were often springboards to launch a word or idea that needed to be delivered. Asbury saw little difference between exhortation and preaching. Asbury and his fellow preachers often pressed home truths, doctrines, warnings, and instructions on themes that were quite different from the announced passages of Scripture. Asbury had things that he wanted to say, and he knew that it would be a long time before he returned to a particular audience. His experience on June 7, 1774, may not have been an isolated event: "[M]y ideas left me, though I felt myself spirited in addressing the people by way of exhortation" (1:118). Especially in the latter years of his life, Asbury became less systematic and more impromptu. Ezekiel Cooper, noting this, stated that

> [h]e was, however, sometimes rather abrupt and obscure, owing to the suddenness of his transitions and depressions; and his method frequently bore the appearance of the want of attention, and correct arrangement: this was discoverable, or rather apparent, in his epistolary correspondence and conversations, as well as in his extemporary public preaching; but this supposed neglect and apparent irregularity, or defect, was sometimes made more impressive and more touching, than the most lucid and critical order or the most ingenious and methodical arrangement.[39]

Eternal Urgency

The twin hallmarks of Asbury's preaching were immediacy and inclusiveness. Both were characterized by a radical optimism that formed the heart of Wesleyan theology. Wesley's exhortations in his sermon "The Scripture Way of Salvation" had been: "Do you believe you are sanctified by faith? Be true then to your principle and look for this blessing just as you are, neither better, nor worse: as a poor sinner that has still nothing to pay, nothing to plead but, 'Christ died.' And if you look for it as you are, then expect it now."[40] Alexander Mather had preached "now" sermons: "Believe now! Come to Christ now!"[41] When the Methodist itinerant David Lewis had led a sinner to the Lord, the sinner responded to the promise of pardoning grace by saying, "Mr. Lewis, it can't be possible that so much filth can by purged away in so short time!"[42] When G.G. Goss assessed the effectiveness of Methodism in its first century, he stated its working premise: "Methodism assumes that God is ready at all times to pardon the sinner."[43] When James Jenkins preached at M'Quarter Camp Meeting on Suntee Circuit, South Carolina, the backslidden German Charles Fisher recalled, "I went to de camp meetins and one shinkins breached. He took his tex, you art weighed in de palance, and art found wanting. He vent on weighing off a great many peoples; and old Fisher did come out just noting at all."[44]

Asbury left legacies of astute psychological observation and informal education initiative to his preachers. It was said of Hope Hull, who learned Latin and started a school, that a listener "felt as if he had passed through a process of spiritual engineering which had mapped before him the field of his accomplished life."[45] While Jacob Young, roughhewn and Kentucky bred, was once preaching, he was interrupted by an "ignorant, rich, rude infidel." The old man tried to impress Young by referring to John Locke's *Essay on Human Understanding*. Young recalled, "I had just given Locke's essay a faithful reading; and was enabled to discover that he had not read them at all. He was swamped and became angry. Our combat lasted several hours."[46]

Asbury preached within the prevailing pastoral paradigm, of which he was a foremost molder. It had begun with the preaching of George Whitefield and had been defended by Jonathan Edwards in his *Treatise Concerning Religious Affections*. Of those who embraced the revivalistic paradigm (i.e., New Lights), E. Brooks Holifield writes, "By pastoral care they meant the entire philosophy of clerical duties: preaching, administering the sacraments, governing in the congregation, studying in private, and praying in solitude. They also used the term to mean the private treating of souls, in the great affair of their eternal salvation."[47]

On Sunday, June 16, Asbury wrote a preaching charge that the "great affair" for a preacher was:

> *Warning* or admonishing *every man*, and *teaching every man*, according to the universal commission in the Gospel. In all wisdom: but those who have been taught, and are negligent in *teaching* and giving this warning: O, pity, pity, pity that there are such! Do you work faithfully? Continue to do it in the name and by the authority of Father, Son and Holy Spirit: tell this rebellious generation they are already condemned, and will be shortly damned: preach to them like Moses from Mount Sinai and Ebal, like David—"The wicked shall be turned into hell, and all the nations that forget God", like Isaiah—"Who amongst you shall dwell with devouring fire? Who amongst you can dwell with everlasting burnings?" like Ezekiel—"O, wicked man! thou shalt surely die!" Pronounce the eight woes uttered by the Son of God near the close of his ministry, and ask with him—"Ye serpents, ye generation of vipers, how can ye escape the damnation of hell?" Preach as if you had seen heaven and its celestial inhabitants and had hovered over the bottomless pit and beheld the tortures and heard the groans of the damned (2:784–5).

Methodism's preaching and pastoral care were "next-life" oriented. Eternity with or without God was the ever-present crossroads. With this scythe, Methodism reaped its harvest. The congregation, "saints and sinners, together wept and sobbed" when Timothy Dewey cried out in Plymouth, New York,

> O sinner! Sinner! Are you determined to take hell by storm?
> Can you brave the vengeance of a righteous God? Can you dwell
> in devouring fire? Can you stand everlasting burning? Is your
> flesh iron, and are your hands brass, that you dare to plunge
> into hell fire?[48]

These were urgent, pungent words, especially if they had been prefaced with the gospel song:

> I'm glad that I was born to die, glory halleluiah!
> From grief and woe my soul shall fly, glory halleluiah!
> I long to quit this cumbrous clay, glory halleluiah!
> And reign with Christ in endless day, glory halleluiah.[49]

The Task above All Others

Asbury often preached without food, bath, or sleep, immediately after a ride of forty miles or more. That, combined with his frail physical condition, would for most individuals have rendered preaching an impossibility. The *sitz im leben* made smooth transitions and decorative language difficult, but such adverse circumstances did not deter plain truth to plain people. Neither did they dampen "the Word of the Lord," which was "like fire" within him. For Asbury, preaching was a compulsion ordained and enabled by God. This task above all other pastoral obligations would transform the nation and "spread scriptural holiness over the land."[50]

When Asbury was 68 years old, he preached while plagued with a "swelled face." "I was turned into another man—the Spirit of God came powerfully upon me, and there was a deep feeling amongst the people" (2:742). Three weeks later in the state of South Carolina, he preached on 2 Corinthians 5:11: "If the people say it was like thunder and lightning I shall not be surprised. I spoke in power from God, and there was a general and deep feeling in the congregation: thine, O Lord, be all the glory!" (2:745).

Asbury delighted in the story of two preachers in England, one "smooth and eloquent" and the other "plain and blunt." A revival of growth was occurring in the circuit where both were employed. When asked what was the cause of the revival, the local inhabitants would uniformly answer, "The plain blunt brother."[51] Plainness and bluntness characterized most early American Methodist preaching. Such was John Kobler's description of a preaching incident in Dayton, Ohio, on January 1, 1799: "I lifted up my voice like a trumpet, cried aloud and spared not; laid before them the corruptions of their wicked hearts, and the fearful consequences of a life of sin, in such pressing terms that many of them looked wild, and stood aghast, as if they would take to their heels."[52]

Fast Draw Preaching

Asbury's legacy was a plain straightforward message delivered extemporaneously, which moved the affections and called for action. When a Presbyterian commended the sermon of a fellow Presbyterian preacher, he stated, "Why the doctor preached right at the heart, just like a Methodist preacher."[53] No less accurate was the German lady, who, after hearing Asa Shinn (a founding member of the Methodist Protestant Church), exclaimed that "it was as easy to tell the difference between a preacher vat preached over the spirit, from one vat preached over the letter as it was to tell the difference between pone-bread and pound-cake."[54]

When the itinerant Abraham Whitworth preached in Queen Anne County, Maryland, a local pastor condemned him for preaching "the knowledge of sins forgiven," especially since Whitworth did not have a college education. Whitworth challenged the non-Methodist pastor to choose a text and he would immediately preach on it, provided that the pastor would allow Whitworth to choose a text on which his detractor would immediately preach. "The parson excused himself because of the lateness of the hour."[55] When preaching was reduced to a quick-draw shootout, the Methodists won every time; no wonder they claimed the West. Asbury's preaching philosophy was hammered out on the anvil of trial and error. "It seems strange, that sometimes, after much premeditation and devotion, I cannot express my thoughts with readiness and perspicuity; whereas at other times, proper sentences of Scripture and apt expressions occur without care of much thought. Surely this is of the Lord, to convince us that it is not by power of might, but by his Spirit the work must be done" (1:126).[56]

The positive side of this methodology was noted by Jedediah Morse in 1792: "Their mode of preaching is entirely extemporaneous, very loud and animated. . . . They appear studiously to avoid connection in their discourses and are fond of introducing pathetic stories which are calculated to affect the tender passions. Their manner is very solemn, and their preaching is frequently attended with surprising effect upon their audiences."[57] The underside was a style of preaching that secured results, but was often biblically and theologically rootless. One novice itinerant used an apt metaphor in recalling his use of Scripture:

> I went through the preliminaries and took my text and began operation. It was a text, which I have since found out that I did not understand, but it afforded me a basis for extending remarks. I used it a little like a cowboy uses a stob to which he fastens his

lariat when he wants his pony to graze. It gives him latitude. So I fastened on to that text and grazed about it from all points of the compass. What I lacked in my knowledge of it I more than made up in the length of time I worked at it.[58]

Methodist preachers spoke revolutionary language in a revolutionary age. John Wilkins, a defender of American rights, argued that Americans responded to language that was "manly," "nervous," and even "awkward and uncouth." He went on to say that "the speech which produces the effect you intend in the most forcible manner, in my opinion, [is] the best."[59] Methodist preachers were hardly more dramatic and sensate than Patrick Henry, who knelt as if he were a manacled slave and uttered, "Is life so dear, our peace so sweet, as to be purchased at the price of chains and slavery? Forbid it, Almighty God!" He then sprang to his feet and cried out, "Give me liberty," and then as he plunged an imaginary dagger into his chest, lowered his voice into a solemn "or give me death."[60] Asbury and his followers extended Henry's and Jefferson's "declaration of liberty," a language that according to Andrew Burstein contained "sensory power, that coursed through the nervous system and in fact, made sense."[61]

The one innate talent that Asbury had for preaching was the quality of his voice. His words came out in a deep, sonorous bass, which beckoned attention regardless of its content. The richness of tone easily carried to the back of any church and was especially necessary for the penetration of open air spaces in which Methodist congregations often gathered. James Quinn said, "I have thought that the good bishop was the best reader of the Holy Bible I ever heard. His voice was a deep-tone bass, without a jar. . . . He said it was a shame if not a sin, for a minister to read the Scriptures in a kind of whisper, or dull, monotonous tone, either in families or congregations."[62]

Asbury enjoyed singing, a fondness that was enhanced by a melodious voice, almost never off key. He often broke out in song while on the trail, a song that lifted his own spirit as well as of those who heard him. Asbury's voice commanded attention; it was not easily forgotten. That's the way he wanted it.

19. "I Pity the Poor Slaves"

In Awe of His Mentor

At the age of 68, Asbury had completely lost whatever corpulence he had ever possessed. White hair, shriveled face, gaunt frame, and stiff joints gave him the appearance of a walking corpse, whenever he was able to walk. Rheumatoid arthritis, a wheezing-gasping voice, colitis, and abscessed teeth transmuted every day into a battle against encroaching death. His afflictions did not prevent him from preaching twice in Georgetown, South Carolina, on the first Sabbath of the New Year in 1813. "It was a small time—cold, or burning the dead" (2:721). In spite of an inflamed foot and a high fever, Asbury made the cold ride into North Carolina. Henry Boehm carried him into the churches, where he sat as he preached.

It was not until March 14, 1813, that Asbury failed to preach on a Sunday. On February 4 he was able to put on his shoes after not having worn them for several weeks. The return to partial normalcy elicited a gleeful chuckle and the exclamation, "O, the sufferings I have endured—patiently, I hope!" (2:722). He was still not able to walk without crutches, but managed to preach each day until he and Boehm reached Newbern on February 8. McKendree chaired the Virginia Conference, which was convened on the tenth. Asbury commented, "[W]e had great order, great union, and great despatch [sic] of business" (2:723). Not quite. Jesse Lee preached on Acts 17:6, "These that have turned the world upside down." During the night, some town jokesters turned everything that could be picked up in Newbern, upside down.[1] Jesse Lee's talents did not include the maintenance of order.

In Baltimore, Asbury visited with Philip Otterbein for the last time. Otterbein had assisted in the ordination of Asbury almost three decades earlier and would die in 1813, at the age of 87. The aged friends laughed and chuckled while they discussed the events and persons of the past that had bound them together. They freely exchanged their interpretations of biblical prophecies in light of the war that was presently being fought. Conversation with like-minded friends was Francis Asbury's most enjoyable entertainment.

At the Philadelphia Conference, Henry Boehm was appointed to the Schulkyl District, which meant that he would no longer serve as Asbury's helper and fellow traveler. When the conference asked if there was anything against Boehm's character, Asbury answered, "Nothing against Brother Boehm." He then haltingly rose and emphatically stated, with some nervousness, "[F]or five years he has been my constant companion. He served me as a son; he served me as a brother; he served me as a servant; he served me as a slave."[2]

It was an emotional moment for the bishop. Henry Boehm had spent more private moments with Asbury than any other man. Six weeks later, Asbury appointed him as one of the executors of his will. However, the intimacy between the two had never evolved into familiarity. Henry Boehm was always in awe of his mentor: "Bishop Asbury possessed more deadness to the world, more of a self-sacrificing spirit, more of the spirit of prayer, of Christian enterprise, of labor, and of benevolence, than any other man I ever knew."[3]

Asbury made little mention of the ongoing war between his adopted and native countries. On August 29 he wrote to the widow of Henry Willis, "*I fear! awfully*, and almost presume that we shall hear on our once happy Columbian plains the blood of thousands is shed" (3:494). The next day, several hundred American soldiers were massacred by Creek Indians led by William Weatherford, alias Chief Red Eagle.[4] The event turned the tide of public sentiment against the British. In response to the massacre, a hitherto relatively unknown Tennesseean named Andrew Jackson began to raise a 2,000-man volunteer army.

Asbury's Valedictory

Asbury was too consumed by the future of his own "army" to pay much attention to a skirmish between the Americans and the British. His stakes were much higher, and he was constantly gripped by the thought that his command was in its waning days. During the summer months of 1813, he prepared two documents. The first was his will, officially dated June 6. "Knowing the uncertainty of the tenure of life, I have made my will, appointing Bishop McKendree, Daniel Hitt, and Henry Boehm, my executors" (2:732). It was a brief document: books, horses, and carriage were left to William McKendree; to the executors, two thousand dollars for the publishing of Bibles, "pious" books and tracts; eighty dollars annually to be paid to Elizabeth Dickens, widow of John Dickens. Of most interest was the request that a Bible be bequeathed to each child named after Asbury. The publishing house eventually distributed over a thousand of these Bibles.

Asbury developed another document during the summer. The custom of presenting a "valedictory" was first mentioned at the New York Conference on May 26, 1813. "Our conference concluded in peace, and the bishops, upon reading the stations, gave a valedictory address, in which our brethren were assured that the plan of their future labours were deliberately formed" (2:731). Asbury decided to put the innovation to full use.

The "valedictory" that Asbury penned was not simply a reminder that the organization of the Methodist Episcopal Church had been carefully created; it was a plea that the present form would remain unchanged. "Especially guard against every danger and innovation," he wrote. The "valedictory" germinated over the summer and received its finishing touches August 5, 1813. The farewell was a curious piece that expressed little of sentiment or gratitude. Of approximately nine thousand words, the longest tract written by Asbury on anything, almost half consisted of direct quotes from Thomas Haweis's *History of the Church of Christ*—the same Haweis whom Asbury had heard at Stillingfleet's church.

Asbury's valedictory was an apology for his leadership and an argument for an itinerant superintendency. In Haweis, Asbury found fodder for his argument. In fact, Haweis stated that the Methodist mode of episcopal government was more apostolic than the Church of England ever was, or could be, "without a radical reformation from its essential forms of locality, written sermons and prayers, state laws, and human policy."[5] Asbury echoed Haweis's assertion that the superintendent was chosen from those "who were most distinguished for zeal, wisdom, sufferings, influence, or respectability of any kind."[6]

Haweis noted that the preservation of order by the rapidly growing apostolic church, initiated at Pentecost, had necessitated the election of a president, the apostle James. James was superior to the rest because, according to Asbury, he had not denied Christ. James, as well as succeeding church leaders, in Haweis's interpretation, commanded respect and obedience, "capable of swaying the decisions of their brethren; consulted in all difficult cases, and placed foremost in the hour of danger."[7] It was not long before the apostolic bishops lost the plan of itinerancy, however, and began to settle in the larger cities.

What the Reformation had only partly restored, English and American Methodism had brought into full fruition. In both order and mobility, American Methodism reflected primitive Christianity. Asbury confidently stated, "It is my confirmed opinion that the apostles acted both as bishops and traveling superintendents in planting and watering, ruling and ordering, the whole connection; and that they did not ordain any local bishops, but that they ordained local deacons and elders. I feel satisfied we should do the same."[8] Asbury forthrightly stated his role in Methodism as *primus inter pares*. "If the elders that rule well are worthy of double honor, then the bishops that rule well must be worthy of triple honor, especially when they do so large a part of ruling, preaching, and presiding in conferences."[9] The following charge to McKendree is important, not only in that it explicates the job description by which Asbury lived, but also in revealing the protective and conservative mindset which dominated Asbury's thinking:

> Be diligent to see and know how the different charitable contributions are disposed of. Sign no journals of an Annual Conference till everything is recorded, everything appears correctly and fairly. Should there be at any time failures in any department such as you cannot cure or restore, appeal to the General Conference. Be rigidly strict in all things. Examine well those who come as candidates for the ministry. It is ours to plead, protest, and oppose *designing* men from getting into the ministry [italics mine]. It is the peculiar excellence of our church and the superintendent's

glory and stronghold that the character of every minister among us must undergo a strict examination once a year. Put men into office in whom you can confide. If they betray your trust and confidence let them do it but once. Of all wickedness, spiritual wickedness is the greatest; and of all the deceptions, religious deception is the worst. Beware of men who have a constitutional cast to deception. Let every office, grade, and station among us know his place, keep his place and do his duty; then you need not fear for the ark of God. The Lord Jesus will take care of and support His own cause.[10]

Asbury's Ecclesiology

Asbury increasingly labored under the dual concerns of securing both his own legacy and the future prosperity of the church. Inherent contradictions did not deter him. While he did not appeal to the authority of apostolic succession, yet Asbury felt it important to argue that Thomas Coke, who had ordained him, was ordained deacon and elder by two scriptural English bishops.[11] (Had Asbury forgotten or chosen to ignore the connecting link of Wesley?) "Let any other Church trace its succession as direct and as pure if they can."[12] There was no one biblical order of church government, yet he believed that American Methodism most resembled the system established by the early church.

And, of course, Asbury had redeemed the appellation "bishop" from all the contamination it had collected through the centuries. "Would their bishops ride five or six thousand miles in nine months for eighty dollars a year, with their traveling expense less or more, preach daily when opportunity serves, meet a number of campmeetings in the year, make arrangement for stationing seven hundred preachers, ordain a hundred more annually, ride through all kinds of weather, and along roads in the worst state at our time of life—the one sixty-nine, the other in his fifty-sixth year?"[13]

Asbury's ecclesiology was complete: A church was a group of persons who worshipped in a simple building, in an emotional manner, with a minimum of liturgical rites, led by a nonresidential and informally educated pastor, and who adhered to a hierarchical form of church government. Yet, as Asbury rode through New England during the summer, the stench of spiritual death filled his nostrils. New England Methodists were building churches with pews, steeples, and bells. They were renting out pews and giving money to charitable causes outside of Methodism. New Englanders were incongruent aesthetically, economically, and emotionally with his vision for the church. It was all coming to an impasse. "We have made a stand in the New England Conference against steeples and pews; and shall possibly give up the houses, unless the pews are taken out, and the houses made sure to us exclusively. The conference now pursues a course which will surely lead to something decisive; we will be flattered no longer" (2:736).

Even with American Methodism's escalating respectability, comfortable accommodations were not easy to come by. Hunger, heat, and sickness tracked Asbury throughout eastern New York during the month of July. He passed over into Pennsylvania at Great Bend, south of Binghamton, New York; there he stayed with a family of infidels and paid his lodging bill by lecturing, singing, and praying. "[S]ome stared, some smiled, and some wept" (2:738). Methodism had not completely lost its stigma. As late as 1810, a New Yorker had declared, "The Methodists are not fit to preach—they are a poor, ignorant set, not fit to preach in any public place; but if they can get a lot of ignorant old women together, in some corner of the town, they will do to preach to them."[14]

Suffering from insomnia, Asbury stayed up to hull peas after his host had gone to bed. In the Blue Mountain area, he and McKendree were refused food. The inhospitality was depreciating the travel funds to the extent that Asbury had to borrow five dollars. Current economics allowed both men and beasts to fare sumptuously for sixty cents. On the Sunday of August 1, Asbury was hosted by Henry Boehm at his father's chapel, where he preached twice. Here he tarried for three days to finish composing his valedictory address.

From Lancaster, the bishops made their way to Morgantown, Pennsylvania, where Asbury preached to about "three thousand people." The singing and praying throughout the night allowed him only three hours' sleep. In Carroll County, he stopped at the grave of his one-time traveling companion Henry Willis, a man of intense spirit and constant physical activity. An exception to most of the itinerants, Willis was well educated and an eloquent speaker. Thomas Ware labeled him "preeminent" in extraordinary gifts.[15]

Methodism's Most Critical Problem

During the first week of October 1813, the bishops presided over the Tennessee Conference, with McKendree occupying the chair almost the entire time. Asbury glossed over the proceedings with the following comment: "Our progress daily was great, and made in great peace and order" (2:743). Actually, there was great contention. A quarterly conference had suspended a local preacher for buying a slave. He had appealed his case to the annual conference, where his presiding elder, Learner Blackman, defended him. Blackman argued that the church was inconsistent in its attitude toward itinerant preachers who owned slaves while expelling those who bought them. Furthermore, he said, the condition of a slave in the preacher's possession was much better than that of one owned by a non-Christian. Christians were more likely to assure that the families of slaves they owned would remain intact. The Nashville District Quarterly Conferences had been irregular in enforcing the law against buying slaves and held a double standard for its ministers and preachers. Although the conference did not overturn the quarterly conference's ruling, Learner Blackman's arguments were persuasive; a significant minority of the conference agreed with him. That minority probably included Asbury, who, for the whole of the debate, sat quietly and said nothing.[16]

The issue had come up at least two other times earlier that year. When Asbury was present at the Virginia Conference in Newbern in February, an applicant for a local minister's license was rejected because he was not "sufficiently established in his opposition to slavery."[17] At the Baltimore Conference, which met during the last week of March, Samuel Mitchell passionately pled for overruling the laws of states that prohibited emancipation. If the Methodists really believed that slavery was a great crime, "they would adopt some decisive measures against it, seeing that they let no other sin go unpunished."[18] The conference did record a rule prohibiting the ministers from owning slaves and the laity from trading in slaves. Asbury made no mention of the debates or the results in his journal. For all practical purposes, the voice of Asbury concerning slavery had been silenced.

There can be no doubt about Asbury's genuine empathy for the slaves during his entire ministry. He preached to them time and time again, to which they responded with veneration close to worship. They openly wept when they beheld his feeble, emaciated condition. Asbury consistently showed a genuine concern that the slaves hear the gospel and that they be allowed to worship in company with their white owners. Asbury first openly condemned slavery on June 23, 1776, when some slave masters in Baltimore had not allowed their slaves to attend Methodist class meetings. "How will the sons of oppression answer for their conduct, when the great Proprietor of all shall call them to an account!" (1:190).

Southern Slavery

Asbury's silence on the issue over the next five years may have been because slavery in the middle-Atlantic states was more genteel and less pervasive than in the deep South. Asbury's condemnation became more invective when he rode south. Asbury did not visit South Carolina until he became bishop. On a day when he had ridden twenty-seven miles without eating, the rice plantations were a stark and appalling affront. "If a man-of-war is a 'floating hell,' these are standing ones: wicked masters, overseers, and Negroes—cursing, drinking—no Sabbaths, no sermons. But hush! perhaps my journal will never see the light; and if it does, matters may mend before that time; and it is probable I shall be beyond their envy or good-will" (2:7).

Asbury never did get beyond their "envy or goodwill." He was an elected official of the Methodist Episcopal Church, a church that embraced North and South, rich and poor, Black and white, bonded and free. Prophets usually alienate their hearers, but a prophetic message does not play well in a revivalistic and

rapidly growing church. "Speaking the truth in love" would call for retrench-
ment and redefinition, which is antithetical to a mind constantly seeking the
escalation of numbers, whether they be miles traveled, attendees preached to,
or adherents gained.

Both Rankin and Coke took more radical stands against slavery than did
Asbury. Rankin recalled his 1775 sermon preached in Maryland: "I endeavored
to open up and enforce the cause of all our ministry. I told them that the sins of
Great Britain and her Colonies cried aloud for vengeance and in a peculiar manner the dreadful sin of buying and selling the souls and bodies of the poor
African."[19] He conversed with like-minded Quakers Anthony Benezet and Israel
Pemberton, who became his friends. Rankin did not temper his condemnation
of slavery. We can only guess at what his approach to emancipation would have
been had he stayed in America.

For Thomas Coke, the situation was a bit different. As Coke passed through
Virginia in 1785, he spoke out against slavery, stirring up no little wrath. One
time, when he was staying with a very hospitable slave owner, Captain Dillard,
who treated his slaves kindly, Coke bemoaned the fact that he "could not beat
into the head of that poor man the evil of keeping them in slavery."[20] The hostility intensified to the extent that a mob threatened Coke with flogging. "A high-
headed lady . . . told the rioters (As I was afterwards informed) that she would
give fifty pounds if they would give that little doctor one hundred lashes."[21]
Coke gradually became more discreet and circumspect in his stance. When he
later returned to Virginia, he adopted a different tactic. "Here I bore a public
testimony against slavery, and have found out a method of delivering it without
much offence, or at least without causing a tumult; and that is by first addressing
the negroes in a very pathetic manner on the duty of servants to masters; and
then the whites which will receive what I have to say to them."[22]

Methodism's Civil Response

Asbury's Methodism was slow to adopt the repelling behavior of John
Woolman, the Quaker tailor who walked back and forth between New England
and North Carolina dressed in undyed clothes and refusing to board with anyone
who owned slaves. Even more eccentric was the dwarfed hunchback Benjamin
Lay, who, in order to dramatize mistreatment of slaves, lived in a cave, stood with
one bare foot in the snow, and threw himself across the yearly meeting door. To
illustrate how America was stabbing a sword through the Negroes' heart, he ran
his scabbard through a hollowed-out Bible containing a bladder of red juice, then
sprinkled "blood" all over the parishioners who sat nearby.[23] Even the Quakers
found him a bit too dramatic and expelled him. It is ironic that in 1790 Asbury
wrote to a Quaker and expressed his wish for both Methodists and Friends to
"bear a stronger testimony against races, fairs, plays, and balls" (3:87). He prob-

ably would not have called on Benjamin Lay to join him on the picket line. Asbury's emotional constitution was too delicate and his physical bearing too dignified to hazard the kind of offensiveness and repulsiveness that was required.

Early on, Asbury hoped that Methodism would purge itself of slavery. On February 23, 1779, he wrote;

> My soul was not tormented by satan, as it has sometimes been, but was kept in sweet peace. I have lately been impressed with a deep concern, for bringing about the freedom of slaves in America, and feel resolved to do what I can to promote it. If God in His providence hath detained me in this country, to be instrumental in so merciful and great an undertaking, I hope he will give me wisdom and courage sufficient, and enable me to give Him all the glory. I am strongly persuaded that if the Methodists will not yield on this point and emancipate their slaves, God will depart from them.

And on March 27, 1779 he recorded:

> I have just finished my feeble performance against slavery; if our conference should come into the measure, I trust it will be one of the means toward generally expelling the practice from our Society. How would my heart rejoice if my detention in these parts, should afford me leisure in any measure in so desirable a work.[24]

Contrary to Asbury's idealism, American Methodism never did take an unequivocal stand against slavery.[25] The moral posturing was there, but practical implementation was lacking. The members of the 1780 conference at Baltimore resolved "[t]hat slavery is contrary to the laws of God, man, and nature, and hurtful to society; contrary to the dictates of conscience and pure religion; and doing that which we would not others should do to us and ours." They passed "disapprobation on all our friends who keep slaves and advise their freedom."[26]

The closest that Methodism came to taking action on this issue was at the 1784 founding conference, when the minutes stated that "every member of our society who has slaves in his possession, shall within twelve months after notice given to him by the Assistant . . . legally execute and record an instrument, whereby he emancipates and sets free every slave in his possession who is between the ages of forty and forty-five, immediately or at farthest when they arrive at the age of forty-five."[27] The Assistants were to keep a journal that recorded the names of all the slaves in their district and the dates of their manumission. Violators of the slavery rules were to be denied entrance to the Lord's table. However, there was a qualification: "These rules are to affect the members of our society no further than as they are consistent with the laws of the states in which they reside."[28]

Asbury and his followers wanted to keep the laws of God and the laws of man at the same time. It didn't work. As early as the Baltimore Conference in June 1785 Asbury, because of all the "agitators," agreed to a suspension of "the execution of the minute on slavery."[29] Just after this, on September 2, 1785, a letter to Freeborn Garrettson demonstrated Asbury's ignorance concerning the severity of the slavery problem: "With respect to slavery, I am clear, and always was, that if every Preacher would do his duty we should not need to make any Minutes, use no force, but only loving and argumentative persuasion."[30]

The Methodist leadership decided to "bite the bullet" in the General Conference of 1800. Not that Methodism had been entirely impotent; between 1780 and 1790 Methodists manumitted 834 slaves on Maryland's eastern shore.[31] Even so, the 1800 conference, which opened at Baltimore on April 6, moved that: "The annual conferences are directed to draw up addresses for the gradual emancipation of the slaves, to the legislature of the states in which no general laws have been passed for that purpose. These addresses shall urge, in the most respectful, but pointed manner, the necessity of a law for the gradual emancipation of the slaves."[32] Three other motions, more pointed and urgent, were made but defeated: "[N]o slaveholders shall be admitted into the Methodist Episcopal Church"; "emancipate all children born after July 4, 1800 to slaves owned by Methodists"; "require every member of the Methodist Episcopal Church, holding slaves . . . within a term of one year . . . given instrument of emancipation for all his slaves."[33]

Theological Shallowness

John Harper, stationed in Charleston with George Dougherty, was forced to burn his copies of the mandate, and subsequently wrote Ezekiel Cooper to warn that Asbury would come to Charleston "only at the peril of his life."[34] Asbury stayed out of Charleston until January 1803. Asbury was informed that the South Carolina state general assembly had publicly read the Methodist decision and subsequently passed a law "which prohibited a minister's attempting to instruct any number of blacks with the doors shut; and authorizing a peace officer to break open the door in such cases, and disperse or whip the offenders" (2:272). A line had been drawn, and Methodism retreated.

The cries of dissension were so great that Methodism voted for an accommodation in 1804. "We declare that we are as much as ever convinced of the great evil of slavery . . . and we do fully authorize all the yearly conferences to make whatever regulations they judge proper in the present case, respecting the admission of persons to official stations in our church."[35] The earlier resolution had lost its teeth and would attempt to gum slavery to death. In other words,

Methodism fell in step with the nation, which tried to pursue a gradualist emancipation policy until the 1820s, after Asbury's death.[36]

Historian David Davis states that "[m]en who had acquired an increasing
respect for property and for the intricate workings of natural and social laws
could or would not view, as an unmitigated evil, an institution that had developed through the centuries."[37] "Natural rights" was a concept both thoroughly
American and thoroughly Wesleyan, in spite of Wesley's graphic description of
slavery's brutality in his "Thoughts upon Slavery," published in 1759.[38] For that
reason, Thomas Jefferson could talk about "inalienable rights" and still own slaves.
Neither Wesley nor Jefferson believed in equality between Blacks and whites; nor
did Asbury.

Lewis M. Purifoy argues that Wesley's thoughts upon slavery lacked theological and biblical substance. "It could as well have been written by any intelligent
child of the Enlightenment. . . . The argument as thus is based upon the law of
nature, and the appeal to reason and good will. It is most emphatically not scriptural; no text is invoked and the name of Jesus Christ is never used."[39] The "natural rights" theme was expounded in the bishop's 1800 pastoral address. Slavery, it
said, is repugnant to inalienable rights and personal freedom because the country
would be glorious if "equal liberty were everywhere established and everywhere
enjoyed."[40]

Methodism simply mirrored the inconsistency of a nation that declared that
all men are "created equal" and at the same time held slaves. At the 1804 General
Conference, Freeborn Garrettson moved that the three bishops draft a section of
the discipline "to suit the Southern and Northern States" regarding slavery. Even
though the motion carried, Asbury refused to act on it. Ezekiel Cooper proposed
that a committee be formed by a member from each conference that would create
a report "containing all the motions."[41]

A House Divided

When the debate over slavery reached a fervent pitch on the conference floor,
Asbury slowly rose from his chair. His very change of posture could influence the
temperament of a congregation. In carefully moderated words, Asbury stated
that he had pledged himself in the southern camp meetings to speak on the issue.
He then tersely declared, "I am called upon to suffer for Christ's sake not for
slavery."[42] James Jenkins recalled that "this was a short speech, but it had the
desired effect. Our radical friends were quite calm."[43]

The calm was only a mirage. Asbury's speech suppressed collective rage and
guilt. In 1805, James Keys wrote Edward Dromgoole, "Lord, brother I wish I
never owned or was master of a negro! They are hell to us in this world, and I fear
they will be so in the next. But what to do with them, I know not. We can't live
with them or without them; and what to [do] is a question."[44] When a cruel slave

owner attempted to testify in a Methodist meeting, he developed a cough, to which the presiding preacher responded, "That's right brother; cough up the [slaves] and then you'll have an open time."[45]

Methodism increasingly lost its moral nerve. The 1804 conference removed from the *Discipline* the previous request that the annual conferences prepare emancipation petitions to the respective state legislatures. Abel Stevens concluded that "[t]he tone was more subdued."[46] Asbury had toned down his pronouncements long before this. In 1797, he had confessed to fear "lest I had, or should, say too much on slavery" (2:144). The 1804 conference stated its rules for the emancipation of slaves, which included that "[e]very member of our society who sells a slave, except at the request of the slave, in cases of mercy or humanity, agreeably to the judgement of a committee of three male members of the society, appointed by the preacher who has charge of the circuit or station, shall immediately after full proof, be excluded the society"; the conference then declared that the "states of North Carolina, South Carolina, and Georgia shall be exempted from the operation of the above rules."[47]

The 1804 conference also divided the *Discipline* into two parts (on the motion of Thomas Coke): "The Doctrines and Discipline" and "the Temporal Economy," the latter containing the statement against slavery. Two thousand copies, without the second section, were sent to South Carolina. Asbury stated on August 19, "I revised the *Revised Form* of the spiritual part of our Discipline: I had long wished to separate the most excellent from the excellent" (2:440). The "excellent" was the emancipation of the slave, while the "most excellent" was the salvation of the slave's soul. Asbury was so convinced of this that in the 1808 general conference he moved that the section and rule on slavery be left out of the thousand copies of the *Discipline* sent to South Carolina.[48]

Asbury's Theology of Slavery

The rescinding of Methodism's stand against slavery ultimately became a theological issue, and Asbury believed the best theology was that which was most evangelistically effective. To take an inflexible stand against slavery would cripple Methodism's attempts to reach both Blacks and whites. The preachers rationalized that God was more pleased with individuals who rescued souls than he was with those who liberated bodies.

In 1797, Asbury wrote to George Roberts in Charleston, South Carolina, "What now can sweeten the bitter cup like religion? The slaves soon see the preachers are their friends, and soften their owners towards them. There are thousands here of slaves who if we could come out to them would embrace religion" (3:160). Anesthetization was certainly better than conflagration; toleration, if it didn't allow Blacks to escape hell now, would procure eternal bliss. Good slaveholders were not those who freed their slaves, as had Freeborn Garrettson and Philip Gatch, but those who allowed their slaves to hear the gospel. Methodists increasingly believed that they were to work toward amelioration of the slaves' condition rather than emancipation. They thought a happy Negro would be more receptive to the gospel, and be then even happier, although in chains.

No matter how tightly Asbury constructed his theological house, the scream of a nagging conscience could be heard inside. Even while he depended on the slaves of the Goughs, Remberts, Bassetts, and Hills, a conflicting value system warred within.[49]

> [M]y mind is much pained. O! to be dependent on slaveholders is in part to be a slave, and I was free born. I am brought to conclude that slavery will exist in Virginia perhaps for ages; there is not a sufficient sense of religion nor of liberty to destroy it; Methodists, Baptists, Presbyterians, in the highest flights of rapturous piety still maintain and defend it. I judge in after ages it will be so that poor men and free men will not live among slaveholders, but will go to new lands; they only who are concerned in, and dependent on them will stay in old Virginia (2:151).

In a single broadside, Asbury condemned the kind of religion that he espoused. It was the kind of religion that was absent from New England, a popular religion that demanded a popular leader, popular with both Black and white, rich and poor. When Asbury stepped on the porch of Cal Carter's fine house along the Rappahannock River in Virginia, he may have not been aware that his host was a descendant of Robert "King" Carter, who when he died in 1722 left an estate of three hundred thousand acres and one thousand slaves.[50]

But who can condemn a man who daily endured the torture of heat, flies, fleas, filth, and stench, a man who occasionally slipped into the opulence of clean sheets, even if they were provided by slaves? On November 22, 1813, he recorded, "Rode to Mr. Thebeau's plantation: sweet retreat!" (2:746). Asbury and Methodism had paid an enormous price to convert the rich. Paul Evans's assessment is tragically correct: "[W]hat Asbury failed to recognize, or at least admit, was that he was being won over as much as they. The planter needed the approving stamp of religiosity even more than Asbury needed them."[51] Asbury was not willing to state forthrightly, "Purity and evangelistic success are incompatible."

All the above is not to say that Methodism became completely inept in its stand against slavery. Many preachers continued to be strong witnesses against it. William Colbert retorted to a slaveholder that he "looked upon [slave traders] to be the grandest set of villains on this side of hell."[52] Then there were the slaves themselves who adhered to Methodism and gave powerful testimony to liberty in Christ. When the slave preacher Cuff was repeatedly beaten by his owner "until the blood ran down to the ground" for praying, he responded, "you may kill me but while I live I must pray." Cuff's master cursed God for creating the Negro and spent a sleepless night. At early dawn, he sent for Cuff in order to have the slave pray for him. "What was his astonishment, when he entered, to find his master prostrate on the floor, 'crying for mercy.'"[53] The slaveholder was converted and Cuff was set free. Cynthia Lyerly has succinctly summarized the dilemma of an unbeliever who owned a truly Christian slave. "To kill a defiant slave would mean a capital loss. For the most pious slave, death would mean a spiritual gain; even nonbelieving masters had to be aware of the martyrology in the New Testament."[54]

Perhaps no human on earth ever fully integrated values that are consistently Christian, except Christ himself. Like most men, Asbury was a hodgepodge of values, most of them both temporarily and eternally good. Ultimately, he voted for a growing though incoherent church. It was better to have the largest in America, even if it was divided and afflicted by a malignant tumor. Asbury preferred to compartmentalize—two churches, two races, two *Disciplines*, and in a sense two gospels. Asbury's polarization was complete when he preached at the Virginia Conference at Newbern, North Carolina, in February 1807. "I preached to the whites, from John iii, 16; and to the Africans, on Eph. vi, 5–8" (2:530). He preached the love of God to the whites and obedient servitude to the Blacks.

Asbury's Black theology, if not congruent with a Christian ethic, was consistent with his own lifestyle. His sacrificial labors were propelled by an eschatology that life is short and eternity is long; both he and the slaves could endure a few years of physical torture for an eternity of spiritual bliss. In 1809, Asbury stated a theology that would become Methodism's working premise: "We are defrauded of great numbers by the pains that are taken to keep the blacks from us; their masters are afraid of the influence of our principles. Would not an *amelioration* in the condition and treatment of slaves have produced more practical good to the poor Africans, than any attempt at their *emancipation*? . . . What is the personal liberty of the African which he may abuse, to the salvation of his soul; how may it be compared?" (2:591).

Cultural Concession Complete

Ironically, the founder of the movement that prepared people for the next world had molded a church that would be entrapped in the primal crisis of the century, if not the entire history of the nation's existence. Armageddon would not be fought at Megiddo, but at Gettysburg. There the Methodists of the North and South met and killed one another. Asbury prayed less than three months before his ordination, "I pity the poor slaves. O that God would look down in mercy, and take their cause in hand!" (1:469). He did not realize that God's "hand" would require the death of over one half million men. Henry Boehm recorded, concerning his last visit to Charleston in 1812 with McKendree and Asbury, "(O)ur Bishops were received as angels from God."[55] Things had changed; they always do.

In August 1818 at a camp in Washington County, Maryland, when Jacob Gruber preached to three thousand people condemning slavery, using his usual wit, irony, and sarcasm, he was arrested by the local officials. The Frederick County court indicted and tried him for a felony.[56] Even though he was pronounced not guilty, the subsequent Baltimore Conference reprimanded him and "[r]esolved, that Brother Gruber be advised by the President of the Conference to be more cautious in the future, and to forbear as much as possible from the use of epithets and allusions calculated unnecessarily to irritate, without informing the people."[57] Methodism had traded moral responsibility for civil prudence. Its last abolitionist tooth had been pulled. Unfortunately, Asbury personified a problem that would plague American evangelicals for the next two hundred years, a problem accurately stated in a study by Michael Emerson and Christian Smith: "So, despite having the subcultural tools to call for radical changes in race relations, they most consistently call for changes in persons that leave the dominant social structures, institutions, and culture intact."[58]

At Death's Door

On Friday, January 7, 1814, a letter caught up with Asbury at Fayetteville, North Carolina, that told of Coke's departure for the East Indies. It was the kind of apostolic mission that was fitting for both Coke and Methodism. Coke had married into wealth and had spent the bulk of his wife's inheritance in spreading the gospel. Two days later, Asbury wrote to Zachary Myles, "I hope Dr. Coke will devote the last of his days nobly, not in making many books, but in his apostolic mission in those two vast quarters of the globe, Asia and Africa" (3:499). In that same letter, Asbury said he felt like a man of eighty rather than sixty-nine. The Virginia Conference was troublesome to Asbury as most of the discussion concerned dress. The fervor of the founder was being reduced to the legislation of the second generation. "We have been mighty in talk this session. I dare not speak my mind on the state of this place—its church or its ministry" (2:752).

The cold wind cut Asbury's emaciated body to the quick. In Baltimore, he was sick during the entire conference. "My strength and labour was to sit still" (2:753). On the closing day of the conference, Asbury preached a funeral service for his deceased friend Philip Otterbein. Climbing the Anglican-style pulpit at Otterbein's church (Old Otterbein), Asbury mustered eloquence that was befitting a friend whom he had admired as much or more than anyone else during his American ministry. "Forty years have I known the retiring modesty of this man of God; towering majestic above his fellows in learning, wisdom, and grace, yet seeking to be known only of God and the people of God; he had been sixty years a minister, fifty years a converted one" (2:753-4). The discourse took so much out of the bishop's already enfeebled condition that he retreated to Perry Hall for three days.

Asbury was pleased with the Philadelphia Conference, which began April 11. On Sunday the tenth, he preached both at the Academy and at St. George's. The two churches had split in 1801 along sociological lines, the Academy representing the merchants and artisans and St. George's largely filled with journeymen, laborers, and skilled workmen. The solution for the conflict was not found in applying the gospel, but in separating people. In a strange way, both the rich and the poor legitimized a church come of age. There was room for everybody as long as they knew their proper place.[59]

On April 24, Asbury preached three times: at Penn's Neck, New Jersey; at Salem, New Jersey; and at Cahansey Bridge. The exertion overtaxed him, and there followed a twelve-week sickness that almost took his life. Most of that time he was shut up at Michael Coate's home in Burlington, New Jersey. He never fully recovered from this bout with pleurisy and pneumonia. At least four physicians attended him. He constantly attempted to expectorate the mucus as his body convulsed with an incessant cough. For weeks there was speculation as to whether he was going to strangle or burn up with fever. When there was sufficient breath he would attempt to break out in a hymn of praise. John Wesley Bond recalled that he would frequently cry out, "Praise the Lord! Glory to God. Oh Glory!" and clap his hands together as in an ecstasy of joy. He said afterward that it was "the severest and sweetest affliction" he ever felt.[60] For ten successive nights Henry Boehm, who had been called in to assist Bond, sat up with Asbury. "Last night he seemed to be carried out of himself: all of his conversation was relative to God, Christ, and the great work of redemption."[61]

Helplessness

As soon as Asbury was sufficiently recovered, he was off over the Pennsylvania mountains. "I have been ill indeed, but medicine, nursing, and kindness, under God, have been so far effectual, that I have recovered strength enough to sit in my little covered wagon, into which they lift me" (2:755). There they were: stout, robust-looking John Wesley Bond (who outlived Asbury only by three years) driving a carriage with his frail, wrinkled little passenger, in a broad brimmed hat, bouncing up and down every time the carriage hit a rock or rut as they traversed the Alleghenies. "I groan one minute with pain, and shout glory the next!" (2:756). Along the way, the horse died and one of the shafts on the carriage broke. It was a typical Asbury journey.

The fog of gloom was thickened by news from the East that British troops under the command of Robert Ross had routed a 7,000-man force at Blandsburg, Maryland, and then marched on Washington, setting the capitol on fire. The nation was helpless, and so was Asbury. Two days later he wrote to Nelson Reed, "Well I pant! I cough! I speak hoarsely! I pray, I speak, sitting; . . . Oh, when brought by affliction as low as dribbling infancy, and even now a boy 6 years of age would excel me in strength, and motion. My mouth has failed. I cannot even eat without difficulty, food to supply" (3: 508–9).

William Burke and the Good Old Days

Upon reaching Shelby County, Kentucky, Asbury breathed a sigh of relief that William Burke was now gone; [h]e had moved to Ohio. Burke had at one point refused appointment from Asbury and had agitated for the right of local preachers to become elders. In 1807, Asbury had met with Burke and other local deacons at Burke's house to discuss the proposal. Burke said that Asbury favored the plan (which was not likely, since Asbury favored only itinerant preachers). However, no one labored more strenuously than Burke. In the early days of Kentucky, he sometimes would travel a hundred miles without seeing a living soul. In the entire year of 1798, Burke said, he did not see the face of another Methodist preacher.

William Burke had accompanied Asbury on his first trip through Kentucky, always in peril from the Indians. All those in the traveling party were armed, except Asbury. According to Burke, Asbury suggested tying a rope around the encampment at night with a small opening for escape if the Indians attacked. "The rope to be so fixed as to strike the Indians below the knee, in which case they would fall forward, and we would retreat into the dark and pour in a fire upon them from our rifles."[62] One of the party suggested that continuing to stay ahead of the Indians would kill the horses, to which Asbury responded, "Kill man, kill horse. Kill horse first." The company continued throughout the night and arrived at Stanford, Kentucky, at dusk after having ridden 110 miles in a 40-hour stretch.[63]

In April of 1796 in Jonesborough, Tennessee, Asbury had spoken regarding the examination of Burke's character. "Burke has accomplished two important things this past year. He has defeated the O'Kellyites and he has married a wife."[64] Burke deserved better than Asbury's malediction some eighteen years later: "the gloomy days of William Burke are over" (2:759).

As Asbury sat six hours a day in the Tennessee Conference at Logan County, Kentucky, where McKendree presided, his mind drifted back and forth between yesteryear and the discussions on the conference floor. He thought of Francis Poythress, Henry Burchet, Jacob Lurton, and even William Burke who had paid such a great price, going cold, wet, and hungry to open up the Kentucky wilderness to the gospel. Asbury wished for the days when it was rather easy to find unmarried men who would leave everything behind, except what could be carried in their saddlebags. The frontier revival had stagnated and perhaps had done as much harm as good; Methodism demanded an army with a disciplined mentality rather than emotional passion. The Tennessee Conference had lost members and gained only one itinerant preacher in the last two years. Alas, most of the preachers wanted to marry and locate. As Asbury sat with his eyes closed, looking like a propped-up corpse, he bemoaned the loss of vitality. Methodist preachers had once been willing to beat the bushes to find one soul cut off from both God and humanity. Now they wanted to be sought out, rather than seeking others out.[65]

Past Friends and Laborers

Asbury's one encouragement was John Wesley Bond, who attended the bishop with uncommon tenderness and tenacity. When the pair encountered a tree in the road, Bond jumped out of the carriage and cut off five of the limbs so the carriage could pass. "Is there his equal to be found in the United States? He drives me along with the utmost care and tenderness, he fills my appointments by preaching for me when I am disabled, he watches over me at night after the fatigue of driving all day, and if, when he is in bed and asleep, I call, he is awake and up in the instant to give me medicine, or to perform any other services his sick father may require of him; and this is done so readily, and with so much patience, when my constant infirmities and ill health require so many and oft-repeated attentions!" (2:761).

As Asbury passed through the North Carolina mountains, the foliage was in its full array of colors, but the dryness of the dying leaves aggravated his asthma. In western North Carolina, he slept in camp meeting tents and preached from the back of his carriage. Preaching outdoors to large gatherings of people was now almost impossible. The bishop was hardly able to breathe, much less project his voice. At Bethesda Chapel in Mecklenburg County, Asbury tried to preach, "but the people were so wonderfully taken up with the novel sight of the little carriage, and still more of the strange-looking old man who was addressing them, that the speaker made little impression on his hearers" (2:763). Nevertheless, at Hopewell Church in Newberry County, "truth came in power to the hearts of the people" (2:764).

James Andrew, future bishop of the Methodist Episcopal Church South, encountered Asbury for the first time at the South Carolina Conference in Milledgeville, Georgia, in December 1814. "Bishop Asbury I shall never forget. His venerable countenance, and the deep solemn intonations of his voice affected me greatly, and even now the recollection of him as I saw him and heard him on that occasion is as vivid as though it were only last week. He usually sat on the platform by the side of his colleague, and as occasion offered threw out some of those sensible, pithy remarks, which one could neither misunderstand or forget."[66] Asbury was so feeble that ordinands had to come to his sleeping room for ordination. "Once or twice the venerable Bishop had to rest during the service of ordination and seemed quite exhausted when it was finished."[67]

Asbury's mind remained sharp while his body withered. As he traveled, a tickertape of past friends and laborers in the gospel rolled before him. Most of them were now dead, and America's bishop would soon join them. The year ended with the South Carolina Conference, which sat from December 21–27. "I preached at the ordinations, but with so feeble a voice that many did not hear: I had coughed much and expectorated blood" (2:767). Asbury was ready to step into the last full year of his life. He was keenly cognizant that life's summation was imminent, and he was determined to endure to the end.

20. "My Only Hope of Heaven"

Punch

Accompanied by young South Carolina preachers William Kennedy and James Norton, Asbury journeyed north, inhibited by both the weather and the early stages of tuberculosis. The cold, damp air attacked his asthmatic bronchial tubes with every inhalation and caused expectorations of blood. His hacking and coughing frame convulsed within clothing and under blankets that were never thick enough. Gawkers felt sorry for the frail, Gothic man who was now known by name to almost every passerby, and especially the slaves who could not do enough for him.

Out of guilt and indignation, Asbury inwardly renounced the cruelty of the plantationists blinded by avarice and a provincial spirituality. He sarcastically sneered, "Away with the false cant, that the better you use the Negroes the worse they will use you! Make them good, then—teach them the fear of God, and learn to fear him yourselves, ye masters! I understand not the doctrine of cruelty. As soon as the poor Africans see me, they spring with life to the boat, and make a heavy flat skim along like a light canoe: poor starved souls—God will judge!" (2:772).

At Georgetown, South Carolina, the party tarried for several days. The bishop preached on Sunday, January 15, 1815, with difficulty. In spite of the burning in his chest he continued, with effort, to read from Laurence Echard's *Ecclesiastical History* in his perennial attempt to understand the church and augment his position in it. At Georgetown, he reaped a seed sown some twenty years before. He had spent ten minutes sharing the gospel with a slave; crossing a small bridge, Asbury bid the slave "Good day," and continued to ride. Some distance away, the Holy Spirit nudged the bishop: "You need to speak to that man about his soul." Asbury turned his horse around and rode up to the large and poorly clad Black man. Dismounting, Asbury asked the slave his name, to which he responded, "Sir, I don't rightly know what my name is. They call me Punch because I am always getting into fights." Asbury asked Punch if he ever prayed, to which the slave responded, "No, sir." Sitting down on a rock, Asbury read some Scripture, sang a hymn, and had prayer with Punch, then departed.

Twenty years later there stood Punch, having located the bishop at his Georgetown stop. "Sir, you know that day you stopped and prayed with me; I went back to my cabin and got down on my knees, and my cabin was all filled with light. Since that day I haven't wanted to fight anymore, curse anymore, play cards anymore. I haven't even wanted to fish anymore. There are now three hundred of us, and they want me to be their preacher." Asbury thought to himself,

"Better to witness to one slave than to rule on the highest throne on the face of the earth."

In 1836, a missionary discovered Punch still living on the South Carolina plantation. Punch stated, "I have many children in this place. I have felt for sometime past that my end was nigh. I looked around to see who might take my place when I am gone. I could find no one. I have felt unwilling to die and leave them so, and have been praying to God to send someone to take care of them. The Lord has sent you my child; I'm now ready to go."[1] The missionary stated that he found between two and three hundred persons under Punch's spiritual supervision.

Arriving in Wilmington, North Carolina, on January 20, Asbury found the church building a wreck, with the windows broken out. The War of 1812 had taken its toll, both physically and spiritually. It was a depressing time. "Were I a young man, I should not wish to be stationed in Wilmington" (2:773). The reception at Newbern was emotionally exhausting. "Here is weeping and lamentations for poor me—the leading characters of the society cannot speak to each other, or of each other, without bringing heavy accusations—yet all very glad to see the bishop" (2:773). The only trembling under the Word was from the cold. "Ah! People hard and dull!" The bishop bluntly addressed them concerning their attitudes.

Between Newbern and Greenville, Asbury and Bond lodged in a house with no heat. At Greenville he conducted a simple burial of a hundred-year-old slave. To quiet his shivering frame, he resorted to a shot of brandy (2:773). The bishop intended to forge on to Norfolk, but his meager strength was not able to persevere. He recuperated in a several-day stay at Edward Hall's in Tarboro. "I am occupied in reading, writing, and patching and propping up the old clay house as well as I may" (2:773).

Enemies until Death

Instead of visiting the society at Norfolk, the itinerants headed northwest toward Lynchburg for the Virginia Conference. In spite of a snowstorm, they reached Lynchburg on February 17. The business was tumultuous and the numbers were poor. There had been a loss of members, and Asbury took out some of his indignation on both the veterans and novices. He rebuked several ministers in front of the conference and denied others ordination because of "deficiency in talents." The health of the conference seemed to be on almost the same level as the bishop's; he attempted to preach but was not able to finish. "I have been almost strangled with an asthmatic cough, and vomiting of blood" (2:775). There was good news: the Treaty of Ghent had been ratified by Congress on February 17. The last war between Britain and the United States was over.

An unfortunate incident took place at Lynchburg, an embarrassment to Jesse Lee, who was a member of the Virginia Conference. Asbury was too weak to preside full time and by the final day was so drained that he requested the presiding elder John Early to read the appointments. Jesse Lee's name was left off the list, with the accompanying explanation that he would be later appointed by the Baltimore Conference.

Lee claimed that a constitutional law had been broken. "The Bishops shall appoint the preachers to their circuits."[2] "Their circuits," in Lee's interpretation, was a reference to the circuits of the conference that the preacher presently served. The omission insulted Lee, an injury compounded by the fact that he had not been consulted. Lee further interpreted Asbury's decision as political manipulation, an attempt to preempt the power base that would elect him at the General Conference scheduled for the next year. As a new member of a conference, Lee was not likely to be sent as a delegate. On April 10, Lee wrote to Asbury that it appeared that the bishop had decided to be his enemy until his death:

> It is high time for you to lay aside all anger, wrath and malice. After you have degraded me for years in my appointments, and cannot make a tool of me, or induce me to fall in with all your whims; you at last have trampled Methodism under your feet, and usurped a power that never belonged to you, in refusing to give me an appointment, thinking thereby to sink me. But you are mistaken. Yet I will not say of you and myself, as you once said of yourself and Wesley. When you wrote to Shadford you said, "Wesley and myself, are like Caesar and Pompey: one would bear no equal, and the other would have no superior." I am willing to have a superior; but I never will submit to your unconstitutional proceedings. I wish you to [act] immediately on receipt of this, and give me an appointment (3:513).

Lee was given an appointment by the Baltimore Conference, but he refused to accept it. Asbury made no mention of the breach, and we have no evidence that he ever responded to Lee's letter.

All That Is Necessary to Know

Asbury and Bond rode east toward Washington. The bishop still fretted when he was asked to pay for lodging; it especially hurt when the traveling fund was down to five dollars, the amount demanded for one night. On March 10, the pair arrived at Georgetown, where Asbury attempted to preach in the 40'x62' two-story church. "My mind, perhaps, partakes of the weakness of my body—I let fly a few scattering shot; I keep up a kind of running fire with my small-gun sermonizing" (2:776). His body was as ravaged as the White House and the navy yard that had been wrecked and burned by the British.

On April 20, Asbury attempted to chair the Philadelphia Conference but was overcome by chills and fever. On the twenty-eighth, he endeavored to preach but could only whisper a few words. On May 21 he had gained enough strength to preach a funeral discourse for Thomas Coke at the New York Conference, which met at Albany. Even though Coke had been dead for a year and buried at sea in the Indian Ocean, this was Asbury's first public acknowledgment. His exaggerated eulogy made up for lost time. He described his friend and rival as "a minister of Christ, in zeal, in labours, and in services, the greatest man in the last century" (2:780). On the same day, he wrote to Thomas Douglas, presiding elder of the Nashville District in Tennessee, with words enshrouded in even more sentiment. "Coke, the gentleman, the Christian, the scholar, the writer, the superintendent, the preacher, the missionary, is no more; all immortal, all divine. Take him in every direction, the greatest man of all the Oxonian Methodists. . . . Oh! Jonathan thou was slain on thy high places; very pleasant has thou been to me; thy love surpassed the love of women!"[3] The waning days, at least in Asbury's mind, were healing the rifts of past years.

As Asbury, Bond, and McKendree arrived in southeastern New Hampshire, Asbury was of little help except for ordaining and stationing the preachers. He preached with trembling feebleness. As he traveled on the return trip through Massachusetts, New York, and New Jersey, he reflected on the improved roads, especially the bridges, which had been built during the 45 years of his itinerancy. Bridges were not simply signs of progress; they helped ministers traverse the many dangerous barriers to the spread of the gospel. Human ingenuity was now conquering rivers of obstruction and peril.

Asbury reunited with Henry Boehm at the old home place of Henry's father. As the two rode into Lancaster, Asbury offered affectionate but rambling advice: "Be sure to take care of your health," he paternalistically admonished. As they parted, the patriarch held his gospel son close to his chest and then kissed him. Boehm could hardly speak, and with moistened eyes stood transfixed on Asbury's fading silhouette until it passed out of sight. They would meet no more.[4]

At York there was an opportunity for a ten-day retreat. Staying with Francis Hollingsworth, Asbury spent "seven hours a day" either reading his journal or having it read to him. Extracts from the journal had already been printed and distributed, either in the *Arminian Magazine* or in tract form. In 1807, the existing journal was published by the Methodist Book Concern; but because of the editing that was done, Asbury was not well pleased with the finished product. Several people, included John Dickens, Thomas Haskins, and Ann Willis, sister of Hollingsworth, had extensively edited the original text.[5]

In 1825, Bishop Beverly Waugh assessed Hollingsworth as a man of "eccentricities, but possessing a mind highly cultured" (1:17). Hollingsworth attempted to persuade Asbury that "uninteresting incidents and traveling notices" should be left out in favor of "deep reflections and acute remarks on men, books, and passing events continually afloat in his powerful and observant mind" (1:24). Asbury responded that an abridgment of his extraordinary life would not do. "As a record of the early history of Methodism in America, my journal will be of use; and accompanied by the minutes of the conferences, will tell all that will be necessary to know. I have buried in shades all that will be proper to forget, in which I am personally concerned; if truth and I have been wronged, we have both witnessed our day of triumph" (2:783).

We Are Going Down Stream

In Albany, New York, on May 20, 1815, Asbury ordained John Bangs, brother of Nathan Bangs. As Asbury laid his hands on Bangs and the other ordinands, he prayed, "O Lord, grant that these brethren may never want to be like other people."[6] Methodism had succeeded because it was different—different in spiritual expectations, different in pastoral methodology, and different in moral standards. The difference was fading, the line of demarcation between Methodism and the surrounding culture was becoming more difficult to discern. Upward mobility and accommodation had taken place before Asbury's eyes, and there was nothing he could do about it. Henry Smith recalled, "He expressed a fear that the Baltimorians were departing from the simplicity of the Gospel; he reproved them in the spirit of a father and raised his voice and cried aloud 'Comeback! Comeback! Comeback! Raising his voice higher at every repetition."[7] Methodist ladies in Baltimore were wearing "stiff stays, hoops from six inches to two feet on each side, so that a full dressed lady entered a door like the crab, pointing their obtruding flanks end foremost; high-healed shoes of black stuff, with silk or thread stockings."[8]

By the time Asbury was in Shippensburg, Pennsylvania, he had experienced a revival of physical strength; the warmth of the summer days relieved the pain in his rheumatic joints. The passage over the mountains went better than expected. His sympathy went out to a cattle driver "who had for many days eaten dust like a serpent following his cattle, broke his leg about seven miles below the town: poor man!" (2:785). At Somerset he preached at the courthouse as a "tottering tenement of clay" (2:785). In fact, everything was tottering except the bishop's resolve. "We will not give up the cause—we will not abandon the world to infidels; nay, we will be their plagues—we will find them herculean work to put us down. We will not give up that which we know to be glorious, until we see something more glorious" (2:787).

On July 19, he wrote to Jacob Gruber, presiding elder of the Carlisle District. "Now if ever wrestle, preach, pray, cry aloud, stamp with ye foot, smite with both hands, wake saints, sinners, seekers, preachers also. The Lord help us, we are going down stream" (3:520). Asbury intended to rally the troops as long as breath or pen could be summoned. On August 13, Asbury preached at a campground outside of Zanesville, Ohio, from the text 2 Corinthians 5:2, "Knowing the terror of the Lord we persuade men." His words were rambling and almost incoherent. His lack of rational discourse made him even more the spectacle.

The groundskeepers placed a feather mattress on a table, where Asbury sat for both visibility and comfort. Several hundred listeners strained to catch every word of Asbury's raspy voice. Many were hearing him for the first time. Many who had heard him were gathering around the patriarch for the last time. An eerie silence fell over the congregation as Asbury exhorted with every available breath, "Persuade men, by all that is desirable in religion, and all that the truly pious enjoy— by all the glories of heaven, and all the horrors of remediless perdition in hell." An eyewitness noted that

> his face which beamed with benignancy gave manifest indication of care and exhaustion. His silver locks hung lightly on his shoulders giving to him a most venerable aspect. The tremulous tones of his once rich and mellow voice fell on the nerves of his silent auditors, and as he sat on the table and stretched forth his shriveled hand pointing significantly to the glowing heavens above, he seemed more like some ancient prophet of Israel fresh from the audience chamber of God than a toil worn servant of the church in modern times.[9]

In Chillicothe, Bond drove Asbury to the front door of houses so he could beg for the mite subscription. He was pleased with the response. They departed in the rain, Asbury with a hacking, feverish cough. At a camp meeting in Mechanicsburg he prayed, "*God, give us a chimney that we may have fire*" (2:790).

Closing Admonitions

On September 10, 1815, Asbury preached his last camp meeting sermon at Mechanicsburg, Ohio. The people so gathered around him that he remarked to James Finley, "You might as well have an elephant in your camp as me." His text was "Today hear the voice of God and harden not your hearts." The emphasis of the message was "today"; in reality Asbury longed for yesterday. James Finley accompanied the Bishop to Springfield, where they stayed with a Methodist family.

> As we passed through the parlors we saw the daughter and some other young ladies dressed very gayly. The daughter was playing

on the piano, and as we moved through the room we doubtless elicited from those fashionable young ladies some remarks about the rusticity of our appearance; and the wonder was doubtless excited, where on earth could these old country codgers have come from? The Bishop took his seat, and presently in came the father and mother of the young lady. They spoke to the Bishop, and then followed the grandfather and grandmother. When the old lady took the Bishop by the hand he held it, and looking her in the face, while the tear dropped from his eye, he said, "I was looking to see if I could trace in the lineaments of your face, the likeness of your sainted mother. She belonged to the first generation of Methodists. Your son and his wife are the third, and that young girl, your granddaughter, represents the fourth. She has learned to dress and play on the piano, and is versed in all the arts of fashionable life, and I presume at this rate of progress, the *fifth* generation of Methodists will be sent to dancing school." This was solemn reproof, and it had a powerful effect upon the grandparents.[10]

In Union, Ohio, Asbury stayed with his close friend, local preacher John Sale. He preached on Romans 13:12, "The night is far spent." He listed the patriarchal stars that had been extinguished: Adam, Abel, Enoch, Noah, and Abraham. He might just as well have included himself. He was passing by for the last time; he knew it and his hearers knew it. With a swelled face, inflamed jaws, and aching joints, he bade farewell to a list of Methodist families that stretched *ad infinitum*: the Bucks, Banners, Smiths, Butlers, Owens, Beales, Heaths, Wrights, Fowlers, and Davises. They were the face of nineteenth-century America, the contours of which were known by Asbury more than any other living person. They were his; he had eaten with them, slept with them, laughed with them, and cried with them. He had befriended them when they had nothing and when they had plenty. For some of them, viewing his solitary appearance, mounted regally on horseback and representing far off places and people, had been the most memorable event of each year. With all of its deprivations and hardships, the "West" had endeared itself to him; impoverishment was fertile ground for humility and spirituality.

From house to house, Asbury distributed Bibles from the City Bible Society in Philadelphia. He was America's perennial peddler; no one on the continent could match his success as a colporteur. On September 29, he wrote to Thomas Douglas, "What was the charge in 1784? Fourteen thousand nine hundred and eighty-eight to two hundred and twelve thousand with possible not one, but three millions of souls congregated in the year. Formerly, our people covered only three or four hundred miles, now scattered one thousand or fifteen hundred in width three thousand in length!"[11] The domain of mission determined Asbury's address, a boundary that had been expanding for 45 years.

A Hoary Captain

The Ohio Conference sat in Lebanon, Ohio, on September 14. Asbury's participation was minimal. His presence was archetypical, a cohesive symbol of both call and commitment. Abel Stevens's hagiography is exaggerated but not totally inaccurate: "The great man had become now a wonder to the nation, a hoary captain, with such a prestige as no other clergyman of the Western Hemisphere could claim."[12] Jacob Young recalled his impression of Asbury at the Ohio Conference: "He was seated on the platform in the conference room, called on Brother Bond to read a chapter and give out a hymn, and then this great man of God prayed sitting on his seat, for he was not able to kneel down. He prayed as if speaking to God face to face. While gazing on his pale face, my emotions were painful yet pleasant."[13]

Asbury knew he was dying, but then he had been close to death several times before; thoughts of his own mortality did not thwart his focus on the future. As he and McKendree traveled, they discussed plans for Methodism's advancement. In Cincinnati, Asbury said to his colleague,

> I am now seventy years old and out of health, it can't be expected that I should visit the extremities each year, sitting in eight, it might be twelve, conferences, and travelling six thousand miles in eight months. Even if I am able to visit the conferences, I can't be expected to preside in more than one of them a year. When I submit a plan for the stationing of the preachers it will be complete. I will get all the information in my power, so as to enable me to make it perfect, like the painter who touches and retouches until all parts of the picture are pleasing (2:792).

Indeed, Asbury seemed to be invigorated. In spite of travelling in a carriage, the pace was rapid and the weather cooperative. On Sunday, October 1, he preached in Cincinnati; three days later, he was preaching in the courthouse in Georgetown, Kentucky, 75 miles away. "My soul is blessed with continual consolation and peace in all my great weakness of body, labour, and crowds of company" (2:792). After preaching in Lexington, Kentucky, he and Bond made their way through Logan County, the site of Presbyterian revivalism fifteen years earlier. It seemed the Shakers had prospered more than anyone else. "They are wiser than millions of the children of this world. . . . But why should I say any harm of this people, who am, I suppose, the last man in the world to envy or to imitate them?" (2:793).

There was no greater privilege among Methodists than to be joined in marriage by the senior bishop. Countless times he had performed the ceremony, but he made hardly any mention of it in his journal. At Fountain Head, Tennessee, he married Frances McKendree, niece of the bishop, to Nathaniel Moore. Three days later, Asbury spoke at the funeral of Frances McKendree's nephew; the same day he baptized a child. "So here have been a marriage, a funeral, and a baptism; and must I be honoured and burdened with them all? Well; make the best of me while you have me; it will not be often" (2:794).

At Nashville, Asbury mourned the death of Learner Blackman, 34 years of age, eloquent preacher and missionary pioneer to Mississippi. Blackman was crossing the Ohio River at Cincinnati on June 6 when the hoisting of the sails on the barge startled the horses and they jumped overboard, taking him with them. Asbury, with the rest of the church, keenly felt the loss. William Sprague later lamented, "By this fatal casualty, the church was deprived of one of its most gifted and every way promising young men."[14]

Official Changing of the Guard

Asbury's only official participation at the Tennessee Conference was preaching the service of ordination. He requested that McKendree station the preachers. It was the official changing of the guard at the last conference Asbury ever attended. The road between Nashville and Knoxville charged a toll at which Asbury chafed and complained to Bond. His criticism was not only an indictment of that particular rough, rocky thoroughfare, but a summation of all the jolts his system had endured over the last 45 years. "We came upon the turnpike—a disgrace to the State and to the undertakers, supposing they had any character to lose. It is a swindling of the public out of their money to demand toll on such roads as these. We are told, *Why, they make you pay on the turnpikes to the eastward.* Yes, so they do; and they make them fine roads" (2:795).

On Sunday, November 5, Asbury was asked to preach at Newport, Tennessee, but declined because of weakness. At Bolig's Tavern, the drunkards were so loud that sleep was impossible. The next night he did not fare much better; "at Barnett's, there was a dance—such fiddling and drinking! I delivered my testimony: I am clear from Barnett's blood!" (2:795). Two days later he attempted to preach at a quarterly meeting at Edneyville but could only give a "feeble testimony." The next Sunday he preached from Acts 26:17–18: "Delivering thee from the people, and from the Gentiles, unto whom now I send thee, To open their eyes, and to turn them from darkness to light, and from the power of Satan unto God, that they may receive forgiveness of sins, and inheritance among them which are sanctified by faith that is in me." It was the last message for which Asbury recorded the content. "[T]hese ministers must be *sent*; and to be qualified for this mission, they must, like Paul, be convinced, convicted, and converted, and sanctified" (2:796).

Attempting to reach the conference at Charleston, Asbury fell short about thirty miles because of the build-up of fluid around his heart and in his lungs. On November 26, he recorded the last assessment of a sermon. "I preached, and we had a time of great feeling" (2:796). On December 2, he gave account of the death of a medical doctor named Ivy Finch, who had his skull fractured between the shaft and wheel of his carriage. "How many Gospel sermons had he heard, and how many prayers had been offered up for him!" (2:797).

Asbury had an eschatological mind-set. He rendered humanity eternally accountable; he never ceased crying, "Repent and be saved." Louis Meyers, who as a 30-year-old heard Asbury preach one of his final sermons, recalled that he "sat in a chair and declared the terrors of the law in a more terrific strain than he had ever heard him." After the sermon, Asbury remarked to his colleagues that "he regretted that he had not through his life, thundered out the law more against sin, and that he saw and felt more and more the majesty of declaring the whole counsel of God in plain and pointed terms."[15] The thunder was almost gone. A lady who had heard Asbury preach in a camp meeting in 1815 wrote to a friend:

> [T]he two first [sermons] were delivered by old Bishop Asbury and Bishop McKendree. The infirmities of the former natural to old age rendered him incapable of performing his office to the satisfaction of his audience. This venerable appearance struck me with awe. I saw him ascend the Pulpit with his cane in one hand while on the other side he was assisted by a minister I suppose. He then commenced his discourse—his articulation very much injured from the top of his teeth and his ideas so unconnected that it was impossible to keep the thread of his discourse. This he continued far beyond my expectation—for I thought in a little time he would be so much exhausted from the exertions he evidently made he frequently paused as if the purpose of recovering breath. He occupied a seat all the time.[16]

Theology as a Medical Manual

A systematic doctrine of God does not exist in Asbury's writing; he was interested only in the operation of God within the soul. Theology to him was like a medical manual for understanding the divine activities in one's own life and then enhancing these activities in the lives of others. Theology was profitable only so far as it illuminates the spiritual physician's diagnosis. In 1775, Asbury wrote, "What a noble and delightful employment is ours, to be nursing immortal souls for the realms of eternal glory!" (1:170).

The end of theology is entire sanctification—the full life of God possessing the totality of one's existence. To this extent Asbury, the non-theologian, encompassed everything he did with theology. It was his desire to perceive and act from God's perspective. This would accomplish the salvation of his own soul and the souls of others. For him the purpose of theology was to enhance the divine-human encounter. "[T]he grand doctrines of the gospel" are all the conditions of humankind in response to grace: "man's original rectitude—his fall—the atonement—repentance—justification—sanctification—the resurrection—the last judgment, and final rewards and punishments" (2:210).

Asbury's theology was plain and pointed. To spend time splitting hairs over semantics or argument for the sake of debate was trivializing the call to rescue the perishing. Theology was valid only so far as it could be utilized for evangelistic artillery; beyond that, it became vain jangling, a speculative enterprise for the erudite. At the General Conference in 1804, there was a debate about revising the *Discipline,* which included a review of the Articles of Religion. A member rose and moved to change the word "preventing [grace]" to "assisting." As soon as he sat down, Thomas Coke sprang to his feet and exclaimed in a high-pitched voice, "Where am I? In a Methodist conference? I thought so; but we have turned Pelagians? Do we think we can get along in our natural depravity with a little assistance, without preventing grace? But perhaps our Brother had mistaken the meaning of the word preventing; in taking it in the common acceptation of hindering?" After further remarks on the necessity of grace before salvation, giving appropriate exegetical insight, Coke exclaimed, "Brethren, do not change that word. I would go to the stake—yes—to the stake as soon as any word in the Bible."[17]

Asbury sat quietly. The technicality of theological language was neither his mentality nor his mission. On September 29, Asbury wrote to Thomas Douglas, "Be distinct in doctrines, as growth in grace, conviction, repentance, justification, regeneration, and sanctification distinct from justification."[18] Asbury's theology eventuated in human experience. Theology was not about who God was; it was about what God did. Theology was operative in the hearts and lives of the persons as God acted upon them. Theology was not for the purpose of understanding God and His ways. Instead it was to elicit a response from hearers; in other words, it was preachable. Theological understanding that could not be preached was an exercise in impractical erudition. Theological learning could only be justified within the context of evangelism.

A Line of Decision in the Sands of Human Existence

At the 1810, South Carolina annual conference the usual question was raised: "Is there anything against Joseph Travis?" The presiding elder, Reddick Pierce, answered, "Nothing against him." As Travis was about to leave the room, Asbury spoke up: "I have something against Brother Travis." As Travis turned around Asbury exclaimed, "I hear Brother Travis has been studying Greek this year." Travis countered, "I plead guilty to the charge. I thought in so doing, I was treading in the footsteps of some of our most worthy Brethren, such as George Dougherty and many others." The bishop tersely commented, "There is the danger of preachers neglecting the more important part of their work namely the salvation of souls." The next day Asbury embraced Travis with an affectionate hug. "Don't think hard of my remarks, my only purpose was to whip the others over your shoulders."[19]

To do theology was not to gaze upon the attributes of God, but to draw a decisional line in the sands of human existence. Theology always called for a verdict. Asbury's theology cried out, "[S]ubmit to the conditions of salvation; the use of the means of grace; and to a life of Gospel obedience" (2:788). Theology did its best work when it demarcated a stark dichotomy, a crossroad to the glories of heaven or irrevocable perdition of hell. The practice of theology was an endless exercise in dichotomizing—life or death, heaven or hell, repent or be damned. Theology was the preacher's equipment for invading the spiritual enemy's territory and explaining life's ultimate choice in no uncertain terms. In 1809, William Spencer recalled his past ministry and that of his fellow laborer John Robinson:

> A sad gloom seemed to rest on the minds of the people, when, all on a sudden (as it were) two poor, little, unimproved striplings entered the circuit with nothing scarcely but 'Repent or perish, believe or be damned, turn or burn; Hell fire will be the doom of all the ungodly, etc.' The mighty power of God attended these poor Endeavors. At the sound of these Rams' horns (crooked as they were), the towering walls of Jericho fell flat to the ground!" (3:419–20).

Preach Christ

American Methodism's founding bishop was clearly christocentric in his understanding of redemption. Christ is the meritorious and procuring cause of our salvation. In the middle of January 1816, Asbury spent several days with Joseph Travis at his Marion Academy in Marion, South Carolina. Travis commented to the bishop, "It must be a pleasing reflection for you, now on the verge of the grave, to think that from your youth up, you have been unreservedly devoted to the service of the Lord and Master." Asbury shook his head and emphatically replied, "My only hope of heaven is in the merits and righteousness of the Lord Jesus Christ."[20] On August 26, 1814, he had written to Nelson Reed, "My justifying, sanctifying, practical righteousness all in and from *Christ*; heaven opens *Glory Glory Glory*" (3:509).

Asbury's journal abounds in christological references. Christ is "the way to God by precept, example, and power" (1:772). All that the church does, its ordinances and functions, are worthwhile only as far as they lead us to Christ. Christ is both the author of and model for our salvation. Asbury does not expound on a particular theory of the atonement or even explicate the attributes of Christ. The process of sanctification is the Holy Spirit conforming the believer to the image of Christ. Christ is our mediator and ongoing high priest ever making up the gap between our imperfections and the perfect law of God (1:268). Christ is the one with whom we can have fellowship, ever receiving and returning His love. "O, what sweetness I feel as I steal along through the solitary woods! I am sometimes ready to shout aloud, and make all vocal with the praises of His grace who died, and lives, and intercedes for me" (2:456).

Universal Grace

Everything that John Wesley wrote, Asbury read.[21] For Wesley, God is the initiator of all that is good in human experience, which is primarily justification, sanctification, and eternal salvation. God acts, and thus humankind is acted upon. God extends grace to all human individuals; it is this grace that enables a positive response. Wesley wrote, "Salvation begins with what is usually termed (and very properly), preventing grace; including the first wish to please God, the first dawn of light concerning His will, and the first slight transient conviction of having sinned against Him."[22] Grace enables the faith of justification. If a person will allow grace to quicken faith, the faith of repentance and obedience, one cannot help but be saved.[23]

Faith in Christ is the only prerequisite for salvation for both Wesley and Asbury. This faith is qualified by sincere repentance and the willingness to follow the Savior. Wesley stated that repentance and its fruits are only remotely necessary: necessary in order to have faith: whereas faith is immediately and directly necessary to justification. Faith "is the only thing without which none is justified: the only thing that is immediately, indispensably, absolutely requisite in order to pardon."[24]

Grace is far more than a gift—it is an announcement of human responsibility. Grace renders all humankind accountable, since it is universal. Grace enables a proper faith; a proper faith renders works of righteousness. A faith that does not eventuate in works of righteousness is a dead faith. Righteousness, for both Asbury and Wesley, is not only imputed but also imparted and evidences itself in holy living. To minimize this enablement is to devalue the atonement and to waste the efficaciousness of Christ's shed blood. This waste results in antinomianism—for both Wesley and Asbury, the scourge of true religion. Antinomianism is a belittling of both what Christ offers and what He requires. It is this characteristic of "Calvinism" that Asbury and Wesley adamantly detested.

The Grace of Sanctification

The opposite of antinomianism is sanctification, the experience of holiness in both heart and life. Sanctification is evidenced by the conquering of the flesh; that is, overcoming a pandering to self. Grace can enable humankind to rise above the dictates of comfort, ease, and perverted appetites. The essence of conquering the flesh is putting Christ's cause before one's own cause and the needs of others before one's own needs. To attain victory, the Christian must take full advantage of the means of grace such as prayer, Scripture reading, and daily disciplines of self-denial. Works of righteousness do not merit salvation. Rather, they are a means to salvation, and evidence a genuine relationship to God. This dialectic was not easily articulated by the Methodists. Asbury attempted to strike a balance between faith and works in a response to the Anglican divine James Hervey:

> I like his philosophy better than his divinity. However, if he is in error by leaning too much to imputed righteousness, and in danger of superseding our evangelical works of righteousness, some are also in danger of setting up self-righteousness, and, at least, of a partial neglect of an entire dependence on Jesus Christ. Our duty and salvation lie between these extremes. We should so work as if we were to be saved by the proper merit of our works; and so rely on Jesus Christ, to be saved by his merits and the Divine assistance of his Holy Spirit, as if we did no works, nor attempted anything which God hath commanded. This is evidently the Gospel plan of man's salvation:—St. Paul says in one place, "By grace are ye saved, through faith; and that not of yourselves, it is the gift of God." In another place the same apostle saith, "Work out your own salvation with fear and trembling." But some, who see the danger of seeking to be justified by the deeds of the law, turn all their attention to those passages of Scripture which ascribe our salvation to the grace of God; and to avoid the rock which they discover on the right hand, they strike against that which is equally dangerous on the left, by exclaiming against all conditions and doings, on the part of man; and so make void the law through faith—as if a beggar could not cross the street, and open his hand (at the request of his benefactor) to receive his bounty, without a meritorious claim to what he is about to receive. What God hath joined together, let no man put asunder. And he having joined salvation by grace, with repentance, prayer, faith, self-denial, love, and obedience, whoever putteth them asunder will do it at his peril (1:293–4).

An Intentional Error

Asbury was unwilling to risk this peril. If he was going to err, it would be on the side of making sure he did his part. It was better to expect too much of oneself than to expect too little. The worst failure of life would be to discover that God had required more of us than we required of ourselves. All of life was to be lived with the final judgment in view. Since there is always a gap between human endeavor and God's perfection, salvific anxiety seems to belie Asbury's quest for holiness. Justification was more than simply standing with certainty on the sure foundation of Christ; it was being proclaimed righteous at the Last Day because of our fidelity in executing the trusts committed to us. In other words, "We are justified by the merits of Christ, through faith, in the day of conversion; and by the evidence of works in the day of judgment" (1:206).

This idea of a double or successive justification process Asbury borrowed from John Fletcher, a person he admired almost as much as he did Wesley. As a boy, Asbury had heard John Fletcher preach. The fine-tuning of Asbury's theology had come via Fletcher's *Checks to Antinomianism*, which he thoroughly read. Fletcher taught four degrees of justification: (a) the salvation of an infant; (b) the faith imputed for Christ's righteousness to the believer; (c) the justification that issues in righteousness; and (d) final justification in the Day of Judgment. Fletcher wrote, "By thy words shalt thou be justified, and by thy words shalt thou be condemned. Circumcision and uncircumcision avail nothing, but the keeping of the commandments, for the doers of the law shall be justified."[25]

A person's justification required keeping two sides of a ledger; one side was already filled with the merits of Christ's atonement, and the other side was a running account kept by the individual. The possibility of eternal salvation is supplied by God and God alone. The outcome of salvation is determined by the person who has been justified, and yet is being justified by an ongoing response to the possibilities of grace. In this sense, the individual becomes master of his fate. An active God demands an active servant.

Asbury's understanding of salvation was indeed a synergism, an active cooperation with God to make sure that the divine will was accomplished in one's own life and in the lives of others. In William Cannon's words, "Once you grant to man a power great enough to make itself as a deciding factor in the acceptance or rejection of the means necessary for the bestowal of saving faith, you lift him, whether you will or not, out of a state of mere passivity into one of activity and of cooperation or non-cooperation with the grace of God."[26]

In the Wesleyan theological scheme, the individual is a critical, though not the central, player. Even though Asbury confessed an ongoing dependence on grace throughout his journal, there was also a high degree of self-initiative. His pursuit of spirituality was energetic, aggressive, individualistic, and thoroughly nineteenth-century American. While Nathaniel Taylor juxtaposed human freedom against Jonathan Edwards' determinism, Asbury personified it. No man on the American shore until this time had done more to earn his salvation than had Asbury. He was the new religious hero, a *homo religiosus* for the nineteenth century, a distinct contrast to the Edwardian and Puritan divines of the past.

The religious hero was accustomed not to leisure but to work. Asbury, as much as or more than any other person, removed the pastoral role from the cloistered studies of Jonathan Edwards and Charles Chauncey to the natural surroundings that embraced every walk of life. He believed that ministers were to be no less productive than farmers, artisans, and mill workers. Methodist preachers looked and smelled more as though they had come from behind a plow than from out of a pulpit. Along with the framers of the Constitution, Asbury brought "aristocratic leisure into contempt and turned labor into a universal badge of honor."[27] No one had to exclaim of a Methodist preacher as it was said of a duke who visited America, "A Duke! I wonder what he does for a living?"[28]

In Conflict with God

The new era did not mean that the Puritan face of God had been eclipsed. Asbury's God lacked a sense of humor and could not appreciate the levity that often left the bishop with the sense that he was not sober enough for his auspicious duties. Repression did not always work. At a home in the Genesee Conference, Asbury was entertaining his host with humorous anecdotes when he noticed McKendree sitting with arms folded across his chest, fingers locked, and in a meditative mood. "I suppose the people here will think that Bishop McKendree has a great deal more religion than I have, and so he has; but if I should be as sober as he is I should not live a month."[29] McKendree smiled while the others laughed.

One of Asbury's great delights in life was getting the last laugh. On August 4, 1812, he was traveling with the portly and venerable Father Bidlock of Kingston, Pennsylvania. Upon stopping at a house to dine they were welcomed by the gatekeeper who could not specifically identify Asbury, mistaking Bidlock for the bishop. He said to Asbury, who was leading the party, "You pass on, sir, and open the gate for the Bishop." He then said to Bidlock, "Please alight, Bishop, and I will order your horse to be taken care of and will bring in your saddlebags." Before the mistake could be corrected, Asbury had sprung from his horse, opened the gate, and was bowing to the rest of the party as they passed through. To Bidlock he said, "Walk in, Bishop, I will see that all is right with your baggage."[30]

The sternness that Asbury adopted in public was the persona that he believed was fit for the office and the God he publicly professed. The stakes were high, for God would require a strict account of those who claimed to be His ambassadors. This concept of a stern God, coupled with the intent to model a ministry that demanded self-denial, placed Asbury under double jeopardy. He could be nothing less than the shepherd prototype, an incarnation of asceticism. This was immediately apparent to all who met him. This pastoral model was described by the Puritan pastor Richard Baxter in his work, *The Reformed Pastor*. Baxter, Asbury's favorite non-Wesleyan author, described the ideal pastor as one of tireless energy and unswerving devotion. Baxter warned pastors in no uncertain terms of pride, inordinate desire to rule over others, indiscretion in speech, lack of church discipline, and entanglement in temporal affairs.

The pastor was one who demonstrated a sort of spiritual athleticism. In other words, for both Asbury and Baxter, the leader was to demonstrate a more intense spiritual vigor and commitment than his followers. Baxter succinctly stated Asbury's compelling conviction: "Take heed to yourselves, lest your example contradicts your doctrine and lest you lay such stumbling blocks before the blind as may be the occasion of their ruin; lest you unsay with your lives what you say with your tongues; and be the greatest hinderers of the success of your own labours."[31] To Jacob Gruber, Asbury wrote, "I recommend it to you and wish you to recommend to all the travelling and local preachers. . . . Baxter is excellent, super-excellent and excells the whole" (3:436–7).

A Theological Microscope

Theology fell short if it did not incarnate Christian character. When Asbury examined a ministerial candidate, he first inquired about the applicant's debts, then of his faith in Christ, and last concerning the preacher's pursuit of holiness. Debt was a theological issue of stewardship and delayed gratification. Above all, it indicated the candidate's theology of values. Entering the Methodist ministry under Bishop Asbury was a rite of value clarification. Anybody could say the right words. Only the chosen could embrace the "counting all things but loss."

When a presiding elder had announced two men to be received on trial—one the son of a renowned general, the other the son of a distinguished teacher—Asbury said nothing during the discussion. After almost unanimous approval by the assembly, Asbury suddenly came awake and spoke to himself in a voice that allowed eavesdropping by most in the room: "Yes, yes, in all probability they both will disgrace you and themselves before the year is out."[32] Unfortunately, his prophecy proved true.

Intuiting character was a task requiring knowledge that could not be gained by reading books. Dr. Thomas Bond, brother of John Wesley Bond and later editor of *The Christian Advocate and Journal*, stated of Asbury that "[t]here was not only a sternness of manner, that would forbid a person approaching him with too much freedom, but he appeared when he looked at you, when he lowered his dark heavy eyebrows, as if he could read you, as if he understood your thought and the motives that prompted you to action, as if you were transparent, and he could look through you, or as if you had a window in your bosom and he could see what was there."[33]

The Active Trinity

Asbury was thoroughly Trinitarian. He believed the heavenly Father is working out His providence, Christ is carrying on the work of redemption, and the

Holy Spirit is the ever-present God who provides both common and preventing grace in a sin-cursed world. The one God in three persons represents the effectual collaboration for moving history toward a grand climax of judgment of the lost and eternal salvation of the righteous. The concept was not a theological premise on which to elaborate, but a mystery to accept by faith. "All, hail, eternal Father, coequal Son, and everlasting Spirit in time and forever!" (1:651).

For Asbury, God is always at work. He unceasingly labors to perfect holiness in the life of the believer. Whatever happens, God has a hand in it. The benefits of that "hand" could be realized only through perfect resignation to what it contained. When traveling in the rugged western Pennsylvania foothills in July of 1814, Asbury exclaimed, "What roads! It was the mercy of Providence, or we should have been dashed to pieces. My body is, nevertheless, in better health; and my mind and soul happy and confident in God. Glory, glory, glory be to the Triune God!" (2:756).

Resignation sought to place all events within the optimism of grace, which was directed by the wisdom of God. When the eminent Robert Williams died on September 26, 1775, Asbury mused that "perhaps brother Williams was in danger of being entangled in worldly business, and might thereby have injured the cause of God. So he was taken away from the evil to come" (1:164). Grief and loss could not have been more effectively insulated. Asbury's theodicy served as an impregnable fortress, impervious to the assault of life's daily exigencies.

"Providence" was Asbury's dominant theological motif for God's activity in the world. God was carrying out His agenda to effect salvation for whosoever would respond. God's operation on earth was often highly discernible, and thus understandable. God kept office 24 hours a day, vindicating the righteous and pelting the wicked with various afflictions. The ever-present hand of God often superseded natural causes, cultural context, and scientific explanation. When American ships traded with the yellow-fever-infested West Indies, Asbury anxiously stated that "the Lord will punish us for our sins and prodigality" (2:27). Nothing just happened; all events were for the purpose of carrying out the divine will, which included the weather. "The weather is excessively warm and dry: people are sickly and dying, especially children. . . . [I]t appears to me to be *unhealthy, judgment weather*" (2:95).

God was bent on getting humanity's attention however possible. "The fever is breaking out again in Portsmouth, and it is awful in Philadelphia; it seemeth as if the Lord would humble or destroy that city, by stroke after stroke, until they acknowledge God" (2:171). God aligned himself with forces of righteousness and against unrighteous persons. When a person had threatened to stone a Methodist preacher and subsequently died within a few days, Asbury opined, "Thus it seems, when men slight the mercies of God, he visits them with his judgments!" (1:90). When a "poor, abandoned wretch" visited a brothel and died the next morning, Asbury commented, "Thus we see the vengeance of God frequently overtakes impenitent sinners, even in this life. How awful the thought! that a soul, in such a condition, should be unexpectedly hurried to the judgment-seat of a righteous God!" (1:106).

The Cosmic Battle

Asbury's worldview included a Satan who is as real and personal as is God. God and Satan are the greater and lesser cosmic persons who do battle primarily within the human heart. Asbury often interpreted his bouts with depression as attacks from Satan. The cries of his flesh to fulfill natural expression were temptations from the archenemy of the soul. Satan was constantly on Asbury's heels and could be defeated only through reliance on divine power. "Satan, that malicious enemy of mankind, is frequently striving to break my peace" (1:82). Satan haunted, tempted and assaulted him. He was determined, if possible, "to distract, if he could not destroy me—even blasphemous thoughts have been darted into my imagination" (1:235).

Satan schemed, connived, and assailed, using his complete arsenal to defeat the messenger of God, and thus sabotage the mission. "[S]ome of my friends were so unguarded and imprudent as to commend me to my face. Satan, ready for every advantage, seized the opportunity and assaulted me with self-pleasing, and self-exalting ideas" (1:115). In other words, Satan kept Asbury's ego in a constant dilemma, damned by both praise and criticism. Rest from ominous guilt would come with advancing age, more realistic expectations, a growing sense of divine pleasure, and the inner affirmation that he had fulfilled the divine ought. The carnal temptations attenuated with the decay of the flesh and death of desire.

A Perfect Defense Mechanism

Providence not only arranged the pieces of life correctly, but provided the confidence that one was fulfilling the divine design. Few men have possessed greater certitude of vocational election than Francis Asbury. Failure was never a serious option. God had willed it otherwise. God protected, perfected, and translated every adversity for his ultimate good. If the ego was under double assault by both bane and blessing, it had the double support of both good and bad events. If something adverse happened, God was simply perfecting and purifying via affliction. If something pleasing took place in the way of comfort or success, it was a gift from God.

Asbury believed that everything was beneficial because ultimately God was in control. Every event pointed the believer to the benevolent hand of God. It was the perfect defense mechanism—an unbroken supply of spiritual and psychological energy that Asbury literally traced all the way back to his biological conception. In 1794, he wrote to his parents, "I am well satisfied that the Lord saw fit you should be my parents, rather than the king and queen, or any of the great; also, as to when and where I drew my breath" (3:127).

History was marching toward a cataclysmic showdown, and the result had already been determined. The spoils would go to the victors, which would include a crown of compensation for all that had been endured for the cause of triumph. This hope of future reward keeps the Christian committed in battle. The sleepless nights and endless miles would have a payday. "I hardly bear it, and yet dare not cast it down, for fear God and my brethren should cast me down for such an abandonment of duty. True it is, my wages are great—precious souls here, and glory hereafter" (2:430). The glory could only be appreciated by sharply contrasting the uninterrupted and unceasing presence of God with the transitory and finite nature of human existence. "Here our communion with the Deity is but partial and very imperfect: we dwell in shells of infirmity—exposed to the assaults of wicked spirits, and surrounded with countless numbers of amusing, empty objects; by which means we are in continual danger of forgetting God, or of being too well satisfied without the fruition of him" (1:280). Eternity could only be comprehended by an understanding of life's contrasting temporality. Mortality and its stuff were to be grasped lightly.

Filled with His Holy Spirit

The Holy Spirit is God actively engaged in the world, primarily as an agent of redemption, who convinces, converts, and sanctifies (2:142). Both speaking and receiving the truth can be accomplished only through the Holy Spirit. The confirmation of God's redemptive plan is a supernatural process that renders mere moral suasion inadequate. Both the written Word and the Living Word are delivered by the Holy Spirit. The Holy Spirit enables the believer to live according to the Word, and in turn preserves his/her body as a temple of God (1:182). Asbury knew that any true life found in the church was born of the Holy Spirit. He alone quickens and revives the church, and is its only hope for continuation as a vital organism.

Asbury did not make a technical connection between the work of the Holy Spirit and the experience of entire sanctification. Neither was there any reference to a permanent filling of the Holy Spirit. This reflects Asbury's conviction that present, ongoing experience was far more important than theological explanation. He wrote on September 24, 1778, "My soul at present is filled with his Holy Spirit; I have a glorious prospect of a boundless ocean of love, and immense degrees of holiness opening to my view; and now renew my covenant with the Lord, that I may glorify him with my body and spirit, which are his" (1:281). Asbury was thoroughly Wesleyan in that he believed the Holy Spirit bears witness to the believer as to the experiential and objective reality of present salvation. "[A]ssurance is suspended on an evangelical act of faith, by which we apply the merits of Jesus Christ for the removal of our guilt; and that we then receive the testimony of the Spirit" (1:81–2).

The last 45 years of Asbury's life had been spent "living to God, and enabling others to do so." He had kept the vision. During the confinement of the Revolutionary War, Asbury read theology: Wesley, Doddridge, Bunyan, and Barclay. "I am reconciled to my condition, and in faith and prayer commit all events to my Divine Protector. This is an excellent season for dressing my own vineyard" (1:268). Four decades later, he was ready to present that vineyard to his Master. It is doubtful that God could have hired a more faithful tenant.

Asbury was highly aware that the redemptive mission of Methodism would not be accomplished within a vacuous theology. He was acutely attuned to what his preachers believed, and how those beliefs were implemented. Stith Mead gave an account of a 1792 conference in which

> [a]ll were examined by the Bishop as to their confession of faith and orthodoxy of doctrine, two were found to be tending to Unitarianism. The Bishop requested all the members of the conference to bring forward as many texts of Scripture as they could recollect to prove the personality of the Trinity, and especially that of the Holy Ghost. The two preachers recanted their errors, and were allowed to continue their ministry. Bishop Asbury then preached from Titus 2:1, "But speak thou the things that become sound doctrine."[34]

Theology as a Verb

Theology that could not be preached was worthless. On August 26, 1815, Asbury preached at a camp outside Urbana, Ohio, on Romans 13:11: "It is high time to wake out of sleep; for now is salvation nearer than when we determined." There was not much in the message to arouse attention or capture the imagination. Toward the end of the sermon, however, Asbury was suddenly invigorated and raised his tremulous voice. He returned to a tactic to which he had often resorted: crying aloud in a dramatic staccato, "Awake! Awake! Awake!" as he slapped the pulpit three times with the palm of his hand. The congregation aroused, and one man was so startled that he awoke from his stupor and was eventually converted.[35]

The Asburian paradigm translated the word *theology* as a verb. Both God and Asbury were pursuing anything that had a soul and were fitting the responsive heart for holy living here and eternal happiness hereafter. Asbury's quarrel with Calvinism was not that it overemphasized the sovereignty of God, but that it produced indifference. The "eternal decrees" undermined the necessity for holy living. This led to antinomianism, a passivity about God's requirements which are clearly stated in Scripture. Predestination, which precluded an person's active response, undercut both the active pursuit of holiness and a grace that produced works. Asbury's theology was a highly energized practical divinity. In Edward Lang's words, "Asbury sought to live the devotion of a monastery, while working for God in the world."[36]

On Sunday, May 14, 1815, Asbury preached at the North Church in New York City. He described his discourse as "something between talking and preaching; yet we had a time of much feeling." The sermon, only briefly referenced in his journal, may have been his true valedictory. The bishop recounted the tortures of his long years of ministry: labors, sufferings, swamps, colds, and his latest affliction, which had robbed him of all his flesh and strength. Suddenly, he raised his voice as if it had been empowered by an abundant reservoir of energy. "But glory to God! My heart's not gone—my faith—my love to God is not gone." The words ran through the congregation with a kinetic explosiveness. Tears flowed and shouts of "Glory to God" filled the church, a true moment of triumph for both a prophet and his people.[37]

21. "Die! Die! My Brother!"

The Normally Minute Details

The over one-half century of travel, complicated by asthma, rheumatism, and various other ailments, had left little more of Asbury than skin and bones. The protrusion of his skeletal frame obliged John Wesley Bond to make bandages of soft leather plastered with salve and apply them to the numerous chafes on the bishop's body. At night, he breathed laboriously and almost constantly coughed. During the sleepless hours, he prayed a rambling intercession for persons, churches, and conferences that came to mind. His kidneys and liver became more dysfunctional, giving Asbury's skin a sallow cast. "Get me a mirror," he requested of Bond. The ghastly image brought a smile. "If they want my likeness now they may have it." Several times he commented, "Mr. Wesley requested that he might not live to be idle, but I feel no liberty to make such a request. I must leave it to God; it may be his will that, as the people have seen my strength to let them see my weakness also."[1] Asbury had possibly forgotten that years earlier he had prayed that he would not live long after he was unable to travel (1:423).

Asbury attempted in December of 1815 to reach the South Carolina Conference, but he was unable to do so. He stayed for a week at Mr. Eccles's place at Cyprus Swamp, about thirty miles north of Charleston.[2] On December 7, he made his last journal entry: "We met a storm and stopped at William Baker's, Granby" (2:797).

The first couple of weeks of 1816 were spent at the home of John Whetstone, a plantation owner in Calhoun County, South Carolina. With a premonition that he might not make it to the General Conference in Baltimore in May, Asbury prepared an "Address." It is a curious, rambling document, having mostly to do with validating Methodism's organizational structure, vindicating Asbury in light of past schisms, expediting the denomination's publishing ventures, centrally locating the General Conference, forming new conferences, electing new bishops, and discussing the raising of finances. Overall, the address pleads for conservation and preservation of the American Methodist system. Asbury suggests the creation of a "General committee of safety," which would censor motions brought to the General Conference of a "critical and doubtful nature" (3:532–42).

Methodism's utmost concern, he said, should be to preserve in both practice and belief the tenets that he himself had propagated. Asbury's normally minute details were not absent; no one ever accused Asbury of projecting a vision that lacked particulars:

> How will you keep your press pure? Both from many new publications presented from Europe or America. Will you establish it on

the United States grand Western road, preferable to any other road, where waggoners may drive 20–30 miles a day, no desperate rocks, no dead horses, no broken leg waggoners, horrible! horrible! It is almost a sin to trade on the Pitt road. Will you establish the book concern where in about 280 miles you can have your books landed at Wheeling or elsewhere and shipped in good order to Chillicothe, to Cincinnati, at the mouth of Kentucky River, Louisville, *Nashville*, Natchez, New Orleans, the whole Western country which promises to be the glory of America and a market for one third, if not one half of your books (3:536).

One last time he publicly authenticated his authority, which some had again called into question. It seemed he was still smarting over the criticism he had received over the formation of the Genesee Conference. He mimicked his adversaries, "You can't have a Conference but when the Bishop pleases, and where he pleases, and he is wiser than hundreds of you. He cannot be mistaken. He is so virtuous he will always do right, and O that this could be so said and proved by large and wise bodies" (3:540). This address passed the baton to a movement that would soon be deprived of its leader. It was Asbury's hope that the baton would be passed to a carbon copy of himself:

Let the new bishops be men who have already proved themselves not only servants but mere slaves, *who* with willing minds have taken with cheerfulness and resignation frontier stations, with hard fare, labouring and suffering night and day, hazarding their lives by waters, by lodging indoors and out, and where Indian depredations and murders have been committed once a month or perhaps once a quarter. . . . They ought to be men who can ride at least three thousand miles and meet ten or eleven Conferences in a year, and by their having had a charge of local Conferences from sixty to an hundred Official characters, to have presided in and *to have* directed well all the business of the whole with every member, having received and graduated exhorters, preachers, deacons, and elders in the local line, ready to all the duties of their calling, always pleasant, affable, and communicative (3:541).

Setting the Record Straight

For Asbury, the only true criteria for leadership were battle scars received in the trenches; only those who wore badges of experience were worthy of election. He commented to John Wesley Bond, "It has never been my practice to say to the younger preachers, 'Go boys—but—come.' I have ever set an example of industry, and punctuality; and if ever the young men should neglect their appointments, it must not be by our example."[3]

It was also at John Whetstone's home that Asbury penned the longest letter he ever wrote, an epistle to Joseph Benson, who had fulfilled two terms as president of British Methodism.[4] It served as his official report back home, a dying man's attempt to bring life full circle. Asbury personally remembered Benson, though he was confused on the details. He referred to Benson as being older than Asbury, when he was in fact younger. After giving some explanations of American Methodism's organizational structure, Asbury characterized the ethos of his office. "With us a bishop is a plain man, altogether like his brethren, wearing no marks of distinction, advanced in age, and by virtue of his office can sit as president in all the solemn assemblies of the ministers of the gospel; and many times, if he is able, called upon to labor and suffer more than any of his brethren" (3:544–5).

He then set the record straight about his relationship to John Wesley and Thomas Rankin. "I can truly say for one, that the greatest affliction and sorrow of my life is that our dear father, from the time of the Revolution to his death, grew more and more jealous of myself and the whole American connection; that it appeared we had lost his confidence almost entirely" (3:545). Asbury affirmed that in spite of political misunderstanding and the events of the Revolution, John Wesley continued to be esteemed, "respected and loved by hundreds and thousands in America as a great apostolic man; and hundreds of children continually named after him—yea, thousands" (3:546).

After asserting that a "degree of justice" was due Wesley's memory, Asbury laid the blame for the interpersonal tension at the feet of Thomas Rankin, whom he dubbed "Diotrephes."[5] "It appeared to me that his object was to sweep the Continent of every preacher that Mr. Wesley had sent to it and of every respectable traveling preacher from Europe who had graduated among us, whether English or Irish" (3:547). Asbury then attempted to refute John Whitehead's diatribe against John Wesley, and Whitehead's accusation that the ordinations of Coke and Asbury were spurious. In short, he reasserted that Wesley was an "apostolic man" and Asbury's office was not only validated by the historical church, but also by "pure principles" and the success that had attended the labors of its ministers. "[H]ail Wesley, hail Oxford Methodists, who, seventy years ago, formed an apostolic society and sent forth their traveling preachers in apostolic order!" (3:550).

The letter to Benson expressed a final word of thanks to the faith community that had borne him. It was also an olive branch, recalling the confidence and peace that had been enjoyed between the two Methodist churches over the last fifty years. One wishes that Asbury would have done as well with some of the individuals with whom he found himself crossways. His memory seemed to be keener in recalling the indictments that had been made against him than in reassessing the accusations he had made, which may not have been totally accurate. Whatever sanctification did, it did not remove the biased perceptions that lay between him and persons of the past who had proved to be annoyances. Thomas Rankin had charged him with being suspicious and gloomy. Such attitudes had saved Asbury from naiveté but often had not endeared him to his fellow workers. The paradox of leadership is that almost every virtue of the leader can be misconstrued as a vice. John Wesley Bond said that few men had more unshaken confidence in their friends, though Asbury "seemed determined to be blind to the faults of none."[6]

Two people Asbury never forgave, at least publicly, were James O'Kelly and Thomas Rankin. They had impugned his character and misrepresented his motives, leaving scars he carried for the rest of his life. Personal integrity was to be protected and even defended. Especially in his last days, Asbury was bent on setting the record straight.

Last Journey

Sometime in January 1816, Asbury stopped at a "brother" Young's, where he met with James Jenkins. Jenkins recalled that Asbury, though he was sick, "testified to the Lord being good to him and better now than ever." When Asbury asked Jenkins to pray with him, Jenkins was unable because he "was too full to pray."[7] Asbury's next stop was Rembert Hall, about twelve miles north of Sumter, South Carolina. Even though his emaciated frame convulsed from constant coughs, attempting to expectorate the fluid that formed around his heart, he was not too weak to discuss "pelagianism" with an acquaintance. It was one more occasion to report how he had been saved from a system of morality to genuine conversion, which had enabled his life of service. Constant exposure to the elements had led to colds that had fastened like a "vulture" on his lungs. "Yet I can trust in nothing I have ever done or suffered—I stand alone in the righteousness of Christ—I stand in justifying, and in the sanctifying righteousness of Jesus Christ."[8]

At Rembert Hall, William Capers caught up with the bishop and requested to be changed from a local preacher to an itinerant by being appointed a circuit for the coming year. "I am a dying man or I would give you one. I will never see another conference in Carolina. You had better wait for your Quarterly Conference to recommend you to a presiding elder."[9] To Bond, he commented, "I have experienced an entire death to the flesh, the lust of the eye, and the pride of life. It is due to the sinking powers of my nature."[10] As his sheets were being changed, he glanced down at his withered body and observed with a cheerful countenance, "Ah, It is sown in dishonor—but," as he tilted his eyes up, "it shall be raised in glory."[11]

From Rembert Hall, Asbury traveled to Marion Academy at Marion, South Carolina, where he spent several days with Joseph Travis. Travis recalled that at a conference in Fayetteville, North Carolina, Asbury had taken him in his arms and kissed him. "I always loved him," said Travis, "and expect to love him in the Kingdom of Heaven, world without end."[12] It was painful to see the church's great statesman in such a pathetic condition. Travis noted, "Patience and entire resignation to the will of God were manifestly exhibited by him from day to day; when recovering from a paroxysm he would shout aloud, 'Hallelujah, hallelujah.'" As he was about to leave, Asbury urged Travis to give up his school and reenter the itinerancy, which he did a year later.

Toward the end of February, Bond and Asbury stopped at the home of a Mr. King in Raleigh, North Carolina, where he preached for the first time that year. During the last few days of February, they lodged with William Williams, eighteen miles outside of Louisburg, North Carolina. From here, Bond wrote to McKendree, "It would be a great gratification to me if we could get on to the Baltimore conference, nevertheless, I have constantly opposed making the attempt well knowing that Father Asbury's health would not admit of it."[13] Four days later, he added a postscript which attempted to share some of Asbury's concerns, mainly the support of the missionaries. The mite subscription would make up the difference after the missionaries had done their best to support themselves. He suggested that the preachers' salaries be raised to $260 for the married men and $120 for the unmarried men. The commander was giving final instructions for the welfare of his troops.

Asbury penned his final latter on March 4 in Brunswick County, Virginia. Again, it revealed the whirling mind that tied together the loose ends of a growing ball of yarn. He was always convinced that the ends would become ever more numerous unless attention were given to miniscule details. One could not talk about the task of ministry without a concern for numbers, finances, and placements. One last time he sounded the note of exactitude. "Had I power to be present, the stewards would have a correct account of all we have received at conferences and expended upon road expenses. In 1815 I asked thirty dollars, they sent forty" (3:556). He then allowed Methodism and the world to eavesdrop on a note of personal gratitude. "The incredible toil of Wesley Bond is only known to me; I must reward him. His character is good; he has attempted to moderate his sermons; preaches to acceptance, generally beloved by the preachers and the people" (3:556).

On Saturday, March 16, the pair arrived at Manchester, Virginia, where they lodged with John Potts. At 4 P.M. on Sunday, a congregation gathered at the house to hear Asbury preach. With great struggle and hardly able to be heard, Asbury expostulated and exhorted for over an hour. Bond commented that he "did not appear so exhausted as I expected."

A local preacher, Philip Courtney, en route to his Sunday appointment stopped to see Asbury.[14] Asbury insisted that Courtney stay and sent Bond in his stead.

Asbury then proceeded to unfold a plan whereby a local preacher would not simply be responsible for a local church but would assume responsibility for a circuit at least twice a year. Asbury knew that the percentage of local preachers as compared to itinerants had been increasing. He did not want to lose the itinerancy he so long had cherished. Commissioning local preachers to travel at least part-time would blur the distinction between "locals" and "itinerants." It was Asbury's version of a half-way covenant, compromise for the sake of efficiency.

The great westward migration had peaked, and Methodist preachers wanted to marry and have families, just like everyone else. The paradigm shift had taken place right before Asbury's eyes. The Methodist preachers' sacrificial embracing of two worlds was almost dead. The horse had been traded for a parsonage. In fact, Methodism was on the verge of electing a married bishop to take Asbury's place.[15]

Last Sermon

Asbury and Bond next traveled to Richmond, arriving there on Monday, March 18. They were hosted at the homes of an unidentifiable "Brother Raymond" and of Archibald Foster, whom Asbury had ordained deacon in 1789. During this time he had an interview with the local Episcopal bishop by the name of Moore. Asbury warned him concerning a spurious Wesleyan preacher who had come from England and was seeking ordination in the Protestant Episcopal Church. "Bishop Moore, in passing through your Diocese, you will find but few Episcopal churches, and these in a sad state of decay with but few communicants; but in almost every neighborhood you will find an unpretending little clapboard meeting house, in these, an humble pious people assemble to worship God in spirit and in truth. Go into these houses and preach to the people that gather in them. Recognize them as the children of God, and as true Christians, and you will greatly promote the cause of Christ."[16]

Asbury insisted on preaching at the "Old Church" in Richmond at the corner of Nineteenth and Franklin Streets at 3 P.M. on Sunday, March 24. He was carried from the carriage to the platform of the church in a chair, and the chair was placed on a table. There Asbury sat and preached for the last time. For almost an hour, with gasping breath, rasping voice, and halting speech, he expounded on Romans 9:28: "For He will finish the work and cut it short in righteousness: because a short work will the Lord make upon the earth." An eyewitness recorded,

> To behold a venerable old man, under the dignified character of
> an ecclesiastical patriarch, whose silver locks indicated that time
> had already numbered his years, and whose pallid countenance
> and trembling limbs presaged that his earthly race was nearly fin-

ished: to see in the midst of these melancholy signals of decaying nature a soul beaming with immortality, and a heart kindled with divine fire from the altar of God—to see such a man, and to hear him address them in the name of the Lord of Hosts, on the grand concerns of time and eternity! What heart so insensible as to withstand the impression that such a scene was calculated to produce?[17]

Died as He Had Lived

Asbury was determined to arrive in Baltimore by May 1, the beginning of the General Conference. He had five weeks to make the 145-mile trip; possibly he would be able to forge ahead in small increments. It was not to be. In Robert Bull's words, he, "died as he had lived—*en route.*"[18] John Wesley Bond rendered almost 24-hour-a-day nursing attention. Bond lay on a mat by the bishop's bed and sprang to his feet at Asbury's request, or if he detected any change in his physical condition. On March 26, they traveled 22 miles to Travis Crenshaw's, where they spent Tuesday and Wednesday nights. Asbury asked Bond to make arrangements for him to preach Wednesday afternoon, but when the time came he was too weak and Bond preached in his stead. On Thursday, they traveled to Edward Rouzee's where they spent the night.

On Friday, Asbury and Bond arrived at George Arnold's in Spotsylvania, Virginia. On Saturday morning, Asbury remarked to Bond, "If this should be as good a day as yesterday, we can hardly help traveling."[19] But it rained and the party stayed put, to the relief of Bond. When Bond suggested that they have service at eleven o'clock the next morning and to invite a family some five miles away, Asbury responded, "You need not be in a hurry."[20] Bond concluded that the bishop was thinking he was too weak to bear the noise of a worship service in the house. Asbury was restless throughout the night and was exceedingly weak the next morning. Bond suggested that they send for a physician, a Dr. Louis who lived some ten miles away.

"I shall not be able to tell him what is the matter with me, and the man will not know what to do," said Asbury.

When Bond insisted, Asbury replied, "He could only pronounce me dead."

"Probably he could give you something that would relieve you. I hope you have no apprehension of anything serious taking place, have you?"

"Yes."

"If anything serious should take place, do you have any word to leave with me?"

"I have spoken and written so fully, an additional word is unnecessary."

"I have heard you speak so frequently on the affairs of the church that I believe I understand your sentiments fully."

"Yes."[21]

Asbury had put his house in order. As the 11 A.M. hour approached, the bishop asked if "it was not time for meeting." When told that only the family was present, he responded, "Call them together." The Scripture lesson for the day was Revelation 21, from which Bond read in clear tones, reverberating from the walls of a small room in a small house, "It is done. I am Alpha and Omega, the beginning and the end, I will give unto him that is athirst of the fountain of the water of life freely. He that overcometh shall inherit all things; and I will be his God, and he shall be my son." As Bond sang, prayed, and expounded on the Scripture, Asbury smiled and raised his hand repeatedly in agreement with the sentiments of worship. After the benediction, he called for the "mite subscription" to be read. When told it was not available, he remained silent. It was his last recorded sentence.

Throughout the afternoon, Asbury seemed to remain conscious of his immediate surroundings, yet gradually making his way to the next life. Shortly before his death, he was not able to take the teaspoons of water that were offered him. "[H]e lifted up his hand toward Heaven with an expression which I will never forget. He then without a groan or complaint, fell asleep in the arms of his Savior; at four o'clock on Sunday, March 31, 1816."[22] The "prophet of the long road" had incarnated his exhortation to Nelson Reed six years earlier, "Die! Die! my brother in the field, in the harness!" (3: 425–6).

Double Burial and Funeral

Bond was bewildered as to what to do. Here he was in the middle of nowhere, at a nondescript place, with the corpse of American Methodism's most venerated saint. There was no one to whom he could turn for advice except George Arnold. Arnold persuaded Bond to bury Asbury in the Arnold family plot.[23] Bond immediately wrote to Daniel Hitt, "I feel at a loss how to proceed respecting his burial, as I feel anxious to comply with the wishes of the church, that he should be deposited in some public burying ground belonging to our connection; but considering the distance we are far from any, and after taking the best council I could advise with, I am inclined to bury the remains of our departed father in the family vault of our friend and brother Arnold."[24] The next day Asbury's body was placed in a plain coffin and with a simple ceremony was interred in the family burying ground on George Arnold's farm.

One of the first acts of the Baltimore General Conference was to decide that the body be exhumed, carried to Baltimore, and re-interred at the Eutaw Street Church.[25] On May 6, several delegates, including Bond, arrived at George Arnold's farm. When Arnold was informed of the conference's intention, he responded, "I consider the General Conference to have the right to dispose of the body of Bishop Asbury. I would not part with the remains of my old friend, in compliance with the request of any individual or any other body of men."[26] The delegates opened the coffin and found the corpse fully preserved after 35 days in the ground. The coffin was closed, wrapped in "laced sheets," and transported by a horse-drawn hearse, arriving in Baltimore on May 9. The body was first taken to the house of William Hawkins and then transferred to the Light Street Church.[27]

For the evening of May 9, the body lay in state at Light Street Church. The conference appointed Henry Stead, William Case, Seth Mattson, and Henry Boehm to sit up with the corpse during the night. Boehm recalled that "[f]ive times that night, in imagination, I went with the Bishop around his large diocese, over the mountains and valleys. I thought of his self-denial, his deadness to the world, of his intense labors, his enlarged benevolence, tears—sympathy for the suffering, of the hundreds of sermons I had heard him preach, the prayers I had heard him offer; the many times I had slept with him; how often I had carried him in my arms."[28]

At 10 A.M. on May 10, the horse-drawn hearse with the body made its way through the streets of Baltimore to the Eutaw Street Church.[29] In front of the hearse walked William McKendree and William Black, the "apostle of Methodism" to Nova Scotia. Behind the hearse walked John Wesley Bond and Henry Boehm, leading the entire delegation of the General Conference. Behind the delegation followed thousands of laity, sprinkled with scores of clergymen from the various churches in Baltimore and the surrounding area. An eyewitness account came from Charles Giles, a delegate to the General Conference:

> The municipal officers, the clergy, and citizens without distinction, were invited to unite with the members of the General Conference in the mournful and solemn procession. The affecting occasion excited the public mind and aroused the feelings of thousands to come and sympathize with us. The scene connected with that memorable day was truly imposing: the whole city appeared to be in motion. I was informed that the procession was a mile in length; besides the multitude accompanying us along the walks.[30]

McKendree preached the funeral sermon to the small proportion of persons who were able to pack into the Eutaw Street Church, while a vast crowd stood outside.[31] The body was crypted under the pulpit and a plaque was later placed on the wall of the church with the following inscription:

Sacred
To the memory of
The Reverend Francis Asbury

Bishop of the
Methodist Episcopal Church

He was born in England August 20, 1745,
He entered the ministry at the age of 17
Came a missionary to America, 1771
Was ordained Bishop in this city December 27, 1784
Annually visited the conferences in the United States
With much zeal continued to "preach the Word"
For more than half a century
And
Literally ended his labors with his life
Near Fredericksburg, Virginia
In the full triumph of faith on the 31st of March, 1816
Aged 70 years, 7 months, and 11 days
His remains were deposited in this vault May 10, 1816
By the General Conference then sitting in this city
His journals will exhibit to posterity
His labors, his difficulties, his sufferings,
His patience, his perseverance, his love to God and man.[32]

During the Conference, McKendree, Boehm, and Daniel Hitt had the will executed by local attorneys. Allowances were made for an ongoing subsidy to John Dickens's widow and for Bibles to be distributed to children named after Asbury. Boehm later estimated the number to be about 1,400, many of which he personally delivered. As the news spread that Asbury intended Bibles to be given to all children named after him, applications continued to be sent to the "book room" until the Civil War.

One last time, Asbury's account was carefully recorded. On July 8, 1816, the Baltimore City Station Church listed the expenses for Asbury's Baltimore funeral:

Rev. Mr. Bond for expenses in removal	$66.00
Lambert Thomas for coffin	$40.00
John Curran for Stage and Horse hire	$50.00
Timothy Richards for Horse Hire	$12.00
Linens, etc…	$ 5.80
Total	$173.80 [33]

On the following Sunday, all the Methodist worship services in the Baltimore area consisted of eulogies to Asbury. Henry Boehm and Joshua Soule were among those who delivered funeral discourses. The best-known and longest eulogy had already been delivered on April 23 at St. George's Church in Philadelphia by Ezekiel Cooper. Three years later, Cooper submitted the sermon, which he had delivered extemporaneously, for publication. The product was a 230-page book.

At the actual discourse a thousand people crammed into the church, while another two to three thousand stood outside. Cooper said of his always friend and sometimes foe, "Every day, in every hour, almost every minute, appeared to be employed, and devoted in close application to some excellent work and useful purpose! . . . His manner of life has been equaled by few, perhaps surpassed by none. I am confidently persuaded, to take him all and in all, that no man in America ever came up to his standard."[34]

Representative Men Elected

For the first time, the church elected multiple bishops at one sitting: Enoch George and Robert Roberts. Roberts was the presiding elder of the Schuylkill District of the Philadelphia Conference and, immediately preceding the General Conference, had capably presided over the Philadelphia Annual Conference and thus was riding a wave of popularity. Both Roberts and George were representative men, symbols for the thousands of nobodies who became somebodies. When Roberts was found by Methodist itinerants, he was wearing a "broad rimmed, low-crown, white wool hat, the hunting shirt of low linen, buckskin breeches and moccasin shoes."[35] Roberts did not let the title of bishop go to his head. Though he no longer wore moccasins, he did carry out the episcopal office from a log cabin.

Shortly before 1790, Enoch George had been presented to Asbury by Methodism's travelling book steward, Philip Cox. "I have brought you a boy, and if you have anything for him to do you may set him to work." Asbury's eyes penetrated the uneasy 20-year-old youth who stood before him. "Bishop Asbury looked at me for some time; at length, calling me to him he laid my head upon his knee, and stroking my face with his hand said, 'Why, he is a beardless boy, and can do nothing.'"[36] George believed that his ministerial career was over before it started, but the next day Asbury appointed him to a circuit in South Carolina. There was nothing new about sending boys to do men's jobs; the miracle is that they did it.

The Asbury Legacy

Asbury led the way for thousands of individuals to inscribe their names on the walls of history as transformers of men. In Crane Brinton's words, "[A]ll normal people are metaphysicians; all have some desire to locate themselves in a 'system,' a 'universe,' a 'process' transcending at least the immediate give-and-take between the individual and his environment."[37] The ignorant and poor left a legacy far beyond the span of biological existence because someone enabled them to believe in both God and themselves. Without that enabling vision, poverty and ignorance would have shrouded most of them with oblivion.

William Capers was 26 years old when Asbury died. "Billy Sugar" was elected bishop of the Methodist Episcopal Church South at its first General Conference in May 1846. The trek began on February 9, 1792, when Asbury visited the home of Captain William Capers, whose wife had died that day. Asbury called the two-year-old boy to him, saying, "So this is the baby." Asbury held, hugged, and kissed him. Sixteen years later, Asbury sent him to Sawney's Creek, South Carolina, where he lodged with the former presiding elder James Jenkins, known as "Thundering Jimmy" and "Bawling Jenkins."

Jenkins looked at young Capers and said, "Well, have they sent you to us as our preacher?"

"Yes, Sir."

"What—you? And the eggshell not dropped off of you yet! Lord have mercy upon us. And who have they sent in charge?"

"No one, sir, but myself."

"What—you by yourself, you in charge of the circuit? Why, what is to become of the circuit? The bishop had just as well sent nobody. What can you do in charge of the circuit?"

"Very poorly I fear, sir, but I dare say the bishop thought you would advise me about the *Discipline*, and I am sure he could not have sent one who would follow your advice more willingly, Brother Jenkins, than I will."[38]

Asbury commissioned four thousand striplings to ignite what historian John Wigger calls the "largest social movement of the early republic."[39] In 1775, fewer than one out of eight hundred Americans was a Methodist; by 1812, it was one out of every thirty-six. By 1820, Methodist adherents accounted for nearly 21 percent of the American population. Methodist preachers—who in intellect, education, native abilities, social status, and possessions had little to offer—left their signature on almost every facet of American life. The surprise is not that men of such uncommon sacrifice would make such a difference; they always do. The wonder is that they would make such a sacrifice.

In accepting less of life's comforts, Asbury's preachers became more—more than they would have been without a model and a vehicle by which they could transport the model. The vehicle was guided by an ideology, and that ideology was incarnated in a person. The ideology was laced with the dichotomies of heaven-hell, light-darkness, and now-later. Such dichotomies energized a life-death urgency. The urgency found its energy in the certitude that there is another world from which God definitely speaks and acts. In Erik Erikson's words, "The disinherited (disinherited in earthly goods, and in social identity) above all desired to hear and rehear those words which made their inner world, long stagnant and dead, reverberate with forgotten echoes; this desire made them believe that God, from somewhere in the outer spaces, spoke through a chosen man on a definable historical occasion."[40]

The God of Opportunity

In spite of the geographical, national, and political distance between Asbury and Wesley, the former was a direct extension of the latter. Fully imbibing Wesley's primary working premise, "You have nothing to do but to save souls," caused all differences between the mentor and the student to pale. Wesley defined the primary task of the pastor as evangelism. Asbury embodied in both practice and spirit. He acted out Wesley's reflection, "[W]hat marvel the devil does not love field preaching! Neither do I: I love a commodious room, a soft cushion, handsome pulpit. But where is my zeal if I do not trample all these underfoot in order to save one more soul?"[41] Asbury, more than any other person, transmitted Wesleyan evangelism to thousands of American preachers. One of them, Freeborn Garrettson, later recalled:

> I traversed the mountains and valleys, frequently on foot, with my knapsack on my back, guided by Indian paths in the wilderness, when it was not expedient to take a horse. I had often to ride through morasses, half deep in mud and water; frequently satisfying my hunger with a piece of bread and pork from my knapsack, quenching my thirst from a brook, and resting my weary limbs on the leaves of trees. Thanks be to God! He compensated me for my toil; for many precious souls were awakened and converted to God.[42]

Whatever Asbury's gifts were, whatever his level of commitment, whatever his political savvy, whatever his measure of discipline, he basically had one thing to offer—the God of opportunity. This God found fertile soil in the land of opportunity. In 1798, Asbury said to Epaphras Kilby, who had never preached a sermon but was being sent to the Granville Circuit, "Go my son and God be with you. Do the best you can and an Angel cannot do better."[43]

The quest for identity is universal. One's identity can never be discovered in isolation; it must either produce a collective mind or become part of one. There is only one way to produce a collective mind, and that is to offer an idea around which others are willing to gather. The idea can never be generic; it must be radical and it must be simple. Asbury had this in common with the Christ who had called him; he shared it in turn with the men to whom he reiterated the call. "Again the Kingdom of Heaven is like unto a merchant man, seeking goodly pearls. Who when he had found one pearl of great price, went and sold all that he had, and bought it."[44]

The Dilemma of Success

Success presented Asbury and Methodism with its gravest dilemma, a problem Christianity has never been able to negotiate: The more it wins the world, the more it becomes like the world. Asbury was at least partially aware of this problem. An analysis made almost two centuries later would have enabled him to more fully appreciate the crisis every numerically effective American sect has inherently created:

The sect-church process concerns the fact that new religious bodies nearly always begin as sects and that, if they are successful in attracting a substantial following, they will, over time, almost inevitably be gradually transformed into churches. That is, successful religious movements nearly always shift their emphasis toward this world and away from the next, moving from high tension with the environment towards increasingly lower levels of tension. As this occurs, a religious body will become increasingly less able to satisfy members who desire a higher tension version of faith. As discontent grows, these people will begin to complain that the group is abandoning its original positions and practices, as indeed it has. At some point this growing conflict within the group will erupt into a split, and the faction desiring a return to higher tension will leave to found a new sect. If this movement proves successful, over time it too will be transformed into a church and once again a split will occur. The result is an endless cycle of sect formation, transformation, schism, and rebirth. The many workings of this cycle account for the countless varieties of each of the major faiths.[45]

A Radical Doctrine

Francis Asbury incarnated the joining of belief and action. The theology he espoused, sanctification of heart and life, enabled one to believe that he or she could be totally devoted to God. Entire sanctification is a radical doctrine, radical in its optimism for humankind, radical in its pessimism concerning the destructiveness of sin, and radical in its belief that persons really can love God and humanity. Whether a person can be "perfect in love" in this life is a question for theologians; the historical fact is that the doctrine of Christian perfection prompted Asbury and his followers to live as though it were so. The herculean efforts of Asbury are directly and completely grounded in John Wesley's theology of sanctification, the hallowing of the whole of life.

Asbury did not impose his way of life upon others; but the standards he had adopted for himself were obvious: frugality, chastity, immense work, and tenacious perseverance. In emptying himself, he was able to absorb the plight of others. He may have chosen a throne, but it was an empathetic throne of dis-ease, which was the lot of almost all of his contemporary Americans. For both migrating Americans and Asbury, the road always lay ahead. The bishop issued an invitation: "Follow me." One cannot follow someone who quits moving, so Asbury never stopped.

The Persevering Servant

Asbury's identification with persons in all stations of life led them to overlook the inconsistencies and contradictions in his life. Asbury could be caring and aloof, austere and affectionate, intimate and distant, sober and jovial, congenial and adversarial, leading and serving. No single incident demonstrated his servant-leader mentality better than what took place at the Lyons, New York, Conference on July 22, 1810. While the conference was in session, Asbury observed a farmer attempting to get his hay in before it was ruined by an approaching rainstorm. Asbury adjourned the conference and ordered the attendees to assist the farmer. We can safely presume that the 63-year-old Asbury would have participated in the task.[46]

Leadership requires singleness of focus but not necessarily simplicity of personality. A person with charisma possesses an identifiable matrix of values, transmitted to others. Leadership not only demonstrates accomplishment, it enables others to visualize that such accomplishment can belong to them. Asbury practiced, mentored, nurtured, and enabled measurable accomplishment. The growing numbers in his journal were his gift to a movement that was ever progressing and expanding. His ministers' self-esteem and psychological fulfillment were sufficient reasons for them to overlook the compulsive idiosyncrasies of the captain. These idiosyncrasies somehow coalesced into a persevering determination to expand the work. Robert Coles profoundly states that "[t]he psychology of the martyr, of a certain kind of moral leader who won't be frightened by obstacles and opponents large and vindictive, is the psychology of will—of a decision made and its consequences be damned. In this age of determinisms, emotional and social and historical and economic, there is little room for 'will' in the vocabulary we summon when we try to understand human affairs."[47] God's grace transformed Asbury's will into "infinite toughness."[48]

A Movement's Most Important Factor

Others were greater than Asbury in both gifts and sacrifice but died in obscurity. Asbury possessed ego strength, the ability to adapt to and to overcome whatever life threw his way. Asbury never retreated. Any passivity he may ever have displayed was not out of lack of confidence or a sense of incompetence, but from the perception that the particular situation demanded disengagement. Asbury never hid from a challenge; he paused and reconnoitered. In Paul Johnson's words, "Great events in history are determined by all kinds of factors, but the most important single one is always the quality of the people in charge."[49] For no person or movement is Johnson's statement more true than for Francis Asbury and the preachers who followed him.

The compatibility between Asbury the man and America the country was not nearly as important as that between himself and the task which divine authority had given him. Asbury's natural habitat was not defined by the diverse terrain, but by the security in his own psyche. In the numerous log cabins where Asbury stayed—filled with lice-infested children, flea-infested dogs, and toothless men and women—comfort was not natural; but he willed himself to be at home. He had certainly known better circumstances in childhood, with loving parents who were religious, industrious, clean, and morally upright. Asbury was well aware of the task with which he had been entrusted. Enabled by grace, he determined to live among people who were often unlike him in habit and disposition. He possessed an ability to combine a narrowly defined ideology with wide and inclusive ego boundaries. These boundaries were defined by an all-encompassing theology of grace. Anyone who chose could ride on the Methodist bandwagon.

A Point of Betrayal

In terms of church administration Asbury at times showed little grace toward those who opposed him, even though their efforts now seem well-intentioned. It was hard for him to forget and to forgive. At this point, his ideology betrayed him. He believed that all had to be sacrificed to the cause—the cause as he interpreted it, which allowed little deviation. Asbury knew where he was going and where the church needed to go. This certitude attracted many, but alienated others. Often those who exhibited similar boldness of initiative and equal clarity of insight (such as Rankin, Lee, Cooper, or even O'Kelly) were all caring, committed leaders. Their intensity often resulted in a diversity of opinion; that was the problem with Asbury's leadership.

The New Testament church was no different. Decision-making has its fallout. It is an imperfect world, and this Asbury fully realized; yet his idealized self found it difficult to admit of imperfect relationships. It was not so much that he was never reconciled to his "enemies"; rather, he was never reconciled to the self that failed to love its enemies. Guilt often produces anger, a human weakness that was glaringly apparent in Asbury, even in his last days. A study of Francis Asbury helps us better understand quintessential American leadership. For almost every virtue there is a betraying vice.

The Greatest Gift

"Father Asbury" was not simply an appellation of affection. It was an evolving veneration for the man who had nurtured his offspring through childhood and adolescence into the status of a mature, fully legitimated American institution. Nathan Hatch assesses that "[b]eyond his personal example, what is remarkable about Asbury's career is his success in stamping personal convictions indelibly upon an emerging movement."[50]

Asbury motivated latent energies and talents in his children; his capacities were congruent with the needs of his children. He had both acted and spoken, and they had responded. It is to his credit that he knew which strings to pull, which places to nudge, and which words to speak to enable his family to realize their full potential. And he did love them beyond the pragmatism of measurable accomplishment. The travel, the intercession, and the displays of affection—all of these things characterized a person who found inherent worth in sheer human existence. He sacrificed exclusive sexual intimacy for devotion to a community of offspring whom he had spiritually borne. His "child-rearing" methods may have been questioned, but never his devotion to them. No children have ever had a more doting spiritual father than did early American Methodists.

Asbury's journal exhibited a good deal of anxiety, restlessness, depression, and guilt. However, to attribute his morbidity to a melancholy temperament is mere tautology. We should recognize it is a delicate task to aspire to the office of a bishop within a system presumed to consist of a selfless humility, while at the same time one is expected to take the front seat in the house. There is no simple resolution for such a dialectic.

Inner antagonism is quieted only by what Erikson calls "ego integrity," the overwhelming recognition that life is what it should have been and admits of no substitutes. This does not mean that one cannot embrace his/her humanity with all of its faults and embarrassments. A person of ego integrity has made peace with both failure and achievement. Asbury maintained ego integrity by labeling both the good and the bad as the fortunes of Providence. Wesley said, "God's people die well." Erikson said that "healthy children will not fear life if their elders have integrity enough not to fear death."[51] Both life and death are a triumph of faith, whatever its source.

More than most people, Asbury made history and was victimized by it. For example, the current of slavery swept him and his followers along, just as it did most Americans. Christianity has always attempted both to transcend culture and to influence it. The results can be disappointing.

Asbury incarnated the circuit rider, a major archetype of the American spirit. These dedicated servants offered hope, light, and stability to the thousands that joined the great westward migration. They excelled in harvesting the multitudes, who were spiritually captivated by the Second Great Awakening. No epoch in American history was more in need of a mobile pulpit, and Francis Asbury provided it. He raised up the fastest growing denomination in the most influential nation in the Western Hemisphere. His contribution can be interpreted as historical coincidence or divine providence, or something in between.

Asbury referred to his life as "unordinary" and to his labors as "Herculean." He cloaked his ambitious energy in humility when he wrote to his mother, after having been on the North American continent for one year, "I cannot as of yet seek great things for myself" (3:14). But Asbury could not deny "greatness" any more than he could disclaim being an only child and having nurturing parents, including a mother who practiced an intense relationship with her God. Asbury was highly aware that this same mother dedicated him to God as a unique instrument of Providence. Asbury believed a special space had been carved out for him within God's plan of redemption. Though he was not unaware of the determining forces of heredity and environment, he perceived that he had an unparalleled opportunity, the Christianizing of a new nation. He believed himself to be a major architect of the nation, no less than did George Washington, John Adams, and Thomas Jefferson. What Joseph Ellis has written about them was also true of Asbury: "All the vanguard members of the revolutionary generation developed a keen sense of their historical significance even while they were still making the history on which their reputations would rest."[52]

The confidence that one can be better than he or she has been before (however that "better" is defined) may be the greatest gift that one person can give to another. This confidence was actualized in Asbury's life. What had given him meaning he sought to give away. It is to Francis Asbury's credit that he discovered a more effective delivery system than anyone else had devised. But a methodology is only as good as the passion of the one using it. This passion, which Asbury believed to be from God, drove him to the very end. He never stopped going and doing. Holiness was a never-ending pursuit in which "arrival" always meant having to start again. Rest would come only on the other side.

BIBLIOGRAPHY

PUBLISHED PRIMARY WORKS

American Society of the Wesleyan Methodist Church, *Minutes of the Early Methodist Conferences in America*. (Baltimore: The Baltimore Maryland Conference Methodist Historical Society, 1774–1779).

Asbury, Francis. *The Causes, Evils and Cures of Heart and Church Divisions* (Salem, Ohio: Schmul Publishers, 1978).

_____. *The Journal and Letters of Francis Asbury*, eds. Elmer Clark, J. Manning Potts, and Jacob S. Payton (London: Epworth Press, 1958).

_____. *A Selection of Hymns from Various Authors Designed as a Supplement to the Methodist Pocket Hymn-Book Compiled under the Direction of Bishop Asbury* (New York, N.Y.: John Wilson and Daniel Hitt, 1808).

Bangs, John. *Autobiography of the Rev. John Bangs* (New York, N.Y.: printed for the author, 1846).

Baxter, Richard. *The Reformed Pastor* (Carlisle, Penn.: Banner of Truth Trust, 1983).

Boehm, Henry. *Reminiscences, Historical and Biographical of Sixty-Four Years in the Ministry*, ed. Joseph B. Wakeley (New York, N.Y.: Carlton & Porter, 1866).

Brown, George. *Recollections of Itinerant Life* (Cincinnati, Ohio: R.W. Carroll and Co., 1866).

Brunson, Alfred. *A Western Pioneer or Incidents of the Life and Times of Rev. Alfred Brunson* (Cincinnati, Ohio: Walden and Stowe, 1880).

Cartwright, Peter. *Autobiography of Peter Cartwright*, ed. W.P. Strickland (Nashville, Tenn.: Abingdon, 1956).

Chase, Abner. *Recollections of the Past* (New York, N.Y.: Joseph Longking, 1846).

Coke, Thomas. *Extracts of the Journals of the Rev. Dr. Coke's Five Visits to America* (London: G. Paramore, 1793).

Coke, Thomas, and Francis Asbury. *An Address to the Annual Subscribers for the Support of Cokesbury College and to the Members of the Methodist Society to Which Are Added the Rules and Regulations of the College* (New York, N.Y.: W. Ross, 1787).

Coles, George. *The Supernumerary of Lights and Shadows of Itinerancy Compiled from Papers of Elijah Woolsey* (New York, N.Y.: Lane and Tippett, 1845).

Cooper, Ezekiel. *The Substance of a Funeral Discourse delivered at the request of the annual conference on Tuesday, 23rd of April, 1816, in St. George's Church, Philadelphia, on the death of the Rev. Francis Asbury, Superintendent or Senior Bishop of the Methodist Episcopal Church* (Philadelphia, Penn.: Jonathan Pounder, 1819).

Dow, Lorenzo. *The Life, Travels, Labors, and Writings of Lorenzo Dow* (New York, N.Y.: R. Worthington, 1881).

Emory, John. *A Defense of Our Fathers* (New York, N.Y.: Carlton & Porter, 1827).

Emory, Robert. *The Life of Rev. John Emory* (New York, N.Y.: George Lane, 1841).

Finley, James. *Autobiography of James B. Finley* (Cincinnati, Ohio: Methodist Book Concern, 1858).

_____. *Sketches of Western Methodism: Biographical, Historical, and Miscellaneous. Illustrative of Pioneer Life*, ed. W.P. Strickland, D.D. (Cincinnati, Ohio: The Methodist Book Concern, 1855).

Ffirth, John. *The Experience and Gospel Labours of the Rev. Benjamin Abbott* (Philadelphia, Penn.: D. & S. Neall, 1825).

_____. *Truth Vindicated or a Scriptural Essay wherein the Vulgar and Frivolous Cavils Commonly Used against the Methodist Episcopal Church Are Briefly Considered in a Letter to a Friend.* Second Ed. (New York, N.Y.: Daniel Hitt, 1810).

Fletcher, John. *Third Check to Antinomianism* (New York, N.Y.: B. Waugh and T. Mason, 1833).

Gaddis, Maxwell P. *Footprints of an Itinerant* (New York, N.Y.: Phillips & Hunt, 1880).

Giles, Charles. *Pioneer: A Narrative of the Nativity, Experience, Travels, and Ministerial Labours of Rev. Charles Giles* (New York, N.Y.: G. Lane & P.P. Sandford, 1844).

Glendinning, William. *The Life of William Glendinning* (Philadelphia, Penn.: W. W. Woodward, 1795).

Gurly, L.B. *Memoirs of Rev. William Gurly* (Cincinnati, Ohio: Methodist Book Concern, 1850).

Hammet, William. *A Rejoindre Being a Defence of the Truths Contained in an Appeal to Truth and Circumstances in Seven Letters Addressed to the Reverend Mr. Morrell* (Charleston, S.C.: I. Sulliman, 1792).

Hibbard, Billy. *Memoirs of the Life and Travels of B. Hibbard* (New York, N.Y.: published for the author, 1825).

Jackson, Thomas. *Lives of Early Methodist Preachers* (London: Wesleyan Conference Office, 1871).

Janson, Charles William. *The Stranger in America, 1793–1806* (New York, N.Y.: The Press of the Pioneer, 1935).

Jarratt, Devereux. *The Life of the Reverend Devereux Jarratt, Rector of Bath Parish, Virginia, written by himself in a series of letters addressed to the Rev. John Coleman* (Baltimore, Md.: Warner & Hanna, 1806).

Jefferson, Thomas. *Notes on the State of Virginia.* Ed. William Peden (Chapel Hill, N.C.: The University of North Carolina Press, 1982).

Jenkins, James. *Experience, Labours and Sufferings of Rev. James Jenkins* (printed for the author, 1842).

Lee, Jesse. *A Short History of the Methodists in the United States of America* (Baltimore, Md.: Magill and Clime, 1810).

Lewis, David. *Recollections of a Superannuate or Sketches of Life, Labor and Experience in the Methodist Itinerancy* (Cincinnati, Ohio: Methodist Book Concern, 1857).

Marsden, Joshua. *The Conference; or Methodism* (London: Blauchard, n.d.).

McKay, Michael J., ed. *The Journals of the Rev. Thomas Morrell* (Madison, N.J.: Historical Society of the Northern New Jersey Conference, 1984).

Methodist Episcopal Church. *Baltimore Conference Minutes*, March 14, 1806 (Baltimore, Md.: Baltimore Historical Society, Lovely Lane Museum).

_____. *The Doctrines and Discipline of the Methodist Episcopal Church in America with Explanatory Notes* (Philadelphia, Penn.: Henry Tuckniss, 1798).

_____. *The Doctrines and Discipline of the Methodist Episcopal Church* (New York, N.Y.: T. Kirk, 1804).

_____. *Form of Discipline for the Ministers, Preachers, and Members of the Methodist Episcopal Church in America* (New York, N.Y.: William Ross, 1789).

_____. *Journals of the General Conference of the Methodist Episcopal Church*. Vol. 1, 1796–1836 (New York, N.Y.: Carlton & Phillips, 1855).

_____. *Minutes of the Methodist Conferences Annually Held in America; From 1773 to 1813, Inclusive* (New York, N.Y.: Daniel Hitt and Thomas Ware for the Methodist Connexion in the U.S., 1813).

_____. *Minutes of Several Conversations between the Rev. Thomas Coke LL.D., The Rev. Francis Asbury, and others at a Conference Begun at Baltimore, in the State of Maryland, on Monday the 27th of December, in the Year 1784.* (Philadelphia, Penn.: Charles Cist, 1785).

_____. *The Proceedings of the Bishop and Presiding Elders of the Methodist Episcopal Church in Council Assembled at Baltimore on the First Day of December, 1789* (Baltimore, Md.: William Goddard and James Angell).

M'Lean, John. *Sketch of Phillip Gatch* (Cincinnati, Ohio: Swormstedt and Poe, 1854).

Morrell, Thomas. *A Vindication of Truth Discovered Designed As an Answer to the Reverend William Hammet's Rejoindre* (Philadelphia, Penn.: Parry Hall, 1792).

Nelson, John. *Extract From the Journal of John Nelson Being an Account of God's Dealing with Him from His Youth to the Forty-Second Year of His Age* (New York, N.Y.: N. Bangs and J. Emory, 1824).

Newell, Fanny. *Memoirs of Fanny Newell* (Springfield, Mass.: Merriam, Little and Co., 1832).

Norwood, Frederick, ed. "Coke's Sermon at Asbury's Ordination," *Sourcebook of American Methodism* (Nashville, Tenn.: Abingdon, 1982), 90–96.

O'Kelly, James. *The Author's Apology for Protesting against the Methodist Episcopal Government* (Richmond, Va.: Central Publishing Company, 1829).

_____. *A Vindication of the Author's Apology with Reflections of the Reply and a few Remarks on Bishop Asbury's Annotations on his Book of Discipline* (Raleigh, N.C.: Joseph Gales, 1801).

Paddock, Z. *Memoir of Rev. Benjamin Paddock* (New York, N.Y.: Nelson and Phillips, 1875).

Peck, George. *The Life and Times of George Peck, D.D.* (New York, N.Y.: Nelson and Phillips, 1874).

Pilmoor, Joseph. *Journal of Joseph Pilmoor, Methodist Itinerant* (Philadelphia: Message Publishing Company, 1969).

Richey, Russell E., Kenneth E. Rowe, and Jean Miller Schmidt. Eds. "Bishop Coke Details His Episcopal Mission to North America, Describes Christmas Conference In Baltimore," *The Methodist Experience in America* (Nashville, Tenn.: Abingdon, 2000) 73–8.

Smith, Henry. *Recollections and Reflections of an Old Itinerant* (New York, N.Y.: Lane and Tippit, 1848).

Snethen, Nicholas. *Discourse on the Death of the Reverend Francis Asbury, Bishop of the Methodist Episcopal Church in the United States of America* (Baltimore, Md.: B. Edes, 1816).

_____. *Snethen on Lay Representation* (Baltimore, Md.: John J. Harrod, 1835).

Soule, Joshua. *A Sermon on the Death of the Rev. Francis Asbury* (New York: J. C. Tatten, 1816).

Telford, John. *Wesley's Veterans* (Salem, Ohio: Schmul Publishers, 1976).

Thrift, Minton. *Memoir of the Rev. Jesse Lee with Extracts from His Journals* (New York, N.Y.: N. Bangs & T. Mason, 1823).

Travis, Joseph. *Autobiography of the Rev. Joseph Travis A.M.* (Nashville, Tenn.: E. Stevenson and F.A. Owens Agents, 1856).

Treffry, Richard. *Memoirs of the Rev. Joseph Benson* (New York, N.Y.: G. Lane & P.P. Sanford, 1842).

Venn, Henry. *Letters of Henry Venn* (Carlisle, Tenn.: Banner of Truth Trust, 1993).

Wallis, Charles L. *Autobiography of Peter Cartwright* (Nashville, Tenn.: Abingdon, 1956).

Ware, Thomas. *Thomas Ware, A Spectator at the Christmas Conference: A Miscellany of Thomas Ware and the Methodist Christmas Conference*. Eds. William R. Phinney, Kenneth E. Rowe, Robert B. Steelman (Rutland, Vt: Academy Books, 1984).

Watters, William. *A Short Account of the Christian Experience and Ministerial Labours of William Watters Drawn up by Himself* (Alexandria, Va.: S. Snowden, 1806).

Wesley, John. *John Wesley's Sermons: An Anthology* Eds. Albert C. Outler and Richard P. Heitzenrater (Nashville, Tenn.: Abingdon, 1991).

_____. *The Journal of the Rev. John Wesley, A.M.* Ed. Nehemiah Curnock (London: Epworth Press, 1913).

_____. *The Letters of the Rev. John Wesley, A.M.* Ed. John Telford (London: Epworth Press, 1931).

_____. *A Plain Account of Christian Perfection* (Kansas City, Mo.: Beacon Hill Press, 1971).

_____. *Primitive Physic* (London: Epworth Press, 1960).

_____. *The Works of John Wesley.* Ed. Thomas Jackson (Kansas City, Mo.: Beacon Hill Press, 1978).

_____. *The Works of John Wesley.* Vol. 9 Ed. Rupert E. Davies (Nashville, Tenn.: Abingdon, 1989).

_____. *The Works of John Wesley, Journal and Diaries.* Vol. 19. Ed. Richard P. Heitzenrater (Nashville, Tenn.: Abingdon, 1990).

Wesleyan Methodist Church. *Minutes of the Methodist Conferences from the first held in London by the Late Rev. John Wesley, A.M. in the year 1744.* Vol. 1 (London: John Mason, 1862, courtesy of John Rylands Library, Manchester, England.)

Wilkins, Henry. *The Family Adviser or A Plain and Modern Practice of Physic for the Use of Families Who Have Not the Advantages of a Physician and Accommodated to the Diseases of America* (Philadelphia, Penn.: Henry Tuckniss, 1795).

Wright, John. *Sketches of the Life and Labors of James Quinn* (Cincinnati, Ohio: Methodist Book Concern, 1851).

Young, Rev. Jacob. *The Autobiography of a Pioneer: The Nativity, Experience, Travels, and Ministerial Labors of Rev. Jacob Young* (Cincinnati, Ohio: L. Swormstedt and A. Pace, 1857).

PUBLISHED SECONDARY WORKS

Ahlstrom, Sydney E. *A Religious History of the American People.* Vol. 1 (Garden City, N.Y.: Image Books, 1975).

Ambrose, Stephen, and Douglas Brinkley, eds. *Witness to America: An Illustrated Documentary History of the United States from the Revolution to Today* (New York, N.Y.: HarperCollins Publishers, 1999).

Andrews, Dee E. *The Methodists and Revolutionary America, 1760–1800. The Shaping of an Evangelical Culture* (Princeton, N. J.: Princeton University Press, 2000).

_____. "The People and the Preachers at St. George's: An Anatomy of a Methodist Schism," in *Rethinking Methodist History.* Eds. Russell E. Richey and Kenneth E. Rowe (Nashville, Tenn.: Kingswood Books, 1985), 125–33.

Armstrong, James. *History of the Old Baltimore Conference* (Baltimore, Md.: King Brothers, 1907).

Asbury, Herbert. *A Methodist Saint* (New York, N.Y.: Alfred A. Knopf, 1927).

Atkinson, John. *Centennial History of American Methodism, Inclusive of its Ecclesiastical Organization in 1784 and its Subsequent Development under the Superintendency of Francis Asbury* (New York: Phillips & Hunt; Cincinnati: Cranston & Stowe, 1884).

Baker, Frank. "Francis Asbury," in *Blackwell Dictionary of Evangelical Biography.* Vol. 1. Ed. Donald M. Lewis (Cambridge: Blackwell, 1995), 31–3.

_____. *From Wesley to Asbury* (Durham, N.C.: Duke University Press, 1976).

_____. *The Methodist Pilgrim in England* (London: Epworth Press, 1961).

Bangs, Nathan. *A History of the Methodist Episcopal Church.* Vols. 1–3 (New York, N.Y.: T. Mason and G. Lane, 1838).

Barclay, Wade Crawford. *History of Methodist Missions: Early American Methodism 1769–1844.* Vol. 1 (New York, N.Y.: The Board of Missions and Church Extension of the Methodist Church, 1949).

Bassett, Ancel. *A Concise History of the Methodist Protestant Church From Its Origin* (Pittsburgh, Penn.: Wm. McCracken, 1887).

Bennett, William Wallace. *Memorials of Methodism in Virginia* (Richmond, Va.: Published by the Author, 1871).

Bilhartz, Terry. *Urban Religion and the Second Great Awakening* (Rutherford, N.J.: Fairleigh Dickinson University Press, 1986).

Boorstin, Daniel J. *The Americans: The Colonial Experience* (New York, N.Y.: Vintage Books, 1958).

Brekus, Catherine A. "Female Evangelism in the Early Methodist Movement," in *Methodism and the Shaping of American Culture.* Eds. Nathan O. Hatch and John H. Wigger (Nashville: Abingdon, 2001), 135–73.

Briggs, F. W. *Bishop Asbury: A Biographical Study for Christian Workers* (London: Wesleyan Conference Office, 1879).

Brown, Kenneth O. *Holy Ground, Too: The Camp Meeting Family Tree* (Hazelton, Penn.: Holiness Archives, 1997).

Bucke, Emory Stevens, D.D., ed. *The History of American Methodism.* Vol. 1 (Nashville, Tenn.: Abingdon, 1964).

Buckley, James M. *Constitutional and Parliamentary History of the Methodist Episcopal Church* (New York, N.Y.: Eaton and Mains, 1912).

Burstein, Andrew. *Sentimental Democracy* (New York, N.Y.: Hill and Wang, 1999).

Butterfield, Herbert. "England in the Eighteenth Century," *A History of the Methodist Church in Great Britain.* Eds. Rupert Davies and Gordon Rupp (London: Epworth Press, 1965), 3–33.

Byrne, Donald E., Jr. *No Foot of Land* (Metuchen, N.J.: The Scarecrow Press, 1975).

Cannon, William. *The Theology of John Wesley* (Nashville, Tenn.: Abingdon, 1946).

A Century of Population Growth, 1790–1900 (Baltimore, Md.: Genealogical Publishing Company, 1989).

Clark, D. W. *Life and Times of Rev. Elijah Hedding, D.D.* (New York, N.Y.: Carlton & Phillips, 1855).

Clark, Elmer T. *An Album in Methodist History* (Nashville, Tenn.: Abingdon, 1952).

——. *Francis Asbury's Last Journey* (Greensboro, N.C.: Christian Advocate, 1955).

Cleveland, Catharine C. *The Great Revival in the West, 1797–1805* (Gloucester, Mass: Peter Smith, 1959).

Coleman, Robert. *Nothing to Do But Save Souls* (Grand Rapids, Mich.: Francis Asbury Press, 1990).

Coles, Robert. *Lives of Moral Leadership* (New York, N.Y.: Random House, 2000).

Conkin, Paul. *Cane Ridge: America's Pentecost* (Madison, Wis.: The University of Wisconsin Press, 1990).

Conrad, Henry. *Samuel White and His Father Judge Thomas White* (Wilmington, Del.: The Historical Society of Delaware, 1903).

Cook, Don. *The Long Fuse: How England Lost the American Colonies* (New York, N.Y.: Atlantic Monthly Press, 1985).

Cooke, Parsons. *Century of Puritanism* (Boston, Mass.: S.K. Whipple and Co., 1855).

Coolidge, Calvin. *Foundation of the Republic: Speeches and Addresses by Calvin Coolidge* (New York, N.Y.: Scribner, 1926).

Court, W.H.B. *The Rise of the Midland Industries, 1608–1838* (London: Oxford University Press, 1938).

Davis, David Brion. "The Emergence of Immediatism in British and American Antislavery Thought," *Religion in American History: Interpretive Essays.* Eds. John M. Mulder and John F. Wilson (Englewood Cliffs, N.J.: Prentice Hall, 1978), 236–53.

Drinkhouse, Edward. *History of Methodist Reform* (Baltimore, Md.: Board of Publications, Methodist Protestant Church, 1899).

Du Bose, Horace. *Francis Asbury* (Nashville, Tenn.: Methodist Episcopal Church South, 1916).

Duren, William Larkin. *Francis Asbury* (New York, N.Y.: The Macmillan Co., 1928).

_____. *The Top Sergeant of the Pioneers* (Atlanta, Ga.: Banner Press, 1930).

Edwards, Maldwyn. "John Wesley," in *A History of the Methodist Church in Great Britain.* Eds. Rupert Davies and Gordon Rupp (London: Epworth Press, 1965), 37–79.

Eller, Paul. "Francis Asbury and Phillip William Otterbein," *Forever Beginning, 1766–1966. Historical Papers presented at American Methodism's Bicentennial Celebration* (Lake Junaluska, N.C.: Association of Methodist Historical Societies, 1967), 3–13.

Elliot, Charles. *The Life of Robert Roberts* (Cincinnati, Ohio: J.F. Wright and L. Swormstedt, 1844).

Ellis, Joseph, J. *Founding Brothers* (New York, N.Y.: Alfred A. Knopf, 2000).

Ellul, Jacques. *The Technological Society* (New York, N.Y.: Vintage Books, 1967).

Emerson, Michael O., and Christian Smith. *Divided by Faith: Evangelical Religion and the Problem of Race in America* (New York, N.Y.: Oxford, 2000).

Emory, Robert. *History of the Discipline of the Methodist Episcopal Church* (New York, N.Y.: G. Lane & P. P. Sandford, 1844).

Erikson, Erik H. *Childhood and Society* (New York, N.Y.: W.W. Norton and Co., 1963).

_____.*Young Man Luther: A Study in Psychoanalysis and History* (New York, N.Y.: W.W. Norton and Co., 1962).

Faulkner, John Alfred. *Burning Questions in Historical Christianity* (New York, N.Y.: Abingdon, 1930).

Feeman, Harlan. *Francis Asbury's Silver Trumpet* (Nashville, Tenn.: Parthenon, 1950).

Finke, Roger, and Rodney Stark. *The Churching of America, 1776–1990. Winners and Losers in Our Religious Economy* (New Brunswick, N.J.: Rutgers University Press, 1994).

Foster, Charles. *An Errand of Mercy: The Evangelical United Front, 1790–1837* (Chapel Hill, N.C.: The University of North Carolina Press, 1960).

Fowler, C.H. "Francis Asbury," *Lives of Methodist Bishops*. Eds. Theodore L. Flood and John W. Hamilton (New York, N.Y.: Phillips & Hunt, 1882).

Fraser, Walter J., Jr. *Charleston! Charleston!* (Columbia, S.C.: University of South Carolina Press, 1989).

Fry, Benjamin St. James. *The Life of Richard Whatcoat* (New York, N.Y.: Lane & Scott, 1852).

Ferguson, Charles. *Organizing to Beat the Devil: Methodists and the Making of America* (Garden City, N.Y.: Doubleday and Co., 1971).

Gaustad, Edwin. *Historical Atlas of Religion in America* (New York, N.Y.: Harper & Row, 1976).

Goss, C.C. *Statistical History of the First Century of American Methodism* (New York, N.Y.: Carlton & Porter, 1866).

Graham, Stephen R. "Phillip William Otterbein," in *The Blackwell Dictionary of Evangelical Biography 1730–1860*. Ed. Donald Lewis. Vol. 2 (Oxford: Blackwell Publishers, 1995), 846.

Green, Evarts Boutell. "The Revolutionary Generation, 1763–90," in *A History of American Life*. Ed. Mark C. Carnes (New York, N.Y.: Scribner, 1996), 298–408.

Gross, John O. *Methodist Beginnings and Higher Education* (Nashville, Tenn.: Board of Education of the Methodist Church, 1959).

Guirey, William. *The History of Episcopacy in Four Parts from its Rise to the Present Day* (n.p., n.d.).

Gunter, W. Stephen. *The Limits of Love Divine* (Nashville, Tenn.: Abingdon, 1989).

Hackwood, F.W. *A History of West Bromwich* (Birmingham, England: Birmingham News, 1895).

Hanford, Mary Ella Cathey. "Asbury and Hanford Families–Discovered Genealogical Information," *The Historical Trail* (Commission on Archives and History, Southern New Jersey Conference, The United Methodist Church, 1996), 34–49.

Harrison, Lowell H., and James C. Klotter. *A New History of Kentucky* (Lexington, Ky.: The University Press of Kentucky, 1997).

Hatch, Nathan. *The Democratization of American Christianity* (New Haven, Conn.: Yale University Press, 1989).

Hempton, David. "Methodist Growth in Transatlantic Perspective, ca. 1770–1850," *Methodism and the Shaping of American Culture.* Eds. Nathan O. Hatch and John H. Wigger (Nashville, Tenn.: Abingdon, 2001) 41–85.

Henkle, M.M. *The Life of Henry Bascom* (Nashville, Tenn.: E. Stevenson and F.A. Owen, 1856).

Henretta, James A. "The Transition to Capitalism in America," *The Transformation of Early American History: Society, Authority, and Ideology.* Ed. James A. Henretta *et al.* (New York, N.Y.: Alfred A. Knopf, 1991), 218–38.

Heyrman, Christine. *Southern Cross: The Beginnings of the Bible Belt* (New York, N.Y.: Alfred A. Knopf, 1997).

Hofstadter, Richard. *Anti-Intellectualism in American Life* (New York, N.Y.: Vintage Books, 1962).

Holifield, E. Brooks. *Health and Medicine in the Methodist Tradition: Journey Towards Wholeness* (New York, N.Y.: Crossroad, 1986).

———. *A History of Pastoral Care in America: From Salvation to Self-Realization* (Nashville, Tenn.: Abingdon, 1983).

Hooker, Richard J. *The Carolina Backcountry on the Eve of the Revolution* (Chapel Hill, N.C.: The University of North Carolina Press, 1953).

Hopkins, E. *Birmingham: The First Manufacturing Town in the World, 1760–1840* (London: Weidenfeld & W. Colson, 1989).

Hough, Samuel F. *Christian NewComer, His Life, Journal and Achievements* (Dayton, Ohio: Church of the United Brethren in Christ, 1941).

Hughes, Edwin Holt. "An Interview with Francis Asbury," in *Methodism*, ed. William Anderson (Nashville, N.Y.: The Methodist Publishing House, 1957), 85–99.

Hurst, John Fletcher. *The History of Methodism.* Vol. 2 (New York, N.Y.: Eaton and Mains, 1902).

Isaac, Rhys. *The Transformation of Virginia: 1740–1790* (New York, N.Y.: W. W. Norton and Co., 1982).

Johnson, Paul. *A History of the American People* (New York, N.Y.: Harper Perennial, 1999).

Jones, John G. *Methodism in Mississippi* (Nashville, Tenn.: Methodist Episcopal Church South, 1887).

Kilgore, Charles Franklin. *The James O'Kelly Schism in the Methodist Episcopal Church* (Mexico: Casa Unida de Publicaciones, 1963).

Klepp, Susan E. "Zachariah Poulson's Bills of Mortality, 1788–1801," in *Life in Early Philadelphia*, ed. Billy Smith (University Park, Penn.: The Pennsylvania State University Press, 1995), 219–42.

Kloos, John M. *A Sense of Deity: The Republican Spirituality of Dr. Benjamin Rush* (Brooklyn, N.Y.: Carlson Publishing, 1991).

Krout, John Allen, and Dixon Ryan Fox. "The Completion of Independence," in *A History of American Life*, ed. Mark C. Carnes (New York, N.Y.: Scribner, 1996), 409–576.

Lang, Edward M., Jr., *Francis Asbury's Reading of Theology: A Bibliographic Study* (Evanston, Ill.: Garrett Theological Seminary Library, 1972).

Langford, Thomas A. *Practical Divinity* (Nashville, Tenn.: Abingdon, 1983).

Langguth, A. J. *Patriots: The Men Who Started the American Revolution* (New York, N.Y.: Simon & Schuster, 1988).

Lawson, John. "The People Called Methodists: Our Discipline," in *A History of the Methodist Church in Great Britain*, eds. Rupert Davies and Gordon Rupp. Vol. 1 (London: Epworth Press, 1965), 183–209.

Lednum, John. *History of the Rise of Methodism in America* (Philadelphia, Penn.: Published by the Author, 1859).

Lewis, James. *Francis Asbury: Bishop of the Methodist Episcopal Church* (London: Epworth Press, 1927).

Lyerly, Cynthia Lynn. *Methodism and the Southern Mind, 1770–1810* (New York, N.Y.: Oxford University Press, 1980).

Malley, Charles Payson. *Ancient Families of Bohemia Manor: Their Homes and Their Burying Grounds* (Wilmington, Del.: The Historical Society of Delaware, 1888).

Manuel, Fritz, and Frank Manuel. *Utopian Thought in the Western World* (Cambridge, Mass.: The Bellnap Press of Harvard University, 1979).

Marshall, Dorothy. *Eighteenth Century England* (London: Longman, 1962).

Maser, Frederick E. *Robert Strawbridge: First American Methodist Circuit Rider* (Rutland, Vt.: Academy Books, 1983).

Mathews, Donald. "Evangelical America—The Methodist Ideology," *Rethinking Methodist History*, eds. Russell E. Richey and Kenneth E. Rowe (Nashville, Tenn.: Kingswood Books, 1985), 91–9.

_____. "The Second Great Awakening as an Organizing Process, 1780–1830," in *Religion in American History: Interpretive Essays*, eds. John Mulder and John Wilson (Englewood Cliffs, N.J.: Prentice Hall, 1978), 199–235.

_____. *Slavery and Methodism: A Chapter in American Morality, 1780–1845* (Princeton, N.J.: Princeton University Press, 1965).

M'Caine, Alexander. *The History and Mystery of Methodist Episcopacy* (Baltimore, Md.: Richard J. Matchett, 1827).

McCullough, David. *John Adams* (New York, N.Y.: Simon & Schuster, 2001).

Mead, Sidney E. *The Lively Experiment* (New York, N.Y.: Harper & Row, n.d.).

Memorial of Jesse Lee and the Old Elm (Boston, Mass.: James P. MaGee, 1875).

Merrens, H. Ray, ed. *The Colonial Carolina Scene: Contemporary Views 1697–1774* (Columbia, S.C.: University of South Carolina Press, 1977).

M'Ferrin, John B. *History of Methodism in Tennessee*. Vol. 2 (Nashville, Tenn.: Southern Methodist Publishing House, 1875).

Miller, Perry. *The Life of the Mind in America* (New York, N.Y.: Harcourt,1965).

Moede, Gerald F. *The Office of Bishop in Methodism* (Zurich, Switzerland: Methodist Publishing House, 1964).

Moorhead, James. *American Apocalypse: Yankee Protestants and the Civil War: 1860–1869* (New Haven, Conn.: Yale University Press, 1978).

Moore, H. M. *Pioneers of Methodism in North Carolina and Virginia* (Nashville, Tenn.: Southern Methodist Publishing House, 1884).

Moore, Robert L. *John Wesley and Authority: A Psychological Perspective* (Missoula, Mont.: Scholars Press, 1979).

Morrill, Milo True. *A History of the Christian Denomination in America* (Dayton, Ohio: The Christian Publishing Association, 1912).

Mudge, James. *History of the New England Conference of the Methodist Episcopal Church 1796–1910* (Boston, Mass.: New England Conference, 1910)

Nash, Gary. "To Arise Out of the Dust: Absolom Jones and the African Church 1785–95," *Race, Class, and Politics: Essays on American Colonial and Revolutionary Society* (Urbana, Ill.: University of Illinois Press, 1986).

Newby, Henry. *Bishop Francis Asbury, The Father of West Bromwich Methodism* (West Bromwich, England: West Bromwich Methodists, 1916).

Newell, Fanny. *Memoirs of Fanny Newell* (Springfield, Mass.: Merriam, Little and Co., 1832).

Niebuhr, H. Richard. *The Social Sources of Denominationalism* (New York, N.Y.: Henry Holt and Co., 1954).

Norwood, Frederick Abbott. *The Story of American Methodism* (New York, N.Y.: Abingdon, 1974).

Olson, Sherry H. *The Building of an American City* (Baltimore, Md.: The Johns Hopkins University Press, 1980).

Outler, Albert C. *The Wesley Theological Heritage*, eds. Thomas C. Oden and Leicester R. Longden (Grand Rapids, Mich.: Zondervan Publishing House, 1991)

Paine, Robert. *Life and Times of William McKendree: Bishop of the Methodist Episcopal Church* (Nashville, Tenn.: Methodist Episcopal Church South, 1922).

Pattison, Robert E. "The Life and Character of Richard Bassett," *Historical and Biographical Papers*. Vol. 3 (Wilmington, Del.: Historical Society, 1900), 1–19.

Peck, George. *Early Methodism within the Bounds of the Old Genessee Conference from 1788–1828* (New York, N.Y.: Carlton & Porter, 1860).

Pell, Edward Leigh. *A Hundred Years of Richmond Methodism* (Richmond, Va.: The Idea Publishing Co., 1899).

Peters, John. *Christian Perfection and American Methodism* (New York, N.Y.: Abingdon, 1956).

Pheobus, George A. *Beams of Light on Early Methodism in America* (New York, N.Y.: Phillips & Hunt, 1887).

Pilkington, James Penn. *The Methodist Publishing House.* Vol. 1 (Nashville, Tenn.: Abingdon, 1968).

Pipekorn, Arthur. *Profiles in Belief: The Religious Bodies of the United States and Canada.* Vol. 2 (San Francisco, Calif.: Harper & Row, 1978)

Posey, Walter Brownlow. *Frontier Mission* (Lexington, Ky.: University of Kentucky Press, 1966).

Pratt, Alfred Camden. *Black Country Methodism* (London: Charles H. Kelley, 1891).

Prince, Henry. *The Romance of Early Methodism in and Around West Bromwich and Wednesbury* (West Bromwich, England: n.p., n.d.).

Randall, William Sterne. *Thomas Jefferson: A Life* (New York, N.Y.: Harper Perennial, 1994).

Richey, Russell E. *Early American Methodism* (Indianapolis, Ind.: Indiana University Press, 1991).

_____. "Early American Methodist Views of the Nation: A Glass to the Heart," in *Reflections Upon Methodism during the American Bicentennial* (Dallas, Tex.: Bridwell Library Center for Methodist Studies, 1985), 91–104.

_____. "The Formation of American Methodism: The Chesapeake Refraction of Wesleyanism," in *Methodism and the Shaping of American Culture*, eds. Nathan O. Hatch and John H. Wigger (Nashville, Tenn.: Abingdon, 2001), 197–221.

_____. *The Methodist Conference in America: A History* (Nashville, Tenn.: Kingswood Books, 1996).

Rogal, Samuel. "James Dempster," *A Biographical Dictionary of Eighteenth-Century Methodism.* Vol. 1 (Queenston, Ont.: Edwin Mellen Press, 1999), 434.

_____. "Martin Rodda," *A Biographical Dictionary of Eighteenth-Century Methodism.* Vol. 6 (Queenston, Ontario: Edwin Mellen Press, 1999), 156.

_____. "Robert Williams," *A Biographical Dictionary of Eighteenth-Century Methodism.* Vol. 9 (Queenston, Ont.: Edwin Mellen Press, 1999), 411–3.

Rohrbough, Malcolm J. *The Trans-Appalachian Frontier: People, Societies and Institutions, 1775–1850* (New York, N.Y.: Oxford University Press, 1978).

Rosenfeld, Richard N. *American Aurora* (New York, N.Y.: St. Martin's Griffin, 1997).

Rowlands, Marie B. *Masters and Men in the West Midland Metalware Trades before the Industrialized Revolution* (Manchester: Manchester University Press, 1975).

Rowthorn, Anne W. *Samuel Seabury: A Bicentennial Biography* (New York, N.Y.: The Seabury Press, 1983).

Ruth, Lester. *A Little Heaven Below: Worship at Early Methodist Quarterly Meetings* (Nashville, Tenn.: Abingdon, 2000).

Sangrey, Abram W. *The Temple of Limestone* (Lancaster, Penn.: Boehms Chapel Society, 1991).

Scharf, Col. J. Thomas. *The Chronicles of Baltimore; Being a Complete History of "Baltimore Town" and Baltimore County from the Earliest Period to the Present Time* (Baltimore, Md.: Turnbill Brothers, 1874).

Schell, Edwin. "Beginnings in Maryland and America," *Those Incredible Methodists*. Ed. Gordon Baker (Baltimore, Md.: The Baltimore Conference, 1972), 1–31.

Scherer, Lester. *Ezekiel Cooper, 1763–1847: An Early American Methodist Leader* (Commission on Archives and History of the United Methodist Church, 1965).

Schlesinger, Arthur M., Jr., ed. *The Almanac of American History* (New York, N.Y.: Barnes and Noble Books, 1993).

Shipp, Albert M. *The History of Methodism in South Carolina* (Nashville, Tenn.: Southern Methodist Publishing House, 1884).

A Short Historical Account of the Early Society of Methodism Established in the City of New York in the Year 1763 (New York, N.Y.: W. and P. C. Smith, 1824).

Simpson, Matthew. *Cyclopaedia of Methodism* (Philadelphia, Penn.: Everts and Stewart, 1878).

Simpson, Robert Drew, ed. *American Methodist Pioneer: The Life and Journals of the Rev. Freeborn Garrettson, 1752–1827* (Rutland, Vt.: Academy Books, 1984).

Smith, Billy G. *Life in Early Philadelphia* (University Park, Penn.: The Pennsylvania State University Press, 1995).

Smith, George G. *The Life and Letters of James Osgood Andrew* (Nashville, Tenn.: Southern Methodist Publishing House, 1882).

Smith, Page. *The Shaping of America: A People's History of the Young Republic*. Vol. 3 (New York, N.Y.: McGraw Hill, 1989).

Smith, Richard Norton. *Patriarch: George Washington and the New American Nation* (Boston, Mass.: Houghton Mifflin Co., 1993).

Soderland, Jean R. *Quakers and Slavery: A Divided Spirit* (Princeton, N.J.: Princeton University Press, 1985).

Sprague, William. "Francis Asbury," *Annals of the American Pulpit*. Vol. 7 (New York: Robert Carter and Bros., 1865), 13–28.

Stevens, Abel. *The Centenary of American Methodism* (New York, N.Y.: Carlton & Porter, 1866).

_____. *A Compendious History of American Methodism* (New York, N.Y.: Eaton and Mains, 1868).

_____. *The History of the Religious Movement of the Eighteenth Century Called Methodism*. Vol. 4 (New York, N.Y.: Carlton & Porter, 1858).

_____. *Life and Times of Nathan Bangs* (New York, N.Y.: Carlton & Porter, 1863).

_____. *Memorials of the Early Progress of Methodism* (Boston, Mass.: G. H. Pierce and Co., 1852).

_____. *Sketches from the Study of a Superannuated Itinerant* (Boston, Mass.: Charles H. Pierce, 1851).

_____. *The Women of Methodism* (New York, N.Y.: Carlton & Porter, 1866).

Stevenson, George C. *City Road Chapel London and Its Associations* (New York, N.Y.: Methodist Book Concern, 1872).

Strickland, W.P. *Life of Jacob Gruber* (New York, N.Y.: Carlton & Porter, 1860).

_____. *The Pioneer Bishop* (New York, N.Y.: Phillips & Hunt, 1858).

Stout, Harry S. *The Divine Dramatist* (Grand Rapids, Mich.: Eerdmans, 1991).

Stuart, Clara. *Latimer: Apostle to the English.* (Grand Rapids, Mich.: Zondervan Publishing House, 1986).

Sweet, William Warren. *Religion on the American Frontier* (New York, N.Y.: Cooper Square Publishers, 1964).

_____. *Virginia Methodism, A History* (Richmond, Va.: Whittet & Shepperson, 1955).

Taylor, Alan. "The Unhappy Stephen Arnold: An Episode of Murder and Penitence in the Early Republic," in *Through a Glass Darkly*, eds. Ronald Hoffman, Mechal Sobel, and Frederika J. Teute (Chapel Hill, N.C.: University of North Carolina Press, 1997), 97–121.

Tees, Francis H. *The Story of Old St. George's* (Philadelphia, Penn.: The Message Publishing Co., 1941).

Tigert, John J. *A Constitutional History of American Episcopal Methodism* (Nashville, Tenn.: Publishing House of the Methodist Episcopal Church South, 1916).

Tiller, John. "Jeremy Borroughes," in *The New International Dictionary of the Christian Church*, ed. J. D. Douglass (Grand Rapids, Mich.: Zondervan Publishing House, 1978), 169.

Tipple, Ezra Squire. *The Prophet of the Long Road* (New York, N.Y.: The Methodist Book Concern, 1916).

Tyson, John R. *Charles Wesley on Sanctification* (Grand Rapids, Mich.: Zondervan Publishing House, 1986).

Tyerman, Luke. *The Life and Times of the Rev. John Wesley, M.A.* (London, Hodder and Stoughton, 1871).

Vickers, John. *Thomas Coke: Apostle of Methodism* (New York, N.Y.: Abingdon, 1969).

Wakely, J. B. *The Heroes of Methodism* (New York: Carlton & Phillips, 1856).

_____. *Lost Chapters Recovered from the Early History of American Methodism* (New York, N.Y.: Wilbur E. Ketchum, 1889).

Walsh, John. "Methodism at the End of the Eighteenth Century," in *A History of the Methodist Church in Great Britain*, eds. Rupert Davies and Gordon Rupp. Vol. 1 (London: Epworth Press, 1965), 277–315.

Ward, W.R. "The Legacy of John Wesley: The Pastoral Office in Britain and America," *Statesmen, Scholars and Merchants*, eds. Anne Whiteman *et al.* (Oxford: Oxford University Press, 1973).

Wardle, Addie Grace. *History of the Sunday School Movement in the Methodist Episcopal Church* (New York, N.Y.: Methodist Book Concern, 1918).

Watters, D.A. *The First American Itinerant of Methodism: William Watters* (Cincinnati, Ohio: Curtis and Jennings, 1898).

Weisberger, Bernard. *America Afire: Jefferson, Adams, and the Revolutionary Election of 1800* (New York, N.Y.: HarperCollins Publishers, Inc., 2000).

Wesley, Charles. *Richard Allen: Apostle of Freedom* (Washington, D.C.: The Associated Publishers, Inc., 1935).

Wigger, John. *Taking Heaven by Storm: Methodism and the Rise of Popular Christianity in America* (New York, N.Y.: Oxford University Press, 1998).

Wilder, Franklin. *The Methodist Riots: The Testing of Charles Wesley* (Great Neck, N.Y.: Todd and Honeywell, 1981).

Williams, William. *The Garden of American Methodism* (Wilmington, Del.: Scholarly Resources, 1984).

Wood, Arthur Skevington. *Thomas Haweis* (London: S.P.C.K., 1957).

Wood, Gordon S. *The Radicalism of the American Revolution* (New York, N.Y.: Alfred A. Knopf, 1991).

Wrightman, William M. "Francis Asbury, Bishop of the Methodist Episcopal Church," *Biographical Sketches of Eminent Itinerant Methodists*, ed. Thomas O. Summers (Nashville, Tenn.: E. Stevenson and F.A. Owens, 1858) 11–42.

_____. *Life of William Capers, D.D.* (Nashville, Tenn.: Southern Methodism Publishing, 1859).

Yeakel, R. *Jacob Albright and his Co-Laborers* (Cleveland, Ohio: Publishing House of the Evangelical Association, 1883).

PERIODICALS AND JOURNALS

"Account of the Yellow Fever," *The Methodist Magazine* 2 (Philadelphia, Penn.: Henry Tuckniss, 1798), 514–9.

Aikens, Alden. "Wesleyan Theology and the Use of Models," in *Wesleyan Theological Society Journal*, 14 (Fall 1979), 2:64–76.

Andrew, James. "Sketches of Itinerant Preachers," *Southern Christian Advocate* (July 29, 1858).

Baker, Frank. "Early American Methodism, A Key Document," in *Methodist History* 3 (January 1965), 2:3–15.

Beegle, Dewey. "Cokesbury College Excavation," *Methodist History*, Vol. 7 (July 1969), 4:9–14.

Benan, Edith Rassiter. "Perry Hall: County Seat of the Gough and Carroll Families," in *Maryland Historical Magazine* 45 (March 1950), 33–46.

Blankenship, Paul F. "Bishop Asbury and the Germans," *Methodist History* 4 (April 1966), 3:5–13.

Brigden, Thomas E. "Early African Preachers of the Methodist Episcopal Church," in *Wesley Historical Society* 9 (March 1913), 15–17.

Bull, Robert J. "George Roberts' Reminiscences of Francis Asbury," in *Methodist History* 5 (July 1967), 4:25–35.

_____. "John Wesley Bond's Reminiscences of Francis Asbury," in *Methodist History* 4 (October 1965), 3–32.

_____. "Lewis Myers' Reminiscences of Francis Asbury," *Methodist History* 7 (October 1968), 1:5–10.

Calkin, Homer. "Henry Foxall: Foundryman and Friend of Asbury," in *Methodist History* 7 (October 1967), 1:36–49.

Carwardine, Richard. "The Second Great Awakening: An Examination of Methodism and the 'New Measures,'" in *Journal of American History* 59 (1972), 327–40.

Coppedge, Allan. "Entire Sanctification in Early American Methodism," *Wesley Theological Society Journal* 13 (Spring 1978), 24–50.

Crookshank, Charles. "William Hammet," *Wesley Historical Society* 8 (March 1911), 1:75–6.

Day, J. M. "The Francis Asbury Cottage," in *Wesley Historical Society* 32 (December 1959), 4:83–5.

Entwisle, Joseph. "Memoir of Henry Foxall," *The Wesleyan Methodist Magazine* (August 1824), 505–8.

Fletcher, G. Arthur. "Bishop Francis Asbury and Belper Chapel Vestry Collection," *Wesley Historical Society* 16 (September–December 1927), 76–7.

"Francis Asbury," *American and Commercial Daily Advertiser* (Baltimore, Md.: May 10, 1816).

Goodwin, Charles. "Vile or Reviled? The Causes of the Anti-Methodist Riots at Wednesbury Between May, 1743, and April, 1744, in the Light of New England Revivalism," *Methodist History* 35 (October 1996), 1:14–27.

Green, Charles. "Bishop Francis Asbury and Rev. Daniel Asbury: Were They 'Our Cousins?'" *The Historical Trail* (Commission on Archives and History of the Southern New Jersey Conference, The United Methodist Church, 1996), 132–41.

Green, R. "The First Preaching Houses in Birmingham," *Wesley Historical Society* 3 (1902), 96–8.

Grissom, W. L. "Some First Things in North Carolina Methodism," *Historical Papers of The Trinity College Society*, series 9 (New York; AMS Press, 1912).

Holland, Bernard G. "A Species of Madness: The Effect of John Wesley's Early Preaching," in *Wesley Historical Society* 39 (1973), 3:77–85.

"In The Smokies: Along the Asbury Trail," *Together* (August 1958), 35–42.

MacMaster, Richard K. "Thomas Rankin and the American Colonists," *Wesley Historical Society* 39 (June 1973), 25–33.

Maryland Journal and Baltimore Advertiser. "To the Editors of the Maryland Journal and Baltimore Advertiser," 12 (February 15, 1785), 698:1.

May, James W. "Francis Asbury and Thomas White: A Refugee Preacher and His Tory Patron," in *Methodist History* 14 (April 1976), 3:141–64.

McCulloh, Gerald. "Cokesbury College, An Eighteenth-Century Experimental Model," *Methodist History* 7 (July 1969), 4:3–8.

Meacham, James. "The Journal and Travels of James Meacham," *Historical Papers* 191 (Durham, N.C.: 1912), 66–95, 87–102.

Mills, Frederick. "Survey of Published Works on Francis Asbury: A Historiographical Essay," *The Historical Trail* (Yearbook of Conference Historical Society of the Southern New Jersey Conference, The United Methodist Church, 1996), 13–25.

Monk, Robert C. "Educating Oneself for Ministry: Francis Asbury's Reading Patterns," *Methodist History* 29 (April 1991), 3:140–54.

"More Asbury Letters," *World Parish* 8 (Lake Junaluska, N.C.: World Methodist Council, April 1960), 1:16–18.

Morrell, Thomas. "The Morrell Letters," *Christian Advocate and Journal* 26 (January 23, 1851), 4:1 and 26 (February 20, 1851), 8:1.

Moss, Arthur Bruce. "Statements on Historical Priority in Asbury's Writings," *World Parish* 9 (February 1961), 25–33.

Norwood, Frederick. "Some Newly Discovered Unpublished Letters, 1808–1825," *Methodist History* 3 (July 1965), 4:3–24.

"Obituary," *The Methodist Magazine* 39 (London: Thomas Cordeux, 1816), 478–80.

Peluso, Gary. "Francis Asbury on American Public Life," *Methodist History* 30 (July 1992), 4:206–16.

Purifoy, Lewis M. "The Methodist Antislavery Tradition 1784–1844," in *Methodist History* 4 (July 1966), 4:3–16.

Schell, Edwin. "1792 Journal of Francis Asbury," *Methodist History* 9 (January 1971), 2:54–7.

_____. "Extracts from 1792 and 1802 Journals," *Methodist History* 9 (January 1971), 2:34–43.

_____. "Methodist Traveling Preachers in America 1773–1799," *Methodist History* 38 (July 2000), 4:307–8.

_____. "Support of the Bishops in Early American Methodism," in *Methodist History* 4 (Apr. 1966), 4:42–50.

Scherer, Lester. "Ezekiel Cooper and the Asbury-Lee Dispute of 1793–94," in *Methodist History* 6 (July 1968), 4:44–6.

Sheldon, W.C. "The Birmingham Magistrate Who Suppressed the Rioters," *Wesley Historical Society* 4 (1904), 61–4.

_____. "The Landmarks of Bishop Asbury's Childhood and Youth," *Wesley Historical Society* 12 (1920), 97–103.

_____. "Travelling in Wesley's Time," *Wesley Historical Society* 7 (1910), 2–8.

Simon, John S. "Elections to the Legal Hundred," *Wesley Historical Society* 13 (1922), 14–21.

Simpson, Robert. "Lost Letters of Bishop Asbury," *Methodist History* 32 (January 1994), 2:99–105.

Smith, Warren Thomas. "The Christmas Conference," *Methodist History* 6 (July 1968), 4:3–27.

_____. "Harry Hosier: Black Preacher Extraordinary," *Journal of the Interdenominational Theological Center* 7 (Spring 1980), 2:111–28.

Steelman, Robert Benis. "Learner Blackman (1781–1815)," *Methodist History* 5 (April 1967), 3:3–17.

Stockham, Richard J. "The Misunderstood Lorenzo Dow," *The Alabama Review* (January 1963): 20–34.

Swift, Wesley F. "Five Wesley Letters," *Wesley Historical Society* 33 (March 1961), 11–16.

"To the Editors of the Maryland Journal and Baltimore Advertiser," *Maryland Journal and Baltimore Advertiser* 12 (Feb. 15, 1785), 698:1.

"Unpublished Letters of Francis Asbury," *Methodist History* 1 (1962–1963), 39–63.

Vickers, John. "Francis Asbury in the Wiltshire Circuit," in *Methodist History* 16 (April 1978), 3:185–189.

UNPUBLISHED PRIMARY WORKS

Colbert, William. "Journal" (Evanston, Ill.: The United Library, Garrett Evangelical Theological Seminary).

Duke, William. "The Journal of William Duke, 1774–1776. A Preliminary Study Edition Abstracted by Edwin Schell from the Original in Diocesan Library, Peabody Institute, Baltimore, Maryland." (Baltimore, Md.: Baltimore Conference Methodist Historical Society, 1958).

Haskins, Thomas. "Journal of Thomas Haskins," vols. 4–6 (Chicago, Ill.: Regenstein Library, University of Chicago).

Letter of Francis Asbury to Freeborn Garrettson, Sept. 2, 1785 (courtesy of Robert Simpson).

Letter of Francis Asbury to Freeborn Garrettson, Nov. 6, 1791 (courtesy of Robert Simpson).

Letter of Francis Asbury to Freeborn Garrettson, Jan. 24, 1811 (courtesy of Robert Simpson).

Letter of James Coleman to Francis Asbury, May 11, 1810 (United Methodist Archives, Drew University).

Letter of John Dickens to Francis Asbury, Jan. 16, 1797 (United Methodist Archives, Drew University).

Letter of Mary Pocahontas Gabele to Mary Hubard, Mar. 21, 1815. Hubard papers, #360, Fol. 36 (Southern Methodist Collection. The Library of the University of North Carolina at Chapel Hill).

Letter of G. Gillespie to Francis Asbury, Mar. 1805 (United Methodist Archives, Drew University).

Letter of William Monroe to John McClintock, Nov. 26, 1848 (United Methodist Archives, Drew University).

Rankin, Thomas. "Journal" (United Methodist Archives, Drew University).

Reed, Nelson. "Diary" (Regenstein Library, University of Chicago, Chicago, Ill.).

UNPUBLISHED SECONDARY WORKS

Brannan, Emora Thomas. "The Presiding Elder Question: Its Critical Nature in American Methodism, 1820–1824, and Its Impact upon Ecclesiastical Institutions" (Unpublished Ph.D. Dissertation, Duke University, 1974).

Clark, Allen B. "The Judge Thomas White Site" (1990, On file–Barrett's Chapel, Frederica, Del.).

Coleman, Robert. *Factors in the Expansion of the Methodist Episcopal Church from 1784–1812* (Unpublished Ph.D. Dissertation, University of Iowa, 1954).

Cowan, Raymond. "The Arminian Alternative: The Rise of the Methodist Episcopal Church, 1765–1850" (Unpublished Ph.D. Dissertation, Georgia State University, 1991).

Evans, Paul Otis. "The Ideology of Inequality: Asbury, Methodism and Slavery" (Unpublished Ph.D. Dissertation, Rutgers University, 1981).

Lang, Edward. "The Theology of Francis Asbury" (Unpublished Ph.D. Dissertation, Northwestern University, 1972).

Lloyd, Mark. "A Rhetorical Analysis of the Preaching of Bishop Asbury" (Unpublished Ph.D. Dissertation, Michigan State University, 1967).

Spellman, Norman. "The General Superintendency in American Methodism 1784–1890" (Unpublished Ph.D. Dissertation, Yale University, 1961).

Thornton, Robert Fulton. "The Home Life of Asbury" (Unpublished Bachelor of Divinity Thesis, Southern Methodist University, 1935).

Wigger, John, H. "Taking Heaven by Storm: Methodism and the Popularization of American Christianity 1770–1820" (Unpublished Ph.D. Dissertation, Notre Dame University, 1994).

Notes

Chapter 1: "Behold Me Now a Local Preacher"

1. See Dorothy Marshall, *Eighteenth Century England* (London: Longman, 1962).

2. W.H.B. Court, *The Rise of the Midland Industries 1608–1838* (London: Oxford University Press, 1938), 22.

3. Ibid., 172.

4. Alfred Camden Pratt, *Black Country Methodism* (London: Charles H. Kelley, 1891), 3.

5. John Wesley, *The Works of John Wesley, Journal and Diaries,* ed. Richard P. Heitzenrater, (Nashville: Abingdon, 1990), 19:345.

6. Pratt, *Country,* 3.

7. John Walsh, "Methodism at the End of the Eighteenth Century," in *A History of the Methodist Church in Great Britain,* eds. Rupert Davies and Gordon Rupp, (London: Epworth Press, 1965), 1:278. The first regular preaching place for Methodist itinerants was located in a theatre which had been built on Moor Street around 1740. The Methodists took possession of this theatre in the early 1750s. Indeed it seemed that the Methodists would take over everything. When a painting gallery was built, a Miss Hulton wrote as late as 1848 that it would "serve for a Methodist meeting house. That society is flourishing enough to take possession of all public edifices whatever." See R. Green, "The First Preaching Houses in Birmingham," in *Wesley Historical Society* (1902), 3:96–98.

8. Frank Baker, *The Methodist Pilgrim in England* (London: Epworth Press, 1961), 73.

9. Franklin Wilder, *The Methodist Riots: The Testing of Charles Wesley* (Great Neck, N.Y.: Todd and Honeywell, 1981), 44.

10. John Wesley, *The Works of John Wesley,* vol. 9, ed. Rupert E. Davies (Nashville: Abingdon, 1989), 151.

11. John Wesley, *The Journal of the Rev. John Wesley, A.M,* ed. Nehemiah Curnock, (London: The Epworth Press, 1913), 4:442.

12. Herbert Butterfield, "England in the Eighteenth Century," in *A History of the Methodist Church in Great Britain,* eds. Rupert Davies and Gordon Rupp (London: Epworth Press, 1965), 29–30.

13. Charles Goodwin, "Vile or Reviled? The Causes of the Anti-Methodist Riots at Wednesbury between May 1743 and April 1744, "In the Light of New England Revivalism," in *Methodist History* 35 (October 1996), 1:20. Wesley condemned the unnecessary provocation of the inhabitants of Wednesbury by Methodist preachers, writing in 1758, "Contempt, sharpness, bitterness, can do no good. 'The wrath of man worketh not the righteousness of God.' Harsh methods have been tried again and again (by two of three unsettled railers) at Wednesbury, St. Ives, Cork, Canterbury. And how did they succeed? They always occasioned numberless evils; often wholly stopped the course of the Gospel." *The Works of Wesley,* ed. Thomas Jackson, 14 vols. (London: The Wesleyan Methodist Book Room, 1831), 13:229; hereinafter cited as *Works*.

14. Ibid., 22.

15. Ibid., 26.

16. John Nelson, *Extract From the Journal of John Nelson Being an Account of God's Dealing with Him from His Youth to the Forty-Second Year of His Age* (New York, N.Y.: N. Bangs and J. Emory, 1824), 107.

17. Ibid., 225.

18. Ibid., 109.

19. Ibid., 146.

20. Ibid., 149.

21. Ibid., 138.

22. Ibid., 138.

23. F.W. Hackwood, *A History of West Bromwich* (Birmingham: Birmingham News, 1895), 90.

24. Herbert Asbury claimed that he was a direct descendant of Joseph Asbury, because Joseph was father to a son by a previous marriage. Charles Green researches this claim in his article "Bishop Francis Asbury and Rev. Daniel Asbury: Were They 'Our Cousins?'" Green makes at least two conclusions: Herbert Asbury's claim that Daniel Asbury's father was a half-brother to Francis Asbury has no foundation in fact, and secondly, there is not sufficient genealogical evidence to state whether Francis Asbury was related to any of the Asburys who migrated to America. The best historical evidence that Francis Asbury may have had some blood relatives in America comes from a Henry Asbury (1810–1896) of Quincy, Illinois. "The original stock of the Asburys in this country were Church of England people—my father having been baptized in that church before the revolution. On moving to Kentucky, he became a Methodist. He informed me that the so called Methodist Bishop Francis Asbury had visited him, and they traced back their kinship to about second or third cousin through their English ancestry. Francis Asbury did not come to America till some time after my great-grandfather—he, you know, left no descendants [*sic*]. I am myself a churchman and never was anything else in religion." Charles Green, "Bishop Francis Asbury and Rev. Daniel Asbury: Were They 'Our Cousins?'" in *The Historical Trail* (Commission on Archives and History: Southern New Jersey Conference, The United Methodist Church, 1996),132–141. Also see Herbert Asbury, *A Methodist Saint* (New York, N.Y.: Alfred A. Knopf, 1927). Daniel Asbury was a long-time Methodist preacher friend of Francis Asbury. He lived in Lincoln County, North Carolina, and presided over the South Carolina Catawba District. There is no proof for or against Francis Asbury and Daniel Asbury's being related. Daniel Asbury's ancestry has been traced to a Francis Asbury who arrived from England in 1665. See Mary Ella Cathey Hanford, "Asbury and Hanford Families—Discovered Genealogical Information," in *The Historical Trail* (Conference Historical Society, Southern New Jersey Conference, The United Methodist Church, 1996), 34–45.

25. According to W. C. Sheldon, this "Wirtly" Birch is the John Wryley Birch who served as the magistrate of Birmingham. "It is easy to point out some places, only one-third the magnitude of Birmingham, whose frequent breaches of the law, and quarrels among themselves, find employment for half-a-dozen as magistrates and four times that number of constables: whilst the business of this was for many years conducted by a single Justice." See W. C. Sheldon, "The Birmingham Magistrate Who Suppressed the Rioters," in *Wesley Historical Society* 4 (1904), 63.

26. Butterfield, *England in the Eighteenth Century*, 19.

27. In 1809 the site was destroyed when nearby construction changed the course of the Tame River. See W.C. Sheldon, "The Landmarks of Bishop Asbury's Childhood and Youth," in *Wesley Historical Society* 12 (1920), 97–103. For an excellent bibliographic essay on Francis Asbury, see Frederick V. Mills, "Survey of Published Works on Francis Asbury; A Historiographical Essay," in *The Historical Trail: Yearbook of Conference Historical Society* (Southern New Jersey Conference, The United Methodist Church, 1996), 13–25. Mills lists fifteen biographies on Francis Asbury, most of which are referenced in this book.

28. Court, *Midland Industries*, 195.

29. Ibid., 197.

30. E. Hopkins, *Birmingham: The First Manufacturing Town in the World, 1760–1840* (London: Weidenfeld & W. Colson, 1989), 6.

31. Goodwin, *Vile or Reviled?*, 18.

32. Robert J. Bull, "John Wesley Bond's Reminiscences of Francis Asbury," in *Methodist History* 4 (October 1965), 10.

33. This experience may have dictated a later regulation at Cokesbury, the school founded by Asbury and Thomas Coke: "We prohibit Whipping and Striking." See Thomas Coke and Francis Asbury, *An Address to the Annual Subscribers for the support of Cokesbury College and to the Members of the Methodist Society to Which Are Added the Rules and Regulations of the College* (New York, N.Y.: W. Ross, 1787).

34. Bull, *Bond's Reminiscences*, 25.

35. Bull, *Bond's Reminiscences*, 25.

36. The first full-time Methodist itinerant for the Staffordshire Circuit, which included West Bromwich, was James Jones, although he served the circuit for almost ten years, including a good part of the 1740s. I have discovered no contact between him and the Asburys. See Baker, *Methodist Pilgrim*, 79.

37. John Wesley, *The Letters of the Rev. John Wesley, A.M.,* ed. John Telford, (London: Epworth Press, 1931) , 6:271.

38. Thomas Jackson, *Lives of Early Methodist Preachers* (London: Wesleyan Conference Office, 1871), 2:169.

39. By this time Birmingham would have been very accessible to the Asburys because a "turnpike" had been built between Birmingham and Wednesbury. See W. C. Sheldon, "Travelling in Wesley's Time," in *Wesley Historical Society* 7 (1910): 2–8.

40. John Telford, *Wesley's Veterans* (Salem, Ohio: Schmul Publishers, n.d.), 2:105.

41. Ibid., 189.

42. Ibid., 211.

43. Hackwood, *West Bromwich*, 90.

44. Henry Venn, *Letters of Henry Venn* (Carlisle, Tenn.: Banner of Truth Trust, 1993), 13–14.

45. Ibid., 473–4.

46. Robert Bull, "George Roberts' Reminiscences of Francis Asbury," in *Methodist History* 4 (July 1967), 27.

47. See J.M. Day, "The Francis Asbury Cottage," in *Wesley Historical Society* 32 (December 1959), 83–85.

48. Hackwood, *West Bromwich*, 90.

49. F.W. Briggs, *Bishop Asbury: A Biographical Study for Christian Workers* (London: Wesleyan Conference Office, 1879), 17.

50. Hackwood, *West Bromwich*, 90.

51. Day, "Cottage," 83–85.

52. Marie B. Rowlands, *Masters and Men in the West Midland Metalware Trades before the Industrialized Revolution* (Manchester, England: Manchester University Press, 1975), 132.

53. Sheldon, "Landmarks," 100.

54. Hackwood, *West Bromwich,* 90.

55. Homer Calkin, "Henry Foxall: Foundryman and Friend of Asbury's," in *Methodist History,* Vol. 6, No. 1 (Oct. 1967): 38.

56. Ibid., 47.

57. Joseph Entwisle, "Memoir of Henry Foxall," in *The Wesleyan Methodist Magazine* (Aug. 1824): 69 and 505–8.

58. Ibid., 91.

59. Ibid., 91.

60. Henry Prince, *The Romance of Early Methodism in and around West Bromwich and Wednesbury* (West Bromwich, England, n.d.), 43.

61. G. Arthur Fletcher, "Bishop Francis Asbury and Belper Chapel Vestry Collection," in *Wesley Historical Society* 16 (September–December 1927), 76–77.

62. James Lewis, *Francis Asbury: Bishop of the Methodist Episcopal Church* (London: The Epworth Press, 1927), 19–20.

63. Edward Lang, "The Theology of Francis Asbury" (Unpublished Ph.D. Dissertation, Northwestern University, 1972), 254.

64. Ibid., 254.

65. John Vickers, "Francis Asbury in the Wiltshire Circuit," in *Methodist History* 16 (April 1978), 186.

66. Ibid., 186.

67. Hopkins, *Birmingham*, 5.

68. Frank Baker, "Francis Asbury" *Blackwell Dictionary of Evangelical Biography,* vol. 1, ed. Donald M. Lewis (Cambridge: Blackwell), 31–33.

69. Day, "Cottage," 85.

70. Henry Newby, *Bishop Francis Asbury, The Father of West Bromwich Methodism* (West Bromwich, England: West Bromwich Methodists, 1916), 10.

71. J.B. Wakely, *The Heroes of Methodism* (New York: Carlton and Phillips, 1856), 72.

72. Briggs, *Bishop Asbury*, 18.

Chapter 2: "I Will Show Them the Way"

1. Nathan Bangs, *A History of the Methodist Episcopal Church* (New York: T. Mason and G. Lane, 1838), 1:54.

2. Ibid., 58. See Frank Baker, "Early American Methodism, A Key Document," in *Methodist History* 3 (January 1965), 2:3–15. Frank Baker argues that Francis Asbury would have heard Taylor's letter read to him, because Wesley sent the epistle to all forty of his assistants, those who were in charge of the circuits.

3. Wesley, *Journal*, 5:290.

4. Joseph Pilmoor, *Journal of Joseph Pilmoor, Methodist Itinerant* (Philadelphia: Message Publishing Company, 1969), 15. Tipple states that entreaties to Wesley were also made by Thomas Webb and Thomas Bell, the latter a trustee of John Street Church. Ezra Squire Tipple, *The Prophet of the Long Road* (New York, N.Y.: The Methodist Book Concern, 1916), 71. Joseph signed his name Pillmoor, Pilmoor, and Pilmore. Edwin Schell, "Beginnings in Maryland and America," in *Those Incredible Methodists*, ed. Gordon Baker (Baltimore, Md.: The Baltimore Conference, 1972), 28.

5. For an excellent discussion of Wesley's organizational structure and Methodism's relationship to Anglicanism, see W. Stephen Gunter's "Treading on the Boundaries," in *The Limits of Love Divine* (Nashville: Abingdon, 1989), 156–180. Gunter states, "At the Conference of 1749, Wesley restricted the title 'assistant' to those whom he made responsible for the oversight of a circuit. In these 'assistants' resided a certain amount of day-to-day authority, but it was always subject to the ultimate episcope of Wesley" (161).

6. Ibid., 134.

7. See *A Short Historical Account of the Early Society of Methodism Established in the City of New York in the Year 1763* (New York, N.Y.: W. & P.C. Smith, 1824).

8. J.B. Wakely, D.D., *Lost Chapters Recovered from the Early History of American Methodism* (New York, N.Y.: Wilbur E. Ketchum, 1889), 114.

9. Ibid., 148.

10. Matthew Simpson, *Cyclopaedia of Methodism* (Philadelphia, Pa.: Everts and Stewart, 1878), 906.

11. John Lednum, *History of the Rise of Methodism in America* (Philadelphia, Pa.: Published by the Author, 1859), 17.

12. All of Asbury's personal papers plus the original full copy of his Journal were lost when the New York publishing house burned in 1836. Fortunately, the entire journal had been published in 1821, but because the original was lost, interpolations by editors are much more difficult to detect. For instance, did Asbury include the "and America" in granting Strawbridge's church chronological priority over the John Street Church founded

by Phillip Embury? The preface to the 1790 *Discipline,* which Asbury would have written or personally oversaw, states that the churches were founded "about the same time." See Arthur Bruce Moss, "Statements on Historical Priority in Asbury's Writings," in *World Parish* 9 (Feb. 1961), 1:25–33. At least eight persons worked on the journal during Asbury's lifetime, including John Dickens, Henry Wilkens, Joseph Langston, and Francis Hollingsworth. (Moss, 30–31).

13. Frederick E. Maser, *Robert Strawbridge: First American Methodist Circuit Rider* (Rutland, Vt.: Academy Books, 1983), 2.

14. See Francis H. Tees, *The Story of Old St. George's* (Philadelphia: The Message Publishing Co., 1941). According to Tees, the church was first named "George Church" after the King of England. At Pilmoor's suggestion, the name was modified to "St. George's," "after the patron Saint of England, who was martyred during the Diocletian persecution." (39).

15. British Methodism, *Minutes of the Methodist Conferences from the first held in London by the late Reverend John Wesley A.M. in the year 1744* (London; John Mason, 1862), 1:98.

16. William Guirey, *The History of Episcopacy in Four Parts From Its Rise to the Present Day* (no publisher, no date), 185; Ezekiel Cooper, *The Substance of a Funeral Discourse delivered at the request of the annual conference on Tuesday, 23rd of April, 1816, in St. George's Church, Philadelphia, on the death of the Rev. Francis Asbury, Superintendent or Senior Bishop of the Methodist Episcopal Church* (Philadelphia: Jonathan Pounder, 1819), 75.

17. Gordon Wood, *The Radicalism of the American Revolution* (New York, N.Y.: Alfred A. Knopf, 1991), 190.

18. Lednum, *Rise of Methodism,* 42.

19. Pilmoor, *Journal,* 134.

20. Billy G. Smith, *Life in Early Philadelphia* (University Park, Pa.: Pennsylvania State University Press, 1995), 6.

21. Ibid., 7.

22. Ibid., 183.

23. Bernard Weisberger, *America Afire: Jefferson, Adams, and the Revolutionary Election of 1800* (New York, N.Y.: Harper Collins Publishers, Inc., 2000), 96.

24. The society leader gave the "rules" to anyone admitted into membership. *Minutes of Several Conversations between Mr. Wesley and Others from the year 1744–1789* contained the "rules." The "rules" included prohibitions on dram drinking, snuff dipping, Sabbath breaking, unprofitable conversation, and anything else thought to be detrimental to spiritual growth. Wesley, *Works,* 8:299–338.

25. Wakely, *Lost Chapters,* 78.

26. Ibid., 81.

27. Robert Drew Simpson, *American Methodist Pioneer: The Life and Journals of the Rev. Freeborn Garrettson 1752–1827* (Rutland, Vt.: Academy Books, 1984), 41.

28. Ibid., 41.

29. Schell, "Beginnings," 14.

30. See *A Century of Population Growth 1790–1900* (Baltimore, Genealogical Publishing Company, 1989), 20–22. Mail at the time was delivered by stage, and postage was according to distance. For example, in 1795 the rates were 6 cents for 30 miles, 8 cents for 30 to 60 miles, etc. George Washington did not learn of his election as President until a week later. The news of Washington's death at Mt. Vernon on December 17, 1799, reached Boston on December 24.

31. Pilmoor, *Journal*, 10.

32. A quarterly conference governed a district, the annual conference governed a conference; for example, the Western Conference, a much larger geographical jurisdiction; and eventually, the General Conference held jurisdiction over the whole denomination. Quarterly conferences were often festive occasions and scenes of intense revivals. After 1784 presiding elders utilized the occasion to serve the eucharist and baptize new believers, since many of the local preachers were not ordained. See Russell E. Richey, *The Methodist Conference in America* (Nashville, Tenn.: Abingdon, 1996).

33. Gerald Moede argues that "the full authority to administering the sacraments made necessary a special administration, so that a class of administration of the Lord's supper would stand above the class of preacher, and that the ordination was not a mere human confirmation but included an essentialist authority . . . this was an Anglican Catholic inheritance which Wesley never rejected." Gerald F. Moede, *The Office of Bishop in Methodism* (Zurich: Methodist Publishing House, 1964), 43.

34. Lednum, *Rise of Methodism*, 106.

35. Ibid., 109.

36. Wesley, *Letters*, 6:23.

37. Thomas Rankin, "Journal" (United Methodist Archives: Drew University), 7.

38. Wesley, *Letters*, 6:57.

39. Ibid., 57.

40. Richard K. MacMaster, "Thomas Rankin and the American Colonists," in *Wesley Historical Society* 39 (June 1973), 25–33. Rankin had visited Charleston, South Carolina, in 1757 as a "merchants factor."

41. Rankin, "Journal," 77.

42. Ibid., 84.

43. Ibid., 93.

44. Ibid., 102.

45. Ibid., 29.

46. Methodist Episcopal Church, *Minutes of the Methodist Conferences Annually Held in America; From 1773 to 1813, Inclusive* (New York: Daniel Hitt and Thomas Ware for the Methodist Connexion in the U.S., 1813), 5–6.

47. See Paul Eller, "Francis Asbury and Phillip William Otterbein," in *Forever Beginning, 1766-1966. Historical Papers presented at American Methodism's Bicentennial Celebration* (Lake Junaluska, N.C.: Association of Methodist Historical Societies, 1967), 3–13.

48. Methodist Episcopal Church, *Minutes 1773 to 1813*, 8.

49. Evidently, Rankin could be short-tempered. When Wesley was cheered while he was preaching at Oxford, Rankin jumped up and cried out, "In the name of God, gentlemen, what can ye mean, to interrupt and insult a servant of the Lord, about to preach salvation?" Wesley responded to Rankin, "Sit down, Tommy, sit down," and continued preaching. On another occasion, Wesley rebuked Rankin for rebuking someone else. Luke Tyerman, *The Life and Times of the Rev. John Wesley, M.A* (London, Hodder and Stoughton, 1871), 3:510, 567.

50. James Dempster was educated at Edinburgh and ministered in northern Ireland before coming to America. He seems to have dropped out of sight after his return to England from America. Samuel Rogal, *A Biographical Dictionary of Eighteenth-Century Methodism* (Queenston, Ont.: Edwin Mellen Press, 1999), 1:434. Martin Rodda's ill-advised loyalist activities while in America undermined his credibility as a Methodist minister in both America and England. (Rogal, 6:156).

51. Rankin, "Journal," 96.

52. Ibid., 88.

Chapter 3: "I Am Determined Not to Leave Them"

1. See Harry S. Stout, *The Divine Dramatist* (Grand Rapids: Eerdmans, 1991).

2. William Duke, "The Journal of William Duke, 1774–1776: A Preliminary Study Edition Abstracted by Edwin Schell from the Original in Diocesan Library, Peabody Institute, Baltimore, Maryland." (Baltimore: Baltimore Conference Methodist Historical Society, 1958), 16. But it should not be assumed that all of the American preachers disliked Rankin. William Watters recalled, "I always thought him qualified to fill his place as general assistant amongst us, not withstanding his particularities. He was not only a man of grace but of strong and quick parts." William Watters, *A Short Account of the Christian Experience and Ministerial Labours of William Watters Drawn up by Himself* (Alexandria: S. Snowden, 1806), 35.

3. Wesley, *Letters*, 4:142.

4. Ibid., 143.

5. Tipple, *Prophet* , 314.

6. Ibid., 126.

7. Maser, *Strawbridge*, 57.

8. Quoted in Dee E. Andrews, *The Methodists and Revolutionary America, 1760–1800. The Shaping of an Evangelical Culture* (Princeton, N. J.: Princeton University Press, 2000), 213.

9. Wesley, *Letters*, 6:150.

10. Asbury insinuated that it was Rankin that defied Wesley's order to ship him back to England. See letter to Joseph Benson, Jan. 15, 1816 (3:553).

11. MacMaster, "Rankin," 31.

12. Ibid., 27.

13. Ibid., 32. John Littlejohn was a Methodist preacher.

14. Wesley, *Letters*, 6:173.

15. Schell, "Beginnings," 18.

16. William Sterne Randall, *Thomas Jefferson: A Life* (New York: Harper Perennial, 1994), 254.

17. Abel Stevens, *The Women of Methodism* (New York: Carlton and Porter, 1866), 241.

18. W.C. Sheldon states that Henry Gough was from this same family but gives no historical evidence for his conclusion. Sheldon, "Landmarks," 99.

19. See Edith Rassiter Benan, "Perry Hall: County Seat of the Gough and Carroll Families," in *Maryland Historical Magazine* 45 (Baltimore, Maryland Historical Society, March 1950), 33–46. Also see Col. J. Thomas Scharf, *The Chronicles of Baltimore; Being a Complete History of "Baltimore Town" and Baltimore County from the Earliest Period to the Present Time* (Baltimore, Md.: Turnbill Brothers, 1874), 43. The Goughs furnished a room for hosting preachers that included "one high-post and one low-post bedstead, two chests of drawers, two tables, two washstands with two pitchers and two basins, two carpets, and for the occasions when the members of the household came to join them in prayer, five walnut chairs." Andrews, *The Methodists*, 216.

20. Emory Stevens Bucke, ed., *The History of American Methodism*, vol. 1, (Nashville, Tenn.: Abingdon, 1964), 162.

21. Wesley, "Calm Address to Our American Colonies," *Works*, 11:84.

22. During 1775, the Brunswick Circuit grew from 800 to 2,664 members. Wade Barclay, *History of Methodist Missions*, vol. 1 (New York: The Board of Missions and Church Extension of the MethodistChurch, 1949), 58.

23. Wakely, *Heroes*, 28.

24. John Atkinson, *Centennial History of American Methodism, Inclusive of its Ecclesiastical Organization in 1784 and its Subsequent Development under the Superintendency of Francis Asbury* (New York, N.Y.: Phillips & Hunt, 1884), 225.

25. Richard N. Rosenfeld, *American Aurora* (New York, N.Y.: St. Martin's Griffin, 1997), 258.

26. Ibid., 274.

27. Ibid., 263.

28. American Society of the Wesleyan Methodist Church, *Minutes of the Early Methodist Conferences in America.* (Baltimore: The Baltimore Maryland Conference Methodist Historical Society, 1774–1779), 6.

29. Robert C. Monk states that "Asbury's *Journal* and *Letters* record comments or notations on some 194 different pieces of literature—most of them books. Of these 164 are credited to 125 different authors. The others are uncredited and simply list titles."

Robert C. Monk, "Educating Oneself for Ministry: Francis Asbury's Reading Patterns," in *Methodist History,* 29 (April 1991), 3:145. Also see Edward M. Lang, Jr., *Francis Asbury's Reading of Theology: A Bibliographic Study* (Evanston, Ill.: Garrett Theological Seminary Library, 1972), 5. The following summary paragraph from Lang is helpful: "It might be expected that Asbury would read a great many books written by English Puritans. He was an Englishman, working in a church which was a transplant to America from England. He was concerned about the restoration of the pure church of the apostles. And he lived at a time when Puritanism had been of great importance for nearly two hundred years. Puritan writings were common. And yet, Asbury read many others besides. He read Church of England divines, Catholics, Quakers. But again, these had something in common with the Puritan Calvinists whom Asbury preferred. If not Calvinists, generally the authors he read were all evangelicals. Robert Barclay, John Brandon, Richard Burnham, William Cave, Samuel Clarke, George Faber, John Fothergill, George Fox, Mark Frank, David Hartley, Ezekiel Hopkins, Alexander Knox, David Simpson, Jeremy Taylor, Richard Watson, and Charles Wesley were men who urged others to follow a holy life. An important ingredient of Asbury's thought was not only that the church should be purified, but even more important, people's lives should be purified. Sanctification was the basic concern of Asbury's work."

30. Atkinson, *Centennial History*, 25.

31. Burgoyne had little military experience. He was better known for his play, "Maid of the Oaks," which had been staged in London by David Garrick. See A.J. Langguth, *Patriots: The Men Who Started the American Revolution* (New York, N.Y.: Simon and Schuster, 1988), 273.

32. See Don Cook, *The Long Fuse: How England Lost the American Colonies* (New York, N.Y.: Atlantic Monthly Press, 1985).

33. Telford, *Wesley's Veterans*, 2:208.

34. Ibid., 209.

35. Bucke, *History*, 1:165.

36. James W. May, "Francis Asbury and Thomas White: A Refuge Preacher and His Tory Patron," *Methodist History* 14 (April 1976) 3:141–164.

37. Cook, *The Long Fuse*, 306.

38 Ibid., 308.

39. Methodist Episcopal Church, *Minutes, 1773 to 1813*, 16–17.

40. Lednum, *Rise of Methodism*, 204.

41. Allen B. Clark, "The Judge Thomas White Site" (Frederica, Del.: Barrett's Chapel, 1990), 2. Also see Henry Conrad, *Samuel White and His Father Judge Thomas White* (Wilmington, Del.: The Historical Society of Delaware, 1903). Samuel White, Thomas White's son, became a U.S. Senator.

42. Ibid., 10.

43. Robert Simpson, *Garettson*, 98.

44. Bucke, *American Methodism*, 1:167. Bangs, *Methodist Episcopal Church*, 1:127.

William Williams, *The Garden of American Methodism* (Wilmington, Del.: Scholarly Resources, 1984), 36.

Chapter 4: "The Spirit of Separation"

1. Thomas Ware, *Thomas Ware A Spectator at the Christmas Conference: A Miscellany of Thomas Ware and the Methodist Christmas Conference,* eds. William R. Phinney, Kenneth E. Rowe, Robert B. Steelman (Rutland, Vt.: Academy Books, 1984), 251.

2. Methodist Episcopal Church, *Minutes, 1773 to 1813*, 20.

3. American Society of the Wesleyan Methodist Church, *Minutes*, 10.

4. Ibid., 10.

5. Nelson Reed, "Diary" (Regenstein Library, University of Chicago), 62.

6. Williams, *Garden*, 35-36. There is no record that Hartley was ever licensed by Methodism. Williams states that he "married into modest wealth and, in 1781, settled permanently in Talbot County." 36.

7. Rosenfeld, *American Aurora*, 377.

8. Robert E. Pattison, "The Life and Character of Richard Bassett," in *Historical and Biographical Papers,* vol. 3 (Wilmington, Del.: Historical Society, 1900), 13.

9. See Charles Payson Malley, *Ancient Families of Bohemia Manor: Their Homes and Their Burying Grounds* (Wilmington: The Historical Society of Delaware, 1888).

10. Matthew Simpson, *Cyclopaedia*, 93–94.

11. Methodist Episcopal Church, *Minutes*, 1773 to 1813, 26.

12. Watters, *A Short Account,* 119.

13. James M. Buckley, *Constitutional and Parliamentary History of the Methodist Episcopal Church* (New York, N.Y.: Eaton and Mains, 1912), 30.

14. Arthur M. Schlesinger, Jr., ed., *The Almanac of American History* (New York, N.Y.: Barnes and Noble Books, 1993), 132.

15. Devereux Jarratt, *The Life of the Reverend Devereux Jarratt, Rector of Bath Parish, Virginia, written by himself in a series of letters addressed to the Rev. John Coleman.* (Baltimore, Md.: Warner & Hanna, 1806), 25.

16. American Methodism took an early stand against the use of snuff or tobacco, but the prohibition was left out of the 1792 *Discipline.* Jesse Lee commented, "Some of them say it is an advantage for their teeth, and others say it is good for their health." Jesse Lee, *A Short History of the Methodists in the United States of America* (Baltimore, Md.: Magill and Clime, 1810), 190–191.

17. W.L. Grissom, "Some First Things in North Carolina Methodism," in *Historical Papers of The Trinity College Society*, Series IX (New York, N.Y.: AMS Press, 1912), 23.

18. Richard J. Hooker, *The Carolina Backcountry on the Eve of the Revolution* (Chapel Hill, N.C.: University Press of North Carolina, 1953), 56.

19. Lednum, *Rise of Methodism*, 265.

20. Robert Simpson, *Garrettson*, 182.

21. See Thomas E. Brigden, "Early African Preachers of the Methodist Episcopal Church," in *Wesley Historical Society* 9 (1914), 15–17. Also see Warren Thomas Smith, "Harry Hosier: Black Preacher Extraordinary" in *Journal of the Interdenominational Theological Center* 7 (Spring 1980), 2:111–128. The first reference by the New York secular press to any Methodist preacher was to Harry Hosier. It was said that when Hosier tried to learn to read, he lost the gift of preaching. When asked about the secret to his preaching, Hosier responded, "I sing by faith, pray by faith, preach by faith, and do everything by faith; without faith in the Lord Jesus, I can do nothing." William Colbert stated that Hosier was "not a man-made preacher."

22. Langguth, *Patriots*, 299–300.

23. Henry Boehm, *Reminiscences Historical and Biographical of Sixty-Four Years in the Ministry*, ed. Joseph B. Wakeley (New York, N.Y.: Carlton & Porter, 1866), 91.

24. The editors of the *Journal* did not think that Asbury ever referred to Benjamin Franklin. However, Asbury recorded the following entry on September 11, 1776: "Here I saw the son of the famous Dr. Franklin; but how unlike his father both in respect to grace and good sense!" (1:199).

25. Rosenfeld, *American Aurora*, 359.

26. Ibid., 312.

27. For three consecutive years (1782–1784) American Methodism followed the pattern of meeting first in Virginia and then in Baltimore, but the "Minutes" were recorded as one conference. The "Minutes" recorded "Held at Ellis's Preaching House . . . and adjourned to Baltimore." Methodist Episcopal Church, *Minutes*, 1773–1813, 33, 38, 43. I agree with Russell Richey that this dichotomy is somewhat superficial. In reality, most of American Methodism was located in one geographical area, the Chesapeake Bay. See Russell E. Richey, "The Formation of American Methodism: The Chesapeake Refraction of Wesleyanism," in *Methodism and the Shaping of American Culture,* eds. Nathan O. Hatch and John H. Wigger (Nashville, Tenn.: Abingdon, 2001) 197–221.

28. John J. Tigert, *A Constitutional History of American Episcopal Methodism* (Nashville: Publishing House of the Methodist Episcopal Church South, 1916), 130.

29. Evarts Boutell Green, "The Revolutionary Generation, 1763–90," in *A History of American Life,* ed. Mark C. Carnes (New York, N.Y.: Scribner, 1996), 366.

30. C.H. Fowler, "Francis Asbury," in *Lives of Methodist Bishops.* eds. Theodore L. Flood and John W. Hamilton (New York, N.Y.: Phillips and Hunt, 1882), 75.

Chapter 5: "What Mighty Magic"

1. Wesleyan Methodist Church, *Minutes of the Methodist Conferences from the first held in London by the Late Rev. John Wesley, A.M., in the year 1744*, vol. 1 (London: John Mason, 1862), 184. This is a strange inclusion, since there is no mention of this decision in the 1783 *Minutes*. The 1785 *Minutes* state that this decision was made at the Bristol Conference in 1783.

2. Asbury's name was not on the original deed. However, before the end of 1784 his name replaced Robert Lindsay's, who declined to travel. It was decided by Wesley that

a non-traveling preacher was unworthy to be listed with the "legal hundred." See John S. Simon, "Elections to the Legal Hundred," *Wesley Historical Society* 13 (1922), 14–21.

3. Sidney E. Mead, *The Lively Experiment* (New York, N.Y.: Harper & Row), 52.

4. John Vickers, *Thomas Coke: Apostle of Methodism* (New York, N.Y.: Abingdon Press, 1969), 119.

5. William Warren Sweet, *Religion on the American Frontier* (New York, N.Y.: Cooper Square Publishers, 1964), 28–29.

6 . Thomas Coke and Richard Whatcoat would play a prominent role in American Methodism. Thomas Vasey would soon return to England and serve as the pastor of Wesley's Chapel, City Road, London. John Fletcher Hurst, *The History of Methodism,* vol. 2 (New York, N.Y.: Eaton and Mains, 1902), 987. James Creighton was one of the few of Wesley's preachers ordained by the Church of England. He spent much of his time as a clerical assistant to John Wesley, was named on the 1784 Deed of Declaration, and was stipulated in Wesley's will to be a member of the committee that would superintend Methodist publishing. Rogal, *Biographical Dictionary*, 1:379. Also see George C. Stevenson, *City Road Chapel London and Its Associations* (New York, N.Y.: Methodist Book Concern, 1872). Included are biographies of Richard Creighton and Thomas Vasey (pp. 146–152). Creighton wrote 18 separate publications. Strangely, Thomas Vasey was ordained by Bishop White of the Episcopal Church in Philadelphia, but returned to England to serve Methodist circuits for 22 years.

7. Wesley, *Works*, ed. Jackson, 4:288.

8. Wesley, *Works*, ed. Jackson, 13:252.

9. Moede, *The Office of Bishop*, 35. Coke was correct in the number of priests needed for ordaining a bishop. He conveniently ignored the Anglican requirement that bishops are required to ordain bishops.

10. John Alfred Faulkner, *Burning Questions in Historical Christianity* (New York, N.Y.: Abingdon Press, 1930), 213.

11. Vickers, *Thomas Coke*, 23.

12. Wesley, *Works*, ed. Jackson, 4:83.

13. Vickers, *Thomas Coke*, 41.

14. Ibid., 43.

15. Ibid., 81.

16. Ibid., 82.

17. Tipple, *Prophet*, 145.

18. Coke did not assess Asbury's reaction as "shocked." Coke claimed that Asbury expected some kind of momentous news and had formed a committee to formulate appropriate action. See "Bishop Coke Details His Episcopal Mission to North America, Describes Christmas Conference, Baltimore," *The Methodist Experience in America*, eds. Russell E. Richey, Kenneth E. Rowe, and Jean Miller Schmidt (Nashville, Tenn.: Abingdon, 2000), 76. Coke recorded, "Mr. Asbury has himself *for some time* expected me" (p. 75).

19. Vickers, *Thomas Coke*, 111.

20. William Warren Sweet, *Virginia Methodism, A History* (Richmond, Va.: Whittet & Shepperson, 1955), 96.

21. Ibid., 97.

22. Edwin Holt Hughes, "An Interview with Francis Asbury," *Methodism*, ed. William Anderson (Nashville, Tenn.: The Methodist Publishing House, 1957), 91.

23. Ware, *Miscellany*, 272.

24. Methodist Episcopal Church, *Minutes of Several Conversations between the Rev. Thomas Coke, LL.D., the Rev. Francis Asbury, and Others at a Conference Begun in Baltimore, in the State of Maryland, on Monday, the 27th of December in the Year 1784*. (Philadelphia, Pa.: Charles Cist, 1785), 3.

25. Ware, *Miscellany*, 247.

26. Ware, *Miscellany*, 84.

27. Phillip Otterbein, a close friend of Asbury's, came to America in 1752. He founded the second Evangelical Reformed church in Baltimore, which later became part of the United Brethren in Christ, the denomination founded by Otterbein and Martin Boehm. Stephen R. Graham, "Phillip William Otterbein," *The Blackwell Dictionary of Evangelical Biography 1730–1860*, ed. Donald Lewis, vol. 2 (Oxford: Blackwell Publishers, 1995), 846.

28. Thomas Haskins, "Journal of Thomas Haskins," vol. 6 (Chicago, Ill.: Regenstein Library, n.d.), 7–8.

29. Ibid., 6:10.

30. Vickers, *Thomas Coke*, 101–102.

31. John Faulkner convincingly argued that Wesley intended to "dovetail" the American Methodist organization into the Anglican Church in America. Faulkner also claimed that the "little sketch" drawn up by Wesley was a separate document, which expressed Wesley's views for the American church to remain within the Anglican-Episcopal fold. He accused Coke and Asbury of destroying this document. The letter sent with Coke read, "In this peculiar situation some thousands of the inhabitants of these states desire my advice; and in compliance with their desire I have drawn up a *little sketch*" (italics mine). Faulkner, *Burning Questions*, 219. For further interpretation see W.R. Ward, "The Legacy of John Wesley: The Pastoral Office in Britain and America," *Statesmen, Scholars and Merchants,* eds. Anne Whiteman et al. (Oxford: Oxford University Press, 1973), 323–350. Ward states that Wesley "seems to have envisaged an extension of the system operating in Ireland with the American Methodists linked nationally with the Church of England by the superintendency of Thomas Coke and substantially by a modernized prayer book" (p. 331).

32. Warren Thomas Smith, "The Christmas Conference," in *Methodist History,* Vol. 6, No. 4 (July 1968): 25.

33. On October 31, 1784, Wesley wrote to Asbury, "As to your having a Bishop from England in every province, it will be long enough before that plan is brought into execution." To what letter Wesley was responding is unknown, and whether he meant

Anglican Bishops or American Methodist Bishops is a mystery. See Wesley F. Swift, "Five Wesley Letters," *Wesley Historical Society* 33 (March 1961): 11–16.

34. "To the Editors of the Maryland Journal and Baltimore Advertiser," *Maryland Journal and Baltimore Advertiser* 12 (Feb. 15, 1785), 698:1.

35. Methodist Episcopal Church, *Minutes of Several Conversations*, 10.

36. The best explanation of the name Cokesbury comes from John O. Gross, *Methodist Beginnings and Higher Education* (Nashville, Tenn.: Board of Education the Methodist Church, 1959), 18. "When it was proposed to name the college, different names were proposed, New Kingswood and others after places in England. Some proposed to call it Coke College and others Asbury College. On which, Dr. Coke to end the discussion, suggested that they might unite the names and call it Cokesbury."

37. W. P. Strickland, *The Pioneer Bishop* (New York, N.Y.: Phillips and Hunt, 1858), 179.

38. Anne Rowthorn, *Samuel Seabury: A Bicentennial Biography* (New York, N.Y.: The Seabury Press, 1983), 62.

39. Joseph J. Ellis, *Founding Brothers* (New York, N.Y.: Alfred A. Knopf, 2000), 139.

40. Bucke, *History*, 214.

41. However, the controversy over personal titles was within the spirit of the times. After Washington was inaugurated President in 1789, the Senate, under the chair of John Adams, spent a two full weeks debating the President's proper title. Should he be called "Mr. Washington," "Mr. President," "Sir," "Your Excellency," or "His Highness the President of the United States of America and Protector of the Rights of the Same"? See David McCullough, *John Adams* (New York, N.Y.: Simon & Schuster, 2001), 405–408.

42. See Frank Baker, *From Wesley to Asbury* (Durham, N.C.: Duke University Press, 1976), 134.

43. Thomas Coke, "Coke's Sermon at Asbury's Ordination," *Sourcebook of American Methodism*, ed. Frederick A. Norwood (Nashville, Tenn.: Abingdon, 1982), 90–96.

44. Wesley, *Letters*, 7:294.

45. Wesley, *Letters*, 8:91.

46. Moede, *The Office of Bishop*, 40.

47. Ibid., 18.

48. Joshua Soule, *A Sermon on the Death of the Rev. Francis Asbury* (New York, N.Y.: J. C. Tatten, 1816), 14.

49. Jarratt, *Life*, 66.

50. Ibid., 68.

51. The final cleavage between Wesley and American Methodism may be interpreted as a logical result of the ecclesiastical bifurcation that lay deep within Wesley's own psyche. For a psychological history of this bifurcation, see Robert L. Moore, *John Wesley and Authority: A Psychological Perspective* (Missoula, Mt.: Scholars Press, 1979). Moore

argues that just as Susanna Wesley had disguised her earlier rebellion against Samuel, John could rationalize the allegiance to the church and his rebellion as being consistent. Wesley compartmentalized his religious innovations and the laws of the church he claimed to serve. One of Wesley's key compartmentalizations differentiated priests and prophets, the latter not ordained to offer the sacraments (a neat theological construct for the societies). At eighty-six years old, Wesley had constructed a house without windows, an edifice to shut out any light that would illuminate the glaring contradictions in his own thinking. "I hold all the doctrines of the Church of England. I love her Liturgy. I approve her plan of discipline, and only wish it could be put in execution. I do not knowingly vary from the rule of the church unless in those few instances where as far as I judge there is absolute necessity." All this from a man who created the greatest schism (walkout) that the Anglican Church had ever experienced. John Wesley, *John Wesley's Sermons: An Anthology,* eds. Albert C. Outler and Richard P. Heitzenrater (Nashville, Tenn.: Abingdon, 1991), 545. Arthur Pipekorn summarizes the contradiction in Wesley's actions: "In 1784, Wesley irrevocably severed himself and Methodism from the Church of England. In that year, he legally incorporated Methodism as a distinct denomination, prepared and published drastic revision of the Anglican Thirty-Nine Articles and Book of Common Prayer and embraced ordination by Presbyters in practice as well as theory, but still he denied characteristically that an irrevocable breach had been made." Arthur Pipekorn, *Profiles in Belief: The Religious Bodies of the United States and Canada*, vol. 2 (San Francisco, Calif.: Harper & Row, 1978), 549.

52. Ware, *Miscellany*, 130.

53. Wesley, *Letters*, 8:25.

54. Ibid., 73. The leaving of Wesley's name off the Minutes caused such calumny that Thomas Morrell wrote a tract defending the American action. "Truth Discovered by Rev. Thomas Morrell, Methodist Episcopal Church" is the most concise historical document that sums up the American attitude to the Wesley-Asbury conflict. "'But you have struck Mr. Wesleys name from your minutes, in1787,' said Mr. Hammet, in his controversy with this gentleman. 'Yes,' said Mr. Morrell, 'and the reasons were substantial; and for the same causes, we struck it again, in 1789. Early in 1787, Mr. Wesley intimated a design of removing Mr. Asbury from America to Europe, and of sending us a superintendent of his *own* nomination. When the conference assembled, some of the eldest and most sensible of the elders observed that Mr. W. had no authority to remove Mr. A. much less could he *impose* a superintendent on us without our choice; for it was written in our constitution, that no person should be ordained a superintendent over us, without the *consent* of the majority of the conference; that no such consent had been given; that though they highly venerated Mr. Wesley, and were willing to receive his advice, and preserve and premote our union with him and our Methodist brethren in Europe, as far as the political interest in our country would authorize us; yet, they could not give up their rights to any man on earth.'"

55. Wesley, *Letters*, 3:183. Albert Outler states, "Despite the Anglican affiliations of John Wesley, Thomas Coke, Joseph Pilmore, and others, Francis Asbury and the bulk of American Methodists in the early decades understood themselves in terms of modified non-conformity that set them quite apart from the Episcopalians on the one side and other American Protestants on the other." Albert C. Outler, *The Wesleyan Theological Heritage,* eds. Thomas C. Oden and Leicester R. Longden (Grand Rapids, Mich.: Zondervan Publishing House, 1991), 146. Outler argues that Wesley miscalculated both the American temper and Asbury's temperament.

56. Wesleyan Methodist Church, *Minutes.*

57. Moede, *The Office of Bishop*, 21.

58. Vickers, "Wiltshire Circuit," 187.

Chapter 6: "Live or Die I Must Ride"

1. Thomas Coke, *Extracts of the Journals of the Rev. Dr. Coke's Five Visits to America* (London: G. Paramore, 1793), 45.

2. Ibid., 305.

3. DuBose, Horace. *Francis Asbury* (Nashville, Tenn.: Methodist Episcopal Church South, 1916), 55.

4. It seems that plans for a school at Abingdon, Maryland were well under way at least a couple of years before the Christmas Conference. Thomas Haskins recorded on November 11, 1782, "This morning went to view the ground where Conference is about to erect an Academy and Chapel. Noble design if accomplished., I suppose there is about 1,000 pounds subscribed—but I think it will take 2,000 pounds to complete it." Haskins, *Journal*, 2:2. On June 19, 1780, Asbury discussed with John Dickens prospects for a "Kingswood School." Asbury later stated, "[T]his was what came out a college in the subscription printed by Dr. Coke" (1:358).

5. Coke, *Extracts*, 51.

6. Coke and Asbury, *Address.*

7. See Dewey Beegle, "Cokesbury College Excavation," in *Methodist History* 7 (July 1969), 4:9–14, and Gerald McCulloh, "Cokesbury College, An Eighteenth-Century Experimental Model,"*Methodist History* 7 (July 1969), 4:3–8.

8. Vickers, *The Wiltshire Circuit*, 188.

9. See Addie Grace Wardle, *History of the Sunday School Movement in the Methodist Episcopal Church* (New York, N.Y.: Methodist Book Concern, 1918).

10. Ibid., 46.

11. Scharf, *Chronicles of Baltimore*, 245.

12. Wardle, *Sunday School Movement*, 48.

13. Albert M. Shipp, *The History of Methodism in South Carolina* (Nashville, Tenn.: Southern Methodism Publishing House, 1884), 330.

14. Letter of John Dickens to Francis Asbury, Jan. 16, 1797 (United Methodist Archives, Drew University).

15. Malcolm J. Rohrbough, *The Trans-Appalachian Frontier People, Societies and Institutions, 1775–1850* (New York, N.Y.: Oxford, 1978), 35.

16. Ibid., 51.

17. See C.C. Goss, *Statistical History of the First Century of American Methodism* (New York: Carlton & Porter, 1866), 59, and *Minutes 1773 to 1813*, 75.

18. Wesley, *Works*, ed. Jackson, 13:276.

19. Boehm, *Reminiscences*, 293.

20. H.M. Moore, *Pioneers of Methodism in North Carolina and Virginia* (Nashville, Tenn.: Southern Methodist Publishing House, 1884), 75.

21. Lowell H. Harrison and James C. Klotter, *A New History of Kentucky* (Lexington, Ky.: The University Press of Kentucky, 1997), 49.

22. Thomas Jefferson, *Notes on the State of Virginia*, ed. William Peden (Chapel Hill, N.C.: The University of North Carolina, 1982), 25.

23. Nathan O. Hatch focuses on Lorenzo Dow as the prototype of the crude, uneducated Methodist preacher who captivated the populist imagination. "A bold and bluff preacher of daring originality, Dow combined an explicit ideology of mass communications, a rare genius for communicating that bordered on a cult of personality at a relentless pace that made his name a household word from the streets of New York to the wilds of Alabama." Nathan O. Hatch, *The Democratization of American Christianity* (New Haven, Yale University Press: 1989), 130. Hatch quotes Asbury as speaking favorably of Dow (130). Hatch quotes from Richard J. Stockham, "The Misunderstood Lorenzo Dow," *The Alabama Review* (January, 1963), 20–34. Stockham quotes from John G. Jones, *Methodism in Mississippi* (Nashville, Tenn.: Publishing House of the Methodist Episcopal Church South, 1887). I can find no reference to Asbury's commenting on Dow in Jones. There is good evidence that Asbury and Dow were in the presence of one another, but Asbury made no mention of him. He evidently shared the same fear of Dow's aberrations as did others. Dow was "received on trial" but never ordained. Dow seemed to assign his rejection to Jesse Lee and Nicholas Snethen rather than Asbury. See Lorenzo Dow, *The Life Travels, Labors, and Writings of Lorenzo Dow* (New York, NY.: R. Worthington, 1881), 29, and James Mudge, *History of the New England Conference of the Methodist Episcopal Church 1796–1910* (Boston, Mass.: New England Conference, 1910), 60–431.

24. George Peck, *Early Methodism Within the Bounds of the Old Genessee Conference from 1788–1828* (New York: Carlton & Porter, 1860), 199.

25. Methodist Episcopal Church, *Minutes of Several Conversations*, 19.

26. Sweet, *Frontier*, 214.

27. Haskins, *Journal*, 2:23.

28. Boehm, *Reminiscences*, 449.

29. Charles William Janson, *The Stranger in America, 1793—1806,* (New York, N.Y.: The Press of the Pioneer, 1935), 86.

30. The oft-repeated statistic of Asbury's traveling 270,000 miles and preaching 16,500 times originated in all probability with Nathan Bangs, who estimated that Asbury traveled 6,000 miles per year and averaged preaching once a day during a 45-year American ministry. See Bangs, *History,* 1:399-400.

31. What is even more puzzling is how Asbury came up with the mileage for a single trip. "I have ridden eighty-four miles to attend this meeting at Bethel" (2:522).

32. At least part of the time Asbury scheduled his appointments several weeks in advance. The following may be regarded as a normal travel plan. See Thomas

Morrell, "The Morrell Letters," *Christian Advocate and Journal* 26 (January 23, 1851), 4:1.

Brother Asbury's Plan to Lynn

Tues., June 24, Ride		Sun. July 13, rest	
Wed., 25, Wilmington		Mon. 14, Hartford, ev. meet.	
Thurs. 26, ride to Philada		Tues. 15, Coventry do	
Fri. 27,	} Philadelphia	Wed., 16, Pomfret do	
Sat. 28,		Thurs. 17, Millford do	
Sun. 29,		Fri. 18, Needham. 3 O'clock	
Mon. 30. Trenton		Saturday 19, Waltham do	
Thurs. July 1, Elizabethtown		Sunday 20,	} Boston
Wed. 2, preach there		Monday 21,	
Thursday 3,	} New York	Tuesday 22,	
Friday 4,		Wednes. 23,	
Saturday 5,		Thursday 24, ride	
Sunday 6,		Friday 25,	} Conferences at Lynn
Monday 7, Morgan's		Saturday 26,	
Tues. 8, Lawyer Hatfield's.		Sunday 27,	
Wednesday 9, Bedford.		Monday 28,	
Thursday 10, Reading		Tuesday 29,	
Friday 11, Bristol		Wednes. 30,	
Saturday 12, Middletown		Thursday 31,	

33. Asbury spent more days (1,707) in Virginia than in any other state. Second to Virginia was South Carolina (1,662 days). The days in South Carolina were more sedentary than the days in Virginia. Many of his days in Virginia were spent crossing the state, whereas South Carolina (except for the years that he ventured to Georgia) was his stopping place (Courtesy of Edwin Schell, Director of the Baltimore Conference Methodist Historical Society, August 10, 1959).

34. Getting lost was a constant threat. The itinerant Abner Chase received the following directions when he asked a German how to get to "Sapbush": "Dat I can—you muss take up about a quarter of half a mile yet uff dis roat, an den you will come py a little pritge, an dat pritge you muss turn over, and when you have turnt dat pritge over, you will come py a little roat on dat site (raising his left arm) dat gose right up de hill, and dat hill you muss take up, and when you haff took dat hill up, you will come to a roat *where dare iss no roat*, and dat you muss take." Abner Chase, *Recollections of the Past* (New York, N.Y., Joseph Longking, 1846), 52–53.

35. Tipple, *Prophet*, 158.

Chapter 7: "All Men Do Not See Alike"

1. See *Century*.

2. Randall, *Thomas Jefferson*, 275.

3. Lee, *Short History*, 151–152. Asbury says Dec. 3.

4. Tigert, *Constitutional*, 248.

5. Ware, *Miscellany*, 130.

6. In this, Methodism simply mirrored the tension in the new U.S. government that was especially prevalent at that time. In Bernard Weisberger's words, America was

faced with finding the balance between "runaway legislatures controlled by a single inter-est or paralyzed legislatures torn among factions, with no firm leadership to restrain or guide them." Weisberger, *America Afire*, 25. Robert Coleman states, "Typical of eigh-teenth-century political attitudes, the Methodist ecclesiastical policy reflected a fear on the one hand of monarchial tyranny and on the other, the consequences of unrestrained democracy. Yet the autocratic government of the Methodist Episcopal Church even in its strictest manifestation did not prevent the church from being identified with the popular egalitarian feeling emerging at this time." Robert Coleman, *Factors in the Expansion of the Methodist Episcopal Church from 1784–1812* (Unpublished Ph.D. Dissertation, Univer-sity of Iowa, 1954), 227.

7. Methodist Episcopal Church, *The Proceedings of the Bishop and Presiding Elders of the Methodist Episcopal Church in Council Assembled at Baltimore on the First Day of December, 1789* (Baltimore, Md.: William Goddard and James Angell), 6.

8. Joshua Marsden, *The Conference; or Methodism*, (London: Blauchard, n.d.), 78.

9. Robert Simpson, *Garrettson*, 401.

10. Soule, *Sermon on the Death of the Rev. Francis Asbury*, 17–18.

11. Ibid., 328.

12. Buckley, *Constitutional and Parliamentary History*, 85.

13. Robert Paine, *Life and Times of William McKendree: Bishop of the Methodist Episcopal Church* (Nashville, Tenn.: Methodist Episcopal Church South, 1922), 159.

14. Boehm, *Reminiscences*, 451.

15. Nicholas Snethen, *Discourse on the Death of the Reverend Francis Asbury, Bishop of the Methodist Episcopal Church in the United States of America* (Baltimore, Md.: B. Edes, 1816), 6.

16. James Finley, *Autobiography of James B. Finley* (Cincinnati, Ohio: Methodist Book Concern, 1858), 254.

17. Wakeley, *Heroes*, 67.

18. Robert Emory, *The Life of Rev. John Emory* (New York, N.Y.: George Lane, 1841), 66. John Emory was elected as a bishop in 1832 and met an untimely death in 1835. His mother's ambition was that he would be like Francis Asbury.

19. Strickland, *Pioneer Bishop*, 316–317.

20. Henry Smith, *Recollections and Reflections of an Old Itinerant*, (New York, N.Y.: Lane and Tippit, 1848), 9.

21. Ibid., 37.

22. Rev. Jacob Young, *The Autobiography of a Pioneer: The Nativity, Experience, Travels, and Ministerial Labors of Rev. Jacob Young* (Cincinnati, Ohio: L. Swormstedt & A. Pace, 1857), 205–206.

23. Boehm, *Reminiscences*, 303.

24. William Sprague, "Francis Asbury," in *Annals of the American Pulpit*, vol. 7 (New York, N.Y.: Robert Carter and Brothers, 1865), 20.

25. Letter of James Coleman to Francis Asbury, May 11, 1810 (United Methodist Archives, Drew University).

26. Letter of G. Gillespie to Francis Asbury, March 1805 (United Methodist Archives, Drew University).

27. Boehm, *Reminiscences*, 444.

Chapter 8: "Enough to Make the Saints of God Weep"

1. Michael J. McKay, ed., *The Journals of the Rev. Thomas Morrell* (Madison, N.J.: Northern New Jersey Conference Historical Society, 1984), 17.

2. Randall, *Thomas Jefferson*, 503.

3. Weisberger, *America Afire*, 89.

4. Wesley, *Letters*, 8:196.

5. Wesley, *Journal*, 7:46.

6. Quoted in Elmer T. Clark, *An Album in Methodist History* (Nashville, Tenn.: Abingdon 1952), 148.

7. There was disagreement as to whether Williams' native land was Ireland or England. See Barclay, *Methodist Missions*, 29, and Rogal, *Biographical Dictionary* , vol. 9, 411-413.

8. Wesley, *Letters*, 12:331.

9. Matthew Simpson and others give his birth date as 1757. Edward Drinkhouse says that at the 1792 Conference O'Kelly was 58 years old. In all likelihood, Drinkhouse is correct, since Jesse Lee referred to him as the "old man." The 1757 date would have made O'Kelly only 35 years old at the time of his succession, not an "old man."

10. Rhys Isaac, *The Transformation of Virginia: 1740–1790* (New York, N.Y.: W. W. Norton & Company, 1982), 212.

11. Randall, *Thomas Jefferson*, 36.

12. Terry Bilhartz calls Baltimore the capital of the young republic. "Between 1790 and 1830, Baltimore grew more (497 percent) than any other city in the United States." Terry Bilhartz, *Urban Religion and the Second Great Awakening* (Rutherford, N.J.: Fairleigh Dickinson University Press, 1986), 12.

13. Walsh, "Methodism," 279.

14. Charles Franklin Kilgore, *The James O'Kelly Schism in the Methodist Episcopal Church* (Mexico: Casa Unida de Publicaciones, 1963), 19.

15. James O'Kelly, *The Author's Apology for Protesting Against the Methodist Episcopal Government* (Richmond, Va.: Central Publishing Company, 1829), 22.

16. Ibid., 22.

17 Lee, *Short History*, 177.

18. O'Kelly, *Apology*, 21. Gordon Wood states that "many of the eighteenth-century migrants from the British Isles—Scotch-Irish and Irish—came with bitter grievances against the English government. They had been pushed about and persecuted by the

English government and Anglo-Irish landlords for so long that they could not feel much loyalty to the English crown." Gordon Wood, *Radicalism*, 110.

19. Ibid., 15.

20. Lee, *Short History*, 159.

21. James O'Kelly, *A Vindication of the Author's Apology with Reflections of the Reply and a few Remarks on Bishop Asbury's Annotations on his Book of Discipline* (Raleigh, N.C.: Joseph Gales, 1801), 56.

22. Lee, *Short History*, 178.

23. Ware, *Miscellany*, 220–221.

24. Guirey, *Episcopacy*, 374.

25. Ware, *Miscellany*, 220–221.

26. See Kilgore, *O'Kelly Schism*, 26, and Edward Drinkhouse, *History of Methodist Reform* (Baltimore, Md.: Board of Publications, Methodist Protestant Church, 1899), 442.

27. Alexander M'Caine, *The History and Mystery of Methodist Episcopacy* (Baltimore, Md.: Richard J. Matchett, 1827), 64.

28. Lee, *Short History*, 180.

29. Ibid., 205.

30. Guirey, *Episcopacy*, 380.

31. Bucke, *History*, 1:452.

32. Lee, *Short History*, 204.

33. O'Kelly, *Apology*, 16.

34. Even the positive historian of the Christian denomination said of O'Kelly that he "was a man of dictatorial spirit and unbending will, occasionally manifesting some impatience when crossed in his purpose. He could not organize, and for that reason played a losing game." Milo True Morrill, *A History of the Christian Denomination in America* (Dayton, Ohio: The Christian Publishing Association, 1912), 20.

35. Paine, *McKendree*, 39.

36. Ancel Bassett, *A Concise History of the Methodist Protestant Church From Its Origin* (Pittsburgh, Pa.: W.M. McCracken, 1887), 32.

37. Paine, *McKendree*, 40.

38. Ibid., 82.

39. Henry Smith, *Recollections*, 59.

40. Harlan Feeman, *Francis Asbury's Silver Trumpet* (Nashville: Parthenon, 1950), 38. In 1835 Snethen wrote, "Mr. A's favorite and common place maxim 'local men have local ideas' proves how little he was versed in atomic philosophy. He had often seen amongst us the worst kind of selfishness, which, instead of tracing to its shrewd cause, misguided and misplaced ideas; he strongly attributed to local views. . . . [T]he delegates of the preach-

ers, and of the ministers of our church, in General Conference assembled, would make the important discovery, which was hid from the sagacious minds of our Wesleys and Cokes and Asburys, that there can be no universal church liberty without particular freedom." Nicholas Snethen, *Snethen on Lay Representation* (Baltimore: John J. Harrod, 1835), 117. In spite of Snethen's disagreement with Asbury, he stated that if the continuance of Asbury's office was predicated on a vote by the Conference, he would have voted for him.

41. Ibid., 53.

42. Ibid., 39.

43. For the verbiage that was fired in the schism see William Hammet, *A Rejoindre Being a Defence of the Truths Contained in an Appeal To Truth and Circumstances in Seven Letters Addressed to the Reverend Mr. Morrell* (Charleston: I. Sulliman, 1792), and Thomas Morrell, *A Vindication of Truth Discovered Designed as an Answer to the Reverend William Hammet's Rejoindre* (Philadelphia: Parry Hall, 1792). Also see Charles Crookshank, "William Hammet," in *Wesley Historical Society*, Vol. 8, Part 1 (March 1911): 75-76. Coke said of Hammet, "The two most flourishing societies in the West Indies, Anglicans excepted, were raised by his indefatigable labours; and there are few in the world with whom I have been acquainted that possess the proper apostolic spirit in an equal degree with him," 76.

44. W.R. Ward accuses Coke of never growing up. "[T]owards the end of his life his colleagues rescued him on the brink of matrimony with a woman whose record of business fraud was so bad that 'if one of our travelling preachers were to marry such a woman he would be censured, if not excluded from the Connexion. The woman's creditors were exulting in the prospect of arresting the Doctor immediately on his marriage with her.'" Ward, *Legacy*, 331. Ward cites Luke Tyerman.

45. Vickers, *Wiltshire Circuit*, 189.

46. Guirey wrote the book *The History of Episcopacy From its Rise to the Present Day*. See Drinkhouse, *Methodist Reform*, Chapter 10.

47. Methodist Episcopal Church, *Minutes, 1773 to 1813*, 148, 165.

48. John Tiller, "Jeremy Borroughes," in *The New International Dictionary of the Christian Church*, ed. J.D. Douglass (Grand Rapids: Zondervan, 1978), 169.

49. Francis Asbury. *The Causes, Evils and Cures of Heart and Church Divisions* (Salem, Ohio: Schmul Publishers, 1978), 222.

50. Ibid., 222.

51. Ibid., 11.

Chapter 9: "It Is for Holiness My Spirit Mourns"

1. H. Ray Merrens, ed., *The Colonial Carolina Scene: Contemporary Views 1697–1774*, (Columbia, S.C.: University of South Carolina Press, 1977), 220.

2. James A. Henretta, "The Transition to Capitalism in America," *The Transformation of Early American History: Society, Authority, and Ideology*, ed. James A. Henretta et al. (New York, N.Y.: Alfred A. Knopf, 1991), 230.

3. Walter J. Fraser, Jr., *Charleston! Charleston!* (Columbia, S.C.: University of South Carolina Press, 1989), 127.

4. Ibid., 111.

5. Ibid., 129.

6. Ibid., 181.

7. Goss, *Statistical History,* 66.

8. Indeed, Asbury feared that Lee would join the O'Kellyites. On July 13, 1793, Asbury wrote to Thomas Morrell that if he sent Lee to Virginia he would "join the faction." Thomas Morrell, "The Morrell Letters," *Christian Advocate and Journal* 26 (Feb. 20, 1851), 8:1. On January 22, 1794, Asbury again wrote to Morrell, "My friend L(ee) has lately written to Fonarden, in Baltimore, of me, as having no religion. Lord help me, I have but little." Morrell, "Letters," *Christian Advocate and Journal* 26 (Jan. 23, 1851), 4:1.

9. Fugue tunes called for persons to sing different words from one another at the same time. Wesley addresses this in his *Journal,* August 9, 1768. "I was much surprised in reading an 'Essay on Music,' wrote by one who is a thorough master of the subject, to find that the music of the ancients was as simple as that of the Methodists; that their music wholly consisted of melody, or the arrangement of single notes; that what is now called harmony, singing in parts, the whole of counterpoint and fugues, is quite novel, being never known in the world till the popedom of Leo the Tenth. He farther observes that, as the singing different words by different persons at the very same time necessarily prevents attention to the sense, so it frequently destroys melody for the sake of harmony; meantime it destroys the very end of music, which is to affect the passions." Wesley, *Journal,* 5:290.

10. Pheobus, George A. *Beams of Light on Early Methodism in America* (New York, N.Y.: Phillips and Hunt, 1887), 169–170.

11. Methodist Episcopal Church, *Minutes of Several Conversations 1784,* 27.

12. John Peters, *Christian Perfection and American Methodism* (New York, N.Y.: Abingdon, 1956), 82.

13. Methodist Episcopal Church, *Form of Discipline for the Ministers, Preachers, and Members of the Methodist Episcopal Church in America* (New York, N.Y.: William Ross, 1789), 25.

14. John Wesley, *A Plain Account of Christian Perfection* (Kansas City, Mo.: Beacon Hill Press, 1971), 37.

15. Wesley's doctrine of entire sanctification evolved, which means that his views of the subject have to be chronologically understood. Some of his early claims were greatly exaggerated. In 1740, Wesley wrote, "So that God is to them all in all, and they are nothing in his sight. They are free from self-will, as desiring nothing but the holy and perfect will of God. . . . They are freed from evil thoughts, so that they cannot enter into them, no, not for a moment. . . . They are in one sense freed from temptation, for though numberless temptations fly about them, yet they trouble them not." Quoted in Gunter, *Love Divine,* 208–209.

16. Ibid., 50.

17. See John R. Tyson, *Charles Wesley on Sanctification* (Grand Rapids, Mich.: Zondervan Publishing House, 1986). Also see Gunter, *Love Divine,* 202–226. Gunter quotes a letter of John to Charles in 1768 : "But what shall we do? I think it is high time,

that you and I, at least, should come to a point. Shall we go on in asserting perfection against all the world? Or shall we quietly let it drop? We really must do one or the other; and, I apprehend, the sooner the better. What shall we jointly and explicitly maintain, and recommend to all our preachers, concerning the nature, the time (now or by-and-by), and the manner of it? Instantaneous or not? I am weary of intestine war; of preachers quoting one of us against the other. At length, let us fix something for good and all, either the same as formerly, or different from it."

18. The first extant reference that we have of Wesley to Asbury regards entire sanctification. Wesley, *Letters*, 6:13. There is confusion on the date, since Wesley refers to Asbury's being in Salisbury, England, on January 26, 1773. At that time he had been in America for over a year. Wesley wrote to a Mrs. Pywell: "[Y]our own soul will be quickened if you earnestly exhort believers without fear or shame to press after full salvation as receivable now and that by simple faith. At all opportunities encourage Mr. Asbury to do this with all plainness. Then the Lord will be with him wherever he goes, and he will see the fruit of his labour."

19. John M'Lean, *Sketch of Phillip Gatch* (Cincinnati, Ohio: Swormstedt and Poe, 1854), 16–17.

20. Ibid., 18.

21. John Ffirth, *The Experience and Gospel Labours of the Rev. Benjamin Abbott* (Philadelphia, Pa.: D. & S. Neall, 1825).

22. For an introduction to William Colbert as an early Methodist circuit rider, see Peck, *Genessee Conference*, 272–275. "Mr. Colbert was a small slender man about one hundred and twenty five pounds, not more; wore buckskin breeches, or small clothes, which he furnished up and repaired with yellow ochre, with which he was always supplied" (p. 275).

23. William Colbert, "Journal," vol. 9 (Evanston, Ill.: The United Library, Garrett Evangelical Theological Seminary, n.p.), 60.

24. Nelson Reed, "Diary" (Chicago, Ill.: Regenstein Library, University of Chicago, n.p.), 37. Reed was one of the original twelve ordained at the Christmas Conference. He served Methodism for sixty-five years.

25. Haskins, "Journal," 4:11–12. Haskins studied both law and mathematics, was a Methodist in Philadelphia, served as a local preacher, and helped edit Asbury's journal. See the several references to Haskins in Andrews, *The Methodists*.

26. 2:174, 210, 279.

27. 1:66, 69, 388.

28. 1:22, 293.

29. Compared to Wesley, who often used the terms "full sanctification," "entire sanctification," "wholly sanctified," and "sanctified throughout." See Wesley, *Works,* ed. Jackson, 4:138; 5:169; 6:46, 488, 490; 7:205, 485; 8:47, 284–286, 293–295; 9:111; 10: 202, 275, 276; 12:380. I thank Herbert McGonigle, a genuine Wesley sleuth, for these references.

30. Compare December 29, 1804, August 25, 1805, September 27, 1806, with March 18, 1780, October 2, 1807, March 10, 1814.

31. February 7, 1782; October 1806.

32. For instance, after stating his "determination to seek it [sanctification] more frequently and seek it more diligently" on April 14, 1779, there are only two discernable instances when Asbury preached on sanctification within the next two years.

33. Hebrews 10:38-39; Isaiah 55:6–7, 1 Corinthians 5:7–8, Revelation 20:11–15; 1 Peter 4:18; Hebrews 9:27; and his favorite text, 1 Timothy 1:15.

34. Wesley, *Plain Account*, 42. He may also have been aware of Wesley's advice to the society members of Canterbury. "But I dislike several things therein. . . . Your affirming, people will be justified or sanctified just now; the affirming they are, when they are not; the bidding them say, 'I believe.'"

35. William Larkin Duren, *Francis Asbury* (New York, N.Y.: The Macmillan Company, 1928), 77.

36. Atkinson, *Centennial History*, 253.

37. Boehm, *Reminiscences*, 343.

38. Snethen, *Funeral Discourse*, 14.

39. Methodist Episcopal Church, *Minutes of Several Conversations*, 18. The first Methodist *Discipline* addressed both the physical and spiritual concerns of fasting as follows: "There are several Degrees of Fasting, which cannot hurt your Health we will instance in one. Let us every Friday (beginning on the next) avow this Duty throughout the Continent, by touching no Tea, Coffee or Chocolate *in the morning*, but (if we want it) half a Pint of Milk or Water-Gruel. Let us dine on Vegetables, and (if we need it) eat three or four Ounces of Flesh in the Evening. At other Times let us eat no Flesh-Suppers. These exceedingly tend to breed nervous Disorders."

40. Atkinson, *Centennial History*, 218.

41. Asbury noted that when he lodged with a Mr. Henry, a Jew, they read Hebrew most of the night. Tipple, *Prophet*, 90.

42. E. Brooks Holifield, *A History of Pastoral Care in America: From Salvation to Self-Realization* (Nashville, Tenn.: Abingdon, 1983), 66.

43. Wesley, *Works*, 5:187.

44. Daniel J. Boorstin, *The Americans: The Colonial Experience* (New York, N.Y.: Vintage Books, 1958), 189.

45. Andrew Burstein, *Sentimental Democracy* (New York, N.Y.: Hill and Wang, 1999), 172.

46. Finley, *Autobiography*, 253.

47. In using analogies and metaphors that were partially but not completely true to "experience," the American holiness movement was faithful to Wesley. E.H. Sugden commented that Wesley "never quite shook off the fallacious notion that sin is *a thing* which was to be taken out of man, like a cancer or a rotten tooth." While "rotten tooth" language may enhance communication, it does not sharpen theological and philosophical precision. See Alden Aikens, "Wesleyan Theology and the Use of Models," *Wesleyan Theological Journal* 14 (Fall 1979), 2:64–76. For the Sugden quote see p. 68.

48. Coleman, *Factors*, 413.

49. There is a wide divergence in interpreting the continuing emphasis of "entire sanctification" within Methodism between Asbury's death and the Phoebe Palmer restoration of the late 1830s. Coleman argues that as Methodism's emphasis on "Christian perfection" attenuated, so did its growth. Coleman, *Factors*, 418. John Peters contends that by the 1830s, "Christian perfection was, in fact, well nigh swallowed up in a welter of other considerations." Peters, *Christian Perfection*, 100. In asking us to reconsider evidences against declension, Allan Coppedge argues that studies of sermons, biographies, and journals demonstrate a concentrated and sustained emphasis of both the experience and teaching of "entire sanctification" from 1812 to 1835. Allan Coppedge, "Entire Sanctification in Early American Methodism," *Wesleyan Theological Journal* 13 (Spring 1978): 24–50.

50. Wesley, *Works*, ed. Jackson, 8:337–338.

51. Atkinson, *Centennial History*, 254.

52. Ibid., 255.

Chapter 10: "Go into Every Kitchen and Shop"

1. John Allen Krout and Dixon Ryan Fox, "The Completion of Independence," *A History of American Life*, ed. Mark C. Carnes (New York, N.Y.: Scribner, 1996), 418.

2. Bucke, *History*, 502.

3. Ibid., 502.

4. Fraser, *Charleston! Charleston!*, 196.

5. Barclay, *Methodist Missions*, 1:200

6. Ibid., 202

7. Bangs, *History*, Vol. 2, 45.

8. Ibid., 55. However, this ruling was overturned in the 1804 General Conference when a "motion to prevent preachers from using spiritous liquors, etc.," was lost. Methodist Episcopal Church, *Journals of the General Conference of the Methodist Episcopal Church*, vol. 1 (New York, N.Y.: Carlton & Phillips, 1855).

9. Wesley, *Letters,* 12:304.

10. Wesley, *Journal*, 4:295.

11. Wesley, *Works*, ed. Jackson, 2:113.

12. Wesley, *Works*, ed. Jackson, 8:270–271.

13. Wesley, *Works*, ed. Jackson, 10:487.

14. Methodist Episcopal Church, *Minutes of Several Conversations*, 4.

15. Ibid., 17.

16. Cooper, *Funeral Discourse*, 40–41, 51–52.

17. James Finley, *Sketches of Western Methodism: Biographical, Historical, and Miscellaneous. Illustrative of Pioneer Life*, ed. W.P. Strickland, D.D. (Cincinnati, Ohio: The Methodist Book Concern, 1855), 98.

18. *The Doctrines and Discipline of the Methodist Episcopal Church in America with Explanatory Notes* (Philadelphia, Pa.: Henry Tuckniss, 1798), 62–66.

19. Bucke, *History*, 319.

20. Wakeley, *Heroes*, 145

21. Abel Stevens, *Life and Times of Nathan Bangs* (New York, N.Y.: Carlton & Porter, 1863), 130.

22. James Jenkins, *Experience, Labours and Sufferings of Rev. James Jenkins* (printed for the author, 1842), 67.

23. Coke, *Extracts*, 85.

24. Williams, *Garden*, 14.

25. Ibid., 16.

26. Fraser, *Charleston! Charleston!*, 134.

27. Randall, *Thomas Jefferson*, 137.

28. Ibid., 38.

29. Quoted in W.T. Smith, "Christmas Conference," 4.

30. Maldwyn Edwards, "John Wesley," *A History of the Methodist Church in Great Britain*, eds. Rupert Davies and Gordon Rupp (London: Epworth Press, 1965), 58. When Asbury arrived in America, class distinctions were very much a part of societal understanding. John Adams referred to the "common herd of mankind" and George Washington used the phrase, "the grazing multitude." Gordon Wood, *Radicalism*, 27.

31. William M. Wrightman, "Francis Asbury, Bishop of the Methodist Episcopal Church," *Biographical Sketches of Eminent Itinerant Methodists*, ed. Thomas O. Summers (Nashville, Tenn.: E. Stevenson and F.A. Owens, 1858), 22.

32. Ibid., 22.

33. Atkinson, *Centennial History*, 284–285.

34. Pilmoor, *Journal*, 122. See Alan Taylor, "The Unhappy Stephen Arnold: An Episode of Murder and Penitence in the Early Republic," *Through a Glass Darkly*, eds. Ronald Hoffman, Mechal Sobel, and Frederika J. Teute (Chapel Hill, N.C.: University of North Carolina, 1997), 96–121. Taylor states that there were twelve thousand present for Arnold's scheduled execution, which Karen Halttunen labels "the pornography of pain," a self-indulgent voyeurism that perceived these public events as entertainment. As a ten-year-old, George Peck, the future Methodist preacher and historian, made the trip with his father to Cooperstown for the event. George Peck, *The Life and Times of George Peck, D.D.* (New York, N.Y.: Nelson and Phillips, 1874), 30–31.

35. Wakeley, *Heroes*, 190, 193.

36. Minton Thrift, *Memoir of the Rev. Jesse Lee with Extracts from His Journals* (New York, N.Y.: N. Bangs & T. Mason, 1823), 246.

37. Methodist Episcopal Church, *Minutes of Several Conversations*, 5.

38. Abel Stevens, *The History of the Religious Movement of the Eighteenth Century Called Methodism*, vol. 4 (New York, N.Y.: Carlton & Porter, 1858), 239.

39. Ibid., 239.

40. Methodist Episcopal Church, *Minutes of Several Conversations*, 12.

41. John Lawson, "The People Called Methodists: Our Discipline," *A History of the Methodist Church in Great Britain*, vol. 1, eds. R.E. Davies and E.G. Rupp (London: Epworth Press, 1965), 188.

42. Bucke, *History*, 1:308.

43. For a treatment of Fanny Newell, see Catherine A. Brekus, "Female Evangelism in the Early Methodist Movement," in Nathan O. Hatch and John H. Wigger, eds., *Methodism and the Shaping of American Culture* (Nashville, Tenn.: Abingdon, 2001), 135–173. Fanny Newell herself did not preach but often exhorted a congregation after her itinerant husband, E.F. Newell, preached. She faithfully stated, "I will go with you and hold up your hands and join to preach the acceptable year of the Lord to perishing sinners" (p. 151).

44. Fanny Newell, *Memoirs of Fanny Newell* (Springfield, Mass.: Merriam, Little and Co., 1832), 98–99.

45. Stevens, *Bangs*, 219.

46. Finley, *Sketches*, 181.

47. Haskins, *Journal*, 2:34.

48. Christine Heyrman, *Southern Cross: The Beginnings of the Bible Belt* (New York, N.Y.: Alfred A. Knopf, 1997),132.

49. Tipple, *Prophet*, 305.

50. Letter of Francis Asbury to Freeborn Garrettson, Nov. 6, 1791 (courtesy of Robert Simpson).

Chapter 11: "The Remedy Worse Than the Disease"

1. James Penn Pilkington, *The Methodist Publishing House* (Nashville, Tenn.: Abingdon Press, 1968), 1:114.

2. Krout and Fox, "Completion," 480.

3. Sherry H. Olson, *The Building of an American City* (Baltimore, Md.: The Johns Hopkins University Press, 1980), 49–53.

4. "Account of the Yellow Fever," *The Methodist Magazine* 2 (Philadelphia, Pa.: Henry Tuckniss,1798), 518.

5. Rosenfeld, *American Aurora*, 227.

6 Ibid., 235.

7. John M. Kloos Jr., *A Sense of Deity: The Republican Spirituality of Dr. Benjamin Rush* (Brooklyn, N.Y.: Carlson Publishing, 1991), 11.

8. Weisberger, *America Afire*, 81.

9. Kloos, *Sense of Deity*, 75.

10. Ibid., 73.

11. Ibid., 105.

12. Page Smith, *The Shaping of America: A People's History of the Young Republic*, vol. 3 (New York, N.Y.: McGraw Hill, 1989), 432–3.

13. Boorstin, *The Americans*, 215.

14. At least five other portraits of Asbury were painted in his lifetime: One in June 1794 by Polk, two by Thomas Barber in 1797, and one at the General Conference of 1808 by Bruff. In his last stop in Strasburg, Pa., he posed for John Frank. Asbury would have been 67 years old for the last sitting.

15. What Asbury meant by "dim-sighted" is that he could see objects at a distance but needed reading glasses. In 1803 Jacob Young saw Asbury for the first time, his head "white as a sheet. . . . The bishop raised his head, *lifted his spectacles* and asked who I was" (italics mine). Young, *Autobiography*, 90.

16. Boehm, *Reminiscences*, 438.

17. Henry Smith, *Recollections,* 72.

18. Scharf, *Chronicles of Baltimore*, 224.

19. Letter of Francis Asbury to Freeborn Garrettson, Jan. 24, 1811 (courtesy of Robert Simpson).

20. Scharf, *Chronicles of Baltimore*, 123.

21. Langguth, *Patriots*, 226.

22. Boehm, *Reminiscences*, 255.

23. Snethen, *Discourse*, 12.

24. Sweet, *Frontier*, 149.

25. Wakely, *Lost Chapters*, 378. This story may be suspect, because the same anecdote was told of Francis Poythress.

26. Henry Wilkins, *The Family Adviser, or a Plain and Modern Practice of Physic for the Use of Families Who Have Not the Advantages of a Physician and Accommodated to the Diseases of America* (Philadelphia: Henry Tuckniss, 1795).

27. E. Brooks Holifield states that, during a period of Wesley's life, he spent each Friday seeing the sick, and that during a five-month period he "dispensed medicines to about five hundred patients." E. Brooks Holifield, *Health and Medicine in the Methodist Tradition: Journey Towards Wholeness (*New York: CrossRoad, 1986), 30.

28. John Wesley, *Primitive Physic* (London: Epworth Press, 1960), 8.

29. Billy Hibbard, *Memoirs of the Life and Travels of B. Hibbard* (New York, N.Y.: Published for the author, 1825), 215–6.

Chapter 12: "I Am a Man of Another World"

1. Lee, *Short History*, 306.

2. Janson, *Stranger*, 210. Washington had been bought up by land speculators hoping to make a profit. In 1794 the city's commissioners sold 6,000 lots to a syndicate headed by a Robert Morris. The syndicate went broke and Morris landed in debtors' prison. Major Pierre-Charles L'Enfant, a Frenchman who had joined the Americans during the Revolutionary War, had laid out the city. He charged $95,000 for his services, but was paid only $2,500. See Weisberger, *America Afire*, 3–8.

3. Buckley, *Constitutional and Parliamentary History*, 212.

4. Thrift, *Jesse Lee*, 268.

5. Goss, *Statistical History*, 67.

6. For an excellent essay on Absolom Jones, see Gary Nash, "To Arise Out of the Dust: Absolom Jones and the African Church 1785–95," *Race, Class, and Politics: Essays on American Colonial and Revolutionary Society* (Urbana, Ill.: University of Illinois Press, 1986) 323–55. As Richard Allen recalled, "Jones was born in slavery and purchased his freedom. Jones's former owner said that he was a faithful and exemplary servant, re- markable for many good qualities, especially for his being not only of peaceable de- meanor, but for being possessed of the talent of inducing a disposition of it to others" (p. 330). The Black historian W.E.B. Du Bois called the Free African Society founded by Jones and Allen "the first wavering step of a people toward an organized social life" (p. 321).

7. Charles Wesley, *Richard Allen: Apostle of Freedom* (Washington, D.C.: The Asso- ciated Publishers, Inc., 1935), 53.

8. Ibid., 139.

9. Ibid., 147.

10. Lee, *Short History*, 272.

11. Boorstin, *The Americans*, 244.

12. Actually, Asbury, during his lifetime, would have had more in common with John Adams than with any other President. When Adams was twenty-one years old he wrote, "I'm resolved to rise with the sun and to study Scriptures on Thursday, Friday, Saturday, and Sunday mornings, and to study some Latin author the other three morn- ings." Adams was the product of a devout Puritan heritage. He wrote to Benjamin Rush, "I believe it is religion, without which they would have been rakes, fops, sots, gamblers, starved with hunger, or frozen with cold, scalped by Indians, etc., etc., etc., been melted away and disappeared. . . . " McCullough, *Adams*, 41, 30.

13. For Washington's religious commitments, see Paul Johnson, *A History of the American People* (New York, N.Y.: HarperCollins Publishers, 1997), 205–6. Washington's exact statement on the issue is found in his 1796 "Farewell Address." It reads, "Of all the dispositions and habits which lead to political prosperity, religion and morality are indis- pensable supports. . . . And let us with caution indulge the supposition that morality can be maintained without religion. Whatever may be conceded to the influence of refined education on minds of peculiar structure, reason and experience both forbid us to expect that national morality can prevail in exclusion of religious principle." Stephen Ambrose and Douglas Brinkley, eds. *Witness to America: An Illustrated Documentary History of the United States from the Revolution to Today* (New York, N.Y.: HarperCollins Publishers, 1999), 36.

14. Page Smith, *Shaping*, 286.

15. Rosenfeld, *American Aurora*, 163.

16. Ibid., 262.

17. Randall, *Thomas Jefferson*, 542.

18. Ibid., 543. David McCullough succinctly states the irony of the 1800 election: "Jefferson, the Virginian aristocrat and slave master who lived in a style fit for a prince, as removed from his fellow citizens and their lives as it was possible to be, was hailed as the apostle of liberty, the "Man of the People." Adams, the farmer's son who despised slavery and practiced the kind of personal economy and plain living commonly upheld as the American way, was scorned as an aristocrat who, if he could, would enslave the common people. McCullough, *Adams*, 544–5.

19. McCullough, *Adams*, 537.

20. Weisberger, *America Afire*, 39.

21. Nathan Hatch argues that newspapers were so crude and vulgar that many people refused to read them. Asbury may have identified with Timothy Dwight, who equated the reading of newspapers "with tavern-haunting, drinking and gambling." Hatch, *Democratization,* 25.

22. Boorstin, *The Americans*, 326.

23. Ibid., 327.

24. Charles Foster, *An Errand of Mercy: The Evangelical United Front, 1790–1837* (Chapel Hill, N.C.: The University of North Carolina Press, 1960), 7.

25. Methodist Episcopal Church, *Doctrines and Discipline* (1798), 28.

26. Strickland, *Pioneer Bishop*, 233.

27. Ibid., 234. The government of the U.S. resided in New York, and Washington had been inaugurated President the month before at the corner of Wall and Nassau streets in New York.

28. Roger Finke and Rodney Stark, *The Churching of America, 1776–1990. Winners and Losers In Our Religious Economy* (New Brunswick, N.J.: Rutgers University Press, 1994), 1.

29. Ware, *Miscellany*, 236.

30. Donald Mathews, "Evangelical America—The Methodist Ideology," in *Rethinking Methodist History*. eds. Russell E. Richey and Kenneth E. Rowe (Nashville: Abingdon, 1985), 91.

31. See Gary Peluso, "Francis Asbury on American Public Life," in *Methodist History* 30 (July 1992), 4:206–16.

32. Russell Richey, "Early American Methodist Views of the Nation: A Glass to the Heart," in *Reflections upon Methodism during the American Bicentennial* (Dallas, Tex.: Bridwell Library Center for Methodist Studies, 1985), 94.

33. Methodist Episcopal Church, *Minutes of Several Conversations*, 3.

34. Richey, "A Glass," 101.

35. Rosenfeld, *American Aurora*, 270.

36. Nathan Hatch states that "[t]he Methodists under Francis Asbury, for instance, used authoritarian means to build a church that would not be a respecter of persons....The most fascinating religious story of the early republic is the signal achievement of these and other populist religious leaders—outsiders who used democratic persuasions to reconstruct the foundations of religious authority." Hatch, *Democratization,* 11.

37. Johnson, *History*, 204.

38. Wesley, *Works*, ed. Jackson, 7:408.

39. James Moorhead, *American Apocalypse: Yankee Protestants and the Civil War: 1860–1869* (New Haven, Conn.: Yale University Press, 1978), 145.

40. Sweet, *Frontier*, 216. Sweet states that the new River Circuit "was a four-week circuit, between four and five hundred miles around, and extended on both sides of the Allegheny Mountains, much of the surface lying at high altitudes." 63. Michael Halfacre's large log house outside of Saltville, Virginia, served as the site for early Methodist conferences in this area (1:572n).

41. Ware, *Miscellany*, 251.

42. Charles Ferguson, *Organizing to Beat the Devil: Methodists and the Making of America* (Garden City, N.Y.: Doubleday and Co., 1971), 8.

43. Frederick Norwood, *The Story of American Methodism* (New York, N.Y.: Abingdon, 1974), 146.

44. In the spring of 1811, Asbury recorded, "Doctor Logan called upon me; he has lately returned from England, he speaks favorably of *my nation*" (2:670, italics mine). Dr. George Logan had taken the personal initiative to travel to Paris in an attempt to persuade the French to stop attacking U.S. ships. His personal negotiations resulted in Congress passing the "Logan Act" which prohibited individualistic intervention by American citizens with foreign countries without proper legislative permission. Weisberger, *America Afire*, 195.

45. William Duren persuasively argued that Asbury was a citizen of the United States because he became a citizen of Delaware. "I was at this time under recommendation of the Governor of Delaware as Taxable" (Duren, 196). However, as late as 1809 Asbury wrote Thomas Coke's wife: "I am now sitting in room in conference with you, altho 3000 miles apart. And a sudden pang went through my heart, farewell my country, my dear friend, oh my dear, my paper, my heart, my eyes! My tears!" (3:409). Whatever the technical status of Asbury's citizenship, he possessed emotional ties to both his mother country and his adopted country until the day he died.

Chapter 13: "Running Like Fire"

1. Walter Brownlow Posey. *Frontier Mission* (Lexington, Ky.: University of Kentucky Press, 1966), 98.

2. John H. Wigger. *Taking Heaven by Storm: Methodism and the Rise of Popular Christianity in America* (New York: Oxford University Press, 1998), 98.

3. Abel Stevens. *Sketches from the Study of a Superannuated Itinerant* (Boston: Charles H. Pierce, 1851), 238-9.

4. Simpson, *Cyclopaedia*, 415.

5. Ibid., 351.

6. Sweet, *Virginia Methodism*, 111.

7. The most accurate available historical account of Cane Ridge is given by Paul Conkin, *Cane Ridge: America's Pentecost* (Madison: The University of Wisconsin Press, 1990). Conkin States that "the upper range of people present at any one time could hardly have been more than 10,000. At least on Sunday afternoon, this many may have been on the grounds or in the general area. But it is quite possible that 20,000 were at Cane Ridge at some time during the next six days" (p. 88).

8. Finley, *Sketches*, 78.

9. Finley, *Autobiography*, 167.

10. Catharine C. Cleveland, *The Great Revival in the West, 1797-1805* (Gloucester, Mass: Peter Smith, 1959), 39.

11. Ibid., 39.

12. Ibid., 57. Also see Kenneth O. Brown, *Holy Ground, Too: The Camp Meeting Family Tree* (Hazelton, Pa: Holiness Archives, 1997). Brown argues that John McGee played an even more strategic part in the initiation and spread of the western revival than did McGready. It is Brown's thesis that John McGee proposed the idea of a camp meeting "in order to facilitate and spread the revival spirit that broke out in the summer of 1800, and he probably suggested the plan at the Red River meeting in June." 41.

13. Finley, *Sketches*, 74-5.

14. Ibid., 75.

15. Ibid., 80.

16. Ibid., 81.

17. Ibid., 82.

18. And it could be said that British Methodism was no stranger to these phenomena as well. See Bernard G. Holland, "A Species of Madness: The Effect of John Wesley's Early Preaching," in *Wesley Historical Society*, Vol. 39, Part 3 (1973): 77. Holland quotes Wesley's "Men of Reason and Religion:" "It is my endeavor to drive all I can into what you may term (a) species of madness . . . and which I term repentance or conviction. . . . While the word of God was preached, some persons have dropped down as dead; some have been, as it were, in strong convulsions; some roared aloud, though not with an articulate voice; and others spoke the anguish of their souls" (p. 77). The brothers John and Charles Wesley were divided over the early ecstasies of the Wesleyan revival. Charles was more skeptical than John about emotional displays. Charles described the following scene, which took place in 1743: "I went on at five expounding the Acts. Some stumbling blocks, with the help of God, I have removed, particularly the fits. Many, no doubt, were at our first preaching, struck down, both soul and body, into the depth of distress. Their *outward affections* were easy to be imitated. Many counterfeits I have already detected. Today, one who came from the alehouse, drunk, was pleased to fall into a fit for my entertainment,

and beat himself heartily. I thought it a pity to hinder him; so, instead of singing over him, as had been often done, we left him to recover at his leisure. Another, a girl, as she began to cry, I ordered her to be carried out. Her convulsion was so violent, as to take away the use of her limbs, till they laid and left her without the door. Then immediately she found her legs, and walked off." Quoted by Gunter in *Love Divine*, 153.

19. Abel Stevens, *A Compendious History of American Methodism* (New York: Eaton and Mains, 1868), 128.

20. Robert Simpson, *Garrettson*, 77.

21. Matthew Simpson, *Cyclopaedia*, 10.

22. Ffirth, *Benjamin Abbott*, 85.

23. Ibid., 89.

24. Edward Leigh Pell, *A Hundred Years of Richmond Methodism* (Richmond: The Idea Publishing Co., 1899), 87.

25. Hibbard, *Memoirs*, 160-4.

26. Quoted in Finke and Stark, *The Churching of America*, 3.

27. Ware, *Miscellany*, 252.

28. Ibid., 254.

29. Vickers, "Wiltshire Circuit," 187.

30. Pilmoor, *Journal*, 97.

31. By the early 1790s Methodists were regularly attacked both in print and by physical abuse for their worship irregularity. In 1790 John Ffirth, a Quaker, negatively responded to the falling down and "tears and cries that seemed enough to pierce the heavens." In spite of his prejudice Ffirth converted to Methodism, and in 1794 he wrote a full-length treatise defending Methodist preaching and worship. Asbury reported lodging at John Ffirth's in Salem, New Jersey, on April 22, 1806. See Bucke, *History*, Vol. 1, 328, and John Ffirth, *Truth Vindicated, or a Scriptural Essay wherein the Vulgar and Frivolous Cavils Commonly Urged Against the Methodist Episcopal Church are Briefly Considered in a Letter to a Friend*, 2d ed. (New York, N.Y.: Daniel Hitt, 1810).

32. Rankin, "Journal," 84.

33. Ibid., 93.

34. Coke, *Extracts*, 109.

35. Ibid., 109.

36. Finley, *Sketches*, 84.

37. Boehm, *Reminiscences*, 32.

38. Wigger, *Heaven*, 188.

39. Young, *Autobiography*, 126.

40. Benjamin St. James Fry, *The Life of Richard Whatcoat* (New York: Lane & Scott, 1852), 57.

41. George Coles, *The Supernumerary of Lights and Shadows of Itinerancy Compiled from Papers of Elijah Woolsey* (New York, N.Y.: Lane and Tippett, 1845), 40.

42. Heyrman, *Southern Cross,* 49.

43. Janson, *Stranger,* 107–8.

44. Heyrman, *Southern Cross,* 65.

45. Colbert, "Journal," 26.

46. Heyrman, *Southern Cross,* 7.

47. Bangs, *History,* 1:112.

48. Robert Simpson, *Garrettson,* 188.

49. Thrift, *Jesse Lee,* 295.

50. Lee, *Short History,* 98.

51. Ibid., 120.

52. Ffirth, *Benjamin Abbott,* 92.

53. Tipple, *Prophet,* 199-200.

54. Ibid., 224.

55. See Donald Mathews. "The Second Great Awakening as an Organizing Process, 1780–1830," in *Religion in American History: Interpretive Essays,* eds. John Mulder and John Wilson (Englewood Cliffs, N. J.: Prentice Hall, Inc., 1978).

56. See Nathan Hatch, "Redefining the Second Great Awakening: A Note on the Study of Christianity in the Early Republic" in Hatch, *Democratization,* 220-6. Of the "perennial tendency of enthusiastic religion toward sectarian division and subdivision," Richard Hofstadter states that "the authority of enthusiasm, then, tended to be personal and charismatic rather than institutional; the founders of churches which, like the Methodist, had stemmed from an enthusiastic source needed great organizing genius to keep their followers under a single institutional roof." Richard Hofstadter, *Anti-Intellectualism in American Life* (New York: Vintage Books, 1962), 57.

57. See Richard Carwardine's essay, "The Second Great Awakening: An Examination of Methodism and the 'New Measures,'" *Journal of American History* 59 (1972): 330.

58. See David Hempton, "Methodist Growth in Transatlantic Perspective, ca. 1770–1850," in *Methodism and the Shaping of American Culture* (Nashville, Tenn.: Abingdon Press, 2001), 41–85.

59. The combination of revival fervor and administrative order continues to be one of the supreme ironies of early Methodism. David Hempton states, "The paradox at the heart of Methodism in the United States in this period is of the creation of an authoritarian religious structure empowered by the authority of the people—an egalitarian spiritual message that did not result in democratic ecclesiastical structures. Methodism in the United States after the Revolution was therefore a form of popular religion that successfully attacked social, ecclesiastical, and professional elites rather than a genuine movement of political or ecclesiastical democracy." Hempton, "Transatlantic," 55.

Chapter 14: "We Are Impartial"

1. Robert Coleman states that "The membership of the Western Conference alone had increased more than 1,500 percent during the period from 1800 to 1812." Coleman, *Factors,* 157.

2. Methodism reported 64,894 members in 1800, 151,995 members in 1808, and 195,357 in 1812. Bangs reports 174,560 members in 1810. See Goss, *Statistical History.* Also *A Century of Population Growth 1790–1980.* The U.S. population in 1800 was 5,308,483 and in 1810 was 7,239,881.

3. For an excellent analysis of the early nineteenth-century population of the U.S., see Gordon Wood, *Radicalism,* 308–11.

4. William Wallace Bennett, *Memorials of Methodism in Virginia* (Richmond, Va.: Published by the Author, 1871), 379.

5. Ibid., 402.

6. Frank Manuel claimed that "the eighteenth century probably produced as many utopian experiments as the sixteenth and seventeenth put together, and the nineteenth quadrupled that number." See Fritz and Frank Manuel, *Utopian Thought in the Western World* (Cambridge, Mass.: The Bellnap Press of Harvard University, 1979), 5.

7. Ferguson, *Organizing,* 149.

8. Williams, *Garden,* 75.

9. See Dee Andrews, "The People and the Preachers at St. George's: An Anatomy of a Methodist Schism," in *Rethinking Methodist History,"* eds. Russell E. Richey and Kenneth E. Rowe (Nashville, Tenn.: Abingdon, 1985), 125–33.

10. Cooper, *Funeral Discourse,* 179.

11. M.M. Henkle, *The Life Of Henry Bascom* (Nashville, Tenn.: E. Stevenson and F.A. Owen, 1856), 207.

12. Ibid., 58.

13. Young, *Autobiography,* 125.

14. Bangs, *History,* 2:153.

15. Lee, *Short History,* 300.

16. Lednum, *Rise of Methodism,* 197.

17. Rosenfeld, *American Aurora,* 16.

18. Peck, *Genessee Conference,* 43.

19. Quoted in Finke and Stark, 52. This was a fear for both Wesley and Asbury. Wesley wrote in1785, "I am become, I know not how, an honorable man. The scandal of the cross is ceased and all the kingdom, rich and poor, Papists and Protestants behave with courtesy and seeming good will!" Walsh, 277.

20. Bennett, *Methodism in Virginia,* 598.

21. Wakely, *Heroes,* 59.

22. Letter of Francis Asbury to Freeborn Garrettson, January 24, 1811 (courtesy of Robert Simpson).

23. Strickland, *Pioneer Bishop*, 377.

24. Boehm, *Reminiscences*, 448.

25. Quoted by Robert Fulton Thornton in "The Home Life of Asbury" (Unpublished Bachelor of Divinity Thesis, Southern Methodist University, 1935), 32.

Chapter 15: "Millions Where Millions Are"

1. Nathan Hatch states of the early nineteenth-century popular religious movements of which Methodism was exemplary that "[h]owever diverse their theologies and church organizations, they all offered common people, especially the poor, compelling visions of individual self-respect and collective self-confidence." Hatch, *Democratization*, 4.

2. Bennett, *Methodism in Virginia*, 485–6.

3. Ibid., 483.

4. Haweis (rhymes with pause) may have been the most effective preacher among the evangelical Anglicans. His extemporaneous preaching emphasized holiness of heart and life. See Arthur Skevington Wood, *Thomas Haweis* (London: S.P.C.K., 1957).

5. Methodist Episcopal Church, *Church in America*, 107.

6. Finley, *Sketches*, 90.

7. Bennett, *Methodism in Virginia*, 495.

8. Methodist Episcopal Church, *Baltimore Conference Minutes* (Baltimore, Md.: Baltimore Historical Society, Lovely Lane Museum, March 14, 1806), 23.

9. Ibid., 30.

10. Ibid., 31.

11. M'Caine, Alexander. *The History and Mystery of Methodist Episcopacy* (Baltimore, Md.: Richard J. Matchett, 1827), 30.

12. Tigert, *Constitutional*, 296.

13. Lee, *Short History*, 345.

14. Bennett, *Methodism in Virginia*, 513.

15. Ibid., 519.

16. This number would have been over one-half of the 1810 population of the United States, which was reported to be 7,239,881. Methodism may have been the optimal entertainment and worship choice, but not to that extent.

17. Richey, *Methodist Conference*, 60.

18. Edwin Gaustad's graph demonstrates that between 1800–1810 Methodists were growing at a faster rate than any other denomination. The Methodists passed the Baptists and became America's largest denomination sometime around 1820. What is remarkable is that the Baptists represented several theological persuasions, compared to the cohesiveness of Methodism. In other words, Methodism as a single denomination

numerically surpassed all of the Baptist sects combined. Edwin Gaustad, *Historical Atlas of Religion in America* (New York, N.Y.: Harper & Row, 1976), 52. Robert Coleman claims that the Methodists numerically passed the Baptists at least by 1812. Coleman, *Factors*, 157.

19. W.R. Ward stated that "Asbury was an entrepeneur in religion, a man who perceived a market to be exploited, one of the most remarkable men of this kind there has ever been." Ward, "Legacy," 345.

20. Emora Thomas Brannan, "The Presiding Elder Question: Its Critical Nature in American Methodism, 1820–1824 and Its Impact Upon Ecclesiastical Institutions" (Durham, N.C.: Duke University, Unpublished Ph.D. Dissertation, 1974), 56.

21. Ibid., 56.

22. Methodist Episcopal Church, *Church in America*, 98, 96.

23. Methodist Episcopal Church, *Journals* (1796–1836), 3:7.

24. Jacques Ellul, *The Technological Society* (New York, N.Y.: Vintage Books, 1967), 20.

25. Remember that in 1810 the population of the states was reported to be 7,239,881. Asbury's estimate would have meant that one out of two Americans annually attended a Methodist camp meeting. Evangelistically speaking, Asbury never underestimated.

26. Williams, *The Garden*, 84–5.

27. Robert Simpson, "Lost Letters of Bishop Asbury," in *Methodist History* 33 (January 1994), 4:102.

28. Bucke, *History*, 1:264–5.

29. Lester Ruth, *A Little Heaven Below: Worship at Early Methodist Quarterly Meetings* (Nashville, Tenn.: Abingdon, 2000), 189.

30. Russell Richey, *Early American Methodism* (Indianapolis, Ind.: Indiana University Press, 1991), 32.

Chapter 16: "Esteem Him as a Father"

1. *A Century of Population Growth 1790–1900*, 29.

2. Edwin Schell statistically dismantles Abel Stevens's claim that of the 737 preachers who died between 1773 and 1845 nearly half "fell before they were 30 years old." Abel Stevens, *Memorials of the Early Progress of Methodism* (Boston, Mass.: G.H. Pierce and Company, 1852), 22. "The list of the earliest Methodist preachers in the USA was first published January 1964 and is now refined by four decades of further study. Birth and death dates are now known for 263 or 33% of these 811 preachers. Surprisingly, the average lifespan of these was 65 years. This was an era when the average lifespan of the average American male aged 20 probably would be dead by age 45. Of the remaining early preachers, 13 lived 70 or more years, another 66 attained 50-plus, and 87 more exceeded 30 years of life. Dying between the ages of 19 and 29 were only 17 of the 263 whose age is known. This puts to rest the oft-repeated assertion that early preachers usually died before age 30." See Edwin Schell, "Methodist Traveling Preachers in America, 1773-1799," *Methodist History* 38 (July 2000), 4:307.

3. Thrift, *Jesse Lee*, 337.

4. Ibid., 284. Also see *Memorial of Jesse Lee and the Old Elm* (Boston, Mass.: James P. MaGee, 1875).

5. Boehm, *Reminiscences*, 291.

6. Letter of William Monroe to John McClintock, Nov. 26, 1848 (United Methodist Archives, Drew University).

7. Peck, *Genessee Conference*, 156.

8. On January 21, 1796, Asbury estimated that he wrote 1,000 letters a year.

9. Francis, Asbury, *A Selection of Hymns from Various Authors Designed as a Supplement to the Methodist Pocket Hymn-Book Compiled under the Direction of Bishop Asbury* (New York, N.Y.: John Wilson and Daniel Hitt, 1808).

10. Stevens, *Religious Movement*, 4:78.

11. Ibid., 100.

12. Ibid., 101.

13. Bennett, *Methodism in Virginia*, 532–3.

14. Stevens, *Women*, 238.

15. Ibid., 237–8.

16. See Lester Scherer, *Ezekiel Cooper, 1763–1847: An Early American Methodist Leader* (Commission on Archives and History of the United Methodist Church, 1965).

17. See Lester Scherer, "Ezekiel Cooper and the Asbury-Lee dispute of 1793–94," *Methodist History* 6 (July 1968), 4:44–6.

18. Cooper, *Funeral Discourse*, 122–3.

19. Norman Spellman, "The General Superintendency in American Methodism, 1784–1890" (Unpublished Ph.D. Dissertation, Yale University, 1961), 162.

20. Tigert, *Constitutional*, 302–6.

21. Ibid., 316.

22. Ibid., 310.

23. Ibid., 313.

24. Ibid., 311.

25. Ibid., 314–5.

26. H. Richard Niebuhr, *The Social Sources of Denominationalism* (New York, N.Y.: Henry Holt and Co., 1954), 173.

27. Paine, *McKendree*, 120–1.

28. Tigert, *Constitutional*, 323.

29. Ibid., 323.

30. Spellman, "General Superintendency," 111–2.

31. Asbury did wear a wig, at least part of the time, up until 1796 (2:81). On June 6, 1777, he decided to put aside his wig but evidently did not maintain the decision.

32. Hooker, *Carolina Backcountry*, 3.

33. Ibid., 52.

34. John Emory, *A Defense of Our Fathers* (New York, N.Y.: Carlton & Porter, 1827), 95.

35. Ffirth, *Benjamin Abbott*, 91–2.

36. William Wrightman, *Life of William Capers, D.D.* (Nashville, Tenn.: Southern Methodist Publishing, 1859), 133.

37. Hibbard, *Memoirs*, 68.

38. D.W. Clark, *Life and Times of Rev. Elijah Hedding*, D.D. (New York, N.Y.: Carlton & Phillips, 1855), 120–1.

39. Charles L. Wallis, ed., *Autobiography of Peter Cartwright* (Nashville, Tenn.: Abingdon, 1956), 75.

40. Tipple, *Prophet*, 313.

41. Boehm, *Reminiscences*, 189.

42. Ibid., 308.

43. Samuel F. Hough, *Christian NewComer, His Life Journal and Achievements* (Dayton, Ohio: Church of the United Brethren in Christ, 1941), 149.

44. Snethen, *Discourse*, 9.

45. Wrightman, *William Capers*, 114.

46. Spellman, "General Superintendency," 173.

Chapter 17: "Live and Die a Poor Man"

1. See Paul F. Blankenship, "Bishop Asbury and the Germans," in *Methodist History* 4 (April 1966), 3:5–13.

2. What Asbury understood as his mission to the Germans is something of a historical controversy. Was he envisioning a German-speaking church under Methodist auspices, or Germans assimilated into the predominantly Anglo-Methodist Episcopal Church? When Asbury in 1809 attempted to entice John Dreisbach to leave the Evangelical Association (a German-speaking church founded by Jacob Albright), in order to minister to German Methodists, Dreisbach refused. According to Dreisbach, Asbury replied that "the German language could not exist much longer in this country." When Dreisbach stated the conditions of "German circuits, districts and conferences," Asbury responded by saying, "That cannot be-it would be inexpedient." R. Yeakel, *Jacob Albright and his Co-Laborers* (Cleveland: Publishing House of the Evangelical Association, 1883), 295-6.

3. Boehm, *Reminiscences*, 215.

4. Bennett, *Methodism in Virginia*, 551.

5. Ibid., 555.

6. Ibid., 555.

7. Boehm, *Reminiscences,* 236.

8. Chase, *Recollections,* 97.

9. Letter, Monroe to McClintock.

10. For a full yet pejorative account of Methodism in Lynn, see Parsons Cooke, *Century of Puritanism* (Boston: S. K. Whipple and Co., 1855). Cooke stated, "If mesmerism, biology, phrenology, necromancy, spiritual rapping, and any of the thousand and one of that class of the tricks is to be played off, it must go out from Lynn, the great mart of humbugs" (275).

11. "Unpublished Letters of Francis Asbury," *Methodist History* 1 (1962–63), 43–4.

12. Boehm, *Reminiscences*, 253.

13. Ibid., 254.

14. Ibid., 255.

15. W. P. Strickland, *Life of Jacob Gruber* (New York, N.Y.: Carlton & Porter), 76–7.

16. Alfred Brunson, *A Western Pioneer or Incidents of the Life and Times of Rev. Alfred Brunson* (Cincinnati, Ohio: Walden and Stowe, 1880), 45.

17. James Armstrong, *History of the Old Baltimore Conference* (Baltimore, Md.: King Brothers, 1907), 167.

18. Boehm, *Reminiscences*, 262.

19. Moore, *North Carolina*, 256.

20. Boehm, *Reminiscences*, 274

21. Ibid., 275.

22. Ibid., 294.

23. Ibid., 316.

24. See "In The Smokies: Along the Asbury Trail," *Together* (August 1958): 35–42.

25. Taylor was friendly to the Methodists, and since his house stood empty while he was in Washington it was an open hospice to Methodist preachers. Boehm, *Reminiscences*, 330.

26. "Unpublished Letters," 46.

27. "More Asbury Letters," *World Parish* 8 (Lake Junaluska, N.C.:, World Methodist Council, April 1960), 1:18.

28. Finley, *Sketches*, 41.

29. Wigger, *Heaven*, 69.

30. Boehm, *Reminiscences*, 446.

31. Lee, *Short History*, 107.

32. Bull, "Roberts' Reminiscences," 33.

33. Tipple, *Prophet*, 322.

34. Wakely, *Heroes*, 68

35. Ibid., 31.

36. Methodist Episcopal Church, *Church in America* (1798), 79.

37. Robert Simpson, *Garrettson*, 397.

38. Atkinson, *Centennial History*, 272.

39. "More Asbury Letters," *World Parish* 8 (April 1960), 1:18. Also see Edwin A. Schell, "Support of the Bishops in Early American Methodism," *Methodist History* 4 (April 1966), 3:42–50.

40. Hibbard, *Memoirs*, 219.

41. Watters, *A Short Account,* 107.

42. Strickland, *Pioneer Bishop*, 197.

43. The Preacher's Fund was established in 1784 to provide for superannuated preachers as well as their widows and orphans. The Chartered Fund was established in 1786 and superceded the Preacher's Fund because of its wider scope. It included active itinerant preachers who had been insufficiently paid. See Matthew Simpson, *Cyclopaedia*, 199–200.

44. Charles Elliot, *The Life of Robert Roberts* (Cincinnati, Ohio: J.F. Wright and L. Swormstedt, 1844), 101–2.

45. Wakeley, *Lost Chapters*, 378.

46. Tees, *St. George's*, 72.

47. Schell, "Bishops," 47.

48. Wakeley, *Heroes*, 392.

49. Atkinson, *Centennial History,* 271.

50. See Scharf, *Chronicles of Baltimore*, 226. All of his adult life, Asbury wore pants which came to the knees and held up stockings with a buckle. He frowned on the more fashionable "pantaloons" which were tucked into the boot tops. Chase, *Recollections*, 83.

51. Bull, "Roberts' Reminiscences," 33.

Chapter 18: "Preach and Live and Live and Preach"

1. Boehm, *Reminiscences*, 336.

2. Ibid., 338.

3. William Glendinning, *The Life of William Glendinning* (Philadelphia, Pa.: W. W. Woodward, 1795), 19–20.

4. Ibid., 53.

5. Ibid., 74.

6. Ibid., 104. Asbury's last reference to Glendinning was Jan. 16, 1814: "William Glendinning and I met, and embraced each other in peace" (2:752).

7. Scharf, *Chronicles of Baltimore*, 304.

8. Marsden, *Conference*, 78.

9. Boehm, *Reminiscences*, 356.

10. Ibid., 368.

11. Cartwright, *Autobiography*, 181.

12. Ibid., 376.

13. Abram W. Sangrey, *The Temple of Limestone* (Lancaster, Pa.: Boehms Chapel Society, 1991), 77.

14. Paine, *McKendree*, 159.

15. Abel Stevens, *The Centenary of American Methodism* (New York, N.Y.: Carlton & Porter, 1866), 91.

16. Bennett, *Methodism in Virginia*, 584.

17. Marsden, *Conference*, 78.

18. Frederick Abbott Norwood, "Some Newly Discovered Unpublished Letters, 1808–1825," *Methodist History* 3 (July 1965), 4:3–24.

19. Tigert, *Constitutional*, 330.

20. "Unpublished Letters," 49.

21. Paine, *McKendree*, 157.

22. Finley, *Sketches*, 233.

23. Marsden, *Conference*, 78.

24. John Wright, *Sketches of the Life and Labors of James Quinn* (Cincinnati, Ohio: Methodist Book Concern, 1851), 103.

25. Boehm, *Reminiscences*, 410.

26. Methodist Episcopal Church, *Church in America* (1798), 28.

27. Boehm, *Reminiscences*, 396.

28. Bangs, *History*, 2:398.

29. Ibid., 398.

30. Quoted in Tipple, *Prophet*, 225.

31. Mark Lloyd, "A Rhetorical Analysis of the Preaching of Bishop Asbury" (Unpublished Ph.D. Dissertation, Michigan State University, 1967), 270.

32. These statistics are courtesy of Edwin Schell, Director of the Baltimore Methodist Historical Society at Lovely Lane Church, Baltimore.

33. Again, this assessment probably originated with Nathan Bangs and was continued by Abel Stevens. See Stevens, *Memorials*, 220. See Bangs, *History*, 2:400.

34. Bull, "Roberts' Reminiscences," 31.

35. Cooper, *Funeral Discourse,* 120.

36. Snethen, *Discourse*, 5.

37. Boehm, *Reminiscences*, 440.

38. Sweet, *Frontier*, 141.

39. Cooper, *Funeral Discourse,* 121.

40. Wesley, *Sermons*, 380.

41. James Lewis, *Asbury*, 18.

42. David Lewis, *Recollections of a Superannuate or Sketches of Life, Labor and Experience in the Methodist Itinerancy* (Cincinnati: Methodist Book Concern, 1857), 39.

43. Goss, *Statistical History*, 175.

44. Jenkins, *Experience*, 118.

45. Shipp, *South Carolina*, 166.

46. John B. M'Ferrin, *History of Methodism in Tennessee*, vol. 2 (Nashville, Tenn.: Southern Methodist Publishing House, 1875), 74.

47. Holifield, *Pastoral Care,* 82.

48. Peck, *Genessee Conference*, 293.

49. Ibid., 359.

50. Perry Miller offered the sweeping but mostly accurate statement on Asbury and early Methodist preaching, "The first generations, Asbury and his paladins....They simply cut the Gordian knot of historic Protestantism with the scimitar of their unabashed Arminianism, and so turned to 'practical' preaching with a zeal that required others to imitate them as rapidly as possible in the pulpit, the camp meeting, or on the hustings, and to catch up as lamely as they could with the theology." Perry Miller, *The Life of the Mind in America* (New York, N.Y.: Harcourt, 1965), 61.

51. Bull, "Myers' Reminiscences," 10.

52. Maxwell P. Gaddis, *Footprints of an Itinerant* (New York, N.Y.: Phillips and Hunt, 1880), 509.

53. Goss, *Statistical History*, 66.

54. George Brown, *Recollections of Itinerant Life* (Cincinnati, Ohio: R.W. Carroll and Co., 1866), 73.

55. D. A. Watters, *The First American Itinerant of Methodism: William Watters* (Cincinnati, Ohio: Curtis and Jennings, 1898), 68.

56. In speaking of the evangelical preachers of this era, Hofstadter noted that "they would have been ineffective in converting their moving flocks if they had not been

able to develop a vernacular style in preaching, and if they had failed to share or to simulate in some degree the sensibilities and prejudices of their audiences—anti-aristocracy, anti-Eastern, anti-learning." Hofstadter, *Anti-Intellectualism*, 80.

57. Finke and Stark, *Churching*, 85.

58. Quoted by Donald E. Byrne, Jr., *No Foot Of Land* (Metuchen, N. J.: The Scarecrow Press, 1975), 217.

59. Burstein, *Sentimental Democracy*, 5.

60. Johnson, *History*, 148.

61. Burstein, *Sentimental Democracy*, 5. Edmund Randolf, who had been in Patrick Henry's presence, wrote, "Here was a form of sermonic chant intended primarily to arouse moral fervor. . . . His figures of speech were often borrowed from the Scriptures." Isaac, *Virginia*, 268.

62. Wakely, *Heroes*, 25.

Chapter 19: "I Pity the Poor Slaves"

1. Wakely, *Heroes*, 259.

2. Boehm, *Reminiscences*, 414.

3. Ibid., 469.

4. Schlesinger, *Almanac*, 197.

5. Paine, *McKendree*, 189.

6. Ibid., 189

7. Ibid., 195.

8. Ibid., 199.

9. Ibid., 195.

10. Ibid., 197.

11. Ibid., 187. This contradiction is also true of Wesley. John Nuelson wrote, "[T]hough Wesley rejected uninterrupted episcopal succession as a basis for the validity of ordination, he continued to hold to some kind of theory of succession which passed authority to expend the sacraments from one presbyter to another." Moede, *The Office of Bishop*, 42.

12. Ibid., 188.

13. Ibid., 166.

14. Lewis, *Recollections,* 40.

15. Ware, *Miscellany*, 184.

16. Paine, *McKendree*, 172.

17. Bennett, *Methodism in Virginia*, 587.

18. Donald G. Mathews, *Slavery and Methodism: A Chapter in American Morality, 1780–1845* (Princeton, N. J.: Princeton University Press, 1965), 27.

19. MacMaster, "Rankin," 27.

20. Vickers, *Thomas Coke*, 95.

21. Ibid., 95.

22. Ibid., 96.

23. Jean Soderland, *Quakers and Slavery: A Divided Spirit* (Princeton, N. J.: Princeton University Press, 1985), 16.

24. Neither of these quotes is included in the 1958 edition of the *Journal*. Both of these quotes are furnished by Edwin Schell, "Extracts from 1792 and 1802 Journals," *Methodist History* 9 (January 1971), 2:35–6.

25. For the regression of Methodism's stand against slavery see Robert Emory, *History of the Discipline of the Methodist Episcopal Church* (New York, N.Y.: G. Lane & P. P. Sandford, 1844), 274–9. For instance, the 1796 statement of "more than ever convinced" was changed in 1804 to "as much as ever convinced," 277.

26. Paul Otis Evans, "The Ideology of Inequality: Asbury, Methodism and Slavery" (Unpublished Ph.D. Dissertation, Rutgers University, 1981), 106.

27. Methodist Episcopal Church, *Minutes of Several Conversations*, 14.

28. Ibid, 14–5.

29. Methodist Episcopal Church, *Minutes*, 1773–1813, 55.

30. Letter of Francis Asbury to Freeborn Garrettson, Sept. 2, 1785 (courtesy of Robert Simpson).

31. Evans, *Ideology*, 227.

32. Tigert, *Constitutional*, 291.

33. Andrews, *The Methodists*, 127.

34. Pheobus, *Beams of Light*, 333.

35. Methodist Episcopal Church, *The Doctrines and Discipline of the Methodist Episcopal Church* (New York, N.Y.: T. Kirk, 1804), 215.

36. David Brion Davis, "The Emergence of Immediatism in British and American Antislavery Thought," in *Religion in American History*, ed. John M. Mulder and John F. Wilson (Englewood Cliffs, N. J.: Prentice Hall, 1978), 239.

37. Ibid, 234.

38. Wesley, *Works*, ed. Jackson, 11:59–79.

39. Lewis M. Purifoy, "The Methodist Antislavery Tradition 1784–1844," *Methodist History* 4 (July 1966), 4:12.

40. Ibid, 15.

41. Stevens, *Compendious History*, 422.

42. Jenkins, *Experience,* 142.

43. Ibid., 142.

44. Sweet, *Frontier*, 159.

45. Ruth, *A Little Heaven*, 110.

46. Stevens, *Compendious History*, 423.

47. Methodist Episcopal Church, *Journals*, 1796, 63.

48. The difference between the Disciplines sent to South Carolina in 1804 and in 1808 was that the whole section of the "temporal economy" was left out in 1804, and in 1808 the prohibition of slavery was left out of the "temporal economy." Tigert, *Constitutional*, 294, 323. Methodist Episcopal Church, *Journals*, 1796, 93.

49. It is safe to say that most Methodist preachers were aware of the jarring incongruity between the good news of the gospel which neglected the slavery of black persons. James Meacham wrote in 1791, "Members who have been professors of the religion of Jesus Christ for ten or twelve years would come to me and apparently be as happy as saints in Heaven, and follow them home and you will see their slaves in the field and kitchens cruelly oppressed, half starved, and nearly naked. O! my Lord, is this the religion of my adorable master Jesus? How can I keep grieving over these cruel oppressions who are in error? And I fear they will be slaves to the devil in Hell forever." James Meacham, *Historical Papers of Trinity College Historical Society* (New York, N.Y.; AMS Press, 1914), 92–3.

50. Evans, *Ideology*, 222.

51. Ibid., 411.

52. Andrews, *The Methodists*, 130.

53. Finley, *Sketches*, 388.

54. Cynthia Lynn Lyerly, *Methodism and the Southern Mind 1770–1810*, (New York: Oxford University Press, 1980), 169.

55. Boehm, *Reminiscences*, 409.

56. An entire transcript of the trial is included in Strickland, *Gruber*.

57. Armstrong, *Baltimore Conference*, 185.

58. Michael O. Emerson and Christian Smith, *Divided by Faith: Evangelical Religion and the Problem of Race in America* (New York, N.Y.: Oxford University Press, 2000), 21.

59. See Andrews, "St. George's," 125–33.

60. Bull, *Bond's Reminiscences*, 12.

61. Boehm, *Reminiscences*, 412.

62. Finley, *Sketches*, 35

63. Ibid., 35.

64. Ibid., 49.

65. In 1815 Asbury wrote, "The Methodist preachers who had been sent by John Wesley to America came as missionaries . . . and now behold the consequence of this mission. We have seven hundred preachers and three thousand local preachers." Coleman, *Factors*, 177.

66. George G. Smith, *The Life and Letters of James Osgood Andrew* (Nashville, Tenn.: Southern Methodist Publishing House, 1882), 59.

67. Ibid., 60.

Chapter 20: "My Only Hope of Heaven"

1. Wakely, *Heroes*, 29–34.

2. W.L. Duren, *The Top Sergeant of the Pioneers* (Atlanta, Ga.: Banner Press, 1930), 105–51.

3. "Unpublished Letters," 55.

4. See Sangrey, *Temple*, 78. "[T]his parting scene occurred at the corner of West King and Charlotte streets, Lancaster, where the Plow Tavern stood. . . . "

5. The original 1792 volume included both an advertisement and disclaimer. They are found in an extract from the Journal furnished by Edwin Schell. The disclaimer reads, "I. This Journal contains the simple exercises of the author's mind and life in the way of a private diary; there having been no intention for many years, of making it public: his charge, as well as labours and travels having become lately, more extensive, he looks upon himself as more responsible than before. II. It was written in much haste. III. To transcribe and dress it up with greater elegance would materially alter its original designs. IV. A brief history of Methodism in America may be communicated through this medium. V. Those for whom it is chiefly intended, are plain and simple people, who will look for nothing elaborate or refined; but for genuine experience and naked truth."

6. John Bangs, *Autobiography of the Rev. John Bangs* (New York, N.Y.: Printed for the author, 1846), 47.

7. Wakely, *Heroes*, 35. Asbury had reason to be concerned. According to Terry Bilhartz, "In both 1804 and 1815 a greater percentage of Methodists was found within the wealthiest ten percent of the property holders than that of any other denomination." Bilhartz, *Urban Religion,* 12.

8. Scharf, *Chronicles of Baltimore*, 225.

9. L.B. Gurly, *Memoirs of Rev. William Gurly* (Cincinnati, Ohio: Methodist Book Concern, 1850), 241–2.

10. Finley, *Autobiography*, 276.

11. "Unpublished Letters," 56.

12. Stevens, *Religious Movement*, 239.

13. Young, *Autobiography*, 318.

14. Quoted in Robert Benis Steelman, "Learner Blackman, (1781–1815)," *Methodist History* 5 (April 1967), 3:15.

15. Bull, "Myers' Reminiscences," 9–10.

16. Letter from Mary Pocahontas Gabele to Mary Hubard, March 21, 1815. Hubard papers, #360, Fol. 36 (Chapel Hill, N.C.: University of North Carolina Library).

17. Raymond Cowan, "The Arminian Alternative: The Rise of the Methodist Episcopal Church, 1765–1850" (Unpublished Ph.D. Dissertation, Georgia State University, 1991), 225.

18. "Unpublished letters," 57.

19. Joseph Travis, *Autobiography of the Rev. Joseph Travis A.M.* (Nashville, Tenn.: E. Stevenson and F.A. Owens, Agents, 1856), 65.

20. Ibid., 94.

21. Sydney Ahlstrom writes, "There is no justification for the conclusion of many historians (including most fervent Methodists) that the Methodist message was a 'democratic theology' or a 'frontier faith.' In the earlier part of the nineteenth century, at least, its theology was derived not from American democracy of the frontier but from John Wesley—a very different source indeed." Sydney E. Ahlstrom, *A Religious History of the American People*, vol. 1 (Garden City, N.Y.: Image Books, 1975), 532.

22. Wesley, *Works*, ed. Jackson, 6:509.

23. Thomas Langford is essentially correct in that Asbury did not make a theological contribution beyond preserving the chief themes of Wesley. Thomas A. Langford, *Practical Divinity* (Nashville, Tenn.: Abingdon, 1983), 79.

24. Wesley, *Works*, ed. Jackson, 5:62.

25. John Fletcher, *Third Check to Antinomianism* (New York, N.Y.: B. Waugh and T. Mason, 1833), 161–2.

26. William Cannon, *The Theology of John Wesley* (Nashville, Tenn.: Abingdon, 1946), 115.

27. See Gordon S. Wood's excellent essay, "The Assault on Aristocracy," in Wood, *Radicalism*, 271–86.

28. Ibid., 278.

29. Peck, *Genessee Conference*, 425.

30. Ibid., 425.

31. Richard Baxter, *The Reformed Pastor* (Carlisle, Penn.: Banner of Truth Trust, 1983), 63.

32. Bennett, *Methodism in Virginia*, 630.

33. Wakely, *Heroes*, 22.

34. Shipp, *South Carolina*, 178.

35. Bull, "Bond's Reminiscences," 21.

36. Lang, *Theology of Francis Asbury*, 246.

37. Bull, "John Wesley Bond's Reminiscences," 27.

Chapter 21: "Die! Die! My Brother!"

1. Bull, "Bond's Reminiscences," 25.

2. James Andrew, "Sketches of Itinerant Preachers," in *Southern Christian Advocate* (July 29, 1858).

3. Ibid., 11.

4. See Richard Treffry, *Memoirs of the Rev. Joseph Benson* (New York, N.Y.: G. Lane & P.P. Sanford, 1842).

5. Diotrephes, according to 3 John 1:9, was one who "loved to have the preeminence."

6. Ibid., 24.

7. Jenkins, *Experience*, 177.

8. Ibid., 26.

9. Wrightman, *William Capers*, 185.

10. Bull, "Bond's Reminiscences," 24.

11. Ibid., 24.

12. Travis, *Autobiography*, 91.

13. Paine, *McKendree*, 180.

14. Bennett, *Methodism in Virginia*, 610–11.

15. Itinerancy more than any other factor had distinguished Methodism from other denominations. For this principle, Asbury stated upon arriving in America, he was willing to suffer and die. Itinerancy was the "Methodist plan" (1:10). Yet by 1815, only seven hundred Methodist preachers remained in itinerancy, as opposed to three thousand who had located. Coleman, *Factors*, 177.

16. Bennett, *Methodism in Virginia*, 612.

17. Ibid., 613.

18. Bull, "Bond's Reminiscences," 3.

19. Ibid., 6.

20. Ibid., 6.

21. Ibid., 6.

22. Ibid., 7.

23. This plot can be located on Courthouse Road about ten miles east of Spotsylvania, Virginia, approximately two hundred yards from a historical marker bearing the following inscription: "A short distance southeast is the site of the George Arnold House where Bishop Francis Asbury died, March 31, 1816. Asbury, born in England in 1745, came to America in 1771 and labored here until his death. He was ordained one of the first two bishops of the Methodist Episcopal Church in America at the Baltimore Conference of December, 1784."

24. "Obituary," *The Methodist Magazine* 39 (London: Thomas Cordeux, 1816), 478.

25. The minute of May 1, 1816, reads, "Moved and seconded, that a respectful letter be addressed to brother George Arnold, on whose premises Bishop Asbury's body is deposited, expressive of our thanks for his attention to our venerable father during his illness, etc., and requesting his permission to have his remains moved." The committee

responsible for the removal consisted of Phillip Bruce, Nelson Reed, Freeborn Garrettson, Lewis Meyers, and George Pickering. Methodist Episcopal Church, *Journals, 1796–1836*, 124–5.

26. Bull, "Bond's Reminiscences," 27.

27. Elmer T. Clark, *Francis Asbury's Last Journey* (Greensboro, N.C.: Christian Advocate, 1955), 12.

28. Boehm, *Reminiscences*, 432.

29. On Thursday, May 9, Steven Roszel "[a]nnounced to the conference that the remains of Bishop Asbury had arrived and were at the house of Wm. Hawkins; whereupon the conference resolved to adjourn until three o'clock P.M. to-morrow in order to attend the funeral in the forenoon." Methodist Episcopal Church, *Journals, 1796–1836*, 139. On May 10, 1816, *The American and Commercial Daily Advertiser* published John Wesley Bond's account of Asbury's death. According to Edwin Schell, no newspaper account of Asbury's funeral has been discovered.

30. Rev. Charles Giles, *Pioneer: A Narrative of the Nativity, Experience, Travels, and Ministerial Labours of Rev. Charles Giles* (New York, N.Y.: G. Lane & P.P. Sandford, 1844), 231.

31. Abner Chase reported that thirty thousand people lined the streets and that McKendree preached only fifteen to twenty minutes because of his own poor health (Chase, *Recollections*, 95).

32. Bangs, *History*, 2:396. This plaque is now displayed in the Mount Vernon Place Church in Baltimore.

33. Schell, "Bishops," 48.

34. Cooper, *Funeral Discourse*, 111.

35. Stevens, *Compendious History*, 397.

36. Shipp, *South Carolina*, 220.

37. Erik H. Erikson, *Young Man Luther: A Study in Psychoanalysis and History* (New York, N.Y.: W.W. Norton and Co., 1962), 110.

38. Shipp, *South Carolina*, 235.

39. Wigger, *Heaven*, i.

40. Erikson, *Luther*, 179.

41. Wesley, *Journal*, Vol. 4, 325.

42. Robert Coleman, *Nothing to Do But to Save Souls* (Grand Rapids, Mich.: Francis Asbury Press, 1990), 16–17.

43. Stevens, *Compendious History*, 378.

44. Matthew 13:45–6.

45. Finke and Stark, *Churching*, 42.

46. Z. Paddock, *Memoir of Rev. Benjamin Paddock* (New York, N.Y.: Nelson and Phillips, 1875), 87.

47. Robert Coles, *Lives of Moral Leadership* (New York, N.Y.: Random House, 2000), 202.

48. This phrase I borrowed from W.R. Ward, *Legacy*, 345.

49. Johnson, *History*, 128.

50. Hatch, *Democratization*, 86.

51. Erik Erikson, *Childhood and Society* (New York, N.Y.: W.W. Norton and Co., 1963), 269.

52. Ellis, *Founding Brothers*, 18.